SCENARIOS OF POWER

STUDIES OF THE HARRIMAN INSTITUTE

Columbia University

The Harriman Institute, Columbia University, sponsors the Studies of
the Harriman Institute in the belief that their publication contributes
to scholarly research and public understanding. In this way, the Institute,
while not necessarily endorsing their conclusions, is pleased to make available
the results of some of the research conducted under its auspices.
A list of the Studies appears at the back of the book.

SCENARIOS OF POWER

Myth and Ceremony in Russian Monarchy

VOLUME TWO

FROM ALEXANDER II

TO THE ABDICATION OF NICHOLAS II

Richard S. Wortman

PRINCETON UNIVERSITY PRESS · PRINCETON, NEW JERSEY

Library of Congress Cataloging-in-Publication Data

Wortman, Richard.
Scenarios of power : myth and ceremony in Russian monarchy /
Richard S. Wortman.
p.   cm. — (Studies of the Harriman Institute)
Includes bibliographical references and index.
Contents: v. 2. From Alexander II to the Abdication of Nicholas II.
ISBN 0-691-02947-4
v. 1. From Peter the Great to the death of Nicholas I.
ISBN 0-691-03484-2
1. Russia—Court and courtiers.   2. Russia—Kings and rulers.
3. Russia—Social life and customs—1533–1917.
I. Title. II. Myth and ceremony in Russian
monarchy.   III. Series.
DK127.W67   1995
394'.4'0970903—dc20   94-21537 CIP

This book has been composed in Sabon

The paper used in this publication meets the minimum requirements of
ANSI/NISO Z39.48-1992 (R1997) (*Permanence of Paper*)

www.pup.princeton.edu

Printed in the United States of America

1   3   5   7   9   10   8   6   4   2

TO MARLENE

CONTENTS

ILLUSTRATIONS

ACKNOWLEDGMENTS

I WOULD LIKE to express my appreciation to the many individuals and institutions whose generous assistance has made this volume possible. The International Research and Exchange Board enabled me to resume research trips to the Soviet Union at the end of the 1980s, ending a ban in force since the early 1970s. The Columbia University faculty research program has funded my numerous trips to Russia in the last decade as well as the preparation of illustrations. I am particularly grateful to the librarians and archivists who have acquainted me with little-known sources that opened new possibilities of interpretation and understanding of Russian monarchy. Edward Kasinec was a generous mentor and guide to the treasures of the Slavic and Baltic Division of the New York Public Library, especially visual materials and the Romanov holdings. Sergei Mironenko and Alia Barkovets both assisted me with the many fonds of the Winter Palace collection at the State Archive of the Russian Federation and shared with me their vast knowledge of the Russian imperial family. Cynthia Coleman provided indispensable information on the Alexander Palace in Tsarskoe Selo that made it possible to gain a sense of Nicholas II's life there. I also thank Ellen Scaruffi, formerly of the Bakhmeteff Archive, and Eugene Beshenskovsky, former Slavic bibliographer of the Columbia Library, for the help they have given me.

I am most grateful to the organizers and participants of the scholarly conferences that have been important raising questions and developing ideas on my subject. These include the International Colloquium on the Internal Policy of Tsarism and the Economic Development of Russia, in Leningrad in June 1990; the conference, Imperial Russia, Borders, Frontiers, Identities, in Kazan in August 1994; and two Social Science Research Council conferences—Architecture and the Expression of Group Identity in Russia, in Chicago in May 1996, and Self and Story in Russian History, in La Jolla in September 1996. Two conferences dedicated to Iurii Lotman (*Lotmanovskie chteniia*) in December 1997 and December 1998 in Moscow were particularly helpful in shaping my thinking at the final stages of my work.

I owe special gratitude to those who read and commented on parts or all of my manuscript. James Cracraft, Laura Engelstein, Daniel Field, Leopold Haimson, and Dr. George Moraitis provided me with astute criticisms and comments on particular sections. Mark Steinberg, Ronald Suny, and Mark Von Hagen raised central issues in the revision of the manuscript and made crucial suggestions. Marlene Stein Wortman read more drafts than bear mention and gave me both comments and encouragement. Her insights into comparative history and problems of interpretation, based on her reading and experience as an American historian, inspired new ways of approaching my subject. She was at once the indispensable collaborator, stern critic, and governing Muse.

BAR   Bakhmeteff Archive of Russian and East European
Literature and History, Columbia University

BE   *Entsiklopedicheskii slovar' Brokgauz i Efron*, 41 vols
(St. Petersburg, 1890–1914)

GARF   Gosudarstvennyi Arkhiv Rossiiskoi Federatsii, Formerly
Tsentral'nyi Gosudarstvennyi Arkhiv Oktiabr'skoi
Revoliutsii

IGK, ts. Nik. I   *Stoletie Voennogo Ministerstva: Imperatorskaia
glavnaia kvartira; istoriia gosudarevoi svity; tsarstvovanie
Imperatora Nikolaia I* (St. Petersburg, 1908)

IGK, ts. Al. II   *Imperatorskaia glavnaia kvartira; istoriia gosudarevoi
svity; tsarstvovanie Imperatora Aleksandra II* (St.
Petersburg, 1914)

MV   *Moskovskie Vedomosti*

NV   *Novoe Vremia*

PSZ   *Polnoe sobranie zakonov Rossiiskoi imperii*

RGIA   Rossiiskii Gosudarstvennyi Istoricheskii Arkhiv, St
Petersburg. Formerly Tsentral'nyi Gosudarstvennyi
Istoricheskii Arkhiv

RNB   Manuscript Division, Russian National Library, St.
Petersburg

TsTM   Tsentral'ni Teatral'nyi Muzei imeni A. A. Bakhrushina

ZKT   *Zhurnaly komitet dlia ustroistva prazdnovaniia
treksotletiia Doma Romanovykh*, RGIA, 1320-1-30

SCENARIOS OF POWER

A glance at the records of past coronations in [Russia] leads to the
conclusion that the pomp and circumstance attending them have not
diminished with the advance of modern ideas, but rather increased. Not
only do the rare coronation ceremonies of other countries pale before the
religious inauguration of the Russian Czar, but there are other powerful
monarchies at present in Europe, like Germany, for instance, where the
reigning sovereign has never yet undergone a coronation and does not
appear to require one.

In Russia, however, it appears to be indispensable to the Government and
the nation. Their great love of display and purely Eastern traditions may
also be reckoned among the causes; but the machinery of government is
not supposed to get into proper working order until after a new Czar has
been crowned, and it is only then, as a general rule, that the personal
policy of the imperial autocrat becomes a known quantity both to his
own people and to the world at large.

New York Times, May 31, 1896[1]

THE LEAD ARTICLE on page 1 of the May 31, 1896, *New York Times* opened
with a statement that Nicholas II had been crowned "with the most gorgeous
ceremonies the world has ever seen." Further on, an article on past coronations (cited in the epigraph to this chapter) pointed out the continued and
even increasing lavishness of these ceremonies. By way of explanation, the
author quoted "a well-known Russian," who referred to "ten thousand
miles of Asiatic frontier." But the magnificent coronation rites and celebrations had their origins in eighteenth-century Western models and sought first
of all to impress Russian and European audiences.

Symbolic display served as an essential mechanism of rule in Imperial Russia. Ceremonies and celebrations—the coronation only the foremost among
them—demonstrated the character and efficacy of the monarchy in different
ways. They showed the emperor's capacity to marshal vast wealth. They
revealed the extent of his realm and the variety of nationalities that he and
his forbears had conquered and ruled. Elaborately choreographed parades
and dignified processions displayed the monarch's powers of control and

---

[1] *New York Times*, May 31, 1896, 14. Wilhelm II held no coronation. Wilhelm I, however,
was crowned in Königsberg in October 1861, though in a ceremony considerably less elaborate
and with less publicity than Russian coronations.

direction—a simulacrum of a state directed by the ruler's will. Crowds lining avenues and filling squares attested to his capacity to maintain "exemplary order" and to win popular support. Altogether these events illustrated what Clifford Geertz described as "the power of grandeur to organize the world."[2]

The coronation and other ceremonies of the autocracy presented a cognitive map of the political order, one of the "particular models or political paradigms of society and how it functions" which, Steven Lukes has argued, distinguish political ritual.[3] Ceremonies and pageantry made clear that the Russian emperor was not bound by the limits of everyday life or subject to mundane judgment. They lifted him into various realms of the sublime free from disagreement and strife, a process I have described as "elevation." The exercise of absolute power and the public presentation of the mythical image of the ruler were reciprocal processes: Absolute rule sustained an image of transcendent monarch, which in turn warranted the untrammeled exercise of his power. In the eighteenth and early nineteenth centuries, the lifting of the monarch into a higher realm was a ceaseless endeavor, compensating for the fragile legitimacy of monarchical authority in Russia. Poetry, art, and architecture were mobilized to represent an otherworldly universe dominated by the monarch's persona. By the same token, the failure of the ruler to make appearances at ceremonies and festivities or to prevent breakdowns in the organization of public events—as occurred during the reigns of Alexander II and Nicholas II—appeared as derelictions of his symbolic obligations. Such lapses cast doubt on the monarch's superhuman capacities and portended a broader loss of authority and control over the political order.

This two-volume study is an exploration of the role of symbolic representation in elevating and perpetuating Russian monarchy from the reign of Peter the Great until the abdication of Nicholas II. It approaches Russian monarchy as a symbolic system that persisted over time but took different forms to adapt to new demands and exploit new possibilities. It examines the dominant myths and the various ceremonial expressions of the myths that defined the monarchy for its servitors. It argues the importance of image and symbol for the maintenance of absolute monarchy and suggests how they affected the responses of Russian monarchy to the challenges of institutional reform, economic change, and popular participation. It seeks to illuminate the symbolic aspects of rule in a culture where symbolic expressions were pervasive and, I argue, often the decisive ones in determining the destinies of the state. Most important, this work seeks to restore the monarchy as an active, conscious factor to the history of Russia's political evolution before 1917. Examined with the same care as other institutions, Russian monarchy emerges as an institution with its own political culture, dominated

---

[2] Clifford Geertz, *Negara: The Theatre State in Nineteenth-Century Bali* (Princeton, N.J., 1980), 102.

[3] Steven Lukes, *Essays in Social Theory* (London, 1977), 68.

by myth, its own specific goals, as an agent creating the scene of struggle and breakdown in the early twentieth century, an agent of its own doom.

Volume 1 described how the presentations of Russian monarchy lifted the ruler and his servitors above the ruled, from Peter the Great through the reign of Nicholas I. Those who participated in the ceremonies and culture surrounding each ruler constituted what I refer to as the elite of Russian monarchy. The presence of the elite at court ceremonies demonstrated the solidarity between the upper ranks of the nobility, military, officialdom, and crown. The elite exemplified the forms of obedience the monarch expected and represented his ideas and tastes to the state administration, the armed forces, and, on occasion, to the population at large.

At the beginning of the nineteenth century, the Russian emperor ruled what Ernest Gellner has described as a horizontally organized society. The elite comprised noblemen from other national areas, such as the Baltic and Tartar provinces and Georgia, as well as Russian nobility. They shared a common bond of service with the emperor and a common domination over a population bound to the land.[4] Under Nicholas I (1825–55), the imperial court, previously the preserve of the highest officials, officers, aristocrats, and favorites of the tsar, admitted increasing numbers of middle- and lesser-level officials.[5]

The elite joined the monarch in two types of ceremonies: First, social occasions, such as soirées, balls, and receptions, defined the inner circle of the monarchy; second, public presentations—coronations, public processions, trips—displayed the preeminence of the elite and its sharing in the transcendent qualities of the monarch. Whether behind the walls of the palace, or before crowds of people, as Max Weber argued, they performed ceremonies principally for themselves, for it was the performance and its representation in text and image that proved the truth of their preeminence.[6] The ceremonies confirmed the myths, justifying elite domination as the culmination of the heroic history of the monarchy. The common people remained outside these heroic narratives, in a realm of "historylessness," unconsciously complying with the terms of the myth.[7] When they appeared at ceremonies, they made up a human backdrop, at times joining in choruses of acclaim for their ruler.

Myth endowed the monarch with an epic persona, placing him in what Michael[8] Bakhtin describes as an epic world of absolute truths, "a transferral

---

[4] Ernest Gellner, *Nations and Nationalism* (Ithaca, N.Y., 1983), 11.

[5] See Volume 1: 303–4, 322–25.

[6] Max Weber pointed out that the various strata of the elite create myths, first and foremost, to justify their collective domination to themselves (Max Rheinstein, ed., *Max Weber on Law in Economy and Society* [New York, 1967], 335–37).

[7] On the concepts of heroic history and historylessness, see Marshall Sahlins, *Islands of History* (Chicago, 1985), 35–51.

[8] Note on transcription of Russian names: I have followed the practice of using Western equivalents of Russian names when those names are common equivalents of Western names

of a represented world onto the past." The presentations were "monologic," banishing doubt and compromise, permitting no responses but admiration and affirmation.[9] The emperor appeared as demiurge, who by a gesture or the printed words of a manifesto accomplished prodigies of conquest or transformation. The principle of "le secret du roi" preserved the sense both of the mystery and the authoritative certainty of rule.[10] Divergent understandings of the myth or of how the heroism of the past should be realized in current circumstances could be voiced only behind closed doors and did not mar the harmonious unity of imperial presentations.

Two overarching myths, a European and a National myth, framed the presentation of political power in Russia from Peter the Great until the abdication of Nicholas II. From the fifteenth to the late nineteenth century, the animating myth of Russian monarchy associated the rulers and their elites with foreign models of sovereignty. The source of sacrality was distant from Russia, located in the images of Byzantium, Rome, France, or Germany. By appearing like foreigners, the monarch and the elite affirmed the permanence and inevitability of their domination of subject populations, both Russian and other nationalities. Peter the Great made Europe the referent of foreignness and superiority, and taught his servitors to act like Europeans.

The European myth elaborated a heroic history of godlike figures, either coming from the West or ruling in the West, antecedents and exemplars of Russian rulers and their elites. While many rulers of early modern Europe had emulated foreign models to enhance their authority when consolidating monarchical power, the appropriation of borrowed signs of sovereignty remained a symbolic imperative for Russian rulers long after it had disappeared in Europe. Only with the assassination of Alexander II in 1881 did the emperor and his advisers introduce a myth to preserve absolute power that emphasized the monarch's national character.

The European myth expressed the motifs of empire and conquest. Empire provided the model of sovereignty for Russia, as for other early-modern monarchies. Empire connoted supreme power, extensive territories, and diversity of subject peoples. Unity came from acts of conquest and was perpetuated by military rule.[11] The themes of conquest and usurpation, enacted spectacularly in the first years of Peter the Great's reign, underlay authority in Russia, and were constantly reaffirmed in performances of ceremonies displaying the Western character of the elite. First literal reenactments of conquest in the Petrine triumphs, then ceremonial displays of European char-

---

(e.g., Alexander, not Aleksandr; Nicholas, not Nikolai). On the other hand, I have kept the Russian original when this is the common practice (e.g., Stepan, not Steven; Iurii, not George).

[9] M. M. Bakhtin, *The Dialogic Imagination* (Austin, Tex., 1981), 13–16.

[10] On "le secret du roi" and monarchical policy in France, see Keith Michael Baker, *Inventing the French Revolution* (Cambridge, 1990), 169–70.

[11] On the varied meanings of empire in early-modern Europe, see Anthony Pagden, *Lords of All the World: Ideologies of Empire in Spain, Britain, and France c. 1500–c. 1800* (New Haven, 1995), 12–15. On the image of empire in early Russia, see Volume 1: 6, 26–30.

acter, dramatized the supremacy of an elite claiming foreign antecedents or associations.[12] The ceremonies sustained what Ronald Suny has described as the distinguishing principle of empire—"inequitable rule," the dominion of one group over another.[13]

In the West, national monarchies developed their own symbols to replace the early-modern model of empire. In Russia, the European myth perpetuated and reinforced the principle of imperial domination, making it the vital center of the monarch's self-image and the unity of the multinational elite. The expressions of European were displayed by a diverse group composed of noblemen from the various people of the empire but with the Russian nobility predominant. The difference between the Russian ethnic heartland, which gave rise to the unity of the Russian lands, and the Russian empire that succeeded it, was expressed in the words *Rus'* and *Rossiia*. *Rossiia* was greater Russia, which emerged in the sixteenth and seventeenth centuries as an imperial state that engulfed *Rus'*. *Rossiia* was the multinational empire ruled by a Westernized sovereign, through a Westernized bureaucracy, and dominated by cosmopolitan nobility united by a common European culture.

The European myth identified the emperor with the secular state, the administrative institutions and laws that Peter the Great began to introduce according to Western models. While the rulers' power continued to be sanctified by God, they displayed their sacral qualities most visibly by the progress, expansion, and strengthening of the state. The Russian state never assumed an existence independent from the person of the monarch as it did in France or England. The notion of the state as an impersonal institution, operating according to laws of its own, remained an ideal of enlightened officials through the early twentieth century, but it could not take hold in the highly literal and personalized symbolic world of Russian monarchy.[14]

After Peter, Russian monarchs appeared not only as the rulers but as symbolic exemplifications of the secular state. The result was an image of secular transcendence expressed in terms of illustrious heroes or pagan gods. Neither religious sanction nor force of tradition was sufficient to justify the monarch's secular pretensions. The emperor and his family faithfully performed the rituals of the church, but his plenitude of power required him to display godlike attributes that were demonstrated in an ongoing ceremonial drama of efficacy and omnipotence.

Although the European myth canonized and perpetuated the existing system of absolute monarchy based on a serf-holding elite, it also expressed a dynamic of change. The epic image of ruler that consecrated his unlimited

---

[12] See Volume 1: 42–51, 82–86, 91–100, 113–15, 171–75, 267–69, 298–99.

[13] Ronald Suny, "The Empire Strikes Out: Imperial Russia, National Identity, and Theories of Empire," in Ronald Suny and Terry Martin, eds., *A State of Nations: Empire and Nation-Making in the Age of Lenin and Stalin*, forthcoming.

[14] On Peter's failure to develop an abstract conception of the Russian state, see Michael Cherniavsky, *Tsar and People: Studies in Russian Myths* (New York, 1969), 82–90.

domination, together with the principle of conquest, dramatized his power and intention to transform Russia. The goals of reform and transformation were symbolically inscribed in Peter the Great's succession law, which made utility along with heredity a justification of monarchical power. Thereafter, each ruler came to the throne posing as the heroic defender of the general welfare—the deliverer of Russia who would inaugurate an era of renovation.[15]

Myth could and did accommodate new policies when they were understood to enhance the resources and power of the monarchy. But it could not accommodate dissent or politics in the public sphere. The antithesis of the monologic world of myth was the modern politics of organized groups, a world of bitter contestation over important policies and compromises that were incompatible with an absolute, superordinate truth. It was the failure of the European myth in the reign of Alexander II to preserve the ideals and practice of absolute power in parts that led Alexander III to ground his authority on national symbols and imagery.

•

The performance of the governing myth was a symbolic obligation of each Russian emperor when he ascended the throne. In the first decade of his reign, the new sovereign revealed his version of the myth, which displayed how he would embody the office of emperor and how he would exemplify the dominant political and cultural ideals of his era. I call these individual realizations of the myth "scenarios of power." The scenarios cast the new emperor as a mythical hero in a historically sensitive narrative that claimed to preserve the timeless verities underlaying the myth. It is in the scenarios of successive reigns that one observes both the transformations and the persistence of myth as it interacts with personality and history.

Ceremonies were episodes in the current scenario, and they received their meaning from the scenario. A ceremony as fundamental as the crowning of each emperor could emphasize a humble acceptance of divinely conferred authority, as in the seventeenth century; the affirmation of supreme moral and political authority, as in the eighteenth century; the identification of the emperor with nation and state as at Nicholas I's coronation in 1826. The coronations of Alexander II in 1856, Alexander III in 1883, and Nicholas II in 1896 presented a changing relationship between the monarch and the Russian people. A trip by the emperor or the heir through the empire could appear as a ceremonial conquest of the land by evoking love and approbation, as in the trips of Catherine the Great and Alexander II, or as an intimidating tour of inspection, as under Paul I and Nicholas I. Parades remained a dominant form of imperial presentation through the nineteenth and early

---

[15] On the centrality and persistence of the reform ethos in Russian monarchy, see Cynthia Whittaker, "The Reforming Tsar: The Redefinition of Autocratic Duty in Eighteenth-Century Russia," *Slavic Review* 51, no. 1 (spring 1992): 77–98.

twentieth century. The discipline and symmetry of military reviews could be taken as proof of the personal power of the emperor, as with Paul I; of the loyalty and beauty of the elite, as with Alexander I; of the power and organization of the autocratic state, as in the displays of Nicholas I. In the late nineteenth and early twentieth centuries, parades would reflect the elegance and sympathy of Alexander II, the national aspirations of Alexander III, and Nicholas II's needs for cameraderie and political support. After 1881 religious ceremonies, particularly processions of the cross, assumed a new prominence in the representation of monarchy, demonstrating the national role of the Orthodox Church. Under Nicholas II, new ceremonies, informal meetings of the tsar with the common people and mass historical celebrations, showed the tsar's bonds with the people and his claim as leader of the nation to the heritage of Russia's heroic past.

The themes of each scenario were set forth in imperial manifestoes issued by the tsars in the first years of their reigns, with the exception of the reign of Nicholas II. The themes were elaborated in ceremonial texts, verbal and visual, that presented the emperor's appearances at public events that made known his persona as ruler. The elite took their cues from these initial statements and performances: their participation was a sign of solidarity with their sovereign, or minimally of outer adherence to the monarchy in its present embodiment. The inner feelings of members of the elite were occasionally expressed in diaries, memoirs, and letters.

The scenarios sought to approximate the epic unity of the myth. But the European models that the monarchy strove to appropriate were diverse, fluid, and open to varied interpretations that permitted complete accord. As a result, scenarios often revealed contradictory aspirations that were submerged in the drama of the performances. For example, the striving for legality and regularity conflicted with godlike images of omnipotence; displays of sentiments and humility contradicted claims to superhuman rationality. The alternative visions of Western monarchy provided antitheses that might revitalize the monarchy and the myth. Such visions informed the training of heirs to the throne. In some cases it was the grandmother or mother, in others the tutors who acquainted the heir with ideas and images of authority that diverged from his father's. The new scenario germinated even as the heir performed his role in his father's scenario. Only Nicholas II's education sheltered him from divergent conceptions of rule.[16]

The scenarios followed a symbolic dynamic that governed imperial presentations until the reign of Nicholas II. A scenario begins each reign with the prospect of energetic change. It takes form in the shadow of events discrediting the previous scenario, such as an uprising, a military defeat, an assassination, which make a new conception of monarchy urgent and unavoidable.

---

[16] I discuss the empresses and patterns of upbringing of the heirs in my article, "The Russian Empress as Mother," in David L. Ransel, ed., *The Family in Imperial Russia: New Lines of Historical Research* (Urbana, Ill., 1978), 60–74.

The emperor brings a new manner of rule, appoints new figures to key positions. But after a period of vigorous, innovative government, obstacles begin to appear, the initial inspiration is lost: The scenarios become frozen, "routinized." The formal and ritualized repetitions increasingly lose touch with the changing views of the time and the needs of the state. Disappointment with the high hopes of transformation sets in. The performance of the world *in potentia*, always in a state of becoming, loses credibility once the potential is not met and opens the mind to new designs and more current settings of the myth.

•

The political symbols and language introduced by the French Revolution challenged the very grounds of the early modern European models that had given Russian rulers moral and cultural preeminence. The revolution overthrew both the religious and utilitarian justifications of monarchical government, denying both its divine designation and its claim to work for the good of its subjects. Festivals of the revolution effected what Mona Ozouf called "a transfer of sacrality," celebrating a new charismatic source of authority in the people.[17] Where the political symbolism of absolute monarchy had stressed the distance from subject, now closeness, the demonstration of affinity between government and governed, marked European political systems as legitimate.

In the first half of the nineteenth century, the word *nation* took on the sense of a political order constituted by the people themselves—a community of equal individuals whose belonging to the nation was expressed in the notion of citizenship. This idea, what Eric Hobsbawm called "state-based patriotism," gave rise in the second half of the nineteenth century to ethnic concepts of the nation, based on a people's common history, language, and religious beliefs. The "ethnic nation" helped to unite newly emerging social groups with the political order and engendered new "invented" traditions that provided rituals and symbols of historical continuity.[18]

While European monarchs initially fought the manifestations of an awakening national spirit, they eventually drew upon such sentiments. These developments were part of a broader process whereby monarchies, conceived of in the image of empires, began to present themselves as nation-states. In the seventeenth and eighteenth centuries, France and Great Britain, which had consisted of separate *nations*, began to apply the term to a unified monarchical nation. The state merged with the nation, that is, with the people,

[17] See Lynn Hunt, *Politics, Culture and Class in the French Revolution* (Berkeley, 1986), 23; Mona Ozouf, *Festivals and the French Revolution* (Cambridge, Mass., 1988), 262–82.

[18] E. J. Hobsbawm, *Nations and Nationalism Since 1780: Programme, Myth, Reality* (Cambridge, 1990), 84–87; Eric Hobsbawm, "Introduction: Inventing Traditions," and "Mass Producing Traditions: Europe, 1870–1914," in Eric Hobsbawm and Terence Ranger, eds., *The Invention of Tradition* (Cambridge, 1983), 1–14, 263–308.

who possessed a sense of civic or ethnic unity.[19] By the middle of the nineteenth century Prussian kings and Hapsburg emperors were posing as leaders of their people. Later, they came to accept parliamentary institutions that could express the needs of conservative society. In the Hapsburg Empire, conservative representatives of various national groups received a modicum of power, and a moderate parliamentary system enabled the old aristocracy to maintain its authority. Franz Josef reigned as a symbol of stability of a multinational elite that could be used to diffuse national conflict.[20]

The symbolic development of Japan shows another evolutionary pattern. In the second half of the nineteenth century, a group of modernizing oligarchs adopted a parliamentary and legal system on European models to unite the regions of Japan, which previously had only loose ties to the center. After studying Western forms of political presentation, they unabashedly reshaped old myths and ceremonies and invented new ones that presented the Japanese emperor as symbol of a Japanese nation.[21]

Russian imperial myths emphasized conquest and domination, rather than the harmonious accommodation of monarchy to a civic nation. The imagery of conquest persisted in the representations of imperial power through the nineteenth century and was renewed, in more bellicose form, in the presentations of the national myth after 1881. The contrast to the mythical histories of Hapsburg and Hohenzollern emperors is striking. The Hapsburg myth was one of dynastic right glorifying the expansion of the realm through marriage. The dominant symbols of the Hapsburgs were variants of family trees and portraits: The figures of the members of the house and their distant roots were enshrined in magnificent art and given mythic grandeur by the tale of Trojan descent.[22] After the Prussian king assumed the mantle of German emperor in 1871, he took on new historical pretensions derived from a mythical medieval empire, to embody the pretensions of both monarchy and nation.[23] While both of these myths were anti-parliamentary, neither glorified

[19] See Alain Guéry, "L'état monarchique et la construction de la nation française," *Revue de la Bibliothèque Nationale*, no. 32 (summer 1989): 6–17; Linda Colley, *Britons: Forging the Nation, 1707–1837* (New Haven, 1992).

[20] See Daniel Unowsky, "Creating Patriotism: Imperial Celebrations and the Cult of Franz Joseph," *Öesterreichische Zeitschrift für Geschichtswissenschaften* 9, no. 2 (1998): 269–93.

[21] T. Fujitani, *Splendid Monarchy: Power and Pageantry in Modern Japan* (Berkeley, 1996); Carol Gluck, *Japan's Modern Myths: Ideology in the Late Meiji Period* (Princeton, N.J., 1985).

[22] See the interesting comparison by Orest Subtelny between Hapsburg and Romanov empires in "The Hapsburg and Russian Empires: Some Comparisons and Contrasts," in Teruyuki Hara and Kimitaka Matzuzato, eds., *Empire and Society: New Approaches to Russian History* (Sapporo, 1997), 86–90. The prominent symbolic role of dynasty in Hapsburg imagery is vividly described in Andrew Wheatcroft, *The Hapsburgs: Embodying Empire* (London, 1995). On Trojan myths of derivation, see Marie Tanner, *The Last Descendant of Aeneas: The Hapsburgs and the Mythic Image of Emperor* (New Haven, 1993), 1–4, 67–118.

[23] On Germany, see Elizabeth Fehrenbach, "Images of Kaiserdom," in John C. G. Röhl, *Kaiser Wilhelm II: New Interpretations* (Cambridge, 1982), 270–85; Isabel V. Hull, "Prussian Dynastic Ritual and the End of Monarchy," in Carole Fink, Isabel V. Hull, and MacGregor

force as the key determinant of the relationship between monarch and subject. The theme of conquest in Russian imperial myth, on the contrary, maintained an image of irresistible domination and a disposition to conflict that precluded compromise with even moderate plans for participation. In the period covered in this volume, it encouraged instead direct confrontation with the most radical enemies of the regime. The violent outcome of the early twentieth century was inscribed in the myths of the ruling house.

Rather than accommodating the monarchy to the demands for a civic nation, Russian emperors, beginning with the reign of Nicholas I (1825–55), redefined the concept of nation to make it a mythical attribute of the monarch. Their scenarios dealt with the challenge of nationalism by conflating the nation with the monarchy and the empire. Official doctrine played on the ambiguous meaning of the Russian word *narod*, which connotes both the Russian people in its broadest, democratic sense and the nation as a collective political entity. The monarchy seized on the concept of *narodnost'*, the translation for the French *nationalité*, which was coming into usage in literary circles at the time, to designate the distinctive historical spirit that informed both Russian institutions and the Russian people.[24] "Official nationality" defined the Westernized empire as national and thus distinguished it from Europe, which had been corrupted by the influence of the French Revolution.[25]

After 1825 nationality was identified with absolutism, "autocracy" in the official lexicon. Russian nationality was presented as a nationality of consensual subordination, in contrast to egalitarian Western concepts. The monarchical narrative of nation described the Russian people as voluntarily surrendering power to their Westernized rulers. The tale of the invitation of Varangians by the town of Novgorod in 862 became the paradigm for the Russian political order, establishing the people's propensity to obey rulers from afar. Immediately after Nicholas I's accession in 1825, imperial manifestoes attributed the failure of the Decembrist uprising to the distinctive spirit of the Russian people, who remained devoted to their tsars. At Nicholas I's coronation in 1826, the "people," "*narod*" became for the first time an active participant in the Kremlin ceremonies. At the close of the coronation rites, Nicholas, returning in full regalia to the palace, stopped on the landing of the Red Staircase and bowed three times to the people gathered

---

Knox, *German Nationalism and the European Response, 1890–1945* (Norman, Okla., 1985), 13–41.

[24] On the meanings of *narodnost'*, see Maureen Perrie, "*Narodnost'*: Notions of National Identity," in Catriona Kelly and David Shepherd, eds., *Constructing Russian Culture in the Age of Revolution: 1881–1940* (Oxford, 1998), 28–32; Nathaniel Knight, "Ethnicity, Nationality, and the Masses: *Narodnost'* and Modernity in Pre-Emanciption Russia," in David Hoffman and Yanni Kotsonis, eds., *Russian Modernity* (London, 1999).

[25] See Volume 1: 379–81. On the western intellectual roots of the doctrine, see Andrei Zorin, "Ideologiia 'Pravoslaviia-Samoderzhaviia-Narodnosti': Opyt rekonstruktsii," *Novoe Literaturnoe Obozrenie* 26 (1996): 71–104.

on Kremlin square. The bow was an initial sign of mutual recognition between tsar and people, expressing an unspoken bond of devotion. Later in the century, the triple bow came to be regarded as an "ancient tradition" distinctive to Russia, expressing the popular and personal character of the monarchy.

Writers and officials in subsequent years systematized these ideas. The empire, in these statements, was portrayed as the Russian people writ large, worshiping their tsar. One of the spokesmen of "official nationality," the historian Michael Pogodin, wrote, "Occupying an expanse that no monarchy on earth has attained, not the Macedonian, the Roman, the Arab, the French, the Mongol, [Russia, *Rossiia*] is settled predominantly by tribes that speak one language, have consequently one form of thought, practice one Faith, and, like an electric circuit, react suddenly to a single contact."[26]

The refashioning of the presentation of the monarchical nation is a central theme of this volume. After 1855, the principal subject of Russian imperial representation shifts from the bonding of monarch and elite to showing the bonding of the monarch and the Russian people. Part 1 deals with Alexander II's presentation of an affectionate bond, based on benevolence and gratitude, as a way to preserve the European myth and the structure of "official nationality." Part 2 analyzes the propagation of a national myth during the reign of Alexander III when imperial presentations strove to display an ethnic and spiritual bond between a Russian tsar and the Russian people. Part 3 treats the reign of Nicholas II in terms of his quest for his own embodiment of the national myth in the face of broad political opposition and the development of modern forms of publicity and representation.

The elevation of the monarch as a figure enjoying a form of popular mandate required new forms of ceremony and imagery to appeal to an expanding public. Beginning with the reign of Alexander II, the enthusiasm of crowds hailing the tsar was taken by journalists, foreign and Russian, as well as by the tsar and his entourage, as a reliable indication that Russian monarchs rivaled or surpassed their European counterparts in popular devotion.[27] After the emancipation of the serfs in 1861, the peasants more frequently appeared as participants in imperial ceremonies to show the democratic character of the monarchical nation and the progress toward civic equality. From 1909 to 1913 the jubilees of Poltava and Borodino, and the election of Michael Romanov, increased the magnitude and changed the nature of imperial celebrations. These were mass gatherings, rivaling or exceeding in numbers the coronation celebrations, that allowed the tsar to make direct contact with the people. Nicholas II viewed them as a symbolic mandate

---

[26] M. P. Pogodin, *Istoriko-kriticheskie otryvki* (Moscow, 1846), 2; P. Miliukov, *Glavnye techeniia russkoi istoricheskoi mysli* (Moscow, 1898), 1:365.

[27] A Japanese journalist seeking models for imperial appearances in Japan observed, in 1889, that European people greeted their monarchs or presidents when they approached. "All wave their hats, wave their handkerchiefs and shout a congratulatory 'hooray' [English in original] in unison" (Fujitani, *Splendid Monarchy*, 165).

more indicative of the people's feelings than the electoral mandate of the Duma.

The incorporation of large numbers of peasants into the presentations of the monarchy revealed the incongruities of using the imperial myth to govern a mass society. The problem of organizing such ceremonies while protecting the security of the members of the imperial family often led to extreme and conspicuous police measures that belied the claims of popularity. The peasants' responses were often orchestrated. Their perceptions of such events are difficult or impossible to measure. The great majority lived outside the ambit of imperial ceremonies. Historical works have suggested that the peasants thought of the tsar in terms of unchanging symbols, as the little father (*batiushka-tsar'*), and that such "peasant monarchism" declined under the influence of the economic and political changes of the early twentieth century.[28] This study is concerned not with peasant mentalities but with peasants as representations in imperial scenarios that the tsars believed were characteristic of the Russian peasantry as a whole.

In the late nineteenth and early twentieth centuries, the growth of literacy and the development of a mass-circulation press, led the monarchy to make increasing use of the media of modern publicity. By 1914, urban literacy had reached 45 percent. Rural literacy had also risen, to about 25 percent. But literacy was higher in areas near industrial cities, such as Moscow Province where it was over 70 percent. By World War I, 68 percent of army recruits were literate. Circulation of newspapers and books rose rapidly, especially after the reform of the censorship laws in 1906. Newspapers and particularly books began to reach the villages, where peasants would sit in groups listening to a reader, frequently an adolescent boy.[29]

---

[28] On the phenomenon of "peasant monarchism," see Daniel Field, *Rebels in the Name of the Tsar* (Boston, 1976); and Terence Emmons, "The Peasant and the Emancipation," in Wayne Vucinich, ed., *The Peasant in Nineteenth-Century Russia* (Stanford, 1968), 41–71. On peasant utopias, see K. V. Chistov, *Russkie sotsial'no-utopicheskie legendy XVII–XIXvv.* (Moscow, 1967); and Maurine Perrie, *The Image of Ivan IV in Russian Folklore* (Cambridge, 1987). Jeffrey Brooks argues on the basis of popular literature that the peasants in the early twentieth century increasingly sought their national identity in the empire, in various forms of superiority to other nationalities, rather than in allegiance to tsar and orthodoxy (Jeffrey Brooks, *When Russia Learned to Read: Literacy and Popular Literature, 1861–1917* (Princeton, N.J., 1985), 241–45.

[29] On urban literacy, see Gregory Guroff and S. Frederick Starr, "A Note on Urban Literacy in Russia, 1890–1914," *Jahrbücher für Geschichte Osteuropas* 19 (1971): 520–31. On rural literacy, see Brooks, *When Russia Learned to Read*, 3–4, and passim. The figures show great increases in numbers of newspapers and in circulation, but the various statistics are inconsistent in terms of specific numbers for the most important newspapers (Caspar Ferenczi, "Freedom of the Press under the Old Regime, 1905–1914," in Olga Crisp and Linda Edmondson, eds., *Civil Rights in Imperial Russia* [Oxford, 1989], 205–7; Louise McReynolds, *The News under Russia's Old Regime: The Development of a Mass Circulation Press* [Princeton, N.J., 1991], Appendix A; and Charles A. Ruud, *Russian Entrepreneur: Publisher Ivan Sytin of Moscow, 1851–1934* [Montreal, 1990], 41, 88, 106, 114, 127). On the censorship law of 1906, see

The press and popular books were used to spread the image of the tsar to the population and to demonstrate the people's support for Nicholas's rule. Newspapers, both official and commercial, brought knowledge of imperial ceremonies and the tsar's person into the everyday lives of the people. But modern publicity could also be detrimental to the monarchy. Not only was it harder for the government to control the content of proliferating newspapers, but the greater variety of newsworthy items and celebrities diminished the relative space devoted to the imperial family. After 1905 Nicholas used the press to compete with the Duma and the political parties for the people's allegiance. For the first time a Russian tsar descended into open political struggle and sacrificed the epic distance that had elevated imperial power. Seeking to defend his autocratic prerogatives, Nicholas alienated traditional supporters of the monarchy, as well as those promoting the new institutions, and jeopardized the sacrosanct image of tsar.

Charles Ruud, *Fighting Words: Imperial Censorship and the Russian Press, 1804–1906* (Toronto, 1982), 207–26; and Ferenczi, "Freedom of the Press," 191–205.

PART ONE

Alexander II and the
Scenario of Love

CHAPTER ONE

The Emergence of the Scenario

Just as our Dear lamented Parent devoted all His Efforts, all the hours
of His life, to labors and cares for the welfare of His subjects, so We . . .
take the sacred vow to have as a single goal the well-being of Our Fatherland. Guided and protected by Providence, which has called us to this
Great service, may we establish Russia at the highest level of might and
glory, and may we realize the constant wishes and intentions of Our
August forbears, Peter, Catherine, Alexander the Blessed, and our
Unforgettable Parent.

—*Manifesto on the Accession of Emperor Alexander II,*
February 18, 1855

ACCESSION

As heir, Alexander Nikolaevich grew up a worshipful and obedient son. He
regarded Nicholas I as the embodiment of the Russian state and tried to
meet his father's high expectations. He fully shared Nicholas's military predilections and delighted in beautiful uniforms, fancy drill, and the spectacle of
the drill field. He was thrilled to learn of his appointment as flügel-adjutant
in his father's suite before his sixteenth birthday. On his wedding day in
1841 he was named to the State Council. At the birth of his first son, Grand
Duke Nicholas Aleksandrovich, in 1843, his father proudly honored him
with the braid of general-adjutant in the imperial suite. Nicholas also appointed him to high state offices. He served on the Committee of Ministers
and other important governmental committees, several of which dealt with
the problem of serfdom. In all these capacities, he remained a submissive
lieutenant, faithfully expressing his father's views.[1]

Alexander was the first heir to play a prominent role in his father's scenario. He symbolized the triumph of the principle of dynastic succession,
the possibility of the first untroubled father-son succession since the mid-
seventeenth century. From the beginning of Nicholas I's reign, public presentations identified the son's devotion to autocracy with his devotion to his
father. This bond became enshrined in a new ceremony of the oath, introduced by Nicholas in 1834 on his son's sixteenth birthday.

---

[1] For a detailed discussion of Alexander II as tsarevich, see Volume 1: 343–78.

But playing the son also set Alexander apart from the intimidating image of his father. Nicholas's displays of power presented the emperor as paterfamilias. The family appeared in his scenario as an epitome of the nation, the heir and empress cast in the passive roles of objects of the people's love. While the emperor's visage evoked awe and submission, the heir and empress excelled at the arts of endearment. During Alexander's eight-month tour of Russia, including Siberia in 1834, he had been received jubilantly as the "hope" of Russia. Vasilii Zhukovskii, who accompanied him, described it as an "all-national betrothal with Russia."[2] Alexander had been moved by the enthusiastic reception, betraying a susceptibility to public acclaim quite uncharacteristic of his predecessors on the throne—his father, Nicholas I, or his uncle, Alexander I.

Alexander's education imbued him with the tenets of the doctrine of official nationality. He believed in autocracy's historic mission and the Russian people's devotion to their Westernized rulers. He conducted himself as a member of European royalty and took on the tastes and manner of the many young German princes who were his comrades. His tutors carried on the eighteenth-century faith in the education of the heir as a means to wise and beneficial rule. They gave him an education of the sentiments, trying to make of him a "human being" who had sympathy for the sufferings of others. He came to see himself as a national leader, who had to win the sentiments of his people by taking their needs and feelings into account. When military defeat undermined the rationale of Nicholaean absolutism, Alexander II increasingly presented this image in the ceremonial mode of official nationality. It was an image of autocrat as beloved national ruler that both made possible his acceptance of reforms and established their limits.

•

Alexander's scenario emerged under the impetus of military defeat. When he ascended the throne in February, 1855, Russia was in the midst of a losing war against Turkey, France, and Great Britain, with a large Austrian army threatening intervention from the West. Russia's weapons were outmoded, the army was short of ammunition and the Black Sea fleet was unequipped to engage new British and French steamships of war. When the allies staged a landing in the Crimea, in September 1854, Russia found itself diplomatically isolated and facing defeat on its own territory.[3] The presentation of the Russian monarch as the exemplar and invincible defender of Western monarchy crumbled with growing evidence of incompetence, corruption, and backwardness.

---

[2] S. S. Tatishchev, *Imperator Aleksandr II, ego zhizn' i tsarstvovanie* (St. Petersburg, 1903), 1:89.

[3] William C. Fuller Jr., *Strategy and Power in Russia, 1600–1914* (New York, 1992), 259–64; W. Bruce Lincoln, *Nicholas I: Emperor and Autocrat of All the Russias* (Bloomington, Ind., 1978), 343–47; Jacob W. Kipp, "The Russian Navy and Technological Transfer," in Ben Eklof,

The news of the initial reversals and the revelations of the corruption and bureaucratic incompetence set in motion a dynamic of symbolic change. In the last months of Nicholas's reign, memorandums began to circulate in the administration that opened a dialogue about the meaning of the official nationality doctrine. The historian, Michael Pogodin, an adherent and ex-postulator of that doctrine, now challenged one of its basic contentions, which he himself had previously elaborated: that Russia's domination of Western Europe was a sign of the nation's strength and the tsar's unity with his people. Pogodin now blamed Russia's meddling in European affairs for the neglect of Russia's internal problems. He condemned Russian foreign policy as a betrayal of the national spirit, brought about by the manipulation of European powers, leading Russia to do their dirty work and crush revolution in the West. Russia, Pogodin contended, had been historically free from violence, conflict, and insurgency. He called for attention to internal needs—the press, education, the economic condition of the peasantry. He appealed for openness of expression, *glasnost'*, that would allow the emperor to penetrate a bureaucracy that shielded him from the truth. Pogodin's observations met with general approval in St. Petersburg, even from Alexander himself.[4]

But in the first year of his reign, Alexander found it difficult to break with his father's memory and image of power. The accession manifesto, cited above, asserted that he would follow the "intentions of his August forbears." His father loomed particularly important. In his case, the phrase "Our unforgettable father" (*Nezabvennyi Nash Roditel'*) was more than a convention. He was unable to separate the office of emperor in his mind from his father's memory. He found it painful to hear himself addressed as "sovereign" (*gosudar'*).[5] When he appeared before the State Council to formalize his accession, on the day after his father's death, he could not contain his tears. He spoke of Nicholas as the source of his strength and recalled their final conversation. Nicholas had told him that he was turning over his command, but not in the good order he had wished, and had left him "many labors and cares."[6]

On February 20 Alexander received the members of the diplomatic corps and announced his decision to continue the war. The addresses delivered on subsequent days to the guards' officers, the cadets corps, and to military schools dwelled on his love of the late tsar and ended in tearful embraces.[7] In the months following Nicholas's death, obituaries and elaborate obsequies carried on the tradition of glorifying a deceased monarch that Nicholas him-

John Bushnell, and Larissa Zakharova, eds., *Russia's Great Reforms, 1855–1881* (Bloomington, Ind., 1994), 115–17.

[4] M. P. Pogodin, *Sochineniia* (Moscow, 1874), 4:251–69, 286–87, 312–13; A. A. Kornilov, *Obshchestvennoe dvizhenie pri Aleksandre I* (Paris, 1905), 4–8.

[5] Anna Fedorovna Tiutcheva, *Pri dvore dvukh imperatorov. Vospominaniia, dnevnik, 1853–1882* (Moscow, 1928–29), 1:186.

[6] Tatishchev, *Imperator Aleksandr II*, 1:139–41.

[7] Ibid., 1:145–46; Kn. A. P. Vadbol'skii, "Iz vospominanii byvshego gvardeiskogo ofitsera," *Russkaia Starina* 114 (June 1903): 545.

self had initiated after his accession. Nicholas's funeral procession from the Winter Palace to the imperial burial site, the Peter-Paul Cathedral, was described in the press and an elaborate *Opisanie* (Description), with a supplement depicting each figure in the procession, individually in silhouette.[8]

At first, Alexander retained Nicholas's ministers and undertook no departures from his policies. He continued to appear in the braid of adjutant of his father's suite and, to the astonishment of his servitors, wore it to the memorial service on the first anniversary of Nicholas's death. Alexander seemed to be mainly preoccupied with introducing new, more fancy and colorful uniforms for the armed forces. Indeed, nearly one-quarter of the decrees addressed to the War Ministry in the year of accession, while Russia was fighting a war, were devoted to changes in uniform.[9] Officials were incredulous that in the midst of military and fiscal crisis, the War Ministry was expending enormous sums and energies to introduce uniforms that would suit the emperor's taste.[10] If the image of Nicholas I in 1825 and 1826 was one of ruthless confidence to preserve the autocracy, Alexander betrayed humility and self-doubt; he constantly spoke of the need for the higher authority of his father to guide him at the moment of crisis. Rather than standing above and intimidating his servitors, he shared common human emotions with them. Such a manner hardly impressed noblemen used to an aura of certain and intimidating authority. Many officers sneered at him as an "old woman" and thought him too gentle and yielding to direct a consistent policy.[11] Writers and intellectuals had the same misgivings. The historian Boris Chicherin wrote that Alexander II had neither the "enchanting manner of Alexander I" nor the "outward majesty of Nicholas I." "Mild, kind, understanding, inspired by the best intentions, he trusted neither himself nor others, and so was unable to win anyone's attachment."[12]

Alexander was tall and handsome and his figure graceful, but his mannerisms betrayed weakness to those accustomed to an authoritarian presence. The eyes of a sovereign disclosed his authority to his servitors. Nicholas eyes were prepossessing and daunting. Alexander's gaze called out for pity and help. "A calf's eyes," Chicherin remarked. The Kamer-Fraulein Anna Tiutcheva wrote, "The eyes are large and blue but the gaze is uninspiring." The diplomat Prince Nicholas Orlov declared that he had not feared to speak his

---

[8] See Volume 1: 272, 413–17.

[9] P. A. Zaionchkovskii, "Vyshee voennoe upravlenie. Imperator i tsarstvuiushchii dom," in L. G. Zakharova, Iu. S. Kukushkin, and T. Emmons, eds., *P. A. Zaionchkovskii, 1904–1983 gg. Stat'i, publikatsii i vospominaniia o nem* (Moscow, 1998), 87.

[10] D. A. Obolenskii, *Dnevnik*, BAR, Folder 1: 51–53; Folder 2: 4.

[11] Friedrich Diestelmeier, *Soziale Angst; konservative Reaktionen auf liberale Reformpolitik in Russland unter Alexander II (1855–1866)* (Frankfurt am Main, 1985), 97–98; F. Latynin, in his memoirs, recalled how the cadets liked Alexander for his kindness to them but felt "none of the child's worship for Nicholas Pavlovich." They "treated him freely without the respectful fear" they had shown Nicholas, who "had forced one willy-nilly to cherish every kind paternal word" (F. Latyninin, "Otrvyochnye vospominaniia," *Istoricheskii Vestnik* [June 1909]: 831).

[12] B. P. Chicherin, *Vospominaniia: Moskovskii Universitet* (Moscow, 1929), 131.

mind with Nicholas, who might become angry, but would not hold it against him. But before Alexander II, "words die on my tongue, when he fixes on me his dull, lifeless gaze, as if he isn't hearing what I am saying."[13]

To make matters worse, Alexander began his reign with a relaxation of court etiquette that was perceived even by reform-minded members of the court as a dangerous weakening of his authority. He reduced the period of lying in state and the period of mourning from six weeks to three. This change followed Nicholas's own instructions, but it seemed part of a general disregard of the rules of etiquette in the opening months of Alexander's reign. Anna Tiutcheva wrote, "The prestige of authority to a large degree is sustained by the etiquette and ceremonial surrounding it, which has a strong impact on the imagination of the masses. It is dangerous to deprive authority of this aura." The shortening of the period of lying in state made it impossible for subjects from the outlying areas of the empire to pay final respects. "Such manifestation of feelings served as a powerful bond between the tsar and his subjects."[14] Dmitrii Obolenskii, a young reform-minded jurist serving under Constantine Nikolaevich in the Naval Ministry, deplored the breakdown of the forms that he believed preserved the court from impropriety. With such changes, he noted in his diary in November 1855, "all those charms (prestige) with which power should surround itself are destroyed." Scandals then became known to the public, and respect for the principles the court represented disappeared.[15]

But Alexander's statements and policies in the first year of his reign suggested his new style of rule. His accession manifesto failed to list his grandfather, Emperor Paul I, who had been exalted in the last years of Nicholas's reign as the exemplar of the dynasty. The manifesto mentioned Catherine the Great, whom Nicholas had despised for her liberalism, morals, and treatment of Paul and whose name he banned from governmental decrees.[16] Although Alexander seemed indifferent to reform, he began to permit a freer, more open atmosphere. Memorandums and plans for reform circulated in society and the bureaucracy and reached the emperor's desk. Pogodin, in May 1855, called upon Alexander, who had been "met with such love," to pronounce "the great word," and summon a Duma, which would bring the Russian people to life. "[The people] will certainly be resurrected, will rise like one person, throw off the shackles of their hereditary and acquired vices. They will be ready for all sacrifices and will abandon petty calculations." Constantine Aksakov's memorandum calling for freedom of speech and an Assembly of the Land came to Alexander's attention.[17]

---

[13] Ibid.; Tiutcheva, *Pri dvore dvukh imperatorov,* 1:82; E. M. Feoktistov, *Vospominaniia E. M. Feoktistova; za kulisami politiki i literatury* (Leningrad, 1927), 217–18.

[14] Tiutcheva, *Pri dvore dvukh imperatorov,* 1:188. The entry is from February 20, 1855.

[15] Obolenskii, *Dnevnik,* Folder 1: 123.

[16] Ibid., Folder 5: 269.

[17] Pogodin, *Sochineniia,* 4:314–17; Kornilov, *Obshchestvennoe dvizhenie pri Aleksandre I,* 21–23.

Controls on the press slowly loosened and periodicals other than *Russkii Invalid* were permitted to print dispatches from the front. In December 1855 Alexander closed the Supreme Censorship Committee, established by his father, and accepted the view of Baron Modest Korf that its extreme measures resulted only in the clandestine circulation of works in manuscript. Leading figures in educated society were allowed to found journals and express their views in print. The Westernizer Michael Katkov received permission to open *Russkii Vestnik*, a journal proposing a broad consideration of the problems of state. The Slavophiles, among them Iurii Samarin, Alexei Khomiakov, and Ivan Aksakov, who had been regarded as subversive under Nicholas I, founded a new journal, *Russkaia Beseda*. Nicholas's ban on foreign travel and the high fees for passports were abolished. Other measures lifted controls over the universities and ended policies of forcible recruitment of Old Believers and Jews into the army.[18]

The progressive deterioration of the military situation induced Alexander increasingly to assume an image of leader of the people that would sustain his pretensions as national monarch. His upbringing had trained him for the role of popular monarch who could mobilize the population in support of autocracy. Like his predecessors, Alexander emulated the model of his chief international rival, in his case Emperor Napoleon III, whom Pogodin described in 1856 as "the leading person in Europe." Napoleon III had risen to the throne by rallying popular support on tours through France. In preparation for the plebiscite confirming the restoration of the empire, he was greeted by organized demonstrations where the people shouted "Vive l'Empereur! Vive Napoléon III!" He had been elected "emperor of the French," "the emperor of the people";[19] Alexander II had no intention of conducting elections or a plebiscite, but the French emperor provided a model of a monarch who was able to rally popular support. Such an example could be used to call upon the Russian people's devotion to their Westernized sovereign without challenging his prerogatives.

The symbolic rupture between reigns took place despite Alexander's reverence for the principle of dynasty and his powerful emotional attachment to his father. He presented himself in a scenario that claimed fidelity to Nicholas's principles at the same time as it repudiated the entire basis of Nicholaean authoritarianism. Alexander strove to adapt a form of popular, national leadership to the Russian mythic tradition and to encompass the people in the monologic universe of imperial ceremony. The people would give their assent to the monarch in explosions of enthusiasm, whether staged or spontaneous. The trope of love, likening monarchy to a romance between monarch and people, would show the national character of the empire. It

[18] Kornilov, *Obshchestvennoe dvizhenie*, 14; L. G. Zakharova, "Alexander II," in *Rossiiskie samoderzhtsy, 1801–1917* (Moscow, 1994), 178–79.

[19] J. M. Thompson, *Louis Napoleon and the Second Empire* (New York, 1983), 111, 135–38; James F. McMillan, *Napoleon III* (London, 1991), 43, 50–51; Pogodin, *Sochineniia*, 4:357.

would indicate that the Russian emperor could win popular support without granting the constitutional reforms instituted in Prussia.

To renew the sense of rapport with the people that he had experienced on his journey in 1837, Alexander embarked on a ceremonial trip through the empire. In September and October 1855 he traveled to Moscow, New Russia, and the Crimea. His visit to Moscow was staged as a repeat performance of Alexander I's dramatic appearance after Napoleon's invasion. But the reenactment of 1812 took place under the shadow of irreversible defeat, after the fall of the fortress of Sevastopol. The enthusiastic reception of Moscow consoled him. He wrote to Prince I. F. Paskevich, "In the midst of these painful circumstances, it was a joy to my heart to meet such a warm and sincere reception."[20]

The reports of Alexander's trip to the south emphasized the feelings of cordial and mutual devotion between tsar and people. The semiofficial *Severnaia Pchela* couched its accounts in the rhetoric of personal devotion and religious reverence. In Odessa and Kherson the troops greeted him with rapture (*vostorg*). When he ventured closer to the front, the soldiers, the report tells us, stopped his carriage, kissed his hands and feet. The cries of the troops "reached the soul of the TSAR. They caressed his soul and repaid the August Voyager for his labors and cares." When Alexander stood at the bedside of soldiers in a military hospital in Nikolaev, the correspondent A. Garainov reported that the injured soldiers responded with tender pity (*umilenie*), another expression of deep feelings of love for and religious devotion to the tsar.[21]

The report maintained an elevated tone of worship, alternating between ecstasy in the presence of the tsar (*vostorg*) and tender sympathy for him (*umilenie*). Garainov invoked a parental metaphor but presented Alexander as a kindly rather than wrathful father. He was the parent (*praroditel'*) who "comforts his sons, and they crowd around him to catch every glance and every word. Father!"[22] Comparing Alexander as popular monarch to Napoleon III, Garainov concluded that not only Alexander but all Russian monarchs showed greater concern for their people. The French emperor Louis Napoleon, he wrote, had promised to go to the front but instead had indulged himself in celebrations. He sat above the nation, exhausting the treasury for his own whims, while the Russian tsars steered the helm of government. The upbringing of the Romanov tsars had trained them to feel responsibility for their subjects. Alexander had showed his concern for the people and spirit of self-sacrifice by visiting the front.[23]

[20] Tatishchev, *Imperator Aleksandr II*, 1:161–62; "Lettres de Th. I. Tjutsheff a sa seconde épouse née Baronne de Pfeffel," *Starina i Novizna* 19 (1915): 146.

[21] A. Garainov, *O vysochaishem puteshestvii i neskol'ko slov o poleznykh sobytiiakh* (St. Petersburg, 1855), 7–8. This pamphlet was a reprint of articles in *Severnaia Pchela*; Tatishchev, *Imperator Aleksandr II*, 1:168–70.

[22] Garainov, *O vysochaishem puteshestvii*, 8.

[23] Ibid., 10.

To the satisfaction of the public, Alexander replaced Nicholas's favorite General Peter Kleinmichel, who was held generally responsible for the breakdown of war supply and organization. But this scarcely affected the course of the war. Despite the seemingly hopeless situation in the Crimea, and Austria's threat to enter on the side of England and France, he remained determined to fight on. His visit to the armies in the Crimea only strengthened this resolve. He helped to formulate campaign plans and expected that disorders among the French lower classes would force France to withdraw from the conflict. He confidently rejected terms proposed by the allies. It was only after Austria gave an ultimatum and even Prussia hinted at intervention that Alexander relented. Nicholas's most trusted advisers, Count P. D. Kiselev, Count K. V. Nesselrode, Count M. S. Vorontsov, and Count A. F. Orlov pointed out that the situation could only deteriorate. In March 1856 Alexander signed the Treaty of Paris. He agreed to the neutralization of the Black Sea and the cession of Southern Bessarabia, acquired in 1812. This deprived Russia of control of the mouth of the Danube. Many figures in the government and the liberal intelligentsia considered the concessions excessive. Though he had no other choice but to sign the treaty, Alexander regarded it as a personal humiliation.[24]

•

The Crimean defeat and the Treaty of Paris irreversibly altered the relationship between Russian monarchy and its European counterparts. Rather than the dominant military force in Europe, the Russian empire had been proved wanting in the organization and technology of warfare. Massive and elaborate parades suggested armed might and irresistible authority but were also diversions from the more serious tasks of government and military strength. On April 29, 1856, Prince Obolenskii, while watching the May Day parade on Mars Field in Petersburg, noted in his diary:

> In the old days, the sight of a huge mass of an army at its most brilliant conquered the imagination and seemed the incarnation and guarantee of the power and invincibility of Russia. Now this specter has vanished and the crowd of armed men saddens the heart with the memory of catastrophes that have befallen us. I wanted this Field of Mars, upon which our army spent all its military prowess, to be covered with buildings so that it could never again be the scene of a parade.[25]

The decisiveness of the defeat forced Alexander II to separate his image from his father's and to proceed with the elaboration of his own scenario of power, a scenario that sought to evoke love. He chose to emulate Western rulers who earned the love of their peoples by working for their benefit. He

---

[24] W. E. Mosse, *The Rise and Fall of the Crimean System, 1855–71* (London, 1963), 19–33; E. S. Shumigorskii, "Iz zapisnoi knizhki istorika," *Istoricheski Vestnik*, no. 138 (November 1914): 629.

[25] Obolenskii, *Dnevnik*, Folder 2: 24–25.

declared his intentions in his Manifesto of March 19, 1856, on the signing of the Treaty of Paris. With the words, "May each, under the canopy of laws equally just for all, equally protective of all, enjoy the fruits of honest labor in peace," Alexander augured a departure from the principle of tightened administrative surveillance, the nostrum for governmental problems during the previous three reigns.[26] The manifesto announced the beginning of the reform era, when the monarch in the interests of his people, would try to change the social, institutional, and legal bases of his power.

The scenario of love adapted the concepts of official nationality to a program of reform. The Russian people's devotion to their sovereigns expressed not only their immemorial subservience to authority, but their love and gratitude for the benefactions bestowed by their rulers. The scenario described a relationship that permitted social and institutional change to take place peacefully under an absolute monarchy, without the divisive conflicts associated with Europe. The bonds of sympathy, the shared lot of the Crimean disaster, now replaced the bonds of awe and devotion of Nicholas's reign.

In foreign policy, too, Alexander appeared as an exemplar of sympathy and conciliation. The new policy was announced with the appointment of Alexander Gorchakov, in April 1856, to the position of foreign minister. The appointment of a diplomat with a Russian name to the position held by Carl von Nesselrode for forty years was itself regarded as a sympathetic gesture to the Russian nation, even if Gorchakov spoke little Russian. Gorchakov announced, "The emperor wishes to live in good harmony with all governments." Alexander, he declared, had decided to devote himself to the well-being of his subjects and "concentrate on the development of the internal means of the country." He continued with his famous words, "They say that Russia sulks. Russia does not sulk. Russia is collecting herself" ("La russie se recueille").[27]

The policy known as "recueillement"—collecting or composing oneself—went along with accueil, a manner of graciousness and amicability. Gorchakov strove, by diplomatic means, to change the restrictions imposed by the Treaty of Paris. He was not averse to supporting nationalist designs in Europe, especially if they came at the expense of Austria. This began with overtures to Prussia, but Gorchakov looked first of all to France for help in undoing the territorial concessions the treaty had made to Austria. Under Napoleon III, France no longer represented a revolutionary menace and seemed a likely ally against Russia's territorial rivals—Austria in the West, England in the East. The rapprochement was marked by the dispatch of Count Morny, Napoleon III's illegitimate half-brother and closest adviser. Alexander declared that the war showed "the mutual sympathies of both peoples for each other and mutual respect of both armies." Appointing Count Kiselev, the eminent former minister of state lands, and calling for

[26] PSZ, 30273, March 19, 1856.
[27] Tatishchev, Imperator Aleksandr II, 1:227–29; V. O. Kliuchevskii, Sochineniia (Moscow, 1958), 5:381–82.

harmony (*soglasie*) between the nations, he insisted that "this was the policy of my father." He claimed that Nicholas had great sympathy for Napoleon III and had welcomed his coup.[28] Morny attended Alexander's coronation as a special envoy of France and was made the center of attention by the Russian officialdom and press.

Rumors of reform began to spread in March 1856. On March 30, 1856, during a brief visit to Moscow, Alexander gave a speech to the marshals of the Moscow nobility pronouncing serfdom an evil. He uttered his famous words that it would be better if emancipation of the serfs "came from above, than below," and through his minister of the interior, A. I. Levshin, asked the nobility to submit petitions for reform.[29] The jurist and historian Constantine Kavelin wrote to his former mentor, Michael Pogodin, on April 3, 1856, that "love for the tsar grows with each day," but he indicated that everyone still feared for the future. "I confess to you that the kindness and sincerity of the tsar has begun to stir even me, and to attach me to him personally, so that if it continues long this way, I will buy his portrait and hang it in my room. Still one should not hurry. What did Alexander I degenerate into?"[30]

Alexander II indeed seemed to promise a return to the mildness and reform spirit of his uncle's reign. His scenario of love recalls the sentiments that Alexander I had evoked in the first years of his reign.[31] But the scenarios presenting the displays of public affection expressed divergent conceptions of the relationship between the sovereign and his subjects. Alexander I's charm and beauty exalted him above ordinary mortals, distancing him as an elusive, angelic figure who awakened affections but could not be approached. He was a figurine who avoided public displays of approval or love from his subjects. Alexander I's reform efforts went on in secret, whereas Alexander II opened them to public involvement and scrutiny. Alexander I played the role of enlightened despot, Alexander II of national leader.

On his thirty-eighth birthday, April 17, 1856, Alexander replaced other ministers remaining from his father's reign and issued a manifesto setting the date of his coronation. The war having been concluded with a beneficent peace, the manifesto declared, his intention became "according to the example of the pious tsars, our forbears," to "crown myself, and receive the proper anointment." Whereas Nicholas I's coronation manifesto expressed retribution and the consecration of order, Alexander's announced a humanitarian ideal. "May the All-Powerful help us, with the taking of the crown, to take a vow before the entire world to live only for the happiness of the peoples under our authority, and with the inspiration of His Most Holy Life-

[28] Tatishchev, *Imperator Aleksandr II*, 1:231–34; Barbara Jelavich, *St. Petersburg and Moscow: Tsarist and Soviet Foreign Policy* (Bloomington, Ind., 1974), 133–35.

[29] Tatishchev, *Imperator Alexander II*, 1:302.

[30] N. Barsukov, *Zhizn' i trudy M. P. Pogodina* (St. Petersburg, 1900), 14:217.

[31] See Volume 1: 193–214.

Giving Spirit may he direct all our thoughts, all our efforts to that end."
The word *happiness* placed Alexander in the tradition of Alexander I, of
dedicating himself to advance his subjects civil and economic well-being. In
the following weeks the government introduced measures further relaxing
censorship restrictions, eliminating admission quotas to the universities, and
establishing government stipends for students to study abroad.[32]

The coronation manifesto referred to the happiness of the *peoples* under
the emperor's authority, indicating that he had in mind all the nationalities
in the empire. In this way, the scenario of love identified the Russian nation
(*Rus'*) with the empire (*Rossiia*) uniting all in a bond of affection with the
emperor who worked for the benefit of all. On his trips in the spring of 1856
Alexander brought the elites of Finland, Poland, and the Baltic provinces
into his scenario.[33] His visits to the Baltic cities were occasions to reaffirm ties
with the Baltic nobility, *Ritterschaft*, who dominated the local government of
the Baltic provinces and sought confirmation of the special privileges granted
by Peter the Great. He received an especially warm reception from the nobility and townspeople of Riga, much as Catherine the Great and Alexander I
had after their accessions.[34] Reports in the Riga newspapers, reprinted in the
German edition of *Sankt-Peterburgskie Vedomosti* and in *Russkii Khudozhestvennyi Listok*, explained the cordiality of the reception as an expression
of personal sentiment. The articles emphasized the outpouring of love from
all parts of the population. "Feelings of reverence poured forth in the cur-
rents of love that surrounded the monarch during his visit." The elaborate
decorations, flowers, and flags were signs of personal feeling. "The lowliest
pauper in the most distant shack" expressed his love with an ornament near
the candle he lit for the emperor. *Russkii Khudozhestvennyi Listok* carried
illustrations of several receptions in Riga and a full-page print showed the
emperor's entry to the city (fig. 1).[35]

CORONATION

The Russian imperial coronation culminated the inaugural events of each
reign. The emperor acceded to the throne on his predecessor's death and
received the oaths from the civil authorities and heads of the military. The
coronation gave the emperor's power the consecration of the Orthodox
Church. The lavish celebrations made it clear that the monarch had taken
on the secular attributes of Russian rulers. It remained the central ceremonial

---

[32] Tatishchev, *Imperator Alexander II*, 1:209–10.

[33] Ibid., 1:210–15.

[34] Ibid., 1:215; MVMDRV, May 31, 1856, 576; June 2, 1856, 576–77; June 5, 1856, 583–
84; June 7, 1856, 592; June 14, 1856, 613; Edward C. Thaden, *Russia's Western Borderlands,
1710–1870* (Princeton, N.J., 1984), 170; Edward C. Thaden, ed., *Russification in the Baltic
Provinces and Finland, 1855–1914* (Princeton, N.J., 1981), 23, 34, 124.

[35] *Russkii Khudozhevennyi Listok*, no. 23 (August 10, 1856): 1–4.

РУССКІЙ ХУДОЖЕСТВЕННЫЙ ЛИСТОКЪ В. ТИММА

1856.   N: 23.

1. *Alexander II's Entry into Riga, May 25, 1856.* Lithograph by Vasilii Timm.
Russkii Khudozhevennyi Listok. Slavic and Baltic Division, New York Public
Library. Astor, Lenox, and Tilden Foundations.

event of Russian monarchy, distinguishing it in this respect from its continental counterparts—Prussia, Austria, and Spain.[36]

The coronation ceremonies consisted of four discrete parts: the procession
from the Kremlin palace to the Assumption Cathedral, the investiture with
the regalia, the liturgy, and the procession in full regalia to the Archangel

---

[36] In Prussia the coronation had little significance and could be foregone. The Habsburg
emperor, after the end of the Holy Roman Empire, was no longer coronated (except as king of
Hungary from 1867).

and Annunciation Cathedrals before the return to the palace. The investiture ceremony was a personal drama that exalted and glorified each monarch. The metropolitan of St. Petersburg and Novgorod conferred the mantle upon the emperor, then handed him the crown, which he placed on his own head. The emperor then received the orb and scepter. He proceeded to place the small crown on the empress, who knelt before him. After the crowning ceremony, he fell to his knees and delivered the prayer of Solomon, a supplication for divine illumination and guidance and vowed to devote himself to his "high service." The entire congregation then knelt, and the metropolitan beseeched God to help the tsar serve Russia. A protodeacon declaimed the full imperial title, enumerating the numerous domains that made up the empire.

The second part of the ceremony, the liturgy, included the anointment and the communion. The anointment in the Russian coronation, unlike in the French, English, and late Byzantine coronations, followed the conferral of regalia and played no role in the consecration of his authority. Rather, it conferred a special, if undefined, grace on the tsar that set him apart from ordinary mortals and approximated him to Christ. The emperor then received communion at the altar with the clergy. But communion was administered to him as if to a lesser member of the clergy, again singling him out as the most holy of laymen but not one ordained to the office of priest.[37]

In the accounts of imperial coronations before 1896 the crowning, with the drama of the emperor's direct address to the Lord, overshadows the liturgy, which showed the tsar's uncertain ecclesiastical status as a member of the Orthodox hierarchy. The emperor was anointed into the clergy yet was legally "head of the church," a title declared explicitly by Paul at his coronation in 1797. Paul saw himself as a highly ranked member of the clergy and even administered communion to himself at the altar during his reign. But his successors took communion at the altar only at the coronation. During the coronations of Catherine the Great and Alexander III, and likely those of Alexander I and Nicholas I, the monarch customarily received communion with the "imperial doors" (tsarskie vraty) open, in view of the congregation, rather than closed as was required of the priesthood. The show of public display revealed the sovereign as the most favored of the lay population rather than as a member of the clergy. The doors were probably open at Alexander II's coronation. The illustrations for the album of Alexander III's coronation include a color plate by I. N. Kramskoi showing the emperor receiving communion before open doors. This practice would end with Nicholas II's coronation in 1896 (see chapter 10).[38]

The coronation ceremony traditionally was an elite event. It took place in the Assumption Cathedral in the Kremlin, the principal see of the Russian

---

[37] For a general discussion of the role of the anointment and the liturgy in conferring "charisma" on Russian monarchs, see B. A. Uspenskii, *Tsar' i patriarkh: kharizma vlasti v Rossii (Vizantiiskaia model' i ee russkoe pereosmyslenie)* (Moscow, 1998), passim, especially 15–29.

[38] Ibid., 151–86.

Orthodox Church, which contained the graves of the first metropolitans of Moscow. The Assumption Cathedral is small, the interior occupying about one-quarter the space of Reims Cathedral or Westminster Abbey. The building, the British correspondent Charles Lowe wrote, "does not at all correspond to the general idea of a cathedral, being rather a superb and exquisitely finished imperial chapel."[39] The Kremlin square, however, permitted a larger audience to experience, if not attend, the ceremony. Lesser dignitaries watched from grandstands erected on the square. A throng of people and guards regiments stood between them and the Red Staircase at the entrance to the palace. Those in the square witnessed the processional to the Assumption Cathedral and heard the bells of the churches and the salvos of cannons at key moments in the ceremony. Then they beheld the imposing recessional, as the tsar, the imperial family, the dignitaries of the court and the state left the cathedral in full regalia and proceeded first to the Archangel Cathedral to pay homage to his ancestors, then to the Annunciation Cathedral. They returned by the Red Staircase to the Palace of Facets.

After the reign of Peter the Great, the ambit of the coronation was extended to include lavish festivities—lasting weeks, sometimes months—before and after the actual rites. The gala entry of the tsar into Moscow, the balls, the audiences, the parades, the people's feast, the fireworks, turned the coronation into a great secular celebration. As well as being a consecration, it was a ritual of union: union between Petersburg and Moscow, between the Westernized elite and the shrines of old Moscow, between the elite and the people. Representatives of national elites were invited in increasing numbers to witness the grandeur and magnificence of the ceremonies and to display to visitors from abroad the extent of the empire and variety of peoples under the emperor's rule.

Nineteenth-century coronation celebrations opened with the emperor's festive entry into the capital. This was a symbolic enactment of Petersburg meeting Moscow, old Russia greeting new Russia, the European elite taking symbolic possession of the old capital. The effect was synergic—a fusion of opposed images of Western splendor and ancient sanctity. The elite Cavalier-Guards regiments led in the court, the emperor on horseback and other members of the imperial family riding in gilded eighteenth-century carriages. Crowds of people lined the streets. Along the way priests blessed the procession, and spectators watched from apartments on Tver Boulevard often rented at considerable cost. The emperor stopped at five points on his route to receive formal greetings from merchants holding prominent positions in the city government, the Moscow marshal, noblemen, officials at the head of the Moscow governmental administration, generals of the Moscow garrison, and the Synod. The procession concluded in the Kremlin, "that shrine and cradle of the Russian state," where the tsar was welcomed and blessed at a prayer service in the Assumption Cathedral.

[39] *The Times of London*, May 28, 1883, 7.

Because of the war, Alexander II's coronation took place eighteen months after accession, the longest period to elapse before crowning since Peter the Great. If Nicholas I's coronation had consecrated the Russian emperor as the incarnation of the principles of legitimacy and absolute authority, Alexander II's presented him as the focus of his subjects' love and hope for the future. Broader publicity in Russian and foreign periodicals sought to bring news of the events to new groups in the population. Detailed accounts appeared in the journals *Russkii Khudozhestvennyi Listok* and *Russkii Vestnik*, and in newspapers such as *Severnaia Pchela* and *Moskovskie Vedomosti*. Vasilii Timm's popular *Russkii Khudozhestvennyi Listok* printed comments of an official character about the ceremony, and lithographs of important moments in the cathedral. Foreign correspondents were welcomed, among them representatives of *L'Independance Belge* and *Le Nord*, organs of the Russian government abroad, but also William Russell, of *The Times of London*, famous for his reports from the Crimea.[40] The descriptions in the Russian periodicals drew heavily from these correspondents' reports, proudly indicating the attention and admiration that the ceremonies had evoked in the West.

The lavish coronation album exemplified the effort to impress Western opinion. It was the largest and most ostentatious of the albums printed to date, an expression of the unity of rulers and aristocracy to whom Alexander sought to appeal at a moment of diplomatic isolation. Four hundred copies were published—two hundred in Russian, two hundred in French—to be given to figures in the court and foreign guests attending the ceremony. The volume was "of such immense size" that the English man of letters Sacherevell Sitwell wrote, "The term *elephant folio* has no meaning, and, indeed, this may be the largest book that ever issued from the printing press."[41]

The Academy of Arts, under the direction of its vice president, Prince G. G. Gagarin, spared no expense in the production of the album, which cost 123,000 rubles and took more than four years to complete. Special large type was cast and Chinese paper imported for the volume. The title was printed in large, old-Church-Slavonic script in gold leaf, red, and black. Alexander personally rejected the editor's proposal to use old-Slavonic script in the text. The album contains fifty-two illustrations, fifteen printed in color lithography at the Paris firm of LeMercier under the close supervision of Gagarin himself. The illustrations gave visual confirmation to the scenario

---

[40] *BE*, 64:184; *Russkii Vestnik* no. 5 (September 1856): 88.

[41] *Opisanie sviashchenneishago koronovaniia Ikh Imperatorskikh Velichestv Gosudaria Imperatora Aleksandra Vtorago i Imperatritsy Marii Aleksandrovny Vseia Rossii* (St. Petersburg, 1856); "Koronatsionnyi sbornik i khudozhestvennyi al'bom," RGIA, 472-65-113, 1. The 1856 publication date is fictional; the work was not published until 1861 ("O rasporiazheniiakh dlia sostavleniia opisaniia koronovaniia," RGIA, 472-64-69, 203–4; Sacherevell Sitwell, *Valse des fleurs: A Day in St. Petersburg and a Ball at the Winter Palace in 1868* [London, 1941], 64).

of love. Figures of people from all classes cluster in the foreground watching raptly and greeting the tsar with rapture.[42] The introduction to the album affirmed that this coronation was distinguished from all others by its magnificence: "The splendor accompanying this ceremony, has never been equaled, in any other land, at any other time." A five-page summary of the history of the coronation emphasized its Byzantine roots by referring to the legend of Monomakh.[43]

Foreign governments went out of their way to send highly ranked, prominent, and aristocratic representatives to confirm the healing of the antagonisms of the past decade. France and England dispatched extraordinary ambassadors, Count Morny and Lord Grenville. Prussia sent Prince Friedrich-Wilhelm, the son of Crown Prince Wilhelm. Prince Paul Esterhazy represented the Hapsburg Emperor. The sumptuousness of their attire and livery evoked astonished comments in the press and in memoirs. *Russkii Vestnik* reported that Grenville had spent twelve hundred rubles per day during his stay at Demuth's Hotel in Petersburg and cited a huge wardrobe budget for his servants. The ambassadors' carriages were an especial object of talk, particularly Count Morny's, which was decorated in red and gilt. The number of foreign emissaries present was extraordinary; there were missions from Brazil and, for the first time at a Russian coronation, from the United States, which, it was reported, included Samuel Colt, the inventor of the revolver.[44]

Alexander's entry procession on August 17, 1856, displayed an opulence that could offset the impressions of weakness and backwardness left from the war. A description from *L'Independance Belge* was printed in translation in four issues of *Russkii Khudozhestvennyi Listok* as well as in *Severnaia Pchela*. The text thus identified the official view of the celebration with the response it ostensibly evoked abroad. The report of *L'Independance Belge*, printed in *Russkii Khudozhestvennyi Listok*, described the brilliance and luxury of the uniforms and costumes. The glittering golden livery of eighty servants of the court, the correspondent observed, cost three hundred to four hundred rubles apiece. His imagination was stunned by the twenty-eight lavish carriages covered by felt and gold, painted in the style of Francois Boucher and occupied by holders of court rank and members of the State Council. The braided uniforms and the chain of carriages carrying court ranks and members of the State Council gave Tver Street "the appearance

[42] "O rasporiazheniiakh dlia sostavleniia opisaniia koronovaniia," RGIA, 472-64-67, 60, 139, 428; 474-64-69, 78; V. A. Vereshchagin, *Russkie illiustrirovannye izdaniia XVIII i XIX stoletii* (St. Petersburg, 1898), 625. For a complete list of illustrations, see N. S. Obol'ianinov, *Katalog russkikh illiustrirovannykh izdanii, 1725–1860* (Moscow, 1915), 2:384–85.

[43] *Opisanie sviashchenneishago koronovaniia . . . Imperatora Aleksandra Vtorago i Imperatritsy Marii Aleksandrovny*, 3–8.

[44] Tatishchev, *Imperator Alexander II*, 1:217; N. Beloozerskaia, "Tsarskoe venchanie v Rossii," *Russkaia Mysl'*, no. 5 (1883): 37; "Vnutrennee obozrenie," *Russkii Vestnik*, no. 4 (August 1856): 276–77; no. 5 (September 1856): 88–89.

of a golden river." The author described the approach of the Cavalier-Guards "in which sons of the first Russian families consider it an honor to serve." The sun rays glittered on their silver arms and helmets. "The sight of this magnificent cavalry evoked cries of astonishment from all." The Horse-Guards appeared in white uniforms, and on black horses, recalling legendary German knights who roamed through the woods at night.[45]

The pictures accompanying the texts confirmed the rhetorical evocations of exotic splendor and popular enthusiasm. Lithographs depicted the groups of the guards regiments, leading the emperor on horseback, the sumptuous carriages bearing members of the imperial family and the chief marshal of the court. In the foreground, people gaze admiringly at the spectacle. Alexander himself was the cynosure. *Russkii Khudozhestvennyi Listok* proudly quoted the *London Times'* correspondent's remarks on Alexander's "majestic looks," his close facial resemblance to Nicholas, and his imposing appearance on horseback. "He rode his horse, a perfect model of stateliness, lightly and attractively." He was so touched by the shouts of the crowd that tears appeared in his eyes, a sign of recognition of the acclaim.[46]

The coronation album printed a montage conveying the excitement of the various parts of the procession. The plate of the entry by M. A. Zichy, Alexander's favored court painter, gives a vivid rendering of the Moscow population ecstatically welcoming the tsar and the court (fig. 2). Both educated society and the people are encompassed in the frame. From the grandstand, a group of famous writers give animated welcome to the emperor, among them Feodor Tiutchev, Ivan Turgenev, Fadei Bulgarin, Alexei Tolstoi, and Vladimir Odoevskii. In the foreground are the people: A peasant woman in folk dress and a tiara hat faces the tsar; a man raises his arms in greeting. Before the spectators we see large figures of the last row of the Cavalier-Guards, proud mustachioed men dressed in elegant white uniforms and golden helmets. Alexander appears in middle ground riding toward us in his green general's uniform and cape, the center of the picture, before the many blue figures of his suite.[47]

The accounts cited in the Russian press dwelled on the pageant of colorfully dressed representatives of the various Eastern peoples in their native costumes who participated in the procession—Bashkirs, Cherkessy, Tatars, Armenians, Georgians, and a variety of Cossacks. The reporters saw them as a demonstration of the extent and diversity of the empire and the forging of bonds between the Asian peoples and the tsar. *Russkii Khudozhestvennyi Listok* presented the people from Central Asian khanates as "tangible proof of the vastness of our state, which some justly call a special kind of planet." Their appearance in procession "eloquently attested to all the one whose

---

[45] *Russkii Khudozhestvennyi Listok*, no. 27 (September 20, 1856).

[46] Ibid., no 28 (October 1, 1856): 1–2; no. 30, (October 20, 1856).

[47] See the reproduction of the watercolor and identification of the writers in *Literaturnoe Nasledstvo*, Vol. 97, Book 2: *Fedor Ivanovich Tiutchev*, 478–79.

2. Coronation of Alexander II: Entry procession. Color lithograph from painting by M. A. Zichy. *Opisanie sviashchenneishago koronovaniia . . . Aleksandra Vtorago i Imperatritsy Marii Aleksandrovny Vseia Rossii.* Slavic and Baltic Division, New York Public Library. Astor, Lenox, and Tilden Foundations.

authority they recognize and whom they came from their own lands to worship."[48] William Russell of the *Times of London* marveled, "What a recollection of the majesty and might of Russia will these people bring back to their distant tribes! They flashed by us in all their brilliance, a dream from *A Thousand and One Nights.*[49] Foreigners' reports cited in *Russkii Vestnik* and *Russkii Khudozhestvennyi Listok* emphasized the civilizing mission of the Russian state. *L'Independance Belge* observed the vigor of the deputies from Central Asia and their rearing horses "with smoking nostrils, foam in the

    [48] *Russkii Khudozhestvennyi Listok*, no. 29 (October 10, 1856): 1.
    [49] "Sovremennaia letopis'," *Russkii Vestnik* (September 1856): 171. V. V. Grigor'ev, who was serving in Orenburg at the time of the coronation, arranged to have several Kirgiz deputies invited. In addition to the effect of their colorful costumes, he emphasized the "governmental significance" of their presence. "I do not doubt that this measure will be ten times more effective in instilling a favorable disposition toward and respect for Russia in the members of the [Kirgiz] horde than ten military expeditions to the Steppe and all possible circulars from the Commission" (I. I. Veselovskii, *V. V. Grigor'ev po ego pis'mam i trudam, 1818–1881* [St. Petersburg, 1887], 146; I thank Nathaniel Knight for directing my attention to this citation).

mouth, "a striking symbol of the triumph of the power of the well-ordered over the power of disorder."[50]

Along the way Alexander stopped to receive traditional speeches of welcome. At the Voskresenskii Gate into Red Square, he met Moscow's governor and city officials. Then he dismounted, helped his mother out of the carriage, and, with his other family members, entered the chapel of the Iberian Mother-of-God to pay his respects to the popular icon of Moscow, as had been traditional at imperial entries since 1797. He then continued the procession to the Spasskii Gate of the Kremlin, where he was welcomed by the commander of the Moscow Garrison and his staff. Thousands of spectators in the stands on Red Square greeted him with great feeling, and then he proceeded into the Kremlin. At the portal of the Assumption Cathedral he was welcomed by the Synod, while the highest ranks of the government, the Senate, and the ministers awaited him inside the cathedral. After the service he proceeded to the Archangel and Annunciation cathedrals, to the cadences of "God Save the Tsar!" and then ascended the Red Staircase, where he turned and made the now traditional, triple bow to the jubilant cries of the people.[51]

The press focused on the mutual love of tsar and people displayed during the procession. "What a treasure the Tsar will find in this love of the people!" the *Russkii Vestnik* reporter exclaimed.[52] *Severnaia Pchela* described the moment with rhetorical flight. "All gazes fixed on the Most August Visitor, arriving to receive the tribute of the people's love and the legacy of His ancestors. The sensitive heart of the people looking into the cordial smile of the Sovereign Emperor, it seemed, guessed the treasures of love and mercy filling the heart of the Monarch who so loved his children. Many of those present made the sign of the cross and shed tears of tender pity." The people also gazed with love on "the young Tsaritsa, ornamenting the life of her Sovereign Spouse."[53] V. I. Daehn, who marched in the procession, echoed these sentiments, writing that he was most impressed with the "universal love of the people for their tsar . . . that unbreakable religious bond between the people and the single ruler of all Russia."[54]

The bowing from the Red Staircase brought the climax of the people's adulation. The reporter in *Severnaia Pchela* wrote, "These minutes were most joyous and most tender. The heart nearly leaped from joy. Tears were on the eyes of all." When the tsar bowed to the people, one foreign corre-

---

[50] "Sovremennaia letopis'," *Russkii Vestnik* (September, 1856): 170–71; *Russkii Khudozhestvennyi Listok*, no. 27 (September 20, 1856): 1–2.

[51] *Russkii Khudozhestvennyi Listok*, no. 28 (October 1, 1856): 2; Tatishchev, *Imperator Aleksandr II*, 1:216.

[52] *Russkii Vestnik* (August 1856): 282.

[53] *Severnaia Pchela*, August 31, 1856, 973.

[54] *Russkii Khudozhestvennyi Listok*, no. 30 (October 20, 1856): 1; no. 31 (November 1, 1856): 1–2; V. I. Den', "Zapiski," *Russkaia Starina* 65 (1890): 592–93.

spondent found the cries of the people "frightening." The reporter replied that "for the Russian heart they are joyous, because we know their source and meaning."[55]

The *Russkii Khudozhestvennyi Listok* article elaborated on the "source and the meaning" of the outburst.[56] The author turned the pageant into a symbolic equivalent of popular sovereignty.

> And that is true! Russia has valuables, lost by the decrepit powers of the West. The young feeling of infinite love and devotion for the anointed of the Lord and for the sovereign guardians of the earthly fate of the beloved fatherland has been preserved in Russia.

At the same time, he put a religious construction on the expressions of popular feeling, maintaining the identification of political sentiment with Orthodoxy, characteristic of official nationality.[57] He asserted that the people crossing themselves everywhere during the procession confirmed the words of the scriptures, "Blessed be he who comes in the name of the Lord"—the words evoking Christ's entry into Jerusalem that were repeated during sermons at various coronations.[58]

The following days were devoted to a series of parades. A review of the first battalion of the Preobrazhenskii Regiment took place the day after the entry on the Kremlin Square. Alexander thus showed his homage to Nicholas's favorite battalion, which had stood at his side on December 14, 1825. The article in *Russkii Khudozhestvennyi Listok* pointed out that present at the review were all the foreign princes attending the festivities and military officers from foreign embassies. "The martial look, the gigantic height, the broad shoulders, heroic poise, and virile expression of the faces of this select army stirred attention and an innate, proud sympathy in the crowd that swelled by the minute." The emperor greeted the regiment, which shouted the traditional wish for his health.[59]

But the journal's description of the immense parade of the guards regiments on August 20 on Khodynskoe Field before an estimated two hundred thousand spectators dwelled not on the military might of the empire but on the kindly aspect of the tsar—"our good-hearted Tsar, an angel of gentleness, mercy, and love, shown with benevolence in the midst of these frightening forces attesting to His might." This was the last review before the coronation. Alexander spent the remaining four days in seclusion at the Sheremetevo estate at Ostankino and prepared himself for the ceremonies with prayer and meditation.[60]

---

[55] *Severnaia Pchela*, September 1, 1856, 981–82; September 5, 1856, 995–96.

[56] *Russkii Khudozhestvennyi Listok*, no. 31 (November 1, 1856): 1–2.

[57] Cited also as part of Russell's report in "Sovremennaia letopis'," *Russkii Vestnik* (September 1856): 170.

[58] See Volume 1: 220.

[59] *Russkii Khudozhestvennyi Listok*, no. 31 (November 1, 1856): 2.

[60] Ibid., No. 32 (November 10, 1856), 2.

The procession of the imperial family and official delegations to the cathedral for the first time included representatives of the peasantry. Village elders of the state peasants—one from each province in the empire, the kingdom of Poland, and the Grand Duchy of Finland—followed the Cavalier-Guards, the pages, and the masters of ceremonies. Their participation, however, was limited in order to preserve the nature of an elite ceremony: The coronation album specified that they were only permitted to "walk around" the cathedral and await the end of the ceremony in the Synodal Chamber.[61] But their mention augured a new era when peasants would join the members of other estates in public ceremonies.

Metropolitan Filaret's address of welcome at the portals of the Assumption Cathedral expressed the theme of hope and love. "Russia accompanies You. The Church meets You. Russia sends You off with a prayer of love and hope," he declared.[62] The invocation of love and hope was taken up in the press. The account in *Russkii Khudozhestvennyi Listok* asserted that faith and love were "unshakeable principles on which power, unity, and prosperity rest; *hope*, the third daughter of heaven, is the radiant companion of the new star, the present reign." Hope expressed the expectations of Alexander at this moment. Nicholas had come to his coronation fresh from a triumph; Alexander's tasks, far more complex and imponderable, awaited him in the future.[63]

After Alexander crowned himself came the dramatic moment of his supplication, when he fell to his knees to beseech God to help him govern the realm. Alexander implored the Lord to teach him, to give him understanding, and to guide him in "his great service" (*vysokoe sluzhenie*). He asked for help in governing "for the welfare of the people entrusted to me and to your great glory." Then he rose, and, as the entire coronation knelt, the metropolitan delivered the prayer "from the entire people." He called on the Lord to instruct Alexander to work in "his great service" to God. A brochure later published by an archimandrite present at the coronation recalled the pathos of the moment and revealed how this religious statement of enlightened rule was understood in the context of the scenario of love. "One could not hear the tsar's prayer to the Supreme Tsar of Tsars about the bestowal of the necessary wisdom to improve his realm without tender pity (*umilenie*)." The metropolitan's prayer, he recalled, "confirmed the union of the beloved Tsar with his faithful subjects." In this way "the bonds of love are further

---

[61] *Opisanie sviashchennneishago koronovaniia . . . Imperatora Aleksandra Vtorago i Imperatritsy Marii Aleksandrovny*, 41; In Nicholas I's coronation procession, the merchantry followed the masters of Ceremonies. "Istoricheskoe opisanie Sviashchennogo Koronovaniia i Miropomazaniia ikh Imperatorskikh Velichestv Gosudaria Imperatora Nikolaia Pavlovicha i Gosudaryni Imperatritsy Aleksandry Feodorovny," *Otechestvennye Zapiski* 31 (1827): 177–78.

[62] Metropolitan Filaret, *Slova i rechi, 1859–1867* (Moscow, 1885), 5:384–85; Tatishchev, *Imperator Aleksandr II*, 1:218.

[63] Nikita Chakirov, *Tsarskie koronatsii na Rusi* (New York, 1971), 190, 192; *MV*, August 30, 1856, 913; *Russkii Khudozhestvennyi Listok*, no. 31 (November 1, 1856).

strengthened by a vow before the God of mutual love, a vow of the Tsar's service to the good of the people, and a vow of the subjects obedience to their God-given Sovereign."[64]

Those in the cathedral remarked on Alexander's sadness and on the empress's delicate, childlike appearance in comparison with the stately figure of the dowager Alexandra Fedorovna. When Alexander placed the small crown on Maria Aleksandrovna's head, many in the cathedral wept. Alexander then respectfully embraced his mother, shook his wife's hand, and embraced the other members of the imperial family.[65] The moment of marital devotion was captured in Zichy's painting of Alexander's crowning of Maria Aleksandrovna in the coronation album (fig. 3). The album contains no illustration of the emperor crowning himself. We see the scene across the bare shoulders of the ladies of the court. In the foreground, guardsmen, cadets, and a young lady in a bright pink dress watch intently. Zichy succeeds in placing the imperial couple and the spectators in the same frame, capturing the emotions that presumably united Alexander with his elite. We can understand what Sitwell meant when he wrote of these: "not works of art, but fascinating in their improbability."[66]

After congratulations from the clergy, the metropolitan proceeded to the liturgy, when the emperor and empress were anointed and the emperor took communion at the altar. Alexander made two departures from the accepted ritual. He did not allow the metropolitan of Novgorod and Petersburg and the archbishop of Lithuania to hold the train of his mantle, giving it instead to the deacons. This was taken as a gesture of respect for the clergy as a whole. Then, instead of having his lips dried by one of the priests, Alexander knelt before the icon of the savior and, while the empress received communion, wept passionately. The tsar implored help from Christ for his own weaknesses at the moment of tribulation. His image was of the fallible human being evoking compassion, whereas his father's had been that of a man conquering weakness with an exterior of godlike strength.[67]

The ceremonies were marred by several unfortunate mishaps, which taken together symbolized the loss of precision, order, and authority. At one point in the ceremony the empress's crown became detached from her hairdo, slipped from her head, and may have fallen to the floor. The empress declared

[64] S.A.T., *Vospominaniia o sviashchennom koronovanii ikh imperatorskikh velichestv v boze pochivshikh Gosudaria Imperatora Aleksandra Nikolaevicha i Gosudarynia Imperatritsy Marii Aleksandrovny* (Tver, 1882), 14–15.

[65] A. I. Del'vig, *Polveka russkoi zhizni* (Moscow-Leningrad, 1930), 2:59; *Russkii Khudozhestvennyi Listok*, no. 35 (December 10, 1856): 3; Tiutcheva, *Pri dvore dvukh imperatorov*, 2:119; M. A. Patkul, "Vospominaniia," *Istoricheskii Vestnik* 89 (1902): 49. The correspondent of *le Nord* wrote, "At this solemn moment a spiritual upsurge seized all present. I saw how more than one tear fell from the eyes of distinguished generals onto their gray mustaches" (citation is from "Sovremennaia letopis'," *Russkii Vestnik* [September 1856]: 180).

[66] Sitwell, *Valse des fleurs*, 65.

[67] V. I. Zhmakin, "Koronatsii russkikh imperatorov i imperatrits, 1724–1856," *Russkaia Starina* 38 (April 1883): 17–18.

3. Coronation of Alexander II: Alexander II crowns Empress Maria Alexandrovna.
Color lithograph from painting by M. A. Zichy. *Opisanie sviashchenneishago
koronovaniia . . . Aleksandra Vtorago i Imperatritsy Marii Aleksandrovny Vseia
Rossii.* Slavic and Baltic Division, New York Public Library. Astor, Lenox,
and Tilden Foundations.

that it meant she would not wear it long. Anna Tiutcheva wanted to withdraw to her room and weep. The incident was widely considered an evil
omen. The large number of guests created an embarrassing crush. Angry and
even unseemly remarks were made by those in the rear of the cathedral who
could not see the ceremony. Tiutcheva noticed that almost no one in the
court was praying during the religious service. Indeed, some of the ladies
had brought food to sustain themselves as they stood through the four or
five hours of ritual.[68]

When Alexander stepped out of the cathedral into the view of the throng
on Kremlin Square, in full regalia, wearing the heavy crown, he appeared
weary and sad, overwhelmed by the task that awaited him.[69] The crowd on

[68] Tiutcheva, *Pri dvore dvukh imperatorov,* 2:121–22; Patkul, "Vospominaniia," 50; V. L.
Meshcherskii, *Moi vospominaniia* (St. Petersburg, 1897–1898), 1:66; Del'vig, *Polveka russkoi
zhizni,* 2:59; Den', "Zapiski," 66:594.

[69] Tatishchev, *Imperator Aleksandr II,* 1:220; "Lettres de Th. I. Tjutsheff a sa seconde épouse
née Baronne de Pfeffel," 158; Obolenskii, *Dnevnik,* Folder 2: 47.

the Kremlin Square responded with shouts of adoration when the emperor and empress in full regalia bowed three times to them, indicating their recognition of the Russian people's devotion. The account in the coronation album abandoned its reserved tone to give full expression to the moment.

> No description can convey the solemnity of the moment when, in view of the monuments of ancient Rus', before the huge mass of the crowd of rapturous and deeply touched people, two crowned heads, the crowns reflecting the rays of the sun, as if a visible sign of their majesty, gratefully bowed before the love and hope of the state. The cry of the people drowned out the cannon salvos and the sound of the bells.[70]

Those present at Alexander's coronation were convinced that these shouts expressed genuine feelings of love for the monarch. Prince Obolenskii, who was close to the Slavophiles, sensed a powerful bond between the tsar and the people. To his dismay the people were kept at the edge of the square, behind a cordon of guardsmen, and gave the spectacle "an official look" (*kazennyi vid*). Nonetheless he perceived that all the peasants (*muzhiki*) were "full of love and deep compassion for him." They asked Obolenskii, "Why is he so sad . . . Why is he gloomy . . . He has lost weight . . . He has many cares. He was not that way when his father was alive."[71]

Like the author of the commentary in *Russkii Khudozhestvennyi Listok*, Obolenskii described this response as a reflection of the Orthodox faith, which "invested the sign of spiritual truth and teaching in external ceremonies." "I sincerely confess that in my eyes, which have already been spoiled by cerebration, the ceremony for the Tsar placed Him still higher than before. I cannot explain this feeling, but I feel what the people must feel."[72] This feeling lasted into the evening and was particularly evident during the illumination of Moscow.

> Their faces glowed, a smile appeared on their lips. The look of the most passionate lover recounting a meeting with his beloved could not be more expressive and vivid than the speaker when he told how the Tsar bowed, walked, or rode. This feeling of the people for the Tsar is very poetic. It is completely selfless and does not ask to be reciprocated, for it is understood and based on nothing. It is not a theoretical or abstract devotion or submissiveness to authority. No, it is an unconscious drive that has neither bounds nor limits.[73]

"When you hear expressions of love from the source, the lips of the people," Obolenskii wrote, "you feel ashamed that you don't feel this love yourself."[74] The belief that Alexander was beloved by the people remained

---

[70] *Opisanie sviashchenneishago koronovaniia . . . Imperatora Aleksandra Vtorago i Imperatritsy Marii Aleksandrovny*, 61–62.

[71] Obolenskii, *Dnevnik*, Folder 2: 46–47.

[72] Ibid., 47–48.

[73] Ibid., 48–49.

[74] Ibid., 49.

an article of faith and sustained his and many other officials' and writers' vision of reform as a display of altruism and generosity.

Alexander's manifesto, promulgated on the day of the coronation, showed exceptionally generous consideration to all estates of the realm. He was profuse in his thanks to the nobility, which, he declared, "has long led the other estates (*sostoianiia*) as an example on the field of honor and sacrifices for the fatherland." The manifesto also granted unprecedented clemencies and favors. Most important, the exiled Decembrists were allowed to return from Siberia to European Russia and to regain their previous titles and rights, ending the bitter resentment that had clouded Nicholas's reign. Other political prisoners were also released, and nine thousand individuals were freed from police surveillance. Some arrears were forgiven, and political sentences were reduced. Alexander declared the recruit obligation suspended for three years, unless peace came to an end.[75]

Filaret's words of congratulations after the coronation emphasized the emperor's civic responsibilities. He stated the hope that "from the tsar's crown, a life-giving light will spread, as from a central point to the whole tsardom, the most honorable of rare stones, state wisdom" and that the tsar's scepter would lead his people to the public good. The imperial standard should "gather the millions of people together in strict order and the labor and vigilance of the tsar should serve to stir and elevate their activity and ensure their tranquillity."[76]

In keeping with the inclusive spirit of the celebration, Alexander insisted that the reception the day after the coronation include new groups of the population. Instead of the traditional gathering of the highest four ranks of officers and officials, marshals of the nobility, and mayors, as was traditional, the reception was thrown open to all hereditary nobles in the capital along with their wives and daughters, including the district marshals of the nobility. A delegation of peasant elders, one from each province, presented Alexander with bread and salt on a silver plate, purchased from funds from the peasant estate. Alexander thanked them for their devotion and zeal, especially during the war. Altogether he received a total of eighty-one gold and silver plates with bread and salt, from the noble, merchant, and peasant estate organizations.[77] Numerous gala occasions—parades, theatrical performances, dinners, and balls—took place on the following days. The Moscow Merchantry gave their traditional ceremonial dinner for the lower-ranking guards, but, unlike his father, Alexander did not attend.

The gala performance that opened the new Bolshoi Theater on August 30 expressed the effervescent spirit of the beginning of Alexander's reign. A special arcade, holding lights, was constructed around the square for the

[75] Tatishchev, *Imperator Aleksandr II*, 1:221–24; *IGK, ts. Al. II*, 169–78; Zakharova, "Aleksandr II," 179–80.

[76] Filaret, *Slova i rechi*, 5:385–87; Tatishchev, *Imperator Alexander II*, 1:219–20.

[77] Tatishchev, *Imperator Aleksandr II*, 1:224–25; *IGK, ts. Al. II*, 180–81.

celebration of the theater's opening.[78] The performance included Donizetti's *L'Elisir d'Amore* (The elixir of love). The opera was the kind of frothy diversion that the emperor enjoyed, expressing a sentimental faith in the magical power of love, creating good feelings and healing wounds—joy and infatuation conquering disbelief and making for a sense of common humanity.

At the sumptuous coronation balls, the Russian court aristocracy reaffirmed their identification with Western high society. Petersburg ladies ordered gowns from Paris; their husbands rented expensive quarters and carriages in Moscow. Dancing was far more to Alexander's taste than his father's.[79] Prince Obolenskii was shocked by the extravagance of events that he saw only as an additional drain on the treasury at a moment of fiscal duress. "This celebration was truly imperial," he wrote of a magnificent supper at one of the Kremlin palaces. "No money is spared, and the desire to throw dust in the eyes of foreigners demands enormous outlays." He claimed that the coronation had cost almost as much as the war.[80]

The masquerade in the Kremlin palace repeated the pageantry of the ball of 1849 that celebrated the palace's opening.[81] Indeed, it was more a theatrical presentation than a social occasion. Eight thousand tickets were given out. The correspondent of *Le Nord* remarked on "the public of the streets, the rabble of society, trampling on the marvelous mosaic of the parquets with their dirty boots and quenching their Homeric thirst from the golden and silver goblets of the imperial buffet." In no democratic country, including his own Belgium, would such a "mixture of citizens of all estates" be allowed.[82] The British journalist Henry Sutherland Edwards observed that the ball presented the emperor among his people, who behaved with restraint and did not crowd around him. Alexander, Edwards wrote admiringly, spoke freely with peasants and particularly guests from the distant parts of the empire.[83]

At the masquerade the ladies of the court appeared in the traditional, formal "Russian dress." They wore the Russian-style tiaras (*kokoshniki*)—

---

[78] Color lithographs of the moment by the architect of the arcade and theater reconstruction Albert Cavos show crowds of well-dressed ladies and gentlemen enjoying the enchanting scene of the brilliantly lit theater. These lithographs were shown at an exhibition organized in 1996 by Moscow's Shchusev Museum of Architecture. They are reproduced in black and white in the exhibition catalog, *Moskva v dni koronatsii: katalog vystavki* (Moscow, 1996), 12–13, 16–18.

[79] Den', "Zapiski," 66:591; Gr. G. A. Miloradovich, *Vospominaniia o koronatsii Imperatora Aleksandra II kamer-pazha dvora Ego Velichestva* (Kiev, 1883), 10–25.

[80] Obolenskii, *Dnevnik*, Folder 2: 55.

[81] See Volume 1: 400–401.

[82] V. Komarov, *V pamiat' sviashchennago koronovaniia Gosudaria Imperatora Aleksandra III i Gosudaria Imperatritsy Marii Fedorovny* (St. Petersburg, 1883), 31–33. The introduction to this work contains details of Alexander II's coronation.

[83] [Henry] Sutherland Edwards, *The Russians at Home: Unpolitical Sketches* (London, 1861), 240–44.

now made closer to the peasant originals. The empress and grand duchesses wore national costumes bedecked with diamonds and other jewels. The emperor and the grand dukes appeared for the first time at a major function in the uniform of His Majesty's Rifles, the regiment Nicholas formed in 1853 out of the peasant militia from the imperial family's Moscow domains. The uniform of His Majesty's Rifles was in national style: wide trousers—*sharovary*—over high boots, a Russian-style kaftan, a black lambskin cap.[84]

Fedor Tiutchev, who attended the ball as a chamberlain, thought the masquerade expressed Russia's Asiatic character. It allowed him to imagine himself in the realm of dreams—it was the dream of Russia embracing the East. Tiutchev saw old aristocrats in costumes he knew besides "quite authentic" Mingrelian, Tatar, and Imeretian princes in their magnificent costumes, and two Chinese, "living and real." "And two hundred steps from these halls, resplendent with light and filled with this very contemporary crowd, lay the tombs of Ivan III and Ivan IV." He wondered how they would react if they saw this scene. "Ah, how much dream there is in what we call reality."[85]

The traditional feast for the people, which took place on Khodynskii Field at Alexander's coronation, symbolized both the new reign's largesse and the dangers of its inclusive spirit. It was staged on a grand scale, and the problems of organization and control, which would have a tragic outcome at the coronation of Nicholas II in 1896, were already testing the administrative capacities of autocracy. Rather than order food from a contractor, the government assigned each of the regiments a dish to prepare. The dishes, however, were prepared too early and lay rotting under covers for two days, filling the air with aromas that attracted stray dogs from around the city. Although the dinner was scheduled to begin at noon with the arrival of the tsar, mobs of people began to appear at eight in the morning, undaunted by a driving rain. Hundreds of thousands covered the field. By noon, most of the food had been consumed. Apparently the commission in charge of the event, embarrassed by the condition of the food, had raised the white flag—the signal to start—an hour early.

When the tsar arrived to open the feast, surrounded by a splendid suite of foreign princes, he was startled that nothing remained. He rode around the field for about fifteen minutes and then left. When he had reached his pavilion, the white flag was raised again and the fountains poured forth with white Crimean wine and mead. The people flattened the trees near the fountains and in a few minutes had emptied the fountains. They then were enter-

[84] Count G. A. Miloradovich wrote, "This purely Russian form of clothing very much became the tsar" (*Vospominaniia o koronatsii Imperatora Aleksandra II kamer-pazha dvora Ego Velichestva*, 16–17); Sutherland Edwards remarked that "at the national fête, he wore a national costume" (*The Russians at Home*, 243). On the Imperial Rifles, see E. E. Bogdanovich, *Strelki imperatorskoi familii* (St. Petersburg, 1899).

[85] I. S. Aksakov, *Biografiia Fedora Ivanovicha Tiutcheva* (Moscow, 1886), 262–63; "Lettres de Th. I. Tjutsheff a sa seconde épouse née Baronne de Pfeffel," 160–61.

tained by acrobats, jugglers, stunt riders, and carousel rides.[86] Zichy's painting of the feast is in the genre of rollicking peasants, merry children enjoying the emperor's largesse.

The festivities concluded with a spectacular fireworks' display at Le Fortovo Field on September 17, which, however was marred by rain. A flaming dove took flight from the balcony of the Lefortovo Palace, with a bower of flowers that turned into a rose bush. The outlines of the new monument in Kostroma to Ivan Susanin appeared to a rendition of the "Cavatina" from Glinka's *Life for the Tsar*. This was followed by a display of the Arch of Triumph in St. Petersburg. During the illumination, Prince A. L'vov led one thousand singers and two thousand musicians in a rendition of his *God Save the Tsar*, the first performance of the anthem at a coronation. As L'vov directed, he, by means of galvanic batteries, set off forty-nine cannons, one by one, sometimes on the beat. At the conclusion, hundreds of Roman candles and rockets soared into the sky.[87]

L'vov had conceived his anthem as an expression of the people's fervent love for their tsar, and the performance of September 17 was a realization of his vision.[88] In F. Blanchard's painting, clouds of red and white provide a background for the group of peasants and tribesmen at the side of the tsar's pavilion. A bearded man raises his hand in wonder, a horse rears, some look with interest or wonder, and others mill about and engage in conversation.[89]

•

At the coronation the scenario of love was addressed principally to educated society. The rhetoric of love expressed the tsar's desire for conciliation with intellectuals, who had been the object of the monarch's suspicion and fear since the Decembrist revolt. It indicated his intention to make them allies in his work for reform, particularly the emancipation of the serfs. Educated individuals could once more join the elite that shared the monarch's glory.

Appealing to romantic sensibility, the scenario was greeted with an effusive response. Writers extolled the tsar's paternal role. An ode by the former chief procurator of the Senate and poet Michael Dmitriev called upon Alex-

[86] Komarov, *V pamiat' sviashchennago koronovaniia*, 28–31; M. A. Patkul', "Vospominaniia," *Istoricheskii Vestnik* 89 (1902): 53–54; Miloradovich, *Vospominaniia o koronatsii Imperatora Aleksandra II kamer-pazha dvora Ego Velichestva*, 12–15.

[87] Sutherland Edwards, *The Russians at Home*, 232–35; Miloradovich, *Vospominaniia o koronatsii Imperatora Aleksandra II kamer-pazha dvora Ego Velichestva*, 25–26.

[88] "Decidedly there was more noise than melody," Sutherland Edwards commented. But he acknowledged, "It was an illuminated, out-of-door concert for the masses and an impressive one" (*The Russians at Home*, 235).

[89] Blanchard's painting is reproduced in Teofil' Got'e, *Puteshestvie v Rossiiu* (Moscow, 1988), 162.

ander to "love your subjects like offspring!"—and receive their love in return.[90] Rather than an intimidating patriarch, he was the kindly protector of his flock who, filled with Christian sentiment, could view his people as brothers.[91] Alexei Khomiakov's poem, "August 26, 1856," presented Alexander as the bearer of fraternal love.

> And kneeling at the foot,
> Of the altar of prayer,
> We believe that God will show grace,
> To the Orthodox Tsar. . . .
>
> And we believe, and will believe,
> That He will give a gift, the crowning gift,
> The gift of fraternal love for brothers and people,
> The love of a father for his sons.[92]

Stepan Shevyrev, the Slavicist and spokesman for official nationality, signaled the beginning of an alliance between throne and university. He declared that university professors could help the tsar by bringing him "truth" (*istina*). But these scholars, he insisted, had to combine truth with love, reason with the heart. "Truth of the reigning power was confirmed and took root as a faith, in the life of the Russian people, by [the governmental] power's acts of love." In Russian history, he concluded, government had been a force for peace, acting to reconcile warring divisive elements.[93]

On September 3 the writer Nicholas Pavlov, whose stories had been personally censored by Nicholas I, delivered a toast to a gathering of writers, scholars, and artists. Pavlov's words were printed in the journal *Russkii Vestnik* and then widely cited.[94] His thoughts, the journal's editor observed, showed that the coronation ceremony had prompted not only official replies but also a response "in the hearts of people serving society outside the sphere of the state." Pavlov declared, "In two days, in two issues of the newspaper, what a wealth of fruitful impressions! Since Peter the Great we can name no epoch of our history where so much was done in so little time." Pavlov hailed the shift from military triumphs and conquest to civil progress and popular approval as the new standard of governmental success. It was not the deafening sounds of weapons but "exploits more in tune with the demands of the century."

---

[90] On the use of Christian symbolism to present the emancipation in terms of redemption and apocalypse, see Irina Paperno, "The Liberation of the Serfs as a Cultural Symbol," *The Russian Review* 50 (October 1991): 417–36.

[91] *MV*, September 1, 1856, 443. The poem was also printed in an appendix to the September 1856 issue of *Russkii Vestnik*.

[92] A. S. Khomiakov, *Polnoe sobranie sochinenii* (Moscow, 1900), 259.

[93] *MV*, September 4, 1856, 447–48; Tatishchev, *Imperator Aleksandr II*, 1:225.

[94] "Sovremennaia letopis'," *Russkii Vestnik* (September 1856): 166–67.

Pavlov believed that the new era permitted the promptings of the heart to fuse with the reason of the state. The preservation and raising of Russia to new heights was "a sacred duty, imposed by reason." But "happy is the time in which the fulfillment of duty fuses with the wishes of the heart . . . happy is life if you don't distinguish between the commands of duty and the promptings of love." It was the tsar's clemency that had permitted this fusion, and Pavlov raised his goblet in the name of Christian love. Alexander had taken on a new role, the bearer of good feelings, uniting educated society, the clergy, and the state. The metaphor of rule as love created the bond between monarch and people without narrowing the distance between them or sacrificing monarchical prerogatives. The myth of a supreme Western monarch, in its new form, would animate a heroic spirit of reform.

NEW IMAGES OF AUTHORITY

After the coronation Alexander began to reveal his own personifications of imperial authority consonant with the scenario of love. Alexander took on this persona without repudiating his father. The equestrian statue of Nicholas I, designed by August Montferrand and executed by Peter Klodt, was an initial sign of continuity between father and son.[95] Alexander proceeded swiftly with its execution: The cornerstone was laid in June 1857, and the monument was dedicated on St. Isaac's Square in Petersburg in June 1859. The figure of Nicholas on the statue appears preened for a parade in the uniform and eagle helmet of the Horse Guards, one of the most aristocratic of the regiments (fig. 4). He is executing a fancy riding exercise. However, his famous strong and piercing gaze is not visible, because his head is fastidiously averted. The statue established continuity with Nicholas's reign by showing the *ceremonial* elegance of his bearing rather than his stern, superhuman presence. An emperor who never was a skillful rider and did not like to ride appears to posterity performing an equestrian stunt. The comparison with the soaring figure of Falconet's Peter was evident to contemporaries.

[95] Alexander specified that he wanted a statue that would render "the features of his immortal parent in the military outfit (*vooruzhenie*) in which the late *Tsar* was most majestic" (*Russkii Khudozhestvennyi Listok*, no. 21 [July 20, 1958]: 1; no. 3 [January 20, 1858]: 1). He was concerned most of all with details of style. He asked for modifications after the first revisions of the plan: "to change the gait of the horse from left to right, to make the plume on the helmet smaller, to place the helmet farther back on the head, to make the boots softer, the epaulets and right sleeve fuller" (Janet Kennedy, "The Neoclassical Ideal in Russian Scuplture," in Theofanis George Stavrou, ed., *Art and Culture in Nineteenth-Century Russia* (Bloomington, Ind., 1983), 205–6. That he continued to watch over the progress of the monument was made clear to the public by an engraving by Vasilii Timm printed in *Russkii Khudozhestvennyi Listok*. Alexander inspects the statue in the studio of the sculptor Peter Klodt with Montferrand, Klodt, and several officials standing behind him (*Russkii Khudozhestvennyi Listok*, no. 19 (July 20, 1857).

Scoffers in the nineteenth century remarked that Nicholas I was galloping after Peter the Great but couldn't catch up.[96]

On the pedestal, Robert Zaleman's large allegorical figures of the virtues—Justice, Strength, Faith and Reason—have the features of Nicholas's three daughters and the dowager empress Alexandra Fedorovna. The statue thus expressed Nicholas's identification of virtue with the family and with the cult of the pure and idealized wife.

The bas-reliefs on the socle by Nicholas Ramazanov and Zaleman spelled out Nicholas's achievements. Two of the four reliefs show him appearing before his people to oppose insurgency: Nicholas presents his son Alexander to the Sapper Battalion on December 14, 1825, and quells the cholera insurrection in St. Petersburg in 1831.[97] The others depict his civic accomplishments—the opening of the Vereiskii Railroad Bridge and Nicholas decorating Michael Speranskii for the completion of the Digest of Laws. In each relief Nicholas is the largest and most prominent figure, towering over uniformed officials with faces resembling his, who look upon him with admiration.[98]

The dedication of the statue, on June 25, 1859, was an act of familial devotion. Alexander wrote to his brother Constantine insisting that he and his wife return from Europe in time for the event. The ceremony, described in *Russkii Khudozhestvennyi Listok*, presented a dramatic entry of the imperial family. Alexander arrived on horseback accompanied by the Grand Dukes and his suite and, after reviewing the troops, returned to the palace to escort the empress Maria Aleksandrovna and the grand duchesses, who rode to the square in carriages. The clergy in their holiday vestments moved in a procession of the cross from St. Isaac's Cathedral to the statue. A hush fell over the square, only the sound of the church choir was heard, and the brilliant chasubles of clergy gave the impression of "a ribbon of gold." When the protodeacon had declaimed the prayer for eternal rest, the troops, at the emperor's command, saluted; a salvo came from the guns of the Peter-Paul Fortress and the boats lined up along the Neva, and then were echoed by the guns of the troops on the square. After the salvo the members of the family, followed by the ladies of the court, all in their holiday "Russian

---

[96] H. W. Janson, *The Rise and Fall of the Public Monument* (New Orleans, La., 1976), 29; Louis Réau, *Saint Petersburg* (Paris, 1913), 41. Later in the century, when the Kiev City Duma announced a competition for a monument to Nicholas I, they insisted that it not be an equestrian statue. "It is required that the monument be an exact expression of the deeds of the late emperor, and, in so doing, the emperor should not be represented on a horse" (*MV*, November 7, 1886).

[97] *Russkii Khudozhestvennyi Listok*, no. 3 (January 20, 1858): 2; no. 19 (July 1, 1859): 52–53, 62.

[98] A. E. Leonov, ed., *Russkoe iskusstvo; ocherki o zhizni i tvorchestve khudozhnikov; seredina deviatnadtsogo veka* (Moscow, 1958), 327–28; Del'vig, *Polveka russkoi zhizni*, 2: 52–53.

4. Nicholas I Monument, St. Petersburg. Design by August Montferrand.
Sculptor, Peter Klodt. Photograph by William Craft Brumfield.

dress," and the leading officials and members of the merchantry proceeded
to the statue. "At this moment the square took on another but no less solemn
character. The measured procession of the imperial family, the thousands of
people, all in silence, the uninterrupted salvos, and the ringing of bells—
all fused in some kind of extraordinary picture, full of majesty." After the

regiments passed by in ceremonial march, the imperial family returned to the Winter Palace.[99]

Alexander understood the ceremony as an expression of filial love. In a letter to his mother, the dowager empress, written after the ceremony, he described sentiments that he would express throughout his reign. Everyone was overwhelmed with tears, he wrote. "As for me, my heart was choking from [the dedication] and at the same time I was happy to be able to achieve this holy design in memory of my emperor, of my father, of the one who treated me not only as a son but as a true friend and whom I continue to serve in my heart as if he were still alive."[100]

The imperial court under Alexander II continued to represent the ceremonial center of the administration, where highly ranked and especially favored officials could pay homage to their sovereign and receive his personal recognition. Alexander followed his father's practice of drawing an increasing number of government officials into the court.[101] By the end of his reign a significant number of those with court ranks served in high positions in the administration.[102]

But court ceremonies assumed a new aura of elegance and cordiality in the first years of Alexander's reign. They presented not an inspiring exaltation of authority but an aesthetic experience meant to enchant and disarm. The Marquis de Custine and Lord Londonderry had described the balls of the 1830s as events that demonstrated Nicholas's capacity to awe his guests with his power to impose order and discipline.[103] The spectacle of Alexander II's court was captured in the famous evocation of a Winter Palace ball in 1859 by the French writer Théophile Gautier in his *Voyage en Russie*.[104]

The opening polonaise, in Gautier's description, was no longer a parade displaying the luminaries of the court and state but a show of color and

[99] *Russkii Khudozhestvennyi Listok* no. 22 (August 1, 1859): 70–71; L. G. Zakharova and L. I. Tiutiunnik, eds., *1857–1861: Perepiska Imperatora Aleksandra II s Velikim Kniazem Konstantinom Nikolaevichem; Dnevnik Konstantina Nikolaevicha* (Moscow, 1994), 101, 175.

[100] GARF, "Pis'ma Aleksandra II imp. Aleksandre Fedorovne," 728-1-2496, 97.

[101] Alexander was generous in awarding court appointments. The number of chamberlains and junkers of the chamber increased from 382 in 1855 to 536 in 1881. Officials holding court "ranks" at the highest level of the court rose from 24 in the mid-nineteenth century to 74 in 1881 (L. E. Shepelev, *Otmennennye Istoriei; chiny, zvaniia i tituly v Rossiiskoi imperii* [Leningrad, 1977], 112, 121, 123).

[102] In 1875 ten governors, nine vice governors, sixty-nine officials in the ministry of the interior, and sixteen in the ministry of finances held ranks of chamberlain or chamber-junker (from *Pridvornyi kalendar'* and *Adres-kalendar'* for 1875).

[103] On Custine's and Londonderry's accounts of Nicholas I's balls, see Volume 1: 326–30.

[104] Théophile Gautier, *Russia* (Philadephia, 1905), Vol. 1; and Théophile Gautier, *Oeuvres complètes* (Geneva, 1978), Vol. 1. Gautier's sketches first appeared in journal articles in Paris from October 1858 to January 1860. They were also published in periodicals and, in 1867, in book format, as *Voyage en Russie*. For an informative discussion of Gautier and his journey, see the introduction to the stylish Russian edition, A. D. Mikhailov, "Teofil' Got'e—pisatel' i puteshestvennik," in Teofil' Got'e, *Puteshestvie v Rossiiu* (Moscow, 1988), 5–13.

beauty.[105] The emperor was the exemplar of grace. The author marveled at the sight of Alexander leading the procession with a grand duchess or court lady on his arm. He wore a uniform "that showed to good advantage his tall, svelte, lively figure." His white jacket was braided with gold and bordered with blue Siberian fox, his breast covered with jeweled medals. "Tight-fitting blue trousers, revealing the contours of his legs, ended in thin boots." His hair was cut short, "leaving exposed his full, smooth, well-formed forehead." Alexander seemed made for artistic depiction. "His perfectly regular features, of an absolute purity, seem modeled for a gold or bronze medal." Gautier thought Alexander's mouth a fit subject for a Greek sculptor.[106] Zichy's iridescent watercolor of the scene places Alexander at the bottom center, the most graceful and gallant of the dancers on the floor.[107]

The refined elegance extends to the Asian guests, making the ball an expression of the cordiality that unites the empire. Gautier notes the turbaned heads in the hall. He remarks on what he described as a peculiarity of the Russian court—Circassian princes and Mongol officers, walking with grand dames of the Orthodox faith. "Under the white glove of civilization is concealed a little Asiatic hand, accustomed to play with the handle of a dagger, grasping it with his nervous, dark, fingers." And yet no one seemed surprised: "And isn't it natural that a Mohammedan prince marches the polonaise with a *grande dame* of St. Petersburg, a Greek Orthodox (*sic*)! Are they not both subjects of the Emperor of all the Russias?"[108]

Alexander gave another striking display of the bonds of cordiality between himself and "Asian peoples" after the capture of the imam Shamil later that year, in August 1859. He received the fierce leader of the Chechens and of other mountain peoples as a friend. He exhibited the leader at balls and parades, as a living trophy of conquest.[109] When Alexander met Shamil at the military camp at Chuguev, in Kharkov Province, the newspaper *Syn otechestva* reported that he embraced and kissed his captive and invited him to stand at his side and to wear his sword during the review of troops. Shamil's biographer wrote, "The former Imam, astonished by this tenderness, this soft, ineffably kind greeting, the like of which he had never heard, understood at this moment the true majesty of the mighty tsars." The ruler

[105] For Gautier's description of the ball, see *Russia*, 1:209–18; and *Oeuvres complètes*, 1:138–47.

[106] Gautier, *Russia*, 1:211; Gautier, *Oeuvres complètes*, 1:141.

[107] Unfortunately a black and white reproduction does not do justice to the painting. The scene is a ball of 1859, but perhaps a different ball since Alexander wears a blue jacket. For a color reproduction, see Got'e, *Puteshestvie v Rossiiu*, 121.

[108] Gautier, *Russia*, 1:212–13; Gautier, *Oeuvres complètes*, 1:142–43. Compare the description by Custine, in Marquis de Custine, *La russie en 1839* (Brussels, 1843), 2, 140–48, which only mentions a Kirghiz khan and an ugly Georgian princess "languishing without honor in the court of her conquerors."

[109] See the description of Shamil's reception in Thomas M. Barrett, "The Remaking of the Lion of Dagestan: Shamil in Captivity," *Russian Review* 53, no. 2 (July 1994): 353–66.

of Russia "gave the wild man of the mountains a touching example of dealing with one's foe," Shamil later recalled with tears in eyes."[110]

The press made clear that Shamil bore witness to the love evoked by the tsar. After the emperor left Kharkov, *Sankt-Peterburgskie Vedomosti* reported, Shamil remarked to the marshal of the nobility, "Everything I have seen here has interested me a great deal, but especially how the highest estate, the nobility, loves its young sovereign!" In return, Shamil himself became an object of popular acclaim, officials making sure to follow their emperor's lead. In Kharkov he was entertained with a circus and illuminations. When he reached Petersburg he was escorted to see the sites of the city, among them the monument to his erstwhile foe, Nicholas I. Shamil and his family were presented as wondrous specimens from a lesser civilization, objects of curiosity for anthropological study, and proof of the empire's civilizing mission in the East. They were installed at Kaluga, where Shamil, his sons, and his sons-in-law were exhibited in full tribal dress. By order of the war minister Dmitrii Miliutin, all officers passing through the town were obliged to visit him.[111]

Shamil's reception was a prelude to the imperialist rhetoric of the subsequent decades, which presented expansion to the East as a sign of Russia's belonging to the common civilization of imperial powers. In his circular of November 14, 1864, Gorchakov justified the advance into Central Asia as the pattern of "all civilized states that are brought into contact with half-savage nomad populations possessing no fixed social organization." Such states "in the interests of security" had to defend their frontiers and reduce their foe to submission, for "it is a peculiarity of Asiatics to respect nothing but visible and palpable force." The other countries, "forced by imperious necessity into this onward march," were the United States, France, Holland, and England. The civilizing of Russia's Asian neighbors had been assigned as "her special mission."[112] Gorchakov's words anticipated the conquests of the subsequent decade—Michael Cherniaev's seizure of Tashkent, Constantine Kaufmann's of Samarkand in 1868, and the reduction of Bokhara, Khiva, and Kokand to the status of Russian protectorates.

•

At the beginning of his reign, hunting excursions became occasions to display Alexander's imperial persona. Alexander I and Nicholas I had disliked hunting—for them a poor substitute for the glory of the battlefield and discipline of the parade ground. Alexander II expanded the staff of the hunting administration, founded a new preserve at Belovezh in Grodno Province,

---

[110] Ibid., 355–56; M. N. Chichakova, *Shamil' na Kavkaze i Rossii* (St. Petersburg, 1889), 107.

[111] *Sankt-Peterburgskie Vedomosti*, October 3, 1859, 929; Barrett, "The Remaking of the Lion of Dagestan," 356–57.

[112] Cited in James Cracraft, ed., *Major Problems in the History of Imperial Russia* (Lexington, Mass., 1994), 410–11.

5. *Alexander II Shoots a Bear*, Lithograph by Vasilii Timm. *Russkii Khudozhestvennyi Listok*. Slavic and Baltic Division, New York Public Library. Astor, Lenox, and Tilden Foundations.

which held some of the last of the European bison (*zubry*) surviving in the empire, and introduced a band to perform suitable music at hunts.[113] He built or rebuilt palatial hunting lodges where he, the grand dukes, and his guests made the event a ceremony of Russian monarchy.[114]

By mid-century the British aristocracy had set the example of the noble sporting life for all of Europe and had made hunting the recreation of the true aristocrat.[115] Hunting was also a sign of the prowess and courage of the leaders of a colonizing nation. The huntsman demonstrated individual daring and sangfroid to subdue other kingdoms, animal as well as human. Harriet Ritvo observed, "the hunter emerged as both the ideal and definitive type of the empire builder." Hunting narratives told of fearless sportsmen confronting big game and dwelled on the epic scenes of the death of mighty

---

[113] N. Kutepov, *Okhota na Rusi* (St. Petersburg, 1911), 4:54–55, 96–102, 153–57; A. I. Mikhailov, "Imperator Aleksandr Nikolaevich na zverinykh okhotakh (s 1849go po 1876 g.); Zapiski okhotnika ochevidtsa," *Russkaia Starina* 58 (1888); 105–10, 118–21.

[114] "Otryvok iz odnogo dnevnika," *Russkii Arkhiv* 53 (March 1915): 406; General von Schweinitz, *Denkwürdigkeiten* (Berlin, 1927), 1:190–92.

[115] Dominic Lieven, *The Aristocracy in Europe, 1815–1914* (Houndmills, 1992), 152–54.

animals. Illustrations portrayed hunters, standing alone, firing point-blank at a leaping animal.[116]

An article published in the February 1, 1857, issue of *Russkii Khudozhestvennyi Listok*, "His Imperial Majesty Shoots a Bear," placed the tsar at the center of a hunting narrative.[117] The bear, the article explains, was discovered only five or six paces away when the emperor fired. Timm's lithograph shows the scene, the bear at close proximity to the emperor (fig. 5). Alexander himself takes aim and fires. But he is not the individual man confronting the beast; the artist clearly did not wish to give the impression that the emperor's life had been endangered. At his side are a Cossack sergeant and an equerry holding a spear and a rifle.

The hunt also provided opportunities for Alexander to be seen in the company of his aristocratic servitors and foreign princes who were numbered in his suite. Another picture of the episode shows his entourage looking on admiringly after the kill. Hierarchy reigns even in the forest. His Flügel-Adjutant, Prince Wittgenstein, and the director of the imperial hunt bring the emperor two bear cubs. Beside and behind him stand other intimates: Baron Lieven, Count Baranov, both members of the suite, the duke of Mecklenburg, and the keeper of the hunt Count P. K. Ferzen. In the background, peasants and equerries drag the bear from the woods. Like other hunters, the emperor had his quarry stuffed and exhibited to display his prowess.[118]

In Russia, hunting was far more difficult and expensive than in contemporary England. Game was scarce and not regulated by laws.[119] Staging large-scale hunting excursions to game preserves became a sign of the emperor's preeminence, as well of his exemplification of European aristocratic life. The opening of the Belovezh Game Preserve on October 6 and 7, 1860, was celebrated as an important moment in Alexander II's scenario. The event was attended by members of the suite, including Prince Karl and Prince Albert of Prussia, Prince August of Württemberg, and the Duke of Saxe-Weimar. A commemorative album with color lithographs by Zichy described the hunt. Local officials, the volume explains, had made arrangements to force the animals into an enclosed area of about five square miles. At the signal the battue commenced. The hunters fired from cover, and spectators watched from a new amphitheater. The album detailed the exact number of bisons, wild boar, deer, and rabbits shot by the participants in the two days. Alexan-

---

[116] Harriet Ritvo, *The Animal Estate: The English and Other Creatures in the Victorian Age* (Cambridge, Mass., 1987), 254–56, 263–64, 268–70.

[117] *Russkii Khudozhestvennyi Listok*, no. 4 (February 1, 1857).

[118] Alexandre Dumas described one stuffed bear that he had seen during a visit to Petersburg in 1858, which "had the favor of being killed by the imperial hand of His Majesty Alexander II, who is famous as a very brave, very skilful hunter of this species of big game" (*Adventures in Czarist Russia* [London, 1960], 63).

[119] Lieven, *The Aristocracy in Europe*, 154–55.

6. Alexander II plants a sapling at the opening of the Belovezh preserve. Color lithograph by M. A. Zichy. From *Okhota v belovezhskoi pushche.*

der, of course, had the greatest success. On the second day he shot twenty-one animals, including six bisons; all the foreign princes together bagged seventeen, and the members of the suite fourteen. The hunters then received a joyous reception from crowds outside. The local population was treated to wine, vodka, and pirogi and reveled through the night. The hunt closed with the dedication of a plot of land for a monument of a bison, to recall the occasion. Alexander and several of the visiting princes planted saplings in a clearing made for the statue. The title page of the book shows the scene: Alexander stands proudly watching the planting to commemorate the opening of an imperial hunting ground. The local peasants look on from behind (fig. 6).[120] Such outings were important social events during Alexander's reign, bringing together the imperial family, Western royalty, diplomats, and Alexander's ministers in an atmosphere of sport and good fellowship.[121]

[120] *Okhota v belovezhskoi pushche* (St. Petersburg, 1861), 43–70.
[121] See, for example, von Schweinitz, *Denkwürdigkeiten*, 1:190–92, 390–91.

The Tsar-Emancipator

You have seized your day . . . Marked in its time,
By the Lord's great blessing—
He lifted the image of slave from man,
And returned the little brother to his family . . .

—*F. I. Tiutchev, "To Alexander II," March 1861*[1]

A great day: the manifesto of the freedom of the peasants. I received it
about noon. I read the document with a joyous feeling, probably the most
important document in the thousand-year history of the Russian people. I
read it aloud to my wife, children, and one friend in my study before the
portrait of Alexander II, upon which we all gazed with deep reverence
and gratitude. I tried to explain to my ten-year-old son the essence of the
manifesto as clearly as possible and told him to imprint the date, March
5, and the name of Alexander II, the Emancipator, on his heart forever.

—*A. V. Nikitenko, diary entry for March 5, 1861*[2]

THE PRESENTATION OF EMANCIPATION

Alexander's motives for embarking on the emancipation of the serfs have
eluded the historian. As heir, he had been known as a defender of serfdom,
and his personal papers give few hints to the considerations that led him
to change his mind. The Crimean War and the state of Russia's army, the
corruption of the administration, the weakness of finances—all this undoubtedly influenced him, but Alexander never explicitly indicated how. He
was reticent in expressing specific views, a problem that often left his advisers
without the necessary guidance to pursue his policies.[3] But once he decided
on the emancipation, he pursued the goal with determination and promoted
it in the government and at public appearances. The emancipation of the
serfs and the other great reforms became central themes of his scenario, elevating him as the champion of justice and humanitarian ideals in Russia.

[1] F. I. Tiutchev, *Polnoe sobranie sochinenii* (St. Petersburg, 1913), 197.
[2] A. V. Nikitenko, *Dnevnik* (Leningrad, 1955), 2:179.
[3] Daniel Field, *The End of Serfdom: Nobility and Bureaucracy in Russia, 1855–1861* (Cambridge, Mass., 1976), 60–62.

The problem of understanding Alexander's motives for emancipation reflects the difficulties of assessing a ruler's intentions while ignoring their symbolic dimension. Alexander's commitment to emancipation arose not only from the specific shortcomings of a serf system and the backwardness revealed by the Crimean War; it resulted as well from the symbolic imperative instilled in him as tsarevich, which ordained that the Russian sovereign should exemplify certain Western ideals, should play a vanguard role, should be an incarnation of absolute values of the educated elite serving the emperor and the state.[4]

Like his predecessors, Alexander strove to embody a humanitarian image of rule. In 1855 a European monarch, who represented an ethical and cultural model for his elite, could no longer appear as a defender of serfdom. In 1857 Russia remained the only major European power with a serf system. European monarchs now posed as champions of the liberal, humanitarian values identified with civilized government. More specifically, the abolition of serfdom or slavery had become a sign of political progress during the nineteenth century. The leading figures in Russian government remained fully Westernized in their culture and, Daniel Field has observed, shared "a common system of values that had no place for Russia's fundamental institution," namely, serfdom. They displayed a mentality of "Westernism," and the tsar, if he was to continue to exemplify the values of the elite, could hardly defend an institution which the historian Sergei Solov'ev described as "this sore, this shame lying on Russia, excluding her from the society of European, civilized peoples."[5]

For Nicholas I, "Westernism" had been expressed in the love for Western military order and the principles of monarchical legitimacy. He, too, had intended to deal with the injustice of serfdom, which he considered an "evil, palpable to all," one that could not continue to exist in Russia. He convened no fewer than ten secret committees to work on improving the condition of the serfs. But fearing that emancipation would bring a noble coup or a peasant insurrection, he concluded that "to attack it at this point would be even more destructive."[6] Alexander presented emancipation as the realization of Nicholas's intentions. Such a rationale enabled him to play the role of a son obedient to the paternal precept, while dismantling his father's system. It allowed him to remain faithful to the principles of autocracy while attacking its social basis, serfdom.

Historians disagree about the extent of Alexander's influence on the formulation of emancipation.[7] But whatever part he played in particular deci-

---

[4] See Volume 1: 345–51.

[5] Field, *The End of Serfdom*, 96–100; S. M. Solov'ev, *Izbrannye trudy; Zapiski* (Moscow, 1983), 339. Solov'ev wrote this section of his memoirs toward the end of the 1870s.

[6] Lincoln, *Nicholas I*, 187–89; Field, *The End of Serfdom*, 57–60.

[7] P. A. Zaionchkovskii and L. G. Zakharova for the most part present Alexander as a passive figure bowing before the menace of peasant rebellion or the crisis of the serf system. Field shows that though Alexander made key decisions leading to emancipation, he never revealed

sions, he assumed the task of presenting the reform and winning the compliance of noble landholders, most of whom were hostile to the reform. He characterized the emancipation as an expression of the feelings of love that impelled both the monarch and the nobility. Freeing the serfs was not to be understood as an administrative imposition furthering the interests of the state but rather as an act of general sacrifice in which all gave for the common good. Emancipation was the first step toward a renovation of monarchy, a popular autocracy linked with the estates through bonds of affection and mutual gratitude.

Like previous scenarios, Alexander's imposed the obligatory forms of deference that conformed to the idealized relationship between sovereign and servitors. Self-interest did not figure in this script nor did the protection of what noble landowners regarded as legal rights to the land. Alexander presented the emancipation in the rhetoric of altruism, as a voluntary sacrifice borne by the nobility in response to the summons of their sovereign to advance the good of Russia. In March 1856 Alexander had requested the nobility to come forth with proposals for emancipation, but they had not responded; instead, many took the opportunity to increase the size of their demesne lands at the expense of the plots of their serfs. When at the time of the coronation A. I. Levshin discussed the serf question with marshals of the nobility, they accepted emancipation in principle but refused to assume responsibility for renouncing the rights of their fellow noblemen.[8]

The appeal to the spirit of sacrifice remained a central fiction in the presentation of the emancipation, but only pressure from above could induce the nobility to respond. In 1857 Alexander convened a Secret Committee of leading officials, to consider the question of emancipation. In August, to move the reform forward, he appointed his brother, Constantine Nikolaevich, chairman. The interior minister S. S. Lanskoi then contrived an initiative that opened the way to noble involvement in the work of emancipation. He replied to requests of the nobility of three western provinces—Vilnius, Grodno, and Kovno. These were instigated by the governor-general of the provinces V. I. Nazimov. The "Nazimov rescripts," issued on November 20, 1857, granted the nobility the right to elect committees to consider serf reform. The rescripts, circulated to all provincial governors and to marshals of the nobility, provided for such committees, "if the nobility of the provinces

---

his reasons and left trusted officials, especially the chairman of the Chief Committee Iakov Rostovtsev, to lead the reform effort. On the other hand, Alfred Rieber and Norman Pereira present the emperor as a leader of reform, taking the initiative at key points to press reform forward (P. A. Zaionchkovskii, *Otmena krepostnogo prava* [Moscow, 1968]; L. G. Zakharova, *Samoderzhavie i otmena krepostnogo prava v Rossii, 1856–1861* [Moscow, 1984]; Field, *The End of Serfdom*, 92–97; Alfred J. Rieber, *The Politics of Autocracy: Letters of Alexander II to Prince A. I. Bariatinskii, 1857–1864* [The Hague, 1966]; N.G.O. Pereira, "Alexander II and the Decision to Emancipate the Russian Serfs, 1855–1861," *Canadian Slavic Papers* 22, no. 1 [March 1980]: 99–115).

[8] Field, *The End of Serfdom*, 63–64.

entrusted to you should express a similar desire." These words were a politely expressed command from the central government, and the nobility had no choice but to comply. They formed provincial committees that began deliberation on the terms of emancipation in their provinces in 1858 and the first half of 1859.[9]

The establishment of committees to consider emancipation represented an unprecedented step—the involvement of noble society in the discussion of an act of state, a breach of the principle of secrecy that had cloaked all discussions of reform since the reign Alexander I. Although opponents of emancipation commanded a majority in most provincial committees, the government found allies among the liberal noble intelligentsia, such as Alexander Unkovskii and other members of the Tver zemstva, and Slavophiles, such as Alexander Koshelev, Vladimir Cherkasskii, and Iurii Samarin, who defended a landed emancipation in their provincial committees.[10]

The fiction of noble initiative enabled Alexander to include the nobles in his scenario of love and lend the emancipation a personal and moral rather than legal character. He displayed his scenario on two trips in 1858. The first, in June, took him to northern provinces, which, except for Vologda, had few noble landlords. The second, in August and September, included six central serf-owning provinces and four western provinces. As in 1837, the announced intention of Alexander's travel was to acquaint him with conditions in the empire and particularly with the emancipation work of the committees. The metropolitan Filaret welcoming Alexander to the Moscow Assumption Cathedral on August 25, the second anniversary of the coronation, explained the purpose of the trip: "It stands to reason that You wish to know Your Tsardom, not only from information that reaches Your Throne, but from direct personal observations, and in this we see that effective Tsarist truth, that to govern trustworthily, one must know exactly the country governed."[11]

But another main purpose was to make his own goals known and to rally the country behind the government in the work of reform. Alexander abandoned the stately silence of the heroic myth to deliver speeches that either persuaded the landowners or cajoled and shamed them to support emancipation. One contemporary wrote, "Until this time, it was not the custom of our tsars to speak with the estates about general national interests. They usually flew with lightning speed across the vast expanse of the empire and rarely even bestowed a gracious word or glance upon the subjects who gathered to greet them."[12]

The reports in the press presented the Russian emperor as a leader of a broad process of national renewal. Glowing accounts of the emperor's recep-

[9] Ibid., 77–86.

[10] Ibid., 211.

[11] Zakharova, *Samoderzhavie i otmena krepostnogo prava*, 113; MV, August 28, 1858, 965.

[12] *Materialy dlia istorii uprazdneniia krepostnogo sostoianiia pomeshchich'ikh krestian' v Rossii v tsarstvovanie imperatora Aleksandra II* (Berlin, 1860), 1:366.

tion in official publications emphasized the play of personal feeling. *The Journal of the Ministry of the Interior* characterized his visits as "triumphal processions of the beloved of the people (*narodnyi liubimets*)." It reported the reaction of an old peasant who walked up to Alexander's carriage and asked him how he could see the tsar. When Alexander pointed to himself, the peasant bowed low before him, and said, "Permit me, little father, to shout 'Hoorah.' "[13] During the June trip through the northern provinces, Alexander was shown inspecting canals in Olonets Province and the Aleksandrov Cannon Factory in Petrozavodsk. In Vologda he met the nobility and visited an exhibition of local handiwork. All along the way he reviewed the local battalions and gave open signs of his approval at their order and condition. In each town he made the usual visits to hospitals, schools, and orphanages, demonstrating his support for education and enlightenment. In Vologda he even made an appeal to the pupils of the gymnasium: "Children, study. I hope you will be useful to the fatherland." To this the students pronounced the traditional reply: "We will do our best, Your Imperial Majesty."[14]

The June trip also displayed his reverence for religious tradition and the church. He stopped at numerous monasteries and made substantial donations for maintenance and repairs. The official press describing these visits made little of Alexander's piety. Rather, it considered notable the presence of the imperial family, their bestowal of recognition on the monastery, and the warm welcome by the brethren. A monk described the joy at receiving the emperor's attention in an account printed in the Olonets provincial newspaper. The crowd gathered around the imperial family and followed them, "like children of one great family. And only a heart full of devotion and love could understand this benignly paternal look, that angelically tender, truly and completely maternal gaze with which our August Mother and Father bade farewell to their subject children."[15]

According to the description of the imperial family's visit to Valaam Monastery in the illustrated *Russkii Khudozhestvennyi Listok*, they joined the procession of the cross to the cathedral and then, after the service, spent two hours meeting the monks and sharing in their repast. An accompanying illustration showed the emperor, the empress, their sons Nicholas and Alex-

---

[13] *Zhurnal Ministerstva vnutrennikh del* 8 (1858): part 2, 27; *IGK, ts. Al. II*, 571.

[14] *IGK, ts. Al. II*, 567–80. In August and September, before the assembled students of the Tver *gimnazium*, he declared, "I hope, my lords, that you will do your best in your studies," and the students shouted the same reply (*MV*, August 30, 1858, 978; September 13, 1858, 1035.

[15] Shvarts Collection, Folder 2, part 4: 57–59, Bakhmeteff Archive, Columbia University. On the northern tour he worshiped at the Solovetskii Monastery and, on his return trip to St. Petersburg, was joined by the empress and the grand dukes Nicholas and Alexander Aleksandrovich for visits to the Svirskii, Konovetstskii, and Valaam monasteries. He also stopped at many monasteries during his trip to central Russia, among them the Trinity Monastery at Zagorsk, the Ipat'evskii Monastery in Kostroma, and the Voskresenskii Monastery in Vladimir.

ander, and members of the imperial suite being rowed by ten monks, in full habit, on an excursion around the island. Newspaper accounts of his visit to the Solovetskii Monastery told how three thousand worshipers crowded around him as he entered the Transfiguration Cathedral.[16]

The journey to the northern provinces greatly impressed the emperor. On his return, he wrote to his mother, "Oh, how glad dear Papa would have been if he could have made the tour we have just finished. Every time one sees our good people up close, one gains new strength, and that gives us new courage to dedicate all our existence to them, as was the goal of our dear Papa's entire life." Then he added, "I am also far from taking all these demonstrations as something personal, for *me*, but rather as a certain indication of the prestige and the *bond* that, thank God, survives here between the people and their sovereign, which was so precious to our dear Papa and which he was so confident I would share."[17]

Alexander's visit to the central Russian provinces in August and September gave him additional evidence of the people's affection. In Kostroma he stepped out onto the hotel balcony three times to bow to the cheers of the people on the square. Huge crowds prevented the progress of his carriage. In Nizhnii-Novgorod the crush of the crowd broke the carriage windows and injured three women. "Everywhere their majesties go the crowd is like a raging sea," Anna Tiutcheva wrote. Clearly the members of the imperial family took the acclaim as a sign of personal affection. Even the little grand duchess Maria, Tiutcheva's charge, enjoyed the scene. It showed, she said, "that the people know her."[18]

The response appeared to confirm Alexander's scenario. He wrote to Constantine Nikolaevich from Kostroma, "We are received everywhere with ineffable cordiality, sometimes rising, one may say, to madness, particularly in Iaroslavl, and here, so much so that it becomes frightening on the streets." Constantine Nikolaevich claimed not to be surprised by the response. He replied, "Thank God, our people have not changed in their attachment to their White Tsar, and in You, dear Sasha, they still see the one who conceived the great deed of the reform of serfdom!"[19]

The popular acclaim lent force to Alexander's particular appeal to the nobilities of the central provinces. He approached them personally, securing the sympathetic intervention of provincial marshals, conversing with individual noblemen, playing on their feelings in public addresses. In this context

---

[16] *Russkii Khudozhestvennyi Listok*, no. 1 (January 1, 1859): 1; *MV*, July 1, 1858, 717.

[17] Alexander II to Alexandra Fedorovna, GARF, 728-1-2496, June 25, 1858.

[18] *MV*, August 30, 1858, 976; A. F. Tiutcheva, *Pri dvore dvukh imperatorov*, 2 vols. (Moscow, 1928), 2:159–60.

[19] L. G. Zakharova and L. I. Tiutiunnik, eds., *1857–1861: Perepiska Imperatora Aleksandra II s Velikim Kniazem Konstantinom Nikolaevichem; Dnevnik Konstantina Nikolaevicha* (Moscow, 1994), 65–66. The golden horde was known as the "white horde," and when the tsar of Russia became ruler of the khanates' territory he was regarded as their successor and called the "white tsar" (George Vernadsky, *The Mongols and Russia* [New Haven, 1953], 388).

he began to encourage a measure of openness and publicity. Publicity permitted Alexander to generalize the personal relationship he had established with the individual gentry assemblies. His addresses to the nobility, as well as descriptions of his reception, were published in the *Journal of the Ministry of the Interior* and then reprinted in the major newspapers of the capitals. Tiutchev wrote to his wife, "All these addresses prove that the emperor sincerely wants the emancipation of the peasants."[20]

These addresses presented the traditional service relationship between tsar and nobility in terms of a personal emotional bond that existed between him and the noblemen of each province.[21] To the Tver nobility, which had already announced its desire for a more extensive reform than the government had proposed, Alexander announced his intention to summon deputies from the noble committees to the capital in order to consult on the terms of the emancipation. Their efforts during the war, he said, had proved their "devotion and readiness, together with other provinces, always to promote the general good." He assured them that their well-being was always close to his heart and asked them to regard the interests of the peasants as equally dear: "We must not diverge in our actions. Our goals are the same: the general welfare of Russia." It was during the emperor's visit that the chairman of the Tver committee Alexander Unkovskii gained the ear of Count Adlerberg and suggested that the whole peasant allotment be called the *usad'ba*—the land and appurtenances immediately around the homestead. Adlerberg brought the proposal to Alexander, who, he said, was "delighted with the idea." Unkovskii, elated with his success, then tried to move further toward his goal of obligatory redemption of peasant lands in the Tver committee.[22]

In Kostroma Alexander appealed to the nobility by evoking the historical memories of the province, the original patrimony of the Romanov dynasty. Kostroma, he declared, "is close to my family and we regard it as kindred." He thanked the people of Kostroma for their reception and for their readiness to assist with the work of ameliorating the peasants' lives. He asked them to observe the terms of the Nazimov rescripts and to justify his trust in them. The Kostroma provincial newspaper wrote, "His words, spoken from the depths of his soul and with deep conviction, inspired the nobility. A loud, enthusiastic, unanimous 'Hoorah!' was the general sincere response. Tears of tenderness (*umilenie*) involuntarily revealed what was happening in everyone's soul."[23]

---

[20] "Lettres de Th. I. Tjutsheff a sa seconde épouse née Baronne de Pfeffel," 189.

[21] According to L. G. Zakharova, the provinces Alexander chose to visit were where noble committees had taken clear positions on the serf reform (Zakharova, *Samoderzhavie i otmena krepostnogo prava v Rossii*, 113–14).

[22] *Zhurnal Ministerstva vnutrennikh del* 8 (1858): part 2, 33–34; Tatishchev, *Imperator Aleksandr II*, 1:335–36; Terence Emmons, *The Russian Landed Gentry and the Peasant Emancipation of 1861* (Cambridge, 1968), 105–7.

[23] *Zhurnal Ministerstva vnutrennikh del* 8 (1858): part 2, 38; Tatishchev, *Imperator Aleksandr II*, 1:336; account from *Kostromskie Gubernskie Vedomosti*, printed in *MV*, August 30, 1858, 976–77.

Alexander spoke sharply to the Nizhnii-Novgorod nobility, whose marshal, S. V. Sheremet'ev, had organized a majority against emancipation. "You know that my goal is the general welfare. Your business is to harmonize your individual advantages with the general welfare. But I hear with regret that personalities (*lichnosti*) have arisen among you, and personalities spoil everything. It is a shame. Remove them." He urged them not to depart from the principles set forth in his rescript. In this way they would prove their "love and devotion and also the selfless striving for the general good."[24]

Alexander celebrated the second anniversary of his coronation in Moscow, where the nobility were among the most vocal critics of the Nazimov rescripts. He armed himself with the moral support of the church. During the religious service, the metropolitan Filaret—known as an opponent of emancipation—praised his sovereign's efforts in behalf of the general welfare: "Your exploits are our hopes. You laboriously sow, so that we can reap the longed-for fruits."[25]

Alexander met the Moscow nobility on the last day of his visit to the city and complained of their betrayal of his affections. The governor-general A. A. Zakrevskii greeted him with a memorandum attacking the government's program and even the peasants' right to redeem their own garden plots. Alexander replied, barely containing his anger, that after issuing the rescripts in 1857 he had expected the Moscow nobility to respond first. But Moscow had not responded. "This was grievous for me, because I am proud that I was born in Moscow, have always loved her when I was heir, and love her now as my native city." He declared that he had set forth principles in his rescripts that he would never renounce. After repeating these principles he said, "I love the nobility, consider it the chief support of the throne. I want the general good, but I do not want it at your expense. I am always ready to stand up for you, but you, for your own welfare, should strive for the good of the peasants. Remember all Russia is watching Moscow Province. I am ready to do everything I can for you . . . I repeat once more my lords, act in a way that I can stand up for you. In this way you will justify my trust in you."[26]

In Smolensk Alexander recalled that Nicholas, on his deathbed, had expressed special thanks to the nobility for their sacrifices during the Crimean War. Tears moistened his eyes. "I too love you," he declared. During the Crimean War, the noble women of Smolensk Province had presented his mother, the dowager, with an icon of the Smolensk Mother of God, to protect Alexander on his visits to the soldiers at the front. Alexander declared that the icon served as a "new bond, which ties you with me even

[24] *Zhurnal Ministerstva vnutrennikh del* 8 (1858): part 2, 43–45; *Materialy dlia istorii uprazdneniia krepostnogo sostoianiia pomeshchich'ikh krestian'*, 1:371–74; Tatishchev, *Imperator Aleksandr II*, 1:336–37.

[25] *MV*, August 28, 1858, 965.

[26] *Zhurnal Ministerstva vnutrennikh del* 10 (1858): part 2, 4–5; Tatishchev, *Imperator Aleksandr II*, 1:338; Field, *The End of Serfdom*, 157–58; *Materialy dlia istorii uprazdneniia krepostnogo sostoianiia pomeshchich'ikh krestian'*, 1:374–76.

more strongly." In subsequent months the Smolensk nobility sought to play on these feelings of mutual affection in order to convince the tsar to support their claims for compensation for the loss of their serfs' land as well as their own.[27]

Alexander's speeches were not distinguished by eloquence or even precision of expression; one commentator doubted that they had been prepared beforehand.[28] But they made clear his resolve to proceed with emancipation. His appearance dispelled the equivocal impression about the tsar's resolve left by the state secretary V. P. Butkov and the deputy minister of the interior A. I. Levshin during their visits to the provinces.[29] An opponent of the reform in Nizhni Novgorod exclaimed, "Ah my friend, there is no more hope. The tsar is a red." By presenting emancipation as an expression of the emotional and personal bond between the monarch and the nobility, Alexander made the reform irresistible: To oppose it they would have to challenge or violate the love and devotion the nobility were supposed to feel for their sovereign. An opponent of reform removed from the Tambov Provincial Committee lamented in a letter to the minister of justice, "The greatest misfortune in life for a faithful subject is the wrath of the beloved Monarch." Such statements, which undoubtedly contained elements of fawning and hypocrisy, also expressed sentiments appropriate for the loyal nobleman.[30]

The trip also affected Alexander's own attitudes toward the emancipation. Before he left, relations between him and the reformers in the Ministry of the Interior had been strained. During his visits he learned that opposition to the reform was weaker than he had been led to believe and that the peasants thought emancipation was imminent. As Larissa Zakharova has suggested, he returned with a new resolve to proceed with the emancipation. He now assured the minister S. S. Lanskoi, "We began the peasant matter together, and we will take it to the end, hand in hand."[31] He turned increasingly to the reform party in the government, which was arguing for an emancipation that would provide the peasantry with land.

An important role in changing the tsar's mind in this respect was played by a member of his suite, Ia. I. Rostovtsev, who served as a member of the Secret Committee, now called the Main Committee. Rostovtsev's four letters from abroad, arguing for a landed emancipation, impressed Alexander. On December 4, 1858, the Main Committee adopted a program for emancipa-

---

[27] *Zhurnal Ministerstva vnutrennikh del* 10 (1858): part 2, 7–8; *IGK, ts. Al. II*, 589; Field, *The End of Serfdom*, 196–99.

[28] *Materialy dlia istorii uprazdneniia krepostnogo sostoianiia pomeshchich'ikh krestian'*, 1:379.

[29] Rieber, *The Politics of Autocracy*, 43; *Materialy dlia istorii uprazdneniia krepostnogo sostoianiia pomeshchich'ikh krestian'*, 1:361–66.

[30] Zakharova, *Samoderzhavie i otmena krepostnogo prava*, 114; Tiutcheva, *Pri dvore dvukh imperatorov*, 2:157; Field, *The End of Serfdom*, 186.

[31] Zakharova, *Samoderzhavie i otmena krepostnogo prava*, 114; Tatishchev, *Imperator Aleksandr II*, 1:339–40.

tion with land, acceding to Alexander's wishes. On February 17 the emperor established the Editing Commission, with Rostovtsev as its chief, to work out the provisions to permit peasants to buy some of the land that they worked on the landlords' estates. The emperor allowed the commission considerable autonomy, which contemporaries considered was "without precedent in Russia."[32]

The assignment of the reform to the Editing Commission placed control in the hands of the liberal Westernized bureaucrats who had been preparing themselves for reform since the last decade of Nicholas's reign. Most of them had a university education, and many had belonged to the Imperial Geographical Society, where they had discussed reform and began gathering demographical data and information on the Russian countryside. Several, including the commission's leading figure, Nicholas Miliutin, had participated in a preliminary effort at emancipation on the Karlovka estate of the grand duchess Elena Pavlovna, the widow of Alexander's uncle, the grand duke Michael Pavlovich, in Poltava province. Several had been associated with the grand duke Constantine Nikolaevich's reform activity in the Naval Ministry. The "enlightened bureaucrats" had connections with noble intelligentsia circles of the 1840s. They envisioned the reform as the beginning of a civic transformation of Russia that would result in the peasants becoming full citizens and in the institution of a legal order led by the monarchy yet consonant with European juridical principles.[33]

The Editing Commission determined the range of the size and payments for peasant allotments according to local conditions in the various provinces. In all cases it increased the size of the allotments recommended by the provincial committees. When the reform encountered its final obstacle in the State Council, which was dominated by conservative landholders, Alexander again invoked his personal bond with the nobility to move the reform forward. In a rare speech to the council, on January 27, 1861, he acknowledged that the landowners' fears were understandable, "since they concern the nearest and most material interests of each." But, he continued, "I have not forgotten, and will not forget, that the initiative on the task was undertaken by the summons of the nobility, and I am fortunate that I am destined to attest to this before posterity."

Assuring the members of the council that everything possible had been done to protect the landlords' interests, Alexander reminded them that "the basis of the entire task must be the amelioration of the lives of the peasants—and amelioration not only in words and on paper but in reality." He then called on the memory of his ancestors, tracing the origins of the reform back to Paul's decree of 1797, which limited peasants' labor obligations to three

---

[32] Larissa Zakharova, "Autocracy and the Reforms of 1861–1874 in Russia: Choosing Paths of Development," in Eklof, Bushnell, and Zakharova, *Russia's Great Reforms*, 27–29.

[33] W. Bruce Lincoln, *In the Vanguard of Reform: Russia's Enlightened Bureaucrats* (De Kalb, Ill., 1982), 91–92, 105–7.

days, and Alexander I's law on Free Agriculturists, which introduced terms
for voluntary emancipation. He recalled that Nicholas had been "constantly
preoccupied with the thought of freeing the peasants."[34] The majority of
the council made numerous proposals to modify the projects in a manner
advantageous to the landlords, but in most cases Alexander approved the
minority opinion, defending the reformers' position.

N. S. Musin-Pushkin's famous painting on the occasion of the emancipation shows Alexander kneeling at his father's catafalque in the Peter-Paul
Fortress on the eve of the promulgation of the reform (fig. 7). Wearing a
greatcoat that conceals most of his uniform, the emperor kneels in the shad-
ows and in the background light streams through a window. His head rests
in his right hand as he leans on the grave; his left hand touches it tenderly.
His face wears an expression of inconsolable loss; his eyes are closed. The
emancipation is depicted as the fulfillment of a paternal precept, a propitia-
tory gift from the son to allow his father's tormented soul to rest in peace.[35]

THE EMANCIPATION AND THE PEASANTS' RESPONSE

The terms of the emancipation of the serfs represented a compromise between peasant and landlord interests. The peasants, after an obligatory period of two years, were to be completely freed from their landlords' authority. They gained possession of the small household plots near their house,
but the landlords' retained property rights to their demesne lands. The peasants could purchase their portion of these lands, through agreements with
their landlords, on the basis of norms set in the emancipation statutes. These
agreements were negotiated by peasant communes. The government advanced most of the purchase price, which they would repay over forty-nine
years in annual redemption payments. The communes were assisted by a
contingent of "peace mediators," a group of educated and, for the most
part, fair-minded officials who did their best to protect peasant interests. But
overall, agreements in European Russia deprived the peasants of 10 percent
of the land they had farmed before emancipation. Most peasants believed
the land was theirs and did not accept the reform as a true emancipation.

The emancipation maintained the separation between the peasants and
other estates intrinsic to the serf order. Officials in Petersburg feared the
consequence of allowing peasants free movement, which would make tax
collection and keeping order in the villages considerably more difficult. Such
fiscal and police considerations took precedence in the decision to maintain
the commune as an administrative and legal organization, under the ultimate
power of the Ministry of the Interior. As a result, the peasants remained

---

[34] Tatishchev, *Imperator Aleksandr II*, 1:376–77; Field, *The End of Serfdom*, 351–56.

[35] *IGK, ts. Al. II*, 671. *Niva* (February 19, 1911), cover picture. The painting later hung on
the walls of the Page Corps.

7. *Alexander II at the Grave of Nicholas I, 1861.* Painting by
N. S. Musin-Pushkin. Niva, 1911.

bound to the commune. They could sever their ties only in rare cases, since
only a few could meet the requirements laid down by the statutes. They had
to gain the agreement of the commune itself and discharge all taxes and half
the principal of the redemption payments on the plots.[36]

That the government had no illusions about the reaction of the peasantry
is clear from the precautions taken to avert unrest. The manifesto was dated
February 19, 1861—the sixth anniversary of Alexander's accession—but
promulgation was delayed until Lent, when, it was hoped, the peasants, out
of respect for religion, would remain compliant. The carnival fair was moved

---

[36] A. Gerschenkron, "Agrarian Policies and Industrialization: Russia 1861–1917," *Cambridge Economic History of Europe* (Cambridge, 1966), vol. 6, part 2, 752–53. For a good
discussion of the administrative implications of the emancipation, see Daniel Field, "The Year
of Jubilee," in Eklof, Bushnell, and Zakharova, *Russia's Great Reforms*, 48–53.

from a square close to the Winter Palace to one a safe distance away. In Petersburg and Moscow the manifesto was promulgated on Sunday, March 5, the last day of carnival. During March and April the peasants heard it pronounced from church pulpits across Russia. Many reacted with incomprehension and anger, and cried, "So, two more years!" when they heard mention of the two-year obligatory period.[37]

The Emancipation Manifesto was written in the grandiloquent rhetoric of the scenario of love by the metropolitan Filaret. An earlier version composed by Nicholas Miliutin and Iurii Samarin had presented the reform as a step in the civic transformation of Russia, the continuation of the practice begun by Alexander's predecessors, of granting "to all estates, rights and institutions secured by firm and protective laws."[38] The metropolitan removed the legal references and made no mention of civil rights extended to the population. He praised the emancipation as the realization of the tsar's oath "to embrace with our tsarist love and care all our loyal subjects, of every calling and condition, from the noble wielding the sword in defense of the fatherland to the humble person, working with the tool of his trade, from one reaching high state service to the person making a furrow on the field with his *sokha* or plough."[39]

Filaret stressed the nobility's spirit of sacrifice and altruism, and extended thanks to them for their "unselfish conduct." "Russia will not forget, that [the nobility], moved only by respect for the dignity of man and Christian love for one's neighbor, voluntarily renounced their serf right, which now has been abolished, and laid the foundation for the peasants' economic future." He expressed the hope that each landowner would accomplish "the great civic exploit of the entire estate in the bounds of his own domains," and thus help to establish advantageous conditions for the peasantry and an example of precise observance of the law.

At the same time the manifesto delivered a forceful reply to the peasantry's hopes for a "true" emancipation and betterment of their lot. The conclusion addressed the peasantry directly, warning them not to be misled by false rumors. It called on them to heed their obligations to society, quoting Paul's epistle to the Romans, that "every soul should obey the powers that be." The manifesto affirmed that the nobles' legally acquired rights could not be taken from them without compensation and the hope that the peasants would understand their landlords' sacrifice for the betterment of their lives. No law, it argued, could spread prosperity unless people labored to build for their own benefit and cultivated their land under the protection of the law. The last words were, "Cross yourself, Orthodox people, and with us

[37] Zaionchkovskii, *Otmena krepostnogo pravo*, 158–60, 164–65.
[38] P. A. Valuev, *Dnevnik P. A. Valueva* (Moscow, 1961), 1:68; N. P. Semenov, *Osvobozhedenie krestian' v tsarstvovanie Imperatora Aleksandra II* (St. Petersburg, 1892), vol. 3, part 2, 811–25.
[39] Tatishchev, *Imperator Aleksandr II*, 1:380.

summon God's blessing of your free labor, the guarantee of your domestic prosperity, and the social good."[40] On February 17 the Holy Synod sent out a secret circular, also written by Filaret, instructing local priests to encourage the peasants to seek rectification of misunderstandings with their landlords "through legal means" and to encourage "good deeds in the moral as well as the civil sense."[41]

Thus emancipation was presented not as an extension of law and rights but as a demonstration of Christian love and devotion, undertaken by the nobility and demanding gratitude from the peasants. Love in this context meant obedience to a higher law introduced by the tsar and sanctioned by religion. It answered the religious appeals of peasant rebels, like Anton Petrov, who preached an apocalyptic Christian myth of revolution. After an initial wave of disturbances in the first five months of 1861, peasant discontent ebbed, in part because of the beginning of the work of the peace mediators. But rumors of a "true emancipation" continued to circulate. The peasants resumed their posture of outer compliance and faith in the authorities.[42]

While the peace mediators took over the work of propitiating the peasants, the Ministry of the Interior provided ceremonial confirmation for the scenario. The first report of the minister Lanskoi, after the promulgation of emancipation, informed Alexander that the peasants were avoiding noisy expressions of joy. They did not content themselves with what they called "the official prayer service (*kazennyi moleben'*)" at the time of the reading of the manifesto. Dispatches from provincial officials described prayer services of thanksgiving for the tsar purportedly held in response to requests of individual peasants and peasant communes.[43] At the beginning of 1862 the Ministry of the Interior, now under the direction of Peter Valuev, began publishing *Severnaia Pochta*, a newspaper intended to influence public opinion, a Russian counterpart to the French *Moniteur universel*. The newspaper evoked the image of a grateful peasantry adoring of their tsar. Articles described the peasants' simple prayers: "Attentive eyes could note how great was the love of the tsar in the simple hearts of the people."[44]

---

[40] Ibid., 1:381–82.

[41] Zaionchkovskii, *Otmena krepostnogo prava*, 156.

[42] Paperno, "The Liberation of Serfs," 428–32. On the peasant response and peasant monarchism, see Field, "The Year of Jubilee," 40–50; Daniel Field, *Rebels in the Name of the Tsar* (Boston, 1976); and Terence Emmons, "The Peasant and the Emancipation," in Wayne S. Vucinich, ed., *The Peasant in Nineteenth-Century Russia* (Stanford, Calif., 1968), 41–71.

[43] In Moscow, Lanskoi reported, a subscription had opened to build a cathedral to Alexander Nevskii, the tsar's patron saint. Collections were begun in peasant villages for their own Alexander Nevskii shrines or churches, poor houses named after the tsar, and other charitable and religious purposes (S. N. Valk, ed., *Otmena krepostnogo prava; doklady ministrov vnutrennikh del o provedenii krest'ianskoi reformy, 1861–1862* [Moscow-Leningrad, 1950], 7, 8, 11–12).

[44] *Severnaia Pochta*, September 16, 1862, 805; September 19, 1862, 813; and September 22, 1862, 829. On the newspaper's founding, see V. G. Chernukha, *Pravitel'stvennaia politika v otnoshenii pechati 60–70-e gody XIX veka* (Leningrad, 1989), 87–91.

Alexander appeared at carefully staged public demonstrations in St. Petersburg and Moscow. Workers, still legally classified as peasants, made up most of the audience at the demonstrations. The first took place before the Winter Palace on Sunday, March 12, one week after the issuing of the manifesto. Alexander, on his way to his weekly review of the guards, met a crowd of chosen peasants and workers on the Palace Square. A delegation of artisans and factory workers presented him with bread and salt. Alexander asked whether they understood what he had done for their "general welfare." They answered obediently, "We thank your imperial majesty with feeling for your great deeds by which you have renewed our life." Alexander replied, "This task had already been started by my father, but he did not succeed in finishing it during his life." He urged them to thank God and pray for Nicholas's eternal memory, then called on them to be useful for the well-being of society.[45]

A similar meeting was organized in Moscow in May. A delegation of factory workers approached Alexander with the traditional bread and salt, and declared their gratitude. He described the scene and his feelings in a letter to the heir Nicholas Aleksandrovich. "Nearly four thousand of them gathered and, when I went out before them in the courtyard before the palace, they fell to their knees and responded to a few words with unceasing cries of 'Hoorah.' " When the empress appeared on the balcony, there were more shouts of "Hoorah." "You understand that it is impossible to look upon such scenes coolly, and inside I thanked God with all my heart for the consolation and reward for our cares."[46]

The demonstrations were also represented in popular prints, lubki, showing the workers' devotion to the tsar.[47] The pictures bring sovereign and people into the same physical space, but only magnify the symbolic distance between them. The lubok of the Moscow meeting depicts the workers kneeling humbly while their elected headman (*starosta*) faced the emperor and heir, both standing stiffly impassive in their guards' uniforms, apart from and somewhat above them (fig. 8). The empress looks down from the balcony. Their leaders, the caption explains, presented the bread and salt "four times." The *starosta* declared to Alexander, "We thank YOUR IMPERIAL MAJESTY and all YOUR Most-August House! God is in the Heavens and YOU are on earth! We take on the obligation to pray to God for YOU!" The emperor thanked them, three times, then added, "Remember only that now your first duty is to obey the law and to fulfill religiously the established obligations." The emperor then passed through the rows of workers, who shouted a rapturous "Hoorah!"[48]

[45] Tatishchev, *Imperator Aleksandr II*, 1:387–88.

[46] Letter to Nicholas Aleksandrovich, May 21, 1861, GARF, 665-1-13.

[47] Six of them were reproduced in the journal *Niva* on the fiftieth anniversary of the emancipation (*Niva* [February 19, 1911]: 156).

[48] GARF, 678-1-1027.

8. Moscow workers bring bread and salt to their Father-Sovereign. *Lubok* (popular print), 1861. GARF.

Other lubki depicted the reception of the emancipation in the country-side. One, entitled "February 19, 1861, in the Village," shows a group of peasants crossing themselves as they listen to a priest reading the manifesto.[49] Several of the pictures evoke the feeling of worship and devotion for the tsar that the peasants were supposed to feel, or appear to feel, on hearing of the emancipation. The lubok issued on the "unforgettable day of February 19" presents the emperor as a distant, almost religious figure, whom the peasants worshiped as their benefactor (fig. 9). Alexander stands in full regalia on a platform beneath Christ in heaven raising his hands in blessing. At his right are military symbols; at his left are signs of culture and en-lightenment, and a scroll with the words *law and justice*. The peasant men kneel below, some holding their hands in prayer. The verse says that they kneel to praise their "blessed Father." It calls on him to see their "tears of tenderness (*umilenie*)" and their joy. He had been blessed by the creator and the "Redeemer, himself." "You, our powerful Ruler, have given us a new life."[50] A long ode on the occasion of the emancipation, written by the peasant poet A. Cheremkhin expressed the same theme of the tsar as Christ's servant and praised emancipation as "the first Easter," bringing the peasants' rebirth.[51]

[49] *Niva* (February 19, 1911): 156, lower left.

[50] GARF, 678-1-1027.

[51] A. Cheremkhin, *Chest' i slava Tsariu osvobodivshchemu krest'ian ot krepostnoi nezavisimosti, 19 Fevralia, 1861 goda* (St. Petersburg, 1863).

He Himself was unswerving,
Fulfilling the precept of Jesus Christ,
And bearing the yoke of the cross
For His beloved Fatherland.

He was strengthened by the spirit of grace
His gaze fixed on the heavenly Father
And himself descended into the deep pit,
To save the dying lamb.[52]

THE POLITICAL MOVEMENT AND THE CELEBRATION OF THE MILLENNIUM OF RUS'

The reception of the emancipation in educated society was mixed. On the one hand, many, like Tiutchev and Nikitenko, greeted it as an important step forward, a great humanitarian gesture by the tsar. Nikitenko, after reading the manifesto, was too excited to remain at home. He wandered the streets and saw people everywhere "content, but calm." He heard complaints about the two-year waiting period, but when he met a friend, Alexei Galakhov, a historian of Russian literature, they embraced and exchanged Easter greetings: "Christ is risen!" "Truly, he is risen!" The metaphor of emancipation as resurrection was common at the time. Michael Pogodin, too, met his friends with Easter greetings. He wrote, "Twenty-three million Christian souls are being summoned to a new life, to the consciousness of their own human dignity."[53]

Tiutchev the courtier, Nikitenko the censor, Pogodin the official historian were all part of the intellectual elite, believers in Alexander's scenario. His example also inspired feelings of altruism in society, a sense that the educated should devote themselves to educating and assisting their poorer brethren. The elite of the town of Mozhaisk, for example, formed a charitable society in the late 1860s, taking the reforms as an example when "Russia was called to new life" by Alexander and "something good, brighter, kinder, and more pure stirred in everyone's heart."[54]

Others, like Pogodin's friend F. P. Elenev, were troubled about the peasants' response. Peter Valuev noted only apathy and dissatisfaction among the officials and population of Petersburg. He observed that "God Save the Tsar!" was sung in theaters with little feeling and mentioned that foreigners remarked on the apathy of the people. The senators resolved not to thank or congratulate the tsar in their response to the manifesto.[55] Noblemen began

---

[52] Ibid., 26.

[53] Nikitenko, *Dnevnik*, 1:179; Paperno, "The Liberation of the Serfs," 426–27.

[54] Adele Lindenmeyr, *Poverty Is Not a Vice: Charity, Society, and the State in Imperial Russia* (Princeton, N.J., 1996), 124.

[55] Valuev, *Dnevnik*, 1:80.

9. *The Unforgettable Day of February 19, 1861.*
Lubok, 1861. GARF.

to voice their dissatisfaction with what they regarded as inadequate payments for their land. They felt the effects of the elimination of governmental credit with the abolition of the Loan Bank in 1859.[56]

The leaders of the noble opposition demanded representative institutions that would allow them to voice these grievances and that would compensate them for the loss of their patrimonial rights over the peasantry. The movement began among the Tver gentry, whose leader, Alexander Unkovskii, had given the tsar early support for a landed emancipation. An address of the Tver nobility in 1862 sharply criticized the terms of the emancipation, particularly the absence of a provision for obligatory redemption to end the uncertain relations in the countryside. The nobility did not doubt the tsar's desire to serve the well-being of Russia, they claimed. The reforms had failed because they were "undertaken without the people's permission or knowledge." The solution was the "summoning of elected representatives from all the Russian land," which would include deputies from all estates of the population. Other noble assemblies followed with demands for public participation, though none accepted renunciation of noble rights. Members of the Moscow and Petersburg nobility advanced projects that favored wealthy landholders.[57]

Initially leaders of the nascent radical intelligentsia expressed sympathy with noble demands for representative institutions. Nicholas Chernyshevskii, Nicholas Serno-Solov'evich, and various anonymous proclamations condemned the terms of emancipation and called for a popular legislative assembly. Then, in May 1862, a series of fires lasting for several weeks leveled large areas of St. Petersburg. Rumors of arson spread. P. G. Zaichnevskii's *Young Russia*, published in the summer of 1862, called for the extermination of "the emperor's party" by axe and fire. The government blamed revolutionaries and arrested those suspected of involvement with radical organizations.[58]

So broad was the sentiment for some form of representative government that several leading officials, *sanovniki*, drafted their own plans for limited public participation in the government, intended to diffuse noble opposition and radical discontent. Peter Valuev introduced the first of a series of proposals to include a small number of representatives of conservative society in the institutions of government. By early 1862 many in Petersburg thought that political reform would inevitably follow emancipation. Dmitrii Tolstoi,

[56] On the fiscal crisis and the emancipation, see Steven Hoch, "The Banking Crisis, Peasant Reform, and Economic Development in Russia, 1857–1861," *American Historical Review* 96, no. 3 (June 1991): 795–820.

[57] Emmons, *The Russian Landed Gentry*, 340–50; A. A. Kornilov, *Obshchestvennoe dvizhenie pri Aleksandre II (1885–1881)* (Moscow, 1909), 113–17; N. G. Sladkevich, *Ocherki istorii obshchestvennoi mysli Rossii v kontse 50-kh—nachale 60-kh godov XIX veka* (Leningrad, 1962), 87–136.

[58] Emmons, *The Russian Landed Gentry*, 382–85; Franco Venturi, *Roots of Revolution* (London, 1952), 290–94.

then director of the Department of Police, predicted in 1861 that Russia would have a representative government within five years.[59]

Alexander allowed the talk to continue and waited for tempers to cool. In October 1862 he noted on one of Valuev's projects that he wanted "above all, for governmental authority to continue to represent authority and not allow any weakening and for everyone to fulfill his sacred obligation." He agreed with the need to correct the shortcomings of the administration "but without touching the basic foundations of monarchical and autocratic government." Nonetheless Alexander did not forbid such projects, which, many thought, indicated that he might change his mind.[60]

Alexander, however, would not engage in the type of politics that had allowed his German cousins to forge a powerful alliance with conservative landholders to fortify monarchical power. He still viewed his prerogatives in terms of a direct personal relationship with the people, which representative institutions would destroy. He said to Bismarck in November 1861 that the people see in the monarch "a paternal and unlimited lord, placed there by God." This feeling, he claimed, had "the force of religious belief and does not at all depend on the personal attachment that they may nurture to me, and which, I would like to think, I enjoy." He concluded that to renounce this power would deal a blow to "that mystique ruling among the people." "The deep respect with which the Russian people, from their innate feelings, surround the throne of their emperor cannot be divided. I would only decrease government authority without benefit, if I recognized any participation of representatives of the nobility or the people. God knows what the business between nobles and peasants will come to if the power of the emperor is not full enough to realize unconditional supremacy."[61] He trusted the privileged classes still less than the peasantry, whom he described as "the most reliable bulwark of order in Russia." Alexander felt that the privileged classes had not acquired "that level of education necessary for representative government."[62]

In 1862 Alexander took steps to quell the constitutional movement among the nobility. He issued warnings against future demands, which were followed in February 1862 by the arrest of thirteen Tver peace mediators for issuing a statement strongly condemning the terms of emancipation.[63] Then

---

[59] The Prussian ambassador Bismarck, in contact with influential figures in court and society, concluded in April 1861: "On the idea that 'all must change,' all unite—the aristocrat, the democrat, the Panslavist, the orientalist, and the existing order—can scarcely find a few adherents among the old bureaucrats, for the most part without influence or ambitions, primarily Germans" (Emmons, *The Russian Landed Gentry*, 395; V. G. Chernukha, *Vnutrenniaia politika tsarizma s serediny 50-kh do nachala 80-kh gg. XIX v.* [Leningrad, 1978], 24–26; Baron B. E. Nolde, *Peterburgskaia missiia Bismarka, 1859–1862* [Prague, 1925], 253–55).

[60] Chernukha, *Vnutrenniaia politika tsarizma*, 26.

[61] Nolde, *Peterburgskaia missiia Bismarka*, 259.

[62] Zakharova, "Alexander II," 190–91.

[63] Emmons, *The Russian Landed Gentry*, 344–45.

he embarked on trips through the provinces to draw the disaffected nobility back into a bond of mutual affection. Just as Alexander's 1858 trips had made known his commitment to emancipation, those of 1862 showed his determination to preserve the prerogatives of the autocrat. He addressed the nobility directly, evoking sentiments of personal devotion that could submerge oppositional feeling. The emperor's appearance in the provinces revived feelings of devotion to the throne that had been tested by an emancipation imposed from above.

In July, after a trip to the Baltic provinces, Alexander visited Tver and Moscow. In Tver he expressed his sadness that he had been misunderstood and that noblemen in the province had opposed rather than supported him in the work of emancipation. This feeling, he declared, had forced him to punish the peace mediators. Alexander used the occasion of the anniversary of his coronation to play his scenario to Moscow. Crowds shouted rapturously and rushed through the streets following his carriage. The metropolitan Filaret greeted Alexander with a speech that announced the celebration of the anniversary of the millennium of the Russian state and extolled the role of the church in the education and development of the civic spirit in Russia.[64]

•

The celebration of the MILLENNIUM of Russia took place in Novgorod on September 8, 1862. It commemorated the legendary beginning of the Russian land in 862—the summoning of the three Viking princes to Novgorod "to come and rule over us." Alexander actively participated in planning the millennium monument and in organizing the festivities. But during the summer of 1862 the atmosphere in Novgorod, a stronghold of the noble constitutional movement, became tense. The nobility made known their intention to refuse to address the tsar and to give a ball in his honor. The Ministry of the Interior, apprehensive about the situation, sent ahead the director of the Department of Police Dmitrii Tolstoi.

The newspaper, *Severnaia Pochta*, carried a series of editorials on the anniversary and accounts of the celebration written by the minister of the interior Peter Valuev.[65] The articles in *Severnaia Pochta* reveal the commitment of

---

[64] N. Barsukov, *Zhizn' i trudy M. P. Pogodina*, 22 vols. (St. Petersburg, 1905), 19:260–67; *Severnaia Pochta*, September 2, 1862, 766.

[65] Valuev mentions his visit in his diary and directs the reader to his *Severnaia Pochta* article. P. A. Zaionchkovskii identifies the September 11, 1862, article "Pis'ma iz Novgoroda" as his (Valuev, *Dnevnik*, 1:189, 393). Even the official, unpublished journal of the Imperial Court (*Kamer-fur'erskii Zhurnal*), which rarely recorded events occurring outside the precincts of imperial residences, included a detailed account (*Kamer-fur'erskii tseremonial'nyi zhurnal za 1862 g.*, RGIA, 516-28/1618-179, 391–402. On the ethos of officials loyal to the autocracy, see Daniel T. Orlovsky, *The Limits of Reform: The Ministry of Internal Affairs in Imperial Russia, 1802–1881* (Cambridge, Mass., 1981), 102–3. See also Richard Wortman, *The Development of a Russian Legal Consciousness* (Chicago, 1976), 70–78.

loyal officials to the tsar and autocracy. The calling of the Varangians represented to them, as it had to the theorists of official nationality, a primal acceptance of rule and order by the Russian people. An unsigned article described the summons to the Viking princes to "come and rule over us" as a sign of the Russians' "submissiveness to authority" and devotion to "the great idea of order." The drama of the growth of autocratic power, one of the articles contended, overwhelmed even "the most inveterate pessimist," inspiring the feeling of *umilenie*, that sense of gratitude and love for the irresistible power of the monarch.[66]

Valuev's and Dmitrii Tolstoi's accounts of the celebrations give poignant expression to the loyal officials' dedication to the tsar and their suspicion of independent political action among the nobility. In *Severnaia Pochta*, Valuev described the feelings he experienced as the emperor arrived by boat along the Volkhov. At the embankments men stood under the large decorative initials of emperor, women under the empress's initial. Alexander, with the imperial family and the suite, stepped off the boat onto the red carpet on the wharf. "Mothers with babies at the breast, decrepit old men, all came out to meet, to behold (*litsezret'*) their adored tsar!" The shouts of welcome were unusually impassioned. "Persons of all callings and ages greeted him in like manner."[67]

Tolstoi's memoir describes the change in mood that overcame the Novgorod noblemen at the sight of the tsar. They stood at the wharf, defiantly awaiting a confrontation. They wore flamboyant capes over their uniforms and "some kind of crazy caps" to shock those present and make clear their oppositional feelings. "Their movements and poses, in other words everything, indicated people who were dissatisfied and somehow aware of their autonomy."[68] As the tsar's boat approached, their hostility melted, to Tolstoi's great delight. "Their faces expressed not only curiosity. No, in their eyes one could see love. Many, looking on at the ship, crossed themselves, and crossed themselves not from cowardice. They were all overcome with a feeling of love, joy, enthusiasm!"[69] The emperor's appearance brought out what for Tolstoi were the true feelings of rapture and devotion of Russian noblemen. "So much for the opposition of our nobility!" he added triumphantly.

The next day the Novgorod nobility showed their change of heart at a reception before morning mass. The provincial marshal Prince Myshetskii welcomed Alexander with bread and salt to "the cradle of the Russian tsardom" and declared the Novgorod nobility's "unchanging feelings of warm love and devotion, about which they have always prided themselves and

---

[66] *Severnaia Pochta*, September 8, 1862, 786; September 14, 1862, 801. On Valuev's notion of a progressive autocracy, see Orlovsky, *The Limits of Reform*, 70–75.

[67] "Pis'ma iz Novgoroda," *Severnaia Pochta*, September 8, 1862, 785.

[68] Graf D. N. Tolstoi, "Zapiski," *Russkii Arkhiv* (1885), 2:56–57.

[69] Tolstoi, "Zapiski," 2:57–58.

always will pride themselves." The tsar then spoke of the emancipation as "a new sign of the indestructible bond of all the estates of the Russian land with the government, with one goal, the happiness and well-being of our dear fatherland." Alexander thus identified himself with the government and took the feelings for himself as feelings for the government as a whole.

Then he addressed the nobility: "I am accustomed to regarding you, milords the nobility, as the chief support of the throne, the defenders of the unity of the state, the comrades-in-arms of its glory, and I am sure that you and your descendants, following the examples of your ancestors, will, with me and my descendants, continue to serve Russia with faith and justice." The Novgorod noblemen responded with vows to serve tsar and fatherland. Alexander assured them that he believed their feelings of devotion, and they replied, "Believe us tsar, believe!" The falling out of partners had ended in tearful reconciliation.[70]

•

The Millennium Monument in Novgorod was intended to celebrate the political and cultural progress of Russia under the rule of its monarchs since the ninth century. But Alexander and government officials also conceived it as meaning something larger, as commemorating the Russian nation as well as the monarchy. The history of the monument reveals an impulse for a representation of the elusive term *nation* that would encompass groups outside the state and suggest the unity of monarchy and people. But as the state remained central to Alexander's conception of nationality, the monument emerged as a representation, above all, of the ambiguity of the concept of nation in his scenario.

The initial plans, drafted at the beginning of Alexander's reign, were for a statue of Riurik. In 1857 the Committee of Ministers decided on "a national (*narodnyi*) monument to the MILLENNIUM of the Russian state." The terms also specified that the monument clearly depict Orthodoxy "as the principal basis of the moral grandeur of the Russian people." It was to commemorate six principal events of the Russian past: the founding of Rus' in 862, with the figure of Riurik; the conversion of Vladimir in 989; the battle of Kulikovo in 1380; the founding of the unified Russian state with Ivan III; the election of Michael Romanov in 1613; and the reform of Russia and the founding of the empire by Peter the Great.[71]

According to P. N. Petrov's official account, the monument was intended to reflect the common feeling for progress held by both the Russian emperor and the people. It would correspond to the emperor's majestic intentions and "those feelings the Russian people always shared, and will share, in

[70] Tatishchev, *Imperator Aleksandr II*, 1:403–4.
[71] E. N. Maslova, *Pamiatnik "Tysiacheletiiu Rossii"* (Leningrad, 1977), 14–17.

the present case with His Majesty."[72] This was a restatement of the official nationality precept of the eternal devotion of the Russian people to their sovereigns. The committee's program for the monument accordingly reflected the conception of Russian history as a series of achievements of tsars and emperors. On the other hand, many of the fifty-three projects interpreted the conception of a "national monument" broadly. Several contestants took the opportunity to memorialize the emancipation. A physician submitted a sketch of a statue of the tsar next to a goddess of freedom who was removing a chain from a peasant, all placed on top of an enormous column. The architects I. I. Gornostaev and P. I. Antipov won second prize with a monument depicting allegorical figures of Russia.[73]

The winning project interpreted the requirements more literally (fig. 10). Its author, the painter M. O. Mikeshin, won the competition because his design reproduced the six scenes requested by the committee and provided a pictorial synopsis of the Russian past that showed the ruling house as builders of the Russian state.[74] He gave the statue the general shape of a bell. The upper section, above the six groups, on the other hand, was in the form of an orb, the symbol of monarchical rule. Above the orb, the figure of an angel held the cross, showing the primacy and, according to Petrov's account, indicating the providential character of the Russian past. The angel holds a cross, blesses an allegorical figure of Russia, and "points to her glorious future under the protection of Orthodoxy."[75]

Following the prescribed narrative program, the Millenium Monument allows the subject matter to prevail over aesthetic canons. Classical allegory alternates with realism, heroic images of tsars with attempts to capture actual features. The statues, many of them executed rapidly, are scarcely finished or graceful and evoked the sharp condemnation of classical artists like Peter Klodt who noted "a similarity with caricature" and found in the work of Mikeshin and I. N. Shreder "clear proof of the sharp decline of art at the present time." Nicholas Pimenov declared that the statues themselves "represented a slander on the level of perfection of Russian sculpture of our era."[76]

The armored figures from Riurik to Peter, executed by Shreder with almost identical faces, strike grandiloquent classical poses while figures of enemies or subjects kneel beneath with realistically depicted expressions of submission or fear. The effect is to emphasize the heroic, legendary character of the

---

[72] P. N. Petrov, *Pamiatnik tysiacheletiiu gosudarstva rossiiskogo v Novgorode* (St. Petersburg, 1862), 3. The brochure was printed at the presses of the Second Section of the Imperial Chancellery.

[73] Maslova, *Pamiatnik "Tysiacheletiiu Rossii"*, 17–18, 23, 26.

[74] Ibid., 23–29.

[75] Petrov, *Pamiatnik tysiacheletiiu gosudarstva rossiiskogo*, 10–11.

[76] Ibid., pp. 32–33, 54–55, 61.

10. Millennium Monument, Novgorod. Design by M. O. Mikeshin, 1862.
Niva, 1872. Slavic and Baltic Division, New York Public Library.
Astor, Lenox, and Tilden Foundations.

rulers and those they defeat or rule, though the combination of styles struck some critics at the time as discordant and anomalous.[77]

The ensemble of historical scenes endeavored to show the unity of the periods as well as the territories of the Russian state: Riurik and Vladimir face south to Kiev; Donskoi to the southeast, the Tatar frontier; Ivan III east

[77] Maslova, *Pamiatnik "Tysiacheletiiu Rossii"*, 31–35, 61.

to Moscow; Minin and Pozharskii to the west, against the Polish threat; and Peter the Great, north to Petersburg. The monument thus portrayed unbroken development from the ninth century to the present: Shifts of capital, cultural style, and political orientation were encompassed in an overall political unity. The harmonizing of disparity is exemplified by the form of the bell, which could represent either the Novgorod bell, a sign of the town's freedoms until the fifteenth century, or the great Tsar bell, a sign of central domination by the prince of Moscow.[78]

Yet it is the grandiose conception of fusing unrelated elements and styles in a visual sweep of history that is so intriguing. It is an example of the confusion of sculptural styles in the second half of the nineteenth century that art historian Maurice Rheims designated "positivist art."[79] In the era of realism, many regarded the loss of grace and harmony as a small price to pay to escape the sterile repertory of classicism. The journal *Niva*, admitting the monument's faults, praised it as "the single monument in which the artist-designer did not submit to the idea of classical traditions and repetition of Roman monuments. For this we extend the most majestic thanks to our compatriot."[80]

The statue made the invitation to the Varangians and the authority of the Russian state appear as part of an ineluctable, providential sweep—a theme that had a strong appeal for governmental officials. Valuev particularly liked the figures of Riurik and Peter the Great. Riurik seemed tranquil and still, to be looking into the distance and from the distance. "Centuries are before him. He personifies the inception, in the cloudy depths of these centuries, of the Rus' that was destined slowly to develop, strengthen, solidify, and expand before Peter." Peter, on the other hand, was in movement, scepter in hand, representing the triumph of Riurik's vision. He personified "the renewed, transformed Russia, finally subduing her neighbors and, together with Peter, submissively stepping out onto the terrain of universal history."[81]

The broadening of the concept of the elite of the Russian state was reflected in the bas-reliefs encircling the statue. These gave realistic depictions of "the great figures (*deiateli*) of the Russian land"—which included representatives of culture and science as well as monarchs, officials, clerics, and military leaders. A volume of biographical sketches of all 109 individuals honored on the reliefs was published to mark the event.[82] Sixteen artists, composers, and writers, among them Derzhavin, Karamzin, Zhukovskii, Pushkin, Gogol, and Lermontov, as well as Glinka and K. P. Briullov, converse at their leisure as if in a salon. They were followed by thirty-one "en-

[78] See Fedor Buslaev's sardonic observations on this ambiguity (*Moi dosugi* [Moscow, 1886], 208).

[79] Maurice Rheims, *19th Century Sculpture* (New York, 1977) 85.

[80] *Niva* (May 8, 1872): 300.

[81] P. A. Valuev, "8ogo sentiabria 1862 goda," *Russkaia Starina* 57 (January 1888): 8–9.

[82] Ibid., 8; N. Otto and I. Kuprianom, *Biograficheskie ocherki lits izobrazhennykh na-pamiatnike tysiacheletiia Rossii vozdvignutom v g. Novgorode* (Novgorod, 1862.)

lighteners," that is, those who spread the Orthodox faith, including Princess Olga, the saints Cyril and Methodius, and the metropolitans of Moscow. A group of twenty-six men of state began with Iaroslav the Wise and Vladimir Monomakh and included several Catherinian magnates, Michael Speranskii, and Nicholas I, whose likeness Alexander had insisted appear on the statue. Thirty-seven figures were military heroes, among them several princes, and generals and admirals of the imperial period. Ivan Susanin, the only peasant represented on the statue, appeared in this group.

The space allotted to great men outside the government is limited, almost grudging. Crowded into one segment of the relief, they serve as minor embellishments to the heroic figures creating Russia. The monument presents the nation as a mélange of different historical periods, aesthetic principles, and cultural traditions united by the monarchy and placed in a single composite by the devices of monumental art. It expresses the spirit of the reform era, of common effort without common principles, animated by the will of the monarch and the power of the state.

The monument provoked critical remarks from writers holding the Slavophile view that the Russian people, not the Russian state, represented the nation. When a lithograph of the monument was published in the official calendar, the *Mesiatseslov*, for 1862, the philologist Fedor Buslaev wrote an angry critique reflecting their objections "This is a monument to the millennium *not of Russia in general, but of Russian state life, Russian politics.*" The monument had omitted the people, Buslaev claimed. To be true to the spirit of the era, a statue should satisfy the principal demands of the era, which were demands for nationality (*narodnost'*). Even the figures chosen on the bas-relief, he asserted, had advanced only the glory of the Russian state. From top to bottom Buslaev found the monument in conflict with Russia's national past. He could see no reason why the allegory at the tip should characterize Orthodoxy. The wide dress with a scarf, the arms bare to the elbow had nothing in common with Orthodox tradition. Such a monument, he argued, should make known the national past to those who were uneducated, yet the common people could not understand these figures.[83]

The supplement to the 1862 *Mesiatseslov* contained an article by the historian Platon Pavlov of Kiev University giving a liberal interpretation of Russia's political history. Pavlov extolled the efforts of Russian monarchs in behalf of the state, their subjects, and cnlightenment. But he presented the progress of the Russian state not in terms of heroic sacrifices for the fatherland or mutual affection but as the result of the evolution of national "*self-understanding*" (*samoponimanie*). Pavlov elaborated a Hegelian vision of a

---

[83] Buslaev, *Moi dosugi*, 187–208. Buslaev pointed out that the religious "enlighteners" such as Saint Sergei of Radonezh and Anthony and Feodesii of Pechersk were presented as ordinary historical figures, yet the people would not recognize them without their halos, nor would Alexander Nevsky, Dovmont of Pskov, or Michael of Tver be recognized without their crowns. Andrei Rublev and Simon Ushakov were not numbered among the artists, and Ivan the Terrible, much admired by the people in their *byliny*, was not included.

state based on the idea of law and civic equality. Alexander II, he argued, brought the reform tradition to its culmination by making the state's goal all groups in society, not particular estates. According to "the Most Gracious Manifesto of February 19, 1861, the lower estate should be as free as the higher and middle classes."

Literature and art also flourished under the monarchs of the eighteenth and early nineteenth centuries, but now, he claimed, the Russian public should take its place at the Eastern flank of European culture. Then Russia could fulfill its destiny as the "enlightener of the ignorant barbarians of Asia." Most important, intellectual activity had now reached its final stage of "public activity, in actual life, in practice." Now all of society was engaged in such questions as the development of cities, the improvement of the condition of Jews, and, most important for Pavlov, education. "All right-thinking people try to take part in such public activity, and it must be only those who have egotistical, animal-like characters who do not sympathize with this noble movement."[84]

Pavlov was setting forth a democratic conception of the nation as a political entity, not the personal bond between monarch and people. When he tried to pursue his ideas, he tested the limits of the government's tolerance. He presented his article, which had been approved by the censors, as a lecture before an auditorium of students and political activists at the Free University of St. Petersburg. At the conclusion, he added the words, "Russia now stands above an abyss into which we will all plunge, if we do not turn to our last means of salvation, to a coming together with the people (*sblizhenie s narodom*)." The audience applauded wildly. The police moved in swiftly and arrested the professor, who within three days, on March 5, 1862, was sent into exile in Kostroma Province, where he remained for four years.[85]

•

The dedication ceremony of the statue was a moving performance of the tsar's scenario, confirming the bond of affection he felt for the estates of the empire. It took place on September 8, 1862, the anniversary of the battle of the Don as well as the heir's birthday, connecting the theme of liberation of Russia with the festivities of the imperial family. After a service in St. Sofia Cathedral, the clergy and the emperor proceeded to the monument. Before lines of troops and spectators who filled the stands, Isidore, the metropolitan of Petersburg and Novgorod, blessed the statue with holy water. All present

---

[84] P. Pavlov, "Tysiacheletie Rossii," supplement to *Mesiatseslov na 1862 god* (St. Petersburg, 1862), 3–70; P. V. Pavlov, "Tysiacheletie Rossii," *Russkii Khudozhestvennyi Listok*, no. 1 (1862): 3–4. The summary was accompanied by a montage of Russian history, showing the various principal events clustered around a figure of Peter the Great.

[85] Alan Kimball, "Russkoe grazhanskoe obshchestvo i politicheskii krizis v epokhu Velikikh reform, 1859–1863," in Ben Eklof, John Bushnell, and Larissa Zakharova, eds., *Velikie reformy v Rossii, 1856–1874* (Moscow, 1992), 271; BE, 44:571; Venturi, *Roots of Revolution*, 229.

fell to their knees, and, in a booming voice, the court deacon, Vereshchagin, delivered thanksgiving and memorial prayers written by the metropolitan Filaret.

Filaret's prayer, at Alexander's request, mentioned not only members of the ruling house but "all chosen sons of Russia" who "over the course of centuries loyally worked for her unity, well-being, and glory, on the fields of piety, enlightenment, government, and victorious defense of the fatherland." He concluded with an allusion to the spirit of rebirth and reform. "May the ancient plant of good not wither and may the new stem of good be grafted onto it and from it grow a new flower of beauty and fruit of perfection." A 101-gun salute and cries of "Hoorah!" followed the prayer.[86]

Deeply moved, Alexander wrote to his brother Constantine, "The reception by all the estates was exceedingly joyous. The dedication of the monument could not have been more marvelous or touching; especially the three prayers, composed specifically for this occasion by Filaret at my instance, which were pronounced so clearly by our Vereshchagin that the words were heard over the whole Kremlin Square."[87] In an article in *Severnaia Pochta*, Valuev wrote that he was overcome with tender pity (*umilenie*). "This prayer breathes such spiritual warmth, such pure heartfelt loving tenderness (*umilenie*), such deep religious moral feelings that reading it, you unconsciously forget your surroundings and are transported into another world, a celestial world."[88]

The warm feelings continued during the festivities. In the evening the imperial family attended a dinner for the Novgorod nobility, which Alexander opened with a toast to the well-being of Russia. Afterward he rode out to the ancient residence of the Novgorod prince, the "village" (*gorodishche*) on the edge of lake Ilmen, where Riurik presumably had lived. There he was greeted by the usual joyous reception. According to *Severnaia Pochta*, "The people met their beloved monarch with unbelievable joy and enthusiasm." Since the ground was damp, several peasants spread their caftans on the ground before the tsar's carriage. They called the tsar "heavenly angel." "One might say that the air trembled with the sound of 'Hoorah.'" The emperor wrote to his brother Constantine that this joy appeared "unfeigned." "The peasants' zeal deeply touched me," the empress remarked to Dmitrii Tolstoi.[89]

But the next day, Alexander, taking no chances, admonished official deputations from the peasantry about the widespread rumor that the emancipa-

[86] N. V. Sushkov, *Zapiski o zhizni i vremeni sviatitelia Filareta, Mitropolita Moskovskogo* (Moscow, 1868), appendix, 88; Barsukov, *Zhizn' i trudy M.P. Pogodina*, 19:268, 275–76; Tatishchev, *Imperator Aleksandr II*, 1:404.

[87] "Perepiska Aleksandra II s Velikim Kniazem Konstantinom Nikolaevichem," *Dela i Dni* 3 (1920): 82.

[88] *Severnaia Pochta*, September 14, 1862, 801.

[89] Barsukov, *Zhizn' i trudy M.P. Pogodina*, 19:277; Tatishchev, *Imperator Aleksandr II*, 1:405; "Perepiska Aleksandra II s Velikim Kniazem Konstantinom Nikolaevichem," 3:82.

tion did not represent true freedom. "Do you understand me?" he asked. "We understand," they replied obediently. Valuev described the scene in his newspaper report. "We saw the rapturous tenderness (*vostorzhennoe umilenie*) of the Russian peasant when he crossed himself at the sight of his tsar. We saw women falling to their knees and kissing the spot where the tsar walked. We heard the following words from old men. 'Just to see our Little Father the Tsar, then I don't mind dying!' "[90]

The Novgorod nobility gave their ball on the second day. Feelings were cordial. Spirited toasts proclaimed the mutual loyalty of tsar and nobility. When he was not dancing, the tsar used the opportunity to chat graciously with local noblemen. The next day, after visiting the Iur'ev Monastery, the emperor and empress returned to Petersburg.[91]

Those responsible for the organization deemed the celebration a great triumph. Valuev, who had worried about both the noble sentiment and the threatening weather, wrote that "everything was fine and successful." In *Severnaia Pochta* he recorded his sentiments, which were the appropriate feelings of a loyal official devoted to authority. As the boat disappeared from view to the accompaniment of the tolling of bells and band music, the inhabitants stood on the wharf. "Everyone was deep in tenderness (*umilenie*) and warm feelings for the Father-Tsar, for his August Family." Novgorod, he believed, would long remember the visit of Alexander, "The Monarch-Emancipator, the Monarch-Benefactor, the Monarch-Friend of Humanity."[92]

But those who understood the nation in a broader sense were less happy with the ceremony. Fedor Tiutchev found the millennium celebrations "very beautiful" but admitted that "the one thing that was lacking for me, as for many others, was a religious feeling of the past and only it could give true meaning to this festival. The millenium did not look down upon us from the summit of this monument." In an article entitled "Moscow, September 8," the Slavophile Ivan Aksakov observed that the millenium had been an official celebration that had excluded the simple people. "They do not know our archaeological calculations. They do not share Western jubilee sentimentality." The people stood outside the external periods and breaks of "external History," though they had been a part of that history when the state and land had been one before the Petrine reforms. The people had its own history of "the unbreakable historical succession of the people's soul." Aksakov concluded that the celebration had raised hopes that the state represented more than an external presence and had bonds with the traditions of the Russian people, but these ideas had been expressed neither by the monument

[90] "Perepiska Aleksandra II s Velikim Kniazem Konstantinom Nikolaevichem," 3:82; *Severnaia Pochta*, September 16, 1862, 805.

[91] *Severnaia Pochta*, September 16, 1862, 805; Valuev, "8ogo sentiabria 1862 goda," 1:12–13.

[92] Valuev, "8ogo sentiabria 1862 goda," 1:12–13; P. A. Valuev, "Pis'ma k A.G. Troinitskomu," *Russkaia Starina* 2 (1898): 212–13; *Severnaia Pochta*, September 18, 1862, 808.

nor the dedication ceremony. It is interesting that Alexander himself noted on a copy of Aksakov's article, "Much is just."[93]

The role of the *narod* in the celebration is also questioned in a curious lubok of the ceremony issued in 1867 (fig. 11). The western side of the monument is depicted where Minin offers the crown to Michael. In the foreground the emperor stands tall, saluting, behind him grand dukes of almost the same height. The guardsmen parading in the rear are somewhat shorter. The clergy, marching in the procession of the cross before the emperor, are dwarflike. The people, miniscule figures, crowd to the left of the monument which overshadows them. The anonymous artist thus represents the hierarchy of the celebration in a visual hierarchy, allowing position and space to express the assignment of power and importance. It contrasts with another, more conventional scene of the ceremony dated 1866. In this lubok, Peter the Great faces the viewer and we see the parade around the monument, with people milling in the streets.[94]

The scenario of love kept the common people apart, in a posture of distant adoration. But at the end of 1862 and during 1863 the hoped for reconciliation of the monarch and the state with the nobility appeared to have succeeded. The Novgorod ceremony ushered in one of the few periods of serenity and confidence during Alexander's reign, Valuev recalled. In the winter the emperor visited Moscow, where oppositional feeling remained strong. Alexander repeated the appeal he had made in Novgorod to the Moscow nobility and apparently won their trust. The round of gala festivities concluded with a ball given by the Moscow nobility for the heir on his name day, December 6, where, Valuev wrote, Alexander's "gracious cordiality" enraptured everyone, as it had in Novgorod. Tolstoi, too, judged the visit a triumph: "Everyone, even if they did not forget their abnormal situation, at least fell under the charm of the enchanting kindness of the Tsar so much that they were ready to give their life for him."[95]

The tsar's position was further enhanced by the uprising in Poland. The massacre of the sleeping Russian soldiers in their barracks in January 1863 produced an outpouring of patriotic sentiment that focused on the throne. The government swiftly crushed the rebels, but the savagery of the revolt, which began during a period of liberal reform in Poland, and the threatened

---

[93] "Lettres de Th. I. Tjutsheff a sa seconde épouse née Baronne de Pfeffel," *Starina i Novizna* 21 (1916); 197; Barsukov, *Zhizn' i trudy M. P. Pogodina*, 19:280–84; Aksakov's remarks correspond to those of the anonymous correspondent from *MV*, September 12, 1862, 1597, who concluded that the peasants understood nothing about the celebration except the immensity of the number, one thousand, when applied to the number of years of the existence of the Russian state.

[94] This lubok is also in the Print and Photograph Division of the New York Public Library, MEWG, 143.

[95] Tatishchev, *Imperator Aleksandr II*, 1:406–8; Tolstoi, "Zapiski," 2:59; Valuev, "8ogo sentiabria 1862 goda," 1:13.

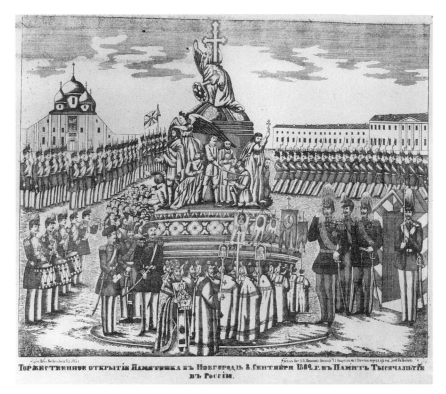

11. Dedication Ceremony of the Millennium Monument, September 8, 1862.
Lubok Print Collection. Miriam and Ira D. Wallach Division of Art, Prints,
and Photographs. New York Public Library. Astor, Lenox,
and Tilden Foundations.

intervention of England and France on the side of the insurgents, inflamed
public opinion. The tsar was enraged, determined not to repeat the capitula-
tion of the Treaty of Paris. "I signed the treaty of Paris, and that was an act
of cowardice," he exclaimed. When his advisers seemed surprised, he
pounded on the table. "It was an act of cowardice, and certainly I will not
do it again."[96] The uprising ended the entente with France and led Russia to
draw close to Prussia once again.

The Polish rebellion, showing the dangers of liberalism and tolerance to
the empire, brought punitive measures against Polish and other national
movements that might threaten imperial unity. These measures won sympathy in public opinion. It was at this time that Michael Katkov, who formerly
had supported liberal concessions, began to champion policies of Russification in the pages of his newspaper, *Moskovskie Vedomosti*. In 1863 the

[96] Shumigorskii, "Iz zapisnoi knizhki istorika," 629.

government forbade the use of the Ukrainian language, just as it was imposing the Russian language throughout administrative and educational institutions in Poland.[97]

The heir, the grand duke Nicholas Aleksandrovich, became another focus of anti-Polish sentiment and imperial patriotism during his tour of the empire in the spring of 1863 (see chapter 3). Alexander understood the acclaim for his son as a sign of the persistent sentiment for him and the dynasty. He wrote to Nicholas Aleksandrovich, expressing delight with the "joyous reception" everywhere. "The expressions in addresses and especially the money donations you have sent have touched me to the depths of my soul, for they are deeds that show the true Russian patriotism that one must take pride in and that constitutes our strength."[98]

The government won additional support with the enactment of reforms of the court system and local self-government in 1864. Both these reforms brought into being institutions with an unprecedented degree of autonomy in their activity. The court reform introduced the elements of a modern judiciary—independent courts, an open, adversarial system of justice, and a professional bar. Against the opposition of conservatives in the government, the reformers even succeeded in bringing the jury system to Russia. The local government reform established *zemstva* assemblies in the districts and provinces of Russia, with deputies elected from all estates, to deal with local "economic" needs. In the second half of the nineteenth century the *zemstva* became the principal institution promoting the development of primary education, medicine, and agronomical expertise in rural Russia.[99]

The court reform maintained the separation between the elite and the masses characteristic of Russian monarchy; it did not reach the peasants. Instead, a system of local, *volost'* (cantonal) courts, under the purview of the Ministry of the Interior, dispensed justice according to the customary law that ostensibly was preserved by the peasants. The peasants, however, did participate in *zemstvo* institutions, though these would be dominated by the nobility and were largely dependent on the peasants themselves for their sources of revenue.

Despite these limitations, the new institutions represented a great advance toward the protection of rights and the development of public life in Russia.

---

[97] On the revolution and the subsequent repression, see Theodore R. Weeks, *Nation and State in Late Imperial Russia: Nationalism and Russification on the Western Frontier, 1863–1914* (De Kalb, Ill., 1996), 94–103; on Katkov, see V. A. Tvardovskaia, *Ideologiia poreformennogo samoderzhaviia* (Moscow, 1978), 48–61.

[98] GARF, 665-1-13; letters to Nicholas Aleksandrovich of July 3, July 15, July 28, 1863.

[99] On the court reform, see Jörg Baberowski, *Autocratie und Justiz: Zum Verhältnis von Rechtsstaatlichkeit und Rückständigkeit im ausgehenden Zarenreich 1864–1914* (Frankfurt am Main, 1996), 39-121; and Wortman, *The Development of a Russian Legal Consciousness*, 235–67. On the *zemstvo* reform, see S. Frederick Starr, *Decentralization and Self-Government in Russia* (Princeton, N.J., 1972); and Terence Emmons and Wayne Vucinich, eds., *The Zemstvo in Russia: An Experiment in Local Government* (Cambridge, Mass., 1982).

The reformers had argued that they would create a conservative grounding for the monarchy in law and legal responsibility and that the *zemstva* would give the nobility the possibility they sought to participate in local government. In the short run their expectations were fulfilled. A revival of the noble constitutional movement in 1865 and 1866 proved weak and short-lived. Many noble assemblies advanced proposals "to crown the edifice" of the *zemstvo* institutions with a national *zemstvo* assembly. The most detailed plan, from the Moscow gentry assembly issued on January 11, 1865, called for dual assemblies, one elected from the *zemstvo*, the other from the nobility, "*for discussion of the common needs of the entire state.*"[100]

Alexander, now confident of his position, dissolved the Moscow assembly. In a rescript of January 29, 1865, he came forth with his only open reply to demands for political participation. He declared that the reforms the government had introduced "sufficiently attest to my constant concern to improve and perfect, to the extent of possibility and in the order prescribed by me, the various branches of state administration." He insisted that the right of initiative for reform belonged to him exclusively "and is inseparably connected with the autocratic power entrusted to me by God." His subjects did not have the right to anticipate his "incessant care for Russia's well-being. . . . No estate has the right to speak with the name of other estates. No one can take it upon himself to petition me about the general welfare and needs of the state." He expressed his belief that he would meet no further "hindrances" of this type from the nobility, "whose centuries-long service to the throne and fatherland remain in my memory and have always been and always will be unswerving."[101]

In a letter to the heir Nicholas Aleksandrovich, who was then traveling in Europe, Alexander expressed the close connection he believed linked the system of absolute monarchy with the survival of the empire. Constitutional demands, he wrote, thwarted the initiatives of the government toward "the gradual development of the prosperity and power of our Mother Russia. Constitutional forms on the model of the West would be the greatest misfortune here and would have as their first consequence *not the unity of the State but the disintegration of the Empire into pieces.*"[102]

---

[100] Emmons, *The Russian Landed Gentry*, 408–9; Kornilov, *Obshchestvennoe mnenie*, 171–72.

[101] Emmons, *The Russian Landed Gentry*, 410–11.

[102] GARF, 665-1-13, January 30, 1865. Alexander expressed the same view in a conversation with D. D. Golokhvastov in September 1865 (Tatishchev, *Imperator Aleksandr II*, 1:534).

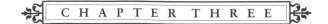

CHAPTER THREE

The Loss of Conviction

In this early grave were buried my best dreams and hopes for the well-being and the glory of the fatherland. Russia risked having an educated tsar, with lofty goals, able to understand her needs and to win for her the hearts of her most noble sons. Providence judged otherwise. Perhaps the Russian people had to learn to rely upon themselves alone.

—Boris Chicherin, Memoirs[1]

The most powerful of all sovereigns of Russia, the most beloved and popular of Tsars, no longer believes in his power or in the benefit of the reforms he has accomplished. Instead he relies upon and seeks salvation from the conspiracies presumably surrounding him on all sides and from the opposition in the spy system of the Third Section and bases the program of his entire administration on this system.

—Prince D. A. Obolenskii, Diary, December 2, 1870[2]

THE EDUCATION OF GRAND DUKE NICHOLAS ALEKSANDROVICH

At the beginning of 1865 Alexander seemed to have weathered the worst of the reform era. The mythical dramatization of the might and popularity of the imperial house seemed to have triumphed; the official nationality doctrine had been recast in more humane liberal terms. But two events, in 1865 and 1866, dispelled this euphoria. The death of Nicholas Aleksandrovich in April 1865 at the age of twenty-one deprived Alexander II of a symbol of unity and renewal. A year later, in April 1866, an attempt on his life indicated that elements among the educated remained antagonistic to the monarchy, despite the reforms. In the late 1860s and the early 1870s Alexander withdrew from his scenario, seeking personal gratification, leaving a general sense of dereliction—of both the national leadership and the moral obligations associated with the Russian monarch.

The grand duke Nicholas Aleksandrovich represented the emperor's hope of finding a common ground with educated society. His history teacher,

---

[1] B. P. Chicherin, *Vospominaniia; Moskovskii Universitet* (Moscow, 1929), 162.
[2] Obolenskii, *Dnevnik*, Folder 3: 114.

Michael Stasiulevich described him as "a living image" of what had long been the object of his tutors' dreams.[3] The heir's instructors continued to nurture the ideal of an educated monarch, prepared to assume the burden of rule for the benefit of the people. The spirit of the reform era, the exceptional intelligence and curiosity of Nicholas Aleksandrovich, seemed to give substance to the hope that they could realize this ideal in a nineteenth-century form—a national reawakening led by a talented monarch drawing on the considerable intellectual resources of Russian universities.

Nicholas Aleksandrovich's exceptional instructors and curriculum were introduced not at the initiative of the heir's parents but in response to the public criticism of his upbringing after 1855. Before 1855 neither his father, the grand duke Alexander II, nor his mother, the grand duchess Maria Aleksandrovna, had regarded Nicholas Aleksandrovich's education as a matter of serious concern. Nicholas I had taken charge of Nicholas Aleksandrovich's education and trained his grandson to follow his own example as a military officer. Nicholas Aleksandrovich learned to assume the military attributes that exemplified European monarchy in the first half of the nineteenth century. When he reached the age of seven Nicholas I chose not a philosopher or a poet but one of his adjutants to supervise Nicholas Aleksandrovich's education. He appointed General Nicholas Zinoviev, the director of the elite Page Corps, who had distinguished himself at the battle of Varna in 1829. Zinoviev was a rigid, religious person of strict rules. His assistant, General Grigorii Gogel', who had daily contact with Nicholas Aleksandrovich and his brother Alexander, had been recommended by the grand duke Michael Pavlovich. Both Zinoviev and Gogel' emphasized military drill above all other subjects in the education of the two grand dukes and forced them to stand at attention for long periods.[4]

After Nicholas I's death Alexander made few changes in the previous arrangements. The empress, nominally in charge of the heir's education, exerted little influence. In her correspondence she described her children's growth and achievements with great pride and mentioned the books she read about pedagogy, referring favorably to Rousseau's *Émile* and Dupanloup's *De l'éducation*. But she felt unable to challenge the authority of the officers in charge. For example, she disapproved of the dance hours Zinoviev introduced for the boys, but went along, she wrote, because it was the general's fondest wish to give them *tournure* and to teach them to bow—to give them the grace and charm of their father.[5] In addition, she, too, enjoyed parades. She doted on the dashing appearance of her sons dressed up in uniform,

[3] M. K. Lemke, ed., *M. M. Stasiulevich i ego sovremenniki v ikh perepiske* (St. Petersburg, 1911), 1:423.

[4] S. S. Tatishchev, "Imperator Aleksandr III; ego zhizn' i tsarstvovanie; chast' I: 1845–1865," RGIA, 878-1-4, 18–23.

[5] Hesse State Archive, D23, 32/4 October 30, 1850, December 15, 1850; D23 32/5, July 15, 1852, August 25, 1853, November 17, 1854.

particularly Nicholas Aleksandrovich, who was her favorite. She commented admiringly about his broad shoulders and his resemblance to her.[6]

The education of Nicholas Aleksandrovich became a serious matter only when educated opinion forced the emperor and empress to attend to it. After the signing of the Treaty of Paris, prominent figures in the government and society, such as the foreign minister Alexander Gorchakov, the diplomat and courtier Vladimir Titov, and the historians Michael Pogodin and Constantine Kavelin, deplored the heir's teaching staff and education. They pointed out the discrepancy between the boy's narrow, military education and the image of national leader of social and economic progress presented in Alexander's scenario. They called on Maria Aleksandrovna to take on the task of ensuring a Western, enlightened education for the heir.

The memorandums on the heir's education diverged on specifics but agreed on several basic points. They emphasized that the heir was isolated in the palace from educated society and the Russian people. Hence they urged he be sent to the university, like Western princes such as Crown Prince Frederick of Prussia and the Prince of Wales. In the first of the memorandums submitted to the empress on Nicholas Aleksandrovich's education, Gorchakov proposed university study and argued that the heir should grasp the principle that Russia "in spite of its vastness and peculiarities is not an exception but contains everything that is good or bad in the rest of the world." "It is subject to the same basic laws," he continued, "because men are the same everywhere in spite of different stages and forms." Gorchakov gave a categorical statement of Russia's national identity. "Being a Christian and European power, Russia constitutes a part of Europe."[7]

The authors agreed that trips through the country could remedy the heir's isolation. Kavelin and Pogodin emphasized the importance of leaving Petersburg to meet the people, as Kavelin put it, to come "face to face with life" and "to learn to understand their needs and sufferings."[8] Pogodin wanted Nicholas Aleksandrovich to "live one life with [the people], to grieve, rejoice, make merry with them, to feel the same hunger and thirst, to give thanks and pray together."[9]

In December 1856 the empress appointed Vladimir Titov, a protégé of Gorchakov, director of the heir's study. An ambassador and contributor in

---

[6] Hesse State Archive, D23, 32/34, letters of March 18, 1845, September 23, 1849, March 16, 1850, December 15, 1850, January 3 and July 15, 1851, and January 8 and October 8, 1859. The Count of Reiset described how in 1853 Maria Aleksandrovna watched tenderly from the window as Nicholas Aleksandrovich assumed guards' duty in an army greatcoat during a teeming rain (see Constantin de Grunwald, *Le tsar Alexandre II et son temps* [Paris, 1963], 197).

[7] The original was in French. It is reproduced in Russian in Tatishchev, "Imperator Aleksandr III," 83–88.

[8] D. A. Korsakov, "Konstantin Kavelin; Materialy dlia biografii iz semeinoi perepiski i vospominanii," *Vestnik Evropy* (August 1886): 548, 554.

[9] Nicholas Barsukov, *Zhizn' i trudy M. P. Pogodina* (St. Petersburg, 1901), 15:86.

the 1840s to Pogodin's journal, *Moskovskii Vestnik*, Titov had the social and intellectual credentials for the position. But he made only limited changes in the curriculum and could not combat the influence of the "generals." His projects for a completely new educational program frightened conservative figures in the court, particularly the dowager empress Alexandra Fedorovna.[10] Kavelin, who had begun to teach the heir jurisprudence, was discharged when his memorandum on the redemption of the serfs with land was published in *Sovremennik*.[11]

In 1858, without removing Titov, the empress appointed the confidant of Alexandra Fedorovna, August Theodore Grimm, to the grand dukes' teaching staff. Grimm had been tutor to the grand dukes Constantine, Michael, and Nicholas Nikolaevich, as well as the grand duchess Alexandra Nikolaevna. He believed that Germans had a civilizing mission. Not only was he unable to speak Russian but his books were openly scornful of Russia and Russians.[12] He reduced the number of hours devoted to Russian language and literature. Grimm insisted that Russian history contained no principle of organic development and did not represent a proper object of study.[13]

Grimm's pedagogy created a scandal that quickly went beyond the bounds of the court and brought the issue of the heir's education into debates on Russia's destiny. Alexander Herzen, conducting a steady critique of the government from London in his journal, *The Bell*, showed that the fate of reform depended on the heir's education. In November 1858 he published an open letter to the empress, taking her to task for neglecting her responsibility to train Russia's future ruler. "We have no present," Herzen began, "so it is scarcely surprising that we are concerned above all with the future of our native land." Maria Aleksandrovna had disappointed hopes of seeing the heir at a university desk. She had fallen under the influence of "the black cabinet"—the enemies of progress in Russia who opposed open courts, publicity, and emancipation. Instead, the grand dukes received a military education. "The military uniform, like a monk's habit, cuts a man off from other people," Herzen asserted. "The title of Russian tsar is not a military rank." Yet the young grand dukes were playing at war—a practice, he remarked, of Prussian and petty German princes. Meanwhile, he wrote, "the Prince of Wales . . . sits over a microscope and studies zoology." The heir was compelled to learn the details of the uniforms of each regiment, the

---

[10] Titov planned to establish a special elite school where the heir could study with aristocratic boys (see the Gershel'man-Shvarts fond, BAR, part 4).

[11] Tatishchev, "Imperator Aleksandr III," 154–59. F. A. Oom asserts, in his "Vospominaniia," *Russkii Arkhiv* (1896), 2:248, that Kavelin was asked to resign because he had taught that no one can be punished without the verdict of a court, a view interpreted in higher circles as an infringement on imperial prerogatives which brought pressure for his resignation. I have found no evidence of dissatisfaction with the content of his lessons.

[12] Tiutcheva, *Pri dvore dvukh imperatorov*, 2:180–81.

[13] B. Glinskii, "Nastavnik tsarskikh detei," *Istoricheskii Vestnik* 63 (January 1896): 261–63; Shvarts, BAR, part 4, 75–77; Oom, "Vospominaniia," 2:251.

"secrets" of the presentation of arms, and the commanding of different detachments, but he knew nothing of governmental procedure, the limits of the authority of different offices, and the economic conditions of the various parts of Russia. "Teach your son to wear a tailcoat, register him in the civil service," Herzen urged.[14]

Herzen's letter reached its mark. Within a month, it was circulating in the court. Grimm's pedagogy succeeded in uniting all those concerned with the grand dukes' education—the court, the generals, the teaching staff, the liberal intellectuals—in a demand for a change in the heir's program. Maria Aleksandrovna, greatly distressed, showed the letter to Anna Tiutcheva, her lady-in-waiting. "Herzen is a scoundrel," Tiutcheva wrote in her diary. "But, alas, on this question as on many others, he is right."[15] The scandal resulted in the appointment of the highly esteemed Count Sergei Grigorevich Stroganov as director of Nicholas Aleksandrovich's education. The preceptor of the Moscow educational district from 1835 to 1847, Stroganov had protected Moscow University and helped to develop it as a center of learning. He was a devotee of history and archaeology and had served as president of the Moscow Society of Russian History and Antiquities and as director of the publication of a series of Russian historical documents, *Drevnosti Rossiiskogo Gosudarstva*. He was the author of a study of St. Dmitrii's Cathedral in Vladimir.[16]

Stroganov assumed his position immediately after the celebration of the heir's majority in September 1859. He believed that Nicholas Aleksandrovich should attend university courses, but political tensions accompanying the emancipation thwarted his plans. The heir attended lectures at Kazan University during his trip through the central Russian provinces in the summer of 1861. There he sat on benches beside other university students and heard lectures on physiology, physics, criminal law, mathematics, and aesthetics. But in 1862 student unrest and the fires in Petersburg kept Nicholas Aleksandrovich from attending lectures at St. Petersburg University and precluded such plans in the future. Russian universities harbored forces bitterly opposed to autocracy, and the fear of conflict that underlay the Russian political order kept Nicholas Aleksandrovich, as well as subsequent heirs to the throne, apart from Russian society.[17]

Instead, distinguished scholars from the university came to teach the heir in the palace. Stroganov separated Nicholas Aleksandrovich from his younger brother Alexander and, in 1861, started him on an exacting pro-

[14] [Alexander Herzen], "Pis'mo k imperatritse Marii Aleksandrovne," *Kolokol*, no. 27 (November 1, 1858): 217–19.

[15] Tiutcheva, *Pri dvore dvukh imperatorov*, 2:181–82.

[16] *BE*, 62:804.

[17] Barsukov, *Zhizn' i trudy M. P. Pogodina*, 18:201–5; Chicherin, *Vospominania; Moskovskii Universitet*, 87; Tatishchev, "Imperator Aleksandr III," 317–18. On the student movements at Russian universities in this period, see Abbott Gleason, *Young Russia: The Genesis of Russian Radicalism in the 1860s* (New York, 1980), 114–72.

gram of study that would last three and one-half years.[18] From Moscow University he recruited Fedor Buslaev to teach Russian literature; Sergei Solov'ev, Russian history; Boris Chicherin, public law and political philosophy; Constantine Pobedonostsev, jurisprudence; and I. K. Babst, statistics. V. D. Kudriavtsev from the Moscow Religious Academy was responsible for the history of philosophy. The economist A. I. Chivilev from the Appanage Department and N. Bunge, the rector of Kiev University, taught, respectively, political economy and the history of finance. M. M. Stasiulevich of St. Petersburg University was appointed the heir's instructor in world history.[19] The result was a growing closeness between the teachers and the heir. They gave him the guidance in understanding his future obligations that he had not received from his parents or the generals and filled the emotional gap left by the emperor and the empress.

Under Stroganov's direction, Nicholas Aleksandrovich's instructors brought a sense of intellectual excitement and inquiry into the classroom. For the first time in a grand ducal education, knowledge and study became values in themselves and not subject to the education of the sentiments or morals—as had been the case with Alexander II. Stroganov explained his approach in a letter to Buslaev in October 1859: "I think you should pay attention principally to training your pupil in independent initiative (*samodeiatel'nost'*), acquainting him with the daily life (*byt*) and intellectual development of Russia in the history of her literature." Buslaev taught by discussion, which he based on literary texts. He acquainted Nicholas Aleksandrovich with the selections from religious and literary works from old Russia in his *Reader*, which served as a standard secondary-school text in late tsarist Russia. Buslaev explained the various Byzantine sources of Russian religion and acquainted his pupil with the tradition of Orthodox patericons and the heroic exploits of the Byzantine past. A follower of the German philologist Jacob Grimm, Buslaev presented a unified Russian literary tradition, which included heroic poems (*byliny*) and lyrics, as well as the epics *The Lay of the Host of Igor* and *Zadonshchina*.[20]

Buslaev's lessons taught Nicholas Aleksandrovich to seek Russia's national character in the creative forces of all groups of Russian people rather than only in the monarchy. He emphasized that "the necessity for the *correct study* of the Russian people in all its estates and classes is the principal and

---

[18] In the first year, in addition to theology, the heir would study history of philosophy, universal and Russian history, Russian geography, and encyclopedia of law. He would hear no more than three lectures a day and would spend the rest of his time preparing his subjects, reading, and practicing fencing.

[19] Tatishchev, "Imperator Aleksandr III," 221, 281–83.

[20] F. I. Buslaev, *Moi vospominaniia* (Moscow, 1897), 330, 334, 337, 339–41. Buslaev's lessons were published at the beginning of the twentieth century (Fedor Buslaev, *Russkaia Khrestomatiia* [Moscow, 1904]; F. I. Buslaev, *Istoriia russkoi literatury; lektsii, chitannye Ego Imperatorskomu Vysochestvu Nasledniku Tsesarevichu Nikolaiu Aleksandrovichu, 1859–1860 g.* [Moscow, 1904], 3).

substantive conclusion we have drawn from the history of Russian literature." By conducting his lessons as discussions rather than lectures, he engaged his pupil in his own quest for a national literary tradition. Nicholas Aleksandrovich requested additional meetings with Buslaev and read such works as Kiril Danilov's song book on his own. He borrowed a manuscript of Russian saints' lives, studies of the history of the Russian Church, and the Law Code of Alexei Mikhailovich. Nicholas Aleksandrovich was the first heir to the Russian throne to interest himself in the pre-Petrine literary tradition and Russian folk poetry.[21]

Sergei Solov'ev taught the heir that the Russian state had a mission that went beyond territorial aggrandizement and national defense. Nicholas Aleksandrovich's classroom notes transcribed the principles that Solov'ev had set forth in the opening sections of his *History of Russia from Ancient Times*. He learned that "Russian history is the history of a European Christian State. Russia must not be regarded as a colossus composed of conquests. It is a new Christian state." Solov'ev's model was not absolute monarchy, but Western civil society and juridical institutions. Russia differed from the "educated West" because of its eastern situation and its lack of population. "All the stagnation, all the poverty of Russian life, all the inadequacy of industry was the result of a sparse population on so vast a territory," Nicholas Aleksandrovich wrote in his notes. Russia developed by moving, like the West, from the clan to higher stages of social organization embodied by the state.[22]

Michael Stasiulevich presented European history in terms of the progress of freedom and individualism, rather than as a succession of just and evil kings. He asked Nicholas Aleksandrovich not to believe that the French Revolution was the result of evil passions but to understand that it arose from a striving for freedom produced by the organic development of society. He quoted Thomas Babington MacCaulay's comparison of freedom with a good fairy, who first appeared in an ugly form of insurrections. To prevent revolution, Stasiulevich taught, it was necessary to understand the real conditions of life, "and so education and not military power saves governments from catastrophes."[23]

In 1862 and 1863 Nicholas Aleksandrovich began the serious study of political economy. Three prominent economists, Nicholas Bunge, Ivan Babst, and Alexander Chivilev, joined his teaching staff and taught courses that presented Europe as a model of economic development that could increase the wealth of the population. Though their views differed, they all rejected the view dominant in Nicholas I's reign, that industrial growth led to the impoverishment and social dislocation of the population. The heir's classroom notes in political economy, probably from Bunge's lectures, con-

---

[21] Buslaev, *Moi vospominaniia*, 330, 349.

[22] "Zapisi lektsii po istorii," GARF, 665-1-1.

[23] M. K. Lemke, *M. M. Stasiulevich i ego sovremenniki v ikh perepiske*, 1:423, 410; Oom, "Vospominaniia," 2:253.

tain a transcription of a classical liberal argument for the productive benefits of technology: Machines in the long run increased wages and increased employment, and to resist technological change was to risk returning to a state of savagery and hinder the perfection of humanity. The development of the English and Irish cotton industries from 1745 to 1807 served as an example of how the introduction of machinery brought a great increase in employment and production.[24]

Boris Chicherin's lectures on the history of European political philosophy acquainted the heir with the basic concepts of liberal idealism in the teachings of Kant and Hegel. Chicherin presented what he described as essentially the same course as he delivered at the university. Stroganov attended all lectures and the empress appeared two or three times. On his examination, Nicholas Aleksandrovich showed that he had mastered Kant's categorical imperative and many difficult concepts of Hegelian philosophy. Chicherin recalled that he presented them all "so clearly, logically, and even elegantly that one couldn't have wished for more." Unfortunately court and military functions left little time for reading the actual texts, and Nicholas Aleksandrovich finished reading only Machiavelli, who impressed him greatly. Chicherin was not allowed the time to deliver his final lectures, but he left his lecture notes for the heir to study. He looked forward to the day when Nicholas Aleksandrovich would have more time to finish the course.[25] Nicholas Aleksandrovich wrote to his mother about his passion for the study of philosophy.[26]

As a result of his education, the heir had taken on the features of the Western ideal that his instructors had hoped Russian monarchs would exemplify. His correspondence indicates that he fully sympathized with the cause of reform, and he played a role in the abolition of corporal punishment in 1863. The diplomat Nicholas Orlov enlisted Nicholas Aleksandrovich in support of this reform as early as 1861 and claimed that the reform had been the heir's initiative. He wrote to Nicholas Aleksandrovich in 1863, "In your still young mind, the idea was born of a reform that was nearly the most important for our morals and the morality of the people."[27]

---

[24] "Zapisi lektsii po politicheskoi ekonomii, 1862," GARF, 665-1-5.

[25] Chicherin, Vospominaniia; Moskovskii Universitet, 87–88; G. M. Hamburg, Boris Chicherin and Early Russian Liberalism, 1828–1866 (Stanford, Calif., 1992), 266–69; Oom, "Vospominaniia," 3:35–37.

[26] Nicholas Aleksandrovich wrote to his mother on September 27, 1861 (the letter is misdated August 27): "Aristotle, Aristotle alone gives me enormous pleasure. We have finished Plato, Socrates, a while back, but they have not died for me. Their names are repeated at each step. All my serious lectures now are related to one another and have a philosophical character." He had withdrawn to his studies, living in his own special world, a world that was "higher and purer than the actual, real world" ("Pis'ma syna Nikolaia Imperatritse Marii Aleksandrovny," GARF, 641-1-33, 16).

[27] "Pis'ma N. A. Orlova v. k. Nikolaiu Aleksandrovichu," GARF, 665-1-27, letter of March 4, 1863. On Orlov's role in the abolition of corporal punishment, see Gr. Dzhanshiev, Epokha velikikh reform (Moscow, 1896), 173–76.

THE SON AS SYMBOL

Acceding to the throne, Alexander II felt himself the devoted son rather than the father, a role he still identified with Nicholas I. His relations with his sons, including Nicholas Aleksandrovich, were distant. On the other hand, he continued to present his family as the incarnation of the monarchy and Nicholas Aleksandrovich as the hope of the dynasty, who would carry on the work of transformation that he had begun. Alexander frequently reminded Nicholas Aleksandrovich of Nicholas I's deathbed exhortation to "serve Russia."[28] Lubki published in the first years of Alexander's reign reproduced the motifs of those published after Nicholas's accession. The heir joins his father with other grand dukes on horseback (fig. 12). He stands with the emperor and the empress in the presence of the regalia, after the coronation (fig. 13).[29]

Nicholas Aleksandrovich's majority ceremony on September 8, 1859, was an occasion to celebrate Russia's impending national rebirth. The account in *Russkii Invalid* noted that Nicholas's birthday, September 8, fell on the anniversary of the Battle of Kulikovo in 1380 and on the holiday of the birth of the Mother of God, which, it stated, signified the beginning of mankind's salvation. The battle of Kulikovo was presented not as a sign of military power, as in the past, but of liberation, the day "when Russia cast off the last survivals of error and readied herself by the summons and direction of the worshiped Tsar to move along the path of citizenship (*grazhdanstvennost'*)." Citizenship suggested the appearance of a civil society, of educated individuals, equal under the law, who were taking part in the life of the people. The struggle now was to be waged against "ignorance and its direct heritage, intolerance and fanaticism."[30]

Nicholas Aleksandrovich's preparation for the ceremony stressed the ties of love between the people and the tsar. The precept delivered to him by V. I. Klassovskii, his teacher of literature, emphasized the source of strength to be found in "the powerful bond of love and faith uniting all Russia and the whole good people of Russia with the Tsar and the Tsar's House. You have experienced this so many times, and so many times still experience it, whenever you have appeared among the people what a chorus of love and sympathy meets you." Klassovskii, however, urged him not to take this affection for granted. "It expresses the striving of the entire people for the unity which

---

[28] For example, on Nicholas Aleksandrovich's fifteenth birthday, in 1858, Alexander wrote that he prayed to God to preserve the heir for "the happiness of Russia." "But remember that to achieve this it is necessary to make yourself *worthy* by all the means available to you and to make use of the time that still remains to study and work, and not only by compulsion but *by inclination* and with constant application. Don't forget Grandpa's words: *Serve Russia!*" ("Pis'ma Aleksandra II Nikolaiu Aleksandrovichu," GARF, 665-1-13, letter of September 8, 1858).

[29] See the collection of lubki in GARF, 678-1-1027.

[30] *Russkii Invalid* (September 8, 1859): 790–91.

Его Императорское Величество Государь Император Александръ II Самодержецъ Всероссийскiй и Его Императорское Высочество Наслѣдникъ Цесаревичъ Николай Александровичъ и Ихъ Императорскiя Высочества Великiя Князья Константинъ Николаевичъ, Николай Николаевичъ и Михаилъ Николаевичъ.

12. Alexander II and Grand Dukes after accession. Lubok, 1855.
Print Division, Russian National Library, St. Petersburg.

it finds in the Tsar's House, love, faith in the future, and that limitless devotion has worked and will work miracles in our history."[31]

The ceremony was identical to Alexander's in 1834, reaffirming the solidarity of son with father and of the imperial family as a whole with the highest ranks of the court, the military, and the state. The taking of the civil oath in the Great Church of the Winter Palace was followed by the military ceremony in the Hall of St. George, in the presence of rows of brilliantly dressed guardsmen. Zinoviev, Gogel', and the heir's companion Colonel Otto Richter attended. The heir's tutors did not receive invitations.[32] Again,

[31] [V. I. Klassovskii,] "Privetstsvie starogo vospitatelia Velikomu Kniaziu v den' ego sovershennoletiia," *Starina i novizna* 2 (1907): 1–9. This was definitely addressed to Nicholas Alexandrovich since it specifies at the beginning that it was delivered on the occasion of his majority *on his sixteenth birthday*. Only the heir celebrated their majorities on their sixteenth birthdays; other grand dukes celebrated theirs on their eighteenth. The attribution to Klassovskii was made by Shvarts, BAR, part 8.

[32] *Kamer-fur'erskii Zhurnal* (1859), RGIA, 516-28/1618-175, 370, 380. The event took place before Stroganov's tenure, when the count raised the prestige of the teaching staff. An unusual marginal note in the court journal made their absence apparent: "The teachers of His Highness were not present at the procession." Zhukovskii attended as well as Alexander's

13. Alexander II, Empress Maria Aleksandrovna, and Grand Duke
and Heir Nicholas Aleksandrovich. Lubok, 1857. GARF.

the emotional climax occurred when the son embraced his parents. Nicholas
Aleksandrovich threw himself into his father's arms, bowed before his
mother, and kissed her hand. "Her majesty strongly embraced her beloved
son, who yesterday was still a boy and today completed the first duty of a
man on the expansive imperial field with all its majesty and responsibility,"

mathematics teacher, Edward Collins, who had been present at the 1834 ceremony (I. A. Shliapkin, "Iz bumag odnogo iz prepodavatelei Aleksandra II," *Starina i novizna* 22 [1917]: 15).

Russkii Invalid reported. On this day he was appointed a *flügel-adjutant* in his father's suite.[33] Nicholas Aleksandrovich made an especially favorable impression at the diplomatic reception. The ambassadors were struck by his poise and charm but above all by his knowledge. He proved able to discuss the foreign policy and the rulers of their respective nations and conducted "a brilliant reception."[34]

A people's celebration on Devich'e Pole in Petersburg brought the people into the event, entertaining them with games and refreshments. A montage in *Russkii Khudozhestvennyi Listok* gives glimpses of the amusements, around a lunette with a bust of the heir. Acrobats and magicians performed on four stages. In the middle of the field a machine released balloons. Four regimental bands played songs. *Russkii Khudozhestvennyi Listok* observed that "everything was assembled here to amuse Russian folk, who could not make up their minds what to look at, what to enjoy." In the evening, illuminations spread the carnival atmosphere to the streets of the capital, and the next day the performances and the illuminations were repeated. The emperor marked the occasion with generous donations to the poor, reduction of the service requirement for recruits to the lower ranks in the army to fifteen years and the navy to fourteen years, and termination of new cases of confiscation of estates for those involved in the Polish uprising of 1831.[35]

On his travels in the empire in 1860 and 1861 Nicholas Aleksandrovich established a new type of bond with the Russian people. His contact with them went beyond ceremonial displays. As Kavelin, Pogodin, and Buslaev had urged, he tried to learn about the people and their lives. He revealed a fresh curiosity about the local culture and economic conditions, and an ability to interact with the population. When he visited Riga in 1860, he informed himself about the local economy. He remarked on the difference between the organic, historical appearance of the city and the artificial character of Petersburg. Noting the signs of prosperity and the imposing, beautifully decorated buildings, he observed:

> All this hasn't cost the crown a kopek. It means that the city has a history. In every century the civilization grew in prosperity and intellectual resources, and it asked from the crown only not to be restricted. We in Petersburg, on the contrary, were born yesterday and have no history. As a result, all enterprises must receive money from the crown, and still nothing comes of it.[36]

Economic conditions were at the center of Nicholas Aleksandrovich's attention when he traveled through the heartland of Russia—Nizhnii-Novgorod, Kazan, and Moscow provinces—during the difficult first months of emancipation in the summer of 1861. He met and spoke with the people,

---

[33] Oom, "Vospominaniia," 2:252; *Russkii Invalid* (September 10, 1859): 793; (September 11, 1859): 799.

[34] Oom, "Vospominaniia," 2:252.

[35] *Russkii Khudozhestvennyi Listok*, no. 30 (October 20, 1859): 98–99.

[36] Julius Eckardt, ed., *Baltische Briefe aus zwei Jahrhunderten* (Berlin, n.d.), 124.

trying to understand their feelings and their needs. The writer and ethnographer P. I. Melnikov took him on a tour of the fair at Nizhnii-Novgorod. *Moskovskie Vedomosti* reported the visit, telling how he talked with workers about their lives and work, asked about the boat traffic and commerce on the Volga, and inquired about the processes of baking bread, even going into the smokehouses and a soap warehouse. He visited peasants in their huts and listened to their talk about their lives and their farm animals. He asked the head of household about the icons on the walls, and it was clear he understood the various styles. "A Russian, a real Russian," the peasants exclaimed.[37]

The peasants, the *Moskovskie Vedomosti* account suggested, were amazed to meet a member of the imperial family who shared their interests and knew their culture. He did not play at being Russian but was a "real Russian." Nicholas Aleksandrovich's own observations make it evident that his involvement with their life was keen and genuine. He was troubled by scenes of backwardness and poverty throughout the trip. At the soap warehouse in Nizhnii-Novgorod, he remarked on the potential benefits of increasing production for the well-being of the Russian people, "who, often slovenly, could start to concern themselves with cleanliness, which serves everywhere as a measure of civic progress." He was amazed at an enormous barge laden with sacks of grain. On August 31 he wrote to his mother, "You inevitably begin pondering and think to yourself: Great and rich you are Mother Russia. You scatter your grain around half the world. But holy Rus' is not rich. Your peasant is poor, trade goes badly, there is no money, there is stagnation, and you ask yourself why is this? And from the start you can't understand why, and it is painful for the Russian heart."[38]

In 1863, in the midst of the Polish rebellion, Nicholas Aleksandrovich embarked on his extended tour of Russia. The journey was reported in letters of his instructors, Ivan Babst and Constantine Pobedonostsev, which first appeared in Michael Katkov's *Moskovskie Vedomosti*. Babst and Pobedonostsev presented the trip as a display of the bonds that united the imperial family with a newly awakened Russian nation. The heir displayed these bonds, showing his concern for the development of Russian industry and native Russian culture, as well as sharing the people's patriotic fervor in the struggle against the rebellion.[39]

The economic development of Russian industry was at the center of Babst's interests, and he used the heir's concern with economic conditions

---

[37] Buslaev, *Moi vospominaniia*, 349–55. This account includes extracts from the reports in *Moskovskie Vedomosti*.

[38] Tatishchev, "Imperator Aleksandr" III, 298–99; "Pis'ma syna Nikolaia Imperatritse Marii Aleksandrovny," 22–23.

[39] The authors note in their introduction that they were endeavoring "to satisfy the wish of the heir to learn the needs of the regions through which his trip passed" (K. P. Pobedonostsev and I. Babst, *Pis'ma o puteshestvii gosudaria naslednika tsesarevicha po Rossii ot Peterburga do Kryma* [Moscow, 1864], iv).

to promote his own protectionist views.[40] The letters recount Nicholas Aleksandrovich's visits to factories, canals, and markets, as well as his conversations with manufacturers, marshals of the nobility, and professors. In Kostroma, Babst and Pobedonostsev cited the arguments of local factory owners that the protection of industry by a tariff would help Russian manufacturers to produce more efficiently and reduce prices. The manufacturers were gratified by the heir's interest and attentiveness. " 'You studied,' you modestly declared, and these words delighted us." They stated their wishes bluntly. "We see in this the guarantee of the well-being of our native industry, and we dare to hope that Your Imperial Highness will be the high patron and intercessor for us before the Sovereign Emperor."[41]

Nicholas Aleksandrovich viewed the economy through Babst's eyes and began to take on his teacher's protectionist views. The surviving fragment of his travel diary relates his visit to a rope factory on the Volga, near Rybinsk, and then discusses the future of steamships as freight carriers on the river. He observes a steam-powered grain mill on the Volga with great interest. In Kostroma he inspects a linen factory, then machine and nail factories, and repeats Babst's arguments. "This interesting production," he wrote in his diary on July 1, 1863, "is having difficulties here because of the murderous cheapness of English nails and the newness of the business." A cotton factory also was encountering difficulty, and the lowering of the tariff, the owners assured him, was the principal reason. "There are few orders and the factory is a very useful enterprise. It is nearly the only one on the Volga."[42]

Babst and Pobedonostsev also described how the heir's love for Russian national literature brought him closer to the people. In Petrozavodsk Nicholas Aleksandrovich heard the songs of a ninety-year-old blind singer, Koz'ma Ivanov. With Buslaev's lessons fresh in his memory, he listened attentively and talked at length with the bard, who was surprised by the heir's knowledge of folk traditions. The old man exclaimed, "Look what I have lived to see. The Tsar's firstborn is singing our favorite songs!" It was the high point of the trip for him. In his diary entry of June 15 Nicholas Aleksandrovich wrote, "I was delighted. An ancient epos in person. Pure language. Inspiration. He speaks of ancient heroes (*bogatyri*) as if he lived with them. In addition to songs, he told stories. His face is very expressive and unusual." In Kostroma an old peasant woman presented the heir with three communion wafers, an icon of St. Tikhon Zadonskii, and a crude paper box that emitted a curious rustling sound, which, it turned out, came from cockroaches. The crowd began laughing, but the meaning of the gift was clear. The wafer

[40] On the Slavophiles' economic program and Babst's role in propagating a national economic policy, see Alfred J. Rieber, *Merchants and Entrepreneurs in Imperial Russia* (Chapel Hill, N.C., 1982), 171–75.

[41] Pobedonostsev and Babst, *Pis'ma o puteshestvii gosudaria naslednika tsesarevicha*, 177–80.

[42] "Dnevnik puteshestviia po Rossii naslednika Nikolaia Aleksandrovicha," GARF, 665-1-53, 18–19, 24, 30.

was given to show that the woman had prayed for the tsarevich's soul that morning. Cockroaches were considered a token of good luck by many of the peasants, a symbol of domestic warmth and plenty.[43]

The letters presented the heir's jubilant reception as support for the tsar and his defense of Russian interests against the Poles. They described the reception in Iaroslavl, where people crossed themselves and threw themselves on the heir's carriage; women wept; hats flew into the air. Peasants clutching at the carriage cried, "Tell our father how we love him! Tell him we will go against the enemy, all to the last." Such displays of enthusiasm, the authors warned, might seem strange and crude to one who was not familiar with the popular character. But it was powerful and warm. "These tears and prayers and movements and cries fused into one whole chorus, and the unity of the people's feeling constituted the harmony of this chorus." This feeling, the authors claimed, was conscious. "The people know and feel what kind of time has come." They had heard of the dangers to the unity of the state. As in 1812, as in the 1830s, the threat from outside aroused the image of 1612, and the authors reminded the reader that Iaroslavl was the gathering point of Minin's and Pozharskii's militia, which fought to cleanse Moscow of the foreigner and "to restore Russia's state unity."[44]

The heir's diary and letters indicate that he shared his teacher's views of the patriotic feelings of the people. As he was leaving Petrozavodsk, he wrote in his diary, the people accompanying him shouted that he should tell "the little Father" that they would not give in to the Poles. "For him we will all rise, give everything, lay down everything." On June 29 he wrote to his mother from Kostroma about his sincere "purely Russian" reception and the feelings of gratitude to the tsar for the good deeds he had done for them. Everywhere they were making one assertion: "We want to prove to the little father tsar how grateful we are to him, how we love him, how he can firmly rely on us, his people. This is the character, the sense of cordial feelings of the meetings." In Iaroslavl they declared that they would arise for him and go through fire and water. One peasant came up to him and shouted, "Well, now he will not fear war." These touching words inspired the heir, who now understood Russia fully in terms of his father's scenario. "Their meaning is clear: The government should feel itself strong, relying on the love of the people. It is clear how well the simple people understand this." Hearing the shouts of thanks for freedom, he assured his mother that he could not forget his father's admonition to serve the people.[45]

Determined to be directly involved with the people, Nicholas Aleksandrovich wanted to volunteer and join the struggle, a desire that Alexander

---

[43] Pobedonostsev and Babst, Pis'ma o puteshestvii gosudaria naslednika tsesarevicha, 24, 210; "Dnevnik puteshestviia po Rossii naslednika Nikolaia Aleksandrovicha," 8.

[44] Pobedonostsev and Babst, Pis'ma o puteshestvii gosudaria naslednika tsesarevicha, 85–87.

[45] "Dnevnik puteshestviia po Rossii naslednika Nikolaia Aleksandrovicha," 10; "Pis'ma syna Nikolaia Imperatritse Marii Aleksandrovny," 38–39.

immediately quashed.[46] Instead, he reveled in the patriotic bond between people and tsar. Writing to his mother on July 21, 1863, he expressed his delight at the many letters and donations from the peasantry. "Our trip from the very beginning has assumed a political character and it seems quite appropriately. I have become an intermediary and witness of those feelings for Papa that have penetrated all estates." The inspiration, he wrote, was powerful. "They are aware of their power and their rights and want to prove their gratitude in deeds and their readiness to sacrifice everything for the salvation of the fatherland of which they have become members with full rights."[47]

The heir also perceived the religious significance of the struggle: "It is comforting how the national idea is closely linked with the religious. Holy Rus', we go to die for our shrines, to defend Kiev, the cradle of our Orthodoxy. . . . Holy France, Holy England, sound laughable. There the people do not use such a phrase, but we are reared with it. It is a force for us, an indestructible force." His temper clearly rose as he wrote the letter. At the end, in reference to threats from England and France, he warned, "Let them seriously ponder the *awakening* of these worthless barbarians who *must be crushed*." The letter, written under his tutor's influence, expressed a chauvinistic spirit that went beyond the government's policy and troubled the empress. She cautioned him to look upon things more critically and not to surrender to the impressions of the moment.[48]

As the trip proceeded down the Volga, Pobedonostsev and Babst emphasized the theme of imperial unity around the Russian nation. At the governor's house in Astrakhan, they stood next to the heir and beheld a strange motley throng in national costumes, among them Greeks, Armenians, Persians, Kalmyks, and Tatars. Few Russian faces were in the crowd, but they still felt themselves in Russia, "in one of the remote regions of a great tsardom, united by the powerful bond of state power and a consciousness of state unity." There among the mixture of "dress, faces, and tongues," the basic tone was provided by the "founding and gathering element of the Russian tribe."[49]

The culmination of the heir's trip, like his father's, was his investiture as Cossack Ataman in Novocherkassk. The ceremonies of mutual loyalty and love were the purest expression of personal attachment to the throne, and Nicholas Aleksandrovich, too, was affected by the Cossacks' vigorous expressions of enthusiasm at his appearance. In his letters to his brother and father, he described a spirited reception that contrasted with the dull flatness of the steppe. He remarked that the entire population came out to greet him. "The

[46] "Pis'ma v. k. Nikolaia Aleksandroicha Aleksandru II," GARF, 678-1-814, 58–59; "Pis'ma Aleksandra II Nikolaiu Aleksandrovichu," GARF, 665-1-13, letter of July 15, 1863.

[47] "Pis'ma syna Nikolaia Imperatritse Marii Aleksandrovny," 74–76.

[48] Ibid., 76–77, 86.

[49] Pobedonostsev and Babst, *Pis'ma o puteshestvii gosudaria naslednika tsesarevicha*, 356–57.

Cossacks are for the most part a fine young people. The little boys are really lively and the girls, too," he wrote to his brother, Alexander, on July 24.[50]

Because of the tense international situation, Alexander could not confer the insignia of the ataman office, the mace (*pernach*) of Catherine II, as Nicholas I had bestowed it upon him. Instead, Nicholas Aleksandrovich received it from the hands of the Cossack leaders, "by the will of the Sovereign Emperor," and declared that it was a sign of the trust and love between the Don Cossacks and their Ataman. "I raised the *pernach* to loud cries of 'Hoorah' from all those present," he wrote his father on August 9. But he felt no pride. "I say that all the time I thought only of You, of how we planned and how happy I felt about riding with You into Novocherkassk to take the *pernach* from your hands."[51]

The trip made Nicholas Aleksandrovich aware of the views he shared with the Russian people on industry, Russian culture, and the unity of the empire. This awareness convinced him of the need for the state to play a more active role in advancing economic development and creating a sense of national unity against external enemies. Such views brought him closer to his father, whom he viewed as the focus of the sincere love of the people and the leader of national resurgence and victory. His correspondence with Alexander indicates that he felt the constitutional movement was only an obstacle to the effective use of state power. He wrote to him on January 11, 1864, expressing irritation with people who busied themselves composing addresses to the tsar. "When will we come to our senses and serve the cause and not squander words? Don't we have healthy forces capable of dedicating public activity to the true service of the fatherland. And it is right now that Russia needs people who truly love her, capable of sacrificing their interests for the good of their native land."[52] In a letter of February 7, 1865, he thanked God that "the majority of right-thinking and enlightened people in Russia are completely aware of the impossibility of applying Western constitutional forms to the state life of our fatherland. This consciousness has spread in recent years and, they say, has sunk roots. On the other hand, he did not think that the efforts of a few isolated individuals represented a danger. "So let us hope that the absurd escapades and attempts of *those who are imprudent* will not disturb the peaceful internal development of our dear Russia."[53]

•

In June 1864 Nicholas Aleksandrovich embarked on his tour of Europe, with the goal of finding a bride. Before he left, he set his heart on Princess Dagmaar of Denmark. In August 1863 he had written to his mother of his passionate

[50] GARF, 677-1-918, 29–32; "Pis'ma v. k. Nikolaia Aleksandroicha Aleksandru II," 678-1-814, 78–85.

[51] Pobedonostsev and Babst, *Pis'ma o puteshestvii gosudaria naslednika tsesarevicha*, 496–98; "Pis'ma v. k. Nikolaia Aleksandrovicha Aleksandru II," 87–88.

[52] "Pis'ma v. k. Nikolaia Aleksandrovicha Aleksandru II," 42, 174.

[53] Ibid., 188–89.

love for Dagmaar, whom he had never met.[54] In September 1864, when news came of peace between Denmark and Prussia, he journeyed to Copenhagen where he first met Dagmaar. A week later, amid lavish celebrations, came the announcement of his betrothal.[55] After he left Copenhagen, the symptoms of his disease, first diagnosed as scrofula, returned with new severity. He was in great pain during the maneuvers with the Prussian army, which he joined with his father. His imperial party then toured Italy, where his condition deteriorated. He died in the presence of his family and Princess Dagmaar in Nice on April 12, 1865. The panel of distinguished physicians who performed the autopsy diagnosed the cause of death as spinal meningitis.[56]

Nicholas Aleksandrovich's death deprived the emperor of a son who combined the charm and manner of the court, the intelligence to win the support of educated society, and a love of Russia that drew him to the people. It deprived the empress of her first-born son, whom she worshiped. It deprived his teachers and friends of an heir who realized their hopes for an educated monarch who had escaped the intellectual confinement of the court. Nor was consolation to be found among the living. No one close to Nicholas Aleksandrovich held a high opinion of his younger brother, Alexander (see chapter 5).

Those who attended the burial ceremony at the Peter Paul Fortress had a sense of foreboding. "I felt I was attending my own burial," the emperor said to Peter Valuev. "I never thought I would outlive him." The first sentence was in French, the second in Russian.[57] For Alexander, the heir's death in fact meant the end of a part of him and of his scenario. It made the family a scene of tragedy rather than one of strength and happiness, leaving him without hope for the future of the dynasty.

Nicholas Aleksandrovich's teachers, as Boris Chicherin indicated in the first epigraph to this chapter, saw his death as the burial of hopes for a renewed and transformed monarchy. Pobedonostsev described the moment as "a decisive hour for the destinies of Russia."

> In him lay our hope, and each one of us who knew him cherished this hope all
> the more strongly the darker the horizon became, the stronger the dark powers
> were pressing, the sadder the circumstances of our future appeared to be. He
> was our hope. We saw him as a counteracting force, the opposite pole.[58]

---

[54] On August 3, 1863, he wrote his mother reassuring her that the young ladies, about whom he expressed his admiration in his letters, had not turned his head. The chief reason, he wrote, was the Danish princess Dagmaar "whom I fell in love with without seeing (*zaochno*) a long time ago. I only think of her and that keeps me from a great deal" ("Pis'ma syna Nikolaia Imperatritse Marii Aleksandrovny," 86–87).

[55] Oom, "Vospominaniia," 2:541–51.

[56] The autopsy was performed by a team of physicians including N. A. Pirogov, who disclosed the cause of death as spinal meningitis. A copy of the autopsy is available in Shvarts, BAR.

[57] Valuev, *Dnevnik*, 2:46.

[58] [Iu. Got'e], "Pobedonostsev and Alexander III," *Slavonic and East European Review* 7 (June 1928): 34–35. Letter is dated April 20, 1865.

THE KARAKOZOV ATTEMPT

On April 4, 1866, the sometime student Dmitrii Karakozov, dressed as a peasant, fired at Alexander II as he was about to leave the Summer Garden in St. Petersburg. Karakozov's shot, however, was understood as considerably more important than an isolated act of violence.[59] For Alexander, it belied the fundamental hope of his scenario that granting reforms and a measure of free discourse would create harmony between educated society and the monarchy. The conservative press and influential figures in the government construed the attempt as evidence of powerful inimical forces in Russia, which had only gained strength in the liberal atmosphere of reforms. Although Alexander continued to act and think in terms of his scenario, he did so with a diminishing conviction that undermined confidence in his rule among both liberals and conservatives.

That the faith in the Russians' native devotion to their tsar was not limited to official ideology is clear from the immediate reaction to the shooting. Initially both officials and members of educated society believed that the culprit must be a Pole. When Alexander confronted Karakozov, he asked him if he was Polish, to which he answered, "No, a pure Russian." When the public learned that Karakozov was Russian, and a nobleman, it responded with shame and bemusement. On April 4 Tiutchev, rejoicing at the tsar's escape, was troubled about the meaning of the attack for all Russians.

> Everything, everything in us, has been insulted by this shot,
> And there is no escaping the insult:
> A disgraceful stain lies alas,
> On the whole history of the Russian people![60]

Alexander took consolation in prayer, and public demonstrations of sympathy confirmed the sense of popular devotion and affection. After the shot, he proceeded directly to the Kazan Cathedral for a thanksgiving service before the Kazan Mother-of God. In his diary he wrote that the prayers were "wonderful." The State Council awaited him on his return to the Winter Palace to present their congratulations. From the balcony of the palace, he received shouts of "Hoorah," which, his diary indicates, were deeply gratifying to him. The capital was joyous, and in the evening Nevskii Prospect was lit as on a holiday. In the theaters on subsequent evenings, audiences sang the anthem repeatedly.[61]

The next day, at the Winter Palace, Alexander received congratulations from the Senate and then from the Petersburg nobility, its numbers aug-

---

[59] On Karakazov and the Ishutin circle, see Venturi, *Roots of Revolution*, 331–53; Gleason, *Young Russia*, 324–30.

[60] Tiutchev, *Polnoe sobranie sochinenii*, 202.

[61] Tatishchev, *Imperator Aleksandr II*, 2:4; N. N. Firsov, "Aleksandr II, lichnaia kharakteristika," *Byloe*, no. 20 (1922): 130; N. I. Kostomarov, *Avtobiografiia* (Moscow, 1922), 377–78.

mented by noblemen and representatives of other estates. The empress and grand dukes accompanied them, and all were greeted with loud shouts of "Hoorah" and tears. Count V. P. Orlov-Davydov, Petersburg Marshal of the Nobility and advocate of noble constitutionalism, delivered an eloquent speech of sympathy. He described the grief the Petersburg nobility felt that a criminal or madman had "made an attempt on the life of your supreme person, consecrated by the church and most dear to us," and expressed gratitude that the tsar had been spared by God. Alexander thanked the nobility and declared that, besides God, he was sustained in his service by "that devotion and those feelings that are constantly expressed to me in all difficult cases, from you milords the nobility as from all other estates."[62]

The escape was mythologized as a reenactment of the heroism of Ivan Susanin, the Kostroma peasant who sacrificed his life to save Tsar Michael Fedorovich from the Poles.[63] The peasant who presumably saved Alexander, Osip Komissarov, was, like Susanin, a native of Kostroma Province. Komissarov, had presumably struck the arm of Karakozov, forcing the bullet to go astray, though Karakozov to the end denied that this had happened and claimed that he had been distracted by the cry of a guard of the Summer Garden. The official version of the event was apparently disseminated by General E. I. Totleben, a member of Alexander's suite, and was publicized by Katkov in *Moskovskie Vedomosti*. In his rescript of April 9, 1866, Alexander declared that his life had been spared "through the dispensation of Divine Providence by the hand of Osip Komissarov." The rescript claimed that Komissarov, had come from the exact *volost'* where Susanin lived.[64]

Komissarov, a longtime resident of Petersburg, was rewarded with a grant of hereditary nobility and presented to the tsar, with his wife in the peasant dress of the Kostroma region. A lubok depicting Komissarov was issued with a description of how he had saved Alexander and how Alexander had rewarded him with hereditary nobility. It concluded with a statement, "Strong and mighty are a people who love their Sovereign so warmly and place all their hopes on him for the well-being and prosperity of the state."[65] The escape thus confirmed the precept of the official nationality doctrine that the Russian people were utterly devoted to the tsar. A few days after the attempt, at a special performance of *A Life for the Tsar*, the audience hissed the Polish scenes of the opera, though it had already been made known that Karakozov was Russian. The final procession and "Glory" chorus, as was customary in gala performances of the opera, included the entire company of singers and dancers. "Such a production of *Life for the Tsar* has never, I think, been seen," the heir Alexander Aleksandrovich wrote in his diary.[66]

[62] Tatishchev, *Imperator Aleksandr II*, 2:4–6.
[63] On the Susanin myth, see Volume 1: 390–95.
[64] *PSZ* 2, no. 43164, April 9, 1866. On the Komissarov incident, see Olga Maiorova, "Tsarevich/samozvanets v sotsial'noi mifologii 1860-kh godov," unpublished manuscript, 32–34.
[65] Slavonic and Print Division, New York Public Library, MEWG, 151.
[66] Kostomarov, *Avtobiografiia*, 377–78; Firsov, "Aleksandr II," 131.

At the performance the anthem was sung eight times. The poet Apollon Maikov declaimed a poem which denied that such a person could be a Russian. "Everything that is Russian in our breast is insulted!" he began.

> Who can this villain be? Where did he come from?
> In vain we seek him among us!
> Among Russians—who does not have the dear face of the tsar
> Impressed on his soul in indelible traits?

Maikov hinted that Karakozov was a fugitive, who, "having forgotten his native traditions from beyond the sea, played at starting rebellion in the land of his fathers." Whoever he was, "he is alien to us." Russians should unite around their tsar. In the last lines, the poet invoked the bond of affection.

> Behold old world, rising on blood,
> That the freedom summoning us to life,
> Has not been the ruin of the Russian people,
> But the light of Truth and kingdom of Love.[67]

The response to the assassination attempt provided an occasion for a reaffirmation and formalization of the scenario of love. Letters and telegrams of congratulations were reprinted in a two-volume collection. The preface, by the publisher A. M. Simchenko, stated that the people's messages were "*sincere expressions* of loyal feelings of limitless love and devotion to their *Tsar-Emancipator,* and worship of the blessed Divine Providence."[68] The volume opened with a series of poems, first Maikov's. Another verse, by N. Meshcherskii, announced directly, "No, *he is not Russian!*" Karakozov "doesn't know the enchantment of the Tsar for Russians." The communications of sympathy emanated, for the most part, from provincial officials, marshals of the nobility, and figures in town administrations.[69]

The notion of a Russian people devoted to the tsar was maintained, but only by broadening the notion of alien to include insurgents. As in the poems by Maikov and N. Meshcherskii, the word *alien* stigmatized those who violated the bond of love between tsar and people. Pressed by conservative ministers, especially Michael Katkov whose *Moskovskie Vedomosti* maintained a constant barrage of allegations about the weakness of the government's measures against revolutionaries, Alexander became increasingly suspicious.

Alexander's rescript of May 13, 1866, to the chairman of the Council of Ministers, P. P. Gagarin, indicated a crucial change in the relationship be-

---

[67] A. N. Maikov, *Polnoe sobranie sochinenii* (St. Petersburg, 1914), 2:188–89.

[68] *4oe aprelia 1866g: Polnyi sbornik izvestii, adresov, telegramm i stikhotvorenii po sluchaiu chudesnogo spaseniia zhizni imperatora Aleksandra II. Vypusk pervyi,* (St. Petersburg, 1866), 3. I have not been able to find the second volume of these messages.

[69] Ibid., 38.

tween the tsar and the public and a new conservative direction in educational policy. The change was presented as a confirmation of the scenario of love, prompted in part by the show of sympathy of all estates for their tsar. The public response had provided "an assurance of feelings in which I find the best reward for my labors for the good of Russia." The feelings expressed in the addresses had convinced him of his "obligation to preserve the Russian people from the germs of those harmful false teachings that in time would undermine public order, if no obstacle is created to their development." He declared the need to strengthen the role of morality and religion. He emphasized the respect for "the rights of property" which were "closely linked to the development of private and national wealth, which are closely related to each other."[70]

The most influential figure in the government until 1874 became the dynamic young chief of gendarmes Peter Shuvalov, a wealthy aristocrat who sought to preserve noble privilege and restore the authority of provincial governors. Dmitrii Tolstoi replaced the liberal A. V. Golovnin as minister of education and took the first steps to follow Katkov's program: the imposition of tighter controls on the educational system and a curriculum favoring mathematics and the classics at the expense of natural sciences, history, and rhetoric, which Tolstoi associated with the free thought that had led to the spread of liberal and radical ideas. The minister of justice Dmitrii Zamiatnin, who was responsible for the implementation of the Judicial Reform of 1864, was replaced by Constantine Pahlen, who sought to reassert the power of the police and procuracy in the judicial system.[71]

But the most important result of Karakozov's attempt was to destroy Alexander's confidence in the efficacy of his scenario. Two days after the shot, A. V. Nikitenko wrote in his diary that the tsar was consoled by the devotion of the classes of the population but "his heart wilted: The feeling of security among his people must disappear in him."[72] At the end of the sixties Alexander increasingly withdrew from direct involvement in government, and limited himself to a "managerial" rule between competing governmental factions. The dominant figure was Shuvalov, who purged many liberal reformers from the ministries of justice and education and defended noble privilege at the same time as he pursued a relatively lenient policy toward the press. The aristocratic journal *Vest'* advanced Shuvalov's program to curb the peasantry by propounding respect for noble property and law and strengthening noble supervision over their villages. Shuvalov, allied with Prince A. I. Bariatinskii, resisted the efforts of the minister of war Dmitrii

[70] *PSZ* 2, no. 43298, May 13, 1866; A. Kornilov, *Kurs istorii Rossii XIX veka* (Moscow, 1918), 3:4–6; Tatishchev, *Imperator Aleksandr II*, 2:8–10.

[71] Allen Sinel, *The Classroom and the Chancellery: State Educational Reform in Russia under Count Dmitry Tolstoi* (Cambridge, Mass., 1973), 34–37, 167–70; Wortman, *The Development of a Russian Legal Consciousness*, 277–78.

[72] Nikitenko, *Dnevnik*, 3:24.

Miliutin, who was supported by Grand Duke Constantine Nikolaevich to reform the army. Miliutin envisioned a citizen army without class distinctions, while Shuvalov struggled to preserve noble privileges (see chapter 4).[73]

UNDOING THE IMAGE: ALEXANDER II'S SECOND FAMILY

Nicholas I had made the imperial family the moral symbol of the Russian state and the microcosm of family love and devotion a model for the macrocosm of the state. Nicholas had associated domestic morality with political order, a connection that persisted through the later history of the dynasty.[74] As a boy, Alexander II had heard about the sacrosanct character of family relations from all sides. "Your domestic happiness is the guarantee of the well-being of the Russian Tsardom," Alexander's trusted adjutant S. A. Iur'evich had written to him in 1847.[75]

But Alexander never showed his father's concern for domestic morality, and, after Nicholas's death, the old constraints loosened. In October 1855 Tiutcheva observed that the rulers themselves wanted to be free: They "want to make believe they are private individuals."[76] After the shattering death of Nicholas Aleksandrovich and the Karakozov attempt, Alexander allowed his romantic predilections to take precedence. In the 1870s the emperor's private life became an open travesty of the image of an emperor sacrificing his personal interest for the good of his family and the fatherland.

The empress Alexandra Fedorovna had exemplified the beloved wife in Nicholas's scenario. Alexander II's spouse, the empress Maria Aleksandrovna, was retiring and introverted. She performed her ceremonial functions faithfully but without flair or pleasure. Her severity lent her receptions a cold and forbidding character. Melancholic and withdrawn, she had difficulty showing warmth and affection.[77] She gave birth to eight children, five of them before Alexander's accession in 1855. After Alexander ascended the throne, relations between emperor and empress became increasingly distant, though the couple always retained the pretense of mutual respect. In the late 1860s the strain of childbirth, the responsibilities of the court, and the humiliations of her marriage took their toll on her health. She appeared weak

---

[73] For a discussion of Alexander as "managerial tsar" and of the Miliutin and Shuvalov factions, see Alfred J. Rieber "Interest-Group Politics in the Era of the Great Reforms," in Eklof, Bushnell, and Zakharova, *Russia's Great Reforms*, 72–80; Shuvalov's domination of the government in the late 1860s and 1870s is assessed in T. A. Filippova, "Petr Andreevich Shuvalov," in *Rossiiskie konservatory* (Moscow, 1997), 199–219.

[74] See Volume 1: 326–42.

[75] Iur'evich, "Pis'ma ob Avgusteishikh Synoviakh Aleksandra II," unpublished manuscript, Baltic and Slavic Division, New York Public Libary, 135.

[76] Tiutcheva, *Pri dvore dvukh imperatorov*, 2:75–76.

[77] Ekaterina R. Radziwill (Count Paul Vasilli), *Behind the Veil at the Russian Court* (New York, 1914), 26–27; Tiutcheva, *Pri dvore dvukh imperatorov*, 1:78–79.

at ceremonies and often failed to attend because of illness, which proved to be incipient tuberculosis.[78] The portraits of the time reflect the austere sadness of her manner (fig. 14).

She found solace in religion. From her arrival in St. Petersburg, Maria Aleksandrovna strove to translate her Protestant religious faith into the language and rites of Orthodoxy. On the day of her confirmation in Orthodoxy in December 1840, she wrote to her sister-in-law, Elizabeth, "I do not call it a religious conversion, because the belief remains the same." Her intense personal faith set her apart from the cool sophistication of the court. Her lady-in-waiting, Tiutcheva, compared her to a nun and an icon. Her piety gave her "a meditative and ascetic manner, like a saint's rather than a society lady's." She was regarded as a tragic figure, a martyr accepting her fate with quiet resignation, representative of what Alfred Rieber has described as the "pietistic, sentimentalist, passive type" of empress. She spoke Russian very well for a Russian empress and became knowledgeable in the study of Russian culture and religion. She was attracted to the works of the Slavophiles, especially Alexei Khomiakov and other nationalist and Pan-Slavic authors. Fedor Tiutchev was a frequent visitor, and she admired his verse, especially the poem *Rossiia*. She sponsored collections for the missionary activities of the Orthodox Church in the western provinces and Poland.[79]

Alexander himself continued to cut the figure to be admired, the center of the pageantry, trim and stylish, even as he aged. During the first decade of the reign he appeared at family occasions, affected the proper feelings, and posed for pictures surrounded by children. In a color lubok of 1859 he is shown in red uniform strolling with the heir in a black uniform to his left, Maria Aleksandrovna to his right, and the three younger sons beside her. He loved to decorate his rooms with touching canvases of family happiness.[80] The Prussian military attaché Von Schweinitz was impressed with the stately imperial procession when he arrived in Petersburg in the summer of 1865. "As their majesties came out of the chapel, followed by five sturdy sons and a daughter just developing into a young lady, I felt the comforting impression produced by a combination of power, beauty, and family happiness."[81]

But Alexander's dispositions were not toward the family. His philandering went beyond the breaching of mores and turned into a concerted, if unacknowledged, rebellion against the image imposed by his mythic role of self-denying emperor. Women gave him the adulation he craved, and his exceptional susceptibility was common knowledge. "People close to him,

---

[78] N. A. Gorbunova, "1874–1880 v Livadii," *Nasha Starina* (August 1914): 771–72.

[79] Letter to Elizabeth, December 4, 1840, Hesse State Archive, D 23, 32/34; Rieber, "Introduction to Tiutcheva," n.p.; Tiutcheva, *Pri dvore dvukh imperatorov*, 1:78–79, 2:117; Olga Nikolaevna, *Son iunosti* (Paris, 1963), 131; de Grunwald, "Le tsar Alexandre II . . .," 194–96.

[80] The lubok is reproduced in *Narodnaia kartinka XVII–XIX vekov* (St. Petersburg, 1996), Plate 26. On Alexander's artistic tastes, see O. Ia. Neverov, "Aleksandr II—tsenitel' i sobiratel' predmetov iskusstv," *Myzei Rossii* (St. Petersburg, n.d.), 4:16.

[81] Von Schweinitz, *Denkwürdigkeiten*, 1:180.

14. Alexander II and Maria Aleksandrovna. Lithograph, 1870. GARF.

loving him sincerely, said that in the presence of women he became a completely different person," Chicherin wrote. He enjoyed visiting the young
ladies' "institutes," and chatting with and heaping favors on admiring
school girls who surrounded him. During his daily strolls in the late 1860s
on the embankment near the Winter Palace and in the Summer Garden, he
was usually in the company of a young lady or ladies.[82]

[82] N. N. Lavrova, "Imperator Aleksandr II i deti," *Istoricheskii Vestnik*, no. 139 (February
1915): 438–39; Boris Chicherin, *Vospominania . . . ; Zemstvo i Moskovskaia Duma* (Moscow,
1934), 4:118; Sir Horace Rumbold, *Recollections of a Diplomatist* (London, 1902), 2:290.

Before 1865 Alexander flirted and strayed but kept within the bounds of discretion. The blows of the heir's death and the Karakozov attempt undermined his confidence in his public mission. He turned instead to private pleasures, flouting public morality and violating the biblical injunctions that his parents had epitomized as the cornerstone of monarchy. Immediately after the death and burial of Nicholas Aleksandrovich, in April 1865, Alexander started a romance with Catherine Dolgorukova (Katia), a schoolgirl at the Smolnyi Institute from a poor aristocratic family. The affair with Dolgorukova, with its titillating connivances and overtones of tragedy, transgressed far more than biblical norms. It was an act of violence against the familial ceremony to which Alexander clung as the moral and personal grounding of tsarist supremacy. While at court Alexander was the father, exemplifying probity; in private he pursued the romantic adventure of his youth, the quest for the blue flower, in a show of scorn for the norms of imperial conduct. His love was not the discreet affair that could remain within the bounds of secrecy and not challenge a monarch's bond to his spouse. He made clear that Katia monopolized his affections. During the 1870s he became increasingly open and demanded acceptance of his infidelity from his family and entourage.

In the summer of 1865, after admiring the "family happiness" of the imperial procession at Peterhof, von Schweinitz was enchanted by "a girl full of maidenly charm, dressed in white, waiting for the moment when she would be presented to their majesties."[83] During the next year Alexander had her removed from the institute to her brother's apartment, where he could visit her conveniently. It was immediately clear that this was no fleeting diversion. He succumbed to Dolgorukova, a contemporary wrote, "with the ardor of a boy in love." Their romance appears to have been consummated in the midst of the July festival at Peterhof in 1866, the event Nicholas had introduced to celebrate the sanctity of marriage.[84]

The affair was soon known to all at court. The emperor, nearing fifty, had fallen passionately in love with a girl less than twenty. He arranged for her appointment as a maid of honor of the empress, a humiliation Maria Aleksandrovna accepted with dignity. Rumors held that Alexander even arranged his 1867 trip to France so that he could be with her in Paris. By 1870 Catherine was established in her own quarters in Petersburg. Alexander treated her as a wife, starting a second household. In 1872 Catherine bore him a son, George ("Gogo"), and a year later a daughter, Olga. Alexander treated them openly as his own.[85]

---

[83] Von Schweinitz, *Denkwürdigkeiten*, 1:180.

[84] Alexandre Tarsaidzé, *Katia: Wife before God* (New York, 1970); 89–98. Tarsaidzé bases his conclusion about the date on uncited personal correspondence and conversations (98). It seems that that summer at Peterhof was when Alexander began to speak of her as his "wife before God," whether or not the date is exact.

[85] A. A. Tolstaia, "Pechal'nyi epizod iz moei zhizni pri dvore; zapiski freiliny," *Oktiabr'*, no. 5 (May 1993): 124–25; Tarsaidzé, *Wife before God*, 146–60.

The romance revealed the emperor not as a strong independent personality but as a slave of love. It was another example of his loss of control, of the weakness his mother had warned him of when he was a young man. Society and the diplomatic corps believed that the two women in his life dominated him. The feeling of guilt before the empress, the Prussian ambassador was convinced, allowed her to convince Alexander to embark on a nationalist foreign policy in the last years of his reign. Others believed that major decisions were influenced by Dolgorukova. In the late seventies Catherine became known as a way to reach the tsar for those eager to purchase profitable railway concessions. Such rumors contributed to the widespread sense that the tsar was "feminine."[86]

The emperor's reputation as irresponsible libertine was fatal to his image as transcendent monarch, possessing powers of self-control and vision not given to ordinary mortals. His conduct called into question the primacy of the symbolic sphere, of presentation over individual wish, of public obligation over private pleasure. He destroyed the moral distance that Nicholas I had established between ruler and subject, placing the amorous tsar not above and perhaps beneath his subjects. The ethos of self-sacrifice for the commonweal, which justified the tsar's monopoly of authority, now lost its persuasive power.

The affair appeared as the central episode of an orgy of self-indulgence and self-enrichment carried on by members of the imperial house. The entrepreneurial activity of the grand dukes, and, secretly, of the tsar himself, added to the atmosphere of deceit and corruption. The behavior of his sons, Alexei and Vladimir, who engaged in carousals with gypsies during the family's solemn visits to Moscow, scandalized public opinion. Prince Obolenskii wrote in his diary on March 10, 1874, "The debauchery has actually taken on colossal dimensions and no censorship prohibitions can guard the imperial prestige from debasement when dissolute youth, unconstrained by fear of responsibility, feelings of propriety, or a sense of their own dignity, impudently and publicly drag their imperial calling in the mud." He explained their behavior by a complete absence of family life and occupation, an immunity from prosecution, and lack of responsibility before the public, since their escapades could not be reported in the press.[87]

The scandals reached their height when in the early 1870s the son of Alexander's brother Constantine, Grand Duke Nicholas Konstantinovich, was apprehended with jewels he had stolen from his mother's icon frame to pay gambling debts. Exiled by the emperor to Khiva, the grand duke continued to embarrass the family with his bizarre behavior, including the theft and sale of a set of ancient coins belonging to the imperial family. The grand duke's mistress was an American adventuress by the name of Henrietta

---

[86] See von Schweinitz, *Denkwürdigkeiten*, 1:340, 2:94–95; and D. A. Miliutin, *Dnevnik* (Moscow, 1950), 4:93.

[87] Obolenskii, *Dnevnik*, 5:295–96, 345–46.

Blackford who, after she was banished from Russia, published, in 1875, a revealing and highly sought after memoir under the name of Fanny Lear.[88] Russian diplomatic agents abroad were ordered to buy up and destroy copies of the book, but of course it circulated widely and the scandal became generally known. In a telling scene, she described the grand duke exposing the hypocrisy of his father, Constantine Nikolaevich, who reprimanded him for his behavior. "I am not to blame, it is my blood," and he then went on to mention Peter the Great, Anne, Elizabeth, Catherine, Paul, Nicholas, and then Constantine Nikolaevich himself, all of whom kept lovers. Blackford added an allusion to a high personage, who, it was generally known, "was under the charms of a lady as capricious as she is transparent, who makes, unmakes, remakes ministers just as a clever little girl dresses and undresses her dolls."[89]

In the second half of the 1870s the imperial family increasingly shrank from the public eye, their whereabouts and their ceremonial activity remaining unknown. Obolenskii noted that when the empress spent two months traveling through Europe in the fall of 1874, not a word appeared in the press, making it seem to the public that she had vanished. But the enemies of *glasnost'*, he thought, had achieved their aim. On November 20, 1874, he wrote of the members of the imperial family: "The public even in the provinces has ceased to *be interested in them*. Whether this is good or compatible with dynastic interests, time will tell."[90]

In addition to long periods abroad, the imperial family spent considerable time at the palace of Livadia in the Crimea in the late summer and fall. The semitropical lushness of the area, the exotic scenery, made it an escape from the capital and its responsibilities. Peterhof and Tsarskoe Selo were outside the capital but attached to it by tradition and ceremony.[91] An invitation to Livadia was a sign of imperial grace; when Dmitrii Miliutin failed to receive one, he took it as a sign of disfavor. The lesser courts of the grand dukes also summered at Livadia. The empress lived her own life in the main Livadia palace. From 1872 Dolgorukova resided in convenient proximity, at a cottage less than a mile from the estate.[92]

At Livadia, court functions took place on a smaller scale and with less formality than at the suburban palaces. The languorous isolation of the

---

[88] Fanny Lear [Henrietta Blackford], *Le roman d'une américaine en Russie* (Brussels, 1875).

[89] Ibid., 164–65.

[90] Obolenskii, *Dnevnik*, 5:308.

[91] The Appanage Department had purchased the estate in 1860, and Alexander had given it to the empress as a place where she could rest and recover from her various indispositions. The family began to visit the estate in the second half of the 1860s and vacationed there nearly every year until the outbreak of the Russo-Turkish War (N. N. Kalinin and M. A. Zelianichenko, *Romanovy i Krym* [Moscow, 1993], 36–39; Alexander, Grand Duke of Russia, *Once a Grand Duke* [New York, 1932], 39).

[92] Gorbunova, "1874–1880 v Livadii," *Nasha Starina* (September–October 1914): 838; (December, 1914): 1052; Miliutin, *Dnevnik*, 1:95; Tarsaidze, 155.

Crimea deprived these activities of symbolic meaning. The courtiers, left idle, spent much of their time in intrigue and rumor; the level of mutual antagonism rose. Only the tsar remained above these animosities, and he, absorbed as he was with his mistress, lent no force or unity to the life on the estate.[93] While Alexander was in Livadia, the consideration of serious governmental matters came to a halt. "Every year, the business season starts later," Obolenskii noted in 1875.[94]

THE REPROACH OF THE PAST: RECALLING PETER THE GREAT AND CATHERINE THE GREAT

The early 1870s witnessed commemorations of two of Alexander's forbears who represented the founders of the tradition of reform in eighteenth-century Russia. The bicentenary in 1872 of Peter the Great's birth and the dedication of the first imperial monument to Catherine the Great in 1873 were opportunities for Alexander to present himself within an illustrious heritage of progressive and dynamic rulers. But in neither case did the emperor lay claim to this heritage. Instead, the two events pointed up the evident distance that separated him from the figures of mythic stature and achievement who were his forbears. They celebrated dynamic rulers who drove reforms forward with cunning, energy, and skill. Peter and Catherine were recalled as monarchs with a national sense, who dedicated themselves wholeheartedly to their people.

The celebration of the bicentenary of Peter's birth took place in Petersburg and in Moscow on May 30, 1872. The Petersburg celebration honored his historical relics—"Peter's things" (*Petrovy veshchi*), making of him a quasi-religious figure. The principal attraction was Peter's "little boat" (*botik*), "the grandfather of the Russian fleet," a foreign, probably English boat that Peter discovered and repaired. Other revered relics were his uniform, the hat with a bullet hole sustained at Poltava, his sword, and the Icon of the Savior, which he carried with him on campaigns.

On May 30 a contingent of sailors marched in procession bearing the little boat to the Peter statue, the "bronze horseman." The court clergy carried the Icon of the Savior in a new golden frame, leading a procession with town deputations to the Peter-Paul Cathedral, where the metropolitan, in the emperor's presence, conducted a memorial service. Alexander placed a jubilee medal on Peter's grave to mark posterity's recognition of his service to the fatherland. Then, with members of the imperial family, he rode on horseback to Isaac's Square where regiments of the guards stood assembled.

---

[93] Gorbunova, "1874–1880 v Livadii," *Nasha Starina* (July 1914): 665; (December 1914): 1055–56; letter of Alexander II to Grand Duchess Maria Alexandrovna, October 20, 1878, San Francisco Museum of Russian Culture.

[94] Obolenskii, *Dnevnik*, 5:343 (entry of December 4, 1875).

With his suite, Alexander reviewed the lines of guardsmen, then proceeded to the Neva, where a prayer was pronounced before the icon. After a mass in the cathedral, a religious procession carried the relics back to the river for the ceremony of the blessing of the Peter the Great statue. The final event was the flotilla on the Neva, organized by the Yacht Club, to demonstrate the "evolution of the Russian fleet."[95]

The evening featured popular entertainments, a row-boat race near the Summer Garden, and the usual games, dances, and tricks staged on Tsaritsyn Meadow. Thirty large pictures illustrated episodes of Peter's reign, including Peter learning to use the astrolabe, his visits to schools and poorhouses, and his major military victories. The explanatory captions were read aloud. According to the commemorative album, the people left the pictures, discussing and arguing. They had learned "the crux" of the matter and the image of Peter as the "eternal worker," who "never stopped in the cause of the expected general welfare." Plays about Peter's life were presented at the Petersburg theaters, and, at the end, verses were read before his portrait.[96]

Alexander did not play a prominent role in the celebration, and the ceremonies lacked a gala character. The buildings had skimpy decorations, the journal *Vsemirnaia Illiustratsiia* remarked; Falconet's monument was not even festooned with garlands of flowers. The emperor was not visible to the public, since the square around the Peter the Great Monument was opened only to a small number of the elite in "magnificent attire." Others could watch the ceremony only from the roofs of the Isaac's Cathedral or the Senate.[97] The Yacht Club's participation in the ceremonies was itself an ironical comment on the significance of the events. The exclusive club, habituated by grand dukes and members of Petersburg society, regarded the sea more as a playground than as a means to advance commerce or national power.

Similar official ceremonies took place in Moscow and other cities and towns. In Moscow the central attraction was the return of the "little boat," "the grandfather of the Russian fleet," to sail the Moscow River, as it had almost two centuries earlier. The boat traveled by train after the Petersburg celebration, and the Moscow Yacht Club arranged a special ceremony of welcome at the station. The metropolitan blessed it with holy water. After a cannon salute, it was drawn by tug through the mass of sailboats and other crafts on the Moscow River to the Moscow Politechnical Institute to be

---

[95] *Al'bom 200 letnego iubileia Imperatora Petra Velikogo* (St. Petersburg, 1872), 281–82; *Vsemirnaia Illiustratsiia*, no. 187 (June 29, 1872): 72–73. A double-page spread in *Vsemirnaia Illiustratsiia* shows the stately religious-military procession. The clergy walk in the center of the square carrying their gonfalons and icons. Alexander, riding a white horse and wearing the elegant suite uniform with a white tassel blowing from his hat, is accompanied by members of his suite, also cutting elegant figures on horseback. All along the square and around the statue, guards regiments stand at attention, and a row of guards officers with regimental standards surrounds the statue.

[96] *Al'bom 200 letnego iubileia Imperatora Petra Velikogo*, 282–83.

[97] *Vsemirnaia Illiustratsiia*, no. 179 (June 3, 1872): 382–83.

placed in the exhibition organized for the event. Religious ceremonies honoring Peter took place in Pereiaslavl and Arkhangelsk as well. In Pereiaslavl a monument was dedicated at the location of Peter's residence. During the prayer to his memory a thirty-one gun salute resounded, and local fishermen lined up their boats to commemorate Peter's efforts at shipbuilding. In Arkhangelsk a religious procession bore Peter's relics onto the square.[98]

The official and religious ceremonies celebrated Peter's military and nautical triumphs and his contribution to Russia's political might. For them, the "grandfather of the Russian fleet" was the founder of Russia as a sea power. Another series of ceremonies, which took place at the academy and the university, recalled Peter's contribution to Russia's intellectual and scientific progress. They celebrated not Peter's physical relics but a tradition of enlightenment that Peter had fostered and now symbolized. They memorialized the emperor who had brought Western knowledge and technology to Russia.

An editorial in Katkov's *Moskovskie Vedomosti* contended that it was the cultural significance of Peter's deed that most deserved celebrating. The progress of Russian naval power hardly deserved a celebration, the author remarked. The bicentenary instead was "a celebration of civic achievement." Russia loved to depict Peter "in the smoke of the battle of Poltava or rays of glory of the Peace of Nystadt." But most of all Russia respected Peter "as the ruling reformer in the arduous labor of self-education and the bestowing of his results on his dear people." For the public, Peter was not a mythical figure of the past but a living example of what Russia needed—"the light of knowledge" and the "radiant light" of Peter as a worker.[99]

In Petersburg on May 30 academicians Constantine Veselovskii, Jacob Grot, and Otto Struve addressed a gala convocation of the Academy of Sciences. Veselovskii spoke on Peter's founding of the academy, Grot on his educational goals and accomplishments, and Struve on his contributions to the study of geography. Similar meetings throughout the empire announced plans to found technological schools in honor of Peter. To Russians gathering across the empire, the jubilee album remarked, "occurs the same thought that pervaded all the great undertakings—*the necessity to study.*" With this realization the people, "the humble tool of his mighty will," had finally understood his purpose.[100]

The most important event commemorating Peter's intellectual heritage was the Politechnical Exhibition in Moscow. The historical section of the exhibition comprised objects surviving from Peter's mining, shipbuilding, and industrial enterprises, farm buildings and implements, and portraits of figures from Peter's reign and later periods of Russian history. In conjunction with the exhibition, the Society of the Lovers of Natural Science, Anthropology, and Ethnography organized a series of free public lectures on subjects

[98] *Al'bom 200 letnego iubileia Imperatora Petra Velikogo*, 283–84.
[99] *MV*, May 30, 1872, 1–2.
[100] *Al'bom 200 letnego iubileia Imperatora Petra Velikogo*, 290–91.

ranging from history to astronomy, from flax production to the creation of the world.[101]

Sergei Solov'ev, the director of the historical section of the exhibition, delivered his famous *Public Lectures on Peter the Great* as part of the celebration. Solov'ev's lectures drew an overflowing audience of nearly three thousand at the Moscow Noble Assembly and were a major social and cultural event. Though admission was free, the audience clearly came from the upper levels of Moscow society and included many high officials and scholars. The governor-general of Moscow attended. The lectures were published in part in *Moskovskie Vedomosti*.[102]

For Solov'ev, Peter's major achievement was to bring his people into contact with European knowledge and civilization. He was less the "transformer" (*preobrazivatel'*) than the "teacher" (*vospitatel'*). In Solov'ev's first lecture, he compared nations to human beings. He expounded the organicist view that nations grew through stages of life, like individuals. The transition from childhood to adulthood was marked for him by the acquisition of knowledge. "By means of science, a person and a people pass from one age to the next, from the age when feelings rule to the age when thought rules."[103]

Peter, for Solov'ev, was "the great teacher of his people." He first taught them how to work by providing an example of tsar-laborer, devoting his efforts to the national good. His first labor was leading Russia in war, and war, Solov'ev claimed, was a pedagogical means Peter used to achieve internal reform. "The great tsar looked upon war from a civic viewpoint, as is fitting for a ruler: He looked upon it as a school for a people who wanted to assume an honorable place among other peoples, not to beg civilization as alms but to present its indisputable rights." Solov'ev's Peter was a stern taskmaster who gave difficult assignments. "At the beginning we will be defeated, but we will study diligently. First we will defeat our teachers with superb material forces, then we will be able to defeat them with equal forces, and finally we will acquire such art that we will triumph even with lesser force. Thus war is a school, a practical school, the school of the first necessity."[104]

Solov'ev's conception of Peter in his *Lectures* was quite different from his portrayal in his *History*, which had been published immediately after the emancipation. Then Solov'ev had compared Peter to the French Revolution in bringing a new social and institutional structure to Russia. In the *Lectures* he compared him to the Renaissance and emphasized his pedagogical and intellectual legacy rather than his institutional one, which by the seventies no longer inspired hope in him. Reforms now were not enough. Peter's insti-

---

[101] L. N. Pushkarev, " 'Publichnye chteniia o Petre Velikom' S. M. Solov'eva kak pamiatnik istoricheskoi i obshchestvennoi mysli," in S. M. Solov'ev, *Publichnye chteniia o Petre Velikom* (Moscow, 1984), 179, 183.

[102] Ibid., 181–82; *MV*, June 4, 1872, 3; June 5, 1872, 3–4.

[103] Solov'ev, *Publichnye chteniia . . .* , 37.

[104] Ibid., 77–78, 147, 155, 166.

tutions had to change, but the change could bring about good "only in the presence of his spirit." Solov'ev's concluding words extolled "that incorporeal heritage . . . the unprecedented example of labor, of strength of will in the struggle against obstacles, in the struggle against evil; the example of love for his people, the example of unshakeable faith in his people and their capacities."[105]

Peter as the exemplar of serious work and study, daunted by no obstacle, was an implicit contrast to Alexander, who, elegant and indulgent, basked in his nation's love rather than bestowing his love on the nation. Solov'ev's *Lectures*, widely circulated and commented on in the press, identified progress with the monarch who was attentive to his people's needs, and they made no connection between the contemporary monarchy and the Petrine tradition. The comparison with the millennium celebration is telling. In 1862 Alexander sought to incorporate Russian history in a monument that expressed the common effort of monarch and people working for the betterment of the state. The theme was union. In 1872 the government honored Peter's memory as a heroic ruler whose achievements were in the past; moderate educated society celebrated a monarch who had been dedicated to the cause of progress and people, who was a force for change. But they no longer shared the hope for a bond of love and gratitude between tsar and people.

Solov'ev's *Lectures* were an implicit reproach of the emperor. His memoirs, written at the end of the 1870s, recorded his intimations of disaster and recalled catastrophic breakdowns of the state in Russia's past. He used the image of a carriage, plunging down a slope. Alexander let out the reins but could not stop the carriage on "the swift, convulsive plunge." Reforms required state wisdom. "But it is a disaster when Louis XVIs and Alexander IIs undertake them." They required a Peter the Great. "A reformer like Peter the Great holds the horses with a strong hand at the steepest plunge and the carriage is safe. But reformers of [the other type] let the horses go full speed down the mountain. They don't have the strength to restrain them, and the carriage awaits ruin."[106]

Alexander's weakness, Solov'ev added, made him fear anyone but mediocrities. His weakness had reached disastrous proportions, lurking behind the image of authority. "Respect for power collapsed in an autocratic state: There was no system, no general plan of action. Each minister played the autocrat in his own way, a veritable time of troubles (*smuta*)."[107] The sense that the general absence of authority spelled disaster was widespread among conservatives and nationalists at the end of the seventies. Many of them had begun to look for a new embodiment of authority in the heir to the throne, the grand duke Alexander Aleksandrovich.

---

[105] Ibid., 145; Pushkarev, " 'Publichnye chteniia o Petre Velikom,' " 197.
[106] S. M. Solov'ev, *Izbrannye trudy; Zapiski* (Moscow, 1983), 345–46, 408.
[107] Ibid., 346.

Prince Obolenskii, who had more sympathy for Alexander, felt his failure all the more keenly. After the celebration he wrote:

No one since Peter achieved such reforms as Alexander Nikolaevich. But what a difference. One was himself the Creator and Executor of his transformations, who died while at work, grieving that he had not succeeded in completing everything he had conceived and did not live to see the fruit of his changes. The other, almost accidentally and unexpectedly, by force of circumstance, was drawn into the effort and half-way down the path became weary and ready to renounce the great deeds He had undertaken.[108]

Liberal writers used the occasion to contest the monarchy's claim to the nation's allegiance and to present Peter as the symbol of what the nation represented to them. The newspaper, *Golos*, condemned the monarchy as the "abstract state," one that did not "fuse the population into a single people." It was the "abstract state, isolated from the love of the people," that had been crushed at Sevastopol. Instead, the author advanced his view of a nation-state, the nation as civic entity: "A state assimilates tribes only by relying on the strength of a basic nationality (*narodnost'*), but a nationality can announce its strength only in conditions of public independent action." Not the powerful leader but an independent people strengthened the state. Russia would become powerful when it became a "Russian state, that is, when it [rested] on the strength of a Russian people, acting independently."

The newspaper framed its discussion to show that the present monarch showed not a love of the people but concern for its own interests, "petty egoism." Peter would have been disappointed to see the ignorance of the population. The people admiring the pictures at the exhibit knew next to nothing about Peter; they knew about Peter's victory at Poltava and his building of Petersburg, but they were ignorant of his efforts to better their native land.[109]

•

The monument to Catherine the Great, dedicated in November 1873, presented another historical symbol that could be used to question the national character of the monarchy. Russian emperors since Catherine made little effort to honor her memory. Even Alexander, who admired his great-grandmother, had to be pressed to proceed with the monument and hoped to leave the matter to his successor, in which case it would never have been built. The initiative came from professors of the Academy of Art, who, in May 1859, issued an appeal for contributions for a statue in Petersburg to honor the Academy's "protector." Alexander did not endorse the appeal but could hardly oppose a statue to Catherine, a symbol of enlightenment, culture, and reform among his forbears. Instead, he issued an order for the submission

[108] Obolenskii, *Dnevnik*, 4:214–15.
[109] *Golos*, June 6, 1872, 1–2.

of projects for a statue to be placed at the palace at Tsarskoe Selo. Alexander chose the project of Michael Mikeshin, after visiting the artist in his studio in July 1861. Mikeshin's project presented Catherine holding a lyre, in rococo style. After criticism from the Academy of Art, Mikeshin created a small model of a statue of Catherine in majestic pose decorated with five medallions, of three field marshals, Potemkin, Suvorov, and Rumiantsev, and the poet Derzhavin and Ivan Betskoi, Catherine's principal educational reformer. Meanwhile the St. Petersburg City Duma, in May 1863, argued that the statue of Catherine be placed in Petersburg, on Nevskii Prospect, before the Public Library and the Alexandrinskii Theater. Mikeshin drew up a new project for a monument to be situated in the park bordered by the Anichkov Palace, the Alexandrinskii Theater, the Imperial Public Library, and Nevskii Prospect—a setting designating the meeting place of power, science, and the arts.[110]

The statue, like the millennium monument, strove to show the monarch as the benefactor of culture and intellectual life, as well as the nation's military leader (fig. 15). Catherine is presented neither as legislator nor reformer. Rather, she appears as a symbol of the multifaceted achievement of the monarchy, of its powers of creation and inspiration. She stands garbed in the imperial mantle holding a scepter in her right hand and a laurel wreath in her left. A massive imposing presence, she leans forward in a strained pose. The figures that circle the pedestal beneath give a sense of the breadth of the empress's achievement. Leading figures of the army, court, and culture, in statues by A. M. Opekushin, sit conversing. Alexander insisted on the addition of two more military figures, the admiral Chichagov and Count Orlov, as well as Princess Dashkova and the chancellor Bezborodko. Mikeshin portrays I. I. Betskoi discussing the establishment of his foundling home with Chancellor A. A. Bezborodko, with Princess Dashkova—the first president of the Russian Academy of Letters—seated near the poet Gavriil Derzhavin, who strikes a dramatic posture to declaim his verse. Like the millennium monument, the Catherine statue tried to incorporate education and culture into the realm of power. But the everyday poses of these figures baffled many critics, who found the attempt to combine genre and monumental art jarring.[111]

The construction of the statue took nearly a decade owing to financial exigencies. When completed, it seemed another symbol of unrealized hopes, suggesting the inspiration a monarch could represent. Like the bicentennial celebration honoring Peter the Great, the Catherine monument recalled a tradition that the government had failed to live up to. *Golos* described it as

---

[110] The most complete discussion of the conception and execution of the statue is François-Xavier Coquin, "Le monument de Catherine II à Saint-Pétersbourg," in Anita Davidenkoff, ed., *Catherine II et l'Europe* (Paris, 1997), 16–25; I. M. Suslov, *A. M. Opekushin; zhizn' i tvorchestvo* (Iaroslavl, 1968), 23–25; Obolenskii, *Dnevnik*, 5:269–70; "Pamiatnik Ekaterine II; 24 noiabria 1873 g." *Russkaia Starina* 8 (1873): 641.

[111] See the comments in "Pamiatnik Ekaterine II," no. 12 (1873): 143; V. V. Stasov, *Izbrannye sochineniia v trekh tomakh* (Moscow, 1952), 2:484–85.

15. Catherine the Great Monument, St. Petersburg. Design by M. O. Mikeshin.

paying "a moral debt," as part of the new "heartening direction": "We are becoming more conscious of ourselves and therefore we value the memory of past figures, past deeds, and cannot indifferently regard the memory of those who worked for the benefit of our self-consciousness." The principles of Catherine's Instruction (*Nakaz*) were those propounded by present-day science.[112]

[112] *Golos*, November 24, 1873, 1.

The emperor and his family attended a modest dedication ceremony of the monument on November 24, 1873. The event, which took place in the cool weather of late autumn, Prince Obolenskii remarked, did not sufficiently honor the "Great Tsaritsa." To him, she represented a sovereign who exerted strong leadership in the interests of the people. But Obolenskii was inspired by the speeches on Catherine at a meeting of the Imperial Historical Society. He remarked on "Her sincere and unaffected love for the Russian people." He thought that her advisers were also imbued with this love, which was why their work proved fruitful. Peter was a Russian person who had fallen in love with Germans. "Catherine, being German by nature, fell in love with Russians." As a result, "not in a single degree or word of Hers can one find hypocrisy directed against the Russian Spirit."[113]

[113] *Zodchii* 11 (1873): 126; Obolenskii, *Dnevnik*, 5:269–70 (entry of November 25, 1873).

CHAPTER FOUR

The Crisis of Autocracy

To the general exploit of self-renunciation, the Russian Empire wished to add the personal exploit of self-renunciation, and to the expression of the dignity of the Empire to add the expression of the warm care for her. The reign in the spirit of love makes up the principal feature in the biography of the present Ruler of one-seventh of the globe.

—Prince Vladimir Sollogub, on Alexander II's decision to join the Russian armies on the Danube in 1877[1]

I have seen their imperial majesties. Around them everything is as it was before, but they are not as they were before. Both left me with painful feelings. The Tsar has a tired look and himself spoke of nervous tension, which he is trying to conceal. A crowned semi-ruin. In an era when strength is needed in him, obviously it can't be counted on. . . . You can feel the ground tremble, the edifice is about to tumble, but it is as if the residents don't notice this. The master and mistress of the house vaguely sense evil but hide their inner terror.

—Peter Valuev, Diary Entry, June 3, 1879[2]

THE PARADE GROUND AND THE EUROPEAN IMAGE

Prussia's victory over France in 1871 had momentous consequences for Russia's international standing and foreign policy. First, a united Germany upset the European balance of power. Second, it meant that for the first time since the reign of Peter the Great Russia bordered on a state that threatened its domination of adjacent areas and the security of its frontiers. For the previous half-century Russian foreign policy had been wary of a united Germany, and many in the "Russian party" deplored Prussia's triumph. But Alexander II welcomed it. Bismarck promised him the freedom to revoke the Black Sea provisions—to break free of the stigma of the Crimean War, to take the side

---

[1] V. A. Sollogub, *Dnevnik vysochaishchego prebyvaniia za Dunaem v 1877 godu* (St. Petersburg, 1878), xxxi.

[2] Cited in P. A. Zaionchkovskii, *Krizis samoderzhaviia na rubezhe 1870–1880-kh godov* (Moscow, 1964), 91.

of the victors, and to resume a respected role on the European diplomatic scene. His family and emotions tied him to Prussia, and he felt that the victory was in some way his own. He sent telegrams of congratulations to Wilhelm I and allowed or encouraged Russian officers, doctors, and field hospitals to serve with the German armies. He awarded the Prussian princes Friedrich-Wilhelm and Karl Friedrich, Prince Albert of Saxony, and Field Marshal Helmuth von Moltke the order of St. George, the highest Russian decoration for bravery in war. In November 1871, at a banquet given in honor of Prussian guests, he delivered a toast to the German emperor and to the continuation of the alliance between the empires.[3]

The Prussian victory had a momentous consequence for Russia's internal policy: It ended the stalemate in the Russian government between the supporters and the opponents of the reform of the Russian army. The former were led by the tsar's brother, the minister of the navy Constantine Nikolaevich, and particularly the minister of war Dmitrii Miliutin. They envisioned a citizen army, made up of recruits from all levels of society and commanded by a professional officer corps who earned their rank through talent and expertise. The conservative party, led by Peter Shuvalov, sought to preserve the privileges of the elite aristocratic officers. Peter Valuev, previously an ally of Shuvalov, had observed firsthand Prussia's success in mobilizing a citizen army for a modern war and was converted to Miliutin's views. The struggle between the parties continued in the government until 1873, when the emperor came down on Miliutin's side. On January 1, 1874, Alexander issued the decree for universal conscription and a six-year term of service.[4]

During the 1860s and early 1870s Miliutin took the first steps to produce trained, professional officers—to end the domination of the highest ranks of the army by commanders who owed their positions to birth, genteel education, and connections. Miliutin introduced junker schools and military gymnasiums with rigorous requirements under local commands, and he abolished many of the cadet corps that had provided genteel schooling for young noblemen favored for high officer positions. He raised the admission standards and improved the curriculum in the General Staff Academy. These changes created a path to promotion for talent, regardless of social origin, but they did not eliminate the nobles' advantages in reaching the top ranks of the military. They resulted in what John Bushnell described as a "two-track system," with the nonprivileged entering the regular army and the elite nobility assigned to the exclusive guards' regiments. In the last decades of

[3] S. B. Obolenskaia, *Franko-prusskaia voina i obshchestvennoe mnenie Germanii i Rossii* (Moscow, 1977), 143, 155; F. A. Tal'berg and N. I. Podgornaia, *Kavalery imperatorskogo voennogo ordena sviatogo velikomuchenika Georgiia, I i II stepenei (1769–1916)* (Riga, n.d.), 101–4.

[4] Dietrich Beyrau, *Militär und Gesellschaft im vorrevolutionären Russland* (Cologne, 1984), 277–308; Fuller, *Strategy and Power*, 281–85; John S. Bushnell, "Miliutin and the Balkan War: Military Reform vs. Military Performance," in Ben Eklof, John Bushnell, and Larissa Zakharova, eds., *Russia's Great Reforms, 1855–1881* (Bloomington, Ind., 1994), 150–51; Forrestt A. Miller, *Dmitrii Miliutin and the Reform Era in Russia* (Nashville, Tenn., 1968), 182–230.

the nineteenth century, while educational qualifications rose throughout the officer corps, the majority of commanders continued to win appointment through contacts with the court or the imperial family.[5]

The elite officers participated in parade-ground shows that exasperated Miliutin. He wrote in his diary on March 14, 1874, "It is painful for me to see the autocrat of eighty million subjects occupied with such a paltry matter." One sharp word from Alexander about precision marching "paralyzed all efforts to give the training of the troops a new character, more suited to the true benefit and conditions of war."[6] The matter may have paralyzed Miliutin's efforts but it was not paltry, for it made clear that the tsar and his military elite would never have anything in common with the rest of the officer corps, no matter how well the latter were trained. Most important, military ceremony remained an important sign of the emperor's identity as European monarch. On the parade ground, members of the Russian imperial family associated with European, particularly German, royalty. German princes continued to participate in these parades and held ranks in Russian guards' regiments, just as Alexander II and his sons held ranks in Prussian regiments.

Alexander had shared his father's delight in the military display since boyhood.[7] As emperor, he continued to hold massive and resplendent reviews on the field or at the Mikhailovskii Manège nearby, and the parade ground remained his passion, as it had been his forbears'. His reviews, however, no longer epitomized the effectiveness of the autocrat's will and state discipline, as they had under Nicholas I. Alexander was not the stern commander and showed little conviction in demanding precise fulfillment of his orders.[8] His parades were demonstrations not of the emperor's will but of a community of Western royalty and Russian noble elite, united by magnificent shows of mutual loyalty.

For Alexander II, the parade ground was a sphere of unfailing personal devotion and mutual dedication, of men imbued with the mystique of uniforms, marching, and horsemanship, where the scenario of mutual devotion prevailed even as it lost its credibility in society. The paragon of this stylish military culture was the imperial suite, the array of adjutant-generals at the emperor's side at all major parades and ceremonies. Alexander was the first

[5] Miller, *Dmitrii Miliutin and the Reform Era in Russia*, 88–136; Bushnell, "Miliutin and the Balkan War," 147–49, 154–55; P. A. Zaionchkovskii, *Samoderzhavie i russkaia armia na rubezhe XIX-XX stoletii, 1881–1903* (Moscow, 1973), 186–87.

[6] D. A. Miliutin, *Dnevnik D. A. Miliutina, 1873–1875* (Moscow, 1947), 1:147.

[7] See Vol. 1: 352–57.

[8] When there was confusion in maneuvers, Alexander reacted not with rage but with momentary irritation. Memoirs describe frequent breakdowns of the organization of parades: Once Alexander was left without a horse; another time the troops began to march in the wrong direction. Where Nicholas would have punished severely, Alexander often relented and forgave (Miliutin, *Dnevnik*, passim; V. V. Voeikov, "Poslednie dni Imperatora Aleksandra II i votsarenie Imperatora Aleksandra III," *Izvestiia Tambovskoi Uchenoi Arkhivnoi Komissii*, vol. 54 [Tambov, 1911], 72, 75; *IGK, ts. Al. II*, 600–1; Peter Kropotkin, *Memoirs of a Revolutionist* [Garden City, N.Y., 1962], 96, 113, 132).

emperor to ascend the throne as an adjutant of the imperial suite, and he awarded suite appointments generously. His relations with his adjutants were relaxed and comradely. He addressed them almost as friends, acted as godfather to their children, and visited them when they were sick.[9]

Riding out with the tsar at his parades and reviews, the suite displayed the Russian emperor among European royalty and showed the European identity of the emperor's servitors. Among the generals in the suite were foreign princes, the Oldenburgs from Denmark, the prince of Luxembourg, and many German princes related to the tsar. Many of Alexander's friends, whom he appointed to his suite, such as Alexander Patkul and Alexander and Vladimir Adlerberg, were also of German extraction. Other adjutants came from families who had been close to the throne during Nicholas I's reign, such as the Baranovs and Orlovs.[10]

The Sunday review of the capital guards' regiment at the Mikhailovskii Manège was the highlight of Alexander's military ceremony, an event he particularly cherished. Grand dukes and foreign princes in Russian uniform often took command. Ambassadors and embassy staffs attended, sometimes with their families. The Prussian military attaché and later ambassador von Schweinitz stood at Alexander's side and, over the blare of march music, strained to hear his comments on European affairs and Russian policies. Especially elaborate reviews were staged for the visits of royalty such as Wilhelm I and Franz-Joseph in 1873 and 1874. Indeed, the general's uniform was changed in 1873 because Wilhelm refused to wear its red trousers, which reminded him of French military dress.[11]

At the Sunday reviews, officers from all the guards regiments in the capital presented reports to the tsar. "It was a kind of club," one of them wrote, "in which the officers made one another's acquaintance." They could mingle with their superiors without the formalities of rank and make contacts otherwise denied them. Alexander and his uncle, the grand duke Nicholas Nikolaevich, who was the inspector-general of the cavalry, knew all officers by name and chatted with them, recalling the service of their fathers and other members of their family. Guards officers felt that the tsar knew them and recognized them individually. He called the guards his "little child" (*detishche*) and addressed them with the familiar *ty*; they looked on him as their "leader-father" (*Vozhd'-Otets*). Most important, they were seen by "the vigilant Eye (*oko*) of the Tsar," and they knew "that their service was remembered and appreciated."[12]

[9] The total number of those with such ranks doubled in his reign, rising from 179 in 1855 to 385 in 1881 (*IGK, ts. Al. II*, 777–90; Den', "Zapiski," 66:173).

[10] *IGK, ts. Al. II*, 779, 799. A complete listing of the members of Alexander's suite is contained in *Prilozhenie*, 289–313.

[11] Von Schweinitz, *Denkwürdigkeiten*, 1:201; Voeikov, "Poslednie dni Imperatora Aleksandra II," 73–74.

[12] Voeikov, "Poslednie dni Imperatora Aleksandra II," 71–73; V. Vonliarliarskii, *Moi vospominaniia* (Berlin, 1939), 47.

The guards put on a show to please the tsar, the grand dukes, and European visitors, each squadron or company trying to catch Alexander's eye. "The units on guard vied with one another in posture, the smartness of their uniforms, their presentation of arms, and their ceremonial march past the tsar." He then received the reports from the ordinaries of the various regiments. This, too, was a spectacle, the cavalry officers halting their gallop a few feet before him. When pleased, Alexander shouted "*molodets*," and they replied "Glad to do our best, Your Imperial Majesty." Again, each tried to outdo the other. Most spectacular were the tsar's Caucasian bodyguards drawn from the best horsemen among the mountain tribes. "These wild riders performed various maneoeuvres and feats of horsemanship, culminating in a frantic charge up the centre of the *manège* to the very feet of the Emperor and his brilliant staff."[13]

The summer maneuvers at Krasnoe Selo, meant as training exercises, were turned into a theatrical performance to impress foreign dignitaries with the magnificence of Russia's armed forces. The English ambassador Lord Dufferin left a vivid account. Together with representatives of several other European states, Dufferin joined "a brilliant staff of about a couple of hundred officers in every variety of uniform" and followed the emperor's calèche out to the plain where the exercises took place. The first morning was devoted to inspection of the cavalry. The English ambassador was enchanted by their evolutions, exclaiming that "nothing could be more beautiful than the way [the cavalry] massed themselves into columns, spread out into lines, changed their front, and charged their imaginary foes." Each regiment had uniformly colored horses, which "gave an additional glory to their appearance." The next day he was entranced by the beauty of the military games. He thought "nothing prettier" than to see the puffs of white smoke in the woods and his field of vision "peopled with battalions." The waves of tirailleurs, regiments advancing on one another, filled what he described as an arena, "while the distant horizon became fringed with thunder, smoke, and fire." He admired the beauty of the seizure of the bastion and retired to stand near Alexander on the emperor's mound. "Then, if possible, the spectacle became even more striking." The artillery and the infantry approached, and the cavalry charged at the fleeing foes.

> This last performance was really splendid. There must have been from six to seven thousand horsemen engaged in the operation, and the rapid movement of such warriors, their breast-plates and helmets glittering in the sun, with the shouts of their commanders, produced an effect impossible to describe.[14]

[13] Vonliarliarskii, *Moi vospominaniia*, 47–48; John F. Baddeley, *Russia in the "Eighties"; Sport and Politics* (London, 1921), 14–15.

[14] Dowager Marchioness of Dufferin, *My Russian and Turkish Journals* (London, 1917), 43–47. The citations are quoted from Lord Dufferin's journal.

IMAGES OF THE NATION AND THE RUSSO-TURKISH WAR

The scenario of love presented the emperor as the central unifying element of the nation. He was the embodiment of the state, the ruler of the empire, and the focus of devotion of the Russian people. The atmosphere of relative freedom after the emancipation permitted the expression of contesting views of what the nation represented. Liberal opinion envisioned the nation in terms of public activity and participation. Platon Pavlov and the newspaper *Golos* anticipated a nation-state, with the monarch encouraging the independent action of society. This form of "state-based patriotism" fostered the idea of citizenship, the individual's political self defined by participation in political organs and not by his relationship to the sovereign. It directly challenged the mythical preponderance of the figure of the tsar and prompted rebuffs and police measures from the authorities.

Other writers, like Fedor Buslaev and the Slavophiles, sought the nation in the peasantry themselves. Proponents of this viewpoint shared the Slavophile notion that the peasants preserved a national spirit, lost by the state and educated groups. Many, such as Ivan Aksakov and Nicholas Danilevskii, also expected a broadening of participation, freedom, and the development of political participation. But by identifying the peasantry with the nation they challenged the national credentials of the monarch, who presented himself as kin to European aristocracy and royalty. And by focusing on ethnic character, they identified Russian interests with those of their "Slavic brethren," particularly the Balkan peoples struggling to free themselves from Turkish overlordship. Such a concept of nation challenged the goals of Alexander's foreign policy—to present Russia as a Western monarchy seeking to maintain peace and harmonious relations between rulers.

With the outbreak of uprisings in Bulgaria and Serbia in the 1870s, Pan-Slavist opinion became increasingly widespread and open. Those calling for Russian support of the Bulgarian and Serbian movements against Turkey called into question the monarchy's national character, the degree to which it in fact served the Russian nation and sought its national interests. They demanded not political reform but heroic leadership, like that displayed by General Michael Cherniaev, the conqueror of Tashkent who had gone off to Serbia to take command of a Russian volunteer army in May 1876.

The rise of Pan-Slavism marked a new era in the public life of Russia, when the commercial press, much of it conservative and monarchist in persuasion, became a political force the government had to contend with. Colonel Vissarion Komarov, the editor of *Russkii Mir*, the "voice of Pan-Slavism," accompanied General Michael Cherniaev (the principal owner of the newspaper) in his escapades with the Serbian armies and printed spurious reports of Cherniaev's heroism and victories. One of the most ardent supporters of Russian intervention in the Balkans was Alexei Suvorin, who took over the newspaper *Novoe Vremia* in 1876. Suvorin turned the newspaper into a mass circulation daily whose reports and editorials inflamed nascent Pan-Slavist sentiment. In 1876 he described "the boredom, the melancholy mood that so many people feel; the apathy that makes people shrug their shoulders . . . tells us they are waiting for something."[15] By 1876 sentiment for Russian intervention embraced a broad spectrum of Russian society, from the empress, the heir, and figures in the court to revolutionaries who sympathized with the democratic aspirations of the Balkan peoples.

The tsar and his ministers wanted to avoid war. The war minister Dmitrii Miliutin feared that the army was not ready, the foreign minister Alexander Gorchakov was wary about antagonizing Western governments, and the minister of finance Michael Reitern warned of the disastrous consequences of a war given Russia's precarious financial situation. Armed intervention in the Balkans could bring only heightened suspicions abroad, the possibility of a new coalition of European powers against Russia, and renewed fiscal crises. During the course of 1876 Alexander tried to avoid war and gain the concessions for the rebelling nationalities through negotiations.[16]

In keeping with his scenario, Alexander tried to show himself acting in concert with his people and taking account of public opinion. Again, he stepped forward with public speeches, explaining the situation and government policy. He promised war if Russia's demands were not met but stated his commitment to a peaceful solution. His speech to the estates in Moscow on October 1, 1876, was a strong response to the British prime minister Disraeli's truculent defense of the territorial integrity of Turkey. But he insisted on maintaining peace if Russian demands were met. "I know that all Russia, together with me, is sharing most actively in the sufferings of our brothers by faith and origin. But for me the true interests of Russia are dearer than anything, and I would like to spare dear Russian blood to the greatest extent." He concluded that if the forthcoming meetings in Constantinople did not reach satisfactory agreements, he intended "to act independently," that is, embark on war, and that he looked to Moscow to provide an example. The next day the foreign minister Gorchakov announced mobilization, still professing reluctance to engage in war.[17]

Moscow was the center of Pan-Slavist sentiment and the threat of war brought a warm response. *Moskovskie Vedomosti* welcomed the end of "the rule of deceit." Ivan Aksakov, in his speech before the Moscow Slavonic Benevolent Committee, declared that "in the Kremlin, among the shrines and ancient monuments of Moscow, the "Russian tsar entered into contact (*obshchenie*) with his people, with the spirit of their past and future desti-

[15] McReynolds, *The News under Russia's Old Regime*, 74–79, 82–85; Hans Rogger, "The Skobelev Phenomenon: The Hero and His Worship," in *Oxford Slavonic Papers* (1976), 9:69; Effie Ambler, *Russian Journalism and Politics, 1861–1881: The Career of A. S. Suvorin* (Detroit, 1972), 133–41.

[16] Fuller, *Strategy and Power*, 308–9; Kornilov, *Obshchestvennoe dvizhenie pri Aleksandre II*, 230.

[17] Tatishchev, *Imperator Aleksandr II*, 2:336; MV, November 3, 1876, 1.

nies." Aksakov said that all Russian areas were rejoicing and that Alexander's glory was spreading beyond Russian borders. Alexander was the successor to Ivan III, "who received the Byzantine coat-of-arms from the Paleologues and combined it with the Moscow coat-of-arms," and of Peter and Catherine, "as the crowned protector of ancient customs and the unbroken historical precept."[18]

Aksakov's dream of a national tsar leading the Russian people against the heathen hardly corresponded with Alexander's intentions. But the process of diplomacy failed to take its course. Pressed by his spouse, the heir, his brother Constantine Nikolaevich, the grand duke Nicholas Nikolaevich, as well as the ambassador to Constantinople Nicholas Ignat'ev, Alexander determined to embark on war on April 12, 1877. He found strength the night before, when his father appeared to him in a dream and reassured him.[19] When he visited the Kremlin on April 23, 1877, there was little bellicose in his manner. Unlike his appearance in the autumn of 1855, he did not invoke the memory of Alexander I and 1812. The enemy was not on Russian soil, and clearly he did not regard Russia's fate as linked with the Bulgarians or the Serbs. At his gala welcome in Petersburg, he again referred to his efforts to find a peaceful outcome.[20]

Alexander's performance as national leader followed the narrative of his scenario. He was not the people's tsar, responding to a national upsurge, but the heroic monarch, who justified his supreme position by a show of courage and self-sacrifice for the nation he served. In keeping with his scenario, Alexander gave the grand dukes command posts. He appointed Nicholas Nikolaevich commander-in-chief and placed the heir Alexander Aleksandrovich and the grand duke Vladimir Aleksandrovich at the head of armies at the front, though under close supervision of the generals assisting them. These were not discrete acts of nepotism but public demonstrations of the valor of the members of the imperial family.[21] What later came to be derided as "the grand dukes' war" was proudly presented as a war led by the grand dukes. Numerous pictures circulated at the time portraying the emperor and the grand dukes at the front in heroic poses (fig. 16).

Most important, the emperor insisted on being close to the front himself. Miliutin, his uncle Nicholas Nikolaevich, and the generals looked with dismay on this decision. The "imperial chief apartment," the tsar with his large suite followed by foreign attachés, represented another burden. In addition to the physical danger and unhealthy weather conditions, the emperor's pres-

---

[18] Tatishchev, *Imperator Aleksandr II*, 2:336–37.

[19] Miliutin, *Dnevnik*, 2:183.

[20] Tatishchev, *Imperator Aleksandr II*, 2:372–76; MV, April 24, 1877, 3.

[21] The grand dukes and elite noble officers continued to dominate command positions thwarting Miliutin's goal of advancing officers according to merit. This resulted in the many blunders that made what should have been a relatively easy war into a prolonged, costly, and embarrassing one (see Bushnell, "Miliutin and the Balkan War," 147–56; Beyrau, *Militär und Gesellschaft*, 392–405).

16. Grand Duke and Heir Alexander Aleksandrovich at Front.
Chromolithograph, 1877 (or 1878). GARF.

ence could create disunity in the command structure. Alexander ignored these objections and then shocked his subordinates by announcing that he wished to take command himself. Miliutin wrote, "This suggestion alarmed not only the grand duke [Nicholas Nikolaevich] but his staff and everyone around him."[22]

Alexander thought of himself as a military man and was determined to participate. He declared to the members of his suite, "Growing up with the army from childhood, I could not stand [to remain behind] and came here to share its cares and labors."[23] He was following the example of Nicholas's stay at the front in 1829. When he first arrived near the front he could not sleep from excitement and awaited combat action. Again he dreamed he saw his father, who pressed him to his bosom and blessed him. Alexander recounted his dream to Miliutin and Grand Duke Nicholas Nikolaevich and wept profusely. Despite strenuous efforts to dissuade him, Alexander insisted on moving closer and closer to the theater of action. On July 3, 1877, he followed his father's example and crossed the Danube.[24]

Alexander's presence at the theater of war was widely publicized and dramatized his personal leadership. The official account was a diary by the author of novellas and plays, Count Vladimir Sollogub, which was excerpted in newspapers and published in book form in 1878. Sollogub's diary characterizes Alexander as a sentimental hero, acting purely out of the altruism that inspired his people: "Where other states envy, Russia loves; where other states seek advantage, Russia sacrifices herself." He related how Alexander, "peace-loving" and reluctant to embark on war, was forced to act by Western greed. "The heart of the Emperor, full of love, had to be saddened by meeting black ingratitude in the sphere of his good deeds." The whole Russian people dreamed of freeing the Balkan Slavs, an act, Sollogub argued, that showed no trace of national ambition or hopes of conquest. When compelled to act by the treachery of England, Alexander II therefore led his people in a war unprecedented by Russia's disregard for gain.[25]

Sollogub depicted Alexander not as a military leader but as a moral one, providing psychological support for the troops. This support took two forms: inspiration—the maintenance of morale; and consolation—the compassion for suffering. He maintained morale by participating in the ceremonials of the barrack, the parade ground, and the court that gave his rule its sense of permanence and majesty. He dined with officers and after each dinner enjoyed cigars with them. This showed, Sollogub wrote, that "before the general labors and dangers, if comradeship was unthinkable, a closeness nonetheless comes about, a family bond expressing kindness and cordiality."[26] Sollogub noted admiringly that Alexander wore the uniform of the

[22] Miliutin, *Dnevnik*, 2:166, 173.
[23] Tatishchev, *Imperator Aleksandr II*, 2:392.
[24] Miliutin, *Dnevnik*, 2:182, 194.
[25] Sollogub, *Dnevnik*, i–xxxi.
[26] Ibid., 13–14.

unit he was reviewing or receiving, sustaining a family bond with the troops. On the anniversary of his mother's death, Alexander attended a memorial service dressed in the Cavalier Guards' uniforms. His continued attention to uniforms, the author claimed, helped to inspire and encourage the troops. On review, they responded by shouting "Hoorah," and this cry, Sollogub felt, carried special meaning in wartime. It expressed "a scorn for fatigue, for deprivation, for hunger, for torments, for torture" and showed "a readiness to die a *ferocious death*, to fall in entire regiments under fire."[27]

Alexander maintained the routine of the imperial court to the extent that conditions permitted. He attended church services and observed all the appropriate religious holidays, as well as the birthdays and anniversaries of the members of his family. For Sollogub, these daily habits demonstrated the permanence and regularity of autocratic power. The camp was a simulacrum of the court and the symbolic sphere of the autocrat's will. It was the sovereign's will that energized autocratic power, and "the wavering of arbitrariness vanishes before the bond of habits established within the bounds of humanness and the firmness of granite." The autocrat was "the shrine incarnate of the state order" and so his personal acts were connected with the well-being of the state. By displaying the signs of the ordinary and unchanging in the combat zone, Alexander revealed the strength and security of the governmental order, as well as its superpersonal source.[28]

Alexander began his stay with courtly elegance, but, Sollogub emphasized, from August to December 1877 he lived a spare army life in tents or small country houses, dined simply, and suffered from extreme heat and cold, as well as prolonged bouts of fever. At the beginning of the trip, in July, at the town of Tsarevitsa, when the heat was unendurable, Sollogub marveled, "the master of countless palaces, accustomed to the most luxurious chambers in the world, sentenced himself, in his mature years, and while his health was poor, to lengthy, prolonged, dwelling under canvas, where the heat, cold, and rain turn into true torments."[29]

Alexander, moving closer to the front, exposed himself and the grand dukes to the dangers of war. A lubok issued in 1877 depicts an episode during the emperor's visit to Sistov, when a bomb exploded nearby (fig. 17). The emperor, with the grand dukes Alexander and Vladimir riding behind him, turns with aplomb and, according to the caption, calmly asks, "Has anyone been wounded?" Hearing there were no casualties he crosses himself twice, whereupon he is received by the Russian troops shown at the left and Bulgarians at the lower right "with inspiration and enthusiasm."[30]

Alexander showed his compassion during his numerous visits to hospitals. He approached each soldier in the hospital "not as a person who was insig-

[27] Ibid., 231, 115.
[28] Ibid., 113, 117–18.
[29] Ibid., 8, 10, 107–8.
[30] GARF, 678-1-1027.

17. Alexander II at the Danube Front. Chromolithograph lubok, 1877. GARF.

nificant before him but as a comrade in heroism, as a confrere in painful service." His appearance had an effect Sollogub described as magical: "The groaning ceased almost momentarily. Sufferings were forgotten. Faces beamed with happiness, tenderness (*umilenie*), and gratitude." The visits showed "that the power of love, devotion, and self-renunciation still lives at the bottom of the Russian soul at solemn moments."[31]

Alexander visited the wounded throughout his stay, comforted them, and brought them presents. He watched injured soldiers return on foot, bleeding, in the days after the storming of Plevna and carried some in his carriage. V. A. Cherkasskii, the chief of the Russian Red Cross at the front, was deeply moved at his attentiveness and sympathy to every need of the wounded and his sincere philanthropy. Cherkasskii was reminded of Saint Louis during the crusades. Alexander's personal physician, S. P. Botkin, wrote in his letters that he was moved to tears by the scenes of the emperor visiting soldiers in the hospital. The tsar was warm with the wounded soldiers who lunged for the presents "like children" and showed naive delight.[32]

[31] Sollogub, *Dnevnik*, xliii, 114–15.
[32] Tatishchev, *Imperator Aleksandr II*, 2:394, 398–99, 403.

After the capture of Plevna, Alexander returned to a joyous welcome in Petersburg. The scenario of cordiality and affection continued. He was met on December 10, 1877, at the station by military and civilian ranks and the town deputation, who delivered addresses and presented him with bread and salt. He visited the Kazan cathedral for the traditional prayer before the Kazan icon and then proceeded to the Winter Palace to join the service of thanksgiving. He was met with wild rejoicing, reminiscent, the German ambassador remarked, of a folk festival. The streets were packed with the population of the city, and the line of troops, he observed, "vanished in the throng of jubilant *muzhiki*." A peasant ran behind the carriage shouting, "Hoorah Alexander Nikolaevich! He has beaten them himself!"[33] The correspondent of the London *Daily News* described a throng of all classes of the population in the cathedral, greeting the tsar enthusiastically. It was "a microcosm of the Russian nation." As the emperor rode in a carriage up to the palace, "the clamor of the cheering rent the sky," and "the cheering continued so long and persistently that he had to gratify the people by showing himself again and again at the window of the palace." The correspondent raised the fundamental question—whether this enthusiasm was genuine. He heard assertions on both sides but concluded that the response was sincere, revealing "fervid warmth compared to which the welcome the Berliners gave their Emperor on his return from the Franco-German War was chill." He convinced himself by his own dispassionate study:

> I have seen many displays of popular enthusiasm but never have I witnessed a manifestation which impressed me so deeply as the scene in the Kazan Cathedral on Saturday last. It was no picked throng: the Russians have not arrived at the artificiality of selected representation on such an occasion by tickets of admission. To the extent of its accommodation the cathedral was as free to the *muzhik* as to the *chinovnik*.[34]

The Petersburg nobility welcomed Alexander with a warm address that extolled the heroic feat (*podvig*) of the tsar's extended stay at the front, which Russia would appreciate and "keep for centuries in her memory." His presence, the speech went on, inspired the troops to show the enormous courage that enabled them to resist the Turks. Russia knew "with what humility you renounced the glory you deserve for your deprivations, labors, and cares." From the Balkans to the Neva, his journey had been accompanied by shouts of enthusiasm attesting to the devotion and love of the Russian people.[35]

[33] Ibid., 2:416; von Schweinitz, *Denkwürdigkeiten*, 1:439.

[34] *The War Correspondence of the "Daily News," 1877–78* (London, 1878), 225–29, 232–33.

[35] Tatishchev, *Imperator Aleksandr II*, 2:416–17. The speech confirmed the tsar's image as exemplar of self-sacrificing sympathy. It praised his self-renunciation in enduring "the broiling heat of midday in the summer and all the trials of a harsh winter in a primitive country, where

•

But the difficulties and human costs of the storm of Plevna could not be concealed by the displays of enthusiasm. The army took the fortress only after three attempts, with enormous losses. After the failure of the second attack, the position of the Russian armies had become so precarious that a military council on July 19, 1877, attended by the tsar and the heir, took the extraordinary measure of mobilizing nearly the entire guards' corpus of the capital.[36] The third assault was planned by the grand duke Nicholas Nikolaevich for Alexander's name day, August 30, the day of Alexander Nevskii. The tsar himself wished to witness the battle. On a bluff, with a commanding view of the battle, the tsar, Nicholas Nikolaevich, and the emperor's suite attended a prayer service and then lunched. Those present drank a toast to the tsar, and the tsar toasted "our glorious armies." The attack was pressed despite unfavorable weather conditions, turning the field into mud. The Russian armies fell back after suffering more than fifteen thousand casualties. It was a great blow to Alexander, his Golgotha, his doctor Sergei Botkin wrote.[37] Plevna fell only on November 28, whereupon Russian armies advanced toward Constantinople. But by the time they reached the Sea of Marmora, they had sustained more than two hundred thousand casualties, and their ranks had been devastated by typhus and dysentery. Alexander insisted on pressing forward to Constantinople, but the threat of British intervention and the exhaustion of the Russian armies convinced him to accept the Sultan's offer of an armistice on January 19, 1878.[38]

Sollogub's depiction of the tsar as protector of ritual, order, and stability ill comported with popular demands for daring and national military leadership, which were expressed in the press. The relaxation of official constraints in Alexander's reign had permitted the rapid increase of privately owned newspapers, which took advantage of the latest technological innovations to increase circulation. Mass-circulation newspapers, like Suvorin's *Novoe Vremia*, gave realistic and grim accounts of the hostilities. Journalists were allowed unprecedented freedom to report directly from the front and gave a sense of the difficulties the Russian armies were encountering.[39] Approximately eighty correspondents, thirty from Russian newspapers, mingled with

a tent was your prison and a wretched room your palace." He was "an angel of consolation, who alleviated the suffering of the wounded with that infinite kindness that overflows from your loving heart."

[36] Bushnell, "Miliutin and the Balkan War," 138–42; Fuller, *Strategy and Power*, 311–27; Tatishchev, *Imperator Aleksandr II*, 2:396.

[37] Tatishchev, *Imperator Aleksandr II*, 2:400–401.

[38] Ibid., 2:401–2; Fuller, *Strategy and Power*, 316–22; Bushnell, "Miliutin and the Balkan War," 138–43.

[39] McReynolds, *The News under Russia's Old Regime*, 81–92; Charles A. Ruud, "The Printing Press as an Agent of Political Change in Early Twentieth Century Russia," *Russian Review* 40, no. 4 (October 1991): 379; and G. K. Gradovskii, *Itogi (1862–1907)* (Kiev, 1908), 400–401.

generals and sent reports back by telegraph. These appeared a few days later, in the morning, in Russia and abroad, giving the world the latest news of what came to be called "the breakfast war." The peasants learned the war news, which was read to them at their *volost'* centers.[40] Nicholas I, in 1829, could conceal his distance from combat with elaborate ceremony, while his figure was glorified in rhetorical flourishes and lubki. Alexander's presence at the front only magnified his inability to affect the direction of the war and made his sacrifice appear an empty gesture and his suffering trivial compared to the privation and death around him.

The emperor's symbolic leadership of the war effort now had to contend with a new type of hero—the general-adventurer who showed courage, abandon, and a contempt for the routine that constrained most commanders of the imperial army. The most glamorous of the new generals was Michael Skobelev, who had defied hierarchy by ignoring his superiors' orders to strike out on his own, and took bold tactical initiatives that had brought him stunning victories at Khiva and Kokand. He distinguished himself at Plevna and engaged in a daring attack at the conclusion of the war at the Shipka pass during the battle of Sheinovo.[41]

Skobelev struck a glamorous figure. He was only thirty-three at the time of the war. The son of a general and grandson of a soldier, he also appeared as someone from the people. He skillfully courted the numerous reporters at the front. He kept his photograph and descriptions of his exploits in readiness. V. I. Nemirovich-Danchenko glorified his exploits in *Novoe Vremia* and in his diaries published after the war. Skobelev spoke English and befriended English and American correspondents, who spread his renown abroad. The colorful reports in the popular press contrasted with the lackluster accounts in the official *Pravitel'stvennyi Vestnik*, written by V. V. Krestovskii.[42]

Skobelev was the principal beneficiary of the new political awareness that swept Russia at the time of the war and represented the hope of victory in the midst of the costly stalemate in the Balkans. "We pictured him as a superhero and legends about him were making the rounds," recalled one Petersburg resident of lower-class background.[43] Handsome and prepossessing in his white uniform, astride his white charger, Skobelev became regarded as an epitome of a folk hero by both the common people and the Pan-Slavist intellectuals, who yearned for energetic national leadership. His dashing

---

[40] Rogger, "The Skobelev Phenomenon," 73–74; Brooks, *When Russia Learned to Read*, 28.

[41] Rogger, "The Skobelev Phenomenon," passim.

[42] Januarius Aloysius MacGahan, a correspondent of the *New York Daily News*, wrote of him: "He is a tall handsome man, with a lithe, slender, active figure, a clear, blue eye, and . . . the kind of nose it is said Napoleon used to look for among the officers when he wished to find a general, a face young enough for a second lieutenant although he is a general—the youngest in the army" (McReynolds, *The News under Russia's Old Regime*, 89–90).

[43] Rogger, "The Skobelev Phenomenon," 75; McReynolds, *The News under Russia's Old Regime*, 89.

figure contrasted sharply with the stiff Germanic generals and the grand dukes, who held the chief positions of command. For the masses, he appeared in lubki surrounded by other mythical and historical figures. A peddler in Smolensk Province sold such lubki, declaring, "Here is Skobelev, who took Plevna." Suvorin's *Novoe Vremia* described him in terms of the *bogatyr'*, the burly knights of the Russian folk epics—*byliny*. Educated society began to see him as a true leader of the nation. Vasilii Vereshchagin made him a hero of a cycle of paintings that were otherwise critical of the war. His *Skobelev at Sheinovo*, exhibited in 1880, was reproduced and widely circulated.[44]

In contrast, Vereshchagin's painting, *Near Plevna*, depicts the tsar's party watching the third assault on the fortress while celebrating his name day; when exhibited in Paris it bore the title "The Tsar's Name Day." The tsar sits slouching in a chair on a bluff; an aide bends over, explaining the operations. Behind the tsar, members of his suite stand in what seems almost parade order. The painting emphasizes the group's distance from the action, visible only by clouds of smoke rising from the battlefield. It also makes the figures appear paltry: They are small, dwarfed by the scene around them, the hill and clouds of smoke making them insignificant. The figures peer intently into the distance. They are spectators, not participants, watching a scene they cannot control. The painting is a visual counterpart to Tolstoi's description in *War and Peace* of Alexander I at the Battle of Austerlitz—a diminutive figure wandering through the field, humbled by his ill-fated attempt to command.[45] It caused a storm in conservative circles. The heir remarked, "Vereshchagin is a swine or a person who is completely deranged."[46]

Alexander's prestige suffered a further blow at the diplomatic table. On March 3, 1878, Russia and Turkey concluded the Treaty of San Stefano which created an enlarged Bulgaria under Russian domination and gave Russia control over the Balkans. But under threat of war from Britain, Germany, and Austria, Russia agreed to negotiation in Berlin. The Congress of Berlin, where Bismarck played the role of "honest broker," agreed on a treaty in July 1879 that reduced the size of Bulgaria and ceded Bosnia-Herzegovina to Austria. The terms prompted an outburst of indignation in Russia against

[44] Rogger, "The Skobelev Phenomenon," 46, 55; Brooks, *When Russia Learned to Read*, 107. See I. Solov'eva and V. Shitova, "A. S. Suvorin: portret na fony gazety," *Voprosy Literatury*, no. 2 (1977): 195–96.

[45] After the siege of Plevna, Vereshchagin wandered over the battlefields contemplating in horror the piles of shells and bones of buried soldiers. On the bluff where the emperor had stood, however, he found no bones or shells but piles of champagne corks. "So from this hill of *zakuski* I took a few corks and bits of champagne bottles and from the Grivitskii redoubt, nearby, a soldier's forgotten skull and bones as well as some bits of rusted shell casings" (A. K. Lebedev, *Vasilii Vasil'evich Vereshchagin; zhizn' i tvorchestvo, 1842–1904* [Moscow, 1972], 179–80). I have not been able to find an adequate reproduction of the painting, which is in the collection of the Tretiakov Gallery.

[46] Previously the emperor had purchased several of Vereshchagin's battle scenes (Neverov, "Aleksandr II," 19).

the Germans and the tsar for permitting such concessions. Rumors of betrayal circulated in Petersburg, giving rise to charges that the emperor was derelict in protecting the nation's interests. "There was a general feeling of discontent, almost scorn for the Emperor; quite striking," a French observer reported.[47]

Ivan Aksakov delivered a speech to the Moscow Slavonic Society condemning the government's conduct of foreign policy. He referred to "the shameful news of our concessions, which, having been brought to the knowledge of our people without being denied by the Russian authorities, fill us with shame, pain our conscience, and oppress us with bewilderment." Without mentioning Alexander's name, Aksakov held the tsar responsible for the concessions. His speech represented an unprecedented public critique of a Russian monarch.[48] Alexander ordered Aksakov banished from Moscow. He wrote an angry letter to his uncle, the Kaiser, but did nothing to shed his German predilections.

POLITICAL DISCORD

The first stirrings of a revolutionary movement in the sixties weakened the tsar's faith in his scenario but did not change the nature of his appeals. Alexander's ministers continued to profess the tenet of official nationality, that bonds with the tsar were endemic to Russian people of all estates and that reasonable men would see the revolutionaries' error and rally to the monarchy's defense. The reforms, strengthening feelings of belonging and legality, would build respect for order that would ultimately lead educated society to condemn revolutionary schemes as futile and criminal. Peter Shuvalov, the director of the Third Section and chief of gendarmes from 1866 to 1874, increased police surveillance and favored enhanced administrative power for governors. But he also viewed openness and freedom of the press as goals of the monarchy that in the long run would strengthen the ties between the estates and the monarch. The minister of justice Constantine Pahlen, though a partisan of greater administrative control over the judiciary, believed in open courts, which he thought would condemn the revolutionaries as criminals.

Large segments of educated society, however, continued to envision a political nation, embodied in representative institutions rather than personal bonds with the monarch. For them, such institutions would be the fruits of the love and harmony of the first years of his reign. By invoking personal affections, Alexander risked the anger of those who felt betrayed, and undying love could easily turn to resentment on the part of those whose expecta-

[47] N.G.O. Pereira, *Tsar-Liberator: Alexander II of Russia, 1818–1881* (Newtonville, Mass., 1983), 131–32.

[48] Kornilov, *Kurs russkoi istorii*, 3:211.

tions had been scorned. The arrests of the participants in the "going-to-the-people" movement in 1874 and the show trials of revolutionaries in 1878 won sympathy for the revolutionaries, not for a government that moderate society viewed as derelict in its responsibilities. By the close of the decade, Alexander could no longer delude himself about a bond of love between the throne and Russian society. Love had turned into its antithesis: bitter rage indulgent of violent revolutionary acts. The tsar and his ministers felt completely isolated from Russian society and engaged in a war to the finish with their most ruthless opponents. In January 1880 Miliutin wrote, "It is hard to uproot the evil when the government finds neither sympathy nor sincere support in a single layer of society."[49]

At the beginning of the 1870s Alexander's' ministers still fought the revolutionary movement with preconceptions of the scenario of love. They believed that the new courts would stigmatize the revolutionaries as criminals in the eyes of the public, winning sympathy and support for the monarchy. They therefore insisted that the trials be publicized, making explicit the details of the revolutionaries' deeds. The minister of justice Constantine Pahlen ordered that the stenographic accounts of the trial of the Nechaev group in 1871 be made known to the public, stating that "the most candid and full presentation of the facts should deal the greatest blow to the party sympathizing with the accused." In 1875 the Committee of Ministers affirmed this view. The government, they concluded, had to remedy society's ignorance about the danger of revolutionary doctrines and the extent of their influence. They recommended a public inquiry "in which all the perniciousness of the elaborated teaching and extent of their menace will be exposed."[50]

The show trials that followed, however, had the opposite effect. Government prosecutors had difficulty making their cases, not to speak of stigmatizing the accused before society. The most spectacular—the trial of the 193—which ended in January 1878, assumed the character of a scandal even before it reached the court. The accused were young intellectuals who had gone "to the people" in the summer of 1874. They had hoped to foment a social revolution in the countryside that would overthrow the autocracy and bring socialism to Russia. They remained in prison for more than three years while the government prepared its case. During this period, seventy-five of their number died or went insane. By the time the trial began, it had come to be regarded as an atrocity. The prosecutors prepared their case carelessly, presenting almost no evidence against the accused. The court acquitted more than half the defendants, though the police arrested many upon release and subjected them to administrative punishments.[51]

---

[49] Miliutin, *Dnevnik*, 3:205.

[50] Wortman, *The Development of a Russian Legal Consciousness*, 279–81; Tatishchev, *Imperator Aleksandr II*, 2:594–96.

[51] Wortman, *The Development of a Russian Legal Consciousness*, 281–82.

The final blow to the principle of publicity in political trials was the acquittal of Vera Zasulich in March 1878. Zasulich had, by her own admission, shot and wounded F. F. Trepov, the governor-general of St. Petersburg, in retaliation for his striking one of the imprisoned revolutionaries, A. P. Boboliubov, a member of the organization Land and Freedom. Rather than try Zasulich for a political crime, which required a special tribunal, Minister of Justice Pahlen had her charged with attempted murder, which would be decided by a jury. He hoped in this way to brand Zasulich a common criminal, withholding information of her revolutionary associations in the government's case. But the jury decided the case contrary to fact and, to the audience's wild approval, acquitted her. The press called the verdict an open protest of "public conscience" against governmental oppression.[52]

Initially conceived as a retaliatory measure against the tsarist police, the assassination of important officials won considerable support in educated society and became the revolutionaries' principal tactic.[53] In June 1879 the terrorist wing of the revolutionary organization Land and Freedom formed a new party, the People's Will, which identified the autocracy as the source of inequality and oppression in Russia and issued a death sentence on the tsar. The series of attempts on the emperor's life that followed revealed the helplessness of the security apparatus of the tsarist state. On November 19, 1879, a group under the leadership of Sofia Perovskaia mined what they mistakenly thought was the train carrying the tsar to Moscow. On February 5, 1880, a bomb planted by Stepan Khalturin exploded under a dining room in the Winter Palace, before the tsar arrived, killing eleven people.

The rivalry between the political police in the Third Section and the regular police in the Ministry of the Interior prevented effective security measures. The chief of gendarmes Alexander Potapov, who had replaced Peter Shuvalov purportedly at the insistence of Dolgorukova, was widely regarded as weak and incompetent. To make matters worse, educated society, apparently indifferent to the government's plight, refrained from the displays of relief and sympathy that followed the Karakozov attempt. On the contrary, zemstvo assemblies drafted addresses calling for the government to win the support of moderates and liberals by increasing freedoms and introducing representative institutions.

The terrorist attacks ushered in a "crisis of autocracy." The old form of rule no longer worked, but the tsar and his advisers seemed at a loss to replace it. The scenario of love excluded both despotic repression, which might eliminate the revolutionaries, and the establishment of representative

---

[52] Ibid., 282–83.

[53] In August 1878 Sergei Kravchinskii assassinated the head of the Third Section N. V. Mezentsov; in February 1879 Grigorii Gol'denburg shot and killed the governor of Kiev Province Alexander Kropotkin. On April 2, 1879, Alexander Soloviev fired five times at the emperor as he walked near the Winter Palace.

institutions, which might win the support of moderate society against them. In these circumstances, the government turned from one to another administrative expedient to fight an unseen but ubiquitous menace. First, temporary governor-generals were established and vested with extraordinary powers to dispense summary justice. But they soon abused this authority, exiling 575 individuals between April 1879 and July 1880 and sentencing 16 to death in 1879. The measure led only to further resentment and terrorist activity.[54]

On February 9, 1880, three days after Khalturin's bomb exploded, Alexander approved the formation of a Supreme Executive Commission, with broad powers to coordinate and unify the workings of the government. He appointed General Michael Loris-Melikov as head of the commission. The son of an Armenian merchant, Loris-Melikov had served with distinction in the Crimean War and had proved himself an energetic reformer as governor of the Terskaia Region. He achieved his greatest renown during the Russo-Turkish War, when he led the armies capturing Kars. As governor-general of Kharkov Province, he had both taken forceful measures against the revolutionaries and sought the sympathy of local society. Loris-Melikov assumed extensive powers, uniting all police agencies in a concerted effort to apprehend the conspirators.

•

The feeling of fear through 1879 took its toll on the tsar's confidence and composure, leaving him, in the words of Valuev, "a semi-ruin." Outwardly, this was expressed in heightened security measures. Alexander now had to take his morning strolls through the halls of the Winter Palace rather than outside. When he walked his dog, Milord, in the Summer Garden, a heavy police guard stood at the gates and Cossacks patrolled key points along the Fontanka Canal. In 1879, for the first time, Alexander rode through the streets of his capital under convoy and with the blinds drawn. Two Cossacks rode before him, two rode on the side, and two at the rear, and later a Cossack stood on the coach box as well. The convoy Cossacks wore brilliant red uniforms, but, as one of the tsar's suite observed, "the impression was spoiled by the thought of the circumstances that had brought this about."[55]

The attacks on Alexander destroyed not only the illusion of love but also the impression of the tsar's personal inviolability. The sense of secular transcendence had been reflected in the tsar's capacity to walk, godlike and invulnerable, among his own people. In December 1878 the correspondent of the Daily News remarked on the nonchalance of the police in St. Petersburg and watched with surprise when a peasant approached the tsar during his soli-

[54] Zaionchkovskii, Krizis samoderzhavie, 91–92.
[55] Voeikov, "Poslednie dni Imperatora Aleksandra II," 60–61; Firsov, "Aleksandr II," 134.

tary stroll along the embankment.[56] Now that sense was gone, and both he and the heir felt oppressed by the new rules.[57]

At the same time, the government's increasingly primitive measures of retribution dramatized its own helplessness. The resort to court martials revealed the failure of regular institutional procedures. Not only did the court martials issue summary military justice, but the convicted were put on display in an effort to induce fear and shame. The condemned revolutionaries were carried in a black hearse through the streets of Petersburg. They were dressed in black and wore a white sign with "State Criminal" printed in bold letters. Around them rode Cossacks, their swords drawn and flashing ominously. The sight left a gloomy impression on the observers. The police saw danger everywhere. In January 1881 they arrested a man who shouted "hurrah" in an unusual way. It turned out to be a singer who played the role of Susanin in *A Life for the Tsar*.[58]

The ceremonial presentations of the tsar made known the new sense of his vulnerability. The train explosion of November 1879 cast a pall over the usually festive Moscow meetings. After the procession from the Red Staircase, Alexander asked for the help of the representatives of the estates "to stop the errant youth on that destructive path along which disloyal people are trying to lead them."[59] The annual holiday of the order of St. George on December 8 was held in an atmosphere of sadness. Alexander stood next to the German ambassador and thanked him for the congratulations from the German emperor on his escape—the first he received. The second was from his own Berlin Grenadier-Regiment. His first toast was to Emperor Wilhelm, in a loud voice wishing him, the oldest knight of the order, the best of health. The band then played the Prussian anthem, *Heil dir im Siegerkranz*.[60]

The celebration of the twenty-fifth anniversary of Alexander's accession took place on February 19, 1880, less than two weeks after the explosion in the Winter Palace. The commission insisted on the cancellation of all public

---

[56] *War Correspondence*, 235.

[57] On April, 6, 1879, the heir wrote in his diary: "Today for the first time I had to ride in the carriage with a convoy! I cannot express how sad, painful, and pitiful this was! To ride with Cossacks at our side in our always peaceful and quiet Petersburg as if in wartime is simply horrible, and there is nothing to do about it" ("Dnevniki Aleksandra III," GARF, 677-1-307, 243). Alexander II wrote to his daughter, Maria Aleksandrovna, on December 4, 1879, "I sit home nearly all the time, and I go out only in a carriage with a convoy, which is horribly unpleasant to me; but what is to be done? These are such times that I must submit to necessity" (letters of Alexander II to the grand duchess Maria Aleksandrovna, San Francisco Museum of Russian Culture).

[58] Voeikov, "Poslednie dni Imperatora Aleksandra II," 62; von Schweinitz, *Denkwürdigkeiten*, 2:141–42.

[59] Tatishchev, *Imperator Aleksandr II*, 2:617–18.

[60] Grand Duke Alexander Mikhailovich, *Once a Grand Duke* (New York, 1932), 55; Alexander to Grand Duchess Maria Aleksandrovna, December 4, 1879, San Francisco Museum of Russian Culture; von Schweinitz, *Denkwürdigkeiten*, 2:85–86.

functions, but the celebration proceeded in and around the Winter Palace. The guards regiments participating in the ceremony were informed that they remained on alert in case of disturbances. The confined, beleaguered spirit of the festivities dispelled what was left of the illusion of an affectionate union between tsar and people.

The usual palace procession was attended by a large number of officials and foreign diplomats, who were visibly proud of their courage in attending. Miliutin noted the enormous crowd and especially the large number of women present. Alexander emerged onto the Saltykov balcony of the Winter Palace to hear a concert from the combined bands of all the guards regiments, accompanied by thunderous salutes from Vasilievskii Island and the shout of "Hoorah." He removed his helmet and bowed several times in response. He then received guards regiments who brought him an icon of the Savior. At a reception, members of the State Council and the Senate delivered speeches praising Alexander's role in the Great Reforms. The Senate assured him that the revolutionary violence had not shaken the people's love for their tsar and that it was the mutual love of tsar and people that had made Russia strong.[61]

The heir found the show of support inspiring. The serenade by the guards regiments, ending with a deafening "Hoorah" and a chorus of the anthem, was, he wrote in his diary, "the wonderful beginning of a festive day." But it was at the performance of Glinka's *Life for the Tsar* that the audience gave what he understood as the most sincere and forceful expression of popular-national support for the monarch: "The mood of the public was most enthusiastic and the anthem was repeated more than ten times! In general, this day was most gratifying for us and God blessed this festive and glorious holiday."![62]

Under Loris-Melikov, the government succeeded in locating and arresting many participants in revolutionary organizations, but the leaders remained at large. He attempted to revive the spirit of the reform era by introducing conciliatory measures. He allowed greater freedom of the press, abolished the unpopular salt tax, and involved *zemstvo* delegates in discussions of possible reforms. In August 1880 the commission was abolished, and Loris-Melikov was appointed the minister of interior. He now came to the conclusion that only some form of popular participation could win sympathy. As in 1862, many important officials believed that the introduction of some form of representative government was imminent. Peter Shuvalov, now ambassador to Great Britain, wrote in February 1881, "It is hard to imagine

[61] Tatishchev, *Imperator Aleksandr II*, 2:626–29; Voeikov, "Poslednie dni Imperatora Aleksandra II," 66–67; Dowager Marchioness of Dufferin, *My Russian and Turkish Journals*, 68; Miliutin, *Dnevnik*, 3:222; *Vsemirnaia Illiustratsiia*, no. 582 (March 1, 1880), 194–95.

[62] "Dnevnik Aleksandra III, 1875–1880 g.," GARF, 677-1-307, 326; This section of the diary has been reprinted in Alexander Aleksandrovich, "Dnevnik Naslednika Tsesarevicha Velikogo Kniazia Aleksandra Aleksandrovicha, 1880g.," *Rossiiskii Arkhiv* 6 (1995): 353.

that Russia can long remain the single exception in the family of European states and that she has not earned that trust from her sovereign that he had shown to his Finnish subjects and the Slavs under his protection."[63]

Loris-Melikov argued that the government could best struggle against sedition by calling on society to "participate in the elaboration of the measures needed at the present time." He proposed to establish two preparatory commissions "on the model of the Editing Commissions organized in 1858," which would deal with questions of administrative, fiscal, and economic reform. Their membership would be appointed from officials in central government institutions. Other "loyal persons, in government service and outside it," could be invited to participate, with the sovereign's consent.[64] Loris-Melikov claimed that his project had little in common with popular representation on Western patterns. "Not only are these alien to the Russian people, but they even could shake its basic political outlook and introduce troubles whose consequences are difficult to foresee." Indeed, the proposal contemplated no change in the structure or operation of government, except to open the organs of the administration to representatives most of whom would be chosen by the government. The meeting of a Special Conference considering the proposal, which included the heir, approved the system of commissions unanimously, and it was submitted to the emperor on February 16, 1881.[65]

But in the context of the tsar's political attitudes, the almost insignificant change in the structure of government was not the issue. For him, constitutionalism, or any form of representative participation, meant the institutionalization and formalization of his relationship with the people. The challenge was not abstract or intellectual but an immediate threat to the personal bonds that, in his mind, empowered and connected him to his ancestors, the court, and the estates. These institutions threatened to become intermediaries and to introduce conflict and opposition within the government.

Alexander's doubts were increased by his uncle, the emperor Wilhelm, who beseeched him to stand fast against any form of representation. Alexander placed a question mark over the recommendation to admit delegates into the State Council, the most important part of the reform, in effect killing

---

[63] Pereira, *Tsar-Liberator*, 153–54; Zaionchkovskii, *Krizis samoderzhaviia*, 284, 291. Shuvalov was referring to Alexander's permission to convoke the Finnish Seim, which met regularly in Helsinki since 1863, and his agreement to a constitution and elective assembly for the newly independent Bulgaria after the Russo-Turkish War.

[64] The members of these commissions would then convene in a general commission together with representatives from the *zemstva* and town dumas to discuss measures of local government, the peasants' status, and specific economic measures. Finally, a group of fifteen elective representatives from the *zemstva* and town Dumas would join in deliberations on the reforms in the State Council (Zaionchkovskii, *Krizis samoderzhaviia*, 283–90; Marc Raeff, *Plans for Political Reform in Imperial Russia*, [Englewood Cliffs, N.J., 1966], 132–40).

[65] Raeff, *Plans for Political Reform*, 135; Zaionchkovskii, *Krizis samoderzhaviia*, 292–94.

this provision. In the end the conference approved only the part of the project that created the legislative commissions but gave them no voice in governmental institutions. Alexander then approved the conference's recommendation. The announcement of the reform was prepared for the emperor to sign on Sunday, March 1, 1881.[66]

THE END OF THE SCENARIO

While the revolutionary movement finally dispelled the pretense of rule through affection, Alexander was openly transgressing the familial order that had symbolized the moral supremacy of the autocracy. By the end of the 1870s his affair with Dolgorukova had turned into an open second marriage. In 1878 he secretly had his children by Dolgorukova legitimized with noble status, under the name Iur'evskii, presumably referring to Iurii Dolgorukii, the descendant of Riurik and prince of Vladimir who in fact was not Katia's ancestor. But the name marked his new family as Russian. In 1881 he said of George "Gogo": "This is a real Russian; in him at least there flows only Russian blood." This presumed, of course, that Russian blood flowed in his own veins.[67] After the death of the empress on May 22, 1880, Alexander made preparations to wed Dolgorukova, ignoring the Russian Orthodox Church's prohibition of marriage for a period of one year after the death of a spouse. The ceremony took place in July, less than two months after the empress's death, in secret, with no member of the imperial family in attendance. Six months later, in an unpublished imperial decree, she officially received her new name, Iur'evskaia, and the title Most Serene Highness.

Alexander's justification was the fear for his life and the need to provide for Dolgorukova, a consideration she undoubtedly impressed on him. The marriage was morganatic, giving neither her nor her children rights as members of the imperial family. But Alexander himself knew that morganatic marriages violated the taboo, in force since Peter the Great, against members of the imperial family taking Russian wives. His marriage deprived his image of both the moral and cultural attributes that had come to justify autocratic power.[68] Many considered the marriage blasphemy against the coronation vows, a violation of a sacrament even more sacred than marriage. Unlike Peter's first wife, Evdokiia Lopukhina, Maria Aleksandrovna had been crowned and, as a result, consecrated by the ceremony that gave autocracy divine sanction. One general declared that before the marriage he believed

---

[66] Zaionchkovskii, *Krizis samoderzhaviia*, 294.

[67] Tarsaidzé, *Katia*, 196–97.

[68] According to Alexandra Andreevna Tolstoi, he had warned the heir Alexander Aleksandrovich never to allow morganatic marriages in the imperial family: "That shakes the foundations of the throne" (A. A. Tolstaia, *Zapiski freiliny: pechal'nyi epizod iz moei zhizni pri dvore* [Moscow, 1996], 89).

that no attempt on the tsar's life could succeed. But once he heard the news, he changed his mind. "I told my wife that now I should not be surprised if he were killed!"[69]

Unmindful of such misgivings, Alexander began to bring Iur'evskaia into ceremonial and family functions. On October 4, 1880, she made her first official appearance at the emperor's side during a review of the convoy Cossacks, and their son, George, wore the Cossack uniform. This appearance made a painful impression on everyone, Miliutin wrote. "How sad and pitiful for him."[70] Alexander entreated the heir Alexander Aleksandrovich, to accept her and her children as members of the family. He introduced him to Gogo as his "eldest brother" whom he was to love and obey. He asked Alexander Aleksandrovich to carry out the will for "the young family" and to act as their protector.[71]

Iur'evskaia and her children began to appear at family dinners, where Gogo played with the heir's sons, which, Alexander Aleksandrovich noted in his diary, particularly irritated his wife, the grand duchess Maria Fedorovna. It was known that Iur'evskaia was a supporter of Loris-Melikov, and many members of the family believed that the projected political reforms represented her attempt to take revenge by destroying the monarchy. Rumors that the emperor was contemplating a change in the order of dynastic succession circulated at court. The heir and the other grand dukes kept their opinions to themselves and silently complied with the tsar's wishes, citing their vows of obedience. Alexander Aleksandrovich wrote in his diary, "I confess that sometimes I can't stand it myself, because it positively goes too far and of course shocks everyone." At one point, Loris Melikov wrote, Alexander threatened his son and his family with exile.[72]

At the end of the mourning period, in January 1881, Iur'evskaia appeared with Alexander at a gala imperial ball. The splendor was equal to those of earlier years, with lavish jewelry and glittering uniforms to dazzle the eye. But the appearance of the former mistress at the side of the emperor gave rise to a sense of resentment and malaise. During the supper she played the role of hostess and accompanied the emperor about the tables to chat with the guests, causing general consternation. The grand duke Alexander Mikhailovich recalled that her face twitched and her lips were tightly drawn.

[69] Carl Graf Moy, *Als Diplomat am Zarenhof* (Munich, 1971), 162; Baddeley, *Russia in the "Eighties"*, 173.

[70] Tarsaidzé, *Katia*, 216–22, 229–31; Alexander II to Grand Duchess Maria Aleksandrovna, October 25, 1880, San Francisco Museum of Russian Culture.

[71] Pereira, *Tsar-Liberator*, 141–42; Tarsaidzé, *Katia*, 239.

[72] Elizabeth Narishkin-Kurakin, *Under Three Tsars* (New York, 1931), 66–70; N. N. Firsov, "Aleksandr III; lichnaia kharakteristika, chast'iu po ego neizdannym dnevnikam," *Byloe*, no. 29 (1925): 92; Alexander Mikhailovich, *Once a Grand Duke*, 53–54, 57; "Dnevnik Aleksandra III, 1880–1881," GARF, 677-1-308, 108; B. V. Anan'ich and R. Sh. Ganelin, "Aleksandr III i naslednik nakanune 1 marta 1881g." in *Dom romanovykh v Rossii* (St. Petersburg, 1995), 208.

She well knew that she was detested, and sorrowful Russian music playing in the background increased the atmosphere of gloom.[73]

Knowledge of the breach of the familial order reached beyond the court, spreading doubt about the future of authority. For some, the situation recalled the beginnings of the "Time of Troubles" at the close of the sixteenth century, when dynastic uncertainties bred political and social chaos. The violation of taboos brought to mind ominous legends and superstitions. Two hundred years earlier a peasant prophet had predicted death for any Romanov who married a Dolgorukaia; Peter II had died on the day he was to wed Natalia Dolgorukitaia. The devil figured in the talk of peasants and workers, who said he had lured the tsar "to fool around with a girl and now God will forsake him." Other rumors claimed that the devil had taken the form of a woman and that she therefore must be destroyed.[74] The emperor was desolate about the general disapproval, though he did not allow this to influence his behavior.

Indeed, there is evidence that Alexander was preparing an even greater affront to the moral and legal order he had vowed to defend, by crowning his new wife empress. Alexander took the first steps by sending Prince N. S. Golitsyn and Tertii Filippov, a Slavophile and specialist on church history, to obtain documents from the archives on the coronation of Catherine I. They returned with the materials on March 1. Iur'evskaia herself claimed that Alexander placed the crown of Catherine I upon her head in a private ceremony.[75]

Yet no act could have been more damaging to the prestige of nineteenth-century autocracy than the crowning of Catherine I. Her coronation had been justified by the repudiation of primogeniture and the assertion of the principle of utility as set forth in Peter's Law of Succession. The nineteenth-century coronation had become a crowning of the royal couple, an expression of the sanctity of the marital vow as much as of the throne. Figures close to the tsar, like Alexander Adlerberg and Miliutin, spoke of retiring. The heir, according to the memoirs of A. N. Kulomzin, threatened to leave for Denmark with his family but was deterred when Alexander threatened to replace him with his half-brother, Georgii. Many, including the tsar's adjutant and friend Alexander Adlerberg, came to regard his assassination as an act of providence, bringing a martyr's death to a tsar about to disgrace and destroy autocracy.[76]

---

[73] Alexander Mikhailovich, *Once a Grand Duke*, 55–57.

[74] Ibid., 53; Tarsaidze, *Katia*, 235–37.

[75] Alexander Mikhailovich, *Once a Grand Duke*, 48; Pereira, *Tsar-Liberator*, 143; Chicherin, *Vospominaniia* . . .; *Zemstvo i Moskovskaia Duma* (Moscow, 1934), 4:118–19.

[76] Feoktistov, *Vospominaniia E. M. Feoktistova*, 1:196–97; Miliutin, *Dnevnik*, 4:78–79; B. V. Anan'ich and R. Sh. Ganelin, "R. A. Fadeev, S. Iu. Vitte i ideologicheskie iskaniia 'okhrani-telei' v 1881–1883gg.," in *Issledovaniia po sotsial'no-politicheskoi istorii Rossii* (Leningrad, 1971), 304n; B. V. Anan'ich and R. Sh. Ganelin, "Aleksandr II i naslednik nakanune 1 marta 1881g." 204–13; on Kulomzin's remark, see 208.

•

March 1, 1881, was the day of reckoning, the dénouement of the scenario of love. Alexander began the day in good spirits. News of the arrest of Alexander Zheliabov, leader of the People's Will, indicated that the tide had been turned against the revolutionaries. After attending mass, he gave his approval to what remained of Loris-Melikov's project of governmental reform, which was to be sent to the Committee of Ministers on March 4. He then prepared to proceed to the weekly review of guards regiments at the Mikhailovskii Manège, the Sunday "parade with ceremony," which he loved. The revolutionary situation had caused the parade to be canceled, but, despite strenuous warnings from Loris-Melikov, he insisted that the event go on. He was especially determined because that day Constantine Nikolaevich's son, the grand duke Dmitrii, was to make his first appearance as Alexander's aide-de-camp.[77]

Foreign visitors found the security arrangements in the capital surprisingly loose. Police restrictions on the population were tight, but the policemen themselves seemed apathetic, fulfilling their inspections perfunctorily as formal requirements. The English ambassador reported that expenditures for police in Petersburg were only one-fifth of those in Paris, a city of the same population. Captain V. V. Voeikov, who attended the review, observed that only one policeman guarded the entire length of the Catherine Canal when the tsar was supposed to pass by.[78] The situation, moreover, seemed to provide Alexander an opportunity to show his characteristic bravado. He had escaped death seven times, and many regarded the news of an additional attempt with some indifference, assuming he would escape once more.[79]

At the manège Alexander, with great style, played the role of elegant and magnanimous chieftain. He entered with majestic stride and "took everyone and everything in with his imperial gaze." He mounted and, to the strains of "God Save the Tsar!" reviewed the guard of the Sappers and Reserve Infantry battalions, which were commanded by the heir and the grand duke Vladimir. He received reports from his adjutants and officers of the guards. Then the troops passed by him in the great ceremonial march. He praised them; they shouted the usual "Happy to do our best, Your Imperial Majesty," to which he replied with thanks. "The tsar was happy and satisfied to the fullest extent," according to Captain Voeikov.[80] After the march, Alexander engaged in the gestures of mutual recognition that identified the military with the imperial family. Here he was in his element, displaying his gift of camaraderie, remembering the officers' names, chatting with them, as always

[77] Tarsaidze, *Katia*, 243–45; Voeikov, "Poslednie dni Imperatora Aleksandra II," 75.

[78] Voeikov, "Poslednie dni Imperatora Aleksandra II," 85; Dowager Marchioness of Dufferin, *My Russian and Turkish Journals*, 67, 114–15.

[79] Sollogub, *Dnevnik*, 72; Voeikov, "Poslednie dni Imperatora Aleksandra II," 88; Feoktistov, *Vospominaniia E. M. Feoktistova*, 1:196.

[80] Voeikov, "Poslednie dni Imperatora Aleksandra II," 77–79.

using the familiar *ty*, about their parents and grandparents, their units, and their common acquaintances. The adjutants designated for guard duty that week formed a semicircle in the middle of the manège.

The review concluded with a spectacular show of horsemanship. The Cavalier Guards, the Horse Guards, the Convoy, and the Don Cossacks of the Guard rode in three straight lines, "like a whirlwind," around the manège, never losing their distance, then suddenly came to a halt before the tsar. The Cossack riders brought the afternoon to a rousing climax. They flew by him over hurdles, their sabers raised, or leaped in acrobatic stunts on their horses. The tsar, delighted, shouted "Thank you! Good Fellows (*Molodtsy*)!" After the performance, on his way out, he chatted with his convoy, praising their stunts, leaving the officers and the commanders congratulating one another on the tsar's warm praise.[81]

After the review Alexander briefly visited his cousin, the grand duchess Catherine Mikhailovna, at the Mikhailov Palace. Then he rode along the Catherine Canal on his way back to the Winter Palace. He sat in his "bomb-proof" carriage, a gift of Napoleon III, and was guarded by an escort of six Cossacks of the convoy. The first bomb, thrown by Nicholas Rysakov, shattered the carriage but left the emperor unharmed. Ignoring the warnings of his escort, Alexander boldly stepped forward. He questioned Rysakov, then bent over an injured Cossack, crossed himself, and inspected the pit the bomb had left. He was looking over the scene and about to leave when Ignatii Grinevetskii's bomb landed at his feet. Once the smoke cleared, the crowd of spectators could see the emperor covered with blood, the uniform in tatters, and his legs, the beautifully preserved legs of youth, destroyed, one shorn from his body, the other maimed. Alexander asked to die at the palace, then lost consciousness. He was carried on the sleigh of the police escort to his study in the Winter Palace.

The emperor's death was signaled by the lowering of the imperial standard over the palace at 3:35 P.M. Outside on the Palace Square, crowds milled about awaiting news. The guards' regiments were out in force. The Preobrazhenskii guards had quickly lined up in the halls, in their great coats and with live ammunition. The regiments of the Ataman Cossacks formed a line before the palace. Guards officers and soldiers, still in their bright dress uniforms from the parade, stood at the entrances to the palace. The official announcement from the palace entrance was made by Adjutant-General Alexander Suvorov, the Inspector-General of Infantry. Unnerved by the situation, he breathlessly declared, "Sa majesté, L'empereur est mort." An official statement, circulated the next day, began: "The Will of the All High has been fulfilled . . ." The announcement of the Russian emperor's death in French and then its characterization as an act of God were final manifestations of the uncertainty and incomprehension of the last years of Alexander's reign.[82]

---

[81] Ibid., 79–83.

[82] Ibid., 84–89; Tarsaidze, *Katia*, 247–48; G. K. Gradovskii, *Itogi (1862–1907)* (Kiev, 1908), 78.

Alexander's death dealt the final blow to the myth of secular transcendence. The emperor, the guardian of the integrity of the state, had been deprived even of his physical integrity. Descriptions dwelled on the fragmentation of his body, his torn flesh, the blood staining the pavement. "His legs completely naked, hung in shreds. One foot was completely torn off," the newspaper *Golos* reported.[83] The broken body, shattering the illusion of the demigod, began the transfiguration of Alexander II's image. No longer a beautiful and gracious sentimental hero, sacrificing his own interests courageously in the dispatch of his duty and devotion to his subjects, he was presented as a symbol of suffering humanity. In the subsequent weeks, those close to Emperor Alexander III elaborated a new myth, one elevating a Russian tsar.

[83] Cited in *MV*, March 6, 1881, 3; see also *MV*, March 3, 1881, 1; Miliutin, *Dnevnik*, 4:28–29.

PART TWO

Alexander III and the Inception of a National Myth

The Fashioning of a Russian Tsar

This is the secret of our impotence. We are very strong, our land is
rich and plentiful. Our people are young and fresh and our nature easily
given to mighty spiritual upsurge. But without direction, without
management, all this perishes, just as our *bogatyr'*-soldiers perish in
battle without able officers.

I believe, your highness, and understand that you become sad when you
imagine your high calling with all its importance and weight. Loving you
with all my soul, I too often think of this sadly. Oh, what a great burden
is power and how happy is the one who escapes this painful lot. But, on
the other hand, how lofty and great it is when power is aware of its
strength, knows what it wants, and understands where to go and how
to govern. Then it performs miracles and, feeling itself in unity with
the people, is filled with great force.

*—Letter of Constantine Pobedonostsev to Grand Duke and
Tsesarevich Alexander Aleksandrovich, October 12, 1876*[1]

"THE RUSSIAN PARTY"

The elements of a national myth evolved among circles of the conservative
opposition in the late 1860s and 1870s. An increasingly vocal corps of journalists and officials felt, like Prince Obolenskii, that Alexander II had not
lived up to his role as the nation's beloved and was betraying the people's
trust. They took exception to his Western manner and tastes, his tolerance
of dissenting views, and the weakness and indecision they discerned in his
foreign policy. They sought a national monarch who was in touch with
what they claimed were the beliefs and aspirations of the Russian people,
who could create unity between government and state as they imagined it
in Europe.

We witness the evident paradox of conservative nationalism, that in order
to appropriate the dominant Western doctrine of nationalism, Russian monarchy had to be shown to be non-Western and to derive from beliefs and
traditions rooted in the people. In this way, the emperor could dominate the

---

[1] *Pis'ma Pobedonostseva k Aleksandru III* (Moscow, 1925), 1:53.

national movement rather than follow it as Alexander II had in the 1870s. There was little agreement, however, among these writers about what constituted a Russian nation. "The Russian party" referred not to a single organized group but to diverse writers, journalists, and officials who opposed Alexander II's policies from a conservative national standpoint. Most of them lived and worked in Moscow, which emerged in their writings as a symbol of a national historical tradition that had been lost in the Westernized bureaucracy of St. Petersburg.

The organizational centers of the party were the offices of Michael Katkov's newspaper, *Moskovskie Vedomosti*, and the Moscow Slavic Benevolent Committee. The two principal sources of the new myth were the state nationalism of Katkov and the romantic nationalism espoused by Slavophiles and Pan-Slavists such as Ivan Aksakov. The doctrines themselves were based on different and even conflicting conceptions of historical development, and initially they expressed mutually incompatible political designs. But they converged in their opposition to the equivocating internal and foreign policies of Alexander II after 1865.

Katkov's viewpoint, at first, was oriented to the West. The son of a minor official, he studied literature and philosophy at Moscow University in the 1830s and taught philosophy there in the 1840s. In 1851 he was appointed editor of *Moskovskie Vedomosti*. After the Crimean War he used his influence to gain a degree of freedom for the press to discuss political issues. Until the late 1870s his social and economic attitudes reflected a Hegelian notion of civic development, to be promoted by a state vigorously advancing the cause of progress. He advocated economic development through free trade and opposed the preservation of the peasant commune. His nationalism focused on a dynamic monarchy that would lead the Russian people in strengthening the empire. In his eyes, Russia should follow the examples of Western states, particularly Great Britain and Germany.[2] In 1870 he singled out King Wilhelm I of Prussia as an example of a dynasty identifying itself with a "common national idea and patriotic front," rather than being the instrument of "alien interests."[3]

Katkov argued that the state should lead and dominate public opinion. In 1863 he used his newspaper to create an illusion of national "public opinion," to promote his demand for more vigorous suppression of the Polish rebellion. His extreme ideas brought him into direct conflict with the minister of the interior Peter Valuev.[4] Katkov claimed he was expressing the views of the people, which he counterpoised to those of liberal society. While other

[2] On Katkov's intellectual development, see Martin Katz, *Mikhail N. Katkov: A Political Biography, 1818–1887* (The Hague, 1966); and Tvardovskaia, *Ideologiia poreformennogo samoderzhaviia*.

[3] Cited in Karel Durman, *The Time of the Thunderer: Michael Katkov, Russian Nationalist Extremism and the Failure of the Bismarckian System, 1871–1887* (Boulder, Colo., 1988), 118–19.

[4] Tvardovskaia *Ideologiia poreformennogo samoderzhaviia*, 48–73.

newspapers avoided chauvinistic proclamations during the Polish uprising, *Moskovskie Vedomosti* reported numerous outbursts of patriotism among the common people. Katkov wrote that "simple and dark people, . . . small people, who are poor and impoverished in spirit, [who] in their dark depths, more than . . . people who are enlightened and intelligent . . . heard the voice of the Fatherland and responded to it." Accounts from *Moskovskie Vedomosti* of peasant communes declaring their wish to die for God and Fatherland were reprinted in *Severnaia Pochta* and *Russkii Invalid*, organs of the Ministry of the Interior and the War Ministry, respectively. Descriptions in the newspaper of meetings of communes near Moscow, it was reported, brought tears to the empress's eyes.[5]

Most striking in Katkov's nationalist exhortations was the absence of the sentimental morality that colored both official nationality and Slavophilism. His newspaper had little patience with the scenario of love; the peasants he described were animated by feelings of national solidarity, not by devotion to the imperial family. Katkov was concerned with the state's interests, with political realism, and the instrumentality he considered essential to state interest was the exercise and display of force. "It is as if we have forgotten," he wrote during the uprising, "that the symbol of state spirit is the sword."[6]

In his view, authoritarian rule and the ability to wield force, effectively and ruthlessly, were the principal attributes that the nation expected from their monarch. With this in mind, Katkov sought the administrative Russification of the Western provinces and Poland.[7] In April 1863 he wrote, "There is in Russia one dominant nationality, one dominant language, which was developed by centuries of historical life." There were many tribes with different languages and customs, but they felt united with "the Great Russian world . . . in the unity of the state, in the unity of the supreme authority—in the Tsar, the living, sovereign, personification of this unity."[8] In Katkov's mind, the tsar had to combine the element of nationality and state rule, fusing the various nationalities into a Russian nation, governed by the monarchy. He envisioned an empire united into a single nation, forged by the state, an empire that allowed neither autonomy nor diversity. He believed that the triumph over the Polish revolution had awakened national feeling and created the basis for a unified state. He presented the public response to

[5] Ibid., 49–51.

[6] Ibid., 55–57, 37.

[7] Ibid., 46–48, 63–64. Katkov hoped that the defeat of the Polish rebellion would allow Russian landlords to replace Polish noblemen in the provinces of Lithuania, West Bank Ukraine, and Belorussia. He called this "a crying state necessity." He wanted Russian officials and clergy to be sent into these areas, and he corresponded with such officials and with priests in the western Provinces. In this way, the principal institutions of the Russian state—administration, nobility, and clergy—would be reproduced in provinces populated by large numbers of Russian peasants.

[8] Katz, *Mikhail N. Katkov*, 127.

Karakozov's attempt as evidence of the Russian people's belief in autocracy and demand for repression of opposition.[9]

If Katkov emphasized the state as the expression of ethnic spirit, the various Slavophile and Pan-Slavic writers of the 1870s looked to the religion and culture of the people as the source of a national spirit. Slavophiles such as Ivan Aksakov called upon the tsar to act as defender of Orthodox religion and to return to pre-Petrine culture and political institutions. The Slavophiles rejected the imperial Russian bureaucracy—Katkov's mechanism of national domination—as an artificial Western imposition, introduced by Peter the Great. They looked to an idealized image of pre-Petrine Russia, when the tsar was able to communicate with his people in an Assembly of the Land.

The demands for vigorous support of the Slavic nationalities abroad, expressed most forcefully in Nicholas Danilevskii's *Russia and Europe*, published in 1866, narrowed the distance between the Slavophiles and bureaucratic nationalism. Earlier Slavophilism, with its emphasis on Russian Orthodoxy as the determining feature of the national spirit, had been less concerned with liberation movements of Slavs abroad. Aksakov identified the Russian people with other Slavic peoples and looked to the struggle to liberate their brothers in the Balkans, under the leadership of the Russian tsar, as a way to unite the nation with the monarchy.[10] Katkov saw the Balkans as a region where the Russian state could extend its power, based on the support of the Russian people, and fortify Russia's position in Europe.

By the end of the 1870s Katkov came to accept Slavophile notions of the primacy of Orthodoxy and the need to preserve the peasant commune, while the Slavophiles accepted the bureaucracy as a necessary institution uniting and strengthening the Russian state at least for the current era. Both were convinced that only a strong national tsar could realize their designs, and from the end of the sixties both looked to the heir, the grand duke Alexander Aleksandrovich, as the future embodiment of their hopes. The heir's tutor of law, Professor and Senator Constantine Pobedonostsev, who shared many of their views, brought the heir together with them and began to express the themes of a national myth of Russian monarchy.

THE YOUNG BULL

Nicholas Aleksandrovich's death on April 12, 1865, had deprived Pobedonostsev of "the opposite pole," an antithesis to Alexander II who displayed a vital rapport with the people, a potential Russian tsar. It was not long, however, before Pobedonostsev himself discovered such an antithesis in Nicholas Aleksandrovich's younger brother, Alexander.

[9] Tvardovskaia, *Ideologiia poreformennogo samoderzhaviia*, 61, 72–73.

[10] On Aksakov's influence on Pan-Slavism see Edward C. Thaden, *Conservative Nationalism in Nineteenth-Century Russia* (Seattle, Wash., 1964), 137–42; Michael Boro Petrovich, *The Emergence of Russian Pan-Slavism, 1856–1870* (New York, 1956), 61–62, 256.

The grand duke Alexander Aleksandrovich was ill suited to play the role of cultivated, sensitive heir in his father's scenario. During the 1850s and 1860s he seemed an alien presence—surly, often uncouth and crude in his manner, regarded with evident embarrassment by his parents. He was hardly the handsome young prince conquering the hearts of those who beheld him. His mother, the empress, did not conceal her feelings of aversion toward him. She was particularly distressed by his likeness to Emperor Paul I. In a letter of 1854, when Alexander was nine years old, she mentioned his "hateful" resemblance to Paul in the eyes of the older people.[11] The lady-in-waiting to Maria Aleksandrovna, Alexandra Tolstoi, observed that Alexander III was the most distant from the empress of all her children.[12]

Until the age of thirteen, Alexander Aleksandrovich was educated in the company of his older brother but received much less attention. Constantine Golovin was surprised when he met the grand dukes in 1859 that only Nicholas Aleksandrovich lived under strict discipline and received instruction in etiquette.[13] Both Alexander and Vladimir Aleksandrovich felt themselves neglected by their parents, who doted on their firstborn, Nicholas, and their youngest, Alexei, and Sergei. As middle children, Alexander and Vladimir received neither the respect of the firstborn nor the cosseting of the last. Later in life they would recall what Alexander Aleksandrovich described as the "disgusting memories" of their childhood—their parents' indifference and the meager portions of poor food they were served.[14]

Alexander impressed those who knew him as someone from outside the world of the court. Large and hulking, he inspired animal metaphors. His father referred to him as a young steer (bychok); later in life the word byk, bull or ox, caught on as a fitting term for him. Countess Kleinmichel, seeing him in 1862, compared him to a peasant and a Kalmyk, "with none of the beauty of his brothers." He was always described in terms that emphasized his distance from the norms of genteel behavior.[15] Such opinions can hardly have remained unknown to him, and from childhood he regarded the polite society of the court with suspicion and fear.

Grand dukes were expected to appear in public, either at their parents' side or as representatives of the family at important social functions. The grand duke Alexander disliked being the center of attention. Later in life he often began his diary entries for his birthday, February 26, with underlined exclamations, *"my unhappy birthday,"* or *"my insupportable birthday."*[16]

[11] Tatishchev, "Imperator Aleksandr III," 8; Maria Aleksandrovna to Elizabeth, September 6, 1854, Darmstadt Archive, D23-32/5.

[12] Tolstaia, *Zapiski freiliny,* 43 n.

[13] K. Golovin, *Moi vospominaniia* (St. Petersburg, 1910), 1:38.

[14] A. A. Polovtsov, "Iz dnevnika," *Krasnyi Arkhiv* 33, no. 2 (1929): 187; Polovtsov describes a conversation of March 1878. See also E. A. Perets, *Dnevnik (1880–1883)* (Moscow-Leningrad, 1927), 46.

[15] Charles Lowe, *Alexander III of Russia* (New York, 1895), 18–20; Countess M. Kleinmichel, *Memoirs of a Shipwrecked World* (New York, 1923), 25.

[16] "Dnevnik Aleksandra III, 1867g.," GARF, 677-1-300, 53; "Dnevnik Aleksandra III, 1868g.," GARF, 677-1-301, 129; "Dnevnik Aleksandra III, 1870g.," GARF, 677-1-303, 128.

He found the usual social amenities of the court, like greeting and embracing, repugnant, and he appeared uncomfortable when forced to endure them. At ceremonies he showed none of the poise that distinguished his father or older brother. When the Finnish Guards Battalion came to greet him on his birthday in 1862, he addressed only the general and merely bowed to the officers. General Boris Perovskii, who directed his education, urged him to say a few kind words, but he balked, claiming he did not know the officers or what to say to them.[17] At public ceremonies his awkwardness was often embarrassing. His meeting with the Lifland nobility in 1862 left a bad impression, in contrast to his brother's appearance the year before. He received the loyal cries of the population, but, according to Perovskii's assistant and his adjutant and companion, N. P. Litvinov, he "simply could not greet the people with charm. It is at least good that this comes, apparently, from bashfulness, and not from a lack of goodwill."[18]

Alexander's intelligence also was regarded as deficient. His mother, his teachers, and his governors agreed about his poor aptitude for study. Nicholas learned amazingly fast, Sasha with difficulty, Maria Aleksandrovna remarked in 1853 when Alexander Aleksandrovich was eight years old. Indeed, in their religion lessons, Vladimir Aleksandrovich, two years his junior, was doing better than Sasha, "who is somewhat indolent," his mother wrote. From the start, Alexander found reading and writing extremely difficult. He never mastered grammar, punctuation, or spelling, and the diaries and letters of his mature years have frequently been cited as evidence of limited intellectual endowments.[19]

In 1864 Alexander and Vladimir began their higher courses with a group of distinguished university professors, several of whom also taught the heir. But the materials often had to be made more elementary for them. A. I. Chivilev taught a simplified course on political economy. Alexander had difficulty learning German and French. On the other hand, K. N. Bestiuzhev-Riumin's lectures on Russian history awakened Alexander's interest, and he began to prepare his lessons in history more carefully.[20] In future years Ivan Babst and F. G. Terner taught political economy; Sergei Solov'ev, history; and Constantine Pobedonostsev, jurisprudence. Alexander's curriculum, like

---

[17] N. Firsov, "Vospominaniia o tsesareviche Nikolae Aleksandroviche i Imperatore Aleksandre III v iunosti," *Istoricheskii Vestnik* (January 1909): 68; E. Kamenskii, "Ot detstva do prisiagi: iz zhizni avgusteishikh detei imperatora Aleksandra II," *Istoricheskii Vestnik* (February 1917): 431.

[18] When welcomed by the town fathers, Alexander conversed with them, "though it was noticeable that he felt himself in an awkward situation." But in the end, Litvinov observed, his kindness and "happy look" won their good will (Kamenskii, "Ot detstva do prisiagi," 436).

[19] Letters of Maria Aleksandrovna to Elizabeth, May 8, 1853, and July 16, 1853, Hesse State Archive, D 23-32/5; N. N. Firsov, "Aleksandr III; lichnaia kharakteristika, chast'iu po ego neizdannym dnevnikam," *Byloe*, no. 29 (1925): 85–86; P. A. Zaionchkovskii, *Rossiiskoe samoderzhavie* (Moscow, 1970), 36.

[20] Tatishchev, "Imperator Aleksandr III," 419–22.

Nicholas Aleksandrovich's, stressed economics but with less philosophical content and attention to European conditions.

Alexander showed little grasp of abstract concepts. His companion, Litvinov, wrote in his diary in 1862, "Alexander Aleksandrovich's nature, with his clearly practical aptitudes, is not given to the theoretical intellectualizations of Alexander Ivanovich Chivilev. Still, he can be turned into a person who is mature in a practical sense and useful for society."[21] Early on he developed a respect for practical action and a distrust for the "intellectualization," (*umstvovaniia*) his older brother had loved. This dislike of embellishment, idealization, and abstraction commended him to those who distrusted the sophistication of educated Western society as something alien to the Russian character. His natural, authentic character was often expressed in the word "*iasnyi*," meaning clear, open, direct, denoting an absence of pretense and evasion. His tutor, Jacob Grot, thought he had the "bright (*svetlyi*) and clear (*iasnyi*) common sense of the purely Russian person."[22]

It was this intuitive grasp, along with a willingness to stand stubbornly opposed to accepted views, that created the sympathy between Alexander Aleksandrovich and his instructors. As with Nicholas Aleksandrovich, teachers filled the void left by the distance of the heir's parents. Grot, Perovskii, and other teachers who taught him at the end of the 1850s and the beginning of the 1860s noted other redeeming personal qualities that had gained him little admiration in the Russian court at the time. Rather than intellectual facility, he displayed enormous diligence and determination— the second child's struggle to vie with the firstborn. At the age of two he already had impressed the adjutant Iur'evich with his persistence and diligence. The grand duke Alexander, Iur'evich wrote, spent more than an hour piling up sand, whereas his brother Nicholas, then four, flitted about from one activity to another. The generals Nicholas Zinoviev and Grigorii Gogel' used the words *serious, assiduous,* and *diligent* to describe his schoolwork and his drill practice.[23]

Alexander also showed diligence during his military exercises. He looked stiff and uncomfortable in uniform and had little taste for such show and bravura. But he eagerly participated in military training. In the summer of 1864 he and Vladimir took part in "actual" service at the annual summer exercises at Krasnoe Selo and lived with regular officers. Alexander commanded a company of a model infantry regiment and was delighted at the maneuvers and exercises that lasted from four or five in the morning until noon. He wrote his mother on July 23, "I am very happy that I can serve in the camp. Here it is real service, which is always pleasant if it is well exe-

---

[21] Kamenskii, "Ot detstva . . . ," 430.

[22] Gershel'man-Shvarts fond, BAR, Folder 3, part 2, 29.

[23] S. A. Iur'evich, "Pis'ma ob avgusteishikh synoviakh Imperatora Aleksandra II," manuscript, New York Public Library, 2, 62–63, 138; Zaionchkovskii, *Rossiiskoe samoderzhavie* . . . , 36; Kamenskii, "Ot detstva . . . ," 100.

cuted." On August 8 he wrote, "In general, the whole camp and especially the time we spent with our battalion left the best impression on us." He was the first of his brothers to be decorated with the Order of Vladimir, fourth degree.[24]

While Nicholas Aleksandrovich's relations with his teachers remained intellectual in character and notable for his personal reserve, Alexander openly displayed his feelings, both positive and negative. He embraced his tutors and wept when they left him, displays that were not taken well by his stern military governors. With Grot and Perovskii, he first showed the pattern of attachment to and dependence on a strong tutor that recurred in his later relationship with Constantine Pobedonostsev.[25] His feelings for his older brother were exceptionally warm and open, but the relationship was treacherous. As children, they grew up close to each other, with the younger idealizing and obeying the older.[26] When Nicholas received his own separate chambers in 1850, and again when he began his own class regimen in 1859, Alexander was overcome with feelings of loss and wept violently. In a notebook of 1861 he drew several plans of his and his brother's rooms at Tsarskoe Selo.[27]

Nicholas Aleksandrovich's betrothal in 1865 left him feeling betrayed and desolated. In October 1864 Alexander wrote to his mother, "Now Niks will finally forget me because he has only Dagmaar on his mind."[28] A month later, he wrote to his brother, "It is sad that this happy time of life is over for me and much that is pleasant awaits you and many pleasures. I don't envy you for getting married soon, but I do envy you for getting the matter over with." He recalled the good times they had together and how hard it was for him to witness such scenes—the quiet teas at Tsarskoe Selo in the autumn, the sleigh rides to the Tauride Gardens and sliding down the ice hills—without his older brother. Again the rooms carried close personal associations, signs of loss. He regarded the table where they sat together, their reception room, with sadness. "Everything vividly recalled the good times when we were together." This attachment to chambers as vessels of personal feelings continued through his life. Private rooms served as human sanctuaries from the bustle and artificiality of the court.[29]

Nicholas Aleksandrovich's death on April 12, 1865, was the culmination of these abandonments and disappointments. He had not seen his brother

---

[24] "Pis'ma Aleksandra IIIego k materi, 1864–1879," GARF, 641-1-115, 7, 9, 11, 15.

[25] Kamenskii, "Ot detstva . . .," 104, 123; K. Ia. Grot, *Imperator Aleksandr III v otnosheniiakh svoikh k nastavniku svoei iunosti* (St. Petersburg, 1906), 1.

[26] N. P. Litvinov, "Iz dnevnika," *Istoricheskii Vestnik* (January 1907); 42, 47, 50; Kamenskii, "Ot detstva . . . ," 452–53.

[27] "Zapisnaia knizhka Aleksandra III, 1861–1862g.," GARF, 677-1-250, 20, 22, 24.

[28] "Pis'ma Aleksandra IIIego k materi, 1864–1879," 21.

[29] "Pisma Aleksandra III v. k. Nikolaiu Aleksandrovichu," GARF, 665-1-22; letters of Alexander III to Nicholas Aleksandrovich, July 21, November 21, November 27, December 11, 1864.

for almost a year before the death, a separation he always resented. When he arrived in Nice, Alexander was allowed into the sick room only at the last moment, when Nicholas Aleksandrovich could no longer greet him. "I did not see my brother for nearly a whole year and did not have the consolation of seeing him in his last days," he wrote to his mother. Everyone pitied his father and mother. "But they were deprived only of a son, it is true the most beloved to his mother." Alexander felt the indifference to his own suffering and rejection. But he had lost "a brother, a friend, and what is most horrible, his legacy, which he transmitted to me."[30] He recalled in 1868 that the experience was particularly horrible for him "because I could not imagine that I would become heir and replace my dear friend Niks."[31]

PUBLIC AND PRIVATE SPHERES

The death of Nicholas Aleksandrovich confronted the grand duke Alexander, at the age of twenty, with the painful obligations of being heir to the Russian throne. Boris Perovskii urged him to seek the spirit of his dead brother in himself. He invoked an old-Russian phrase, "*sovlech'sia starogo cheloveka*," exhorting him "to take the old person into yourself." Alexander had to earn the public love and respect his brother had gained. "For this, you must work a great deal on yourself." He told him to remember that not only Russia but all Europe was following his every step and breath. "From the moment the eyes of the late tsarevich closed, you belonged not to yourself but to history." As heir, his role was first as "mediator of the truth, kindness, and mercy between the people and the tsar." Perovskii compared him to Alexander I and Alexander II. He urged him to gain knowledge by reading serious books and to be polite to all in order to win the hearts of his subjects. "Russia lay at the feet" of his brother, because of his "politeness and attentiveness."[32]

Perovskii, following the example of previous mentors of heirs to the throne, urged the heir to overcome his mortal limitations in order to assume the persona of Russian sovereign. But Alexander Aleksandrovich could not rise above himself. He remained uncomfortable and awkward in public. He was nonplused by the ingratiating advances suddenly made to him when Nicholas Aleksandrovich lay dying. He wrote to his teacher, Grot, "No, I already see there is no hope. All the courtiers have horribly changed in their attitude toward me and have started to woo me." In the summer of 1865 he remarked to his friend Vladimir Meshcherskii, "I know there are good and

[30] "Dnevnik Aleksandra III, 1866g.," GARF, 677-1-299, 27. Entry is for April 12, 1866.

[31] "Pis'ma Aleksandra IIIego k materi, 1864–1879," 49, 95.

[32] B. A. Perovskii, "Kratkii ocherk slov moikh Gosudariu Nasledniku Tsesarevichu," *Starina i Novizna*, no. 6 (1903): 344–46.

honest people, but there are also many bad ones. But how does one distinguish, and how will I rule in my time?"[33]

During his first appearances as heir, Alexander Aleksandrovich, made clear that he would not dispose Russia toward him "by politeness and attentiveness." His difficulties became immediately evident at his majority ceremony, which took place on July 20, 1865, a little more than three months after Nicholas Aleksandrovich's death.[34] He stumbled over the words of the oath. As at previous majority ceremonies, the emperor, empress, and son embraced in tears. "A painful moment," a report in *Journal de St. Pétersbourg* declared, "but at the same time endearing. Everyone was overcome by the excitement, everyone had tears in his eyes . . . and everyone prayed God to deliver his parents from greater trials."[35] At the reception, Alexander was "compelled" to say a few words to the members of the State Council, the Senate, and some officers. Apparently it did not go well, "A difficult task without the necessary preparation," Peter Valuev observed.[36] The empress wrote to her sister-in-law, Elizabeth, on the occasion of the oath, "I have lost faith in the future. How difficult it was when Nixa at sixteen took the same oath. Will *this* brother really replace him, or will Nixa's prophesy be fulfilled?"[37]

Alexander's trips through the countryside in the months after the majority ceremonies were lackluster affairs. He traveled to Moscow in August 1865 and a year later in August 1866. The dinners and receptions for members of the noble and merchant estates proved onerous for him. Alexander used every opportunity to avoid such meetings. In Tver he rejected a proposal for a ball from the provincial nobles and merchantry. In Nizhnii-Novgorod he declined to attend a sumptuous reception and urged the donors to use the money instead for public needs.[38]

The other obligation he faced on becoming heir was marriage, and, with little ado, his parents insisted that he take his brother's bride, Princess Dag-

[33] Grot, *Imperator Aleksandr III*, 1–2; V. L. Meshcherskii, *Moi vospominaniia* (St. Petersburg, 1898), 2:1–2.

[34] This ceremony marked his majority as heir, designated by the Law of Succession at age sixteen and celebrated on the heir's sixteenth birthday. The majority ceremonies of other grand dukes took place after their twentieth birthday on the holiday of the Order of St. George, November 26. If Nicholas Aleksandrovich had not died, Alexander would have taken the oath on November 26, 1865 ("O prisiage E. I. Vysochestva Naslednika i Velikogo Kniazia Aleksandra Aleksandrovicha," RGIA, 473-1-1080, 4).

[35] Quoted in *Russkii Invalid* (July 20, 1865): 2.

[36] Valuev, *Dnevnik*, 2:60.

[37] She was alluding to Nicholas Aleksandrovich's prophesy, made when he was five years old, that Vladimir Aleksandrovich would rule, because the name Vladimir means ruler of the earth (letter of Maria Aleksandrovna to Elizabeth, July 17, 1865, Hesse State Archive, D 23-32/5; Tiutcheva, *Pri dvore dvukh imperatorov*, 2:12).

[38] Meshcherskii, *Moi vospominaniia*, 2:57; A. A. Shevelev, "Puteshestviia po Rossii ego Imperatorskogo Vysochestva Naslednika Tsesarevicha Aleksandra Aleksandrovicha," *Russkoe Obozrenie* (July 1897): 46:59; Kamenskii, "Ot detstva . . .," 458; E. Kamenskii, "Naslednik Tsesarevich Aleksandr Aleksandrovich," *Istoricheskii Vestnik* (February 1917): 364–65.

maar of Denmark. But Alexander had found solace for the loss of his brother in a romance with Princess Maria Meshcherskaia, a cousin of his friend Vladimir Meshcherskii. Like his father and other grand dukes, Alexander Aleksandrovich experienced the conflict between his attraction to a Russian woman and the imperative to marry into foreign royalty.

In his diary for 1865 Alexander described the turmoil with a naive honesty. He thought only of Meshcherskaia and when he could meet her, though he knew he should not see her. In June 1865 he informed her they should stop seeing each other, but his infatuation grew only stronger in the subsequent months. Reports of his romance appeared in French and Danish papers and caused consternation at the Danish court. The emperor and empress at first said nothing, perhaps because they remained oblivious to him and his life. In the meantime, he decided not to go to Denmark, to throw everything over, to renounce the throne and marry Meshcherskaia.[39]

There then took place a reenactment of the confrontation of twenty-eight years earlier, when Alexander II faced the wrath of his father over his affair with Olga Kalinovskaia.[40] On May 18, 1866, Alexander II told his son that the matter had reached the Danish newspapers and that the king had expressed concern. Alexander Aleksandrovich confirmed the rumors and told his father that he did not intend to go to Denmark and did not wish to marry. The next day, unable to contain himself, he announced that he felt unable to love Dagmaar and that he had decided to renounce the throne. Alexander did not preach to his son; moralizing did not suit him. He declared that he was not emperor by his wish, (*po svoei okhote*) and that the grand duke should concern himself with his calling ("*prizvanie*"), insisting all the while that he must have gone out of his mind. He then commanded him to go to Denmark and threatened to exile Meshcherskaia from the court.[41]

The last words stunned Alexander Aleksandrovich. He could not contemplate making his beloved suffer. In the following days he cursed his fate and wept but agreed to go to Denmark. His father, commiserating with him, told him about his own youthful infatuation, which had made him, too, think of renouncing the throne, but insisting that "all had turned out for the best." The grand duke bade Meshcherskaia farewell in an empty room in the building of the former lycée at Tsarskoe Selo: "She threw herself toward me. We kissed on the lips for a long time and embraced each other closely." That week he sailed for Copenhagen.[42]

Like his father, Alexander Aleksandrovich submitted to parental pressure and the obligations of his office. But his renunciation followed a different heroic narrative. His father had given up Kalinovskaia but cherished the

---

[39] "Dnevnik Aleksandra III, 1865–1866g.," GARF, 677-1-298, 16–17, 25, 186; this volume of the diary includes love verses and what is apparently a self-portrait drawn by Maria. See also "Dnevnik Aleksandra III, 1866g.," GARF 677-1-299, 36–37, 77.

[40] See Volume 1: 370–71.

[41] "Dnevnik Aleksandra III, 1866g.," 77–81.

[42] Ibid., 83, 92–93.

sentimental dream throughout his life, rebelling against constraints by yielding to romantic transports. Alexander Aleksandrovich gave up his lover to assume a sacred moral obligation to family. In Copenhagen he asked the king for Princess Dagmaar's hand, promising to love her and to answer for her future. Not the individual rebelling for a beloved woman, he now became the member of the family preserving the spiritual heritage of his dead brother. When he proposed marriage, on June 11, 1866, Dagmaar threw herself into his arms. He asked her whether she could still love after the death of his brother. She replied that she could love no one "but his beloved brother, and warmly kissed me." Then he said, "Dear Niks has helped us greatly and of course now he is fervently praying for our happiness. We talked a great deal about my brother, about his death and the last days of his life in Nice." The Queen and King then came into the room and embraced him, and other members of the family congratulated him. "I have never felt so buoyant and joyful as at these moments."[43] Alexander took pride in his act of self-renunciation. He wrote to Meshcherskii in 1867 that he had "stopped before the abyss as one should, without falling in, about which I am proud and happy."[44]

The wedding of Grand Duke Alexander Aleksandrovich to Princess Dagmaar, now rebaptized Grand Duchess Maria Fedorovna, took place on October 28, 1866. He wrote in his diary before the ceremony: "I am now in the most awful mood in the expectation of all the insufferable celebrations and balls that will take place in a few days." "And later they will be surprised and will cry that I am in a bad mood and intentionally do not want to seem merry." He felt sorry for his fiancée, who had to hear all his grumbling, though she was the one, he acknowledged, who had left relatives and home, and had true reason to be sad. As late as the day before the wedding, he had not received the visiting princes of Prussia, Denmark, and Wallachia, who had arrived for the wedding, and had not met their suites. The Prussians were especially offended, and the grand duchess Elena Pavlovna remarked on the heir's discourtesy.[45]

The official account of the event, written by Peter Nikolaevich Petrov, the author of the description of the Millennium Monument, focused on the importance of foreign wives as bearers of cosmopolitanism and the civic spirit. "The conclusion of weddings between members of the families of rulers strengthens the close bond of the mutual friendship between peoples." From the time the Byzantine princess "who bore the name of Wisdom (*Sofiia*)" came from Rome, "the light of European enlightenment was

[43] Ibid., 109.

[44] B. Frank, "Iz neizdannoi perepiski imperatora Aleksandra III i Nikolaia II s V. P. Meshcherskim," *Sovremennye Zapiski* 70 (1940): 179; A. A. Polovtsov, *Dnevnik gosudarstvennogo sekretaria, A. A. Polovtsova* (Moscow, 1966), 2:197; Igor Vinogradoff, "Some Russian Imperial Letters to Prince V. P. Meshcherskii (1839–1914)," *Oxford Slavonic Studies* 11 (1962): 113.

[45] "Dnevnik Aleksandra III, 1866g.," 283–84; Valuev, *Dnevnik*, 2:161.

shed on the capital of Ivan III." Catherine the Great had *"wanted to make people educated"* and to instill in them *"a greater demand to live in an educated society."* The empress Maria Fedorovna had continued Catherine's tradition by encouraging the education of young noble ladies. Russian people, as a result, saw their emperors' wives as their "new guardians." The magnificence of the occasion and the details of the ceremony were worthy of attention, not only because of the gravity of the moment but because they were related to *"them alone, as objects of the people's love (predmetami liubvi narodnoi)."*[46]

It was the grand duchess Maria Fedorovna's personality that offset her husband's brooding presence and enabled the couple to appear as objects of the people's love. She had the magnetism necessary to draw the elite to her, the endearment and kindness (*laska*) that denoted the charm of Western royalty. As with Nicholas I and Alexander II, it was the eyes that established the emotional bond. F. A. Oom, the head of Nicholas Aleksandrovich's chancellery, noted on first seeing her in the fall of 1866, "Her eyes struck us with the expression of endearment (*laska*) and tenderness, and, in addition, her gaze penetrated the person it fixed on."[47] Prince Viazemskii wrote a series of poems welcoming her. His first, on the news of the betrothal, evoked the voice of the people in a common prayer, fusing "in a single love," a "confession of national love."[48] On her arrival in Petersburg, he wrote,

> You are now our own,
> Before God, before people:
> Answering our feelings,
> Accept the gifts of our heart.
> The heart of our people,
> Gives the news of love to your heart:
> Where love flowers and ripens,
> There is the blessing of God.[49]

The grand duchess carried on the rituals of personal graciousness and friendship that were part of the scenario of love. In 1867 the couple traveled to Moscow to introduce her to the second capital. The visit was a major success, her charm winning an enthusiastic response. In 1869 and 1870 Alexander Aleksandrovich took his principal tour of the empire, the first and only such journey of a Russian heir with his spouse. He was accompanied by Pobedonostsev, Babst, as well as Meshcherskii and Perovskii. They followed the course of Nicholas Aleksandrovich's trip in 1863 down the Volga and the Don. Before the party left, an order went out at the emperor's com-

---

[46] P. N. Petrov, *Illiustrirovannoe opisanie torzhestv brakosochetannia Gosudaria Naslednika Tsesarevicha i Gosudaryni Tsesarevny* (St. Petersburg, 1867). 2.

[47] Oom, "Vospominaniia," 548.

[48] Kniaz' P. A. Viazemskii, *Polnoe sobranie sochinenii* (St. Peterburg, 1896), 12:254–56.

[49] Ibid., 12:269. See also "Dve vesny," 12:270–71.

mand that the party not be met or accompanied along the way and that the proposal for gala balls and dinners be refused, except with the agreement of their Highnesses. The acting governor of Nizhnii-Novgorod Province, however, pointed out "all the difficulty of the task" of refusing such requests and, indeed, such dinners and balls were held in several towns.[50]

The receptions were enlivened by the grand duchess.[51] An anonymous account of the trip, published at Katkov's Moscow printing house, contained the standard descriptions of popular acclaim and descriptions of Maria's meetings with the peasants, who "say how much they love Her, they say it with tears." She smiled at them and hugged their children. The peasants brought fish, cups, and dishes, "gifts of simple love which must announce itself in some way." Considerable attention was devoted to the couple's visits to churches. The account mentioned their meeting with an archpriest in Saratov who had organized the local Red Cross and led a campaign against the spread of the Old Belief. The trip ended in Kiev where the couple visited the Cave Monastery. In the evening there were popular amusements, where "happy Russian faces" were visible as well as a Russian spirit. The next day they visited St. Sophia. The author expressed his feelings that this was "the place the Russian land came from. . . . Here is the Russian spirit; Russia is in the air."[52]

A poem published in the journal *Voskresnoe Chtenie* in 1869 dwelled on the national bond as well as the affectionate attachment between the people and the imperial couple.

> Everyone rushes toward Them,
> See Both travel, by the Ruling will,
> Both, to see mother Russia,
> And to show Themselves Orthodox.

The poem expressed both the distance and attraction between the ruling house and the people. The couple had to "show themselves" Orthodox; they had to "see," to "look at" (*posmotret'*), Mother Russia. Two distinct entities, the imperial family and the people, were establishing contact. The people were impressed by the simplicity of the heir and his wife.

> They have no brilliant and gaudy suite,
> But there is cordial sincerity,
> There is tenderness (*laska*) to the people.[53]

[50] "O puteshchestvii Ikh Imperatorskikh Vysochestv v 1869 godu," RGIA, 1339-1-28a, 45–47, 88–89, 93–94.

[51] Kamenskii, "Naslednik Tsesarevich Aleksandr Aleksandrovich," *Istoricheskii Vestnik* (March 1917): 633–40; Shevelev, "Puteshestviia po Rossii," *Russkoe Obozrenie* (February 1898): 821–32.

[52] *Puteshestvie Gosudaria naslednika tsesarevicha i Gosudaryni tsesarevny v 1869 godu* (Moscow, 1869), 15–16, 40–45, 67–68, 75–81.

[53] Cited in Shevelev, "Puteshestviia po Rossii," *Russkoe Obozrenie* (February 1898): 832.

Meanwhile, the tsarevich had continued his brusque ways and offended the merchants of Samara by cutting short their presentation of bread and salt and their statement of affection for the throne.[54] Two moments stirred his feelings—the visit to Sevastopol and his investiture as ataman of the Don Cossacks in Novocherkassk. At Sevastopol General E. I. Totleben, hero of the battle, escorted him on a tour of the ruins of the fortress and showed him the shell casings and bullets lying on the ground fourteen years after the siege.[55] In Novocherkassk, he wrote:

> We liked the Don a great deal and we spent our time very pleasantly on the Don and in Novocherkassk. In every settlement we were met with enthusiasm, and we left (the boat) everywhere and visited their churches. The steamship was accompanied from *stanitsa* to *stanitsa* by Cossacks on horseback firing into the air and doing stunts, and it was pleasant to see that the Cossack spirit and mettle have been kept alive among these men of the Don.[56]

The investiture ceremony and the bestowal of the Cossack ceremonial mace (the *pernach*) in July 1869 moved him deeply. He wrote, "That glorious ceremony made me tremble a lot and become very emotional—but it still was pleasant when it was all over. I was happy without limit and satisfied with everything because I felt the power of the ataman in myself and was aware that this was not a simple title but a power, and a great one." He described the Don country as "a completely different world. Quiet and tranquillity are evident everywhere. No one talks about politics; no one is even interested in it. It is the most patriarchal society and the most democratic because the nobility came about accidentally and there is no hereditary nobility."[57]

Alexander Aleksandrovich's admiration for the Cossacks was in response to his fundamental aversions—to political discussions and to the articulate and assertive members of the nobility. The Cossacks' hearty demonstrations of loyalty, the rough equality that obscured the rifts between their leadership and the lower ranks, gave the impression of a simple world without politics. They were Russians distinguished by martial prowess, displayed in the defense and advance of the empire—which he understood as an ethnic Russian image of conquest. A society, both martial and "democratic," and devoted to the tsar—however atypical they were of the Russian population—was a

---

[54] "Memuara Meshcherskogo V.P.: Razmyshleniia, vpechateleniia, ubezhdeniia, priznaniia," GARF, 677-1-106, 1–4.

[55] Kamenskii, "Naslednik Tsesarevich Aleksandr Aleksandrovich," *Istoricheskii Vestnik* (March 1917): 642, 657; "Dnevnik Aleksandra III, 1869–1870g.," GARF, 677-1-303, 28; *Souvenirs de Sebastopol (recueillis par redigés par s.m.i. Alexandre III, Empereur de Russie)* (Paris, 1894).

[56] Kamenskii, "Naslednik Tsesarevich Aleksandr Aleksandrovich," *Istoricheskii Vestnik* (March 1917): 640.

[57] "Dnevnik Aleksandra III, 1869–1870g.," 14, 16.

perception he cherished and that he would pass on to his son, Nicholas II. When he returned to Novocherkassk in May 1870 for the three-hundredth anniversary of the Don Host, he wrote to his uncle, the grand duke Michael Nikolaevich, of his pleasure "with these nice *dontsy*. It is impossible not to become attached to them and not to respect them after their three hundred years of loyal service to Russia."[58]

•

Alexander Aleksandrovich regarded his family as a sacred personal sphere apart from the obligation of presentation before court and state. His marital constancy developed in opposition to his father's frivolity and fickleness. From the moment of his marriage, he entered into a loving close relationship with the grand duchess. After the wedding, he wrote, "It was such a pleasant and extraordinary feeling to think that finally I am married and the most important step in life had been taken." He described his first night with rare feeling—locking the door, the joys of the embrace, then long conversation and little sleep.[59]

Dagmaar became the kindred, sympathetic soul that had been lacking in his life. His family reflected the romantic Victorian ideal of a sanctuary for humane and tender feelings. His diary entry on New Year's Day, 1867, recalled the bliss he had discovered on his visit to Denmark, when he met his bride-to-be. "I thought that I could love no more, or at least not with such passion, but I now saw and felt something completely different. I then understood the blessing and kindness of God. I then felt the meaning of true happiness."[60]

Returning to St. Petersburg Alexander withdrew into his own family, separating himself as much as possible from his parents' unhappiness and the life of the court. He and the grand duchess Maria Fedorovna settled in Anichkov Palace—the heir's residence since the beginning of the century—and found its intimate surroundings and small rooms more to their liking than the vast reaches of the Winter Palace. The Anichkov also preserved memories of his older brother, on which he loved to dwell. In two halls facing the garden, he kept the same yellow silk wall covering that Nicholas Aleksandrovich had ordered in Moscow.[61] Otherwise Alexander experienced his greatest happiness during his visits to the suburban palaces, Tsarskoe Selo, Peterhof, and Gatchina. He referred to these residences as "dear" (*milyi*), to the Winter Palace and its tedious social functions as the "endless *cotillion*!!!"[62]

---

[58] Kamenskii, "Naslednik Tsesarevich Aleksandr Aleksandrovich," *Istoricheskii Vestnik* (March 1917): 645–46; Robert H. McNeal, *Tsar and Cossack, 1855–1914* (New York, 1987), 4–5, 173–74.

[59] "Dnevnik Aleksandra III, 1866g.," 287–89.

[60] "Dnevnik Aleksandra III, 1866–1867gg.," 23.

[61] A. P. Bogoliubov, *Vospominaniia o v boze pochivshem Imperatore Aleksandre III* (St. Petersburg, 1895), 17.

[62] He notes on November 19, 1875, before his return to the capital for the season, "It is sad to part with dear Tsarskoe Selo and after our quiet and peaceful life here to fall again into

During these years Maria Fedorovna encouraged Alexander's interest in art. In Copenhagen the two visited art collections as well as china and glass factories. Alexander built his collection of painting and began collecting old silver, largely following his wife's taste. He decorated the walls of the Anichkov with paintings and set aside two rooms in the palace as a gallery for his collection, which grew rapidly. At the same time he began his lifelong effort to encourage native Russian art. On his visits to Paris during the 1870s he met the Russian realistic painters of the dissident *peredvizhnik* (itinerant) group and began to purchase their works.[63]

He developed a taste for seascapes, commissioning numerous paintings of ships and providing the artists with precise instructions about the details. He loved the sea, which afforded him the greatest protection from the tumult and menaces on the mainland. When planning a new villa for himself, he asked that it be situated on an island. "Even if an estate is far from cities, [an island] is preferable because it is more serene," he wrote to A. A. Stiuler in 1876. He began the practice, which was continued by his son, Nicholas, of extended yacht cruises in the Finnish archipelagoes. The yacht was not only a form of relaxation but a metaphor of peaceful distance from Russian reality. In his diaries he wrote of his boats with fondness, noting the distances they had traveled and describing the details of his excursions. If Nicholas I's favored reality was the parade ground, expressing political solidarity through discipline and subordination, Alexander II's the hunting preserve, with its bonhomie and bravado, then Alexander III's were the sea and nature, symbols of solitude and remoteness from his subjects.[64]

THE SHAPING OF A NATIONAL IMAGE

The members of the Russian party looked to the heir to provide the national image that would unite the monarchy with the people. Like his older brother, he had been taught to love the Russian people and to see in them the true national spirit. He and the other grand dukes spoke Russian among themselves and at court, unlike Alexander II who, as grand duke, frequently used French in his daily life.[65] But Alexander Aleksandrovich remained

---

Peterburg and what Vladimir calls the 'endless *cotillion*!!!' " ("Dnevnik Aleksandra III, 1875–1880gg.," 34).

[63] John O. Norman, "Alexander III as a Patron of Russian Art," in John O. Norman, ed., *New Perspectives on Russian and Soviet Artistic Culture: Selected Papers from the Fourth World Congress for Soviet and East European Studies, 1990* (New York, 1994), 26–27; Bogoliubov, *Vospominaniia*, 10–15, 24–29, 35–39. His art collection began when his father made him a gift of the collection purchased from the Moscow tax farmer, V. A. Kokorev (Neverov, "Aleksandr II," 17).

[64] "Pis'mo Tsesarevicha Aleksandra Aleksandrovicha A. N. Stiuleru," *Starina i Novizna* 6 (1903): 1; "Pis'ma Tsesarevicha Aleksandra Aleksandrovicha k professoru A. P. Bogoliubovu," *Starina i Novizna* 3 (1900): part 1, 5–7; Bogoliubov, *Vospominaniia*, 14.

[65] Tatishchev, "Imperator Aleksandr III," 103.

European in his education and culture and lacked his brother's intellectual involvement and rapport with the people. Rather than a grand duke who was drawn to the people, his teachers and advisers fashioned in him a symbol of Russianness—an individual who, in spite of appearances, was by nature Russian.

They made the grand duke *appear* Russian by stressing particular features that distinguished him from the Westernized court and that they defined as national. They effected a reversal in the values of signs, attributing positive value to the very features that made him seem out of place at court. They made uncouthness and unsociability signs of the authenticity and candor of the Russian man, untouched by the duplicity of Western culture. In his apparent obtuseness, they discerned an intuitive sense of truth unclouded by intellectualizing; in his sullen obdurate temper, a source of strength and personal authority. Most important, his taciturnity and difficulties with verbal expression became signs of inner certainty, the intimidating silence of the epic hero.

They also attached these traits to historical figures from Russia's medieval past, thus creating the rudiments of a national myth. On Nicholas Aleksandrovich's death, Count Michael Tolstoi, the author of numerous books on medieval saints, composed a precept for Alexander and exhorted him to become a *vitiaz'* (medieval knight) like Alexander Nevskii. This was not Vasilii Zhukovskii's Nevskii, a prince heroic in his humility, which the poet had presented to the young Alexander II.[66] Tolstoi's Nevskii exemplified the national honor by defending Russia's borders from Germans, Lithuanians, and Swedes, and "in his blissful death became the heavenly intercessor for the Russian land." Alexander Aleksandrovich, large and powerful, was frequently described as a *vitiaz'* and *bogatyr'*, and, compared to his namesake, as a protector of Russian culture and unity from Western threats.[67]

It was the heir's Orthodox faith that identified him most clearly as a Russian man. For Alexander Aleksandrovich, worship meant more than compliance with the liturgical requirements of the church. He loved religious services and prayed fervently. He often recorded in his diary the exact number of times he attended church and his feelings of exaltation at the services.[68] Religion provided an emotional bond both with his dead brother and his mother. He noted on March 23, 1866, that he read the Gospel according to John aloud with Meshcherskii: "This is my favorite Gospel and

---

[66] See Volume 1: 347–48.

[67] Gr. M. V. Tolstoi, "Stat'ia po sluchaiu ob"iavleniia Naslednikom prestola Velikogo Kniazia Aleksandra Aleksandrovicha," Gershel'man-Shvarts fond, BAR, Folder 2, part 8, 8; For an example of the later use of the Nevskii image, see S. Petrovskii, *Pamiati Imperatora Aleksandra III* (Moscow, 1894), 320–22. On the image of Nevskii in the nineteenth century, see Benjamin Schenk, "Aleksandr Nevskij und die russische Nation: Geschichtsilder und Entwürfe kollektiver Identität, 1263–1917," masters thesis, Free University of Berlin, 1997, 135–50.

[68] Kamenskii, "Ot detstva . . . ," 431; Firsov, "Aleksandr III; lichnaia kharakteristika," 96.

I came to love it even more when it was read at the death of Niks according to Mama's wish."[69]

Faith in God, he wrote, gave him the strength to carry on after Nicholas Aleksandrovich's death: "Perhaps in the eyes of others I have often forgotten my designation, but the feeling that I should live not for myself but for others was always in my soul; a painful and difficult obligation. But *'May Your Divine Will, be Done.'* I saw these words constantly, and they console and support me always, because whatever happens with us, it is all God's Will, and therefore I am tranquil, and *I place my faith in the Lord!*"[70] Alexander III's national and religious tastes arose from wells of feeling within him: the animosity toward his father and his Western frivolity, but most of all a powerful intellectual and spiritual, if not personal, affinity with his mother.

His mother's brooding and reclusive asceticism provided Alexander Aleksandrovich a model of piety and spiritual dedication. Just as the empress Maria Fedorovna had set the emotional tone for the scenario of Nicholas I, the empress Maria Aleksandrovna provided an image of Orthodox piety that would be enshrined in the scenario of Alexander III.[71] On May 22, 1884, the fourth anniversary of his mother's death, he wrote his wife:

> If there is something kind, good, and honorable in me, I owe it all to my dear nice mama. Mama constantly occupied herself with us, preparing us for confession and prayer. By her example, she taught us to love and understand the Christian faith as she herself understood it. Thanks to Mama all my brothers and Mary (Grand Duchess Maria Aleksandrovna) became and remained true Christians and we loved both the faith and the church. No matter how many very different and sincere conversations there were, Mama always listened calmly and always found something to answer, to calm, to scold, to approve, and always from a lofty, Christian point of view. . . . We loved Papa a great deal, but because of the nature of his obligations and the crushing work, he could not occupy himself with us like nice, dear Mama.[72]

It is clear that love of prayer and worship brought Alexander close to the most influential figure in his development—Constantine Pobedonostsev. A professor of civil law at Moscow University, Pobedonostsev had participated in the drafting of the court reform of 1864. During the Polish uprising of 1863, his patriotic feelings had drawn him into Katkov's circle. A Muscovite by origin and taste, the grandson of an Orthodox priest, he was also close to the Slavophiles and shared their high valuation of the importance of Russian Orthodoxy to the Russian nation. But at the same time he revered the Petrine

[69] "Dnevnik Aleksandra III, 1865–1866gg.," 185.
[70] "Dnevnik Aleksandra III, 1866g.," 27–28.
[71] See Volume 1: 247–55.
[72] "Pis'ma Aleksandra III Marii Fedorovne, 18 aprelia–18 sentiabria, 1884g.," GARF, 642-1-709, 15.

administrative order as the source of law in Russia.[73] The disruptions of the reform era offended both his sense of order and spiritual tranquillity. A reclusive intellectual who preferred contemplation and writing to governmental activity, he found service in the Senate tedious and futile, and increasingly felt alienated from what he saw as a temporizing, immoral governmental policy.[74]

Initially Pobedonostsev shared the general contempt for Alexander's capacities and character. But he soon discovered attractive features in him, the "simple soul" (*prostaia dusha*), which he later associated with the Russian people.[75] The change came about after Alexander's marriage. Pobedonostsev wrote to Anna Tiutcheva, "He has become more steady, cheerful, alert, and independent. When he feels himself at ease, what a kind, clear expression (*dobroe, iasnoe vyrazhenie*) is in his eyes." A month later he wrote, "His heart is really upright—one can feel attached to him. He has a Russian heart."[76] He, like Alexander, loved the beauty of the Orthodox liturgy and enjoyed quiet prayer in small churches.[77]

Pobedonostsev used his position as tutor to develop Alexander's sense of himself as a Russian. On the birth of Alexander's first son, Nicholas, in 1868, Pobedonostsev hoped that the child would resurrect the spirit of his late namesake, the grand duke Nicholas Aleksandrovich. "May the newborn resemble him in manner and mind, and in that native love of Russia, which struck everyone in him, attracted everyone to him, and raised joyous hope in everyone's soul."[78]

To encourage Alexander's interest in Russian history, Pobedonostsev arranged for history lessons from Sergei Solov'ev and sent him works of Pan-Slavist writers such as Michael Pogodin, Nil Popov, Iurii Samarin, and Rostislav Fadeev. He recommended the patriotic historical novels of Mikhail Zagoskin and Ivan Lazhechnikov whom the heir came to regard as his favorite writers. He suggested trips to the monasteries and churches of the Russian

---

[73] Robert F. Byrnes, *Pobedonostsev: His Life and Thought* (Bloomington, Ind., 1968), 106–7, 322–24.

[74] For an explanation of the evolution of Pobedonostsev's views, see A. Iu. Polunov, "Konstantin Petrovich Pobedonostsev—chelovek i politik," *Otechestvennaia Istoriia* (January–February 1998): 43–45.

[75] On *prostaia dusha* as a theme in Pobedonostsev's writings, see O. E. Maiorova, " 'Ia zhivu postoianno v ramkakh . . .' ," in Catherine Evtuhov, Boris Gasparov, Alexander Ospovat, and Mark von Hagen, eds., *Kazan, Moscow, St. Petersburg* (Moscow, 1997), 174–76.

[76] [Iu. Got'e], "Pobedonostsev and Alexander III," *Slavonic and East European Review* 7 (June 1928): 35–36; Iu. Got'e, "K. P. Pobedonostsev i naslednik Aleksandr Aleksandrovich, 1865–1881," in *Publichnaia biblioteka SSSR imeni Lenina; sbornik II* (Moscow, 1929), 112.

[77] Byrnes, *Pobedonostsev*, 286. Pobedonostsev wrote to Catherine Tiutcheva on March 31, 1877: "Our religious service is not only the formula of prayer, which, it is true, would be hard to endure; it is an entire sacred poem, comprising songs, images, sounds, memories, and thoughts. In it the soul not only prays but lives in meditation and feeling, and also relishes a beauty that nothing on earth can approximate" (Olga Maiorova, " '. . . Pishu Ia tol'ko dlia vas. . .': Pis'ma K. P. Pobedonostseva k sestram Tiutchevym," *Novyi Mir* [March 1994]: 218–19).

[78] *Pis'ma Pobedonostseva k Aleksandru III*, 1:7.

north, and, in return, Alexander sent him icons and other religious items for distribution to churches. He introduced Alexander to the nationalist circles of Moscow and invited their leaders to lecture before him. In 1868 Alexander attended political discussions that included, in addition to Pobedonostsev, Ivan Aksakov and Michael Katkov. In the 1870s Pobedonostsev supplied Alexander with publications of the Moscow Slavonic Benevolent Committee, the principal Pan-Slavist organization, and invited leaders of the organization to lecture to him and the empress in the palace. He persuaded Alexander to subscribe to Meshcherskii's *Grazhdanin* and later arranged for Fedor Dostoevskii to read his works before him.[79]

As tutor and adviser of the heir, Pobedonostsev pressed Alexander to assert his national persona in opposition to his father. The first episode of conflict took place on the occasion of the death of the metropolitan Filaret in 1867. Urged on by Pobedonostsev, Maria Aleksandrovna wanted the heir to attend the funeral. "The entire people considers the burial of Filaret an all-national matter," Pobedonostsev wrote to him. "They await and crave your arrival in Moscow." The emperor was unable to go, and Alexander's presence, Pobedonostsev assured him, would "attest to everyone the complete involvement by the imperial family in the feeling of national and state loss, and would make the people's heart beat even more strongly with love for the tsar and for you."[80]

This letter proved decisive in defining Pobedonostsev's relations with the heir and the shaping of their concept of nation.[81] Pobedonostsev viewed the tsar's appearance among the people at a religious event in Moscow as a demonstration of the monarchy's national bond with the people. The failure of the emperor to appear was a dereliction of his obligations as national monarch. The emperor, however, decided to send Vladimir Aleksandrovich and prevent his heir from becoming a focus of national sentiment. Alexander Aleksandrovich was crushed.[82] From this moment, Alexander Aleksandrovich began to regard his father's antagonism to him as contempt for the national spirit.

Under Pobedonostsev's encouragement, Alexander Aleksandrovich increasingly viewed Moscow as a national center and his father as isolated from the popular and spiritual roots of monarchical authority. Ivan Babst showed him the need to protect Russian merchants and industrialists, especially those centered in Moscow, from foreign competition. Babst plied him with anti-German and anti-English memoranda, evoking, Alfred Rieber

[79] Got'e, "Pobedonostsev and Alexander III," 39–40; Byrnes, *Pobedonostsev*, 75–76, 120–21; Meshcherskii, *Moi vospominaniia*, 2:99.

[80] *Pis'ma Pobedonostseva k Aleksandru III*, 1:5–6.

[81] The decisiveness of this moment for Pobedonostsev is argued convincingly by Olga Maiorova ("Mitropolit moskovskii Filaret v obshchestvennom soznanii kontsa XIX veka," in *Lotmanovskii Sbornik* 2 [Moscow, 1997]: 615–16).

[82] K. P. *Pobedonostsev i ego korrespondenty*, vol. 1 (Moscow-Petrograd, 1923), part 2, 1005–6.

writes, "a touching picture of the honest, plain Russian merchants defending themselves (and the interests of the hard-working Russian working man) against the accusations of sloth, greed, and selfishness heaped on them by unfeeling bureaucrats." Although Babst kept the heir informed and brought him to the appropriate meetings, the effort to raise tariffs failed.[83]

Alexander Aleksandrovich actively supported the Moscow industrialists' effort to gain control of the Moscow–St. Petersburg railroad and prevent a takeover by La grande societé des chemins de fers russes, a foreign consortium supported by the grand duke Constantine Nikolaevich. The Moscow group formed a Russian company for this purpose, and in 1868 Alexander Aleksandrovich presented their proposal to the emperor. His father scolded him for believing "the nonsense and slander" of V. A. Kokorev "and former tax farmers like him." By 1870 the heir was openly espousing nationalist industrial policies.[84]

From the late 1860s the heir, as an advocate of national causes, waged a psychological and political duel against the emperor. On the surface Alexander II showed confidence in his son, following the example of Nicholas I. On September 14, 1865, he appointed him to the State Council. In April 1868 he designated him adjutant-general in his suite, and in September of that year lieutenant-general. He made him a member of the Tariff Commission and invited him to meetings of the Committee of Ministers. From the moment of Nicholas Aleksandrovich's death, he insisted that Alexander Aleksandrovich attend ministerial reports and dinners with important guests. He appointed him head of the committee to direct relief for the famine in 1868, the one position in which the grand duke gained public sympathy. When the emperor went abroad in 1875 and 1876 he entrusted the direction of the empire to him.[85]

Alexander Aleksandrovich often took issue with his father's views and advanced those favored by Pobedonostsev, Meshcherskii, and others in the Russian party. Alexander II found himself being doubted by a son whose intelligence he held in contempt. The grand duke, on the other hand, believed that the high offices he had been assigned entitled his views to respect, and

[83] Kamenskii, "Ot detstva . . . ," 444; Rieber, *Merchants and Entrepreneurs in Imperial Russia*, 196–98.

[84] Rieber, *Merchants and Entrepreneurs in Imperial Russia*, 187; Igor Vinogradoff, "Further Russian Imperial Correspondence with Prince V. P. Meshcherskii," *Oxford Slavonic Papers*, no. 11 (1964): 102. Dmitrii Obolenskii saw him at Meshcherskii's home in 1870 and noted: "His sympathies are extremely national, reaching the point of exclusiveness. He has many good instincts. May God permit them to develop sensibly and correctly" (Obolenskii, *Dnevnik*, Folder 3, 58–59; entry is for March 10, 1870).

[85] "Polnyi posluzhnoi spisok Ego Imperatorskogo Velichestva Gosudaria Imperatora Aleksandra Aleksandrovicha," GARF, 677-1-25, 2–10. Alexander Aleksandrovich's diary for 1865 notes his first attendance of ministerial reports; see also his letter to Stiuler of July 10, 1870, RGIA, 878-1-12, 65. On the popular response to his direction of the Famine Relief Committee, see V. A. Tvardovskaia, "Aleksandr III," in *Rossiiskie Samoderzhtsy* (Moscow, 1994), 220–21.

the disregard they encountered struck him as an ongoing indignity.[86] At the beginning Alexander Aleksandrovich tried both to prove himself and to serve his father. But the emperor failed to answer his letters, and his suggestions were ignored. At the beginning of 1869 he joined an effort to expose abuses in the artillery department. He took the side of a group of generals, including Bariatinskii and Fadeev, who opposed Miliutin's efforts at reorganization and reform. But when he tried to discuss the question privately with his father, he was dismissed before he could utter a word.[87]

During the late 1860s and 1870s, encouraged by Meshcherskii and Pobedonostsev, Alexander Aleksandrovich began to entertain the image of a new type of servitor—one animated by a national spirit to assist the tsar in attaining the good of Russia. His criticism increasingly focused on individual officials whom he believed to be hostile to the well-being of Russia, as he and his confidants understood it. He began to condemn such officials for being out of touch with the people, for being antinational. He wrote to Meshcherskii in August 1867 that the main problem of Russian ministers was that "they do not know our Mother Russia." But he realized his own shortcomings as well. "Unfortunately I must confess that I myself know my Dear Native Land poorly, but at least I try to find out, and I am always happy when people write or speak of her sensibly (del'no)."[88]

Del'no, a favorite word of his, meant practical and businesslike, not deluded by intellectualizing, abstraction, or showy sentiment. It meant dealing with reality, and reality could be found only outside Petersburg. In a letter of 1868 he praised the minister of justice Constantine Pahlen, who had just returned from Moscow with an extremely critical report of the Moscow court system. "It is evident that Pahlen goes about his trips in a businesslike way (del'no). . . . He himself admits now that Petersburg views on the matter are often false and that without traveling and seeing everything oneself it is impossible to know Russia."[89]

During the late 1860s and early 1870s Alexander Aleksandrovich increasingly identified the source of Russia's problems in Germans, whether they served in Russia or in Germany. In 1867 Pobedonostsev introduced him to Iurii Samarin's critique of the privileges of the Baltic German nobility and Lutheran church hierarchy in *The Borderlands of Russia*. The book made a strong impression on him. The same year Alexander commented on an article by Samarin in the journal, *Moskva*: "This article is against these *filthy Germans* and is marvelously written." He feared that the author would be brought to trial for speaking the truth about Russia's best interests.[90]

---

[86] Vinogradoff, "Some Russian Imperial Letters," 112; Vinogradoff, "Further Russian Imperial Correspondence," 107.

[87] Firsov, "Aleksandr III; lichnaia kharakteristika," 88–89. On the incident, see P. A. Zaionchkovskii, *Voennye reformy 1860–1870 godov v Rossii* (Moscow, 1952), 289–93.

[88] Vinogradoff, "Some Russian Imperial Letters," 112.

[89] Ibid., 115.

[90] "Dnevnik Aleksandra III, 1867g.," 66.

The heir's anti-German sentiments also reflected the influence of his mother and wife, both of whom feared and detested Prussia. The empress Maria Aleksandrovna, a Hessian princess, had always been suspicious of Prussia's growing power. The grand duchess Maria Fedorovna openly expressed the anti-Prussian feelings of the Danish royal family and the bitterness over the loss of Schleswig-Holstein to Prussia after Denmark's war with Prussia and Austria in 1864.[91] Indeed, a month after her betrothal to Nicholas Aleksandrovich in October 1864, she had written to Alexander II requesting Russian support to help Denmark resist the growing Prussian dominance.[92]

Meshcherskii, in 1870, gave him and Maria Fedorovna a sketch, written in French, of what purported to be his "reflections, impressions, convictions, and confessions" after their trip through Russia. Meshcherskii stressed the harmful influence of the court which, he claimed, "has never been as powerful and as terribly dangerous as in our times." He presented the court as "an occult power" that with "fatal ease" could "slip into the interior of the sovereign's life and establish its power there despite all obstacles."[93]

Meshcherskii warned that the present ministers, with the exception of the minister of education Dmitrii Tolstoi, were allies of Peter Shuvalov, the chief of the Third Section, and kept ties only with the court. They isolated the tsar from the country and promoted the interests of the Poles and Germans. He thus played on the heir's distrust of Poles and Germans as groups with divided loyalties who would betray the empire. He reduced the political scene in Russia to forces of good and evil. There were only two parties in Russia, he wrote, Shuvalov's conservative party representing foreigners and striving to crush the Russian people, and *le parti russe*.[94]

The moral and political split between foreigners and Russians became sharper and more emphatic in the heir's response to two major events of the 1870s: the Franco-Prussian War, culminating in the unification of Germany under Prussian leadership, and the Russo-Turkish War. In both circumstances he blamed his father's ministers for a weak defense of Russia's national interests.

The Franco-Prussian War confirmed his suspicions of Germans. He wrote to Meshcherskii in August 1870, "One has to think seriously of our native land and that soon the filthy Prussians will reach her; even now there are people who still think that [Prussia] is our ally." He recognized the menacing implications of a united Germany for Russia and sharply criticized his father's support of Prussia. "It is sad, very sad to see how we are preparing an

[91] Zaionchkovskii, *Rossiiskoe samoderzhavie*, 37–38.

[92] For her letter to Alexander II, see GARF, 642-1-604, 5–6.

[93] "Memuara Meshcherskogo . . . ," 6–9.

[94] Ibid., 10–15. The memorandum is tentatively dated 1868, but it appears to have been written after Alexander's and Maria Fedorovna's journey of 1869–70.

inevitable danger for ourselves and worry only about making it easier for the Prussians to occupy our Baltic provinces and perhaps even more."[95]

On October 16, 1870, after hearing of the fall of Metz, Alexander wrote to his mother, "Sooner or later we are bound to feel the power of Germany on our own shoulders."[96] When Alexander II raised his glass to toast the German emperor in November 1871 his eyes were directed at the heir.[97] Indeed, none of the grand dukes shared their father's admiration for Prussia. The Prussian ambassador did not fail to note the sullenness and hostility toward him from all but the youngest, Paul Aleksandrovich.[98]

The emperor and the heir came into open conflict on the issue of support for the Bulgarian and Serbian uprisings. The grand duke maintained ties with Pan-Slavist circles in Moscow, approved of their speeches, and joined the clamor for war against Turkey. The issue allied him with his mother, the empress. Pobedonostsev's letters argued the case that war was inevitable in Russia's diplomatic situation and explained the failure to act by the weakness of leadership. The tsarevich replied that he was in complete agreement. He condemned Gorchakov and Miliutin and praised the Pan-Slavist ambassador to Turkey, Nicholas Ignat'ev. He yearned for war and criticized temporizing and conciliatory policies. When the minister of finance Michael Reitern insisted that Russia lacked sufficient resources to wage war, Alexander scoffed and declared, "Moscow will give everything that is needed. All that is required is to tell her of the war's goal and the tsar's decision." His support for the Slavonic cause helped stir war passions and prompted angry rebukes from his father. The police read his mail and kept Pobedonostsev under surveillance. Yet the grand duke continued to attend the emperor's daily meetings with the minister of war Dmitrii Miliutin, the minister of the court Count Alexander Adlerberg, and military leaders.[99]

During the summer of 1876, languishing at Livadia, the heir felt oppressed by the daily routine of social occasions and spoiled for action. The government's indecisiveness, its efforts to reach a compromise and avoid taking the lead of a national movement, angered him. At this point his association of weakness with antinational leadership by those alienated from the people, and his identification of strong, authoritative rule with national character, began to crystallize in a new concept of authority. His letters to his "little soul Mini" express his growing frustration with officials who were not Russian in origin or spirit and indicate what he expected from a national official.

[95] Vinogradoff, "Some Russian Imperial Letters," 118.

[96] "Pis'ma Aleksandra IIIego k materi, 1864–1879," 121–22.

[97] S. B. Obolenskaia, *Franko-prusskaia voina i obshchestvennoe mnenie Germanii i Rossii* (Moscow, 1977), 143, 155.

[98] Von Schweinitz, *Denkwürdigkeiten*, 1:410–11.

[99] Got'e, "Pobedonostsev and Alexander III," 46–47; Byrnes, *Pobedonostsev*, 123; Kamenskii, "Naslednik Tsesarevich Aleksandr Aleksandrovich," *Istoricheskii Vestnik* (March 1917): 664; de Grunwald, "Le tsar Alexandre II . . . ," 194–96; "Pis'ma Aleksandra Aleksandrovich Marii Fedorovne, 1876–1877 gg.," GARF, 642-1-705, 17.

On September 30, 1876, he wrote to her, "It simply nauseates me to think of what has become of us and the kind of petty and pale individuals who are at the head of our government." There were no statesmen. "All this scum (*svoloch'*) of officials who think of their own bellies and nothing else, and no ministers of the Russian Empire. Papa does not have one decent man who would tell him the truth and be his staunch adviser, who would know and love Russia and be a true Russian (*istinnyi russkii chelovek*), who would serve his sovereign and his fatherland out of conviction and not as a hireling. I can't do anything by myself and can't say anything because Papa won't trust me." He reported a discussion with Ignat'ev, who insisted that Russia had to seize the opportunity to declare war or the situation would turn to Russia's disadvantage.[100]

Alexander was particularly incensed at the minister of finance Reitern, a scion of a Baltic German family that had been in Russian service since Peter the Great. When Reitern could not tell him where to find the means to support a war, he wrote, "And this calls itself a Russian minister of finance who understands Russia's interests and dignity; to hell with this heathen German. May God permit us to find at least one genuine minister of finance in Mother Russia among eighty million inhabitants!" He felt that his father, too, had become disillusioned with the ministers. He believed that if he were in Petersburg he could change the foreign policy "and direct the entire matter on a new, fresh, and common sensical path!?!"[101] He conferred with Nicholas Ignat'ev about the crisis. At this meeting the two discussed the possibility of calling an Assembly of the Land, which would allow a meeting of tsar and people. In October 1876 he wrote to Pobedonostsev that the government itself should take on the leadership of the Slavic benevolent committees and the popular movement.[102]

Alexander's letters of these years suggest the type of rule and official conduct he expected in the Russian state. He used the term *true Russian*, indicating that there were false Russians about and that Russian nationality was not simply a matter of origin and language but a specific political persona capable of decisive and forceful action. Alexander II's ministers, Reitern foremost among them, were the antithesis of his ideal: They were vacillating, full of doubt and ambivalence, without the will to act for the benefit of the fatherland. Alexander Aleksandrovich's crude and intemperate language gave a new national expression to the service ethos. It sharply divided those with the ethic of sacrifice, who thought in terms of Russia's well-being, from those weakened by doubts and Western influence, who were ruled by narrow self-interest, namely, "their own bellies."

    [100] "Pis'ma v. kn. Aleksandra Aleksandrovicha v. kn. Marii Fedorovna, 30 iiulia 1876–26 maia 1877 gg.," GARF, 642-1-705, 20, 22.

    [101] Ibid., 26; letter of October 3, 1876.

    [102] P. A. Zaionchkovskii, *Krizis samoderzhaviia na rubezhe 1870–1880 godov* (Moscow, 1964), 450; Got'e, "Pobedonostsev and Alexander III," 47.

Pobedonostsev's letters to Alexander and his writings combined this type of moral-splitting with a vision of new men, distinguished by virtue, firmness of conviction, and will. Drawing on historical rhetoric and legend, he projected such figures into a vague, distant national past, before Peter the Great, when Russians were united in an emotional bond, through religion and a respect for authority. Pobedonostsev's letter of October 12, 1876, cited in the epigraph to this chapter, follows the cadences of the Russian *Primary Chronicle*. The phrase "our land is great and rich" (*zemlia nasha velika i obil'na*) were those of the invitation to the Varangians in 862. It expressed the yearning for unquestioned authority, a rupture with the old order. Pobedonostsev returned to the motif of conquest but changed its central figure. The reference to *bogatyri*, the heroic knights of the epos, called forth a native image of martial strength, in contrast to an effete, European leadership. The national monarch would distance himself from the men ruling Russia in the previous regime, guide himself by ancient example, and dominate through the attributes of a legendary past. Pobedonostsev's historical imagery was an answer to the problems of current Russian monarchy—the legacy of weakness and corruption that he portrayed as coming from blind imitation of Western rationalism and openness.

Pobedonostsev's conservative defense of autocratic prerogatives was profoundly antitraditional and antihistorical.[103] His argument was moral, rejecting existing institutions as well as the legal and political principles governing the monarchy during the previous two reigns. His views grew out of a negative, Augustinian conception of human nature. Men were evil and in need of authority, and Russians, "who were marked by "decomposition and weakness and untruth," required an especially strong hand.[104] But absolute power could perform miracles, he indicated in his letter of October 12, when it did so "in unity with the people." By combining the notion of heroic authoritarian rule with action in unity with the people, Pobedonostsev gave the conquest motif a national and even democratic meaning.

Like Katkov, Pobedonostsev argued that the people themselves yearned for forceful rulers. But unlike Katkov, he identified this with an ancient tradition. The heroic figures were to come from within Russia—native heroes imbued with the spirit of the people. The idealization of the ancient past and the role of a national tsar echoed some Slavophile visions of pre-Petrine Rus', but not their notions of an Assembly of the Land. Nor was this unity between tsar and people the emotional bond of mutual affection that Alexander II sought to exercise. Pobedonostsev described it to Alexander in his letter of October 16 as a moral, spiritual bond inspired by resolute exercise of the power in behalf of the people.

---

[103] On Pobedonostsev's lack of interest in historical studies, see Byrnes, *Pobedonostsev*, 43.

[104] Ibid., 292–93.

Legal benefits and rules mean nothing compared to this feeling. The people fall into despondency and anguish when they feel no governing force. My God, how important this is! Here in Russia there is no governing force but the unity of the people with the state in *moral* consciousness.[105]

THE RUSSO-TURKISH WAR AND THE CRISIS OF AUTOCRACY

Alexander II's decision to embark on war dispelled the heir's frustration and ennui, and filled him with excitement about the national cause. In his diary Alexander Aleksandrovich recorded that he was buoyed and enthused by the reviews of the departing troops and especially by the processions in Moscow on April 26, 1877, when Alexander called for the nation's support. "The meeting in Moscow has always been marvelous, but this time it has exceeded all expectations and the crowd was larger than usual. . . . The Tsar's procession on the Red Porch was marvelous with the wonderful sound of bells and the frightening 'Hoorah!' "[106]

When he went off to meet his father at the front, Alexander wrote to his wife, "I am sure that no matter how sad it is to part for an indefinite time that you are happy for my chance to join a real cause and to prove in that cause to the Tsar and Russia my readiness to serve them not merely in words but in acts as well." As we have seen, Alexander II regarded the conduct of the war as a family matter and assigned his brothers and sons important command positions. Alexander Aleksandrovich hoped to lead a select detachment of the guards but instead was assigned command of the troops to protect the flank of the Russian advance, at Rushchuk on the Danube.

Despite the large forces at his disposal, Alexander's assignment was purely defensive, and this rankled in him. Most of the military decisions were made by the generals assisting him, among them Peter Vannovskii and Ilarion Vorontsov-Dashkov.[107] Alexander felt himself disregarded, as he had been during governmental deliberations. His recommendations were ignored. Like most of the commanders, he vigorously opposed the emperor's presence near the front but to no avail. He objected to the tactics at Plevna, urging more aggressive attacks and suggesting the removal of the grand duke Nicholas Nikolaevich. When the guards were finally mobilized, he again hoped to command them. But when it turned out that he would be subordinate to "a Rumanian prince," he was offended and returned to his detachment at

---

[105] *Pis'ma Pobedonostseva k Aleksandru III* (Moscow, 1925), 1:67.

[106] "Dnevnik Aleksandra III, 1875–1880 gg.," 156–57.

[107] S. S. Tatishchev, "Tsesarevich Aleksandr Aleksandrovich v vostochnuiu voinu, 1877–1878," RGIA, 878-1-9, 1–5; see also Lowe, *Aleksander III of Russia*, 34–38; F. M. Fon-Bradke, "Ocherk boevoi sluzhby Ego Imperatorskogo Vysochestva Gosudaria Naslednika Tsesarevicha i Velikogo Kniazia Aleksandra Aleksandrovicha vo vremia osvoboditel'noi voiny 1877–78 godov na balkanskom ostrove," *Starina i Novizna* 15 (1911): 214–31; Firsov, "Vospominaniia o tsesareviche Nikolae Aleksandroviche i Imperatore Aleksandre III v iunosti," 74–75.

Rushchuk. He felt guilty before the guards regiments and wrote about this to A. P. Oldenbourg, his cousin: "If everyone suffered physically in this campaign, I suffered thirty times more morally."[108]

Symbolically the heir's presence confirmed the emperor's image of the imperial family as leaders of the nation. Alexander II showed his esteem by bestowing on the heir the Cross of St. George, second degree—the highest level of decoration for bravery ever bestowed on a member of the imperial family—as well as a gold saber and the order of Vladimir, first degree, "with swords." Those serving with the heir at Rushchuk were also generously decorated, indeed in a measure far exceeding their modest contribution to the war effort.[109] In the lithograph of the grand dukes, Alexander Aleksandrovich poses heroically, his sword raised, his adjutants looking on admiringly (fig. 16).[110]

The heir's own impressions, recorded in his letters to his wife, indicate that he looked upon war as something less than glorious. He gave simple but moving descriptions of the human costs of war, the waiting, the pain, the injured youths groaning and languishing without beds, in filthy conditions. He wrote of the tragic siege of Plevna: "What is unendurably sad and painful is that we again lost such a great mass of people, that so much dear Russian blood was shed once more."[111] He came to view war as a horrendous ordeal, to be prevented at all costs, which may have influenced him to avoid conflict during his own reign.

At the front he also observed the ineptitude and weakness of many of those in command. When his troops first were forced to retreat, he wrote to Nicholas Nikolaevich and claimed the setback resulted from carelessness (*neispravnost'*) and poor direction (*nerasporiaditel'nost'*) "or, to put it better, from the lack of desire to fulfill what was commanded." He described the headquarters to his wife as "a pit of dirt, intrigue, stupidity, and disorder." All those who visited his detachment remarked on its exemplary order (*poriadok*). He quoted a remark of Vorontsov-Dashkov: "This is the single unit where there is order, where business goes forward as it should, where it is possible to live."[112] Alexander developed a strong sense of solidarity with the officers at Rushchuk. Vannovskii later became his minister of war, and Vorontsov-Dashkov the head of his palace security and minister of the court.

[108] Tatishchev, "Tsesarevich Aleksandr Aleksandrovich," 19–20, 26–27.

[109] Alexander I and Alexander II himself had received only the fourth degree of the Order of St. George, but Alexander II awarded himself the first degree of the order on the hundredth anniversary of the order in 1869 (S. G. Kashchenko and N. G. Rogulin, "Predstaviteli Doma Romanovykh—kavalery ordena Sviatogo Georgiia," in *Dom Romanovykh v istorii Rossii* (St. Petersburg, 1995), 262–63).

[110] "Aleksandr II: lubki," GARF-678-1-1027.

[111] Letters of September 4–5 and November 18, 1877, "Kopii pisem Aleksandra III Imperatritse Marii Fedorovne," GARF, 642-1-707, 70, 197.

[112] Tatishchev, "Tsesarevich Aleksandr Aleksandrovich," 14–15; "Pis'ma Aleksandra IIIego k materi, 1864–1879," 250–51; Got'e, "Pobedonostsev i Aleksandr III," 50; letter of October 10, 1877; "Kopii pisem Aleksandra III Imperatritse Marii Fedorovne," 149–50.

Alexander may have suffered during his command, but he prided himself on a leadership that he believed instilled obedience and discipline. His general's uniform, the Cross of the Order of St. George, always in prominent view, was his favored attire for important celebrations.

The heir's leadership and true coming of age were symbolized by the large beard he grew, in response to an order permitting those at the front to grow beards. "What joy," he wrote to Maria Fedorovna on June 1, 1877, "we have been allowed to stop shaving and wear beards. It is such a pleasure. I just gave an order to take my razors as far away as possible!"[113] After the war he kept the beard. It symbolized the lasting bond that developed among the officers at Rushchuk. In subsequent years they gathered at reunion suppers in their war uniforms—many of them even gluing on false beards—to recall, Alexander wrote in his diary, "a time so dear and glorious in our memories."[114]

The experience of war, revealing the disorder in the system, confirmed Alexander's sense of the dangers of weak authority. As the terrorist movement became his and Pobedonostsev's chief preoccupation, they became increasingly wary of Pan-Slavist efforts to involve Russia with national insurgencies abroad.[115] After the acquittal of Vera Zasulich, Pobedonostsev wrote to Alexander in despair: "There is no government as it should be, with a firm will, with a clear notion of how it wants to defend the basic principles of administration decisively, to *act* everywhere where necessary." The revolutionaries were acting against the will of the people. "Should a handful of young people who have lost their reason be feared, in view of the masses who preserve their common sense and faith in authority?" But, he contended, the masses were losing their faith in a government that was busy composing new rules.[116]

At this time Pobedonostsev introduced Alexander Aleksandrovich to Dostoevskii, who had become a defender of strong governmental authority. Dostoevskii and Pobedonostsev shared the notion of reconstituting the moral influence of the Orthodox Church which had been weakened by the Petrine reforms. Dostoevskii personally presented *The Brother's Karamazov* to the heir and was apparently received at the palace. His vision of a state based on religion, as well as his contempt for foreigners and his ridicule of the progressive press, clearly appealed to Alexander and Pobedonostsev. Shortly before his death in 1881 Dostoevskii advanced his own proposal for an Assembly of the Land—a form of direct consultation with the peasants to discover their needs rather than "chatter houses" (*govoril'ni*) dreamed of by "European Russians."[117]

[113] "Kopii pisem Aleksandra III Imperatritse Marii Fedorovne," 12.

[114] "Dnevnik Aleksandra III, 1875–1880 gg.," 187.

[115] Byrnes, *Pobedonostsev*, 129.

[116] *Pis'ma Pobedonostseva k Aleksandru III*, 1:116–18.

[117] Leonid Grossman, "Dostoevskii i pravitel'stvennye krugi 70-kh godov," *Literaturnoe Nasledstvo*, vol. 15 (Moscow, 1934), 87–92, 114–17.

Alexander Aleksandrovich voiced the national authoritarian views of Dostoevskii and Pobedonostsev in the discussions of governmental reforms that were under way in the commission headed by Loris-Melikov. At the beginning of 1880 he attacked Grand Duke Constantine Nikolaevich's project for a consultative institution of estate deputies to discuss legislative matters. The project would have brought garrulous representatives of educated society into the government; it would not have been an assembly of the land, uniting people and tsar. The heir said,

> It is essentially the beginning of a constitution, and a constitution, at least for a long time, can bring us no good. Chatterbox lawyers will be elected, who will only orate and will not help matters. Even in Western states, constitutions bring misfortunes . . . I think we should not be occupied with constitutions but with something quite different.

In support of his contention, Alexander mentioned Danish ministers who complained to him of "parliamentary chatterboxes" who hampered the operation of the administration.[118]

Freedom of speech and the representation of diverse interests are identified here with a noisy, messy, garrulousness and the clangor of human voices in contrast to the silent force of authority that set the monarch's power above the doubts of ordinary human intercourse. Alexander Aleksandrovich and Pobedonostsev now argued for the concentration of powers in the hands of an all-powerful dictator, who would unite the administration, and they initially supported Loris-Melikov. Alexander worked together with Loris-Melikov and actively participated in the senatorial inspections the minister organized. He initially viewed the general as the determined official that he desired. He wrote to Loris-Melikov praising his program for strong authority, which would promote *the happiness of our dear native land,* and the unhappiness of milords the ministers whom the program and the tsar's decision will probably shake up, but to hell with them?"[119] He obtained Loris-Melikov's backing to secure Pobedonostsev the position of chief-procurator of the Holy Synod and to allow him to attend meetings of the Committee of Ministers, a privilege not usually accorded to a chief-procurator. But relations began to sour when Pobedonostsev criticized the relaxation of controls over the press and university meetings. Pobedonostsev was then excluded

---

[118] Zaionchkovskii, *Krizis samoderzhaviia,* 141–42. On January 25, 1880, he wrote in his diary of the proposals submitted by Constantine Nikolaevich and Valuev: "Both projects were unanimously rejected for many reasons. . . . The chief reason is that this measure would satisfy no one, would tangle domestic matters even more, and still in some way would be one of the first steps to a constitution!" (Alexander Aleksandrovich, "Dnevnik Aleksandra III, 1875–1880 gg.," 312–13; "Dnevnik Naslednika Tsesarevicha Velikogo Kniazia Aleksandra Aleksandrovicha, 1880g"; *Rossiiskii Arkhiv* 6 (1995): 348).

[119] "Perepiska Aleksandra III s Loris-Melikovym (1880–1881gg.)," *Krasnyi Arkhiv* 1(8) (1925): 108.

from the ministers' sessions with the tsar that considered the proposal to involve estate representatives in government.[120]

Alexander appreciated the ceremonies staged on behalf of his father, like the twenty-fifth anniversary ceremonies on February 19, 1880 (see chapter 4), but he remained frightened by the political scene. In an undated diary entry of March 1880 he wrote, "It is terrible to think of what we have lived through during these five years. The troubled years before the Turkish War, then the war itself in 1877 and 1878, and finally the most horrible and disgusting years that Russia has ever gone through. Times worse than these could hardly be!"[121]

These events were followed by his mother's death on May 22, 1880. For Alexander, this was a shattering trauma. He later wrote:

> With her death began all that time of troubles, that living nightmare we lived through that spoiled everything good, the dear recollection of family life. All illusions vanished, all spun around, it was impossible to make sense of this maelstrom, and we didn't understand one another. All the filth swam to the surface and engulfed everything good, everything sacred![122]

From his despair, Alexander Aleksandrovich emerged a tranquil but defiant symbol of strength, made in his mother's image. The change in his personal appearance at the end of the 1870s gave striking expression to his distance from his father's scenario. Photographs of the late 1860s and the early 1870s show a flaccid, overfed young man, clean-shaven except for a thin slanted mustache—a disappointing contrast to his father, who even in his sixties was admired for his shapely figure (fig. 18). The bushy red beard he grew during the Russo-Turkish War gave him what was regarded as a strong, virile, national appearance (fig. 19).

To be sure, by 1877 the beard had long been fashionable in western Europe. But in the context of the European myth, the beard carried negative meanings: It connoted peasants and clergy, the backward and uncouth elements of Russia, revolutionaries and Jews. The clean-shaven faces of the emperor and the nobility showed that they belonged to the advanced culture of the West. That the monarch wore a beard transformed him into a national symbol. The beard designated the tsar as someone from a distant, legendary past. The court historian S. S. Tatishchev wrote, "The majestic simplicity of his bearing, the artless, expressive, and perspicuous speech, even the broad, thick beard that he was the first member of the Ruling House to grow . . . and that so became the manly features of his face, all this gave him the look of a Russian *bogatyr'*, just as internally he was a *bogatyr'* in spirit."[123]

---

[120] Zaionchkovskii, *Krizis samoderzhaviia*, 231–33; Byrnes, *Pobedonostsev*, 144.

[121] "Dnevnik Aleksandra III, 1875–1880 gg.," 332; "Dnevnik Naslednika Tsesarevicha Velikogo Kniazia Aleksandra Aleksandrovicha, 1880g.," 355.

[122] "Pis'ma Aleksandra III Marii Fedorovne, 18 aprelia–18 sentiabria 1884g.," 13.

[123] Tatishchev, "Tsesarevich Aleksandr Aleksandrovich," 29–30.

18. Grand Duchess Maria Fedorovna and Grand Duke Alexander Aleksandrovich.
About 1870. GARF.

Within the new symbolic context, Alexander Aleksandrovich, the ungainly, sullen, and morose young man, was turned into an epitome of national strength and patriarchal authority. As the ministers lost a sense of
control, as the emperor appeared increasingly immoral and helpless, the
heir's appearance and behavior set him apart as one who could defend the
traditional values of autocracy. The national, religious rhetoric he had
learned and the Russian figure he now embodied would become elements of
a new authoritarian myth of power.

19. Grand Duke Alexander Aleksandrovich and Grand Duchess Maria Fedorovna.
About 1880. Page Corps Collection, Bakhmeteff Archive of Russian and
East European Literature and History, Rare Book and Manuscript Library,
Columbia University.

Alexander III's persona as ruler was made known in the first days after
the assassination of Alexander II. Anna Tiutcheva found a transformed individual when she saw him as tsar on March 25, 1881. His lack of confidence
and shyness were gone. "Somehow there appeared in him that calm and
majestic look, that full self-possession in movements, voice, and gaze, that
firmness and clarity in words, brief and defined—in brief, that free and natural majesty, combined with an expression of honor and simplicity, that were

always his distinguishing features." She believed that his shoulders, "those of a *bogatyr'*," would be able to bear the enormous burden of rule "with the simplicity of a pure heart and an honest consciousness of the obligations and rights placed in him by the lofty mission to which God has summoned him. Seeing him, you understand that he is conscious of himself as an emperor, that he has taken upon himself the responsibility and the prerogatives of power." She perceived in Alexander III "that national and popular strain" (*natsional'naia i narodnaia strunka*) that she had found lacking in his father.[124]

[124] Tiutcheva, *Pri dvore dvukh imperatorov*, 2:226–29.

Accession and Coronation

Murdered . . . murdered! Yes the Russian Tsar Murdered,
Our tender . . . kind Tsar! Now bleeding,
He is now a lifeless corpse!
He who with the love of a tsar,
Gave life to Rus', now lies mangled
In his Palace now, as the grave is made ready,
And the bells ring for the deceased. . . .

Oh beloved Tsar! Oh remain after death
Our protector!
May Your bloody image show us our emptiness
Our vacillation and weakness for all time!
And the blood that you shed for our sins,
Your sacred blood, be the salvation
The sobering of all our native land,
Like a sacrifice, like the last pledge of expiation,
The consummation of the exploit of your life!

—*Apollon Maikov, March 3, 1881*[1]

REPUDIATION AND APOTHEOSIS

The gruesome climax of the scenario of love marked the demise of the
Petrine image of monarch as the exemplification of Western monarchical
culture in Russia. As the government under Loris-Melikov struggled to find
a way to institute the reform, Alexander III and his advisers began to set
themselves apart from the old myth and to introduce new ways of elevating
the Russian monarch's authority. The pattern of enthronement and repudiation endemic to Russian monarchy resumed. The new monarch and his entourage sought to break free of the errors and constraints of the previous
reign, which they disavowed. But now they disavowed not only the previous
monarch's scenario but the very grounding of the myth itself, which no

---

[1] Published in *MV*, March 12, 1881, 3. The verse was apparently omitted even from the
prerevolutionary edition of Maikov's works (see his *Polnoe sobranie sochinenii*, 9th ed. [St.
Petersburg, 1914]).

longer was capable of elevating the monarch's authority and making it worthy of reverence and worship.

The break first occurred behind closed doors in the deliberations on Loris-Melikov's reform project, which Alexander III allowed to continue until he was sure of himself. At the March 8, 1881, meeting of the Council of Ministers, Pobedonostsev, now readmitted to the council, burst into a tirade against Loris-Melikov's reform proposals. "Pale as a sheet, clearly agitated," he began by claiming that representatives in constitutional states expressed only their own views, not those of the people. Alexander concurred, referring, as he had the year before, to the assertion by Danish ministers that the deputies in their assemblies did not express the people's real needs (see chapter 5). Pobedonostsev further defined all public political forums as "chatter houses" (*govoril'ni*) like the *zemstva* and the courts.[2] The possibility of the involvement of only a few representatives of the *zemstva* in the work of governmental institutions promised the advent of public politics, a process replete with conflict and recrimination that would reduce the emperor from a figure of mythical grandeur to a mortal engaged in petty and degrading struggle.

Russia was great, Pobedonostsev insisted, "thanks to the unlimited mutual trust and close bond between the people and the tsar." The people were "the preserver of all our valiant qualities, our good qualities. We can learn much from them."[3] The confounding of untrammeled and effective monarchical authority with ethnic Russianness that emerged in Alexander III's correspondence of the 1870s would define the future elite. Alexander II's scenario had sought to expand the elite by seeking the sympathy of Westernized moderate opinion. Alexander III and Pobedonostsev not only excluded these elements but categorized them as bearers of foreign influence antagonistic to the national spirit. The educated were thus split into those who were loyal to the national spirit and those who were disloyal, and the field of distrust expanded to include large numbers of the educated who earlier had been counted on to give at least passive support to the monarchy.

The motif of conquest by foreign rulers, transformed into Westernized Russian monarchs, could no longer exalt authority in an era valuing national participation and origin. The presentations of Alexander III would seek to portray the acts of conquest and domination in national images—to make him, and the past of Russian monarchy, appear native and Russian. Force,

---

[2] Zaionchkovskii, *Krizis samoderzhaviia*, 328–29; Perets, *Dnevnik*, 38–40. On the other hand, Alexander III's father-in-law, King Christian IX of Denmark, tried to convince Alexander, through Maria Feodorovna, to establish "an advisory estate," suggesting that had Alexander II made such a concession it might have saved his life. Such things, he wrote in a letter of April 14, 1881, "have been introduced throughout the entire civilized world and it is to be hoped will be received in Russia with rejoicing and gratitude and destroy infamous nihilism" (Preben Ulstrup, "Maria Feodorovna through Diaries and Letters," in *Maria Feodorovna: Empress of Russia* (Copenhagen, 1997), 144, 146.

[3] Perets, *Dnevnik*, 38.

reinvigorated and omnipresent, was the most prominent aspect of the new regime. As at the accession of Paul I and Nicholas I, guards' regiments invested the capital with a show of armed domination, reaffirming conquest as a motif of imperial presentation. Immediately after the assassination, the Pavlovsk Guards threw a cordon around the new emperor's residence, the Anichkov Palace, assuming responsibility for the security of him and his family. On March 25 the imperial family left the capital for the palace at Gatchina, which became Alexander III's favorite and principal residence, as it had been for Paul. The fortresslike structure of the palace symbolized the forbidding distance Alexander created between himself and the population, the walls of distrust replacing the illusion of personal affection played on by his father.[4]

Extreme measures of security were tight and conspicuous at the funeral procession and burial of Alexander II on March 7. Orders went out forbidding the building of stands and the viewing of the procession from balconies. Special agents from the City Duma inspected all houses along the route, and all windows facing the procession were ordered closed. The large numbers of police and troops along the way made it difficult to see the cortege. But the people succeeded in climbing onto rooftops and watching from the Neva.

There was little attention to discipline or order. State-Secretary E. A. Perets described officials straggling in groups, chatting with one another and even smoking along the way. Adjutants bearing the regalia did so "unceremoniously" (*beztseremonno*); one even held the cushion for the regalia under his arm. Many serving as the honor guard at the coffin failed to appear at the cathedral, and the Bureau of Ceremonies seemed in complete disorder. State-Secretary Perets contrasted the indifference of the court with the reverence of the common people. The newspaper accounts, too, focused on the large group of peasants, appearing for the first time in an imperial funeral procession. In the rear an old peasant was supported by both arms. He was "as white as the moon, in a caftan embroidered with gold." In this way, "even peasants accompanied their Tsar-Liberator to the place of rest from his imperial labors and his terrible grief."[5]

The myth drew on the shock and sense of humiliation that accompanied the assassination. The repudiation of the past was made possible by a general sense of shame for the act: shame that a civilized state could not protect the anointed of God. "This brought everyone to despair," wrote V. V. Voeikov, an officer in the Uhlans' Guards at the time. "Everyone felt some shame."[6] A day after the assassination, in a sermon delivered at St. Isaac's Cathedral, the rector of Petersburg Religious Academy Ioann Ianyshev dwelled on the

---

[4] Tatishchev, "Votsarenie Imperatora Aleksandra III," 10, 12; Voeikov, "Poslednie dni Imperatora Aleksandra II," 100, 114.

[5] Perets, *Dnevnik*, 30, 47; A. V. Bogdanovich, *Tri poslednikh samoderzhtsa* (Moscow-Petrograd, 1924), 48; Voeikov, "Poslednie dni Imperatora Aleksandra II," 107–10; *NV*, March 8, 1881, 1; *MV*, March 10, 1881, 3–4.

[6] Voeikov, "Poslednie dni Imperatora Aleksandra II," 89–90.

shame of an empire populated by many millions that could not protect "this Angel of the Russian land, in his unexampled beauty and purity illuminating the entire world and with maternal love warming the whole Russian land."[7]

In the eyes of the devout, the assassination transfigured Alexander from secular prince to religious martyr. Slavophile writers placed him in the tradition of early-Russian saint-princes who had been sanctified not for their holy lives but for their violent deaths, such as Saints Boris and Gleb, the brothers of Prince Iaroslav the wise, who awaited their murderers and died passively in imitation of Christ. Ivan Aksakov wrote, "His image stands before us now in the radiant glory of a Passion-sufferer. The people praying for the soul of Alexander II count him among the intercessors for the Russian land."[8] Indeed, the spot on the pavement where Alexander lay dying immediately became a popular shrine. Large numbers of people came and tried to wet their handkerchiefs in the blood and seize a shred of clothing, even a fragment of bone, as relics of the tsar-martyr. They placed wreaths of greens and flowers near the spot, sobbed, and uttered prayers, venerating the site as a shrine, just as they had prayed at the tomb of Paul I. A temporary chapel for the pavement, designed by Nicholas Benois, was erected with great speed and dedicated on April 17.[9]

The feelings of the people were expressed in a book of poems, *A Wreath for the Great Martyr-Tsar Sovereign Emperor Alexander the Blessed; Verse of the Common Man (prostoliudin)*, by G. M. Shvetsov. Seven thousand copies of the first two editions, subsidized by private donations, were distributed within two months. Shvetsov, a former serf, declared his gratitude for the emancipation and the other reforms, and his love for the tsar-emancipator, "the Greatest of the monarchs of the whole world and the unforgettable Friend of humanity." In the poems he repeatedly compared Alexander II to Christ and also described the gathering of people who came to weep for the memory of the martyred tsar at the chapel on the canal, which he called Golgotha.

> The evil, perfidious regicide!
> Can he shake Russia?
> The people is grateful to its monarchs,
> For Divine Mercy and Grace.[10]

[7] *MV*, March 4, 1881, 3.

[8] Quoted in Cherniavsky, *Tsar and People: Studies in Russian Myths*, 187.

[9] George P. Fedotov, *The Russian Religious Mind*, (Belmont, Mass., 1975), 2:110; Graf Fon-Pfeil', "Poslednie gody imperatora Aleksandra II; iz vospominanii iz russkoi sluzhby, 1878–1881," *Novyi zhurnal literatury, iskusstva i nauki* (March, 1908): part 2, 44–45; *MV*, April 17 and April 25, 1881.

[10] G. M. Shvetsov, *Venok Tsariu-Velikomucheniku Gosudariu Imperatoru Aleksandru II blagoslovennomu: stikhotvoreniia prostoliudina G. M. Shvetsova* (St. Petersburg, 1882), 7 and passim. Shvetsov thanked Count S. A. Stroganov and the merchant L. F. Militsyn, who was the elder of the commune for the memorial chapel on the canal (see title page, 27).

Shvetsov's stanzas expressed the beginnings of a popular cult of Alexander II, which spread in subsequent years, inspiring processions of the cross with Alexander II's portrait as an icon and nurturing expectations that the church would soon canonize the assassinated tsar.[11] But a cult of the dead tsar hardly sanctioned a break with the previous reign. The message from pulpits and in the publications of those close to the throne expressed the theme of repudiation rather than worship of Alexander. Father Ignatii, the abbot of the Sergiev Hermitage, near Peterhof, a cleric with close ties to the court, made this point in an appeal for contributions for a cathedral to mark the assassination. Ignatii's Christ was the victim of the people themselves. When betrayed by the Jews, Ignatii explained, Christ cried out, asking what the people had done. Alexander's blood also cried out,

My people, what have you done? For my whole life I have cared for you and your well-being, and you condemned me to death. My thoughts and heart were devoted to you . . . I made the expiatory sacrifice—the body and blood of Christ cleansing every sin, and you murdered me.[12]

Maikov's verse in the epigraph to this chapter, appearing in *Moskovskie Vedomosti*, pronounced Russia's sin to be weakness, while Katkov's editorials played on the theme of martyrdom to justify forceful repressive authority. Alexander II, he wrote, had been a "soft-hearted, long-suffering lover of mankind, who depreciated rather than elevated the majesty of his rights." Alexander's great exploit (*podvig*) of working for the benefit of the people had ended with a martyr's death. His kindness and tenderness had kept him from wielding his power. "May the supreme power in Rus' observe its sacred significance in all its plenitude, in all its freedom, in vital unity with the forces of the people."[13]

The word *love* continued to be used in official rhetoric but with a different meaning—Christian faith, identified with political devotion. In Afanasii Fet's "March 1," the poet identified love for the tsar with love for Christ. Love "burned more brightly" and "with new justice."[14] In Alexander III's scenario, "love" expressed faith and self-renunciation, not human sentiment for a kind and feeling human being. Love for the fallen emperor was to be expressed through religion and the church.

The theme was illustrated in a print issued in Moscow the next year, with Fet's poem as the caption, entitled "An Expression of National Grief in Memory of the Tsar'-Liberator and Martyr" (fig. 20). A bust of the late

[11] Polovtsov, *Dnevnik gosudarstvennogo sekretaria A. A. Polovtsova*, 1:392–93; N. A. Epanchin, *Na sluzhbe trekh imperatorov* (Moscow, 1996), 193–94.

[12] *Zhizneopisanie arkhimandrita Ignatiia (Malysheva) byvshego nastoiatelia troitse-sergievoi pustyni* (St. Petersburg, 1899), 92.

[13] MV, March 3, 1881, 1–2; March 5, 1881, 2; March 15, 1881, 3. These editorials are reproduced, with erroneous dating, in M. N. Katkov, *Sobranie peredovykh statei Moskovskikh Vedomostei 1881g.* (Moscow, 1898), 121–22, 124–25, 139–40.

[14] A. A. Fet, *Polnoe sobranie stikhotvorenii* (St. Petersburg, 1912), 397.

ВЫРАЖЕНІЕ НАРОДНОЙ СКОРБИ ПАМЯТИ ЦАРЮ ОСВОБОДИТЕЛЮ и МУЧЕННИКУ ПАДШЕМУ ОТЪ РУКИ ЗЛОДѢЕВЪ 1го МАРТА 1881 г.

20. *An Expression of National Grief in Memory of the Tsar-Liberator and Martyr.* Chromolithograph. 1882. GARF.

emperor set in the Kremlin is surrounded by peasants laying wreaths and weeping. An angel in the form of a young slender woman rising above the Bell Tower of Ivan the Great holds a crown of thorns above the statue.[15]

Alexander III eschewed the emotional appeals of the scenario of love. His accession manifesto, issued on the day of the assassination, repeated the

[15] "Aleksandr II: lubki," GARF, 678-1-1027.

phrases of his father's accession manifesto, but with few of the professions of personal loss contained in all Alexander II's first pronouncements.[16] The central themes of the new myth were announced in his famous manifesto of April 29, 1881, which declared his intention to maintain and wield his autocratic prerogatives.[17] The manifesto, written by Pobedonostsev, declared that it had been God's will to confer upon the new tsar "the Sacred duty of Autocratic rule."[18] Divine sanction now justified not only the tsar's right to rule but the system of rule—autocracy. The people's devotion was now demonstrated not in shows of reverence to the throne and the monarch but in prayers: "The warm prayers of the pious people, who are known in the entire world for the love and devotion to their sovereigns" would bring the blessings of God upon their tsar.

Thus the bond between tsar and people was to be religious. The "Voice of God" had summoned him "to turn vigorously to the task of Ruling, with hope in Divine Providence" after the shameful act of assassination. The use of the word *vigorously* (*bodro*) signified a revitalization and recrudescence of authority reminiscent of Nicholas I.[19] The faith in God, the people's prayers, charged him to act with energetic and ruthless action from above. *Vigor* became a common term in the rhetoric of conservative periodicals calling for reaffirmation of autocratic power.

The last lines of the manifesto provided the historical imagery for the national myth. It was under the protection of hereditary tsarist power and "in unbreakable union of Our land with it" that Russia had "survived great troubles (*smuty*) many times" and had emerged with strength and glory. The reference to the troubles, the *smuty*, made the seventeenth century the symbolic point of beginning, when the reaffirmation of authority ostensibly occurred with the popular backing of the assemblies of the land, leading ultimately to a restoration of order, an expansion of territory, and a strengthening of state institutions. The manifesto referred to Russia not as the Russian state or empire but as "the Russian land" ("*zemlia Russkaia*"), the term

---

[16] *PSZ* 3, no. 1 (March 1, 1881).

[17] Ibid., no. 118 (April 29, 1881).

[18] Pobedonostsev's initial draft read "the burden of supreme rule" (*bremia verkhovnogo pravleniia*). He then changed the words to make divine justification of absolute monarchy unequivocal (O. Maiorova, "Mitropolit Moskovskii Filaret v obshchestvennom soznanii kontsa XIX veka," 617).

[19] The usage may have been derived from Pushkin's poem of 1828, "To My Friends," in which he declared his admiration for Nicholas I.

> I simply love him:
> He rules us vigorously (*bodro*), honorably,
> He suddenly brought Russia to life,
> With war, with hopes, with labors . . .

The dictionary of Pushkin's language defines the word as "an attribute of a guard (*strazh*), hero, leader, tsar, or poet/prophet (particularly connected with Nicholas I)" (*Slovar' iazyka Pushkina* [Moscow, 1956], 1:150. I thank Natalia Mazour for alerting me to this connection.

used in the ancient chronicles, indicating that between the hereditary monarch and the "land," there had been an "unbroken" historical bond. Alexander called on the example of the medieval past to summon his "faithful subjects" to serve "Us and the State," to "eradicate the vile sedition disgracing the Russian land, to strengthen faith and morality, to work for the good upbringing of children, and to eliminate falsehood and depredation."[20]

On the day of the manifesto's promulgation, Alexander held the annual May Parade of the capital's guards regiments on the Field of Mars. The parade, the last in the uniforms of the previous reign, was a show of continuity with military tradition and proof that the autocracy ruled undaunted. The emperor appeared with a brilliant suite, including the German and Austrian ambassadors and extraordinary emissaries from Turkey and Persia. He rode by the arrayed regiments to their loud "Hoorah!" Then the infantry and cavalry units passed by the imperial tent in ceremonial march. The parade, like the tsar's reference to his determination "to turn vigorously to government," was a demonstration of the undiminished force and permanence of autocracy. At the beginning of the parade Alexander declared to the troops, "We, according to the examples of Our grandfather and father, will rule Autocratically and Monocratically (*Samoderzhavno i Edinoderzhavno*)" to which the troops responded with another loud "Hoorah!"[21]

In future years Alexander curtailed military ceremonials in the capital. He discontinued the Sunday reviews in the manége and the spring parades. Instead, he held his major parades in the winter on the Palace Square before the Winter Palace. The effect was to make the colorful spectacle somber and menacing. As one officer recalled, "Most often the skies were gray and, together with the troops' overcoats and the white patches of snow, composed a monotonous picture, like a gouache on gray paper. Only the dull gleam of the cuirassiers' armor and helmets enlivened the scene."[22]

NATIVE SIGNS: THE RETURN TO MOSCOW

The manifesto set forth the historical grounding of the myth, which would be revealed during Alexander's reign in ceremony, church architecture, and the goals of national policy (see chapter 7). In the first months of his reign, Alexander's scenario emphasized traits and signs that would associate him with the Russian people and distinguish him from the Westernized and educated elite. Some of the associations had originated with influential members of the "Russian party." But it was Alexander who identified them with the

---

[20] The close identification of the state with the land, rather than the church or the people, suggests Katkov's influence. See his editorial on Alexander's visit to Moscow, below in this chapter.

[21] Voeikov, "Poslednie dni Imperatora Aleksandra II," 132–41; *MV*, April 30, 1881, 3.

[22] B. V. Gerua, *Vospominaniia o moei zhizni* (Paris, 1969), 1:81, 92.

imperial persona and made them aspects of an image of a ruler who was transcendent because he embodied national traits now defined as intrinsic to Russian monarchy.

Alexander's gruff and surly manner immediately revealed his break with the graciousness of the Westernized elite. If Alexander II was feminine in his graciousness and capacity for endearment, Alexander III was masculine in his capacity to intimidate. The English correspondent Charles Lowe wrote, "His manner is cold, constrained, abrupt, and so suggestive of churlishness as often to deprive spontaneous favors of the honey of friendship for the sake of which they are accorded." He addressed guards' officers with the formal *vy*, rather than the familiar *ty*. He abandoned the traditional embrace with them—when they kissed the monarch on the shoulder—and instead merely shook hands. Many officers regretted the loss of the kindly paternal aura they had felt with Alexander II.[23] He also diminished the importance and prestige of the emperor's suite, which had comprised the emperor's comrades-in-arms. It ceased to be the brilliant assemblage of the tsar's inner circle, the array of European princes, grand dukes, and favorites, which showed that the Russian monarchy belonged to the royal culture of the West.[24]

Following the pattern of previous reigns, Alexander changed the design of military uniforms to show his imperial persona. The details of his uniforms gave them a virile national appearance, rather than a smart European look. The changes first affected the police and gendarmes, whose uniforms were designed to imitate the Russian caftan. Then the guards began to wear high Russian jackboots. Various regiments lost the ornaments that were their pride. The cuirassiers lost their armor and helmets, except for special gala occasions, and the Cossacks their shakos. The Hussars and Uhlans were combined with the Dragoons and deprived of their epaulets, sabers, and sultans. Even the tsar's suite began to wear uniforms resembling caftans, with white lambskin coats and wide *sharovary* with stripes. The tsar's initials on their epaulets were now in Slavonic lettering.[25]

Alexander exemplified the new "Russian style" of the military. He gave a rugged and forceful impression. Large, bearded, wearing jackboots and a

---

[23] Lowe, *Alexander III of Russia*, 322, 330; Voeikov, "Poslednie dni Imperatora Aleksandra II," 102–3.

[24] Voeikov, "Poslednie dni Imperatora Aleksandra II," 103, 143. Gradually, members of the suite were registered in guards' regiments and given civil ranks, which drove many into retirement. The emperor's initial lists of appointments indicated that he would appoint few new adjutant-generals. During the thirteen years of his reign, he appointed only 6 adjutant-generals, compared to 178 in his father's reign and 238 during the reign of Nicholas I. The total number of appointments of adjutants to his suite in his reign was 43, compared to 939 in his father's reign (Shepelev, *Otmenennye istorii*, 45).

[25] V. M. Glinka, *Russkii Voennyi Kostium XVIII-nachala XX veka* (Leningrad, 1988), 86–89; *Illiustrirovannoe opisanie peremen v obmundirovanii i snariazhenii imperatorskoi russkoi armii za 1881 god* (St. Petersburg, 1898); Zaionchkovskii, "Vyshee voennoe upravlenie," 88; Voeikov, "Poslednie dni Imperatora Aleksandra II," 141–43; Epanchin, *Na sluzhbe trekh imperatorov*, 194.

21. Alexander III. Chromolithograph. 1882. Russian National Library, St. Petersburg.

Russian cap, he took on the aspect of the *bogatyr'* (see fig. 21).[26] The officers soon were expected to grow beards as well. A decree issued shortly after Alexander's accession permitted members of the guards to wear beards, extending a right allowed only to the army at the end of the previous reign. (The guards had been allowed to grow beards but only with an unshaven strip on their chins of two finger-widths.) According to Captain Voeikov, everyone immediately grew beards in the guards, though a few considered that beards were only for peasants (*omuzhichanie*). These individuals, however, "vanished from the horizon."[27]

[26] In this respect the imagery of the monarch sought to assimilate the romantic nationalist sense of the popular hero Skobolev, who, until his death in June 1882, was regarded with misgivings as a rival for popular esteem (Rogger, "The Skobolev Phenomenon," 57–65).

[27] Voeikov, "Poslednie dni Imperatora Aleksandra II," 133.

The symbolic role of the guards and officer corps as public expressions of the autocrat's personality had changed, but the elite elements of the military continued to represent the bond between tsar and high nobility. Although he diminished the glitter of the elite, he continued to defend the supremacy of the officers corps and social distinctions in the hierarchy. In 1882 the war minister P. S. Vannovskii restored the more aristocratic sounding name "cadet corps" for the "military gymnasiums" established by Dmitrii Miliutin and replaced civilian instructors for academic subjects with officers. Alexander faithfully participated in the anniversary celebrations of the regiments and invited the officers to his table for breakfast on these occasions.[28] At the end of his reign a decree was prepared that legalized duels in the ranks, a measure taken to restore the élan of the elite guards' units.[29]

Emblems of Muscovite Russia were introduced to show the distinctively Russian character of the bond linking the tsar with his officers corps. Guards' regiments received new standards emblazoned with icons whose saint days corresponded to their regimental holidays. Eight-pointed Orthodox crosses were placed at the top of the flagstaffs. The guards, the principal forces of Petrine secularization and the image of the Westernized Russian military, now assumed a medieval and religious as well as national character.

The omnipresence of icons, the hush of common prayer with the tsar at Krasnoe Selo, the playing of hymns, all this lent the usual religious services at military ceremonies an exalted and inspiring tone in subsequent decades. Some grumbled that the Russian army comprised many who were not Orthodox but were Protestants, Catholics, Muslims, or sectarians and that the new symbols "would bring division and not unity" into the army. But this imperial cosmopolitan conception of the army received little sympathy in the elite officer corps. General Nicholas Epanchin, a general in the guards' regiments and future director of the Page Corps, dismissed such objections as indicating an absence of "a consciousness of state spirit." He recalled the words of General Suvorov: "We are Russians."[30] The sense that Orthodoxy denoted imperial unity and state consciousness began to take hold at the upper levels of the Russian military. General V. I. Gurko wrote that this fusion of "military and religious ceremonies" produced a feeling of elation as the monarch became the symbol of the people's might. Such ceremonies, he wrote, were the distinguishing feature of the Russian court, which he believed reflected the spirit of " 'the ancient Muscovite empire' permeated with religious and secular powers that complemented each other and formed one whole."[31]

Ancient Muscovy now replaced the reign of Peter the Great as the founding period of the Russian monarchy, when an abiding bond formed between tsar and people. This bond had been weakened but not destroyed by Peter

---

[28] Ibid., 133, 141–43, 161, 163.
[29] Zaionchkovskii, *Samoderzhavie i russkaia armiia*, 240–44, 299–307.
[30] Epanchin, *Na sluzhbe trekh imperatorov*, 194.
[31] V. I. Gurko, *Features and Figures of the Russian Past* (Stanford, 1939), 340.

the Great. It lived on incarnate in the shrines of Moscow, which now became a principal symbol of Russian monarchy.[32] Symbolic Moscow did not encompass modern Moscow, the city of factories, the liberal intelligentsia, and often fractious nobility. It was Moscow of the Kremlin and Red Square, epitomizing the spiritual unity between tsar and people and a devotion to the autocratic ruler. The new scenario detached imperial Russia from the imperial city and located it in a new time space, what Michael Bakhtin called a chronotope—a metaphor that identifies a certain time in the past with a particular place.[33]

The relationship between old and new capitals was increasingly stated in terms of struggle and antagonism, the resumption of a narrative of conflict rather than reconciliation between the national and Western elements of Russian life. An article in *Sankt-Peterburgskie Vedomosti,* printed a few days after the assassination, depicted St. Petersburg as a nest of "foreigners thirsting for the disintegration of Russia. . . . In St. Petersburg you meet many people who seem to be Russians but think like enemies of their native lands, like traitors to their people."[34] The Pan-Slavist Nicholas Ignat'ev, who would replace Loris-Melikov as the minister of the interior in May 1881, shared the view that the source of Russia's problems was a "powerful Polish-kike group" in Petersburg that controlled the banks, the press, and the courts. He wrote in a memorandum of March 12, "Every honest voice of the Russian land is drowned out by the cries of the Poles and the kikes, asserting that only the "intellectual" class should be heard and that Russian demands should be rejected as backward and unenlightened." To counter such influence Ignat'ev encouraged secret denunciations to the police and introduced the "temporary regulations" of August 14, 1881, which perpetuated many of the security measures in force since 1879. He urged Alexander to visit Moscow to convene an editing commission on administrative and financial measures. He looked forward to the calling of an Assembly of the Land in Moscow.[35]

In July 1881, during the annual maneuvers at Krasnoe Selo, Alexander unexpectedly announced his decision to travel to Moscow and the towns along the Volga. As Voeikov understood it, the tsar felt he had to leave his isolation "to appear before his people in the heart of Russia."[36] Alexander arrived in Moscow on July 17 and reaffirmed his bond with the people of Russia's national capital. The pictures in *Vsemirnaia Illiustratsia* show his

---

[32] For more on this theme, see my article "Moscow and Petersburg: The Problem of Political Center in Tsarist Russia, 1881–1914," in Sean Wilentz, ed., *Rites of Power: Symbolism, Ritual, and Politics since the Middle Ages* (Philadelphia, 1985), 244–74.

[33] On Michael Bakhtin's notion of the chronotope, see Katerina Clark, "Political History and Literary Chronotope: Some Soviet Case Studies," in Gary Paul Morson, ed., *Literature and History: Theoretical Problems and Russian Case Studies* (Stanford, 1986), 230–46.

[34] Cited in *MV,* March 11, 1881, 3.

[35] Zaionchkovskii, *Krizis samoderzhaviia,* 337–39.

[36] Voeikov, "Poslednie dni Imperatora Aleksandra II," 146.

22. Alexander III welcomed at Khodynskoe pole. Lithograph, Moscow,
July 1881. *Vsemirnaia Illiustratsiia.*

joyous welcome (fig. 22). After the presentation of bread and salt by the
Moscow town delegation, he declared, "The Late Little Father expressed his
gratitude many times to Moscow for her devotion. Moscow has always
served as an example for all of Russia. I hope this will be true in the future.
Moscow has attested and now attests that in Russia, Tsar and people com-
pose one, concordant (*edinodushnoe*) whole."[37] Then after a religious service, he stepped out onto the Red Staircase to bow three times and receive
the crowd's acclaim (fig. 23).[38] Voeikov described what he understood as the
significance of the act:

> This is a custom unique in the world—the autocratic tsar bows to his faithful
> subjects. This custom is the sacrament (*tainstvo*) of the contact (*obshchenie*) of
> the Russian Tsar with his people which conceals the unshakeable consciousness
> of the indestructible power of sacred Orthodox Rus' through all adversity.[39]

The same historical national theme surrounded Alexander's trip down the
Volga. He visited towns "from the most ancient times consecrated by devotion to Russia, where, after the great troubles of the seventeenth century,
true Russian people elected the Romanov house to the throne." Here, Alexander drew on the origins of the Romanov authority in 1613. *Vsemirnaia
Illiustratsia* carried a series of prints of his reception in the various towns

[37] *Vsemirnaia Illiustratsiia*, no. 656 (1881): 102.
[38] Ibid.
[39] Voeikov, "Poslednie dni Imperatora Aleksandra II," 148–49.

23. Alexander III at Red Staircase. Lithograph, July 1881.
Vsemirnaia Illiustratsiia.

showing the joy of the people and the gala spirit of the journey. When they came to Kostroma, "the cradle of the Romanov house," the emperor and empress were met by enthusiastic peasants, going into the water up to their waists, who seized the wheels of their carriages.[40]

Katkov, in *Moskovskie Vedomosti*, interpreted the popular acclaim as the people's resounding affirmation of state power. He welcomed the tsar to Moscow "to come in contact with the Russian Land in the shrine of her past, in her heart, in the very source of her strength." He emphasized that all economic development, philanthropy, and freedom in Russia came from the state, that the state was the mainstay of the people's well-being. In Russia, he insisted, no contradiction, no antagonism, "not the slightest disagreement," could arise between the interests of the people and those of the state. The various estates of the realm, he argued, should assist the state, or, more specifically, the police, in fighting sedition.[41] *Moskovskie Vedomosti* reported on the joyous welcome of the tsar in the Volga towns. This was a display not of personal love but of "that secret spiritual bond that unites the Russian Tsar with his people. A touching, heartening, scene! May [this bond] be preserved like the eternal sun, whose wonderful rays dispel the deluge of enemies alien to the Russian land!"[42]

In the first months of Alexander's reign, a rift opened between the more Slavophile and the more statist of his supporters. The former saw the national characteristics of the monarchy deriving from direct contact with the Russian people, realized in an Assembly of the Land (*zemskii sobor*). The latter regarded the Orthodox Church and the autocratic state as the expression of the people's spirit. The Slavophile viewpoint was represented by such figures as the minister of the interior Nicholas Ignat'ev and such leaders of the monarchist organization "Holy Retinue" (*Sviataia Druzhina*) as Illarion Vorontsov-Dashkov, who had been at Alexander's side at Rushchuk and would become minister of the court, and the Pan-Slavist general Rostislav Fadeev. The statist viewpoint was defended by Katkov and Pobedonostsev.

Those who hoped to establish direct bonds between tsar and people prepared two major initiatives in the first year of Alexander's reign: the establishment of a government newspaper for the people and the calling of an Assembly of the Land. Fadeev promoted the idea of a peasant newspaper in the administration. It was an idea that appealed to Alexander who, as heir, had headed a special conference for the publication of cheap books for the people.[43] *Sel'skii Vestnik* began publication under the auspices of the Ministry of the Interior in the summer of 1881. The newspaper represented the

[40] Ibid., 151–54; *Vsemirnaia Illiustratsiia*, no. 657 (1881): 120–22; no. 658 (1881): 142.

[41] Katkov, *Sobranie peredovykh statei Moskovskikh Vedomostei 1881g.*, 337–39; MV, July 18, 1881, 3. The dating of these editorials in *Sobranie peredovykh statei Moskovskikh Vedomostei 1881g.* is erroneous.

[42] MV, July 26, 1881, 3.

[43] Anan'ich and Ganelin, "R. A. Fadeev, S. Iu. Vitte," 315–23; B. G. Litvak, *Russkoe pravoslavie; vekhi istorii* (Moscow, 1989), 374–75.

monarchy's first attempt to utilize the mass-circulation press for its own purpose. Though it could not rival the principal urban dailies, it was widely distributed in local offices of the Ministry of the Interior. It gained a following among the peasants, and by 1905 its circulation reached 150,000.[44]

Sel'skii Vestnik carried sermons, religious stories, information about agriculture, as well as exhortations to self-help and temperance and featured stories about the tsar's work in government, his celebrations, and his trips. The first issue described the tsar's trip to Moscow, which it called one of the "significant events" of the new reign, and the peasants' joy at seeing him along the way.[45] It presented the tsar and his family as sympathetic human beings, recognizable to the common people. The second issue carried an article, "How the Tsar's Family Spent Their Summer." It told how the imperial family lived in a small house, where the sovereign and his wife (*gosudar' i gosudarynia*) received reports and worshiped. The article made particular mention of their love of church singing and the piety of the heir, the grand duke Nicholas Aleksandrovich. An article in the third issue related the imperial family's meeting with a fisherman, his wife, and children, who welcomed them with bread and salt. They visited his home, and the tsar discussed fishing with the old man and his son. The empress served as Godmother for the child born to the fisherman's daughter-in-law and sent a silver tea service to mark the event.[46] Newspaper surveys indicated that the peasants liked the newspaper largely for the advice on farming.[47] But in official thinking, the rural sales sustained the belief in the basic affinity between peasant and emperor that supported his rule against the educated classes.

Fadeev and Vorontsov-Dashkov continued to press for an Assembly of the Land, and in September 1882 Ignat'ev submitted his project for an assembly to Alexander. Such an assembly, both Ignat'ev and Alexander believed, would enable the tsar to reach beyond the bureaucracy. Allowing direct contact with the people, an assembly would exclude the intelligentsia from state affairs. An assembly meeting in Moscow, Ignat'ev argued, would bring Alexander's rule closer to its ancient historical roots. The project, drafted by P. D. Golokhvastov, an official in the Ministry and an associate of Ivan Aksakov, suggested that the number of deputies be set at about three thousand and that the assembly meet in the Cathedral of Christ the Savior in Moscow, which had finally been completed.[48]

Clearly such an assembly did not contradict the principle of autocratic rule in the tsar's mind. But his principal advisers thought otherwise. When news of the project reached Pobedonostsev, it produced what the historian

---

[44] See James S. Krukones, *To the People: The Russian Government and the Newspaper Sel'-skii Vestnick ("Village Herald"), 1881–1917* (New York, 1987), especially 22, 70–78, 247, 253.

[45] *Sel'skii Vestnik*, September 1, 1881, 3–5.

[46] Ibid., September 8, 1881, 9; September 15, 1881, 13.

[47] McReynolds, *The News under Russia's Old Regime*, 107.

[48] Zaionchkovskii, *Krizis samoderzhaviia*, 450–52.

Peter Zaionchkovskii described as the effect of a bombshell. Pobedonostsev wrote to Alexander, "If *will and direction* will shift from the government *to any kind* of popular meeting it will be *a revolution, the ruin of the government and the ruin of Russia.*" Katkov, horrified, wrote in *Moskovskie Vedomosti* that the demands for a *zemskii sobor* always came from the revolutionary camp, that the revolutionary Nechaev, when being led out of the courtroom, furiously shouted *"zemskii sobor, zemskii sobor."*[49] Alexander quickly withdrew his backing for the project, and at the end of May 1882 Ignat'ev was replaced by Count Dmitrii Tolstoi, the former minister of education whose monarchist views were not beclouded by Slavophile fantasies.

THE CORONATION OF 1883

The historical union with the Russian people and the Russian land took place in the realm of symbol and ceremony. The rites and celebrations of the imperial coronation merged the two themes of the national myth, the conquest from above of a powerful and authoritative native ruler and the expression of a warm bond between him and the Russian people. The cries of the people on the streets were presented as expressions of this bond, and the Orthodox Church appeared as its institutional embodiment, the bearer of the nation's religious and monarchical spirit.

The very fact that the coronation took place was presented as a sign of the recrudescence of the monarchy—showing that the tsar enjoyed a popular mandate. The government waited two years to stage the event, the longest interval between accession and coronation in the dynasty's history. Rumors circulated that there would be no coronation or that it would take place in secret. The manifesto announcing the coronation on January 24, 1883, promised that the celebration would put an end to "those monstrous rumors and gossip that have filled foreign newspapers regarding Russia."[50] Indeed, Fadeev looked on a failed coronation as the last chance for convening an assembly. He hoped, he wrote euphemistically in a letter, for "a not completely successful outcome of the coronation," which would cause panic in the government.[51]

Apprehensions mounted as the preparations began. The emperor's sojourn in the capital was to be brief—only two weeks; Alexander I's had been six weeks, Nicholas I's nearly two months, Alexander II's four weeks. "Everyone feared for the Tsar," Grand Duke Constantine Konstantinovich

---

[49] Ibid., 461–65, 468; Katkov, *Sobranie peredovykh statei Moskovskikh Vedomostei 1881g.*, 233–34; *MV*, May 12, 1882, 2.

[50] *PSZ* 3, no. 1330 (January 24, 1883).

[51] Anan'ich and Ganelin, "R. A. Fadeev, S. Iu. Vitte," 321.

wrote in his diary."[52] During his stay the emperor was surrounded by a large guard, his departure times were kept secret, and crowds who approached him too closely were dispersed by bands of Cossacks.[53] The coronation manifesto on May 16 appealed for the reconciliation of "the entire disturbed order," the enhancement of justice and enlightenment of the people "in the truths of the faith," and the strengthening of "loyalty to duty and law" of all callings in the population.[54]

The coronation events took place without incident, which produced a sense of relief.[55] The authorities skillfully used the native and foreign press to give the impression of broad support. The press coverage of Alexander III's coronation far exceeded previous coronations' and demonstrated the monarchy's determination to show itself as a national, democratic institution. The government invited forty-nine foreign correspondents to the festivities and paid all expenses, including transportation. Five foreign correspondents—from England, France, the United States, and Germany—and seven Russian journalists, including Katkov, Aksakov, Suvorin, and Komarov, occupied coveted places in the cathedral.[56]

Niva and *Vsemirnaia Illiustratsiia* carried descriptions with numerous lithographs of the events. *Sel'skii Vestnik* devoted several issues to the coronation. *Illiustrirovannyi Mir* published a lively report with abundant pictures of the ceremonies and personages involved in the event. The most detailed popular account was published by the Pan-Slavist journalist and general Vissarion Komarov, the publisher of the chauvinistic newspaper *Svet*, with a circulation of more than seventy thousand. Komarov had been associated with Fadeev and the members of the *Sviataia Druzhina*, and his volume clearly enjoyed government support.[57]

The various descriptions reproduced disagreements between the statist and Slavophile conceptions of the national monarchy among tsarist officials.

[52] B. Kn. Constantine Konstantinovich, "Dnevnik, 5 marta-25 iulia, 1883g.," GARF, 660-1-21, 61.

[53] Grand Duke Alexander Mikhailovich, *Once a Grand Duke*, 71; Tvardovskaia, *Ideologiia poreformennogo samoderzhaviia*, 226.

[54] *PSZ* 3, no. 1583 (May 16, 1883).

[55] Regarding the joy in St. Petersburg following the successful completion of the coronation festivities, see K. Golovin, *Moi vospominaniia*, 2:34–36.

[56] "Svod svedenii i dannykh o sv. koronatsii v 1883 godu," RGIA, 472-65–188, 142–43; the correspondent of *Le temps* wrote that sixty-seven correspondents, Russian and foreign, had been authorized to follow the coronation events (*Le temps*, May 29, 1883, 1). The *Times* remarked in an editorial that the Russian government had "the greatest desire to favor the press" (*Times of London*, May 28, 1883, 11; *Koronatsionnyi Sbornik: Koronovanie v Moskve; 14 maia 1896* (St Petersburg, 1899), 151; Lowe, *Alexander III of Russia*, 70.

[57] V. Komarov, *V pamiat' sviashchennogo koronovaniia Gosudaria Imperatora Aleksandra III i Gosudarynia Imperatritsy Marii Fedorovny* (St. Petersburg, 1883); BE, 30:816; Komarov also published a brief, less detailed and evocative account in Moscow (V. Komarov, *Sviashchennoe koronovanie Imperatora Aleksandra III i Imperatritsy Marii Fedorovny* [Moscow,

The coronation album gave the officially approved portrayal of the event.[58] The format of the volume made it clear that it was seeking to evoke the culture of early Russia. The title and much of the text were printed in Slavic revival lettering. It was the first coronation album to contain artistic evocations of Muscovy. Russian folk-style illustrations depict the tsar and boyars as burly *bogatyri*. The text is brief, sixty-five pages, of which only eleven describe the ceremonies of the coronation themselves. The message is blunt and unmistakable. The historical introduction identifies the Orthodox Church as the bearer of the Russian national spirit. It describes the coronation as "this sacred, solemn, and all-national act that expresses the historical union of the Tsar with his State, his precept with his church—that is, with the soul and conscience of his people—and, finally, the union of the Tsar and the people with the Tsar of Tsars, in whose hands rests the fate of tsars and peoples."[59] The church is thus "the soul and conscience of the people," and it is the Orthodox Church that bestows popular sanction. The people themselves are hardly mentioned in the album.

The color illustrations are the work of exclusively Russian painters, including a number of the "itinerants" (*peredvizhniki*). Their contribution to the album makes clear Alexander's intention to encourage a national school of art.[60] Constantine Savitskii (fig. 24) presents the entry procession down Tver boulevard as a mass of guardsmen and a few Asian horsemen with the emperor in their midst. The artist makes no effort to bring the spectators into the scene as Zichy had in Alexander II's entry procession. The entry appears as a triumphal show of force. In Vasilii Polenov's rendering of the greeting at the Assumption Cathedral, Alexander is flanked by his brothers, also wearing beards and presenting strong martial images. The beards bring their appearance closer to that of the clergy, unlike their predecessors whose sleek, clean-shaven faces had denoted the sharp difference between secular and ecclesiastical realms (fig. 25).

1883]). On Komarov and the *Sviataia Druzhina*, see Anan'ich and Ganelin, "R. A. Fadeev, S. Iu. Vitte," 300; BE, 30:816.

[58] *Opisanie sviashchennogo koronovaniia Ikh Imperatorskikh Velichestv Gosudaria Imperatora Aleksandra tret'ego i Gosudaryni Imperatritsy Marii Fedorovny Vseia Rossii* (St. Petersburg, 1883). The album came out in an edition of five hundred copies, three hundred of which were in Russian, two hundred in French. It cost 92,376 rubles to produce the five hundred copies compared to 120,000 rubles for the four hundred copies of Alexander II's album ("Koronatsionnyi sbornik i khudozhestvennyi al'bom," RGIA, 472-65-113, 1). It was published under the Office for the Production of State Papers (*Ekpeditsiia Zagotovleniia Gosudarstvennykh Bumag*), which introduced more advanced technological capacities for state publications and paper money.

[59] *Opisanie sviashchennogo koronovaniia . . . Gosudaria Imperatora Aleksandra tret'ego i Gosudaryni Imperatritsy Marii Fedorovny Opisanie sviashchennogo koronovaniia*, 2.

[60] On Alexander III's encouragement of the Russian realists, see Elizabeth Valkenier, *Russian Realist Art. State and Society: The Peredvizhniki and Their Tradition* (Ann Arbor, Mich., 1977), 123–27, 132–34; Norman, "Alexander III as a Patron of Russian Art," 28–33.

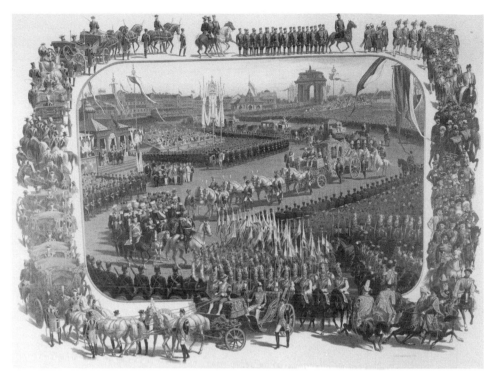

24. Alexander III's Coronation Entry. Color lithograph from painting by Constantine Savitskii. From *Opisanie sviashchennogo koronovaniia . . . Gosudaria Imperatora Aleksandra tret'ego i Gosudaryni Imperatritsy Marii Fedorovny*. Slavic and Baltic Division, New York Public Library. Astor, Lenox, and Tilden Foundations.

Indeed, the coronation album as a whole is a solemn statement of the reign's might, of autocracy reborn through reconquest. This theme was expressed in the numerous depictions of military ceremonies, which appear for the first time in a coronation album. They show the emperor at the consecration of the standards of the Preobrazhenskii and Semenovskii regiments, at various parades, and at the feast for the regiments at Sokolniki.[61] The emperor on horseback, in Russian hat and boots, dominates the scene.

While watching Alexander's entry into Moscow on May 10, the English correspondent Charles Lowe felt as if he were witnessing a triumph. He saw a "scarlet crowd" in the distance that looked like a British regiment but turned out to be the emperor's personal convoy, consisting of "three-squad-

[61] In addition, a special album was published containing the assembling, disposition, and responsibilities of the military units gathered for the coronation (*Opisanie sbora i zaniatii voisk pod Moskvoiu vo vremia sviashchennogo koronovaniia Ikh Imperatorskikh Velichestv v 1883 godu* [St. Petersburg, 1883]).

25. Welcome of Alexander III at Uspenskii Cathedral. Color lithograph from painting by Vasilii Polenov. *Opisanie sviashchennogo koronovaniia . . . Gosudaria Imperatora Aleksandra tret'ego i Gosudaryni Imperatritsy Marii Fedorovny.* Slavic and Baltic Division, New York Public Library. Astor, Lenox, and Tilden Foundations.

rons of Circassians and Don Cossacks, all finely made, handsome men and bravely mounted." He cited a verse:

> What conquests brings he home!
> What tributaries follow him to Rome
> To grace in captive bonds his chariot wheels!

Then came deputies from the numerous "Asiatic tribes" and "Cossack tribes." "All eyes turned on these picturesque strangers from the Far East, who pace along on their richly caparisoned steeds. . . . on they ride before the mighty Monarch."[62]

The coronation played a dual role in the presentation of a nationalist imperialism. Not only did the representatives of colorful Asiatic peoples impress foreign observers, but the coronation impressed those representatives with the power and wealth of the Russian tsar. A delegation of chieftains from Turkestan invited to the coronation were presumably so overwhelmed with the magnificence of the events and the shows of military might that they decided that further resistance was hopeless. They formed a Russian party that in 1884 petitioned for admission to the Russian empire.[63]

Komarov's volume, *V pamiat' sviashchennago koronovaniia*, expressed a feeling of national superiority and colonial disdain for these peoples. The account described the Asian representatives as "a messy crowd, bumping into one another . . . a murderously funny procession of savages." They wore "the most motley robes that were extraordinarily garish and strange costumes in bright colors. Some dress like women, others tightly like ballet dancers." One could not but "give a good laugh" at a Kalmyk mulla who rode on horseback wearing a wide red robe and a yellow cap "like the chorus from *Ruslan and Ludmilla*."[64]

The emperor's approach was announced by a roar that Lowe thought resembled nothing he had ever heard from English crowds. "They do not strike the ear like sharp successive explosions of pent-up enthusiasm but fall on the senses like the steady, continuous roar of an ever advancing sea. . . . every straining Slavonic throat utters a deep and loud 'Hoorah,' " as the "two squadrons of ponderous cuirassiers"—the Cavalier Guards—marched before the tsar himself.[65] Komarov interpreted the roar as the voice of the family of the Russian people welcoming their father and mother. "This family of one hundred million is the basis of the Russian state's existence, the condition for its structure and life, the foundation of general equality before

---

[62] *Times of London*, May 23, 1883, 5.

[63] John P. LeDonne, *The Russian Empire and the World, 1700–1917: The Geopolitics of Expansion and Containment* (New York, 1997), 132; Prince A. Lobanov-Rostovskii, *Russia and Asia* (New York, 1933), 172. On the influence of the new sense of colonial superiority on imperial policy toward newly subjected territories, see Andreas Kappeler, *Russland als Vielvölkerreich; Entstehung, Geschichte, Zerfall* (Munich, 1992), 174–75.

[64] Komarov, *V pamiat' sviashchennogo koronovaniia*, 56–57.

[65] *Times of London*, May 23, 1883, 5.

Tsar and law, the source and preserver of every living atom entering into the composition of the Russian people."[66]

After the traditional prayer at the chapel of the Icon of the Iberian Mother of God, the imperial family proceeded to Red Square, where they entered the scenes of the seventeenth century. When they appeared on the square, a choir of seventy-five hundred singers and an orchestra of more than three thousand musicians performed the "Glory" chorus from Glinka's *Life for the Tsar*, as arranged by Tchaikovsky. The chorus, sung at the conclusion of the opera when the Moscow population is awaiting the newly elected Michael Romanov, elevated the tsar into the theatrical world of legend. Tchaikovsky had simplified the chorus and included a transition to the singing of "God Save the Tsar!" thus linking the presumed seventeenth-century and nineteenth-century expressions of popular devotion.[67] Observers on the square exulted at the crowd's stirring response to the tsar. The *Novoe Vremia* correspondent wrote, "Such shouts of rapture resounded that I never have heard."[68] Lowe concluded that "as far as one can judge from the popular manifestations of this day, there is everything to show that the throne which he ascends on Sunday next is securely based on his subjects' love and devotion."[69]

Such reports heartened Katkov, who believed that the people's cries indicated that Russian monarchy did not work according to the natural law theories of Western liberalism. The telegrams of Western correspondents had told Europe about "the people's unusual patriotic enthusiasm" and "the Russian people's devotion to its autocratic Tsar, who needs no contracts with his people to strengthen his supreme power."[70]

---

[66] Komarov, *V pamiat' sviashchennogo koronovaniia*, 57–58.

[67] Alexander Poznansky, *Tchaikovsky: The Quest for the Inner Man* (New York, 1991), 420; Anthony Holden, *Tchaikovsky: A Biography* (New York, 1995), 226.

[68] *NV*, May 12, 1883, 1. The text sung on the occasion follows:

> Glory, Glory to our Russian Tsar!
> Given us by the Lord a Sovereign-Tsar!
> Moscow awaits you and our sacred Kremlin
> Appear before the people our native father!
>
> Glory, Glory, Holy Rus'!
> Celebrate the festive day of your Tsar!
> Rejoice, make merry, your Tsar comes forth
> The people meet the Sovereign Tsar.
>
> Greetings to the longed-for in his capital,
> Greetings to your most beautiful Tsaritsa,
> Greetings to the longed-for, given by the Lord
> You are strong with the love of holy Rus'
> You are the leader of Orthodoxy, God is with you
> Greetings, Greeting, Hoorah! Hoorah!

[69] *Times of London*, May 23, 1883, 5.

[70] *Sobranie per. st. 1883g.*, 231–32.

Komarov's volume, reflecting a Slavophile viewpoint, expressed a direct bond between people and emperor, an organic fusion. On May 15, the day of the coronation ceremonies, the people appeared as "a vital force, concealing in itself the presence of God." He saw a physical sense of merger of people and sovereign. His key term was *splosh'*, meaning "total," a variant of the verb *splotit'*, meaning "to fuse," etymologically connected with the word used to describe binding longitudinal sections of wood. The national rapture (*narodnyi vostorg*) submerged the individual in the masses:

> This national rapture, this national unity seizing everyone, these ubiquitous gigantic crowds of people, extending without limit as far as the eye can see, these cries of rejoicing, this sincere heartfelt "Hoorah!" rising from the breast—all this fused and united (*splachivali*) in one whole, all and everyone. It elevated and diminished each person.[71]

For Komarov, Moscow was the embryo of Russia's "state existence" (*gosudarstvennoe bytie*) and of Russian and Slavic unity. The Kremlin was the symbolic manifestation of the historical spirit that imbued the people of Moscow. The people of Moscow, "concealing in themselves the presence of God," were "crude and illiterate according to bureaucrats' statistics." But they had in them "something tender, sensitive, impressionable, a great heart in all cases of state life." The people of Moscow were suffused with "a feeling of conscious devotion to the Tsar and state."[72]

Alexander III's entry and the subsequent festivities evoked organic ethnic bonds that united tsar and people, giving new meaning to the Russian coronation. No longer was the coronation presented as the European emperor being greeted and thereby accepted by the population of Moscow, the synechoche of the nation; the Russian tsar demonstrated and thereby validated his national persona by renewing his attachment to the source of the national spirit among the people of Moscow. Alexander III's and Nicholas II's coronations were less the fusion of the Western and Russian polarities of imperial culture than a coming home: a denial of these polarities and an affirmation of the national identity of the Russian emperor. On the day of the coronation, May 15, Alexander III met and made contact with the Russian people. The Kremlin square, holding the crowds following the ceremony, announced by the tolling of bells, seemed to open out to all of Russia. It was as if the cathedral had no walls, Komarov wrote, "as if the coronation occurred on a boundless square, under an open sky, as an all-national event (*vsenarodno*)."[73]

To show the prominence of the people, as at Alexander II's coronation in 1856, a delegation of peasants marched at the beginning of the procession

[71] Komarov, *V pamiat' sviashchennogo koronovaniia*, 109–110.
[72] Ibid., 110–11.
[73] Ibid., 111.

to the cathedral.[74] They appeared almost anomalous amid the brilliant uniforms of the guards and courts. The description in the coronation album read, "*Volost'* elders from all Russian provinces, communal heads (*gminnye voity*) from the Kingdom of Poland, and the elder of the *belopashtsy* (descendants of Ivan Susanin) stood out in the surrounding magnificence with their simple but varied attire."[75] Other accounts used similar words. Komarov focused on the elder who represented the descendants of Ivan Susanin, emphasizing that he would be one of twelve permitted to watch the ceremonies in the cathedral; in 1856, at the coronation of Alexander II, all had waited in a nearby building.[76] The author described how the emperor was seized by the rapture of the crowd in the Kremlin as he was about to enter the Assumption Cathedral: His benevolence was expressed as two great tears that wet his eyes—"the most majestic gift that Russia received." The tears were "the guarantee of the most majestic spiritual purity, the good intentions and goodwill of the Tsar, the guarantee of the firmness of power, this blessedness of the heart, the pledge of love."[77]

During the rites of coronation Alexander's measured, sluggish manner was taken by Komarov as a sign of dignity and strength. He described the drama: The tsar received the crown from the metropolitan and placed it on his own head "with a firm hand, unhurried calm, and a smooth movement." The adjutant-general Edward Baranov brought him the scepter, and Valuev presented the orb "with the low bow of a boyar." "A feeling of spiritual contentment descended on all present." The empress approached the emperor and knelt before him while he placed the small crown on her head. Then he conferred on her the purple and gold chain of Andrew the First-Called. "All this was performed with great feeling and without the slightest hurry." He kissed her with "so pure and elevated a kiss, one that spoke of endless, endless [*sic*] friendship and love." The grand duke Constantine Konstantinovich wrote in his diary, "I cannot describe, cannot express how touching and tender it was to see these embraces of husband and wife and kisses under the imperial crown—this ordinary human love in the glitter and radiance of imperial majesty."

The emperor and empress now sat on their coronation thrones in full regalia and the Protodeacon recited the full imperial title, followed by a loud prayer for "many years" and a 101-gun salute. The tsar then left the throne, fell to his knees, and pronounced the prayer of Solomon, asking for divine help in his "great service." Those present repeated the moving prayer to

---

[74] Only representatives of the state peasants, not of landlords' serfs, had made up the opening delegation at the coronation of Alexander II.

[75] *Opisanie sviashchennogo koronovaniia . . . Gosudaria Imperatora Aleksandra tret'ego i Gosudaryni Imperatritsy Marii Fedorovny Opisanie sviashchennogo koronovaniia,* 17.

[76] Komarov, *V pamiat' sviashchennogo koronovaniia,* 119–20.

[77] Ibid., 125.

themselves. The grand duke Constantine could not hold back his tears. "How many warm prayers were raised at this moment!" he wrote.[78]

The paintings reproduced in the coronation album convey the emperor's overpowering presence. Ivan Kramskoi's rendering of the moment of crowning is close up, focused completely on Alexander who occupies almost two-thirds of the picture (fig. 26). The emperor dwarfs the clergymen at his side, his beard and balding head dominating the picture. The cathedral is a mere blur in the background. Alexander has an intimidating, crushing aspect, but his face is soft and pallid. The full-page portrait by A. P. Sokolov of Alexander on his coronation throne in mantle, holding the orb and scepter, was the first of its kind in a coronation album. Sokolov's painting allows no distance between the viewer and the emperor's looming, impassive figure.[79]

At the coronation Alexander found his ceremonial persona. He towered over everyone; his size, his red hair and beard, his "bright" eyes, all made for an impressive sight. "There is something grandiose in him," the artist V. I. Surikov remarked of Alexander in the cathedral; he was "a true representative of the people."[80] He seemed to fit, to express the notion of a national ruler. D. N. Liubimov, a secondary school student serving in the "Holy Guard" for the coronation, later recalled the great majesty of Alexander dressed in the imperial regalia: "This extraordinary garb that so befit the holy places of the Kremlin became him perfectly: his enormous height, his stoutness, his great beard. A truly Russian tsar, of Moscow and all Rus'."[81] State Secretary A. A. Polovtsov wrote in his diary, "One felt that here it was not a case of an empty formality but of a celebration having a national sense and taking place not without a fierce underground struggle." He noted that the courtiers attending the tsar were nearly all from old-Russian families, while the German noblemen were holdovers from the previous reign.[82]

In Komarov's presentation, the ceremony submerged individual feelings in a spiritual, political union. The key moment of fusion occurred after the tsar had crowned himself, during the "prayer for the tsar." Then Alexander stood, and the entire assemblage knelt before him. At a signal, all those awaiting in the stands of the Kremlin also fell to their knees. Komarov claimed that he later heard that the people outside the Kremlin, along the Moscow River did the same, as did the "Asiatics" among them. "This was so solemn a moment, during which the entire human being fused with an invisible world and ascended to the Creator." Again the people shed tears of

[78] Ibid., 130–33; B. Kn. Constantine Konstantinovich, "Dnevnik, 5 marta–25 iulia, 1883g.," 68.

[79] Opisanie sviashchennogo koronovaniia . . . Gosudaria Imperatora Aleksandra tret'ego i Gosudaryni Imperatritsy Marii Fedorovny Opisanie sviashchennogo koronovaniia, 21, 22, 23.

[80] Tvardovskaia, "Aleksandr III," 258.

[81] D. N. Liubimov, "Russkaia smuta deviatisotykh godov, 1902–1906," BAR, 93.

[82] Polovtsov, Dnevnik, 1:95. Among the Russians, he mentioned Golitsyn, Gagarin, Iusupov, Meshcherskii, and Uvarov; among the Germans, Nesselrode, Grot, Pahlen, and Sivers.

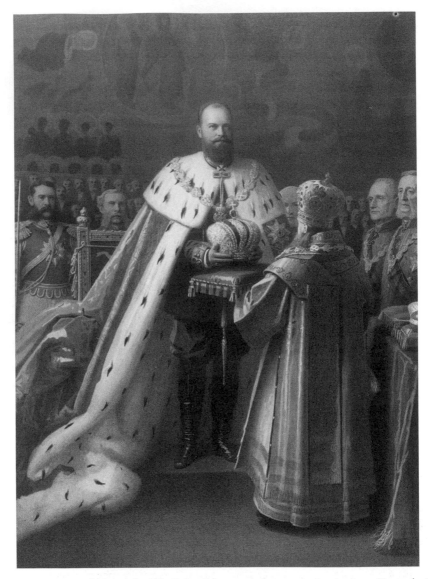

26. Crowning of Alexander III. Color lithograph from painting by Ivan Kramskoi.
*Opisanie sviashchennogo koronovaniia . . . Gosudaria Imperatora Aleksandra
tret'ego i Gosudaryni Imperatritsy Marii Fedorovny.* Slavic and Baltic Division,
New York Public Library. Astor, Lenox, and Tilden Foundations.

gratitude and *umilenie*, but they were an expression not of love but "of a unity and community (*obshchnost'*) of interests."[83]

After the anointment and communion the emperor and empress, in full regalia, walked in procession across the Kremlin square to the Archangel and Annunciation cathedrals, accompanied by the crowd's loud "Hoorah!" "A 'Hoorah' that was unforgettable," Komarov wrote. He, like Lowe, described the Russian shout as distinctive. "Here was expressed all the people's love. All the nature of the Russian man, with his infinite kindness and selfless spirit of sacrifice, unleashed that mighty inimitable cry . . . That 'Hoorah' is unique in the entire world. That 'Hoorah' belongs only to the Emperor, to the leader of Russian might and glory, the bearer of the people's hopes and the people's beliefs." He described the tsar's measured, imposing gait: "The Tsar walked quietly and smoothly. With calm step, his head bowed slightly down, combining an expression of humility with firmness, he moved forward." The comparison now was with a believer going to a religious service, about to undergo a religious experience. " 'The Tsar goes through a sea of sounds,' they said, but it would be more accurate to say that the Tsar walked with the same look and feeling as the first Christians who went to take communion. So much clarity, purity, firmness."[84]

The imperial family followed the procession consisting of delegations from all estates, described conventionally as "all of Russia." After the services in the Archangel and Annunciation cathedrals, the emperor and empress ascended the Red Staircase. They turned, and the square fell silent. They stood side by side, and the emperor bowed three times to the people. "From the Tsar's first bow, tens of thousands of hats flew into the air and the mighty 'Hoorah' resounded through the Kremlin and white-stone Moscow like rolling thunder."[85] *Sel'skii Vestnik* explained the bows' political significance and the people's joyous response to their peasant readers: "These cries expressed the Russian people's unlimited love for their Anointed Tsar with consciousness that in him alone resides the guarantee of national happiness and well-being."[86]

Again we see the contrast between the Slavophile understanding and the official conception of the national meaning of the coronation. Ivan Aksakov believed that Alexander III's coronation marked the beginning of a new epoch.

> What a day! What a great historical day! It is beyond the powers of a person to bear these titanic sensations fully if he experiences them as an individual. But no one experienced the moment as part of his individual life. All merged into

---

[83] Komarov, *V pamiat' sviashchennogo koronovaniia*, 133–34.

[84] Ibid., 138.

[85] Ibid., 138, 150.

[86] *Sel'skii Vestnik*, April 3, 1883, 129; *Koronovanie ikh Imperatorskikh Velichestv* (Moscow, 1883), a lower priced coronation album, described this "ancient Russian custom": "The exultation of the people then reached its apogee, and you will find no words to express it" (136).

one titanic body, into one trembling soul. All felt and understood themselves one Russian people, one in time and space. Two persons, two giants, stood before each other today, Tsar and People, People and Tsar, and achieved the great historical deed. The land groaned from the people's rapture. It was she that spoke, Holy Rus'! These rolls of thunder drowning out the cannon shots and the tolling of the Kremlin bells, these are her rejoicing, her cries of love, her voice.[87]

Michael Katkov's *Moskovskie Vedomosti* gave a less romantic assessment of the ceremonies. Katkov now had come to Pobedonostsev's view that the Orthodox Church embodied the spiritual union of tsar and people. The coronation showed the entirely religious grounds of Russian autocracy, which did not rely on the rational egoism or contractual agreements of the West. The crowning in the Assumption Cathedral consecrated what was for him "the unbreakable union between Russian autocracy and the Orthodox Church." The people joined in this union by observing and sharing the feeling of *umilenie*, of humble joy and sadness with the crowning of their tsar.[88]

•

The postcoronation festivities evoked the dynasty's Muscovite past in art, poetry, and music. The seventeenth-century interior of the Hall of Facets, with the murals of Semen Ushakov, was restored for Alexander's coronation banquet. The director of the Hermitage, Alexander Vasil'chikov, had called for this restoration, hoping that "a new dawn will come for our native art." Artists from the Palekh shop of icon painters re-created Ushakov's figures so exactly, according to Komarov, that the fresh gilt and frescoes would "transport you far back into the historical past, to the very beginnings of Moscow."[89]

At the banquet the emperor and empress occupied the same thrones they had when in the Assumption Cathedral, but they sat apart from the heir and other family members. "The symbolic meaning of the dinner was the unity and uniting (*edinstvo i edinenie*) of the Tsar with the state. Neither relatives nor rank nor foreign interference stands between the Tsar and the people," Komarov wrote. The emperor and empress were served by Alexander's brothers and the chief ranks of the court. The menu included Russian as well as Western dishes: borsch and consommé, pirozhki, steamed sturgeon, veal

---

[87] Ivan Aksakov, *Sochineniia* (Moscow, 1886), 5:118. Printed originally in *Rus'*, no. 10 (1883).

[88] M. Katkov, *Sobranie peredovykh statei Moskovskikh Vedomostei 1883g.* (Moscow, 1898), 228, 234; *MV*, May 11, 1883, 2; May 16, 1883, 5.

[89] The renovations of the Palace of Facets came to nearly half a million rubles ("O vozobnovlenii Granitovoi Palaty, privedeniia eia v tot vid v kakom ona sushchestvovala v drevnee vremia i o raznykh rabotakh, otnosiashchikhsia do eia ubranstva, RGIA, 472-64-20, passim); Aida Nasibova, *The Faceted Chamber in the Moscow Kremlin* (Leningrad, 1978), 13; Komarov, *V pamiat' sviashchennogo koronovaniia*, 89–93.

in aspic, roast chicken and fowl, asparagus, kasha, and ice cream.[90] The menu was designed by Victor Vasnetsov. Ornate floral decorations framed a scene of boyars bearing the tsar's regalia to the feast, next to a shield and helmets draped with gonfalons. The reverse showed a priest and peasants bearing bread and salt, and a player of *gusliar'* with words praising the tsar.[91]

Then an orchestra, soloists, and chorus from the Bolshoi Opera, performed the cantata *Moskva*, with words by Apollon Maikov and music by Peter Il'ich Tchaikovsky. For the occasion Tchaikovsky departed from his usual preference for classical forms and wrote what one authority described as "his only work written in the archaic national style dear to Borodin and Rimsky-Korsakov."[92] At the previous three coronation banquets, choruses had sung the hymn "What Glory Now Shines!" with words of Lomonosov set to music by Giuseppi Sarti—an eighteenth-century expression of ceremonial rejoicing.[93]

To extol and recall Moscow's triumph in uniting Russia, Maikov's cantata, which was reprinted in the coronation album and Komarov's book, used phrases and imagery from the medieval epics *The Lay of the Host of Igor*, which Maikov had translated into modern Russian, and *Zadonshchina*. The program of the cantata, with at least part of the text and an illustration depicting the regalia of Michael Romanov and his coronation, was placed at each individual table setting.[94] The princes experiencing the wrath of God were disunited until the Moscow prince brought them together and overthrew the Tatar yoke. The Russian tsar then appeared as *bogatyr'*, representing the hope of all Slavic nations. The figure of the epic Russian knight combined the principle of armed force with the Russian folk tradition and faith in the providential mission of the Russian state as the leader of all Slavs. The people of "Eastern countries" apostrophize the Russian *bogatyr'*.

> For all eastern countries, You, now,
> Are like the rising star of Bethlehem,
> In Your Sacred stone Moscow!
> The Lord loves and has chosen You,

---

[90] Komarov, *V pamiat' sviashchennogo koronovaniia*, 140–42.

[91] The menu is reproduced in *Veseliashchiisia Peterburg* (St. Petersburg, 1994), 22–23.

[92] André Lischke, *Piotr Ilyitch Tschaikovski* (Paris, 1993), 989–92; T. Frumkis, on the other hand, emphasizes the eclectic character of the work (Frumkis, "Kantata P. I. Chaikovskogo 'Moskva': [Ne]sluchainyi tekst v [ne]sluchainom kontekste," in G. S. Knabe, ed., *Moskva i moskovskii tekst russkoi kul'tury* [Moscow, 1998], 127–28).

[93]
> What glory now shines,
> This city with your coming,
> Has not room for all the joys,
> In its vast edifice.
> But the air is filled with applause,
> And brilliance dispels the darkness of night.

Evgenii Karnovich, "Koronovanie Gosudarei," *Russkii Arkhiv* no. 1 (1990): 62–63.

[94] Frumkis, "Kantata P. I. Chaikovskogo 'Moskva,' "126.

Fasten Constantine's sword to Your side,
And crown Yourself with the crown of Monomakh,
You are to be the defender of orphans,
The deliverer of captives,
The defender of true faiths!
There is this prophesy about Your Moscow:
"Two Romes Fell, The third stands,
There will be no fourth."[95]

The triumph of the Russian nation in the image of the autocrat was the theme of the two parts of the gala performance at the Bolshoi Theater on the evening of May 18. Rather than Donizetti's opera bouffe, *The Elixir of Love*, performed at Alexander II's coronation in 1856, the troupe presented the first and last scenes of Glinka's *A Life for the Tsar*. The opera created a ceremonial equivalence: The year 1613 became a historical setting for what had just occurred in 1883. The finale on Red Square, when Moscow witnesses the procession leading Michael Fedorovich on his way to the Kremlin was a rousing hymn to the new reign. A chorus of almost eight hundred singers, accompanied by musicians playing old horns, sang the Slavsia chorus, as row after row of soldiers marched in to bring the opera, and presumably the troubles of the early 1880s, to a rousing conclusion.[96]

After the intermission the ballet company performed *Night and Day*, choreographed by Marius Petipa to the music of Ludwig Mincus. If *Life for the Tsar* celebrated the resurrection of authority, *Night and Day* allegorized Russia as the dominant nationality in a multinational empire.[97] The ballet returned to the eighteenth-century theme of renovation. The traditional image of the sun represented the monarch who illuminated and gave warmth to everything. The spirits of night gave way to glorious day, with birds, fountains, and flowers ushering in the new reign. Butterflies burst from a hive and alighted on flowers. "All the nationalities of the Russian empire (*Russkoe tsarstvo*) in holiday costumes"—Finns, Georgians, Don Cossacks, Siberian Shamans, Poles—"greet the rising light of day." Each group performed its own dance, then all joined a general Russian round dance and in the center stood "the most beautiful and stoutest woman, that is, Rus'." At the conclusion they came together while a chorus intoned glory to the "beautiful sun, our tsar on earth." The evening ended with the usual singing of the anthem.[98]

The people's feast on Khodnynskoe Field on May 21 assumed a greater scope than previous events. Tables were set for four hundred thousand, though the number attending reached six hundred thousand, the highest yet for a coronation feast. The people were treated to candies, cookies, figs, beer,

---

[95] Komarov, *V pamiat' sviashchennogo koronovaniia*, 143–47; Maikov, *Polnoe sobranie sochinenii*, 2:413–20.

[96] Komarov, *V pamiat' sviashchennogo koronovaniia*, 307.

[97] See Le Donne, *The Russian Empire and the World*, 132–36 for the imperial context.

[98] Komarov, *V pamiat' sviashchennogo koronovaniia*, 308–11.

and mead and received coronation mugs carrying the imperial seal and the year 1883.[99] The feast also presented extensive and elaborate entertainment. For the first time at a coronation, the entertainment included performances of the popular theater, the *balagan*, which had been attracting a growing audience during the 1860s and 1870s.[100] The entrepreneur and impresario M. V. Lentovskii, who had founded the Hermitage and Skoromokh theaters in Moscow, was recruited to organize the feast and entertainments. He proposed to the Coronation Commission that an event taking place in spring have as its theme "the rebirth and dawn of spring, the glory of Russia and her peoples."[101]

Accordingly, the central event of the festivities was Lentovskii's spectacular allegorical procession "Spring," which took place in the central amphitheater on the field. The procession included popular folk heroes from the *byliny* and lubok literature. The audience beheld a bewildering succession of floats, led by heralds in "winged armor and spiked helmets," beetles on horseback and foot, grasshoppers, and frogs. The queen bee sat on a hive, followed by a float with the *bogatyr'* Mikula Selianovich and a globe in front showing the boundaries of the Russian empire. Mikula wore the costume of a ploughman and was surrounded by figures of flies. He held a great golden plough, resting on the Russian land. He embodied, Komarov explained, "the power of the black soil." According to *Koronovanie ikh Imperatorskikh Velichestv*, Mikula enjoyed the greatest success among the people. A Russian peasant dressed in a red shirt and holding a birch branch came next, followed by the float "Spring," with several butterflies and a woman allegorizing spring. Then came four *bogatyri* leading captives. Behind them, the *bogatyr'* Dobrynia Nikitych rode on the back of the snake Gorinych, which he had slain in his legendary exploit. The final floats presented peasants celebrating. A float entitled "Intoxication" held a carousing peasant seated next to a barrel. Then came a cart with a drunken young man, followed by four *skomorokhi*—the popular minstrels of old. The procession concluded with a goat, a bear, a crane, and a Russian chorus and dancers.[102]

The pageant connected the reassertion of authority with pagan sources of rebirth and fertility, and the government of Alexander III with the Antaean might of the people, personified in the *bogatyr'*. The strength of the Russian

---

[99] Ibid., 333, 342. Two hundred thousand had participated at Nicholas I's coronation in 1826. I have no figures for the 1856 coronation. However, since three times the number of tables were set in 1856 as in 1826, it is likely that the number in 1856 approached that for 1883.

[100] A. F. Nekrylova, *Russkie narodnye gorodskie prazdniki, uveseleniia, i zrelishcha, konets XVIII–nachalo XX veka* (Leningrad, 1984), 158–60, 167–71; Neia Zorkaia, *Fol'klor, lubok, ekran* (Moscow, 1994), 49–56, 156–58.

[101] M. V. Lentovskii, "Zaiavlenie v koronatsionnuiu komissiu o plane narodnogo prazdnestva v dni koronatsii [Aleksandra III], TsTM, 144-1-904, 1–6.

[102] Komarov, *V pamiat' sviashchennogo koronovaniia*, 341; *Koronovanie ikh Imperatorskikh Velichestv*, 195.

people had conquered their enemies, internal and external. The *bogatyr'* Do-brynia Nikitych, representing the healthy strength of the Russian people, had struck down the serpent, symbolizing "the annihilation of everything bad and evil." In the illustrated volume *Beautiful Spring*, (*Vesna krasna*) these figures were vividly depicted in watercolors by Fedor Shekhtel'. The concluding verse condensed spring, the people, and the Russian monarch into a single image.

> Everything has returned to life,
> Thank God that you [spring] have breathed into us,
> Justice, strength, power . . .
> So our native land,
> Like the ancient mythical *bogatyr'* Mikula,
> Our dear people could be just as strong and full of vigor![103]

After the pageant and the departure of the imperial family, the merriment began—songs, round dances, carnival games, clowns, and puppet shows. People devoured *pirozhki* and partook of beer and mead, which "poured forth abundantly from hundreds of carts." They spontaneously burst into song. The festivity in Moscow was exemplary for all of Russia. A lubok, entitled "People's Fête in the Village on the Occasion of the Coronation of Their Majesty," showed an old peasant and a woman in folk costume danc-ing merrily to the strains of a balalaika while a round dance goes on in the background. A boy on the side holds a paper, perhaps the coronation mani-festo (fig. 27).

Lentovskii also arranged four other shows with patriotic and national appeal: *A Russian Wedding at the End of the Sixteenth Century*—a play by Peter Sukhonin that had gained great popularity in Moscow—and several *balagan* productions—a folktale, *Ivan-Tsarevich*, in five acts, by Vladimir Rodislavskii; a military pantomime, *Russian Eagles in the Caucasus*; and *The Resurrection of Harlequin*, in seven scenes. Komarov's account dwelled on the perfect order of the crowd and on foreign impressions. "All the for-eigners were delighted with the calm of this awful mass of people, the order, the absence of pushing, noise, and cries. Over the entire day there were no drunks, fights, or scandals." Komarov ascribed the order to the fact that the people had not come for free drinks or entertainment but to have their tsar among them and to be seen by him. He quoted one comment: "The Great Tsar is coming to us hearty fellows, to watch how we make merry."[104] But the authorities did not have the same trust in the docility of the people that had made the security forces inconspicuous at the 1856 feast. Police and soldiers appeared in large numbers, and military bands marched through the crowds when gatherings became too dense.[105]

[103] *Vesna krasna: allegoricheskoe shestvie ustroennoe na narodnom gul'iane v Moskve, 21 maia, 1883 g.* (Moscow, 1883).

[104] Komarov, *V pamiat' sviashchennogo koronovaniia*, 334–35, 342–43.

[105] A. Suvorin, "Malen'kie pis'ma," *NV*, May 24, 1896, 1.

27. Village Celebration of Alexander III's Coronation. *Lubok*, 1883. GARF.

The same day, on the grounds of the Petrovskii Palace in Moscow, the emperor gave a dinner for the peasant elders, numbering more than six hundred, who had been selected to attend the coronation, the first since the peasants had been freed from bondage. The dinner marked the peasants' inclusion, as an honorable estate, in the framework of Russian monarchy. But the elders also represented authority as custodians of order. Alexander warned them to dispel the rumors circulating in the villages that the nobles' land was soon to be divided among the peasants. "Follow the advice and direction of your marshals of the nobility and do not believe the stupid and absurd rumors of a division of land, additions to household land, and so forth. These rumors are spread by our enemies. All property, yours as well, should be inviolable."

The tsar's speech to the elders was printed in all the major newspapers, with the peasants' response, "We are satisfied." *Sel'skii Vestnik* devoted special attention to the meeting. The tsar spoke to the peasants kindly, like "a loving father." But a loving father also must give admonitions, it emphasized, "to prevent mistakes and to point out the true way." It was the wicked people who had distorted the true meaning of the emancipation.[106]

Komarov described the address of the tsar to the peasants as a heroic act (*podvig*). Alexander stood face to face with the peasants and "openly, directly, and honestly delivered a speech to them, destroying illusions and mi-

---

[106] *Sel'skii Vestnik*, June 5, 1883, 227–28. On the rumors circulating among the peasantry at the time of the coronation, see Krukones, *To the People*, 82–84.

28. *Alexander III Receives Peasant Elders in the Courtyard of the Petrovskii Palace in Moscow.* Painting by Ilia Repin, 1886.
Copyright State Tret'iakov Gallery.

rages and advancing law and justice." His speech affected them "with irresistible force." Inspired and joyful, the peasants received the words of the tsar "like a voice from above," and they vowed they would tell their fellow peasants the tsar's words and obey the marshals. Then the imperial family passed by the tables, as the elders drank toasts to their health.[107] The elders were asked to bring twenty thousand sheets with the tsar's statement to their villages for distribution at future *volost'* meetings. They received a picture of the tsar and were presented with an album containing photographs taken of them with the minister of the interior Dmitrii Tolstoi, who expressed the wish that such albums be placed in all local peasant institutions in the empire.[108]

Ilia Repin's famous painting of the scene makes clear the change in the relationship between the emperor and the people occurring in the new reign (fig. 28). The emperor and the peasants are at the same level, facing each other as fellow human beings, in contrast to the representations of Alexander II standing above the peasants who look up worshipfully. Repin, however, conveys an awkward formality. Alexander seems uncomfortable standing before the bearded elders, their heads bared, obediently hearing his words. The peasants occupy the same space as the emperor, but the expressions on their faces are blank and unrevealing. The painting, meant for the coronation

[107] Komarov, *V pamiat' sviashchennogo koronovaniia*, 350–59.
[108] Ibid., 359–60.

album, had been delayed because the authorities at first insisted that Repin present Alexander III as Christ preaching to the people.[109]

After leaving the peasants, the tsar received thanks for his statement from a group of marshals of the Russian nobility. He in turn thanked them for their loyalty and expressed the hope that they would remain "the support of the throne, in everything good for the benefit of the throne and the fatherland." Alexander thus reaffirmed his determination to rely on traditional estate organizations, which he saw as agencies of the Ministry of the Interior.[110]

The unity of tsar and people was to reinforce administrative authority from above. The peasants would remain under the tutelage of the Ministry of the Interior and the marshals of the nobility, rather than participate on their own in a civil and legal system. Katkov welcomed the meeting as a source of hope for the renovation of the nobility and for the protection of the peasants from kulaks and outside influences.[111] The ceremony and speech foreshadowed the schemes to restore noble dominance in the countryside.

•

The coronation gave symbolic expression to the popular spiritual bond between the masses and the tsar at the same time as it presented the church as the institution expressing the nation's spirit. In the final two events of the celebration, the visit to the Trinity Monastery and the dedication of the Cathedral of Christ the Redeemer, the Orthodox Church was elevated as the principal symbol of the national monarchy, a role it would continue to play for the duration of Alexander's reign. On May 22 the imperial family made the traditional postcoronation pilgrimage to the Trinity Monastery to venerate the relics of St. Sergei and to extol the saint and the monastery for their part in Dmitrii Donskoi's defeat of the Tatars at Kulikovo in 1380. After the ceremonies at the monastery, the family visited the hermitage of Gethsemane, which had been founded by the metropolitan Filaret as a retreat for solitude and prayer. Alexander recalled a previous visit to the hermitage, and the imperial family took tea in Filaret's cells, which remained exactly as they had been at the metropolitan's death. Then they venerated the Chernigov Mother of God at the monastery's cave church. The visit also provided an occasion to show the religious unity between the tsar and the people. Komarov described the large numbers of worshipers greeting the emperor along the way and praying for him at the monastery cathedral. The response, he concluded, revealed the rural population's continued devotion to the ruling

[109] For interesting comments, see Elizabeth Valkenier, *Russian Realist Art* (Ann Arbor, Mich., 1977), 126.

[110] Francis William Wcislo, *Reforming Rural Russia: State, Local Society, and National Politics (1855–1914)* (Princeton, N.J., 1990), 102.

[111] Komarov, *V pamiat' sviashchennogo koronovaniia*, 361; Katkov, *Sobranie peredovykh statei Moskovskikh Vedomostei 1883g.*, 244–45.

29. The Cathedral of Christ the Redeemer. Architect, Constantine Thon. 1879.
Lithograph from *Vsemirnaia Illiustratsiia*.

house and to the state. The "common sense" and "firm character" of the Russian people had belied the revolutionaries' propaganda.[112]

The dedication of the Cathedral of Christ the Redeemer set the relationship between tsar and church in the providential narrative of the first half of the nineteenth century. Constantine Thon's immense neoclassical rendering of Moscow-Vladimir church architecture had been built over a period of nearly half a century to commemorate Napoleon's defeat by the Russians (fig. 29). The cathedral symbolized the combined efforts of the monarchy and the church to achieve the unity and preeminence of the Russian state. The wall paintings, completed during the previous reign, placed the growth of the Russian state, assisted by the leaders of the church, in the context of sacred history.[113] The dedication took place on May 26, not the anniversary of an event of 1812 but the Day of Ascension, marking Christ's entry into glory.[114]

---

[112] Komarov, *V pamiat' sviashchennogo koronovaniia*, 366–72; *Opisanie sviashchennogo koronovaniia. . .Gosudaria Imperatora Aleksandra tret'ego i Gosudaryni Imperatritsy Marii Fedorovny*, 53–54.

[113] Nicholas I had laid the cornerstone in 1837 (see Volume 1: 384–86). On the paintings, see, P. Iu. Klimov, "Zhivopisnoe ubranstvo khrama Khrista Spasitelia," in E. I. Kirichenko, ed., *Khram Khrista Spasitelia* (Moscow, 1996), 73–132.

[114] See the discussion of the rhetoric and ceremony of the event in E. I. Kirichenko, *Khram Khrista Spasitelia v Moskve* (Moscow, 1992), 140–42.

The imperial manifesto on the dedication of the cathedral, written by Pobedonostsev, incorporated the triumph of 1812 into the ancient union of tsar and people. The edifice, Alexander declared, was the fulfillment of Alexander I's vow to build a cathedral as an expression of thanksgiving to God for the salvation of the fatherland. The consecration of the church in the midst of the Russians gathered for the coronation attested to "how holy and fast is the centuries-old union of love and faith tying the Monarchs of Russia with the loyal people."[115]

Tchaikovsky's "1812 Overture," commissioned for the occasion, presented the war against Napoleon in the triumphalist spirit of the resurgent autocracy. Tchaikovsky juxtaposed two national anthems that were not in use in 1812. The booming, triumphal cadences of "God Save the Tsar!"—composed only in 1834—play against the fanfares of the "Marseillaise"—banned by Napoleon as "a summons to rebellion." Tchaikovsky himself had contempt for a work he had put together in less than a week and that he considered "very loud and noisy."[116] Like the Redeemer Cathedral, which he also disliked, the overture expressed the glories of the past in the ponderous idiom of nineteenth-century patriotism.

The dedication ceremonies began with massive processions of the cross that covered a large area in central Moscow. Bearing miracle icons, the clergy moved from various churches to the Kremlin to the Cathedral of Christ the Redeemer.[117] The processions established a succession from the Assumption Cathedral, ancient but miniscule, to the immense and ornate new edifice that could hold nearly ten thousand worshipers and whose cupolas were visible across Moscow. The succession between churches symbolized the spiritual continuity between Muscovy and Imperial Russia proclaimed in the new myth. The clergy then arrayed themselves around the cathedral, the priest of each church facing the building before the gonfalons. All awaited the imperial family's arrival.[118]

At ten the emperor, wearing a general's uniform and mounted on a white horse, followed by the imperial family in a carriage, made his way from the Kremlin Palace to the cathedral. Along the way the bands played "God Save the Tsar!" and Tchaikovsky's "1812 Overture" as well as other military music.[119] After the sanctification of the altar, the imperial family, the suite, high officials, and foreign guests joined the clergy in the first procession of

---

[115] Komarov, *V pamiat' sviashchennogo koronovaniia*, 445–46; PSZ 3, no. 1602 (May 26, 1883).

[116] Poznansky, *Tchaikovsky: The Quest for the Inner Man*, 380; Holden, *Tchaikovsky: A Biography*, 203–5.

[117] The ceremony is described in Kirichenko, *Khram Khrista Spasitelia v Moskve*, 144–48; and in Komarov, *V pamiat' sviashchennogo koronovaniia*, 429–45.

[118] Komarov, *V pamiat' sviashchennogo koronovaniia*, 433–34.

[119] The premier of the work, however, was in a concert hall built for the exhibition of 1881 (Poznansky, *Tchaikovsky: The Quest for the Inner Man*, 380; Holden, *Tchaikovsky: A Biography*, 203–4).

the cross around the cathedral, which completed the dedication. The procession moved between the lines of the clergy and the standards of the regiments participating in the event. To the strains of the hymn "*Kol' slaven*" and the ringing of church bells, the artillery launched into a salvo that continued throughout the procession. The music, the parade, and the cannons recalled that "a cathedral was being consecrated that had been erected in memory of the glorious deeds of the Russian army."[120]

The procession then returned to the cathedral for the holding of its first mass. At the conclusion the emperor kissed the cross, whereupon Bishop Ambrosii of Kharkov declaimed a speech emphasizing that Alexander III had completed the work of his forbears, "who sowed that others may reap." With the coronation, the bishop concluded, Alexander took up his labor of caring for the fate of "the great Russian people." Then, addressing the empress, he characterized the emperor as one with the laboring population. "The tiller of the soil, working in the field, weary and needing replenishing of his force, awaits his food from his home, from his wife: May Your love, with all the treasures of the loving heart, be the bread replenishing the forces of the August Toiler of the Russian land."[121]

The dedication of the cathedral concluded the coronation celebrations with a ceremony of incorporation. It brought the Russian past into the present myth, making the defeat of the revolutionaries the equivalent of Napoleon's defeat. It made the clergy, possessing the sacred icons, the guardian of the symbolic national tradition, embodied finally in the tsar, who, by his character, was like the people, the August Toiler of the Russian land. The ceremony inaugurated an era when church architecture would become a symbol of Russia's national past, and processions of the cross a principal public ritual of Russian monarchy.

---

[120] Komarov, *V pamiat' sviashchennogo koronovaniia*, 436–41.
[121] Ibid., 441–44.

CHAPTER SEVEN

The Resurrection of Muscovy

His service as Tsar before Russia,
Was that He—the Tsar Himself—believed in the age-old bases (*ustoi*),
Upon which rests The Russian Land,
He declared them loudly. . . .

Rus' has been resurrected in spirit—the gloom of doubts has vanished,
And what was only feeling and tradition,
Has been tempered, like armor, by consciousness.

—*For the portrait of Emperor Alexander Aleksandrovich,*
Apollon Maikov, 1894[1]

"HOLY, ORTHODOX RUSSIA"

On the first anniversary of his coronation Alexander III wrote to his wife,
Maria Fedorovna, "These days will remain the most gratifying memory and
comfort for my entire life." Two days later he described the coronation as
"a great event for us. And it proved to a surprised and morally corrupt
Europe that Russia is still the same holy, Orthodox Russia as it was under
the Muscovite Tsars and, if God permits, as it will remain forever."[2] For the
emperor and those in his entourage, the success of the Moscow festivities
confirmed the persistence of the past. The coronation expressed not the unity
of the Petrine empire with old Russia but the true Muscovite identity of the
Russian monarchy, despite its Western trappings.

Alexander's words express the synchronic mode of symbolic elevation introduced with the national myth. Since Peter, the distance between emperor
and people had been evoked by tropes, whether metaphorical or metonymi-
cal, that lifted the emperor into a realm of art and imagination. Now the
predominant forms of presentation became historical rather than literary.
The emperor associated himself with a new founding period, the seventeenth
century, denoting the true heritage of autocracy. The synchronic mode was
profoundly antitraditional, for it produced a complete rejection of the recent
past. By exalting the seventeenth century, it diminished the eighteenth and
nineteenth and delegitimized the legalistic bureaucracy, the intelligentsia,

---

[1] S. Petrovskii, ed., *Pamiati Imperatora Aleksandra III* (Moscow, 1894), frontispiece.
[2] GARF, 642-1-709, 24–25; letters of May 14 and May 16, 1884.

and the dynamic of reform that had reached its culmination in the previous reign. It looked back to a timeless heritage untouched by historical change.

The synchronic mode was characteristic of ethnic, racial linguistics and political myths of late-nineteenth-century Europe.[3] It located the real nation in its true form at a particular remote point in history. This stage had ended with inevitable decline, a diachronic step of retrogression. But beneath, in the substratum of national life, lay the dominant values and beliefs that could be resurrected by a determined, ruthless national leadership ready to expunge the nation of alien elements. The people (*narod*) were identified with the nation (*narod*) as it had manifested itself at the moment of foundation. Its idiom was retrospective and legendary, rather than mythical and metaphoric. Its heroes were figures exemplary of the nation's identity, rather than gods descended. Its genres were national epics and saints' lives, vindicating the past and the boundaries of the nation, rather than classic myths, demonstrating the ruler's freedom from the past and mortal bounds.

The synchronic mode introduced a break with official history, as written by Nicholas Karamzin and D. I. Ilovaiskii. Karamzin and Ilovaiskii glorified the dynasty's past to demonstrate the achievements of absolute monarchy in Russia. The synchronic mode presented the monarch not as the maker of history but as its embodiment, as an artifact of a true unchanging past. The Russian emperor might live in Western palaces, consort with Western royalty, rule institutions with Western names, but these superficial overlays concealed a native heritage that could be recaptured by a restoration of the previous political and spiritual order.

The elevation and glorification of the monarch now took place by claiming to inhabit another time frame, when the Russian tsar was in contact with the nation. The distance between the ruler and the ruled was the distance between the monarch and the manifestations of the fallen present that encumbered his power. After Alexander III's death in 1894, *Moskovskie Vedomosti* described him as the initiator of a new period in Russian history, "the *Russian* period"; he was the "great moral gatherer of the Russian land," placing him among the princes of Moscow. He had restored "Russian Autocracy," which had been realized in Muscovy when Byzantine autocracy had gained its distinctively Russian character.[4]

The new myth, confirmed by the coronation, exalted Alexander as Russian tsar—who represented the nation without the summoning of assemblies of the land. The myth designated the policies of Alexander's reign as "national" and exalted them as the realization of historical traditions that had been

---

[3] On the emergence of synchronic paradigms and a "duo-temporal 'mythology of structure' " in linguistic and racial theories of the late nineteenth century, see the interesting remarks in Malcolm Quinn, *The Swastika: Constructing the Symbol* (London, 1994), 26. T. Fujitani describes the invention of numerous timeless "traditions" in late-nineteenth-century and early-twentieth-century Japan. Some of these—for example, funeral ceremonies—involved drawing on a remote pre-Buddhist past (Fujitani, *Splendid Monarchy*, 152).

[4] Petrovskii, *Pamiati Imperatora Aleksandra III*, 175, 286.

betrayed and now were rediscovered in the people. It reflected a doctrine, according to Constantine Golovin, that combined "such disparate words as 'powerful authority' and 'the rights of the national majority.' " "The basic dogma of this religion of a special sort," he wrote, "was autocracy, not only of the tsar but of the purely Russian majority, which presumably could never err."[5]

Alexander's scenario of brooding imperturbable confidence exemplified the identification of nation with power and instilled a sense of confidence in his servitors, many of whom took on his brusqueness and arrogance. He may have felt embattled and frightened by the hostile society that had bred a revolutionary movement, but he conveyed the will to prevail over Westernized society and the belief that Russia would recapture the greatness of Muscovy. The resurgence of the ancient past would be displayed in images of forceful Russification, a revitalized Orthodox Church, a strengthened state administration, and a national industrial policy.

The national myth gave a new meaning to the monarch's rule of empire. Muscovite Rus' provided a model of an ethnically and religiously united people, ruled by an Orthodox tsar. It justified the subjugation of non-Russian nationalities and the effort to turn them into Russians by forcing on them Russian religion, Russian language and culture, and Russian institutions. Alexander III did not originate the policy of "Russification": It had been initiated in Poland and Ukraine during the reigns of Nicholas I and Alexander II.[6] But the policy now was presented as a defense of the national character and sovereign rights of the monarchy and the Russian people. The idealized conception of the empire shifted from a multinational elite serving the Westernized European emperor to an Orthodox, ethnically Russian elite, serving the Russian tsar. The government no longer tried to appear as German in Riga and Tatar in Kazan, but as a Russian master subjecting lesser peoples of the empire.

The symbolic break became clear in the first months of Alexander III's reign, when the term *true Russian* became a synonym for those favoring ruthless pursuit of ethnic and authoritarian policies. The government openly affirmed the principle of ethnic supremacy first in relationship to the rights of Jews after the pogroms of 1881 in Ukraine. Government officials, recent literature has shown, did not instigate the pogroms, which they feared were a threat to the existing order. But the minister of the interior Nicholas Ignat'ev used the occasion to repudiate the relative tolerance of the previous reign. He vowed to return to Russia's ancient tradition and "to follow vigorously the principles, evolved by the monarchy's entire past history, according

[5] Golovin, *Moi vospominaniia*, 2:39.

[6] For discussions of Russification, see Edward Thaden, "The Russian Government," in Edward Thaden, ed., *Russification in the Baltic Provinces and Finland, 1855–1914* (Princeton, N.J., 1981), 15–108; Raymond Pearson, "Privileges, Rights, and Russification," in Crisp and Edmondson, *Civil Rights in Imperial Russia*, 85–102.

to which the Jews must be regarded as aliens." Ignat'ev described the Jews as the "conquered foe" and proposed measures limiting Jewish residence to designated towns in the Pale and barring them from the liquor trade. He issued these as administrative regulations, thus avoiding the State Council, where they faced considerable opposition. The Committee of Ministers approved a somewhat modified version of his proposals, called "Temporary Regulations," which forbade new Jewish settlers and Jewish land ownership outside the major cities of the Pale and prohibited them from doing business on Sundays and Christian holidays.[7]

Anti-Semitic expletives were common in circles close to the tsar, who frequently used the word *kike* to refer to people or types of conduct arousing his anger. Alexander's attitudes were summarized in his remark to the governor-general of Warsaw I. Gurko: "In the depth of my heart, I am always happy when they beat the Jews, but still we must not allow it."[8] The feeling of ethnic supremacy went beyond the Jews to include other nationalities as well. A. A. Polovtsov wrote in his diary that the sense of Russian distinctiveness had become an ideal of Russian political life. This distinctiveness found its expression "in the worship of the samovar, kvas, and baste sandals, combined with a contempt for everything that has grown out of the life of other peoples. It follows from this that everyone who does not bear the Great Russian stamp must be persecuted. The Germans, the Poles, the Finns, the Jews, and the Muslims—all are seen as one common problem and declared to be irreconcilable enemies of the Russians." Sophisticated aristocrats cringed at the tsar's crude antiforeign and anti-Semitic statements, which lent credibility to Western perceptions of Russia as a backward and Asiatic state.[9]

The policy of Russification was pursued most openly and energetically in the Baltic provinces. Alexander became the first Russian emperor to withhold confirmation of the privileges of the Baltic nobility. In 1882 and 1883 Senator N. A. Manasein submitted a blueprint for administrative and cultural centralization and the spread of Orthodoxy in Lifland and Estland provinces. He recommended the extension of the Russian court system to the Baltic provinces and the abridgement of the autonomy of local institutions

---

[7] Michael Aronson, *Troubled Waters: The Origins of the Anti-Jewish Pogroms in Russia* (Pittsburgh, 1990), passim; Louis Greenberg, *The Jews in Russia: The Struggle for Emancipation* (New York, 1976), 2:30–31; S. M. Dubnow, *History of the Jews in Russia and Poland* (Philadelphia, 1918), 2:309–24; Sylvain Bensidoun, *Alexandre III, 1881–1914* (Paris, 1990), 54.

[8] Ignat'ev, in 1881, spoke of a powerful "Polish-kike group" in Petersburg that dominated the banks, the press, and the courts and used its influence to encourage tolerance for themselves and reforms on a western European model. See p. 207(Zaionchkovskii, *Krizis samoderzhaviia*, 337–39; Zaionchkovskii, *The Russian Autocracy*, 16).

[9] Zaionchkovskii, *The Russian Autocracy*, 65; Polovtsov, *Dnevnik*, 2:447. The entry is from April 1892; Dominic Lieven, *Nicholas II: Emperor of All the Russias*, London, 1993, 25–26.

dominated by the German nobility. The governors M. A. Zinov'ev of Lifland Province and particularly S. V. Shakhovskoi of Estland Province energetically supported Manasein's goals. Whereas the system of self-government survived this campaign, the Baltic nobility suffered a "loss of power and status," according to Heide Whelan, that drove many of them to turn inward and cultivate their German identity and family life.[10] I. V. Gurko, the governor-general of Warsaw, implemented Russification policies ruthlessly in Poland, so much so that "the time of Gurko" became synonymous with harsh, brutal oppression.[11] In the Caucasus, policies of Russification were introduced when local elites resisted assimilation into the Westernized nobility and officialdom of the empire.[12]

Alexander believed that he ruled "the same holy Orthodox Russia that it was under the Muscovite Tsar," and he sought to restore to religion the role he believed it played in the seventeenth century. Religion no longer was merely a utilitarian "necessary condition of the state's existence," as it had been under official nationality, but was the goal of the state and a force in itself. The first chief-procurator of the Holy Synod who came from the clerical estate, Pobedonostsev, sought to convert the Russian people and Russian society to a native, religious form of social thought and action, under the aegis of the tsarist administration.[13] He extolled a clergy who would accomplish a great exploit (*podvig*), "toiling in the wilderness, woods, and swamps of endless Russia in great need, suffering from the cold, from hunger and poverty, and often feeling offended." He envisioned an active parish clergy, "priests from the people," who would "stand and fall with the people."[14]

Between 1881 and 1902, under Pobedonostsev's encouragement, the number of parish clergy increased by nearly 80 percent. The monastic clergy also grew in these years. The number of convents doubled. Between 1881 and 1890, 160 new monasteries were established, and monasteries expanded their charitable and educational efforts. At the same time, new religious fraternal organizations were formed that supported churches, hospitals, and poor houses. Alexander Polunov points out that Pobedonostsev, in his effort to activate the church, used techniques of social organization that had originated during the Great Reforms.[15]

---

[10] Thaden, *Russification in the Baltic Provinces and Finland*, 54–69, 324–25; on the Baltic nobility in this period, see Heide Whelan, *Adapting to Modernity: Family, Caste, and Capitalism in the World of the Nineteenth-Century Baltic German Nobility* (Cologne, 1999), 172–73.

[11] Weeks, *Nation and State in Late Imperial Russia*, 105–7.

[12] Austin Jersild, "From Frontier to Empire: The Russification of the Caucasus, 1845–1917," unpublished ms., chaps. 11, 12.

[13] This theme is developed in the important study by A. Iu. Polunov, *Pod vlast'iu ober-prokurora: gosudarstvo i tserkov' v epokhu Aleksandra III* (Moscow, 1996).

[14] Ibid., 46–48.

[15] N. A. Rubakin, *Rossiia v tsifrakh* (St. Petersburg, 1912), 80; Litvak, *Russkoe pravoslavie*, 376; Polunov, *Pod vlast'iu ober-prokurora*, 73–75.

Pobedonostsev believed that simple priests could uplift the people through education, and his most cherished cause was the network of parish schools, where priests taught peasant children reading and the principles of Orthodoxy. In a report of 1883 he presented his plans as a return to the priests of ancient Rus' who had taught children "from the very beginning of the enlightenment of the Russian people by Christianity." From the time of St. Vladimir and Iaroslav, they were "the first and almost the only teachers and educators of the people . . . Their educational activity corresponded to the spiritual needs of the people." The aim of the parish schools was "to strengthen the Orthodox faith and Christian morality among the people and to impart useful elementary knowledge." Their curriculum focused on religion, comprising sacred history, catechism, and explanations of the service. Reading would be taught through religious texts, and arithmetic would be connected with "solving problems immediately related to the peasants' way of life." Between 1880 and 1900 the number of parish schools increased nearly tenfold, and the number of pupils nearly fifteenfold, to 1,634,461.[16] Financial resources for these schools, however, were meager, and the priests were insufficiently trained to teach the curriculum. As a result, in 1891 the Synod reduced the educational requirements for teachers, since half their number had failed to meet them.[17]

Under Pobedonostsev's direction, the Synod sponsored a growing number of publications for the people. These no longer dealt exclusively with the formal details of church activities but tried to "enter every home." Pobedonostsev believed that the common people could choose heroes, like those in saints' lives, presenting "an ideal of strength, virtue, and holiness." Church publications included saint's lives, scriptures, gospels, and the Psalter. In 1885, to commemorate the millennium of St. Cyril and Methodius, publications of saints' lives amounted to 350,000 copies, more than half the volumes published by the church. The Synod also greatly increased the circulation of "Trinity and Athos Sheets," which, its report of 1884 declared, were intended "to provide the simple Russian people with edifying reading and thus promote their religious and moral education. Between 1879 and 1897 more than 76 million of these were circulated. They extolled the simple hardworking life and polemicized against enemies of the church such as Leo Tolstoy.[18]

Pobedonostsev also hoped to make the church hierarchy active participants in spreading religion. But, Alexander Polunov has shown, his vision

[16] Thomas C. Sorenson, "Pobedonostsev's Parish Schools: A Bastion against Secularism," in Charles E. Timberlake, ed., *Religious and Secular Forces in Late Tsarist Russia: Essays in Honor of Donald W. Treadgold* (Seattle, Wash., 1992), 185–89, 198; Byrnes, *Pobedonostsev,* 278–79; S. Iu. Witte, *Vospominaniia* (Moscow, 1960), 1:387–90. In comparison, in 1893 there were about 1,831,400 pupils registered in secular primary schools under the Ministry of Education (*BE,* no. 40: 768–69, Table 6).

[17] Polunov, *Pod vlast'iu ober-prokurora,* 87–89.

[18] Brooks, *When Russia Learned to Read,* 300–301, 307–11.

of dedicated, self-reliant clerics clashed with his determination to subject the hierarchy to central, administrative control.[19] He treated the hierarchs with contempt, when possible appointing mediocrities as metropolitans and moving bishops every two or three years to ensure their dependence on the Synod. No figure of the stature of the metropolitan Filaret of Moscow could emerge after 1881.[20] At the same time, he sought to regulate the observance of holy days, alienating both the court and educated society. He canceled plays and public amusements that offended his sense of probity and rescheduled governmental meetings and ceremonies when they coincided with holy days. Not even the opposition of the Ministry of the Imperial Court could prevent him from closing the Imperial Theater during Lent.[21]

In the first years of Alexander's reign, the Synod tolerated the pastoral movement in the Orthodox Church, which the church hierarchy had previously discouraged. The movement pursued an "internal mission," like that practiced by German Protestant denominations, and fostered preaching and education among the people.[22] The movement gave rise to a new group of charismatic parish preachers among the secular clergy. The most famous, Father Ioann of Kronstadt, attracted a large national following. These priests addressed the personal and moral needs of their flock. They encouraged frequent confession and communion, which most worshipers took only at Lent.[23] The Russian church in this respect began to follow the example of the Roman Catholic Church, which, after the revolutions of mid-century and the Paris Commune, promoted mass appeals and popular cults as a response to the challenges of liberalism, socialism, and nationalism.[24] But in Russia the movement awakened the suspicion of the authorities, including Pobedonostsev, who frowned on the independence and initiative of the new priests, though a figure such as Ioann of Kronstadt continued to preach under the protection of powerful figures in the government and the imperial family.[25]

---

[19] Polunov, *Pod vlast'iu ober-prokurora*, 30–34.

[20] Igor Smolitsch, *Geschichte der russischen Kirche, 1700–1917* (Leiden, 1964), 1:311–12. The metropolitan of Kiev Filofei accused the emperor of becoming isolated from the people, which led Alexander to doubt the metropolitan's mental capacities.

[21] Polunov, *Pod vlast'iu ober-prokurora*, 78–79. V. S. Krivenko, in his memoirs, tells how Pobedonostsev convinced the Ministry of the Court to cancel ballet performances during Lent ("V ministerstve imperatorskogo dvora," RNB, 1000-2-672, 174).

[22] Simon Dixon, "The Church's Social Role in St. Petersburg, 1880–1914," in Geoffrey A. Hosking, ed., *Church, Nation and State in Russia and Ukraine* (London, 1991), 168–73.

[23] Nadieszda Kizenko, "The Making of a Modern Saint: Ioann of Kronstadt and the Russian People," Ph.D. diss., Columbia University (1995), 38–39, 155–56.

[24] See Barbara Corrado Pope, "Immaculate and Powerful: The Marian Revival in the Nineteenth Century," in Clarissa W. Atkinson, Constance H. Buchanan, and Margaret R. Miles, eds., *Immaculate and Powerful: the Female in Sacred Image and Social Reality* (Boston, 1985), 180–86.

[25] See Kizenko, "The Making of a Modern Saint," passim.

•

Pobedonostsev failed to create the selfless and energetic church hierarchy that would bring ancient piety to the people. Instead, great religious commemorations recalled the spirit of Russia's past and made clear the significance of Orthodoxy for the national myth. Seventeen jubilee celebrations marked great religious events of Russia's past during Alexander's reign. The year of the coronation, 1883, also witnessed the five-hundredth anniversary of the Tikhvin Mother of God and the centenary of the death of Tikhon Zadonskii. The millennium of Cyril and Methodius followed in 1885, the nine-hundredth anniversary of the baptism of Rus' in 1888, the fiftieth anniversary of the union with the Uniates of the northwestern region, and the five-hundredth anniversary of the death of Sergei of Radonezh in 1892. These became occasions for immense processions of the cross. Along with the clergy in their glittering vestments, the processions included leading officials and military men in uniforms, as well as schoolchildren: The representatives of state and church demonstrated their unity by following the cross, icons, and gonfalons. The procession for the anniversary of the death of St. Sergei, numbering, according to one source, "several-hundred thousand" of the faithful from towns all over Russia, made its way over the entire distance from Moscow to the Trinity Monastery in Zagorsk.[26]

The most important of the religious celebrations, the nine-hundredth anniversary of the conversion of Rus', in 1888, celebrated the rule of the empire by the Orthodox Great Russian Monarchy. The idea for the commemoration had originated with the metropolitan of Kiev in 1886. But the St. Petersburg Charitable Society, a Pan-Slavist and nationalist organization headed by Nicholas Ignat'ev, insisted that the celebration assume an all-Russian character—namely, that the theme of state unity overshadow the local Kievan observance of the event. Both Ignat'ev and Pobedonostsev attended as honored guests, and Pobedonostsev gave the principal speech for the occasion. Delegates assembled from all parts of Russia and from other Slavic countries, confirming Russia's leadership of the Slavic world, though they were barely mentioned in the official description and Pobedonostsev paid them little attention. William J. Birbeck attended as representative of the Church of England and proposed collaborative ecumenical efforts to the metropolitan Platon. Such plans were quashed by Pobedonostsev, but the Englishman's presence lent international prestige to what was a Russian state event.[27]

The speeches and editorials of the celebration emphasized the importance of the conversion of Rus' for the building of the Russian empire and the development of autocracy. The celebration included the unveiling in Kiev of

---

[26] Polunov, *Pod vlast'iu ober-prokurora*, 75; K. Korol'kov, *Zhizn' i tsarstvovanie Imperatora Aleksandra III* (Kiev, 1901), 79–85. Korol'kov gives the estimate on page 83.

[27] *Prazdnovanie deviatisotletiia kreshcheniia russkogo naroda* (Kiev, 1888), 5–10; other descriptions were published in *Sel'skii Vestnik*, July 24, 1888, 342–47; *MV*, July 18, 1888, 2–3; and Byrnes, *Pobedonostsev*, 211–16.

M. O. Mikeshin's statue of the seventeenth-century Cossack hetman Bogdan Khmelnitskii, whom the text described as "the principal initiator of the unity of Little and Great Russia." Khmelnitskii was shown on horseback, holding the attributes of his office and pointing to Moscow. The inscriptions read, "We want to be under the Tsar of Eastern Orthodoxy" and "A Russia, one and indivisible. To Bogdan Khmelnitskii."[28]

Processions of the cross displayed pageantry that brought the people into the ceremony; according to the official description, the people were "the chief expression" of the celebration. Three processions came from the town, the largest from the Kiev Monastery of the Caves. The sound of singing and band music accompanied the rows of icons and banners to the chapel on the river, where a large crowd awaited the church service held to mark the conversion. Photographs showed the lines of clergy converging before spectators at the edge of the Dnepr.[29] *Moskovskie Vedomosti* described a vast throng of onlookers and the sense of spiritual unity that the spectacle inspired: "The people were everywhere, as far not only as the eyes could see but as far as one could see with binoculars." Everyone felt they were beholding "an all-national Russian festival of our enlightenment by Christianity." Watching the rows of gonfalons, hearing the beautiful sounds of the choirs, "everyone felt the great unifying meaning of this ecclesiastical, historical world celebration, that thread of a single soul, radiance of a single thought, beating of a single heart."[30]

Pobedonostsev's speech extolled the people's love for the Orthodox Church. Again, he enveloped the present in his imagined past. Early Rus' had created the basis for a powerful Russian state. Orthodox Christianity, adopted by St. Vladimir, had given the Russian people the strength to combat the pagans and other foes. The Russian Orthodox Church had nationalized the catholic Byzantine faith. It had combined "the mighty word of the Russian language and the marvelous sound of their native song" with the beautiful liturgy they had received from Byzantium. The church was a protector from the snares of error.

> Fathers and brothers! What is nicer, kinder, what is dearer than the church for all, the great and the small. What beauty is dearer and more sympathetic than the beauty of the church for the Russian heart? The church is our native mother and is kind to the Russian person. We are all her children, and if someone strays far from her, then God will allow him to return to the parental home, to his mother. Our church is the home of the Russian person, the home that is most kindred, where all are equal, all have and find their place, and all may equally drink of joy and consolation.[31]

---

[28] *Prazdnovanie deviatisotletiia*, 14; NV, July, 12, 1888.
[29] *Prazdnovanie deviatisotletiia*, 31–33, 38–40.
[30] Ibid., 39.
[31] Ibid., 136–38.

A popular biography of Alexander III, published by a priest, K. Korol'kov, stated that the celebration "greatly assisted the rise of Russian church life and the development of a national consciousness of self." The anniversary's emphasis on the political significance of the conversion had all but overshadowed its religious significance, the philosopher Vladimir Solov'ev observed.[32]

BUILDING MUSCOVITE CHURCHES

From the beginning of Alexander III's reign the construction of Muscovite churches symbolized the triumph of the age-old foundations of early Rus'. Architects drew on democratic architectural theorists of the 1870s, many of whom, like the French architect and historian Eugène Émanuel Viollet-le-Duc, looked back to the seventeenth century as the flowering of Russian national art and architecture.[33] Russian monarchy utilized revival architecture, as A.W.G. Pugin and Viollet-le-Duc had conceived it, as a means to restore a lost purity, to change attitudes, and to reshape society.[34] After 1881 the tsarist government developed this logic into a kind of inverted archaeology—monuments constructed to resurrect an invisible national past.

Alexander's introduction of the Muscovite style of church architecture was an emphatic statement of the break with the religious culture of the previous reigns. The church announcing this break was the shrine built at the site of Alexander II's assassination, the Cathedral of the Resurrection of Christ, or, as it came to be popularly known, "The Savior on the Blood." The initial projects submitted for the church in 1882 followed the canonical five-cupola, Russo-Byzantine style, fashioned after Thon and exemplified in the cathedral of Christ the Redeemer in Moscow (fig. 29). A few others were patterned on St. Sofia, and several combined various styles of seventeenth-century Russian churches.[35] Alexander was unhappy with all the submis-

---

[32] Korol'kov, *Zhizn' i tsarstvovanie Imperatora Aleksandra III*, 81; Martin George, "Die 900-Jahr-Feier der Taufe Russlands im Jahr 1888 und die Kritik Vladimir Sergeevic Solovevs am Verhältnis von Staat und Kirche in Russland," *Jahrbücher für Geschichte Osteuropas* 36, no. 1 (1988): 15–17.

[33] On the architectural theories of the 1870s, see E. I. Kirichenko, *Arkhitekturnye teorii XIX veka v Rossii* (Moscow, 1986), 152–278; and E. Viollet-le-Duc, *L'Art Russe* (Paris, 1877), 164–71, 178. On Viollet and the controversy surrounding his books, see Lauren M. O'Connell, "A Rational, National Architecture: Viollet-le-Duc's Modest Proposal for Russia," *Journal of the Society of Architectural Historians* 52, no. 4 (December 1993): 436–52; and Lauren M. O'Connell, "Viollet-le-Duc and Russian Architecture: The Politics of an Asiatic Past," conference paper, 1996.

[34] See, for example, Margaret Belcher, "Pugin Writing," in Paul Atterbury and Clive Wainwright, eds., *Pugin: A Gothic Passion* (New Haven, 1994), 115–16; and Thomas R. Metcalf, *An Imperial Vision: Indian Architecture and Britain's Raj* (Berkeley, 1989), 139–40.

[35] The decree of March 25, 1841, ordained that "the taste of ancient Byzantine architecture should be preserved, by preference and as far as possible" in the construction of Orthodox Churches. "The drawings of Professor Constantine Thon, composed for the construction of

sions. His wish, as reported in the press, was for a church to be in the "Russian style" and "in the style of the time of the Muscovite tsars of the seventeenth century."[36] *Nedelia stroitelia* reported that he desired a pure Russian style "of the seventeenth century, models of which are met, for example, in Iaroslavl."[37]

The project that won the tsar's approval was submitted by Father Ignatii, the hegumen of the Sergiev Hermitage at Peterhof who had appealed for contributions for the cathedral shortly after the assassination. Ignatii, who had briefly studied at the Petersburg Academy of Arts, was encouraged by the grand duchess Catherine Mikhailovna, the tsar's cousin. The priest drew the sketch of the church, he claimed, "almost automatically," on the day of Annunciation. But he was not a professional architect and his plans had to be completely revised by the architect Alfred Parland. The final form of the cathedral, Michael Flier has shown, was a mélange of the plans of many architects who were struggling to find a seventeenth-century national style that suited the emperor's taste.[38] The decision to depart from the classical Moscow-Vladimir style was clearly the emperor's. Although the church was built with public donations, the imperial family contributed nearly one-quarter of the total cost, which came to 4.6 million rubles. Alexander continued to watch over the completion of the cathedral and resisted attempts to economize.[39]

Parland answered the tsar's vague wishes by making the Cathedral of the Resurrection of Christ a composite of architectural forms and design motifs of the seventeenth century. At first sight, the cathedral's exterior recalls the kaleidoscopic forms of Vasilii the Blessed; Parland himself noted the resemblance, which was clearly intentional (fig. 30). The flamboyant decorations, the tent roof, the onion cupolas became signatures of the new style. But, as B. M. Kirikov has observed, the resemblance is deceptive. The cathedral's five-cupola cruciform structure, with a large central basilica hall, has little

Orthodox Churches, may prove useful in this regard" (*Svod zakonov rossiiskoi imperii* 12 [St. Petersburg, 1857]: 49). The provision is article 218 of the *Stroitel'nyi Ustav*.

[36] *MV*, April 9, 1882; A. A. Parland, *Khram Voskresenie Khristova sooruzhennyi na meste smertel'nogo poraneniia v Boze pochivshego Imperatora Aleksandra II na ekaterinskom kanale v Sankt-Peterburge* (St. Petersburg, 1909), 2.

[37] Michael S. Flier: "The Church of the Savior on the Blood: Projection, Rejection, Resurrection," in Robert P. Hughes and Irina Paperno, eds., *Christianity and the Eastern Slavs*, (Berkeley, 1994), 2:27; "At Daggers Drawn: The Competition for the Church of the Savior on the Blood," in Michael S. Flier and Robert P. Hughes, eds., *For SK: In Celebration of the Life and Career of Simon Karlinsky* (Berkeley, 1994), 98; Georgii Butikov, *The Church of the Savior on the Blood* (St. Petersburg, n.d.), 29.

[38] Flier, "At Daggers Drawn," 109–11. For the projects of the second competition, see the 1884 volume of *Zodchii*. Ignatii's account of his participation is cited in *Zhizneopisanie arkhimandrita Ignatiia (Malysheva), byvshego nastoiatelia Troitse-Sergievoi pystyn'* (St. Petersburg, 1899), 84.

[39] It remained under the jurisdiction of the Ministry of the Imperial Court until the revolution (Iu. V. Trubinov, *Khram Voskreseniia Khristova [Spas na krovi]* [St. Petersburg, 1997], 33, 54, 94).

in common with the intricate warren of Vasilii the Blessed. The external decorative devices—the tracery, *kokoshniki*, and *shirinki*—borrow from a great number of seventeenth-century churches in the Moscow-Iaroslavl style.[40] Indeed, the official architect Nicholas Sultanov, in an article published in 1881, declared the Moscow-Iaroslavl style the exemplar of Russian national church architecture.[41] The elaborate entwining designs, though deriving from the seventeenth century, verge on the lushness of art nouveau.[42]

Although this cathedral was not consecrated until 1907, its amalgam of the five-cupola form with pre-Petrine ornamentation became the dominant model for church design in the official Russian style from 1881 to 1905. A report of the chief-procurator from the 1890s asserted that Alexander himself reviewed projects for churches and "willingly approved those projects that reproduced the ancient tradition of Russian churches."[43] The monarchy, claiming popular national roots, now sponsored the same undisciplined and flamboyant decorative forms that had been deplored by members of the seventeenth-century church hierarchy.[44]

The Cathedral of the Resurrection of Christ boldly announced the theme of resurrection as central to Alexander III's scenario; indeed, it was the first of five new churches named "Resurrection." The exterior mosaics depict the bearing of the cross, the Crucifixion, the Deposition, the Descent into Hell, and, on the southern pediment, Christ's Resurrection. The Resurrection established Jerusalem as a new beginning point for the sacred narrative of Russian monarchy. Flier has shown that the interior is modeled on the layout of the Church of the Holy Sepulcher in Jerusalem, whose name is also "The Resurrection of Christ."[45] The new cathedral places Russia's beginning not at the Roman Empire—as in the legends of Andrew the First-Called and Prus—or at Byzantium, as claimed in the legend of Monomakh, but at Golgotha itself, now with Christ's martyrdom transposed to Russia.[46]

The iconography and structure echo the popular identification of Alexander II with Christ, expressed in G. M. Shvetsov's poem "At the Russian Golgotha," but they set it in an official myth repudiating the errors of the recent past. The symbolism has a negative thrust—rejecting, clearing away the previous historical narrative, removing Rome, and even Byzantium, as

[40] B. M. Kirikov, "Khram Voskreseniia Khristova (k istorii russkogo stilia v Peterburge)," *Nevskii Arkhiv: istoriko-kraevedcheskii sbornik* 1 (1993): 229–33; I. Grabar', *Istoriia Russkogo Iskusstva* 9, book 2 (Moscow, 1965): 269.

[41] N. Sultanov named the Georgian Mother of God in Moscow and the Church of the Trinity at Ostankino as its best examples ("Vozrozhdenie russkogo iskusstva," *Zodchii* 2 [1881]: 9; E. A. Borisova, *Russkaia arkhitektura vtoroi poloviny XIX veka* [Moscow, 1979], 308).

[42] Trubinov notes this convergence (*Khram Voskreseniia Khristova*, 40–41).

[43] Polunov, *Pod vlast'iu ober-prokurora*, 76.

[44] William Chase Brumfield, *A History of Russian Architecture* (Cambridge, 1993), 165–66, 553–54; George Heard Hamilton, *The Art and Architecture of Russia* (Harmondsworth, 1983), 216.

[45] Flier, "The Church of the Savior on the Blood," 32–43.

[46] On the legends of Byzantine and Roman origins, see Volume 1: 26–30.

30. Cathedral of the Resurrection (Christ on the Blood), St. Petersburg. Architect, Alfred Parland. Photograph by William Craft Brumfield.

forerunners of Russia. It expresses the determination to do away with foreign mediation of the divine, to overcome the derivative character of Russian religious doctrine, and to identify Russia with the source of Christianity. The true Russian spirituality could be manifested only after Russia had thrown off some of the Byzantine trappings and before the nation had fallen under the domination of Western culture, that is, in the seventeenth century. The Muscovite architectural forms—the tent, the *kokoshniki* and *shirinki,* and the elaborate tent-style canopy covering the sacred blood-stained pavement in the center of the cathedral—associated and identified seventeenth-century Russia with the scene of the Crucifixion and the true faith.[47] The achievements of Alexander's II's reign were inscribed in chronological order on twenty granite plates set into the socle, overshadowed, however, by the rich imagery of resurrection.

The references to Jerusalem, like the Muscovite architectural details on the exterior, expressed a powerful admonition about the political evils besetting Russia. The building of the cathedral was an act of expiation to atone for the assassination of Alexander II, the shame of which branded the entire people. The prayer of Vasilii the Blessed, inscribed beneath the central cupola, begged God to forgive them for their sins. Parland placed the prayer there in response to the popular belief that angels standing on crosses atop churches announce the invocations of the faithful to the All-Mighty. The many icons of Boris and Gleb recalled those whose deaths had expiated the sins of the Russian land.[48] The final lines of Fet's "March 1, 1881" pronounced the transformation of the blood into a shrine:

> The snares of the pharisees are powerless,
> What was blood, became a cathedral,
> And the site of the horrendous crime,
> Our eternal shrine.[49]

The Resurrection Cathedral built on the site of the assassination on Catherine Canal is easily visible from Nevskii Prospect. There is nothing understated in its appearance; it is a declaration of contempt for the order and symmetry of the capital, producing what Louis Réau described as "a troubling dissonance."[50] The Muscovite style set in the middle of classical Petersburg was meant to express this rejection. The many Russian-style churches that went up in St. Petersburg in subsequent decades were also placed at prominent sites as visual admonitions to the population. A few that survived

---

[47] Parland based the design for the canopy on the Throne of Ivan the Terrible in the Assumption Cathedral in the Kremlin. It was placed in the cathedral only in 1913 (Trubinov, *Khram Voskreseniia Khristova,* 108–9).

[48] A. A. Parland, "Khram Voskreseniia Khristova," *Zodchii* (1907): 375–76; Parland, *Khram Voskresenie Khristova,* 3; Flier, "The Church of the Savior on the Blood," 43–45.

[49] Fet, *Polnoe sobranie stikhotvorenii,* 397.

[50] Louis Réau, *Saint Petersburg* (Paris, 1913), 67–68.

the militant atheism of the 1930s can still be seen in Petersburg.[51] The Assumption Cathedral of the filial of the Kiev Monastery of the Caves (1895–1900) looks out over the Neva from the Nikolaevskii embankment, an elaborate church in the Moscow-Iaroslavl style. The Resurrection Cathedral on the Obvodnyi Canal (1904–1908) combines a Byzantine central basilica with *kokoshniki* and a tent belfry in plain view from the Warsaw Railroad Station.[52] Sultanov's Peter-Paul Cathedral at Peterhof, completed in the late 1890s, brought the images of the Resurrection Cathedral to the playground of the court. Set on a pond, it reproduced the tent forms and *kokoshniki* of the seventeenth century in brick, which Sultanov considered the building material most suitable for Russian churches (fig. 31). It was in stark contrast to the rococo elegance of the Peterhof palaces.

The churches were acts of visual provocation—flagrant repudiations of the aesthetic, and, by extension, the philosophical and spiritual premises of Russian autocracy since Peter the Great. The organic motifs of these churches—the abundant, bulbous onion domes and profuse *kokoshniki* and *shirinki*—spring mushroomlike from their surface, defying the order and restraint of neoclassicism, and even the eclecticism that had replaced it. The profusion of decoration exemplifies what Randolph Starn and Loren Partridge have identified as the use of redundancy to enhance the totality and expressiveness of monumental architecture: excess as a prerogative of absolute power.[53]

Churches were placed at other sites to inspire contrition and spiritual purification. A fanciful, single-domed Church of the Savior, covered with *kokoshniki* and other decorations, accompanied by a tent-shaped bell tower, went up at Borki near Kharkov, the site of the wreck of the emperor's train in 1888, as a sign of miraculous salvation (fig. 32).[54] Others were built at factory compounds to awaken the religious faith of industrial workers. At the beginning of the 1890s Leontii Benois designed a church for two thousand people near the textile factory of the Hof-meister N. C. Nechaev-Maltsov, in the town of Gusev, near Vladimir (fig. 33). The massive edifice was surmounted by a great tent roof and bell tower at one end, and, at the other, by cupolas and *kokoshniki* in the Iaroslavl style. The image of St. George, the patron saint of Moscow, over the portal was probably the work of Victor Vasnetsov, who executed the paintings on the interior walls.[55] Churches in

[51] More than twenty Russian-style churches went up in Petersburg from 1881 to 1914; at least eighteen of these were demolished or transformed beyond recognition, most of them in the 1930s. For listings of Slavic revival churches built after 1881 and information on their fate, see *Utrachennye pamiatniki arkhitektury Peterburga-Leningrada; katalog vystavki* (Leningrad, 1988), 31–39; S. Shul'ts, *Khramy Sankt-Peterburga: istoriia i sovremennost'* (St. Petersburg, 1994), 52, 79–82, 104, 106, 119–21, 173–74, 177–80, 200, 203–4, 212, 218.

[52] Shul'ts, *Khramy Sankt-Peterburga*, 81–82, 120–21.

[53] See the suggestive remarks on inflation and copiousness in the art of monarchy in Randolph Starn and Loren Partridge, *Arts of Power: Three Halls of State in Italy, 1300–1600* (Berkeley, 1992), 166–74.

[54] *Niva* 24 (1894): 569.

[55] *Zodchii* (1893): 8, plates 1, 2, 6; *Zodchii* (1903): 30–31.

31. Peter-Paul Cathedral Peterhof. Architect Nicholas Sultanov.
Photograph by William Craft Brumfield.

32. Church and Bell Tower at Borki. Niva, 1894.

seventeenth-century style went up in the center of provincial towns across Russia during the reigns of Alexander III and Nicholas II.[56]

Early-Russian architecture also demonstrated Russian domination of the border regions of the empire. It recalled images of a distant past of Orthodox religion and Russian rule, suggesting that the reproduction of the visual artifacts could restore the imagined unity of that earlier time. In the Caucasus, Russian colonists and missionaries expected "to restore" Orthodox Christianity, evoking an era when it was presumably the region's dominant faith.[57] Imposing Orthodox Churches displayed imperial rule over Central Asia. The Cathedral of the Transfiguration, a large neo-Byzantine church completed in 1888, towered over the governor's house on the principal square of Tashkent. It was the most prominent building in the center of the new Russian city. The buildings of the Teachers' Seminary in Tashkent were constructed in the 1880s in Muscovite style. In 1898 a tall, five-cupola, tent-style brick church, designed by A. L. Benois, was built into the walls of the seminary compound, confirming the particular national and ethnic character of the Russian presence in Tashkent.[58] Similar tent-style churches went up in Baku

---

[56] E. I. Kirichenko, *Russkii stil'* (Moscow, 1997), 116–17, shows two of these in Krasnoiarsk and Ural'sk.

[57] Jersild, "From Frontier to Empire," chap. 4; A. Platonov, *Obzor deiatel'nosti obshchestva vozstanovleniia pravoslavnago khristianstva na Kavkaze za 1860–1910gg.* (Tiflis, 1910).

[58] V. A. Nil'sen, *U istokov sovremennogo gradostroitel'stva Uzbekistana: xix-nachalo xx vekov* (Tashkent, 1988), 49–52, 64–65; Robert Crews, "Civilization in the City: Architecture, Urbanism, and the Colonization of Tashkent," conference paper, 1996, 5.

33. Church for two thousand people at Gusev. Architect,
Leontii Benois. Zodchii, 1893.

in the 1880s. Russian missionaries and officials in the Caucasus pointed out the importance of the physical presence of Orthodox Churches for the religious guidance of the mountain peoples. The Viceroy of the Caucasus, Prince Alexander Dondukov-Korsakov, wrote that the "external" aspects of the faith were most important for "Eastern peoples."[59]

The most striking examples of Russian church architecture as political symbols rose in Estland and Poland. The governor of Estland Province, S. V. Shakhovskoi, an ally of Pobedonostsev, promoted a campaign of proselytizing the local population for Orthodoxy and actively encouraged the construction of Orthodox Churches. His pride was the Alexander Nevskii

---

[59] *Zodchii* (1889): plates 35–38; Jersild, "From Frontier to Empire," chap. 12, 493 n. 124.

Cathedral in Revel (present-day Tallin). The cathedral, built in Moscow-Iaroslavl style, was placed, the architect M. Preobrazhenskii boasted in the dedicatory volume, at the "best site," allowing it "to dominate the city" (fig. 34). The site was the Domberg, the city's most prominent square, which Toivo U. Raun called "the traditional bastion of the Baltic German elite."[60] To accentuate the twin feelings of triumph and subjection, the cathedral was named for Alexander Nevskii, the namesake of the tsar and victor over the Teutonic Knights.

The authorities in Petersburg exerted pressure to choose and obtain the site on the Domberg. The deputy minister of the interior Viacheslav Plehve chaired the committee in Revel that made the recommendation. But the confiscation of land on the square violated certain articles of the Baltic civil code and prompted a lengthy correspondence involving the minister of the interior, the minister of justice, and the emperor himself. In the end, the minister of justice N. A. Manasein concluded that it would be intolerable to build the church on any other square because that would have placed it beneath the level of the city's Lutheran churches. The law could not deter the symbolic statement. Manasein wrote in his memorandum of 1893, "An Orthodox cathedral, rising above numerous Lutheran churches, will occupy a beautiful, dominating location that is suitable for an Orthodox shrine in a Russian state."[61] The minister's words typify the boundless confidence of Alexander's officials. It was in the power of the Russian state to create a shrine (sviatynia) and thereby shape the national character and religious faith of the region.

Shakhovskoi also undertook a campaign of church building in rural Estland. The silhouettes of cupolas and tent forms would create the aspect of an Orthodox, and therefore Russian, countryside. The buildings followed the rectangular plan of Lutheran churches but were decorated with the early-Russian motifs. A tent-form belfry beneath an onion cupola was attached by a passageway to the main cubiform church corpus, with a central onion cupola and four small cupolas at the corners. Kokoshniki decorated the bases of the cupola and, in several churches, like the one shown, the tent roofs themselves (fig. 35). An album of photographs of seven churches built between 1887 and 1889 publicized the achievement.[62]

---

[60] M. Preobrazhenskii, Revel'skii Pravoslavnyi Aleksandro-Nevskii Sobor (St. Petersburg, 1902), 3–4; Toivo U. Raun, "The Estonians," in Thaden, Russification, 323–25.

[61] "Po voprosu o postroike sobora v g. Revele, Estliandskoi gubernii," RGIA, 797-91-6.

[62] Al'bom vidov tserkvei Estliandskoi gubernii, sooruzhennykh pod vedeniem Revel'skogo nabliudatel'nogo komiteta po postroike tserkvei, prichtovykh i shkol'nykh zdanii (Revel, n.d.); Adres-kalendar' na 1889g. (St. Petersburg, 1889), 285. The album was issued by the commission supervising the construction, which was chaired by a member of the Governor's Bureau (gubernskoe pravlenie), A. A. Shirinskii-Shikhmatov and consisted of Russian officials and priests. Shirinskii-Shikhmatov later rose to the positions of provincial governor, member of the State Council, official in Nicholas II's court, and chief-procurator of the Holy Synod (A. A. Mosolov, Pri dvore poslednego Rossiiskogo imperatora [Moscow, 1993], 244, 273).

ПРАВОСЛАВНЫЙ СОБОРЪ
ВЪ Г РЕВЕЛЪ

ЗАПАДНЫЙ ФАСАДЪ.

CATHEDRALE ORTHODOXE
A RÉVAL

FAÇADE OCCIDENTALE.

Proj. et exec. par M Préobraꞩensky.

34. Alexander Nevskii Cathedral, Revel (Tallin). Architect, M. Preobrazhenskii.
M. Preobrazhenskii, *Revel'skii Pravoslavnyi Aleksandro-Nevskii Sobor*. Slavic and
Baltic Division, New York Public Library. Astor, Lenox, and Tilden Foundations.

In Poland, too, Russian Orthodox Churches expressed the new resolve to
press Russian language, education, and administrative domination on the
subject population. I. V. Gurko, the governor-general of Warsaw, regarded
the construction of Orthodox Churches as a crucial sign that Poland was
part of the Russian land. Nearly twenty Russian Orthodox Churches were

35. Parish Church. Estland. *Al'bom vidov tserkvei.* . . . Slavic and Baltic Division, New York Public Library. Astor, Lenox, and Tilden Foundations.

built in Warsaw in the 1890s, most of them for Russian army units. These were in the Russo-Byzantine style, following the earlier model of imperial architecture. Like Shakhovskoi, Gurko ended his tenure as governor by planning a great cathedral that would show the Poles the fact of conquest. Leontii Benois's immense Alexander Nevskii Cathedral (1894–1912) combined the Moscow-Vladimir design with abundant *kokoshniki* covering the roof. Its seventy-meter bell tower dwarfed surrounding buildings. It became "the most conspicuous accent of the city skyline," prompting lewd comparisons from the city's residents.[63] Gurko succeeded in gathering funds from a campaign for public donations centered in Moscow. The chancellery of the governor-general appealed to Moscow's residents: "By its very presence . . . the Russian Church declares to the world . . . that in the western terrains along the Vistula, mighty Orthodox rule has taken root . . . The appearance of a new . . . church in Warsaw as a boundary and pillar of Orthodox Russia will animate the hopes of the Orthodox Slavs for unification under the Orthodox cross." The journal of the Warsaw Eparchy boasted in 1912, "Under the dome of this magic temple, we find ourselves as if on Russian soil."[64]

Russian-style churches carried the national image beyond the empire's borders, to Port Arthur, Karlsbad, Vienna, and Florence.[65] The spiritual claims of the new national myth were announced most impressively by the Church of Maria Magdalena in Jerusalem, set prominently on the Mount of Olives at the site of the Orthodox Gethsemane. Alexander III commissioned the church in 1883, in honor of the patron saint of his mother Maria Aleksandrovna, whose memory haunted him. The *kokoshnik* decoration and tent-shaped bell tower are visible from afar, identifying old-Russian imagery and Orthodoxy for all to see across Jerusalem. It directly identifies the two sources of Russian national spirit in Alexander's scenario, the Holy City and old Russia, brick and mortar thus creating the signs and a demonstration of a new sacred history.

THE CONSECRATION OF ADMINISTRATIVE POWER

Under Alexander III, the vigorous and decisive exercise of the tsar's power was a sign of a national monarchy. The historical narrative of seventeenth-century Muscovy associated the origins of the Russian nation with the affirmation of monarchical authority after the breakdown period of "Troubles" at the beginning of the seventeenth century. The seventeenth century was the paradigm for a recrudescence of state power that could reunite an administration divided in the previous reign by considerations of legality and institutional autonomy. Alexander sought to return the Russian state to that historical model by creating a new administration staffed by officials with the features of "true Russians"—men who energetically pursued his vision of national power, who were responsive to his will. Together, he and

---

[63] Piotr Paszkiewicz, "The Russian Orthodox Cathedral of Saint Alexander Nevsky in Warsaw," *Polish Art Studies* 14 (1992): 64–65, 67.

[64] Ibid., 65–66.

[65] The Mary Magdalena Church was built with the donations of the members of the imperial family, and the St. Nicholas Church in Vienna, modeled on the Savior of the Blood, with funds donated by Alexander himself. For an extensive listing, with illustrations, of the properties of the Russian Orthodox Church abroad, see *Bratskii ezhegodnik: Pravoslavnye tserkvi i russkie zagranichnye uchrezhdeniia za granitseiu* (Petrograd [sic], 1906); *Podvor'e russkoi pravoslavnoi tserkvi v Karlovykh varakh* (Prague, 1987); *Zodchii* (1881): 21, plates 49–50.

his symbolic national elite created an image of strength that exalted Russian monarchy when the empire's international standing had declined, its finances were in disorder, and many high officials cherished a sense of legality that challenged the totality of autocratic rule.

A sense of efficacy, based on determined and, if necessary, ruthless exercise of power, without the vacillation and doubt of the previous reign, distinguished Alexander's scenario. The efficacy was demonstrated, first, by the suppression of the revolutionary movement, which was accomplished with unanticipated ease. The imagined vast network of revolutionaries turned out to be small bands that were rounded up, before and after March 1, 1881. The victory ushered in a period of police oppression. The arrests and trials of the revolutionaries continued until after the coronation. On April 3, 1883, the third trial of regicides sentenced seventeen of the accused to heavy punishments. After the coronation the regime arrested the remnants of the revolutionary organizations.[66]

After Alexander III's accession the government introduced swift and harsh measures against the press, closing fifteen major journals. The surviving journals were placed under tight restrictions. Circulars from the main directorate of the Press proscribed all discussion of agrarian and labor questions in periodicals of *zemstvo* and administrative institutions. A report from Petersburg in *Le temps*, on April 11, 1883, concluded that the government had reduced the press to impotence and insignificance, depriving itself of sources of information about the country and public opinion: "A universal silence has descended here."[67] The epic unity of the myth had been restored, expressed by an official monologue echoed in the press. Meshcherskii, in a memorandum to the tsar, argued that such a policy would "force people to get used to the sounds of conservative talk just as readily as they now are accustomed to liberal talk."[68]

Similar measures were introduced in the universities. These were heralded by the appointment of a conservative minister of education, I. D. Delianov, a creature of Pobedonostsev and Katkov. Katkov heralded the change with the words "Rise milords, the government is coming, the government is returning." The University Charter of 1884, which Alexander signed against the recommendation of a majority of the State Council, eliminated the vestiges of university autonomy and gave the ministry the right to draft the teaching programs of the juridical and philological faculties. The ministry established strict governmental controls over the universities, increased inspectors' power over the students, and introduced uniforms and estate quotas, restoring an order similar to that which prevailed in the reign of Nicholas I. But these efforts did not eliminate student discontent. Quite the contrary,

---

[66] Bensidoun, *Alexandre III*, 47.

[67] Ibid., 47–52; Zaionchkovskii, *The Russian Autocracy under Alexander III*, 157–59, 164–75.

[68] Iu. B. Solov'ev, *Samoderzhavie i dvorianstvo v kontse XIX veka* (Leningrad, 1973), 90.

toward the end of the 1880s student disorders led to the closing of five Russian universities (Moscow, Petersburg, Kazan, Kharkov, and Novorossiisk).[69] Indeed, the combination of learning and futile repression created a cauldron that bred criticism and opposition.[70]

Unifying the state by eliminating the spheres of independence created by the reforms, was a more challenging task. Not only did it antagonize moderate public opinion; it also offended the fundamental views of many officials high in the government, in the court system, and in the State Council, who had gained prominent positions during Alexander II's reign and who would resist efforts to undo the institutional heritage of the reforms. Alexander III's scenario set him against this legal state, and his efforts to introduce his own men and policies only further increased the divisions in the bureaucracy, turning it, too, into a scene of struggle between the monarchical and legal state. This occurred when the government began to introduce the counterreforms during the second half of the 1880s. The principal sponsor of the counterreforms was the minister of the interior Dmitrii Tolstoi, a wealthy nobleman who had understood his official role since the 1860s as one of personal obligation and devotion to the tsar. Their foremost ideologist was Alexander Pazukhin, the marshal of the nobility of Simbirsk Province.

Upon his appointment as minister in May 1882, Tolstoi reversed the direction of reform of local peasant institutions being planned in the Kakhanov Commission under Ignat'ev. The majority of this commission hoped to break down estate barriers and establish an all-class *zemstvo* at the level of the county (*volost'*). This would introduce the peasants into institutions governed by law—a first step toward the creation of what Frank Wcislo called a "legal autocracy," which would regulate each level of the state according to the norms of law.[71] Tolstoi augmented the commission with a group of experts, among them Alexander Pazukhin. The experts warned against the rise of an alien class of non-noble and peasant landowners. The strengthening of the state, they argued, depended on the strengthening of estate institutions, for autocracy "could not base itself . . . on organs that [were] subject to constant change and lack[ed] stability."[72]

Pazukhin's article, "The Current State of Russia and the Estates System," described an idealized seventeenth-century autocracy that would serve both

---

[69] Kornilov, *Kurs istorii Rossii v XIXv.*, 3:295–96; Zaionchkovskii, *The Russian Autocracy under Alexander III*, 181–201; Samuel D. Kassow, *Students, Professors, and the State in Tsarist Russia* (Berkeley, 1989), 28–36.

[70] An example is the experience of the future Kadet leader V. D. Nabokov, who recalled that at the end of the 1880s "a bureaucratic spirit depressed everyone, a whole range of subjects had been withdrawn, lecture halls often remained empty" (Brian Boyd, *Vladimir Nabokov: The Russian Years* [Princeton, N.J., 1990], 26–27). Other liberal leaders such as Paul Miliukov and Peter Struve also suffered the excesses of the bureaucratic system in these years.

[71] On the Kakhanov Commission, see Wcislo, *Reforming Rural Russia*, 63–82.

[72] See the extensive analysis in Thomas S. Pearson, *Russian Officialdom in Crisis: Autocracy and Local Self-Government, 1861–1900* (Cambridge, 1989), 135–42; and Wcislo, *Reforming Rural Russia*, 92–94.

as inspiration and blueprint for Tolstoi's counterreforms.[73] Pazukhin saw Russia split into two warring camps: historical Russia, "devoted to ideas bequeathed by her past, the Russia of believers, capable of great sacrifices," and the Russia without history, the Russia that knew no history and had "no ideas, no respect for the past, no care for the future, believing in nothing, capable only of destruction." "Russia without history" was Pazukhin's label for the Westernized educated elite who had moved to the capital, imbibed knowledge from books, and lost their "everyday estate" features and therefore their national identity.[74]

Pazukhin compared contemporary Russia with the situation after the "Time of Troubles" (*smuta*). Russian autocracy arose at this time not from the social conflicts that ostensibly prompted the growth of state power in European states but from a historical feeling of unity between people and sovereign. This feeling spread during the Time of Troubles, when all estates joined to fight the foreign aggressor and to restore the monarchy. The unity came from within, an intrinsic and organic need for authority. The key link in the state structure was the order (*chin*): Every citizen of the Moscow state had his own order, his place in society; he belonged to an estate that had specific obligations. When authority failed, the estates united in the Assembly of the Land to rebuild the state order.[75]

For Pazukhin, the seventeenth century was a period of administrative consolidation and growing state power in Russia. The "land" (*zemlia*) comprised for him not a community of the people, as it did for the Slavophiles, but the "state ranks" that constituted society. He asserted, "The estate organization, in the thinking of the ancient Russian person, was the guarantee of order and tranquility in the country." By the end of the seventeenth century Russia had attained all the necessary conditions for "political might." The autocracy had attained "freedom of action," while the estates served the central power and extended Russia's borders. Peter was not the founder of powerful autocratic rule but its beneficiary. He developed the system to increase state power and bring Russia closer to the West.[76]

The Great Reforms, Pazukhin contended, had sundered the historical unity of the Russian state, bringing disaffection and disorder. He was particularly concerned about the effects on the nobility, which had been deprived not only of its patrimonial rights over the peasantry but of its power over local government. Pazukhin saw the *zemstva* as independent of the state, and, including members of different estates, as destructive of the "organic"

---

[73] A. D. Pazukhin, "Sovremennoe sostoianie Rossii i soslovnyi vopros," *Russkii Vestnik* (January 1885): 1–58. It was also published as a separate brochure in 1885; the text may date from as early as 1881. Alfred Rieber has found an archival copy of the document that archivists have tentatively dated 1881–82, but we do not know what the dating is based on (Rieber, *Merchants and Entrepreneurs*, 95 n.; Pearson, *Russian Officialdom in Crisis*, 149–50).

[74] Pazukhin, "Sovremennoe sostoianie Rossii," 6, 38–39.

[75] Ibid., 41–46.

[76] Ibid., 43, 47.

unity that had existed between the administrative authorities and the nobility. He sought to restore this unity and to replace the existing system with a *zemstvo* that would be an organ of the noble estate. Katkov echoed Pazukhin's arguments for the estate system in *Moskovskie Vedomosti*. He greeted this "native creation of Russian history." The basis for local improvement was noble government in "the Russian tsardom." "May the Russian nobility, as in olden times, be the living link between tsar and people."[77]

The seventeenth century provided Pazukhin and Katkov with a historical paradigm of nobility and monarch uniting in the cause of a powerful state, a vision of Muscovy that, in official thinking, replaced the Slavophiles' notion of a direct union between the masses and a benevolent tsar. Pazukhin's evocation of Muscovy represented what Frank Wcislo has aptly described as "a ceremonial monument throughout Alexander III's reign."[78]

As head of Dmitrii Tolstoi's chancellery, Pazukhin drew up plans to unite nobility and state in the new office of the "land captain" (*zemskii nachal'-nik*), instituted in a law decreed in July 1889. The land captain, a local nobleman, appointed by the Ministry of the Interior, possessed both administrative and judicial powers over local peasant institutions. To remove potential conflicts between administrative and judicial spheres, Alexander, in early 1889, had issued a decree abolishing the Justice of Peace, the office created in 1864 to deal with minor peasant disputes and infractions. For Tolstoi, the Justices of the Peace represented an alien element in a state too sparsely populated and whose population was too backward to understand the meaning of law. The peasants, whom he described as "the dark people, have no concept of the separation of powers." They were "seeking an authority to protect them or at least tell them what to do." The land captain, Tolstoi argued, would raise the damaged prestige of the government among the people by restoring "an authority whose personal directives could redress the violation of law in matters arising from the needs of their simple agrarian milieu."[79]

The projects met strong opposition in the State Council and in January 1889 were defeated in the General Session, thirty-nine to thirteen. Most of the criticisms focused on the merging of administrative and judicial spheres. Even Pobedonostsev opposed it, pointing out that the new official would not be connected with the other district officials. But Alexander approved the minority opinion, apparently influenced by an article by Meshcherskii, "The Voice of a Country Marshal." He also referred to Tolstoi's opinion that, if land captains were not instituted, "peasant mutinies would undoubtedly blaze up during the coming summer."[80]

---

[77] Tvardovskaia, *Ideologiia poreformennogo samoderzhaviia*, 235.

[78] Wcislo, *Reforming Rural Russia*, 101–2.

[79] Pearson, *Russian Officialdom in Crisis*, 169–70; Wcislo, *Reforming Rural Russia*, 105–6.

[80] Zaionchkovskii, *The Russian Autocracy under Alexander III*, 237–39.

Pazukhin hoped that the nobility would, "as in olden times, be the living link between tsar and people." In fact, the land captain was a local representative of the central government's Ministry of the Interior. The Ministry of the Interior regarded the estate system as an administrative category, an instrument for the exertion of state power in the peasant village. The land captain would not only extirpate wrongdoing and correct the abuses of peasant courts, but he would intervene as a benign patriarchal presence to advance prosperity, defend communal landholding against breakdown, and ensure the dominance of the tsar and the landed nobility.[81]

The notion of the nobility as an estate of government administrators in the provinces was counterposed to the nobility as a group vested with rights and privileges, as defined by Catherine the Great's Charter to the Nobility in 1785. The nobility as a whole, in fact, prompted the suspicion of the tsar and his advisers. A few months after the publication of Pazukhin's article, Pobedonostsev wrote to Alexander that the nobility, though more trustworthy than other estates, should remain on their lands. No estate was distinguished by a "special quality of loyalty to tsar and fatherland," and all had in their midst members of the opposition, even the nobility, who included in their number "traitors in Russia's times of trouble."[82]

The rescript of April 21, 1885, on the anniversary of the Charter of the Nobility, composed by Pobedonostsev, reflected these feelings. It thanked the nobility for its devotion and loyalty, and promised credit to the noble estate, "which is inseparable from the history of the state and the Russian people." But there was also an admonition. The emperor announced that "we firmly hope that sons of valorous fathers, who have served the state, will show themselves worthy members of the estate in service to the fatherland."[83]

The celebration of the centenary fell far short of the expectations of conservative leaders of the nobility and of Katkov himself. The credit extended was less than wished, and, to Katkov's dismay, the Noble Bank assumed the obligation of foreclosing on estates whose owners did not meet their payments. A meeting of marshals of the nobility, which was to take place in Moscow, was prohibited by the government. Even such wealthy, conservative stalwarts as provincial marshals awakened fears of opposition in Tolstoi and Pobedonostsev, who saw this meeting as representing another "assembly" (sobor). The rescript was not a return to the time of Catherine, when the representatives of the orders in society could be summoned to Moscow

---

[81] Wcislo, *Reforming Rural Russia*, 114–16. The ministry document cited is from 1902.

[82] Ibid., 101.

[83] *PSZ* 3, no. 2882 (April 21, 1885). Katkov reacted by republishing his articles of 1863, which hailed noble land owning as the basis of a strong state administration. He, too, sought to place this change in a historical tradition going back to Muscovy. He greeted the rescript with a fond look back to the seventeenth century: "After long following errant ways, we are returning to our native, Orthodox, autocratic Rus' " (Tvardovskaia, *Ideologiia poreformennogo samoderzhaviia*, 236).

to write a law code and the empress conferred the first rights on an estate; rather, it was a return to the time of tsar Alexei, who dispensed with assemblies and consolidated the power of the state administration.[84]

By 1886 Alexander and his advisers had dissociated themselves completely from the reform tradition and set themselves against the officials who remained loyal to the principles of legality and the development of civic order in Russia. The open, symbolic repudiation of the most fundamental of the reforms took place in 1886, when the government not only refused to celebrate the twenty-fifth anniversary of the emancipation but issued a special order in February prohibiting its observance. State-secretary A. A. Polovtsov asked in astonishment, "Who would have thought five years ago that the government would forbid the celebration of the twenty-fifth anniversary of this measure!" Apparently Alexander and Pobedonostsev feared political demonstrations, but, more specifically, they wished to discourage any interest in the previous reign that might stir hopes of reforms. General N. A. Epanchin, an admiring and loyal servitor of the tsar, observed, "This order emphasized the negative view of the reforms of the Tsar-Emancipator and even disrespect for His memory."[85] The imperial family's libraries at the end of the century, Marc Raeff noted, contained few books on the Great Reforms.[86]

The counterreforms of the courts and the *zemstva* met ferocious resistance in the State Council when they were submitted at the end of the 1880s.[87] In each case the council forced significant modifications of the original proposals, which intended to curtail the autonomy of these institutions and to ensure the domination of the *zemstva* by the wealthy landed nobility. In the series of laws issued between 1887 and 1892 the courts and *zemstva* retained their autonomy, but with increased authority assigned to the minister of justice over the judiciary, and the governors over the *zemstva*. The representation of deputies from the landed nobility was increased in *zemstvo* assemblies. The most thoroughgoing counterreform was the reform of city government, which virtually eliminated the independence of urban institutions. The tsar and State Council existed in what Heide Whelan called a state of "equilibrium" but it was an uneasy equilibrium, with absolute power functioning in the police and administrative spheres. More significant than the actual changes was the motive that guided the counterreforms—the monarch's abiding determination to reverse the civic development begun in the 1860s.

[84] Solov'ev, *Samoderzhavie i dvorianstvo v kontse XIX veka*, 187–94; Tvardovskaia, *Ideologiia poreformennogo samoderzhaviia*, 237.

[85] Polovtsov, *Dnevnik*, 1:392–93; Epanchin, *Na sluzhbe trekh imperatorov*, 193–94.

[86] Marc Raeff, "The Romanoffs and Their Books: Perspectives on Imperial Rule in Russia," *Biblion* 6, no. 1 (fall 1997): 53.

[87] On the State Council's role in these years, see Heide W. Whelan, *Alexander III and the State Council: Bureaucracy and Counterreform in Late Imperial Russia* (New Brunswick, N.J., 1982).

In practice, the myth elevated administrative authority at the expense of law, which was associated with Westernization and reform. The exaltation of power emboldened officials to use that power with little regard for legal norms and to promote a form of administrative license. The contempt for the legal order was in part fostered by the "Temporary Regulations" of August 1881, which could be used to invest governors and governor-generals with "reinforced" and "extraordinary" discretion in times of political crisis. The regulations, which remained in force until the end of the empire, provided the authorities with extensive powers to jail citizens, close newspapers and commercial ventures, and remove officials from *zemstvo* organizations.

The regulations increased the power of the police and organs of the Ministry of the Interior to conduct surveillance and to exile suspicious individuals. In fact, the governors, whose punitive authority was now given legal sanction, often went beyond the particular provisions to order arbitrary arrests, extort bribes, and intervene in areas of the administration beyond their purview. The political police developed their own practices of administrative exile. The Senate, presumably the guardian of administrative legality, did little to correct these grievances. Indeed, some governors guilty of infractions were appointed senators. The jurist Anatole Koni described several of his fellow senators as "governors who had flogged the 'Yids' and peasants for imagined mutinies, along with a whole string of unsuccessful directors of the Department of Police who, having feathered their nests, were permitted to protect their precious skins as senators."[88]

•

Alexander III also presented a cautious foreign policy as a sign of strength and confidence. Russia's international power position had continued to decline with the rise of a united and powerful Germany on Russia's western frontier and the growing assertiveness of Balkan nations that Russia could no longer control. The government's finances, still in disarray from the Russo-Turkish War, dictated moderation and caution. Alexander's initial statement of foreign policy aims, announced in a circular of March 5 only four days after his accession, stated these goals clearly. Russia, "like all other states," had engaged in a struggle for its own creation during which "her forces and national spirit had developed." Now Russia had attained its

---

[88] Jonathan W. Daly, "Emergency Legislation in Late Imperial Russia," *Slavic Review* 54, no. 3 (fall 1995): 602–19; Zaionchkovskii, *The Russian Autocracy under Alexander III*, 55, 88, 97–103. Daly argues that the "Temporary Regulations" actually formalized many decrees that had been issued and introduced some limits to the governors' arbitrary authority. He writes, on page 602, that the emergency legislation "was not a turning point on the path toward a modern 'police state' but a sign of that country's uneasy transition from an absolutist to a constitutionalist order." But the immediate effect during the next decade seems to have been to legitimize arbitrary acts taken in contravention of the law. Another revisionist interpretation of Alexander's administration is presented in Baberowski, *Autocratie und Justiz*, 208–23 and passim.

full development. "Feelings of envy and dissatisfaction are alien to her." The emperor declared that he would dedicate himself to "matters of domestic development," connected with economic and social problems, "that now constitute an object of special concern to all governments." The foreign policy would be "completely peace-loving," as Russia remained "loyal to her friends." He indicated that Russia was concerned "above all about herself: Only the duty to defend her honor or security can distract her from internal concerns."[89] The foreign minister Nicholas Giers endeavored to maintain the alliance with Germany and Austria, in defense of the common interests of the three monarchs in central Europe. The reign began with the renewal of the Three Emperors' League in June 1881, which was confirmed again in 1884.

Indeed, Alexander, with Giers's guidance, succeeded in resisting pressures to wage wars twice during his reign. By backing Giers, Alexander succeeded in restraining the generals who had penetrated close to Afghanistan during the 1880s. Russian action in central Asia challenged Britain's control of the routes to India and, in 1885, brought the two empires to the brink of war. Giers, backed by Germany, agreed to negotiations that settled the border dispute. Alexander also curbed those in the central Asian department of the Foreign Ministry who had allowed the generals to seize territories on the eastern frontier. At the same time, he gained British acceptance of the vast conquests in central Asia.[90] In 1885 Alexander contained his anger at his "ungrateful" cousin, Alexander of Battenberg, the king of Bulgaria, who had taken the lead of a liberal national movement to unite with eastern Rumelia. Austria began to prepare for war, but Alexander rejected the advice of Russian agents to intervene in Bulgaria.[91]

Alexander was presented as the "peace-loving tsar" (*tsar'-miroliubivets*) or "tsar peacemaker" (*tsar-mirotvorets*). But his commitment to peace was an expedient and not based on principle. His main goal, he noted in a memorandum of 1882, was taking Constantinople, "so that we are once and for all established on the straits and know that they will be constantly in our hands."[92] He allowed Katkov and other nationalists unusual freedom in criticizing the moderation of the Foreign Ministry. Partly under their influence, and against Giers's recommendations, he pursued an alliance with France, which would strengthen Russia's diplomatic position, particularly in the Bal-

---

[89] The circular, printed in *Pravitel'stvennyi Vestnik* on March 6, 1881, is cited in Voeikov, "Poslednie dni Imperatora Aleksandra II," 106–7; Lowe, *Alexander III of Russia*, 77–80.

[90] Peter Morris, "The Russians in Central Asia," *Slavic and East European Review* 53, no. 133 (October 1975): 526–29, 536–38; Jelavich, *St. Petersburg and Moscow*, 198–201.

[91] The Russian government was convinced that its military could not confront Austria at this stage. Alexander wrote in a memorandum, "Thank God, they are still afraid of us!" See Fuller, *Strategy and Power*, 336–38; Dietrich Geyer, *Russian Imperialism: The Interaction of Domestic and Foreign Policy, 1860–1914* (New Haven, 1977), 117; and Jelavich, *St. Petersburg and Moscow*, 204–10.

[92] "Zapiska A. I. Nelidova v 1882 o zaniatii prolivov," *Krasnyi Arkhiv* 46 (1931): 180–81.

kans. Alexander's open anti-German sentiment and the national tariff policy (see below) prepared the way for the dissolution of the Three Emperors' League at the end of the 1880s and the signing of the Franco-Russian alliance in 1894.

Russia, Alexander's manner implied, could and would make its own choice regarding when to go to war. In the last years of Alexander's reign, a brash sense of Russia's national superiority reigned among officials and Petersburg high society. Andrew Dickson White, the American minister to Russia, wrote, in 1893, that "there has never been a time probably when such a feeling of isolation from the rest of the world and aversion to foreign influence of any sort have prevailed in Russia as at present."[93] In May 1896, just before Nicholas II's coronation, a *New York Times* correspondent wrote from London: "No one seems before to have realized what a colossal thing Russia really is or what prodigious results must follow when she begins to move about. Visitors there report with curious unanimity the discovery that the Russians believe they are on the point of becoming a match for all western Europe quite by themselves and independent of allies."[94] A change in the official manner had taken place, from the sentimentality of the previous reigns—shows of humility, sympathy, and tears—to a studied arrogance, giving the impression of invulnerability and certainty.

•

This sense of certainty, derived from a feeling of national historic destiny, made it possible in the last years of Alexander's reign to disregard the social disruptions and political repercussions attendant on a policy of rapid industrialization. The fear that Russia might follow the path of western Europe had dominated high spheres of Russian government since the reign of Nicholas I. After the emancipation the government followed a laissez-faire policy, expecting that increased freedom would stimulate economic growth, whereas conservatives sought to discourage large concentrations of industry. The Ministry of Finance was preoccupied with fiscal concerns, striving to keep down expenditures in order to deal with the deficits incurred by Russia's heavy military expenses.[95]

The principal critic of the government's caution in economic policies was Michael Katkov. Katkov was convinced of the Russian state's ability to cope with industrial unrest and, at least until 1885, believed that Russia could have nothing resembling a European proletariat. He considered industrial development "the basis of state life," and his articles repeatedly emphasized the disproportion between Russia's natural wealth and its economic standing. When the Russo-Turkish War exposed the weaknesses of Russia's fiscal

---

[93] Theodore H. von Laue, *Sergei Witte and the Industrialization of Russia* (New York, 1969), 120–22.

[94] *New York Times*, May 24, 1896, 1.

[95] Von Laue, *Sergei Witte* , 8–17.

and economic policies, he turned against the doctrines of laissez-faire and began to demand increased governmental involvement in the economy.Katkov's attention focused on two questions—the nationalization of the railroads and the struggle for a tariff that would protect Russian industry. He concluded that, in both Russia and France, private ownership of railroads had led to widespread corruption and disregard for the interest of the state as a whole. He admired Bismarck's policy of nationalizing the railroads. "After the bayonet, it is the railways that consummate national cohesion," he wrote.[96]

Katkov's arguments for high protectionist tariffs received a sympathetic ear from the tsar, who had learned the protectionist creed in the 1860s from his teacher, Ivan Babst. Alexander's first minister of finance Nicholas Bunge, however, followed the same policies as his predecessors, while he struggled with the continuing fiscal crisis left by the Russo-Turkish War. Bunge also introduced measures to improve the peasants' condition, such as the repeal of the poll tax and the establishment of a peasant land bank. But Alexander increasingly circumvented his minister. He raised tariffs on his own, in response to pressures from the Moscow industrialists. By 1885, Alfred Rieber concludes, consultations with industrial and trading interests had more influence on tariffs than the chancellery of the minister of finance.[97]

The two ministers who succeeded Bunge, Ivan Vyshnegradskii and Sergei Witte, were spokesmen for Katkov's views. Both had been trained as engineers and had advanced to the position of director of the privately owned Southwestern Railway Company, rather than having come through the official hierarchy. They brought to government an understanding of industry and the needs of entrepreneurs as well as a conviction that industrial development was essential to Russia's future as a great power. Vyshnegradskii had been a professor of mechanical engineering at St. Petersburg Technological Institute. Witte, a member of the Baranov Commission planning the government takeover of the railroads in Russia, published an important book on railroad traffic rates. Both wrote for *Moskovskie Vedomosti*. Their articles condemned Bunge's policies and argued for higher tariffs, greater state intervention in the economy, and active encouragement of industry.[98]

Vyshnegradskii began his tenure as minister in 1887 by sharply raising tariffs on industrial goods. Other increases followed, culminating in the "Mendeleev tariff" of 1890—inspired by the chemist's calls for protectionism—which lifted Russia's rates to the highest in the world. These increases provoked a tariff war between Germany and Russia. The tariff issue, com-

[96] Tvardovskaia, *Ideologiia poreformennogo samoderzhaviia*, 74–81, 100–102.

[97] Rieber, *Merchants and Entrepreneurs*, 111–12, 198.

[98] B. V. Anan'ich and R. Sh. Ganelin, "I. A. Vyshnegradskii i S. Iu. Vitte—korrespondenty 'Moskovskikh vedomostei,' " in N. G. Sladkevich, ed., *Problemy obshchestvennoi mysli i ekonomicheskaia politika Rossii XIX–XX vekov* (Leningrad, 1972), 12–34.

bined with the Russian government's prohibition on acquisition of land by foreigners in the Vistula provinces, led Bismarck in 1887 to forbid the sale of Russian securities on the Berlin stock exchange.[99] Russia now turned to France as its principal securities' market.

Sergei Witte's tenure as minister of finance (1892–1903) marked the turn to a policy of state-subsidized industrialization. His program was the ultimate realization of Alexander's national views. Witte was convinced that the emperor's authority and the people's religious faith and political devotion gave the state vast powers to promote economic development. He maintained a Katkovian faith in the capacity of the Russian state to contain the social dissatisfaction and unrest attendant on industrial development. In his mind the Russian state was a mighty organism standing above society and capable of prodigies. Unlike Pazukhin, he believed that its officials did not have to worry about a social base in the nobility. He wrote in a memorandum of 1897 that the Russian state had not developed on the basis of an existing estate structure. "Having no enemies, the supreme power in Russia has no need of allies."[100]

In his writings of the 1880s Witte grounded his economic ideas on a conception of the Russian people's deep religious faith. His ideas in this respect were close to Pobedonostsev's, whom he regarded as "the most highly cultured and intelligent Russian he knew" and who shared his sense that industrial technology was necessary for Russia.[101]

Economic doctrine, Witte believed, had to be based on Orthodox faith, which protected the Russian people from socialist doctrines. In his first extended work, an analysis of railroad freight rates, published in 1883, Witte presented Orthodoxy as the basis of social morality: Religion would instill love in the lower classes— that is, respect or obedience—and would lead the upper classes to exemplify the ethos of work and simplicity. Such a change in the attitudes of many Russians of all classes, he thought, would result from the ongoing revitalization of the Orthodox Church.[102]

Witte's brochure, *Regarding Nationalism: National Economy and Friedrich List*, published in 1888, set forth List's arguments for the protection of national industry. He found the 1841 work of the German liberal a powerful statement of the importance of industrial development to a nation's greatness. List had looked to Britain as a model, then developed his own arguments for governmental protection of native industry against British competition. Protective tariffs had spared German industry the

---

[99] Geyer, *Russian Imperialism*, 130–33, 153–57.

[100] Solov'ev, *Samoderzhavie i dvorianstvo v kontse XIX veka*, 282.

[101] Witte, *Vospominaniia*, 1:306; Byrnes, *Pobedonostsev*, 360–61, 365.

[102] Von Laue, *Sergei Witte*, 50–52; Steven G. Marks, *Road to Power: The Trans-Siberian Railroad and the Colonization of Asian Russia, 1850–1917* (Ithaca, N.Y., 1991), 24; Sergei Witte, *Printsipy zheleznodorozhnykh tarifov po perevozke gruzov* (St. Petersburg, 1910), 129–33.

effects of British competition, and Witte looked toward Germany as a model for Russia.[103]

His presentation of List is a good example of what may be called the nativization of a Western idea. List had considered the development of representative institutions and increased freedom essential to the growth of a national economy. Witte omitted mention of these points and instead cited List's views of the historical role of Russian monarchy, which corresponded to his own. List had written that Russia owed all its economic development and commercial significance to the authority of the tsar. Witte concluded that "the economic might of Russia is based exclusively on the mightiest national unity, which creates the basis of the economic well-being of the entire people." List's critique of the "cosmopolitanism" in economic thought, the views of classical English economists to advance policies of free trade, served Witte as a powerful defense of the protectionist policies he promoted in the 1880s and 1890s.[104]

When appointed in August 1892 Witte embarked on his tasks as if he were the bearer of a national spiritual mission led by the tsar. His first step was to attend a religious service in the Finance Ministry's chapel. The priest was the popular Father John of Kronstadt.[105] Witte saw the emperor as the single protector of the good of the people. The lofty power of Russian monarchs, he believed, enabled them to avoid "the conditions that twist the soul and close one's eyes to what one doesn't wish to see." The tsars did not harbor the selfish motives of ordinary mortals, "the egotistical and material interests that often spoil the human heart."[106]

This statement of the moral supremacy of the autocracy, echoing the views of Pobedonostsev, justified the state's operation of the railroads because only the monarch could pursue the common good of Russia. "In the hands of the government of the tsar, who belongs to all social classes and to none, railroads cannot and will never consciously serve as the tool of estate or propertied privilege or for the conscious maintenance of inequality." Rather, they served the interests of the whole people "as a means of giving the people access to the highest blessings of culture."[107] Witte recruited a large number of talented, energetic officials from the provinces into his ministry. This younger generation of officials shared his faith in paternalistic state guardianship (*opeka*) to advance the economy and change the social and agrarian order.[108]

[103] Von Laue, *Sergei Witte*, 62–67.

[104] S. Iu. Witte, *Po povodu natsionalizma: natsional'aia ekonomiia i Fridrikh List* (St. Petersburg, 1912), 41–45.

[105] Von Laue, *Sergei Witte*, 67.

[106] Witte, *Vospominaniia*, 1:407.

[107] Cited in Marks, *Road to Power*, 7–10.

[108] On this new generation of bureaucrats and their political and social views, see David Macey, *Government and Peasant in Russia, 1861–1917: The Prehistory of the Stolypin Reforms* (DeKalb, Ill., 1987), 46–51.

Witte admired Alexander III as an embodiment of power and displayed the brash confidence and contempt for formal procedures characteristic of Alexander's scenario. Though noble by birth, Witte was direct and brusque. He had the manners more of a merchant than a nobleman and felt akin to a tsar who did not prize social polish or superficial courtesy. Like Alexander's teachers, Witte regarded the tsar as a person of moral sense, who had "intelligence of the heart" rather than of the mind. The emperor's physical appearance conveyed a sense of power. "He was not handsome but rather had a kind of bearlike manner. . . . He made an impression with his imposing stature, the calm of his manners, and, on the one hand, his great firmness, and, on the other, the good nature expressed on his face." He was a model family man, head of government, and head of household. "With him, there was no divergence between word and deed. . . . If he said something, you could count on him like a mountain of stone."[109]

With Alexander's backing, Witte worked toward balancing the budget, by sharply increasing excise taxes and seeking foreign loans and investment in Russian industry. Against criticisms that such investment would turn Russia into a foreign colony, Witte replied that the Russian state was too strong to be subjected to foreign powers; it would use Western technology and investment to build the Russian economy. Later in his lectures for grand duke Michael Aleksandrovich, Witte gave the tsar credit for this achievement. Alexander, he wrote with uncharacteristic modesty, had "personally been minister of finance, often taking on himself the 'burden of the Ministry of Finance.'" The emperor himself had moderated the demands of all branches, even the military, and refused requests for extraordinary credits. At the same time, his policy of peace had permitted "the significant growth of many branches of the national economy."[110]

The building of the economy, however, depended on enormous exactions from the rural population, which the government used to balance the budget, subsidize industry, and pay off foreign loans. The high excise taxes introduced under Vyshnegradskii led to the further impoverishment of rural Russia and contributed to the great famine of 1891. But when Witte assumed the office of minister of finance in the midst of the famine, he continued the policies of borrowing heavily abroad and taxing the rural population. He maintained that the high tariffs would protect Russian industry, even if it raised the prices of industrial goods for rural landholders.

Witte's policies were based on a Katkovian trust in the autocratic state to contain social unrest and his belief that the peasant population would remain the monarch's humble and faithful subjects. His industrial policies alienated the provincial nobility, who witnessed the government subsidizing and encouraging industry while paying what they regarded as scant attention to

---

[109] Witte, *Vospominaniia*, 1:188–89, 407–08; Von Laue, *Sergei Witte*, 37–38.
[110] S. Iu. Witte, *Konspekt lektsii o gosudarstvennom khoziastve* (St. Petersburg, 1914), 51–52.

their needs. The building of industry both increased the ranks of the opposition among the nobility and led to the growth of an industrial proletariat with a great concentration of workers in the capital. The grandiose designs inspired by the national myth disregarded the apprehensions of traditional conservatives and bred new social and political forces that the government found increasingly difficult to contain.

Witte's major initiative, the Trans-Siberian Railroad, also figured in his vision of a rejuvenated autocracy resuming its status as a dominant power. The railroad sought to advance the goal, long sought by the tsar, of the administrative Russification of Siberia.[111] But for Witte, the Trans-Siberian Railroad promised gains beyond the administrative unification and economic development of the empire. He shared the enthusiasm in high governmental spheres for Russia's cultural tasks in Asia, what Theodore Von Laue described as "imperialist exultation." He viewed the Siberian railroad as a symbol and instrument of Russia's progress and might, allowing Russian penetration into the eastern reaches of the empire and then into Asian markets beyond Russia's borders.[112]

In the 1890s Witte began to propagate a national imperialism that exalted the Russian nation as the bearer of a higher Orthodox cultural tradition beyond Russia's borders into the Far East. He fell under the influence of the Buriat Lamaist healer Peter Badmaev, who boasted that he could foment rebellions in China and inner Asia among the native peoples and convince them to accept the authority of the Russian tsar.[113] He also introduced Badmaev to the heir, Nicholas Aleksandrovich, who listened sympathetically to these schemes. The atmosphere of heady confidence in St. Petersburg lent Russia's mission in the East a sense of destiny, of coming triumphs and conquests. In a dispatch of July 1895 the German ambassador Prince Radolin noted the swaggering confidence reigning in the upper echelons of the Russian officer corps about their mission in Asia: "In short, everything I hear blends into one single voice, which says that in time Russia is destined for world domination, starting with the East and Southeast, which are as yet unspoiled by the cancer of European civilization. . . . These are not just a few single exalted individuals who think and speak this way—this is the general view that one encounters everywhere."[114]

---

[111] Marks, *Road to Power*, 52–54, 69–74, 94–95, 106–7.

[112] Von Laue, *Sergei Witte*, 121–22; Marks, *Road to Power*, 125, 136–38.

[113] Geyer, *Russian Imperialism*, 189.

[114] Cited in David Schimmelpenninck Van Der Oye, "Ex Oriente Lux: Ideologies of Empire and Russia's Far East, 1895–1904," Ph.D. diss., Yale University (1997), 221.

CHAPTER EIGHT

Petersburg and Moscow;
The Death of a Russian Tsar

This was not a mob,
It ignited elemental feelings (*stikhiia*),
Love and sadness,
It summoned native forces;
They trudged from everywhere,
The children of national grief,
Like a solid wall, near the walls,
They stood for whole days;
Whole nights, from the river,
Like an overflow of water,
The Russian people poured
Into the fortress like a powerful wave,
There was rich man and poor,
Equal before that giant,
Who rested in peace, sheltered
By the canopy, magnificent like power,
He lay as if alive,
Pensively silent and tranquil,
This warrior of universal peace,
Silent forever.

—*"The Final Farewell," Apollon Kokhin, 1894*[1]

COURT AND FAMILY

The national myth was made known on the printed page, in ceremonies, and
by the designs and silhouettes of Orthodox Churches. Governmental decrees, programmatic statements, and laudatory accounts of Alexander III's
public appearances announced the redemption of a distant past. Military
and church ceremony displayed religious symbols of Muscovy. Church architecture transformed the landscape, demonstrating the rebirth of old Russia

[1] *Vsemirnaia Illiustratsiia*, no. 1344 (1894): 402.

in the midst of the new. The scenario of Russian tsar unfolded beyond the confines of the imperial court, depriving it of the tsar's sacred aura.

Since the reign of Nicholas I the court had represented the ceremonial center of the Russian administration, an epitome of the Russian state.[2] Court titles or ranks rewarded officials who won the favor of their superiors or the throne. They could appear in the precincts of their sovereign and enjoy the reflected glory in their offices in Petersburg or the provinces. The scenarios of the previous reigns lent a sentimental and personal character to the relationships between sovereign and servitor. The official received the personal recognition of the monarch, who addressed him by name and recalled forebears and relatives, suggesting familiar, family bonds. Alexander II addressed officials, too, with *ty*, the familiar form, and greeted and embraced them warmly. The court ceremonies played out the scenarios of the sovereigns, swelling the participants and the chorus, in displays of a sentimental bond with the throne.

By all appearances the court flourished in Alexander III's reign, its festivities providing the show expected of the Russian monarchy. Social functions resumed in the winter of 1882–83. The court journal for 1884 listed seven balls in January and February—four at the Anichkov Palace, where the imperial family resided during the season, and three at the Winter Palace—in addition to social evenings and other functions. Lavish occasions took place at the Winter Palace, attended by up to eight thousand guests, and at the Anichkov Palace every winter, with the exception of 1892, when they were canceled and two hundred thousand rubles assigned to famine relief.[3]

Gracious socializing replaced the discord of politics. Oppositional salons closed. Society "danced more and criticized less. . . . Politics ceased to interest the public," Catherine Radziwill wrote, "because, it was felt, this was a subject which the Sovereign liked to reserve to himself."[4] The round of balls, breakfasts, and receptions that lasted from New Year's until Lent demonstrated the staying power of the monarchical order in Russia. The return of the social season was publicized in the popular press. The weekly illustrated *Vsemirnaia Illiustratsiia* printed brief descriptions and full-page reproductions of drawings and gravures of court events, beginning with the great winter ball in the Winter Palace of January 19, 1883, attended by twenty-eight hundred members of the court, the military, and the governmental elite, as well as provincial governors and marshals. The journal cited *Pravitel'-stvennyi Vestnik*: "There has not been the glitter, animation, and unconstrained merriment of this first great ball of Their Majesties in the halls of

---

[2] See Volume 1: 322–32.

[3] V. S. Krivenko, ed., *Obzor deiatel'nosti Ministerstva Imperatorskogo Dvora* (St. Petersburg, 1901), part 2, 138–79; *Kamer-fur'ierskii zhurnal* (1884), RGIA, 516-1(206/2703)-36; Véra Galitzine, *Reminiscences d'une émigrée* (Paris, 1925), 70–73; [Anonymous], *Russian Court Memoirs, 1914–1916* (New York, n.d.), 34.

[4] Radziwill, *Behind the Veil*, 159.

the palace for a long time." A two-page spread of black and white drawings by Karl Brozh presented a montage of five scenes from the event.[5]

The national myth introduced a disjuncture between the symbols consecrated by the myth and the ceremonies that united the notables of the administrative and military elite with the Russian sovereign. This disjuncture remained submerged during Alexander's reign. The feelings of devotion to a Russian tsar and Orthodox Church that embodied the Russian national spirit validated the nationality of Westernized noblemen and officials. Their attachment to early Russia was displayed by their predilection for artistic motifs from the distant past, the Russian style, and their interest in the study of early-Russian history.

This predilection was more than an artistic taste: It indicated the Western court's affinity for the Russian national past, without suggesting a renunciation of Western culture. It was reflected in a semiotics of association, through decorative art, dress, and architecture with Russian motifs. Alexander's younger brother, the grand duke Vladimir Aleksandrovich, who was the president of the Academy of Arts, took the lead in favoring the new taste. In 1885 and 1886 he had the lower dining room of his palace on the Neva redesigned as an old-Russian chamber, with painted vaults and ceiling and richly decorated wood panels.[6] The initial display of the Russian style was the gala costume ball Vladimir gave at his palace on January 25, 1883.

Vladimir's Palace was decorated to resemble old-Russian chambers.[7] The 250 guests came in costumes of boyars, Scythians, Varangians, and citizens of Novgorod, and one lady as a *rusalka*, or mermaid, from the Dnepr River. The costumes were designed based on careful historical research. A report in *Vsemirnaia Illiustratsiia* marveled, "It was as if all pre-Petrine Rus' was resurrected and had sent its representatives to the ball."[8] Although the ball followed the traditional sequence of Western dances, and the menu was Western, the grand duke also served chestnuts, cloudberries, cranberries, and black currants to indicate a national taste.

The grand duke Vladimir and the grand duchess Maria Pavlovna, dressed as a boyar and boyar's wife, greeted Alexander and Maria Fedorovna with bread and salt. The scene was presented in a popular lithograph based on a drawing from *Vsemirnaia Illiustratsiia* (fig. 36). The empress wears the bejeweled robes of a tsaritsa of Moscow. But Alexander comes in the gener-

[5] *Vsemirnaia Illiustratsiia*, February 19, 1883, 162–65. On Brozh, see *Nicholas and Alexandra: The Last Imperial Family of Tsarist Russia* (London, 1998), 66–68.

[6] M. N. Velichenko and G. A. Miroliubova, *Dvorets velikogo kniazia Vladimira Alekandrovicha* (St. Petersburg, 1997), 132, 138.

[7] For a good description of the preparations for the ball and of the ball itself, see ibid., 105–22.

[8] *Vsemirnaia Illiustratsiia*, February 18, 1884, 182. The event was also described in *Vestnik Iziashchnikh Iskusstv* 1 (1883): 122.

36. *Grand Duke Vladimir Aleksandrovich and His Spouse Bring Bread and Salt to Their Imperial Majesties.* Chromolithograph, 1883. Russian National Library, Print Division. St. Petersburg.

al's uniform of the Cavalry of the Artillery.[9] He thus follows the early-nineteenth-century manner when men did not wear costumes but were observers of, rather than participants in, the masquerade pageant. We witness, however, a change in manner from the masquerade ball of 1849 in Moscow when a pageant of noblemen and noble ladies in native costume entertained the imperial family and court nobility, who wore their usual formal dress.

Otherwise, the court continued to follow Western patterns, though Alexander did have the musicians at palace balls dress in red Russian-style caftans. Lithographs in *Vsemirnaia Illiustratsiia*, such as the scene of the ball in the Concert Hall of the Winter Palace on January 20, 1884, show the restrained elegance of the Westernized court (fig. 37).[10] The black and white sketch is uncluttered by color or individual features, the antithesis of the profuse decorations of the revival churches. Alexander stands stolidly watching the dancers, the grand duke Vladimir at his side. It is a world of contained pleasures, made possible by the emperor's strong, if joyless, countenance.[11]

[9] The general scene by Karl Brozh shows the guests dancing, obscuring all but the head of the emperor, who stands in the rear (*Vsemirnaia Illiustratsiia*, February 26, 1883, 181–84).

[10] *Vsemirnaia Illiustratsiia*, February 18, 1884, 155–57.

[11] For other drawings of Brozh, see *Nicholas and Alexandra*, 67.

37. Ball at Winter Palace. Lithograph, 1884. *Vsemirnaia Illiustratsiia*. Slavic and Baltic Division, New York Public Library. Astor, Lenox, and Tilden Foundations.

The empress Maria Fedorovna lent the court its éclat, offsetting her husband's brooding presence with her charm. Catherine Radziwill wrote:

Her lovely smile, the gentle look of her eyes—those great luminous black eyes, that seemed to read into one's very soul—brought more friends to her husband than millions spent or years of effort would have done. Whenever she appeared, whether in a ballroom surrounded by imperial pomp and adorned with the crown jewels or in a humble cottage, wherever one saw her she took with her light and joy and consolation.[12]

The empress danced. The emperor deserted the dance floor as soon as he could for a game of whist. She greeted the guests at the tables graciously while he circulated, fulfilling his duty as host, "as any master of the house would do." He toured the tables "with a bored look, rarely addressing a word to anyone, and went finally to sit, as if relieved of his corvée, next to Countess Vorontsova, to whom he owed no such payment." The empress also delighted at giving informal dance evenings at the Anichkov, with no more than three hundred guests and only the Danish ambassador from the diplomatic corps. These would have continued until morning but for the emperor who ordered the musicians to leave one by one until, with one violinist remaining, the amusements came to an end.[13]

[12] Radizill, *Behind the Veil*, 120.
[13] Ibid., 157, 120–21; Galitzine, *Reminiscences*, 71–72.

The social life of the court thrived but it had become the empress's domain, relegated to the female sphere and therefore of secondary political significance. Russian empresses had always presided at such occasions, but the emperor and his suite remained the central figures. The accounts of the court of Alexander III, written principally by women, focus on the figure of the empress. They dwell on the gems, the finery, the receptions and salons at the great houses of the capital.

Alexander's involvement with the court had a custodial character, presented as his fulfillment, like the tsars of old, of the role of master or housekeeper (*khoziain*) of the Russian land. The official history of the court, published in 1901, presented the emperor's observance of his ceremonial obligations as a national tradition. Alexander held court occasions, not out of the Western spirit of hedonism, "not for the amusement of Himself and his family, but as the master (*khoziain*) of the Russian land. He received guests on ceremonial days and greeted them with bread and salt. During his trips through Russia he distributed gifts to local residents who took part in the tsar's reception."[14]

Alexander III tried to give the administration and management of the court a more Russian character. The ministers of the court under Alexander II had been scions of the Baltic nobility, Vladimir Adlerberg and his son, Alexander Adlerberg, Alexander's boon companion. Russians were more prominent in Alexander III's entourage, particularly generals of his suite who had seen combat in the Caucuses and in the Russo-Turkish War. Illarion Vorontsov-Dashkov, Alexander III's minister of the imperial court, had distinguished himself in the Caucuses and Turkestan and was with him at Rushchuk. From a wealthy, Russian aristocratic family, he had collaborated with Rostislav Fadeev in the Holy Retinue and shared the vision of a national monarchy.[15] For his estate in Tambov Province, he built a flamboyant brick Moscow-Iaroslavl–style church, designed by Nicholas Sultanov, which was shown to the public in the journal *Zodchii*.[16]

Peter Cherevin filled the office described as Alexander's *dezhurnyi general*, which in this case meant "the general always on duty." He controlled access to the tsar and was in charge of the tsar's security. Cherevin had achieved distinction during the Russo-Turkish War and served as assistant minister of the interior under Loris-Melikov. He shared Alexander's conceptions of outside reality, splitting the world between good and bad, the emperor and empress belonging to the former, and everyone else, including the ministers, grand dukes, and foreign monarchs, to another sphere, worthy of contempt. Cherevin was Alexander's drinking companion and the individual closest to him. He dazzled "in his Cossack uniform with the Cross of St. George for the Turkish campaign and a large white hat—the *papakha*." The third mem-

---

[14] Krivenko, *Obzor deiatel'nosti Ministerstva Imperatorskogo Dvora*, 17.

[15] V. S. Krivenko, "V ministerstve imperatorskogo dvora," RNB, 1000-2-672, 32–37, 52.

[16] *Zodchii* (1889): 74–77.

ber of this triumvirate, however, was the Baltic nobleman Gen. Otto Richter, who had fought in the Caucuses in the 1850s and, in 1858, had been designated as the companion of the grand duke Nicholas Aleksandrovich and Alexander Aleksandrovich. Richter served as director of the division of the emperor's chancellery in charge of petitions. He prudently refrained from representing the interests of the Baltic nobility, though he passed on information from governors' reports to their corporate leaders. He, too, cut an imposing, majestic figure as he led the imperial suite on parade.[17]

Alexander made known his determination to eliminate waste and reduce expenditures. Memoirs comment on his frugality and his efforts to end the extravagance of court suppers and to curtail excessive personnel. Wherever possible, he declined proposals for major improvements in the palaces and preferred repairs to replacement. He and the imperial family avoided lavish expenditures on their own needs. But other expenses increased. Alexander spent large sums of money on gifts of jewelry, which were administered by the newly reorganized emperor's cabinet.[18] He raised the wages of court servants, who, he insisted, should be only Russians, including the cooks. He introduced electricity both in imperial palaces and on the streets of Peterhof, Gatchina, and Tsarskoe Selo.[19] Alexander's favorites, however, were less frugal than he. At Gatchina, Cherevin was famous for his own "club," which he held at midday for officials arriving from Petersburg to report to the tsar. He welcomed them with his famous wit and sumptuous lunches of food and wine drawn freely from the court storehouses.[20]

Alexander took a hard-headed, economic approach to members of the extended imperial family—his brothers, uncles, and cousins. He evicted the grand dukes living at court expense in the rooms of the Winter Palace and withdrew their right to help themselves to whatever they needed in the way of furniture, dinnerware, and other items from the imperial palaces. In 1886 he approved a law regarding the imperial family, which limited membership to the children and grandchildren of reigning emperors, who would receive an allowance of 280,000 rubles a year from the court lands.[21]

Alexander abandoned his father's cordial family manner, particularly the practice of allowing grand dukes to visit the emperor uninvited. He refused to tolerate the escapades of his uncles, Constantine and Nicholas Nikolae-

[17] Krivenko, "V ministerstve imperatorskogo dvora," 141–46, 151–53; "Cherevin i Aleksandr III," *Golos Minevshego*, no. 5–6 (1917): 96–101; Whelan, *Adapting to Modernity*, 173.

[18] Sergei N. Gontar, "Alexander III's Reforms in the Decorative Arts," in *Maria Feodorovna: Empress of Russia*, 276.

[19] Krivenko, *Obzor deiatel'nosti Ministerstva Imperatorskogo Dvora*, 1–18; part 2, 76–117; Epanchin, *Na sluzhbe trekh imperatorov*, 179–80; Gerua, *Vospominaniia o moei zhizni*, 1:44; Tatiana N. Muntian, "Life at the Court of Alexander III and Maria Feodorovna," in *Maria Feodorovna: Empress of Russia*, 308.

[20] Krivenko, "V ministerstve imperatorskogo dvora," 153–55, 204–5.

[21] Krivenko, *Obzor deiatel'nosti Ministerstva Imperatorskogo Dvora*, part 2, 32–37; Krivenko, "V ministerstve imperatorskogo dvora," 52–53; Mosolov, *Pri dvore poslednego Rossiiskogo imperatora*, 63–67; BE, 53:119.

vich, both of whom started second families with ballerinas. He punished these wayward relatives like a stern patriarch. He barred Constantine Niko-laevich from residence in Petersburg and Nicholas Nikolaevich from service. The young duke Michael Mikhailovich paid for a marriage with a foreign countess against the emperor's wishes by losing his military and court rank in the army and being forced into exile abroad.[22]

On the other hand, those grand dukes whom the emperor respected were promoted to prominent positions. He appointed his uncle, Michael Nikolae-vich, chair of the State Council in 1881. His brother, Vladimir, a connoisseur of art, remained president of the Academy of Art, and Aleksei Aleksandro-vich continued to serve as chief admiral of the fleet. He appointed the poet Grand Duke Constantine Konstantinovich, the oldest son of Constantine Nikolaevich, president of the Academy of Sciences in 1889.[23] Alexander placed his greatest trust in his brother Sergei, who was the most zealous adherent of the national myth and whom he named governor-general of Moscow in 1891 (see below, in this chapter).

•

Alexander was a devoted family man, but he did not present his family as a symbol of the moral supremacy of the monarchy and the imperial court, as had Nicholas I. Alexander, Maria Fedorovna, and the children participated in imperial ceremonies, but they did not take on roles dramatizing the tran-scendent humanity of the emperor. During the winter social season the fam-ily resided in the congenial chambers of Anichkov and not at the Winter Palace. The contrast with Nicholas I is indicative. Nicholas also had loved Anichkov, and he and the empress Alexandra Fedorovna had regarded the move to the Winter Palace at his accession as an expulsion from paradise. Nonetheless, Nicholas resided at the Winter Palace and presented his family there as the centerpiece of the court.[24]

Alexander's private life assumed its own sacred character. His family con-stituted a realm apart from the state, the object of primary loyalty and af-fection. Alexander doted on his children and frequently chopped wood, hunted, and went fishing with them. His one vice was an immoderate love of brandy, which he consumed in large quantities with his companion, the court commandant P. A. Cherevin, hiding his bottle in a jackboot to avoid the empress's suspicious eye. Then, it was said, he broke out of his customary taciturnity, fell to the floor, and rolled about boisterously with the children.[25]

[22] Lowe, *Alexander III of Russia*, 323; Witte, *Vospominaniia*, 1:422–26; Radziwill, *Behind the Veil*, 161–62.

[23] Norman, "Alexander III as a Patron of Russian Art," 29. On Constantine Konstantino-vich, see V. S. Sobolev, *Avgusteishii Prezident: Velikii Kniaz' Konstantin Konstantinovich vo glave Imperatorskoi Akademii Nauk, 1889–1915 gody* (St. Petersburg, 1993).

[24] See Volume 1: 261, 322–28.

[25] "Cherevin i Aleksandr III," *Golos Minevshego*, 99–100.

The imperial family thus took up the middle-class ideal of separation of private from public life. It inhabited its own sequestered settings, apart from the capital. Gatchina remained Alexander's favorite suburban residence, though the family stayed at Peterhof in June and July for the summer social events. He avoided Tsarskoe Selo, which recalled painful memories of his father's affair with Dolgorukova. At Gatchina, he lived a life "more like that of a private country squire than the life a sovereign was generally supposed to lead." The family occupied small, low-ceiling rooms overstuffed with Victorian furniture and bric-a-brac and took advantage of the magnificent parks for shooting, boating, and long walks. Members of the court were not attracted to the town, which they found dull and quiet, and officials suffered the long and tedious trips from Petersburg. For the court and the educated public, Gatchina was a scene of confinement, resembling a prison as well as a fortress, and the emperor was viewed as a prisoner, unable to travel freely in his own domain.[26] To discountenance such thinking and to answer reports in the foreign press that the emperor remained locked in his apartments, newspapers in the first months of his reign described his frequent outings in the parks at the Gatchina Estate and in the surrounding areas.[27]

The feelings and experiences of the imperial family's private life found representation in private objects, miniatures of decorative art. Alexander liked Russian art and collected folk handicrafts—ceramics from Gzhel, clay figures from Dumkogo. He and the empress had a particular taste for the jewelry and decorative art that had been perfected and gained new appeal in fin-de-siècle France. In France, Deborah Silverman writes, objets d'art decorating the household represented "nature against history, private intimacy against public monumentality, feminine caprice against male rationality."[28] At the same time, such objects in the form of high "kitsch" brought great public moments into the comfortable precincts of the home, equating the monumental with the familiar and picturesque. They erased the distinction, Maurice Agulhon wrote, between the "aesthetics of the exterior" and the "aesthetics of the interior."[29]

The opulent Easter eggs fashioned by the jeweler Carl Fabergé expressed the broad themes of Alexander's scenario in the idiom of late-nineteenth-

---

[26] Tvardovskaia, *Rossiiskie Samoderzhtsy,* 243; Petrovskii, *Pamiati Imperatora Aleksandra III,* 318–19; Epanchin, *Na sluzhbe trekh imperatorov,* 174–75; Radziwill, *Behind the Veil,* 152–53.

[27] For example, *MV,* May 2, 1881, carried a report to this effect reprinted from the newspaper *Golos.*

[28] See Debora L. Silverman, *Art Nouveau in Fin-de-siècle France: Politics, Psychology, and Style* (Berkeley, 1989), 21, 30–33, 38. Silverman also shows the political significance of rococo as a cultural grounding for the Franco-Russian alliance (159–71).

[29] Thomas Richards describes high kitsch as "the miniature attempting to signify the gigantic by compressing the public sphere into the narrow compass of small objects designed for private consumption." Thomas Richards, *The Commodity Culture of Victorian England: Advertising and Spectacle, 1851-1914* (Stanford, 1990), 88. Maurice Agulhon "La 'statuomanie' et l'histoire," in his *Histoire vagabonde* (Paris, 1988), vol. 1: 174-75.

38. "Hen" Egg, by Fabergé. 1885. Photograph by Larry Stein.
The FORBES Magazine Collection, New York. © All rights reserved.

century decorative art, turning these familiar Easter gifts into small monuments of the feelings and experiences of the imperial family. Their splendor and importance indicate the shift in the locus of representation from the arena of the court to the private setting, where the symbols and events of the imperial house could become the object of the members' own fascination and adulation. While Alexander continued to give thousands of small porcelain Easter eggs as gifts during the Easter celebrations, in 1885 he began to give a Fabergé egg as an especially meaningful gift to the empress, an imperial keepsake.[30]

The subjects of the Fabergé eggs were chosen to suit the emperor's taste. Fabergé cleared every aspect of their design with the minister of the court who, it is evident, was acting under the instructions of the tsar himself.[31] According to tradition, the Easter egg as a symbol originated with Mary Magdalena, the patron saint of the emperor's mother, Maria Aleksandrovna, and of his wife, Maria Fedorovna. The egg symbolized Christ's resurrection,

---

[30] See Alexander von Solodkoff, "History of the House of Fabergé," in Solodkoff (ed.), *Masterpieces from the House of Fabergé*, (New York, 1989), 56-57. Egg-shaped objets d'art had been produced as Easter presents since the eighteenth century. But only with Fabergé's creations did they become a traditional gift within the family and a symbolic and artistic expression of the family itself; Tamara V. Kudriavtseva, "The Feasts of Feasts; Russian Orthodox Easter," in *Kejslige Daskaeg*; *Imperial Easter Eggs* (Copenhagen, 1994), 14-16.

[31] Marina Lopato, "Fresh Light on Carl Fabergé," *Apollo* (January 1984): 44; Solodkoff, "History of the House of Fabergé," 54–61.

and Alexander chose the egg as the symbol of death and resurrection of the imperial family. Easter eggs identified the family tragedies of the previous decade with the nation's spiritual rebirth. The earliest surviving Fabergé egg, which Alexander gave to Maria Fedorovna in 1885, contained Fabergé's trademark "surprise" in the center—a tiny hen that enclosed a crown—connecting the symbol of rebirth with the monarchy (fig. 38). The "Resurrection" egg of 1889 was a single piece of crystal containing a realistic scene of the Resurrection sculpted within.[32] Fabergé's succession of flower eggs in the 1890s carried on the themes of spring and rebirth. The first of these, the Imperial Spring Flowers Egg, conceals a small egg of red enamel, decorated with rococo-style scroll work. The small egg opens to reveal a bower of flowers of white chalcedony and garnets, which can be removed from its golden base.[33]

•

Beginning in 1883 the imperial family spent two to three months each year away from Petersburg and the suburban estates. They visited Livadia in the Crimea first in 1884 and most years returned for visits lasting from one to several months. They lived in the modest Small Palace, while the larger palace, Massandra, was under construction in Louis XIII style. Despite its baroque exterior and elaborate parks, Massandra had wood-paneled small rooms and low ceilings that gave Alexander a sense of comfort. He also built a small hunting lodge on the estate. For the imperial family, Livadia was a retreat from official Petersburg. The heir Nicholas Aleksandrovich described in his diary the warmth and informality of the celebration in 1891 of the twenty-fifth wedding anniversary of the emperor and empress: "Most pleasant was that there was nothing official about the celebration. Everyone wore frock coats (*siurtuki*), and it was completely patriarchal!"[34]

Other trips included cruises on the imperial yachts through the Finnish archipelagoes and trips to Denmark, which took place nearly every year and lasted for six to ten weeks. Alexander most closely realized his ideal of private life among his Danish relatives, far from the burdens of his office and fears for his security. He felt himself a welcome guest at Fredensborg palace where he enjoyed "romping on the sequestered lawns . . . with the children of his royal relatives who knew and adored him as 'Uncle Sasha.' "[35]

---

[32] Susanna Pfeffer, *Fabergé Eggs: Masterpieces from Czarist Russia* (n.p., 1990), 16–25; A. Kenneth Snowman, *Carl Fabergé: Goldsmith to the Imperial Court of Russia* (New York, 1979), 90–91. The first Fabergé egg recorded in the archives was a white enamel egg, set with diamonds and two egg-shaped rubies, but this example has not survived and has not, to my knowledge, been described elsewhere (Tatiana F. Faberzhe and V. V. Skurlov, *Istoriia firmy Faberzhe* [St. Petersburg, 1993], 19, 61).

[33] Pfeffer, *Fabergé Eggs*, 22–25, 34–37, 54–55, 58–61.

[34] N. N. Kalinin and M. A. Zelianichenko, *Romanovy i Krym* (Moscow, 1993), 58–59.

[35] Krivenko, *Obzor deiatel'nosti Ministerstva Imperatorskogo Dvora*, part 2, 194–200; Lowe, *Alexander III of Russia*, 314.

Like his father, Alexander was a devotee of the hunt. He hunted in the environs of Gatchina, at Lysino and Belovezh, and every other year spent a month at the reserve at Spala in Poland, which he reconditioned and restored. For Alexander III, hunting provided an escape from the official world into nature, which he enjoyed with a few members of his suite and close friends. Alexander carefully recorded the numbers of animals of each type that he shot, the fish that he caught, but his exploits were not publicized in the press as attributes of his heroism. Zichy continued to render the scenes in watercolor, but his pictures were kept in family albums. German princes and generals were among the guests, but Wilhelm II, who yearned to visit Spala, was never invited.[36]

The only extensive ceremonial trip of Alexander's reign occurred from late August to October 1888. The family traveled south through Ukraine to Elizavetgrad for several days of maneuvers and then swung northwest for a week of hunting at the Spala hunting preserve in Poland. They then journeyed east to the Cossack territories, where the heir received his ceremonial induction as Cossack ataman. From September 25 to October 13 they traveled through the Caucuses. They returned by ship to Sevastopol for their trip to Moscow. On October 17 their train derailed near the station of Borki in Kharkov Province.

The appearance of the family reaffirmed the claim that these were lands to be ruled and, where possible, inhabited by ethnic, Orthodox Russians. It provided an occasion to invoke the synchronic mode and disclose traces of an original Russian and Orthodox domination. This was the message of his visit to the Polish town of Kholm, where the family stopped on their way to Spala. Kholm exemplified the goals of the policy of Russification. The nobility of Kholm was Polish and Catholic, the peasantry Ukrainian and adherents of the Uniate faith. In 1875 the Russian government had "united" the Uniates with the Orthodox Church. After that, the local administration had endeavored to force the peasants into Orthodox congregations, but these efforts met with strong resistance.[37]

The account, in *Moskovskie Vedomosti*, of Alexander's visit described Kholm as part of the Russian land. The tsar appeared among the "martyrs" who had suffered "the blind hatred of the apostates from Slavdom." One had to be present to understand the importance of "an event experienced by Kholm Rus', resurrecting her, as once in ancient times a drink of fresh water resurrected the semi-legendary *bogatyr'*." The crowds greeted Alexander on his way to the Kiril-Methodius Church, which had been built in 1875. They awaited the act of "union of the Russian Tsar with the Russian people of the borderland representing part of the ancient Russian-Galician principal-

---

[36] N. A. Vel'iaminov, "Vospominaniia N. A. Vel'iaminova ob Imperatore Aleksandre III," *Rossiiskii Arkhiv* 5 (1994): 268–74.

[37] See the thorough discussion in Weeks, *Nation and State in Late Imperial Russia*, 172–76.

ity." The basis of this union was the popular faith in the Kholm Mother-of-God icon, by tradition painted by the disciple Luke and brought to the region by Saint Vladimir himself. The resurrection of the faith was in response to the people, and the newspaper described the "touching" scene of the tsar worshipping together with peasants. "Everywhere in the vast cathedral you could see simple cloth caftans of the local Russian peasantry; you could see the burnt peasant faces. Crude peasant working hands folded, making the cross and zealously praying with their Tsar. You could see eyes full of tears of joy and divine rapture."[38]

In the Caucuses Alexander reviewed Russian troops in each town and received numerous delegations from the region and from central Asia. In Batum he attended the laying of the cornerstone of an Orthodox Church. The bishop described the conquest of the region as the restoration of Christianity, which he believed dominated the region in the distant past as indicated by the ruins of several old churches. Christianity had been destroyed by "the triumph of the sword," but Alexander's father, "uniting this region with Russia, restored Christianity, and the new cathedral will strengthen it under our power. Here justice and not the sword rules."[39]

The government newspaper, *Pravitel'stvennyi Vestnik*, described a triumphal journey of the Russian tsar, who was welcomed into these territories. In the Caucuses Alexander was the deliverer. The exarch of Georgia welcomed Alexander into "this city, before dark and ignorant of the true God, now bright and enlightened in God. For where there is the light of true Christianity, there is the light of true citizenship, there justice and mercy rule."[40] The newspaper emphasized that Alexander appeared in many towns never visited by a Russian tsar. The exarch declared that all the people of the region who had seen the tsar—Georgians as well as Turkmen and other Eastern peoples—were lovers of the Russian tsar. They would return and tell everyone how they had kissed the emperor's hands. They would become heroes of the day in their tribes. The newspaper concluded, "There is no doubt that the visit of His Imperial Majesty to the Caucuses will fuse into one all the nationalities living there in general love and devotion to the Tsar and to stand for Him and for the whole land, the Russian land."[41]

The Russian land defined the new, national character of the Russian empire. The subjugation of other nationalities elevated Russia to the level of an imperial nation and justified the colorful exploits of the Russian forces. The books the imperial family read about history and geography confirmed the myth. The imperial libraries of the late nineteenth century, Marc Raeff noted,

---

[38] *MV*, September 11, 1888, 2.

[39] Ibid., September 26, 1888, 2. Jersild, in "From Frontier to Empire," chap. 4, discusses the notion of the restoration of Christianity among Russian missionaries and colonists of the area at this time.

[40] Cited in *MV*, October 13, 1888, 2.

[41] Cited in ibid., October 18, 1888, 3.

contained little about other nationalities, except for highly embellished romanticizations.[42] The Eastern regions served as scenes of Russian heroism in exotic settings, adventure stories that gave substance to the traditions of heroic conquest.

THE ALEXANDER II MONUMENT

From the moment of Alexander II's death, public opinion demanded monuments that would memorialize Alexander II as emancipator and reformer. The monument to the tsar-emancipator had to figure in a religious-national scenario that deemphasized his civic accomplishments. The designing of a work that both expressed the themes of Alexander III's scenario and commemorated Alexander II's contribution to reform proved difficult indeed. The problems began with the divergent characters of the patrons of the monument. The monument was the initiative of the mayor of Moscow S. M. Tretiakov and the *zemstvo* activist D. F. Samarin. But the choice of the project and the construction remained under the purview of the Ministry of the Court, that is, within the confines of the imperial family. The architects submitting projects for the competition had to depict a monarch who expressed the spirit of reform without offending the sensibilities of Alexander III and the members of the imperial family.[43]

Six months before the assassination, in September 1880, the literary critic Constantine Leont'ev prophesied the complexities of erecting an appropriate statue to Alexander II.[44] Leont'ev contended that the main problem in designing such a monument was to give elegant artistic expression to the achievements of Alexander's reign, which could not be rendered in the usual classical idiom. Current fashion gave no guide: One should not "disfigure a national monument of gratitude with European frock coat and tails," Leont'ev wrote. He envisioned a grandiose "historical cathedral" situated in Moscow, filled with glittering decoration. Decorations would give the monument its national character. There would be elaborate carvings by native craftsmen in the Russian style. Leont'ev regarded the national as only a particular expression of the universal. "The national has been only *unique combinations* of what is common to all mankind (*obshchechelevecheskogo*)." He urged that the monument include copies of ancient Greek statues in ivory, gold, and enamel.

But Alexander III's scenario did not present the national as an expression of the universal, and the artists had to design a statue that somehow ex-

---

[42] Raeff, "The Romanoffs and Their Books," 63.

[43] The rules of the competition were announced in July 1881. The style was left to the artists' discretion, "but the monument should be a faithful and clear representation of the personality, great deeds, and events of the glorious reign of the deceased monarch." The materials were to be granite, marble, and bronze (*MV*, July 31, 1881).

[44] Constantine Leont'ev, *Sobranie sochinenii* (Moscow, 1912), 7:451–57.

pressed both. The combinations proposed in the projects submitted for the three competitions typified the mélange of "positivist art."[45] The five prize-winning entries for the second competition, reproduced in the journal *Vsemirnaia Illiustratsiia*, offered a variety of solutions. Alexander II is presented in three poses—standing, in general's uniform and mantle, seated on the coronation throne, and finally in the classical equestrian pose. The national character was displayed with decorative forms of the "Russian style," such as the tent (*shatrovye*) roofs and *kokoshniki* designs on the canopies and pedestals.[46]

The project awarded first prize, by Vladimir Sherwood, the architect of the Historical Museum in Moscow, gave one answer to the sculptor's quandary. Alexander is presented standing, in general's uniform and mantle. In an explanatory note published in *Moskovskie Vedomosti*, Sherwood claimed that the principles of autocratic rule and emancipation were complementary. It was the uniform, the emperor's military persona, that marked him as leader of his nation. The mantle was necessary because,

> The monument, first, should express the feelings of the people, and the Russian people are accustomed to respecting not only the person of the tsar but the very principle of power. Second, in spite of all his acts of liberation and indeed because of them, the late tsar revealed himself as a true representative of autocratic power.[47]

Power was the principal referent of the project, which may explain its success in the competition. Sherwood expressed the theme of liberation rather obliquely, confounding it with religion. "The tsar, his head bent, looks down with love and points with his right hand to the sacred Kremlin cathedrals. With this movement, we have expressed the religious feeling inspiring him and making up the true source of freedom."[48] The statues on the bases narrated the themes of liberation and the expansion of empire. Groups of standing figures represented the emancipation, the liberation of the Slavs, and the subjugation of the Central Asian khans and the Caucuses.

But neither Sherwood's nor any of the other prize-winning projects appealed to Alexander III. After the third competition, the grand duke Vladimir Aleksandrovich, president of the Academy of Arts, issued a severe judgment: "Not one of the submitted projects has proved worthy of execution as a monument to the deceased Monarch, for they lack monumental appearance, originality, and the character that penetrated the entire reign of the late Emperor."[49] In 1890 the emperor took it upon himself to commission plans

---

[45] Maurice Rheims, *19th Century Sculpture* (New York, 1977), 85.

[46] Sketches of the projects were reproduced in *Vsemirnaia Illiustratsiia*, June 11, 1883, 468.

[47] *MV*, September 23, 1882, 3.

[48] Ibid., 3–4.

[49] N. Sultanov, *Pamiatnik Imperatoru Aleksandru II v Kremle Moskovskom* (St. Petersburg, 1898), 615–19.

from the architect Nicholas Sultanov and the artist P. V. Zhukovskii, who held no official post but was the emperor's personal friend.[50]

Sultanov resolved the problems by designing a massive structure that dwarfed and to a large extent concealed the figure of the tsar. The monument, two perpendicular galleries meeting at the statue of Alexander II, loomed over the wall of the Kremlin (fig. 39). The ceilings of the gallery presented the history of the dynasty in Venetian mosaic portraits of Russian princes and tsars, based on Zhukovskii's drawings. If the embellishments were meant to fit the statue into the surroundings, the portraits were intended to "explain the historical meaning of the monument." The portraits began with St. Vladimir as the first Christian prince, shown wearing a Byzantine crown and holding a cross, and ended with Nicholas I. The historical meaning was embodied in the ruling house, and Alexander II's achievement was presented as an extension of the dynastic heritage.

Sultanov claimed that the monument, like the Kremlin, combined both Russian and Italian forms. Tent-shaped canopies at the ends of the galleries and above the statue, he claimed, marked it as national. The canopy, Sultanov wrote, "gives the monument a sacred character in the eyes of the people completely appropriate to the late emperor, for our people are used to seeing a canopy only over especially sacred spots, as in churches over altar thrones and over the tsar's and patriarch's places, and in palaces over the throne." The canopy, however, was a common device in late-nineteenth-century design, and Sultanov's is particularly reminiscent of George Gilbert Scott's Albert Memorial, completed in 1876. Just as Scott had utilized the Gothic, which had become the British "national" style, Sultanov followed the now emblematic tent form, which evoked the Muscovite traditions of the national myth. The canopy, crowned with a double-headed eagle, was made of pink granite and decorated with gilded bronze and green enamel work. Sultanov claimed it gave the impression of "a colossal piece of brocade forming a tent. It is a replica of those luxurious cloths that were always used to make the tsars' tents."[51]

The statue by A. M. Opekushin, the sculptor of the Pushkin monument in Moscow, emphasized Alexander II's civic and human virtues. Alexander stood before the viewer as he had appeared at his coronation, wearing a full general's uniform beneath the imperial mantle. His left hand holds the scepter and rests on a cushion supporting the imperial crown, thus giving prominence to the inherited symbols of power (fig. 40). At the same time Alexander's right hand points outward to the people, "signifying the good

[50] For a more detailed discussion of the competition and of the monument itself, see my article, "Statues of the Tsars and the Redefinition of Russia's Past," in Donald Martin Reynolds, ed., *"Remove Not the Ancient Landmark": Public Monuments and Moral Values* (Amsterdam, 1996), 124–30. On P. V. Zhukovskii and Alexander, see Vel'iaminov, "Vospominaniia N. A. Vel'iaminova ob Imperatore Aleksandre III," 280.

[51] Sultanov, *Pamiatnik Imperatoru Aleksandru II*, 584–85; Elisabeth Darby and Nicola Smith, *The Cult of the Prince Consort* (New Haven, 1983), 46–50.

39. Alexander II Monument, Moscow Kremlin. Architect, N. Sultanov.
N. Sultanov, *Pamiatnik Imperatoru Aleksandru II v Kremle Moskovskom.*

deeds bestowed on them."[52] There was general agreement that the likeness was extraordinary. Opekushin captured Alexander's straining to play the roles of autocrat, standing above his people, and the sympathetic human being, the benefactor of his people who evoked not awe but affection. He is not a hero but an emperor, at once a military leader and a ruler struggling to be a civic leader. The pedestal carried the inscription: "To Alexander II, with the love of the people."[53]

Like Leont'ev's scheme, the monument sought to answer the problem of memorializing Alexander II by surrounding the figure of the tsar with an

[52] *MV*, August 10, 1898; Sultanov, *Pamiatnik Imperatoru Aleksandru II*, 569–70.
[53] N. A. Geinike et al., eds., *Po Moskve* (Moscow, 1917), 187.

40. *Statue of Alexander II in Moscow*
Kremlin. Sculptor, A. M. Opekushin.
N. Sultanov, *Pamiatnik Imperatoru*
Aleksandru II v Kremle Moskovskom.
St. Petersburg, 1898.

41. Alexander II Statue. Zlatoust,
Ufa Province. Zodchii, 1887.

immense and variegated structure. Louis Leger described it as "assuredly one of the most colossal monuments ever dedicated to glorify a sovereign."[54] A guidebook of 1917 remarked on the excellent view from the gallery but that "the memorial itself does not have an artistic effect." The canopy was "of very expensive materials, with a mass of gilt that is already tarnished and a Venetian mosaic that is tasteless and devoid of ideas."[55]

[54] N. Sultanov, *Pamiatnik Imperatoru Aleksandru II*, 623–24; K. Baedeker, *Russland* (Leipzig, 1901), 241; Louis Leger, *Moscou* (Paris, 1904), 41. The photo is shown in *Pamiatniki arkhitektury Moskvy; Kreml', Kitai-gorod, Tsentral'nye ploshchadi* (Moscow, 1982), 296–97.

[55] Geinike et al., *Po Moskve*, 187. The Bolsheviks tore the monument down shortly after they moved the capital to Moscow in 1918.

Alexander II's achievements received their true tribute in the statues erected to him in towns and public institutions across the empire. While the Moscow monument hid his figure, these placed it forward for all to see. They stood in court houses, before hospitals, and in the squares of provincial towns. The statues showed Alexander in different guises and emphasized various aspects of his activity. In Zlatoust Alexander holds the emancipation edict and is dressed in a simple uniform (fig. 41). The Petrozavodsk statue has Alexander holding the emancipation edict and wearing a uniform and the imperial mantle. In Samara he stood in army uniform and cap, with his hand resting on a sword. The Kishinev monument shows him holding, in his right hand, the declaration of war against Turkey. In Runeberg's famous statue in Helsinki (1894) he wears a military uniform and stands nobly over allegorical depictions of justice, peace, science, and labor. The date 1863, the year he opened the Finnish Diet, is inscribed on the base. Newspapers published reports of peasant villages making collections for their own statues to the tsar-liberator.[56] These statues were discreet statements of dissent from the ruling myth, expressions of the unrealized hopes of moderate society for a continuation of reforms, civic progress, and public participation. In this respect they were counterparts to the Bismarck statues and towers in Germany, which became symbols of a cult of the patriotic bourgeoisie, in answer to the pathos and vainglory of Wilhelm II's cult of self and dynasty.[57]

BORKI AND THE INVOCATION OF MIRACLE

On October 17, 1888, the imperial train returning from the South derailed at the station of Borki, leaving twenty-one dead and thirty-seven injured. The railroad car carrying the imperial family capsized, but all members escaped without serious injury.[58] The accident drew attention to the vulnerability of the emperor and, at the same time, made him the focus of popular sympathy.[59] The disaster was presented as proof of the miraculous grace God sheds on the tsar and the Russian people. The imperial manifesto of October 23, 1888, stated that the miracle was not only the result of divine intervention;

[56] Accounts and pictures of Alexander II statues are scattered throughout the press. There are many examples in the journal *Zodchii* and in D. N. Loman, *Tsar' osvoboditel', tsar'-muchenik, Imperator Aleksandr II; chtenie dlia naroda* (St. Petersburg, 1898).

[57] Thomas Nipperdey, *Gesellschaft, Kultur, Theorie: Gesammelte Aufsätze zur neueren Geschichte* (Göttingen, 1976), 166–67; Isabel V. Hull, "Prussian Dynastic Ritual and the End of Monarchy," in Carole Fink, Isabel V. Hull, and MacGregor Knox, eds., *German Nationalism and the European Response* (Norman, Okla., 1985), 24.

[58] The investigations never conclusively determined the cause of the accident. Many suspected revolutionary sabotage, though mechanical failure seems the most likely explanation. Witte had warned the officials in charge and the tsar himself that the speed was excessive for the condition of the tracks on that line (Witte, *Vospominaniia*, 1:197–99).

[59] Krivenko, "V ministerstve imperatorskogo dvora," 120. Krivenko, who accompanied the tsar, recalled that the people "greeted [the tsar] sincerely, even went into ecstasy."

it was God's response to "to the fervent prayers, which thousands and thousands of sons of Russia daily make for Us wherever there stands a Holy church and Christ's name is praised." The tsar declared that his survival was owing to the holiness of the Russian people. He called upon Divine Providence to give him the strength to complete his "great service," which he had promised to fulfill in his coronation prayer.[60]

The congratulatory literature elaborated on the themes of this manifesto. General E. V. Bogdanovich wrote a brochure emphasizing both Alexander's heroism in taking charge of the evacuation of the wounded and the popular enthusiasm about his survival. He described the religious celebrations of the event, the dedication of churches, chapels, and icons, and the introduction of an annual memorial church service on October 17 to commemorate the bestowal of divine mercy upon Russia. Bogdanovich concluded by setting the event in the seventeenth century narrative of "troubles." Just as God had preserved the tsar, the tsar was preserving Russia.[61]

The metropolitan Platon of Kiev published an admonitory sermon that stressed the organic unity of the Russian people with their tsar. Not only the tsar and his family were menaced "but our fatherland and all of us, the subjects of His Majesty, who form a single political body with him—the Russian state." The accident itself was an act of God, expressing both God's wrath and his mercy. God's wrath had led him to endanger the tsar and the Russian people, and his mercy had allowed him to escape unharmed. God was angry at the Russian people for their sins. Platon held the Russian people collectively responsible for the disaster, just as the church and conservative press had blamed all of Russia for the weakness and liberalism that had made possible the murder of Alexander II. Platon went on to identify the sins of the Russian people. They comprised not only the everyday sins, resulting from the weakness of mortals, but the more serious ones, attendant on "obstinacy" and "unrepentant hearts"—those who sinned with intention. Sectarians headed the list of intentional sinners, followed by adulterers and atheists.[62]

---

[60] *PSZ* 3, no. 5502 (October 23, 1888). The German ambassador General von Schweinitz observed in his diary that the manifesto could be interpreted in two ways. Some, he noted, predicted that the shock might make him milder and more flexible; others predicted that the miraculous escape would make him all the more firm in the defense of the unity of the faith and the Russian language. The congratulatory literature published after the event confirmed the second interpretation (Von Schweinitz, *Denkwürdigkeiten*, 2:372).

[61] E. V. Bogdanovich, *Sila vsevyshniago chudodeistvenno iavlennaia 17 oktiabria 1888g.* (St. Petersburg, 1889), 20–25. Bogdanovich, an elder of the St. Isaac's Cathedral, had been involved with the publication and dissemination of church sermons in the late 1870s and early 1880s. Inspired by the sermons of the metropolitan Filaret of Moscow, Bogdanovich saw his role as enlightener of the people. Bogdanovich included in the volume the various official descriptions of the event, the tsar's manifesto, and the expressions of congratulation and relief that various organizations and groups sent to the tsar (3–5, 46–47).

[62] Platon, Metropolitan of Kiev, *Beseda po sluchaiiu Krusheniia Tsarskogo poezda*, Kiev, 1890, 6–11.

But Russians, the sermon stated, could propitiate the Lord's anger by repenting and giving thanks for sparing the Tsar's life. They should love and obey their tsar, not "conceive anything bad against him and try in every way to preserve him from anything that might bring him harm. The miraculous escape had shown God's Providential concern for Russia. In return, Russians should "with a tenderness of their hearts (*v umilenii serdets*)" pray all the more zealously to God to protect their tsar and help him in his "imperial labors."[63]

•

The emphasis on miracle reflected a fundamental change of emphasis in the tsar's scenario. Before the accident, Orthodoxy was the agency of Russia's providential history, led by the Russian tsars. The invocation of miracle to support the power of a Russian emperor expressed a loss of trust in the forces of history. Miracle acted in defiance of reason and history, realizing the unbelievable. From 1888 to 1894 the return to Moscow increasingly revealed a monarchy reliant on divine intervention, which placed the tsar's power above the laws of nature and reason.

The emphasis on miracle brought Alexander's scenario closer to the simple faith of the people, reflected in their worship of miracle icons, which had become increasingly popular in the decades after emancipation. During this period, B. V. Sapunov writes, icons "penetrated all spheres of the social and personal lives of people of that time, schools, special educational institutions, state offices, private enterprises, hospitals, soldiers' barracks, even drinking houses." The people turned to icons to help them in their worldly travails and to give solace in disappointment and grief. Mother-of-God icons gained an especial popularity, particularly those with figures of the indigent and suffering filling the edges of the image. The Orthodox Church endeavored to assert its authority and investigate to determine which icons deserved veneration. But it was difficult to constrain the popular desire for direct communion with religious symbols. Sapunov found 288 versions of the Mother of God in late-nineteenth-century icons. These icons were looked to for immediate displays of miracle, for the signs of divine intervention, marking Russia as a chosen holy land, a land of miracles born of prayer.[64]

One of the most popular was the icon of the Mother of God, "The Joy of All the Grieving" (*Vsekh skorbiashchikh Radosti*). During the second half of the century thousands of copies of the icon were circulated, its sides covered with different images of the wretched of the earth. The icon had a long

---

[63] Ibid., 12–14.

[64] B. V. Sapunov, "Nekotorye siuzhety russkoi ikonopisi i ikh traktovka v poreformennoe vremia," in *Kul'tura i iskusstvo Rossii XIX veka: Novye Materialy i issledovaniia* (Leningrad, 1985), 141–42.

association with the monarchy and Petersburg; Peter the Great's sister, Natalia, had brought the original to Petersburg in 1711, the year the city officially became the government seat. The association with miracle was confirmed, on July 23, 1888, when a copy of the icon hanging in a wooden chapel on the grounds of the Imperial Glass Factory survived a fire caused by a bolt of lightening, which destroyed all the other icons. "The Joy of All the Grieving" was found on the ground, with donations from the poor—twelve *polushki* (copper quarter-kopek coins with portraits of Nicholas I and Alexander II)—adhering to its surface.[65]

The survival of the icon attested to its miraculous character, and new copies called "The Joy of All the Suffering with Coins" had *polushki* painted on or attached at the appropriate spot on the board. On the site of the fire the government built a church named "Joy of All the Suffering." Initiative came from the minister of the interior who, in June 1893, requested Synod approval for a church to honor the tenth anniversary of Alexander III's reign. Built in elaborate Moscow-Iaroslavl style, with five cupolas, profuse *kokoshniki*, *girki*, and a tent-style bell tower, it brought a scene of old Russia to an embankment of the Neva. Worshipers came by boat or steamship to what soon became one of the most popular shrines of the capital.[66]

After the Borki accident, miracle icons were presented as both talismans divinely bestowed upon Russia and symbols of the bond between tsar and people. The hegumen Ignatii published a pamphlet connecting the tsar's escape with a miracle that had taken place in Vologda on October 17, 1655. On that date a procession of the cross bearing the miracle icon "All-Kind Christ" was followed by the sudden end of a plague. The residents believed that their prayers before the same icon in 1888 had brought divine intercession.[67] A brochure, *Bright Days*, published in Moscow by one E. Poselianin, described the "miracle of October 17" as an example of "God's love for man," like God's placing Jesus Christ on earth to suffer for man's sins. The entire railroad car was wrecked, Poselianin claimed, except for the wall holding an icon of the savior, which remained untouched. God thus gave evidence of his existence and indicated that the Orthodox Church was "the true path to His service." The "miraculous event took place with the Orthodox icon brought to the Tsar by good Orthodox custom." It was a sign of the presence of God in the Orthodox Church, showing that "the Russian land is a holy land."[68] An icon "The Miracle of God's Grace for the Imperial Family and

[65] Ibid., 142–43.

[66] The architects were Alexander Gogen and A. V. Ivanov (Shul'ts, *Khramy Sankt-Peterburga*, 177–78); "Po otnosheniiu Ministerstva Vnutrennikh Del o postroike tserkvi vo imia Skorbiashei Bozhiei Materi v selenii Imperatorskogo steklannogo zavoda na naberezhnoi r. Bol' shoi Nevy," RGIA, 797-63-225.

[67] Arkhimandrit Ignatii, *17 oktiabria. Dva chuda: pervoe v Vologde, 1655 goda, vtoroe, pod khar'kovom, 1888g.* (St. Petersburg, 1890).

[68] E. Poselianin, *Iasnye dni. 17 oktiabria. 29 aprelia. 28 oktiabria* (Moscow, 1892), 10–13.

Russia, October 17, 1888," showing the patron saints of the members of the imperial family, was widely disseminated in photographic copies.[69]

After Borki, Moscow was increasingly presented not only as the birthplace of the monarchy but as the locus of miracle, to be exalted to preserve the union between tsar and people. Poselianin's *Bright Days* declared that the emperor "should have perished according to natural laws." But the "power that [Moscow] had professed and that had exalted her revoked these laws."[70] In February 1891 Alexander III openly demonstrated the special status accorded to Moscow by appointing his brother, Sergei, to replace the liberal V. A. Dolgorukov as governor-general of the city. The commander-in-chief of the Preobrazhenskii Regiment from 1887 to 1891, Sergei was a tall, handsome, guards officer, completely absorbed in the life of his regiment and the boon comradeship of his subordinates. He was also a fervent believer in the idea of a divinely chosen national autocracy derived from original sources of Christianity in the Holy Land. Sergei visited Jerusalem twice to pray at the Church of the Holy Sepulcher and actively participated in the Russian Orthodox Palestine Society, which encouraged Russian pilgrimages to Middle Eastern holy places. He and his wife, the grand duchess Elizabeth Fedorovna, a princess of Hesse-Darmstadt, who remained a devout Lutheran, attended the dedication of the Church of Maria Magdalena in Jerusalem in 1888.[71]

The appointment of a grand duke to the position of governor-general of Moscow represented an extraordinary intrusion of the family into the state's civil structure. It meant placing the city government under a member of the imperial family with direct access to the tsar. The assigning of such power recalled the fragmentation of the early-Russian appanage system, when uncles and brothers of the tsar preserved rights and authority over particular appanages.[72] It expressed a sense that political power was the private possession of the family. This led Sergei, Grand Duke Alexander Mikhailovich wrote, "to try to turn Moscow into his private domain."[73]

Moskovskie Vedomosti clarified the significance of the appointment. It was a sign that "the principles and ideas that always formed the basis of Moscow's worldview and that correspond to the true good of Russia have begun to predominate in her political life." The appointment would inspire Sergei to fulfill the task "to preserve as sacred the precepts of the ancient

[69] O. Iu. Tarasov, *Ikona i blagochestie: ocherki ikonnogo dela v imperatorskoi Rossii* (Moscow, 1995), 238.

[70] Poselianin, *Iasnye Dni*, 5.

[71] Theophanis George Stavrou, *Russian Interests in Palestine, 1882–1914* (Thessaloniki, 1962), 67–69, 110–11; Robert L. Nichols, "The Friends of God: Nicholas II and Alexandra at the Canonization of Serafim of Sarov, July 1903," in Timberlake, *Religious and Secular Forces in Late Tsarist Russia*, 216–17.

[72] See, for example, Witte, *Vospominaniia*, 2:14–15.

[73] Grand Duke Alexander Mikhailovich, *Once a Grand Duke*, 173.

times of Moscow, which assure that Moscow will always preserve its purely Russian character and provide a model for other Russian cities."[74] Moscow would show its purely Russian character first by ridding itself of its Jewish population.

Alexander instructed the minister of the interior Ivan Durnovo to expel the Jews from Moscow because, he said, "my brother does not want to go to Moscow unless it is cleared of Jews." Durnovo drafted a memorandum in April 1891 and another the following year that led to statutes empowering Grand Duke Sergei to expel large numbers of Jews from the capital. Alexander signed both without the State Council's approval.[75] The first stage, the expulsion of those Jews who might be in the capital illegally, was carried out as an open show of force. The *Times of London* reported: "The whole quarter was ransacked, apartments forced open, doors smashed, every bedroom without exception searched. . . . The indignities which the women, young and old alike, underwent at the hand of the Cossacks may not be described." In subsequent years, two-thirds of the thirty thousand Jews of Moscow were forced to leave the city. Those remaining were subjected to various indignities, including the closing, under government pressure, of a new synagogue built at considerable expense.[76]

On May 5, 1891, the grand duke Sergei and the grand duchess Elizabeth Fedorovna entered Moscow to a full imperial welcome—"A real holiday," the *Novoe Vremia* correspondent wrote. He was received by the governor and mayor of Moscow. Then, in his adjutant's uniform, with the grand duchess at his side, he rode through the streets of Moscow, acclaimed by crowds of people along the way. The buildings were festooned with his and her initials and with garlands and flags. Sergei and Elizabeth paid homage to the Iberian Mother of God and then proceeded to the Assumption Cathedral. At the portal the Moscow metropolitan Ioannikii welcomed them, declaring Moscow's happiness to see the governor-general and his wife, "the Orthodox grand duchess," making known her conversion, which had taken place the month before.[77] After a thanksgiving service and prayers at the shrines of the church, the metropolitan blessed them with icons. Then they moved in procession to the Chudov Monastery. At the monastery they venerated the remains of the metropolitan Saint Alexei and were blessed by his icon. They took up residence in the Nicholas Palace until the renovation of the governor-general's mansion was completed.[78]

[74] *MV*, May 18, 1891, 2.

[75] Zaionchkovskii, *The Russian Autocracy*, 76, 97; *Rossiiskoe samoderzhavie*, 136, 173; Greenberg, *The Jews in Russia*, 2:41–42; Dubnow, *History of the Jews in Russia and Poland*, 2:399–404.

[76] Greenberg *The Jews in Russia*, 2:42–47.

[77] Conversion to orthodoxy had not been obligatory for grand duchesses not married to the presumptive heir. Sergei Aleksandrovich was the fourth living son of Alexander II.

[78] *NV*, May 7, 1891, 1, 2; *Zodchii* 2 (1893): 12–14, plate 9.

Alexander indicated the special importance of Sergei's appointment by coming to Moscow for the first time in more than two and a half years. On May 18 he appeared in an imperial procession to honor his brother.[79] Receiving bread and salt from the Moscow mayor, he declared, "I am very happy that my brother will be my representative in Moscow. I am sure that he will love Moscow and that Moscow will love him. I have loved Moscow from childhood." At the Assumption Cathedral the metropolitan Ioannikii welcomed "your special favor to the ancient-ruling city." The metropolitan also thanked God for miraculously saving the life of the heir after the attack in Otsu, Japan. After visiting the Chudov Monastery, Alexander bowed from the Red Staircase to the cries of the crowd.[80]

During the visit Alexander toured the site of the Alexander II statue in the Kremlin, accompanied by the architect Sultanov and Grand Duke Sergei, whom he had appointed chair of the Construction Commission. He closely examined objects unearthed during the excavations, seeking physical manifestations of Russia's past and the Russian nation. Sultanov wrote, "The Crowned Viewer was especially attracted by things either that were very rare archaeologically or that were important for the history of Russian national art or, finally, were characteristic of the history of Russian everyday life." He found a collection of red tiles with relief designs particularly interesting.[81]

The renovations Sergei ordered in the church in the governor-general's mansion revealed the same archaeological impulse. Sergei insisted that the church be remodeled in the "strictest Russian style of the seventeenth century" and indicated his preference for "the repetition of existing ancient patterns." He reviewed and confirmed all the choices of designs and plans of the church's reconstruction. Its ceiling was replaced by arches to create a vaulted interior like that of Vasilii the Blessed. The vaults were covered with paintings of Russian princes and saints copied from the walls of Novospasskii Monastery in Moscow. The iconostasis, which held many "original ancient" icons, followed simple, early-Russian models, and the royal doors were taken from a decrepit ancient church near Moscow. The choir was a copy of a Pskov church. The lamps, oven, candle box, and other ecclesiastical

---

[79] Another purpose of the tsar's visit may have been to see the French exposition in Moscow. But Alexander did not make an effort to give this visit much importance. Although he and the empress spent three hours examining the various exhibits of French arts and crafts, he made no effort to entertain the French organizing committee. The exhibit had been encouraged by Prince Dolgorukii, and Sergei arrived in Moscow after it had opened and paid no attention to it. See George F. Kennan, *The Fateful Alliance: France, Russia, and the Coming of the First World War* (New York, 1984), 78–81. The French presented Alexander with a jewel-studded ceramic plaque depicting a family tree from Nicholas I that "symbolized the cultural *ralliement* of the two nations forged on the common ground of their eighteenth-century heritage" (Silverman, *Art Nouveau in Fin-de-siècle France*, 164–65).

[80] NV, May 21, 1891, 2.

[81] Sultanov, *Pamiatnik Imperatoru Aleksandru II*, 628–29.

items also reproduced early-Russian models.[82] The locale and decor created the setting to reenact an imagined seventeenth century, among a purely Russian population.

•

The image of a transformed Moscow, under the direction of his brother, provided Alexander with a simulacrum of total control just as he was encountering resistance in his efforts to regain authority over the Russian state. The State Council had stymied the program of counterreforms. The abolition of the privileges of the Lifland and Estland nobility had proved unfeasible owing to the social unrest in these areas. The greatest blow to the national image of efficacy, however, came with the famine of 1891 and the cholera epidemic that followed in its wake. Mass starvation and disease claimed as many as four hundred thousand lives. The government took measures to assist the transport of grain to the stricken provinces, and the tsar appointed a committee, with the heir Nicholas Aleksandrovich as chair, to oversee state and charitable famine relief. But the lack of storehouses and difficulties of organizing supplies exposed the weakness of the administration's own resources and forced the government to rely on charitable and *zemstvo* institutions.[83]

The famine and epidemic exposed the limits of the national monarchy. Doctors and other *zemstvo* workers in the provinces saw that the people regarded any government action with suspicion and began to rely on their own organizations and efforts. In this respect the famine represented a divide as great as that of the Crimean War, revealing the government's failing administrative capacities just as that war had discredited its military abilities. It energized voluntary and independent organizations as well as *zemstvo* work, augmenting the active political groups that would enter the opposition in the next decade.[84]

Once again, ceremony produced a show of national unity and power. In May 1893 Alexander III returned to Moscow to celebrate the tenth anniversary of the coronation and to lay the cornerstone of the Alexander II monument. The press reported an exceptionally warm reception. The grand duke Constantine noted in his diary on May 15 that the newspapers described the rejoicing as greater than that at the coronation itself.[85] The magazines *Niva* and *Vsemirnaia Illiustratsiia* published illustrations of the tsar's procession in the Kremlin. *Niva*, describing the tsar's bowing from the Red Staircase,

---

[82] N. Sultanov, "Tserkov' v dome Moskovskogo General-Gubernatora," *Zodchii* 2 (1893): 12–14; 3 (1893): 17–20.

[83] Bensidoun, *Alexandre III, 1881–1914*, 97–109. On the famine and measures taken, see Richard Robbins, *Famine in Russia, 1891–1892: The Imperial Government Responds to a Crisis* (New York, 1975), passim; on the cholera, see Nancy Mandelker Frieden, *Russian Physicians in an Era of Reform and Revolution, 1856–1905* (Princeton, N.J., 1981), 138–52.

[84] Frieden, *Russian Physicians* , 150–58; Lindenmeyr, *Poverty Is Not a Vice*, 61–63, 79–82.

[85] "Dnevnik V. K. Konstantina Konstantinovicha, 1893g.," GARF, 660-1-40, 65.

insisted one had to be a true Russian to understand this moment. The phrase "bowed to the people" did not convey the sense of what happened in the Moscow Kremlin where

> Every corner, every stone, is a historical memory, dear to the Russian heart. One must be truly Russian to feel all the deep sense of the Tsar's bow, that external sign of the warm unity of the Tsar with his people, and to appreciate fully the greeting of cries, the words uttered through tears, "little father Tsar . . . we will give everything . . . everything for you, we will give our lives." In this unity of the Russian people with their Tsar is our force, our strength, our pride, the touching heritage of the past and the guarantee of our might for future time.[86]

Vsemirnaia Illiustratsiia also took the explosion of enthusiasm as a sign of the tsar's authority. It referred to Alexander's inspection of the Black Sea fleet, before his return to Moscow, and described "colossal battleships," which were "the last word in shipbuilding," speedy cruisers, gunboats. They were "brilliant proof of what could be accomplished in a brief seven-year period by the obedient fulfillment and correct understanding of the sovereign will." The Moscow festivities "powerfully helped the upsurge of the spirit of true Russian people."[87]

Both also described the laying of the cornerstone and printed pictures of the event. The ceremony showed Alexander's abiding attachment to early Russia. The imperial tent, set up on the site in the Kremlin, was designed in seventeenth-century style, of red cloth and gold braid, with enormous golden Russian eagles of the seventeenth-century crest. Even the hammer and trowel for the ceremony were decorated with seventeenth-century motifs. The most sacred icons, it was emphasized, the icon of the Savior and the Iberian Mother of God were brought to bless the monument. After the first stone was consecrated with holy water, Alexander laid it down and struck it with hammer blows in the form of the cross. At this moment the bells of Ivan the Great sounded, echoed by all the churches of the city and answered with a 133-gun salute.[88]

DEATH AND APOTHEOSIS

By 1894 it had become clear that the major triumphs of Alexander III's reign had been the defeat of the revolutionary movement and the maintenance of peace abroad. He had lost his momentum in transforming the state and, according to Epanchin's memoirs, had also lost faith that his ministers could enact his will. He became increasingly dependent on the triumvirate of generals of his suite—Vorontsov-Dashkov, Cherevin, and

[86] *Niva*, May 29, 1893, 528–29.
[87] *Vsemirnaia Illiustratsiia*, May 22, 1893, 378.
[88] Sultanov, *Pamiatnik Imperatoru Aleksandru II*, 632–43.

Richter—to make decisions. He asked them to screen all reports and recommendations coming to him from the ministers. In June 1894 Cherevin received virtually dictatorial powers in all the towns through which the emperor passed, including the right to remove officials and interfere freely in the administration.[89]

Alexander III's untimely death at age fifty-two in October 1894 forestalled the last stage of the scenario, when its appeals would have become irrelevant or hypocritical, prompting different concepts of monarchy. His decline and death became instead an occasion for the monarchy and international press to lament the tragedy of a mighty symbol of nation and peace, struck down prematurely by illness. The tsar's decline and death, and the elaborate observances that ensued, captured the vast international audience of the late-nineteenth-century daily press. Prayer services for his health took place in England, at Notre-Dame in Paris, in the Vatican by Pope Leo XIII, and by President Grover Cleveland, his cabinet, and congressmen in Washington. The death occasioned the most demonstrative expressions in France, Russia's new ally. The French government ordered churches and government buildings draped in mourning. The Chamber of Deputies canceled its session. Condolences were sent to St. Petersburg by the heads of towns visited by Russian squadrons in the previous year and by luminaries no less renowned than Louis Pasteur and Anatole France.[90]

The conveying of the emperor's coffin from Livadia to Moscow and Petersburg broadened the amplitude of the mourning, which the accounts presented as a truly national display of grief. It demonstrated to Europe, and particularly to France, the popularity and viability of the Russian monarchy. Charles Lowe described the ceremonies as "a grand spectacular funeral-drama in five acts with a variety of interludes," during which Alexander "may be said to have been canonized." His body, dressed in the uniform of the Preobrazhenskii Regiment, lay in state for two days at the church at Livadia. The imperial crown and the sword he had worn during the Russo-Turkish War rested on his coffin. To the ringing of church bells and gun salutes, the coffin was carried along the three-kilometer road from Livadia to Yalta, which was strewn with flowers. In Yalta the local population gathered for a memorial dinner, and the archbishop of Simferopol and Taurus held a brief funeral service on the pier. A cruiser brought the coffin to Sevastopol. At the major train stations from Sevastopol to Moscow—Simferopol, Kharkov, Borki, Orel, and Tula—large numbers of people stood holding candles. "The love of the people for the deceased Tsar became apparent with manifestations of the most sincere and deep grief," the priest K. Korol'kov wrote in his popular biography of Alexander III. Deputies from the various

[89] Epanchin, *Na sluzhbe trekh imperatorov*, 165–67; Lowe, *Alexander III of Russia*, 271, 327–28; "Cherevin i Aleksandr III," *Golos Minevshego*, 96–101.

[90] Bensidoun, *Alexandre III, 1881–1914*, 294–95.

42. Alexander III funeral cortege. Moscow, 1894. Lithograph from
Vsemirnaia Illiustratsiia.

estates placed ninety-nine wreaths on the coffin, which filled two cars of the
funeral train.[91]

The most elaborate and impressive observances took place in Moscow.
Thousands gathered along the streets, and houses were draped in black. The
throngs watched in grief and awe as the simple carriage following a procession passed to the tolling of the many bells of Moscow. Lithographs and
photographs of the coffin's entry into Moscow and its approach to the Kremlin were published in *Vsemirnaia Illiustratsiia* and *L'Illustration* (fig. 42).
The new tsar, Nicholas II, led the procession on foot, his head bare, walking
slowly, stopping briefly at the Town Duma and at the Iberian Chapel. "The
whole people, like a single person, bared their heads, as the holy dust of the
deceased emperor approached, the *Vsemirnaia Illiustratsiia* reporter wrote.
"The picture was majestic. From all sides one heard sobbing and weeping."[92]

The Russian people's collective dedication to their sovereign was described in the domestic press as a popular mandate in religious form. Kokhin's verse in the epigraph to this chapter, published in the journal *Vsemirnaia Illiustratsiia*, presented the people's tears and weeping as a display of
national solidarity with their sovereign. *Moskovskie Vedomosti* described
the different types of people, poor and rich, children and elderly, weeping at
the coffin. The tears dropping on the deceased tsar's hand symbolized the
unity of the national spirit.

---

[91] Lowe, *Alexander III of Russia*, 240; K. Korol'kov, *Zhizn' i tsarstvovanie Imperatora Aleksandra III*, 2 0– 1; Kalinin and Zelianichenko, *Romanovy i Krym*, 60–61, 75.

[92] *L'Illustration*, November 24, 1894, 432; *Vsemirnaia Illiustratsiia* (1894): 398; Korol'kov,
Zhizn' i tsarstvovanie Imperatora Aleksandra III, 241–47.

The Ruling hand of the Deceased was damp from the accumulated tears of those kissing him farewell. There blended the tears of the Empress and Her Ruling Son with the tears of all Russian people, beginning with Members of the Imperial Family and ending with the poorest, most outcast sons of great Rus'. And in this mixing of tears, shed over the grave of the deceased tsar, the great mysterious unity of the Russian people was consummated with its great beloved tsar, which is inaccessible to the ordinary mind.[93]

Most significant was the lying in state of Alexander III in the Archangel Cathedral in the Kremlin, the burial place of the pre-Petrine tsars. Foreign correspondents were admitted into the cathedral to witness the glittering gold catafalque and to hear the Service for the Dead. "Many of those present were unable to restrain their emotion," the correspondent of the *Daily Chronicle* wrote. "Tears were seen rolling down the cheeks of noble ladies. Sobs broke on the ear almost rhythmically with the cadences of the sacred music. Evidently the late tsar was deeply esteemed and beloved by those within his circle."[94]

The coffin then returned to Petersburg for the final obsequies in the elaborate neoclassical grandeur of the capital. But the Petersburg procession, though joined by an impressive array of notables, failed to evoke the devotion and exaltation that had appeared in Moscow. The crowds were small, and the procession moved fitfully and irregularly. The inclement Petersburg weather was depressing. A correspondent from Moscow took the weather as a sign of Petersburg's "rottenness," borne on a Western wind. The onlookers, though respectful and reverent, were few and did not display the Muscovites' enthusiasm.[95]

The burial services in the Peter-Paul Fortress took place amid extraordinary splendor and pomp. The cathedral was draped with silver and gold cloths. A large Monomakh Cap was placed atop the catafalque, the crown of the old-Russian tsars thus sitting majestically in the midst of the baroque elegance of Peter's cathedral.[96] The occasion was played primarily to the elite and the large number of foreign princes. Before a largely European audience, the final prayers blessed the all-Russian emperor. The French lavished atten-

---

[93] Petrovskii, *Pamiati Imperatora Aleksandra III*, 86–88.

[94] Quoted in Lowe, *Alexander III of Russia*, 295.

[95] Uncertainties about the change of superiors under the new tsar made official concerns paramount and diminished the pageant's effect. V. N. Lamzdorf, the director of the chancellery of the Foreign Ministry, felt the indifference of the Petersburg population to the death and noted that the tsar was mourned only because the people lacked confidence in the heir (Lowe, *Alexander III of Russia*, 296–98; F. Dukhovetskii, *Dve nedeli v Peterburge; Vospominaniia torzhestva pogrebeniia tela Imperatora Aleksandra III i svetlogo dnia brakosochetaniia* [Moscow, 1894], 6, 23–23, 60; A. V. Bogdanovich, *Tri poslednikh samoderzhtsa*, 183; V. N. Lamzdorf, *Dnevnik, 1894–1896* [Moscow, 1991], 75–76, 84).

[96] A painting of the scene is reproduced in Vladimir Gendrikov and Sergei Sen'ko, *The Cathedral of St. Peter and St. Paul: The Burial Place of the Russian Imperial Family* (St. Petersburg, 1998), 132.

tion on their new ally, sending more than five thousand memorial wreaths, many of them of silver. The French delegation itself brought ten thousand bouquets of artificial flowers, tied with the tricolor, affixed to which were pictures of Alexander and President Carnot, with the legend "United in sentiments and death."[97]

•

The European press reacted to the death with statements of bereavement and admiration for the tsar whom many regarded as a despot.[98] Even the English and German periodicals lauded the tsar's international leadership and preservation of the peace. The most exalted rhetoric came from France. An editorial in *Le temps* was rapt in its praise:

> Inspired by a philosophy that was at once humane and Christian, he disdained the laurels one gains on the battlefield. He wanted to be and he was the emperor of peace, which permitted him to put an end to agitation and to revolutionary organizations in his empire, to restore finances, to penetrate to the heart of Asia and the shores of the Bering Sea with railways, to increase Russia's prestige in the world.[99]

The eulogies printed in the Russian monarchist press presented Alexander as a stalwart figure of legend, an image that would be reproduced in the popular biographies of subsequent decades. A collection of articles published in *Moskovskie Vedomosti* depicted Alexander as a person of saintly self denial who had subordinated his own well-being to labor for the good of the country. L. A. Tikhomirov, the former revolutionary now turned official ideologist, extolled Alexander III's life as a heroic feat (*podvig*) in an article entitled "The Bearer of the Ideal." Alexander had borne the cross of power, the duties of rule. Tikhomirov presented the image of tsar as selfless laborer, set forth in the first years of his reign. The tsar had overcome all difficulties, "troubles, treason, the disorder in the treasury, famine, pestilence, the fear of what seemed an unavoidable war." His reign was "an epoch of unheard of prosperity, tranquillity, plenty, and glory." He gave himself completely to his work. "Never, even under such a worker-tsar as Peter the Great, have we heard of such self-sacrificing and exhausting dedication of all the energies of a tsar for state service." He had slept no more than four hours a night.[100]

Alexander's feat of self-sacrifice, in Tikhomirov's characterization, went beyond utter devotion to his state duties. The tsar had embodied a medieval ideal of self-sacrifice: He represented the monarch who renounced himself to bring social interests and conflicts into accord and imposed justice over

[97] Dukhovetskii, *Dve nedeli v Peterburge*, 38–39; Lowe, *Alexander III of Russia*, 300–301.

[98] For a thorough discussion of these responses, see Bensidoun, *Alexandre III, 1881–1914*, 294–95.

[99] Ibid., 295.

[100] Petrovskii, *Pamiati Imperatora Aleksandra III*, 303–4.

all. Alexander III was the "tsar of justice and peace" who embodied the ideal of the great Christian monarchs of the past, Constantine the Great and Charlemagne. When he died, "the ideal image" that was before them vanished. According to Tikhomirov, his article brought tears to the eyes of Nicholas II, who in his own diary described the death of his father as "the death of a saint."[101]

Many articles in *Moskovskie Vedomosti* stressed the distinctive Russian characteristics of his rule. Again, the analogy with his patron saint, Alexander Nevskii, was drawn, emphasizing the prince's defense of Russia against attack from the West: The Tatar yoke symbolized not bondage but Western influence.[102] The new national monarchy ended what Lev Tikhomirov decried as "the swallowing of the sovereign by the state," characteristic of European absolutism, which was expressed in the phrase "L'état c'est moi."[103] The official nationality under Nicholas I had represented some kind of "official patriotism" (*kazennyi patriotizm*), one Iu. Nikolaev asserted, but "was not embodied in living phenomena." Nicholas I "himself still was not fully conscious of the complete separateness (*otdel'nost'*) of Russia from Europe by its type, was not aware of the complete separateness of Russian autocracy from west European monarchism."[104]

Novoe Vremia, a Petersburg newspaper, was less ready to identify Alexander as Russian. Rather, it emphasized, he reconciled new and old Russia:

> New Russia in His person, as if fraternized in these ancient church walls with old Rus', and recognized in the old Rus' the precepts without which the Russian people would not have distinguished themselves as mightily among the Slavic tribe and the peoples of Europe. From now on, there is no difference between old and new Rus'.

Alexander as an exemplar of Russia's humanitarian, Western character was the theme of the controversial speech that Vasilii Kliuchevskii delivered as chair of the Society of History and Ancient Russian Studies at Moscow University. Kliuchevskii praised Alexander for restoring Russia's prestige in the eyes of Europe. Europe looked upon Russia as an Asiatic despotism, as "representatives of Mongol stagnation (*kosnost'*)." Although Russia had protected Europe from Batu Khan and Napoleon, Europeans regarded Russia as the enemy of freedom, and Russians in turn learned to look suspiciously on Europe. Alexander III had saved Europe from war. "The tsar of the Russian people was the sovereign of international peace and order," which confirmed "the historical calling of Russia." Kliuchevskii then affirmed a central theme of Alexander's scenario, declaring, "In Russia's political organization, the idea of the people is expressed in the will of the Tsar,

---

[101] Ibid., 306–11; L. Tikhomirov, *Vospominaniia* (Moscow, 1927), 428.
[102] Petrovskii, *Pamiati Imperatora Aleksandra III*, 320–22.
[103] Ibid., 306.
[104] Ibid., 288–89.

and the people's will becomes the thought of their Tsar."[105] The speech delivered in a closed meeting immediately reached the public and stirred indignation in liberal circles and particularly among the students, eighteen of whom were expelled.[106]

The press portrayed Alexander as a Russian person sharing the idealized features of his subjects, a man of the people. *Moskovskie Vedomosti* evoked "kind blue eyes with a bright open gaze, his engaging face, framed with a thick bright red beard, the powerful height of the *bogatyr'*." He was direct and honest, accessible and warm, a person who hated everything artificial and pretentious. He renewed Russian customs at court—the *slavlenie*, a Christmas procession of the clergy to the homes of worshipers for prayers and hymns (which had been curbed by Peter the Great in 1724), and *molitvoslovie*, readings from the missal at home at the New Year. He loved Russian art and Russian writers, particularly Dostoevsky and the playwright, Alexander Ostrovsky.[107]

Novoe Vremia extolled his "calm mind," his "straightforward thinking," his love of "truthfulness" (*pravdivost'*) and everything Russian—food, newspapers, literature, art. Alexander III was the first tsar since Fedor and Ioann Alekseevich to wear a beard. For *Novoe Vremia* he, more than any other person, corresponded to the concept of Russian tsar.[108] A *Vsemirnaia Illiustratsiia* columnist vividly characterized the national image Alexander left behind:

> The late Tsar was a complete Russian man. From the good-natured face, polite smile, the blue eyes with their soft glitter, the bright red beard, broad and thick, the powerfully built body, the measured movements, terse speech, the simplicity of manner, directness, the thirst for truth, from all this to the steadfastness in work, loyalty in friendship, and including the wholehearted love of his family— this was a Russian man.[109]

The most striking description of the tsar's last days appeared in the account of his death written by Father Ioann of Kronstadt. The incident was remarkable in several respects. First, the summoning of a charismatic priest,

---

[105] V. O. Kliuchevskii also extolled Alexander's patronage of historical studies and historical restoration, his knowledge of Russian archaeology and iconography, and his work as chair of the Russian Historical Society ("Pamiati v Boze pochivshego Imperatora Aleksandra III," *Chteniia v Imperatorskom Obshchestve Istorii i Drevnostei Rossiiskikh pri Moskovskom Universitete* 4 [1894]: 1–7).

[106] The text was published in the society's *Readings*, reprinted in the newspaper *Moskovskii Listok*, and lithographed and circulated among the students. A group of radical students whistled Kliuchevskii down during a lecture, an event that escalated into protests and petitions. On the incident, see Robert F. Byrnes, *V. O. Kliuchevskii: Historian of Russia* (Bloomington, Ind., 1995), 114–15; M. V. Nechkina, *Vasilii Osipovich Kliuchevskii: Istoriia zhizni i tvorchestva* (Moscow, 1974), 348–52.

[107] Petrovskii, *Pamiati Imperatora Aleksandra III*, 317–19.

[108] NV, October 21, 1894, 2; October 22, 1894, 2.

[109] *Vsemirnaia Illiustratsiia* (1894): 347.

rather than a member of the court clergy, to pray at the tsar's bedside seemed to indicate the tsar's willingness to join his people in receiving the ministration of a humble cleric, beloved by the people. Second, Ioann described his and Alexander's feelings with extraordinary candor, which some felt inappropriate in a published work about a tsar.

Ioann's account, "The Last Hours of Tsar Emperor Alexander III," was printed in *Tserkovnye Vedomosti* and *Novoe Vremia*.[110] The priest presented Alexander as a humble Christian man, who found succor in prayer and the sacrament of communion. At Alexander's bedside he saw himself as a representative of the Russian people, who could pray for the alleviation of the tsar's suffering and for his salvation. When Ioann arrived on October 8 the heir told him that the tsar felt better; Alexander claimed that he felt "the power of the prayers of loyal Russia over Him." When Ioann saw Alexander for the first time on October 11 he assured him that "all of Russia is praying for you." The tsar walked into another room, knelt, and invited him to pray with him. "His Majesty prayed with feeling, bowed his head, and turned deeply inward."[111]

Ioann's text emphasized the great importance of the sacrament of communion, a favorite theme of his sermons.[112] He wrote that he did not consider his mission complete until he had ministered communion to the tsar: "I myself take communion daily," he wrote. "And I consider it a great deprivation if I do not do so." On October 17 Ioann came to the emperor with a goblet and chanted a hymn. Alexander repeated a prayer and sipped from the goblet with reverence. "Tears of tenderness (*umilenie*) fell upon his chest." The tsar, wrote Ioann, received great consolation from Christ's benefaction. The empress took communion later that day, when her future daughter-in-law, Alix of Hess, was anointed into Orthodoxy. Ioann wrote of the empress: "Her soul, oppressed by the grief of the ailing Tsar, thirsted for consolation and comfort in Holy Communion."[113]

In subsequent days, as Alexander's condition deteriorated, Ioann prayed with the imperial family as well as with the tsar himself. On October 20 Alexander's breathing began to fail and the whole family waited at his bed-

---

[110] "Poslednie chasy Gosudaria Imperatora, Aleksandra III," *Tserkovnye Vedomosti* (1894): 1656; *MV*, November 20, 1894, 2. It was reprinted in I. Pobedinskii, *Imperator Aleksandr III, Tsar'-mirotvorets (Ko dniu otkrytiia pamiatnika v Moskve)*, (Moscow, 1912), 14–17. On the doubts raised by the article preceding publication in *Novoe Vremia*, see Kizenko, "The Making of a Modern Saint," 326–28. The summoning of Ioann of Kronstadt probably was not the suggestion of the emperor himself. According to the grand duke Nicholas Mikhailovich, Ioann was brought to Livadia by the grand duchess Alexandra Iosifovna and the Queen of Greece, and Alexander, in weakened condition, reluctantly agreed to see him. On the other hand, Alexander did pray with him twice and the priest was permitted to publish his account of their worship (Vel'iaminov, "Vospominaniia ob Imperatore Aleksandre III," 301–5).

[111] I. Pobedinskii, *Imperator Aleksandr III, Tsar'-mirotvorets*, 15–16.

[112] On Ioann's effort to give greater emphasis to the sacrament of communion, see Kizenko, "The Making of a Modern Saint," 38–40, 155–56, 179.

[113] Pobedinskii, *Imperator Aleksandr III, Tsar'-mirotvorets*, 16.

side. Ioann again prayed near the tsar. He salved the tsar's legs and stomach with holy oil from the icon, then lay his hand on his head and held it for a long time. Ioann asked Alexander if it hurt. He answered that, on the contrary, it made him feel better. Alexander's last words were directed to the priest. "The Russian people love you," he said. Ioann answered, "Yes, your people love me." "They love you," Alexander said, "because they know who you are and what you are." The priest concluded his account by asking the Russian people not to weep because their prayers failed to cure the tsar. Their prayers had brought a quiet, Christian death, "and a good end crowned his glorious life which is all the dearer." He called on the people to love the tsar's heir, who would follow in his footsteps.[114]

Ioann's description focused on the relationship between himself, as the representative of the people, and the tsar, a humble worshiper seeking their prayers. The contrast with Count Bludov's description of the last hours of Nicholas I is revealing. Bludov apotheosized Nicholas as warrior, dying a heroic death. He recounted the drama of the tsar's imposing presence as he held audiences with the leading officials of the state and said his moving farewell with the empress and the heir. Ioann's account said nothing about the Russian state; even the imperial family remained in the background.[115]

The presentation of Alexander's death in the Russian and foreign press created the legend of a beloved and powerful national ruler. Alexander III had come to represent integrity, responsibility, predictability—a ruler whose image of strength had prevented war and restored order in Russia and prestige to the Russian throne. Despite the famine, despite the absence of public participation, these evocations left the impression that Russia was better off and more powerful than in 1881, a feeling widely held among the officials and, most important, by Nicholas II when he ascended the throne.

The power of Alexander's III's image in death was perhaps best appreciated by an anonymous Russian opponent of the regime who wrote a pamphlet published in London that sought to refute the idealization of the tsar. "Finally, he has become the mythological center of that repulsive cult of falsehood that has been conscientiously devised by all those interested in the perpetuation of autocracy and illegality around the presumedly 'peasant tsar' (*muzhitskii tsar'*), and 'peacemaker tsar.' " In the process of grieving, the good-natured Russian man, the author suggested, was willing to accept these characterizations as a rite of mourning. The Russian man was indiscriminating, all-forgiving—tendencies that reflected his lack of self-respect and that grew stronger from "the feeling of honoring the 'deceased' which is so vital in thousands of simple Russian hearts."[116]

[114] Ibid., 16–17.
[115] See Volume 1: 415–16.
[116] *Bolezn' i smert' Aleksandra III: Pravdivye zametki* (London, 1900), 19.

PART THREE

Nicholas II and the Search for
a National Persona

CHAPTER NINE

Childhood and Marriage

A good-natured poet-dreamer once urged the heir "to be a human being
on the throne." These are touching words, but ones that said little. The
throne needs not simply a human being but a sovereign (*gosudar'*). The
rights of the human heart, which are the same everywhere—in the chambers of the tsars, in peasant huts—join on the throne with obligations to
which the promptings and demands of human nature must be subordinate. May faithful and energetic service, above all to Tsar and Fatherland,
prepare the Heir to the Throne for these obligations. May the young
Tsesarevich bloom and ripen, the hope of Russia, and become imbued in
imperial service with the sacred majesty of the calling of Tsar in Russia.

—*Michael Katkov, editorial on the majority of Tsarevich Nicholas
Aleksandrovich, May 5, 1884*[1]

THE FAMILY AND THE CLASSROOM

Katkov's editorial on the eve of Nicholas II's majority ceremony bluntly
stated the aversion to abstract humanitarian principles intrinsic to the national myth. The popular and historical mandate that elevated the God-
chosen monarch dispensed with the pedagogical imperative of previous
reigns. The heir no longer had to be uplifted to suit his office, transformed
into a superhuman embodiment of the ideals of the Russian state. History
endowed him with authority sanctioned by the nation. The importance assigned to formal education correspondingly diminished, reduced to the acquisition of the knowledge and skills required of any young man of high
birth entering governmental service. Presumably, it would be "faithful and
energetic service" (*vernaia i bodraia sluzhba*) to tsar and fatherland that
would prepare the heir for the throne. But even this injunction would be
observed perfunctorily in Nicholas II's upbringing.

As a result, formal education did little to shape the views of Nicholas II
as monarch. The principles and lessons of his education could not provide
viewpoints that diverged in some respects from those of the dominant scenario and provide a dynamic of change. Alexander III did not believe that
the heir had to receive special education and training to prepare him for

[1] M. N. Katkov, *Sobranie peredovykh statei*, 251.

the high office of emperor. Indeed, he tried to protect Nicholas from the consciousness of his destiny and the burdensome obligations that some day he would have to bear. He ruled out a rigorous program of studies. When Nicholas reached the age of eight, Alexander warned his first teacher to limit instruction to spelling and multiplication tables and told her not to allow the boy to think of the throne. While this may have been good advice for a boy of eight, the same principle governed Nicholas's later education as well.[2]

Alexander was concerned more with his children's physical development than with their intellectual advancement. He wanted them to grow up as "normal, healthy children," not "like China dolls" or "hothouse flowers." But Nicholas was not the image of a healthy Russian lad. He was small and had an uncharacteristic delicately feminine appearance, and a girlish laugh and handwriting. His father did not let him forget this. When Nicholas shrank from fistfights or hid after wrongdoings, Alexander declared that he was not his son, not a Romanov, that he would tell grandfather he was a little girl (*devchonka*).[3] Alexander treated his children strictly, allowing no contradiction. Nicholas adored his father but regarded him as a distant and in many ways intimidating figure. Nicholas's uncle, the grand duke Michael Nikolaevich, later said that the heir "fears his parents and won't talk about anything with them"; he could not be asked to bring matters even to the attention of the empress.[4]

Nicholas did take on his father's love for physical activity. His diaries of the 1880s tell of outings together, sawing and chopping wood, horseback riding, and hunting. He also shared Alexander's fascination with the beauty and drama of the Orthodox liturgy. He knew the service well and loved to sing and lead a choir. He was inspired by the stories of the Passion and the Resurrection and would stand gazing at the image of the Mother of God and set candles before the icons. "His cherished wish was to dress himself in a gold stikharion, to stand near the priest in the middle of the church, and, at the time of anointing, to hold the sacred cup."[5]

Nicholas displayed his father's strong feelings of national pride and contempt for other nationalities, particularly Germans. In a letter of 1878 Pobedonostsev described Nicholas, then ten years old, eagerly awaiting popular pictures of the Russo-Turkish War.[6] In 1880, at age twelve, Nicholas wrote a comic story about two Germans, whom he characterized as petty, selfish, stupid, and cowardly. They speak in broken Russian and constantly fight

---

[2] Andrew M. Verner, *The Crisis of Russian Autocracy: Nicholas II and the 1905 Revolution* (Princeton, N.J., 1990), 11–12; Il'ia Surguchev, *Detstvo Imperatora Nikolaia II* (Paris, 1953), 26. Surguchev is the only detailed source we have about Nicholas's childhood. It is an account given to Surguchev, in emigration, by V. K. Ollongren, the son of Nicholas's governess, Alexandra Ollongren, and Nicholas's classroom companion for several years.

[3] Surguchev, *Detstvo*, 26–29, 44–49, 78, 84, 151.

[4] Verner, *The Crisis of Russian Autocracy*, 64; Polovtsov, *Dnevnik*, 2:430.

[5] Surguchev, *Detstvo*, 88, 92, 108–9, 132, 135–36.

[6] *Pis'ma Pobedonostseva k Aleksandru III*, 1:109.

with each other. They duel and are placed in a fetid prison where they feed on mice and breathe the fumes from a nearby toilet. They are terrified by a spider they see at night. The devil takes them to hell, but they escape and continue their squabbling. As a young man Nicholas loved to tell stories about the awkwardness of Germans, who he believed were unable to adapt themselves to Russian manners and customs.[7]

Nicholas's closest relationship was with his mother. By the 1870s the suspicion of close mother-son bonds characteristic of earlier royal pedagogy had given way to an acceptance of emotional nurturing. When she was in childbirth with Grand Duke Michael, Nicholas and his brother, the grand duke George, "seemed to dry up, to become dull. They began to eat and sleep poorly."[8] When he reached manhood, his expressions of love for his mother remained effusive. His letters invariably began with outpourings of affection and professions of sorrow that they were apart, feelings that appear to have been sincere. Maria Fedorovna was both his repository of trust and his model for courteous behavior. He took on her manner of unremitting civility and charm and her capacity to endear without feeling attachment or showing real emotion.

Maria Fedorovna was the first Russian empress in the nineteenth century to take principal responsibility for the heir's education. Above all she feared his teachers, who might compete for the heir's affection and influence his views. She chose instructors who she felt confident would not dominate the heir. To limit contacts, she arranged their schedule so that no instructor taught Nicholas more than two days in succession.[9] When Nicholas reached the age of ten, Gen. Grigorii Danilovich, was chosen to supervise his education. Danilovich was a member of the tsar's suite and a friend of Alexander's brothers, the grand dukes Paul and Sergei. Danilovich, like the generals who had supervised the education of Alexander III and Nicholas Aleksandrovich, was concerned principally with discipline and obedience. He was known for his particularly rigid and intolerant views and his determination to protect the heir from outside influences.[10]

According to the grand duke Alexander Mikhailovich, Danilovich believed that "the mysterious forces emanating during the sacrament of taking the oath on the day of the coronation provided all the practical data required by a ruler." While the grand duke may have simplified Danilovich's viewpoint, the statement captures the general's belief that the Russian monarch's authority was not related to knowledge or experience. Danilovich organized the education within Alexander III's reclusive scenario, protecting the heir not only from the Russian public but from the influences of the Westernized

---

[7] "Iumoristicheskii rasskaz 'Dva nemtsa,' napisannyi v. kn. Nikolaem Aleksandrovichem," GARF, 601-1-162; Lowe, *Alexander III of Russia*, 342.

[8] Surguchev, *Detstvo*, 89–90, 93.

[9] E. Flourens, *Alexandre III, sa vie; son oeuvre* (Paris, 1894), 77–78.

[10] Verner, *The Crisis of Russian Autocracy*, 8; Lieven, *Nicholas II*, 34.

court as well. The heir's day was strictly organized, and he and the other grand dukes were almost always in the presence of a master. Nicholas detested Danilovich but accepted his authority. He obeyed in an exemplary manner, showing none of the willfulness characteristic of earlier grand dukes. "Never was it necessary to make an observation, to subdue resistance, to resort to rule," his French teacher recalled. "Always an equable mood, a surprising spontaneity of obedience." His teacher of tactics declared that the general had made of Nicholas "a moderate, punctilious old man." Nicholas developed an extreme reserve and a shield of disingenuousness that enabled him to deal with conflicting views. Even Pobedonostsev deplored his lack of opinions, noting in 1899 that Nicholas had asked one of those close to him: "Why are you arguing? I always agree with everyone and then do things in my way."[11]

The goal and organization of Nicholas's education was to provide him basic skills and knowledge without distracting him with interests and commitments that could rival the influence of his parents and family. In this respect, Dominic Lieven has observed, his experience diverged greatly from monarchs elsewhere in the late nineteenth and early twentieth centuries, who were allowed to attend schools for part of their education. George V had attended Naval College, Wilhelm II a gymnasium. Even Emperor Hirohito had studied at a "Peers' School."[12] These monarchs had shared some of the experiences of conservative young men outside the military and the court. But such contact threatened the Russian heir's security, and the national myth expressed a distrust of Western education as potentially alien and corrosive to Russia's political heritage.

The curriculum and his higher courses, which Nicholas pursued after 1884, included modern languages, history, mathematics, physics, chemistry, topography, and military science, but no classes on ancient history or ancient languages. The staff, like his father's, included university professors, several of them figures of distinction. Nicholas's history instructor was Egor Zamyslovskii, a specialist in seventeenth-century Russia from St. Petersburg University. Pobedonostsev taught law and Michael Kapustin, a jurist from St. Petersburg University, international law. The former finance minister Nicholas Bunge lectured to him from 1886 to 1889 on political economy, economic policy, and finances. Bunge responded to Alexander's growing sympathy for interventionist policies and presented Nicholas with the arguments for increased, although cautious state involvement in the economy. Nicholas Beketov, a renowned scientist, taught him chemistry, and Michael Dragomirov, military science. Most of Nicholas's instructors were intelligent and accom-

<hr />

[11] Grand Duke Alexander Mikhailovich, *Once a Grand Duke*, 165–66, 178–79; G. Lanson, "Le tsar Nicolas II raconté par son ancien professeur," *Les annales politiques et littéraires* (September 1, 1901): 133; Polovtsov, *Dnevnik*, 2:440; Mosolov, *Pri dvore poslednego Rossiiskogo imperatora*, 17–18, 20; A. A. Polovtsov, "Dnevnik," *Krasnyi Arkhiv* 46, no. 3 (1931): 131.

[12] See the interesting comparisons drawn by Lieven, *Nicholas II*, 41.

plished scholars, if not great minds, and the quality of the instruction can hardly be blamed, as it often is, for the limits of Nicholas's knowledge and judgment. Peter Bark, finance minister from 1914 to 1917, an educated and able official, wrote in his memoirs that Nicholas had received, "from a young age, a thorough training under the direction of the best teachers in Russia."[13] Contemporary accounts emphasized the thoroughness of his education as well as the tsarevich's sharp intelligence and good memory.[14]

But the efforts of his parents and Danilovich to protect the heir from important intellectual interaction deprived his lessons of meaning and influence. The caution and distrust of Alexander III's scenario dominated the classroom. According to one of Nicholas's teachers, his instructors were told to lecture and not to question him, a principle precisely contrary to that followed by the instructors of Nicholas's namesake in the early 1860s. At age twenty-four, two years before his accession, Nicholas wrote to his mother that he and his brother George were overcome with uncontrolled fits of laughter during lectures given by several professors of astronomy. His upbringing translated the distrust of the intelligentsia, expressed in the national myth, into an indifference to or disdain for intellect in general. As a result, Bunge's lessons made little impression on Nicholas. General Epanchin, one of Nicholas's admirers, was amazed that he knew nothing about simple economic terms like *tariff war* yet admitted his ignorance with nonchalance.[15] The one subject that awoke Nicholas's enthusiasm was history, an interest he shared with his father. He studied Solov'ev's works and read historical journals and novels. In 1884, at the age of sixteen, he was appointed an honorary member of the Imperial Historical Society.[16] But his historical reading was more of a diversion than a source for deeper understanding of Russia's past.

Only Pobedonostsev was allowed frequent access to the heir, and he conveyed the principles of government that fit the ideas and images of Russian monarchy which he had helped to construct. Although we have no record of Pobedonostsev's personal conversations with Nicholas, the conspectus of his course on state law from November 1886 to January 1887 gives a sense of the ideas of government he conveyed. Like Michael Speranskii's course presented to Alexander II in 1837, Pobedonostsev's combined a discussion

---

[13] N. N. Firsov, *Nikolai II* (Kazan, 1929), 14–15; *BE*, 23:212; 27:406; N. I. Anan'ich, "Materialy lektsionnykh kursov N. Kh. Bunge 60–80-kh godov XIXv.," *Arkheograficheskii ezhegodnik za 1977 god* (Moscow, 1978), 304–11; B. V. Anan'ich, "The Economic Policy of the Tsarist Government and Enterprise in Russia from the End of the Nineteenth through the Beginning of the Twentieth Century," in Gregory Guroff and Fred V. Carstensen, ed., Entrepreneurship in Imperial Russia and the Soviet Union (Princeton, N.J., 1983), 129–30; Lieven, *Nicholas II*, 35.

[14] See the review of contemporary newspaper accounts in Lowe, *Alexander III of Russia*, 340–47.

[15] Verner, *The Crisis of Russian Autocracy*, 14, 20; Epanchin, *Na sluzhbe trekh imperatorov*, 199.

[16] Polovtsov, *Dnevnik*, 1:188.

of the types of governmental systems with an argument for the necessity of absolute monarchy in Russia. But the two officials presented sharply different conceptions of the goals and meaning of Russian monarchy. Speranskii emphasized the exalted calling of the ruler of "true monarchies" to exercise self-restraint in the interests of the people. The ruler had to respect the laws and treaties of his government, which were to be "immutable and sacred" for him. "Law (*pravo*), and consequently autocratic law," he explained, "is law to the extent that it is based on justice (*pravda*). Where justice ends and injustice begins, law ends and despotism begins." The autocrat was never subject to human courts and judgment but always to the court of conscience and the judgment of God, and the court of conscience continued to haunt Speranskii's pupil, Alexander II, throughout his life.[17]

Pobedonostsev repeated the proposition that monarchy is based on firm principles of law that flowed from the supreme power. But he mentions neither justice nor the importance of conscience in ruling the empire. He identifies law with order: "A firm and rational government cannot exist without a firm principle of state order." Constitutional ideas represented a special danger to Russia. The "ceaseless attempts" to introduce constitutions in Russia came "not from the people but from a few parties, or people who were ambitious or doctrinaire." Western monarchies had degenerated since the second half of the eighteenth century. Only in England had representative institutions emerged from a tradition of local self-government that had produced "a consciousness of social duty and a firm feeling of national unity." Elsewhere such a sense had not developed, and it was the Russian monarch's destiny to learn from the mistakes of continental European states. In Pobedonostsev's evocation, the Russian empire was too diverse to form a nation-state, and only the monarchy could prevent breakdown and turmoil. There was no soil for representative institutions,

> where there is not a whole nationality (*natsional'nost'*), but a motley variety of tribes, dialects, and interests of a heterogeneous population, where fragmented parties, faiths, and sects are in constant struggle with one another, where the notion of civic *freedom* has not developed historically in inseparable unity with the notion of civic and public *duty* (as in England) but has arisen only under the influence of abstract teachings of the *rights* of man and universal equality (as in France).[18]

By all accounts Charles Heath, Nicholas's English teacher, was the instructor he most liked and who had the greatest influence on him. An English public school graduate and a former gentleman farmer, Heath had been a popular instructor at the Aleksandrovskii Lycée. With the easygoing urbane

---

[17] *Gody ucheniia ego Imperatorskogo Vysochestva Naslednika Tsesarevicha* (*Sbornik Russkogo Istoricheskogo Obshchestva*, vol. 31) (St. Petersburg, 1881), 364–71.

[18] K. P. Pobedonostsev, "Konspekt lektsii po kurs 'Gosudarstvennoe pravo' sostavlennyi dlia v. kn. Nikolaia Aleksandrovicha," GARF, 601-1-208, 22–23, 28–30, 42–43.

manner of the English gentleman, he displayed charm and intelligence without touching on matters that might become serious or offensive. Nicholas learned his excellent English from Heath and shared with him a love of the outdoors and sports. He took on his tutor's manner of genteel graciousness and aplomb.[19] While Nicholas I assumed the persona of a Prussian commander and Alexander II that of a German prince, Nicholas II had the nonchalance of an English gentleman. Lieven has observed that he resembled his counterpart, George V, not only in his portraits, with the clipped, sleek beard, but in his reserve, love of family life, sports, and stuffed Victorian interiors.[20]

PUBLIC PRESENTATIONS

Nicholas II's boyhood diaries and compositions have a tone and character quite different from those of previous heirs to the throne. The absence of a guiding intelligence, a Zhukovskii or Stroganov or even Perovskii, tells in the absence of ethical models of rule in his various lessons and writings. His compositions of 1881 describe numerous family parties the thirteen year old attended at Christmas season and other holidays, his joy in the presents, the candies, the champagne, his delight at trained dogs and puppet shows. His diaries dwell on his play and excursions at Gatchina and the other suburban estates. His classes and teachers are barely mentioned.[21]

Andrew Verner has noted the focus on family in Nicholas's diaries. The word *semeistvo*, referring to the larger, extended imperial family, appears on nearly every page, and he frequently refers to activities with the word *we* rather than I as he engages in study and activity with his brother, George, or other members of the family.[22] The family was his world, sheltering him from the stern and brutal necessities of government and the fear of another catastrophe, like the death of his grandfather.

The imperial family's visit to Moscow in July 1881, when Nicholas was thirteen, initiated him into the performance of his father's national scenario. He beheld Russian monarchy as a festive union between tsar and people. A schoolroom composition expresses the excitement he felt as he looked down from the Red Staircase and beheld the shouting people on the Kremlin square. "My God! What a majestic and touching picture!!! Thousands and thousands of bare heads. When Papa and Mama came through the doors and when Papa bowed to the people, such a deafening 'Hoorah' resounded

[19] Alexander Iswolsky, *Recollections of a Foreign Minister* (Garden City, N.Y.), 248; Lanson, "Le tsar Nicolas II," 132; N. Charykov, "Karl Osipovich Khis," *Istoricheskii Vestnik* (April 1902): 422–36.

[20] Lieven, *Nicholas II*, 28–29.

[21] For example, see "Uchenicheskie tetradi Nikolaia Aleksandrovicha po russkomu iazyku," GARF, 601-1-163. "Dnevnik, 1882," GARF, 601-1-217.

[22] Verner, *The Crisis of Russian Autocracy*, 11.

that I shuddered and my ears rang. This 'Hoorah' continued until we reached the entrance of the Assumption Cathedral." He recorded the same impression after his trip to Moscow the following year. He remembered the displays of popular devotion that occurred during the trip along the Volga, the massive welcome of shouting people running through the streets, whole families of peasants greeting him in boats as he approached Kostroma.[23]

Nicholas was fascinated by the shrines of Russia's past in Moscow. His compositions describe his visits to the ancient chambers of the Kremlin palaces and the Cathedral of Christ the Redeemer. He was especially impressed by the immensity and magnificence of the cathedral and could not take his eyes off two of the pictures, the betrayal of Christ by Judas and the death of Vladimir Monomakh. He described his first sight of the towers, walls, and cupolas of the Trinity Monastery and recalled the invasion by the Poles at the beginning of the seventeenth century "and how the Russian people courageously defended themselves and repulsed them."[24]

Like his father, Nicholas regarded the court as an alien realm, and court presentations as painful trials. His majority ceremony on his sixteenth birthday, May 6, 1884, was hardly an imposing or portentous event. Indeed, Alexander III instructed the foreign minister Giers to inform foreign diplomats that the celebration would be reduced in size to spare the heir embarrassment.[25] Pobedonostsev prepared him for the ceremony, visiting him three times in the two weeks before.[26] On the dais of the Palace Church in the Winter Palace Nicholas repeated the oath to serve his father and tsar, with a "childlike but firm voice," and seemed to be very ill at ease. The ceremony was disorganized, in part because Prince Alexander Dolgorukii, the ceremony master, was ill, but in fact, Polovtsov wrote, because "the disorder of the whole Russian land is always reflected in court ceremonies as well." The report in *Vsemirnaia Illiustratsiia* was dry and brief, with no mention of emotion. A lithograph presents the imperial family arrayed to witness Nicholas taking the oath. It casts them in the typical lithographic idiom of *Vsemirnaia Illiustratsiia*—as stonelike figures performing the ceremony faithfully, a living tableau vivant (fig. 43).[27] Nicholas's diary entry on the ceremony is succinct. He mentions that he wore the ataman uniform. "I am very happy that it all went well. I received Prussian, Greek, and Danish orders."[28]

A classroom composition he wrote shortly afterward presents the day as little more than a test of nerves. He viewed the ceremony as a frightening

[23] "Uchenicheskie tetradi Nikolaia Aleksandrovicha po russkomu iazyku (sochineniia)," GARF, 601-1-167, 26–27, 46–47, 57–60, 97.

[24] Ibid., 29–30, 38.

[25] Von Shweinitz, *Denkwürdigkeiten*, 2:272.

[26] He is mentioned in the entries for April 19, April 26, and May 3, 1884 (Nicholas II, "Dnevnik, 1884g.," GARF, 601-1-219, 114, 120, 128).

[27] Polovtsov, *Dnevnik*, 1:215; *Vsemirnaia Illiustratsiia*, May 19, 1884, 426.

[28] Nicholas II, "Dnevnik, 1884g.," 131. Following tradition, Nicholas became honorary ataman of the Cossack host when he became heir to the throne on March 1, 1881.

43. Nicholas II's Majority Ceremony, May 6, 1884. Lithograph from *Vsemirnaia Illiustratsiia*. Slavic and Baltic Division, New York Public Library. Astor, Lenox, and Tilden Foundations.

moment, interfering with the pleasant course of his everyday life. It inspired no awe or sense of the loftiness of the occasion. The anticipation of the moment tormented him ceaselessly. "I found myself in some kind of languorous expectation, which prevented me from giving myself completely to any pleasure, lesson, or anything else. I would have been very glad to postpone my majority to my twentieth birthday." He could not take pleasure even in the birthday presents he received the evening before. But he dreamed of enjoying them at Gatchina once the ordeal was over.[29]

That morning Nicholas breakfasted with his father, but Alexander spoke not a word about the significance of the moment. Once the ceremony began he tried to be calm, but "as the moment to read the oath came closer, my heart beat louder and louder," and when he stood before the throng he feared that the beating of his heart could be heard by all. His attention was riveted on himself. He does not mention the emotional embraces or tears of those present. "I felt that all eyes were fixed on my back and that all gazes penetrated through it." He feared mistakes, his lips grew dry, but he was relieved that he had completed it without an error. He took the military oath with greater confidence and at the end was rewarded with gifts from his relatives. "Of course, I was absolutely delighted by these presents," but in fact, he confessed, he was only truly happy when he returned to his room. "I finally

[29] "Uchenicheskie tetradi v. k. Nikolaia Aleksandrovicha po russkomu iazyku i literature," GARF, 601-1-170, 67–68.

have gone through this important event that wearied me so much." In the evening he dined with his father and mother "which we have been allowed to do only rarely in the past." They then went downstairs to admire a model of the tower of Ivan the Great in Moscow, illuminated as it had been at the time of the coronation.[30]

The next day, May 7, Nicholas received the diplomatic corps. One by one the ambassadors greeted him, but he found the function, and especially the diplomats with whom he had to chat, painful nuisances. He wrote in his diary, "This trying exercise lasted forty minutes. All the ambassadors and emissaries began to present their subordinates to me. It was necessary to talk with these people. But I quickly succeeded in getting away from them. I bowed and left!"[31]

Previous majority ceremonies marked the beginning of a new stage in life when the heir was allowed greater independence and played a more active role in court ceremonies. They celebrated the heir's passing into manhood, taking on the responsibilities of his father's successor. But Alexander III clearly assigned little significance to the ceremony and hardly treated his son with greater regard than before. Indeed, as a measure of economy, he announced that Nicholas would forego the allowance of three hundred thousand rubles to which he was legally entitled after the majority and would continue to be supported by his parents.[32]

Unlike the court, the guards' regiments were sacralized by the national myth, and induction into military training remained a festive and joyous moment in the heir's upbringing. Nicholas was delighted at his contacts with the guards and his first military appointments. In his diary he recorded the uniforms he wore on special occasions. In 1884, the year of his majority, he was thrilled by the summer exercises at Krasnoe Selo, where he watched maneuvers in his ataman uniform. On August 26, after a visit to the camp of the Preobrazhentsy, he underlined the sentence "I commanded half a company." When taken on an outing to a nearby park, his thoughts were only of returning to the bivouac. That winter he participated in the reviews at the Mikhailovskii Manège and attended breakfast with the officers of the guard.[33]

Active military service began only in 1887, when he reached the age of nineteen. Like previous heirs, he eagerly awaited this moment. In January 1887 Nicholas asked his father to allow him to participate in maneuvers at Krasnoe Selo that summer. Alexander agreed but, indicatively, had not thought to suggest it himself. Nicholas wrote in his diary on January 18, "A fine day! For me especially. Today, after breakfast, I announced my wish to

[30] Ibid., 68–71.
[31] Ibid., 71; Nicholas II, "Dnevnik, 1884g.," 132.
[32] Polovtsov, *Dnevnik*, 1:210.
[33] "Dnevnik Nikolaia II, 1884g.," GARF, 601-1-219, 220–27, 345.

Papa to begin service in the camp this year, and Papa, as a result, allowed my dream to come true. Hoorah!!! With all my soul!"[34]

Nicholas's diary records his great enthusiasm in the subsequent weeks. He danced at the court balls "until ready to collapse," attended lively suppers, and overslept his lessons. On February 4 he rode to the barracks in his Preobrazhenskii uniform, then marched to the square. "The *parade* began at seven. I have rarely enjoyed myself so much because I did everything from beginning to end." The *folle journée*, the last day before Lent, was especially merry. "From the ball directly into Lent," he wrote on February 16. "An astonishing change in my life. Again it is quiet and tranquil. But I must say that I recall yesterday's ball with great pleasure. We have begun to fast."

After Lent Nicholas turned to more serious diversions. On February 23 he attended an "interesting meeting" of the Historical Society, where he heard papers on Sergei Solov'ev, Pavel, Nakhimov, and Pushkin. On March 2 he returned with great joy to Gatchina and delighted in sliding down the hills. He attended lessons and read the historical journal, *Russkaia Starina*, nearly every day. The journal, he wrote on April 9, "is extraordinarily interesting to me. I continue day and night to dream of Krasnoe [Selo] and my life in the camp."[35]

On May 5 and 6, 1887, he journeyed to Novocherkassk for his induction as ataman of the Don Cossacks. During the ceremony he received from his father the Cossack regalia—the silver-tipped wooden maces, the *pernach* conferred by Peter the Great and the *naseka* by the empress Elizabeth. In his diary Nicholas described the approach to the town and the scenes of endless steppes with Cossacks at their settlements.[36] He proudly dressed himself in his ataman uniform, and his father in the uniform of the Cossacks of the Guards, for their entry into Novocherkassk. Suffering the oppressive heat of the steppe, he was welcomed at a "beautiful meeting" by the appointed ataman of the Don N. I. Sviatopolk-Mirskii. The Cossack population had converged from their distant settlements and stood along the road, "behind them the endless steppe."

The investiture ceremony took place on May 6, Nicholas's nineteenth birthday. After a church service, he received the *pernach* from his father and raised it into the air. The emperor and archbishop delivered speeches, and Nicholas marched with the *naseka* while the regalia was carried ahead of him. Then he attended a breakfast for the deputies, with toasts. The next day he reviewed a parade with the *pernach* in his hand and visited a Kalmyk hut where he heard "their noisy service." When he returned to Gatchina, he wrote in his diary, "I cannot say what a pleasant impression this trip to Novocherkassk and to the Cossacks made on me!!!" For both Alexander

---

[34] "Dnevnik Nikolaia II, 1887g.," GARF, 601-1-221, 22.
[35] Ibid., 22–103.
[36] Ibid., 129–34.

and Nicholas, the Cossacks represented the Russian tradition of conquest, a group carrying on the role of pacifying and colonizing border regions, extending the empire's frontiers.[37]

Nicholas's military service at Krasnoe Selo began in late June 1887. The elated entries in his diary indicate that his stay at the camp fulfilled all his expectations. He described his excitement during the war games and the merriment at the bivouacs. He wrote to his father, "Here everything is set up so splendidly and everything is so much to my taste that I completely understand Mitia [Grand Duke Dmitrii Konstantinovich] for whom there exists no better place on earth than Krasnoe Selo." He was "completely in love with his wonderful barrack," so much so that he was a little ashamed to be in such a wonderful house, which he described in detail to his mother. The food was excellent. He felt himself at home with his company and knew nearly everyone by face and name. He was amazed at the praise he frequently received during the reviews. Everyone was delighted with him, and he and the officers drank down a goblet of champagne. He defeated one of them in billiards and wrote, surprised, that he was already considered the best player in the division. At the closing of the camp, he wrote in his diary, "I cannot say how sad I am to leave the regiment tomorrow for nearly an entire year!!!"[38]

Nicholas's initiation into the guards' regiments followed the traditions created by Nicholas I in the 1830s. The heir was to experience a personal as well as symbolic bond with the elite of the armed forces who would serve him as emperor. But for Nicholas II these bonds took on an especially significant and almost exclusive importance. Much more than his predecessors, he was allowed to revel with the officers. While he loved the parade ground, he was most taken by the diversion of socializing with officers and young men of his own age, whose flattery he appears to have taken at face value. He enjoyed the raucous life of the officers' mess—staying out in their company until six in the morning, drinking huge quantities of champagne in restaurants with Gypsy orchestras.[39]

In their midst he was a comrade and equal, not a figure comfortable with command. The memoirs about Nicholas in the guards' regiment give a sense of gracious camaraderie rather than a picture of sovereign among servitors. The memoirs of loyal guards' officers tell how the young men looked to

[37] The celebration was described in the press but with only passing attention to Nicholas himself. *Moskovskie Vedomosti* published a description of the various ceremonies, and its editorial of May 14 hailed the emperor's conferral of the *pernach* on his son, "undertaking new obligations in the service of his dear Fatherland. The ceremony of the taking of the regalia, the symbols of this service, by the young Ataman was touching and joyous" (*MV*, May 9–14, 1887; an editorial on the investiture appeared on May 9, 1887, 2).

[38] "Dnevnik Nikolaia II, 1887g." 178–223; letters to Alexander III, June 24 and 25, 1887, GARF, 677-1-919, 107–110; letter to Maria Fedorovna, June 25, 1887, GARF, 642-1-2321, 55–56.

[39] Verner, *The Crisis of Russian Autocracy*, 24; Lieven, *Nicholas II*, 37. See the citations from Nicholas's diary in Edvard Radzinsky, *The Last Tsar: The Life and Death of Nicholas II* (New York, 1992), 19.

the tall, prepossessing grand dukes as idols, men with fine carriage, suave flexibility, and magnanimity. Nicholas earned the guardsmen's affection but not their respect.[40] His father's early death fixed him in this role. On his twenty-first birthday, in 1889, Alexander appointed him flügel-adjutant in his suite, and in 1892, when he turned twenty-four, colonel in the Preobrazhenskii Regiment. But it did not occur to him to promote his son to general's rank, which both he and Alexander II had received from their fathers as a sign of equality and, ostensibly, of fellowship with them.[41] During his own reign Nicholas remained a colonel, a rank that did not enhance the majesty of his image.

Nicholas enjoyed the boon companionship of the barrack, but it remained superficial and did not grow into friendship. When he was about to leave for Krasnoe Selo in June, his mother sent a letter of advice and admonition. She urged him to behave courteously with his comrades but to avoid "familiarity or too much intimacy" and to beware of flatterers. He replied, "I will always try to follow your advice, my dearest, darling Mama. One has to be cautious with everyone at the start."[42] He kept his mother's admonitions in mind, remained cautious in his attachments, and broke off contact with old comrades when he found new ones.[43] The regiments gave freedom from family but within its purview—a pattern of innocuous dissipation, a genteel respite that offered no real personal independence. Nicholas's affair with the ballerina Mathilda Kshesinskaia was another episode in this sanctioned waywardness, another rite of passage in the young man's growing up. He partied with Kshesinskaia in the company of the grand dukes, and the dancer clearly understood that the affair could not lead to marriage.[44]

•

In preparation for the throne, Alexander appointed Nicholas to the State Council and the Committee of Ministers. He also named him chairman of the Committee on Famine Relief and of the Siberian Railroad Committee.

---

[40] See, for example, Gerua, *Vospominaniia o moei zhizni*, 1:84–87, who particularly worshiped Grand Duke Vladimir Aleksandrovich, and Epanchin, *Na sluzhbe trekh imperatorov*, passim.

[41] "Polnyi posluzhnoi spisok Ego Imperatorskogo Velichestva Gosudaria Imperatora, Nikolaia Aleksandrovicha," GARF, 601-1-1, 9–10. Alexander II had been appointed lieutenant-general before his wedding in 1841 on the eve of his twenty-third birthday; he was appointed adjutant-general two years later on the birth of his first child (see Volume 1: 378). Alexander III was appointed adjutant-general on April 17, 1868, when he was twenty-three years old, and lieutenant-general in September of that year.

[42] Edward J. Bing, ed., *The Secret Letters of the Last Tsar* (Toronto, 1938), 33, 36; "Pis'ma imperatritsy Marii Fedorovny Nikolaiu II," GARF, 601-1-1294, 14–17, letter of June 21, 1887; "Pis'ma Nikolaia II imp. Marii Fedorovne," GARF, 642-1-2321, 55–56, letter of June 25, 1887.

[43] A. F. Girs, "Vospominaniia byvshego ofitsera Lb.-Gv. Preobrazhenskogo Polka i Minskogo Gubernatora, A. F. Girsa o svoikh vstrechakh s Gosudarem Imperatorom Nikolaem II," BAR, Giers collection, 14–15; V. N. Lamzdorf, *Dnevnik* (Moscow-Leningrad, 1928–1934), 2:259.

[44] See Verner *The Crisis of Russian Autocracy*, 29–30.

According to General Epanchin, Alexander issued an order that Nicholas attend ministerial reports. He did so, however, only briefly and not at all in the last three years of Alexander III's reign.[45] Nicholas felt out of place at governmental meetings and viewed them with impatience.

Nicholas regarded state institutions and their officials with disdain and did not trouble to disguise his feelings. He shared his father's hostility to the Westernized bureaucracy. But whereas Alexander distinguished among his officials between "true Russians" who upheld his vision of a strong autocracy and those infected with Western ideas, Nicholas distrusted nearly all officials. These feelings became clear when he was appointed to the State Council in 1889. At the reception after his first meeting, he could find nothing to say and offended the senior members. They were then excluded from the religious service for his name day and the breakfast celebration at Anichkov. Such breaches of etiquette in a system based on formal respect for rank and order could only portend a serious rift between the imperial family and the chief legislative organ of state. The State Council was the only institution he attended regularly, one meeting a week, but found preparations for this a tedious chore.[46]

Nicholas rarely expressed opinions in the State Council, the Committee of Ministers, or the governmental committees he chaired. D. N. Liubimov, a member of the Committee on Famine Relief, remarked that Nicholas sat at its meetings quietly, keeping his views to himself, looking younger than his years. On the other hand, when his father appeared unexpectedly, everyone leaped to his feet, stretched to attention, "like a string," especially the heir. The sight of Alexander III was overwhelming. Liubimov wrote, "Neither before nor after have I seen another person who so overwhelmed (*podavlial*) those around him with his majesty as did Alexander III."[47] Alexander's contempt was understood as the impatience of a monarch with more serious things on his mind, whose anger upheld authority. Nicholas's contempt, on the other hand, was ascribed to immaturity or insufficient preparation for the throne.

Alexander Izvol'skii remarked that Nicholas II had never been treated as tsarevich. Alexander neither sought to impress him with his high obligations nor sought to acquaint him with his future tasks as emperor. He continued to look upon him as a child.[48] Nicholas remained juvenile in appearance and tastes, loving sports and games like hide-and-seek. Many in the court and the government made sneering remarks about Nicholas, who did not live up to their masculine ideal. A tsarevich of only five-foot seven and slight of build was cause for distress. Even the American minister's wife Mrs. Lathrop

---

[45] Epanchin, *Na sluzhbe trekh imperatorov*, 204–5.

[46] Verner, *The Crisis of Russian Autocracy*, 26; Polovtsov, *Dnevnik*, 2:197, 243, 369.

[47] Lamzdorf, *Dnevnik*, 2:259; Verner, *The Crisis of Russian Autocracy*, 82–83 nn. 62, 63; D. N. Liubimov, "Russkaia smuta nachala deviatisotykh godov, 1902–1906," BAR, Columbia University, 89–90.

[48] Iswolsky, *Recollections*, 260.

remarked in 1886 that it would be a misfortune if the heir did not grow. "Russians will find it difficult to connect the idea of majesty with one who is so small." Vladimir Lamzdorf, the director of the chancellery of the Ministry of Foreign Affairs, wrote in 1892, "The heir, twenty four years old, is a very strange sight: half infant, half man, short, skinny, insignificant."[49]

JOURNEY TO THE EAST

From the early nineteenth century the last stage of a tsarevich's education was his tour through the empire he would rule. The tour had two purposes: to acquaint the heir with Russia and to strengthen, by means of face-to-face acquaintanceship, the bond of sentiment that linked the future emperor with his people. Nicholas took no such tour. Not only did fears for the security of the imperial family preclude such travel, but the national scenario also made its principal purposes superfluous. The spiritual bond of monarch with his people came through the church and history and required neither exposure to empirical reality nor knowledge of present-day Russia.

Instead, Nicholas embarked on a ten-month voyage to Asia, to parts of the world never visited by a Russian heir or monarch—Egypt, India, Ceylon, Siam, Indo-China, the Dutch East Indies, China, and Japan. The tour announced Alexander III's determination to give Russia a presence in Asia and to make the heir aware of Russia's destiny in the East.[50] For this reason, two of the most articulate advocates of Russia's destiny in the East, Nicholas Przheval'skii and Esper Ukhtomskii, were encouraged to befriend the heir and share their experiences and views with him.[51]

Nicholas Przheval'skii was an explorer, commander, naturalist, and popular writer, who undertook numerous expeditions into inner Asia, three of them as far as Tibet. A military leader subduing Manchurian and Chinese "brigands" along the way to Tibet, he saw his journeys as the beginning of Russian dominion in the regions he explored.[52] His books connected Russia's imperial might with scientific progress. His writings depicted all Asians, but particularly the Chinese, as deceitful and egotistical peoples who spent their lives in idleness consuming opium and tea. They were cowardly and fought only from fear of punishment. He wrote in 1873, "With a thousand of our

---

[49] Lathrop, *The Court of Alexander III* (Philadelphia, 1910), 69; Lamzdorf, *Dnevnik*, 2:259; Alexander Mikhailovich, *Once a Grand Duke*, 173. This is evident in some of the portraits of Nicholas from the 1890s; see especially the painting of Nicholas by Ernst Liphart from the 1890s in *Nicholas and Alexandra: The Last Imperial Family of Tsarist Russia*, 41.

[50] Witte indicates that the idea of an Eastern journey originated with Alexander himself (*Vospominaniia*, 1:438).

[51] The best discussion of the views of Przheval'skii and Ukhtomskii can be found in Schimmelpenninck Van Der Oye's, *Ex Oriente Lux*.

[52] Ibid., 12–59; N. F. Dubrovin, *Nikolai Mikhailovich Przheval'skii: biograficheskii ocherk* (St. Petersburg, 1890), passim.

soldiers we can subdue all Asia from Baikal to the Himalayas. There we can repeat the achievements of Cortez."[53]

David Schimmelpenninck has shown that Przheval'skii's "conquistador imperialism" had great popular appeal. His daring explorations and pride in Russia's superiority showed that the possibility of conquest existed, even if Alexander III was not about to risk international stability to support such romantic adventures. Alexander III and Maria Fedorovna regarded the explorer's example as one suitable for the heir's attention, and, with the empress's invitation, Przheval'skii, at the beginning of the 1880s, came to give lectures to Nicholas about Inner Asia. In 1883 Nicholas presented Przheval'skii with an aluminum telescope before his impending fourth expedition.[54] In August 1883, during Przheval'skii's fourth expedition to Inner Asia, Danilovich wrote a letter asking him to send reports to Nicholas.[55] Przheval'skii's letters gave a vivid account of the difficulties and successes of his expedition, the various native groups, as well as the wildlife and the terrain he encountered. The explorer made clear his belief in the superiority of Russians as true Europeans and his contempt for Asians. His first letter of November 7, 1883, explained how he chose twenty of the best Cossack sharpshooters to accompany him. He explained to Nicholas, "With the well-known cowardice of Asians, such force is sufficient to guarantee our safety."[56]

In a letter of August 10, 1885, Przheval'skii described how the natives along the Cherchen River in Eastern Central Asia welcomed the Russians as saviors from their Chinese tormentors, how they dreamed of coming under Russian rule. They said, "We know about the justice that rules in Russian Turkestan. Here, any Chinese official, even any soldier, can impudently beat us as much as he wants, seize our property, our wives, our children. They take exorbitant taxes. We cannot endure such a situation for long." They had armed themselves for an insurrection. "Give us only one Cossack. Let him be our leader."[57] Przheval'skii wrote in 1888 that the nomadic Mongols, Chinese Muslims, and inhabitants of Eastern Turkestan were ready "to become subjects of the White tsar, whose name, equally with that of the Dalai Lama, appears in the eyes of the Asiatic masses as surrounded with a halo of mystic might."[58]

Esper Ukhtomskii was an official of the Department of Ecclesiastical Affairs for Foreign Confessions and a specialist in Eastern art and Buddhist religion. He published articles and a book on the religious practices of the Buriats and Kalmyks, which he studied during official trips to Siberia and

---

[53] Schimmelpenninck Van Der Oye, *Ex Oriente Lux*, 37.

[54] Ibid., 44–45.

[55] Ibid., 32; Dubrovin, *Nikolai Mikhailovich Przheval'skii*, 361, 381.

[56] "Pis'ma Przheval'skogo, N. M., puteshestvennika, o svoem puteshestvii po Tibetu, dlia doklada v. k. Nikolaiu Aleksandrovichu," GARF, 601-1-1329, 1–2.

[57] Ibid., 40–41.

[58] Schimmelpenninck Van Der Oye, *Ex Oriente Lux*, 42. On the meaning of "white tsar," see chapter 2, n. 19.

Central Asia in the 1880s. Ukhtomskii was chosen to accompany Nicholas during his trip to the Far East.[59] His illustrated six-volume account of the voyage, *The Voyage of His Imperial Highness, Sovereign Heir, and Tsarevich in 1890 and 1891 to the East*, appeared in Russian between 1893 and 1897, and then in French, German, English, and Chinese translations.[60] Ukhtomskii wrote the book in consultation with Nicholas, who personally censored the volumes. Empress Alexandra Fedorovna later purchased several thousand copies which she donated to governmental institutions.[61]

The tone of Ukhtomskii's account was elevated and romantic, and the text was illustrated by many drawings of the exotic sites that the heir and his party visited. The purpose of the trip presumably was the conventional broadening of the heir's "intellectual horizon." He would witness "the entire past of humanity." He would come into contact with "the strangest and most powerful ideas" of Greece, Egypt, and Asia, "incarnated in stone and work, steadfast, undefeated by the chaos of centuries."[62] The first volume opened with a photograph of Nicholas, handsome with a mustache, and a montage of panoramic views of the sites visited. Scenes of European cities and Greek temples alternated with drawings of the ships and Eastern temples, mosques, and obelisques.

Ukhtomskii gave moving descriptions of the many temples and palaces along the way as well as lyric evocations of the beauty of Asia and the sea. These passages were intertwined with comparisons with Russia and turned the travel book into a tract on Russia's Eastern destinies. Russia's history, with its contact with Asian peoples in the empire and abroad, had created a spiritual and political affinity between Russians and Asians. Learning of the court life of early princes of Akhmedabad in India, the author wrote:

> You unwillingly feel yourself in a kindred setting, from which emerged the types of the "terrible Eyes" of the Riurik dynasty, Kalita, Fedor Ivanovich, with their boyars, coming from Prussia and Lithuania, from the nearby Hordes and from far away beyond the Volga. Only our historical figures can personify and fuse Western and Eastern principles, as if the birth of a new race, mixed in blood but distinctive in spirit, begins distinctly to emerge.[63]

Since the Russians were kindred with Asians, they were more sensitive to their needs, treated them as equals, and sympathized with their plight as victims of European greed and exploitation. When the Russian squadron entered the waters of the Pacific, Ukhtomskii expressed his disgust for the "invasion of alien regions for the glory of pitiful egotistical prejudices of soi-disant educated humanity." Russians, on the other hand, had "stayed at

[59] Schimmelpenninck Van Der Oye, *Ex Oriente Lux*, 65–76.

[60] Kn. E. E. Ukhtomskii, *Puteshestvie na vostok ego Imperatorskogo Vysochestva, Gosudaria Naslednika Tsesarevicha, 1890–1891* (St. Petersburg, 1893–1897).

[61] Schimmelpenninck Van Der Oye, *Ex Oriente Lux*, 77–78; Witte, *Vospominaniia*, 1:437.

[62] Ukhtomskii, *Puteshestvie na vostok ego Imperatorskogo Vysochestva*, 1:1–2.

[63] Ibid, 2:104.

home" for more than two hundred years. Russia's expansion, he asserted, did not fall in the same category as Europe's. "One cannot call the natural merger with Turkestan and the Amur region political conquests."[64]

Ukhtomskii made a basic distinction between conceptions of space. Westerners, and particularly the British, regarded Asia as "foreign" and Asians as "cattle" and therefore ripe for easy profits. Russians found Asia like their own native land (rodina). "The more energetically Europe advances into Asia, the brighter shines the image of the White Tsar [of Moscow] in rumors and traditions [of Asia]." Asians were enthused by the "mysteriously attractive amalgam" of the Iranian and Turanian principles, the rational and the spiritual, he concluded, drawing on Alexei Khomiakov's Slavophile notion of Russians' ethnic past. This attraction, he claimed, explained the warm reception given Nicholas by the king of Siam, the Vietnamese, and in China "which regards Europeans with scorn."[65]

•

Ukhtomskii and M. K. Onu, an authority on Asian affairs, were the specialists who accompanied Nicholas on his journey. The party also included Major-General Vladimir Bariatinskii, an adjutant who was supposed to supervise the heir, and four officers of the guards.[66] Nicholas was feted by the local potentates, shown sites, and then given the chance to shop for art objects and curiosities, a passion in which, by his own admission, he indulged freely. In India, Siam, and Indo-China he enjoyed big game hunting, going after antelopes, tigers, and elephants, though usually without great success.

The *Pamiat' Azova* served as his home during the ocean trip, and Nicholas himself admitted in a letter to his father that "my life on this frigate will remain for me the brightest and most pleasant memory of the entire trip." The ship reproduced the setting he had left in Russia. The services on religious holidays recalled his life in the family. The company of aristocratic guardsmen made for nightly carousing, recalling life with the guards in Petersburg. The trip was commemorated with a Fabergé Easter egg in the form of the *Pamiat' Azova*. A dark-green jasper egg embellished with rococo gold work encapsulates a gold and platinum model of the ship, fitted with smokestacks, ladders, and guns, and set on an aquamarine base.[67] The egg marked the trip as a significant event in the life of the imperial family. The sumptu-

[64] Ibid, 3:213–14.

[65] Ibid., 3:214–17.

[66] Flügel-Adjutant N. D. Obolenskii, of the Horse-Guards, V. S. Kochubei of the Cavalier-Guards, and E. N. Volkov of the hussars.

[67] GARF, 677-1-919, 190, letter of June 11, 1891, to Alexander III; GARF, 642-1-2321, 113, letter of December 10, 1890, to Maria Fedorovna. See also "Dnevnik Nikolaia II, 1891g.," GARF, 601-1-225, 66–67, entry of February 13, 1891. Nicholas writes of his joy at being back aboard the ship: "You feel light and free and I, in the full sense of the word, rest on these travels from the busy trips on shore, for example, after the voyage in India" (Pfeffer, *Fabergé Eggs*, 26–27).

ousness of the memento made the frigate a symbol of Russia's sea power, extended to the waters of the Far East.

The journey has often been characterized as frivolous and pointless, a pleasure trip through oriental exotica taken by the heir in the company of aristocratic and none-too-serious comrades.[68] Nicholas may have seen little of Asian life outside the courts he visited, but his diaries indicate that he shared many of Ukhtomskii's attitudes. He took exception to the British colonials' arrogance and highhandedness in India. He was shocked, he wrote to his father, about the crude arrogance the English showed to the Maharajah in Benares. He remarked that English newspapers in Hong Kong and Shanghai were "raging" over his visit to Canton and Hankow. "The articles are so senselessly stupid and impudent that they might have been written by idiots. They all call me 'the imperial globe-trotter' [English in original]—and this is their only successful expression." He admired the neatness of Nagasaki. The people were "cordial and quiet and the main thing I liked was that I saw not a single European."[69]

Nicholas, like Ukhtomskii, observed that as a Russian he felt a special affinity with the Asian potentates and aristocrats he visited. He liked the maharajahs he met and enjoyed their shows of Indian dancing and magic. In Ceylon, "this paradise on earth," he was astonished by a torchlight pageant that included priests, a "devil dance," the dancers wearing terrible masks, bayaderes, and musicians slowly proceeding through the crowd on elephants. He especially took to the king of Siam, "a kind, courteous person, well-educated and worthy of his office." He got on well with shopkeepers when negotiating his countless purchases. Everywhere, he was immensely impressed by Buddhist temples, which awakened in him pious, spiritual feelings that invoked a common spiritual heritage. Visiting a row of temples dedicated to the god Krishna, he wrote, "Each time I see a temple distinguished by grandeur, order, and reverence, as in Russia, as I enter I begin to feel a religious mood, as if I am in a Christian church!" He liked the bright motley colors of Buddhist temples in Siam, which reminded him of Vasilii the Blessed.[70]

He described the Japanese as "such a cordial and polite people, the very opposite of the Chinese." Many spoke Russian. He liked the cleanliness and order of Japanese towns and farms and enjoyed his visits to the market in Japan, where he and his companions amused themselves with parasols. His pleasant visit, however, was brought abruptly to an end when a crazed Samurai struck him on his head with a sword while he was visiting the town of Otsu. Nonetheless Nicholas continued to profess his admiration for the

[68] For example, Grand Duke Alexander Mikhailovich, *Once a Grand Duke*, 167.
[69] Letters of Alexander III to Nicholas II, GARF, 601-1-1139, 30, letter of December 18, 1891; 677-1-919, 144, 172, letters of January 20 and April 1, 1891; "Dnevnik Nikolaia II, 1891g.," 177, entry of April 24, 1891).
[70] "Dnevnik Nikolaia II, 1891g.," 42, 95, 97, entries of January 28, March 8, and March 9, 1891.

Japanese in the days after the attack. He wrote in his diary on May 1, 1891, "I like everything Japanese as much now as before April 29 and I am not at all angry at the nice Japanese for the disgusting act of one fanatic who is their compatriot."[71]

The journey and his lessons confirmed a sense of imperial rivalry and Russia's moral superiority. What he saw heightened his pride in the Russian fleet and military forces, which represented to him the might and majesty of Russia. In the sea of Java, his "heart rejoiced" at the magnificent sight of the Russian squadron in Asian waters, next to what appeared to him shoddy English vessels. He wrote to his mother, "I don't understand how [the English] can send such rotten skeletons, because you can't call them anything else, to their colonies." He was happy to see the surprise and envy of the English at the Russian ships, each of which, he believed, was stronger than two English ships put together.[72]

Both Ukhtomskii and Nicholas felt a swell of national pride when they landed at Vladivostok on May 11. For Ukhtomskii, Siberia was proof of the success of Russia's colonization of the East. British colonials lived in luxury and comfort. Russian settlers, on the other hand, were selflessly devoted to improving their state: "the onerous, wretched, and self-denying conditions, in which innumerable spiritual figures of the Russian land consummate their lofty national deeds on its remote frontiers." "We Slavs unconsciously serve ideals of a tolerant-democratic character, while western Europeans always, and in everything, strive by force to achieve domination over the 'inferior' races, which they spurn on principle."[73]

Nicholas was thrilled by the first sight of Russian guards' battalions, which, he wrote to his father, filled him with "indescribable rapture." His visit to Vladivostok served as a symbolic statement of Russia's new presence in the Far East. There he participated in the dedication ceremonies of a new wharf and a monument to Admiral Gennadii Nevel'skii, who, at the end of the 1840s and the beginning of the 1850s, had explored the Amur River and taken possession of the Amur area for Russia. The most important ceremony for him was the dedication of the beginning of the eastern link of the Trans-Siberian railroad, on May 19, one and one-half miles from Vladivostok. After a prayer service a rocket flew into the air, and a salute sounded from the guns of the ships in the harbor and the shore artillery. Nicholas himself placed a shovel of earth in a wheelbarrow and rolled it to the tracks; the scene was portrayed in a contemporary lithograph (fig. 44). He then joined the governor-general, his own suite, and the chief builder in a railroad car, and, to the shouts of "Hoorah" of the surrounding people and workers

[71] Ibid., 125, 163–64, 172, 184, 195–96, entries of March 24; April 16, 22, and 27; and May 1, 1891.

[72] "Pis'ma imperatora Nikolaia II, imperatritse Marii Fedorovne," 642-1-2321, 123, letter of February 21, 1891.

[73] Ukhtomskii, *Puteshestvie*, 4:210–13.

44. Nicholas II at Dedication Ceremony for the eastern link of the
Trans-Siberian Railroad, 1891. K. Korol'kov, *Tsar-mirotvorets,
Imperator Aleksandr III*. Kiev, 1904.

on the railway, he rode the distance back to Vladivostok. After a prayer
service, he laid the cornerstone, with a silver plaque, for the Vladivostok
train station.

The ceremony was followed by a gala lunch, where Nicholas loudly declaimed Alexander III's rescript on the dedication. "All listened to the Tsar's
words with rapt attention," *Novoe Vremia* reported. The moment the last
word was pronounced, the crowd shouted "Hoorah," the guns of the fortress and the ships gave a thunderous salvo, and the crowds nearby joined
in singing the national anthem. Nicholas wrote to his father, "I and all the
others here were in some kind of feverish mood during all these celebrations,
which are creating something firm, and I thank the Lord God that I could
attend these events!"[74]

As he traveled down the Amur River, the beginning of his long return to
European Russia, Nicholas continued to be moved by national feelings. A
village of settlers from Poltava Province had, he wrote, "a completely Russian look," and the girls performed a round dance before a house. Nicholas
admired the Cossacks who came out to greet him from their settlement. He
liked their lack of formality: They readily crossed the Chinese border to farm

[74] "Pis'ma v. kn. Nikolaia Aleksandrovichu imp. Aleksandru III," 677-1-919, 190–91, letter
of June 11, 1891; "Dnevnik Nikolaia II, 1891g.," 210–24; "Dnevnik Nikolaia II, 1891g.," part
2, GARF, 601-1-226, 1–5; *NV*, May 20, 1891, 1; Schimmelpenninck Van Der Oye, *Ex Oriente
Lux*, 125–26.

lands on the other side. He noticed that they were in a state of readiness, each with his own horse and arms in good order. They kept alive the new image of expansion, conquest, and triumph by heroic Russian warriors. As he sailed down the Amur, Cossacks from settlements along the river brought him gifts and joyously entertained him with equestrian stunts and dances on the shore.[75]

Along the way, Nicholas dedicated a monument to Count Nicholas Murav'ev-Amurskii, who, as governor-general of Eastern Siberia, had pressed Nicholas I to explore and build fortresses on the Amur River. Peasant villages came out on boats to greet him. He read books about Siberia. One of them, by a lieutenant-colonel Vebel', particularly impressed him. Vebel' warned that the Amur region was isolated from other parts of Russia and could not be provided help if necessary: Only the completion of the Siberian railroad could spare the region from ruin.[76] When Nicholas reached Orenburg in July he attended the celebration of the three hundredth anniversary of the Ural Cossack host.[77]

Nicholas's experiences and the Eastern vision reached the public first in the daily press. Detailed reports of his voyage, published in *Pravitel'stvennyi Vestnik*, were reprinted in such mass publication dailies as *Novoe Vremia*. They informed the Russian public of the progress of the voyage, the reception of Nicholas by oriental potentates and diplomats, the acclaim of the people. At the same time, they provided historical and artistic background material about the monuments Nicholas visited and described the exotic dancers, magicians, and others who entertained him.

The summary of the official account bluntly stated the purpose of Nicholas's trip as well as its achievement. It had "directed the attention of all Russian people to the East for an entire year." The heir was welcomed cordially everywhere and "peoples and tribes" were enthused by the "unprecedented visit of the son of the White Tsar, the Heir to his throne." The summary described the journey as a heroic act of sacrifice by the imperial family. The emperor and empress had endured separation from their son. Nicholas had exposed himself to risk, the hardship of spending months in a ship cabin, and homesickness for his parents. "The Tsarevich regarded the visiting of distant parts not as a pleasure trip but as the fulfillment of a duty, as the opportunity to gain experience and knowledge that would later be useful in the service to Tsar and Fatherland."[78]

---

[75] "Dnevnik Nikolaia II, 1891g.," part 2, 10–11, 18–21. In the last decades of the century the government undertook massive resettlement of Cossacks from other regions—the Don, the Kuban, the Urals, and Orenburg—to the new frontier in the East (A. T. Topchii, "Romanovy, kazachestvo i osvoenie vostochnykh territorii Rossii," in *Dom Romanovykh v istorii Rossii*, 134–39).

[76] "Dnevnik Nikolaia II, 1891g.," part 2, 25–44.

[77] Ibid., 140–43.

[78] *MV*, August 5, 1891, 1.

Nicholas came away from his voyage with a conviction of Russia's importance, moral prestige, and potential role in the Far East. Przheval'skii's "conquistador imperialism" had reinforced his belief in the unlimited capacity of armed force and the historical destinies of Russia, elaborated in the national myth, and had suggested that Russia could prevail in the East. The journey through Asia and Ukhtomskii's lessons confirmed the sense of Russians' moral and spiritual supremacy and the empire's capacity to compete with the great colonial powers in Asia. His return through Siberia showed him the exploits of Russian explorers and settlers colonizing the East. Nicholas entertained grandiose perspectives on Russia's destinies that ill comported with the cautious Eastern policy followed by the officials of the Ministry of Foreign Affairs during his father's reign.

MARRIAGE AND FAMILY LIFE

In the nineteenth century, marriage marked the true coming of age of the heir to the Russian throne, the moment when he received his own court, separate residences, and started a family life that gave him some limited independence from his parents. Nicholas II was the only nineteenth-century Russian emperor who came to the throne unwed. When he returned to Russia from his trip in 1891 he was twenty-three and had not even been betrothed.[79] After his return, and especially when the emperor's health began to fail, marriage became a pressing concern.

The delay certainly did not bespeak reluctance. Nicholas had long yearned to marry and shared his parents' idealized conception of the family. In his diaries of the 1880s he expressed his attraction to his German cousins, particularly Victoria and Alexandra, "Alix" of Hesse, and remarked on his pleasure at being with them. He met Alix first in 1884, when he was sixteen years old. She came to Petersburg for the wedding of her older sister, Elizabeth, to the grand duke Sergei Aleksandrovich. Nicholas noted in his diary on May 24 that he sat next to little twelve-year-old Alix and liked her a great deal. He wrote in his diary on November 19, 1884, "The desire to marry lasted until breakfast and then went away."[80] He began thinking seriously of her after meeting her again in Denmark in 1887, and by the time she visited Petersburg at the beginning of 1889 he already felt he was in love. He wrote in 1891, "My dream is to marry Alix of Hesse."[81]

After his return from his Eastern tour, his affair with Kshesinskaia flourished. He arranged for a mansion on the Neva and visited her almost daily.

---

[79] In comparison, Alexander I wed at sixteen, Nicholas I at twenty-one, Alexander II at twenty-three, and Alexander III at twenty-one.

[80] "Dnevnik Nikolaia II, 1884g.," GARF, 601-1-219, 152, 328.

[81] Verner, *The Crisis of Russian Autocracy*, 30.

But he did not seriously consider marriage. In April 1892 he wrote in his diary, "I never imagined that two identical feelings, two loves, could exist in one's soul. . . . Our heart is a wondrous thing!" His love for Alix spared him the painful crisis of the grand duke falling in love with a Russian woman. He found consolation with Kshesinskaia when the plans for marrying Alix met what seemed insuperable obstacles.[82]

Nicholas was attracted to Alexandra not only by her stunning beauty but because the two were kindred spirits. They shared the same predilections, for the family, zealous personal religion, and private life. If Nicholas took on the persona of an English gentleman, Alexandra was English in her upbringing and tastes. Her mother, Princess Alice of Hesse, was a daughter of Queen Victoria. Princess Alice was a woman of deep religious faith and a devotee of the philosopher David Strauss during his period of religious mysticism. Alexandra and her older sister, Elizabeth, grew up in a setting of intense religious commitment. When Alexandra was six years old, she lost both her mother and sister and her playmate, May. She matured under the influence of Queen Victoria, who took a special interest in her and watched over her upbringing. Alexandra took on Victoria's reclusive, grave righteousness as well as her aversion to frivolity.[83] The death of her father, Prince Louis IV, in 1892 was another shattering blow, leaving Alexandra despondent for the subsequent two years.

At first, Alexandra's strong adherence to her Protestant faith kept her from accepting Orthodoxy, the condition for betrothal to the heir that Alexander III refused to waive. From 1891 until April 1894 she adamantly refused to convert. In April 1894 she relented, perhaps under the influence of her sister, the grand duchess Elizabeth, who in 1891 finally accepted Orthodoxy. The resolution of the crisis was a moment of spiritual exaltation. After she announced her decision, Nicholas repented his sins and proclaimed his eternal devotion.[84] On May 25, 1894, Queen Victoria, who feared a marriage that would expose her granddaughter to the hazards of the Russian political scene, wrote to Nicholas that Alexandra needed "great quiet and rest." "Her dear father's death, her anxiety about her brother, and the struggle about her future have all tried her *nerves very much*." She urged Nicholas not to hurry with the wedding.[85]

But Alexander's illness and Nicholas's determination hastened events. The emperor summoned Alexandra hurriedly to Livadia, on October 10, hoping that the marriage would take place before his death. She was baptized into Orthodoxy the day after he died. The timing of the wedding prompted sharp disagreement. Marriage was Nicholas's primary concern. He and his mother

[82] Ibid., 31.
[83] Lieven, *Nicholas II*, 46–49.
[84] Verner, *The Crisis of Russian Autocracy*, 33–34; Lieven, *Nicholas II*, 45.
[85] Andrei Maylunas and Sergei Mironenko, *A Lifelong Passion: Nicholas and Alexandra, Their Own Story* (London, 1996), 70.

wanted the wedding immediately—before Alexander's body left Livadia. The minister of the court Vorontsov-Dashkov earned Nicholas's lasting enmity by arguing that it should occur only after the period of mourning had elapsed. The grand dukes insisted that it be delayed until after Alexander's funeral. Their position won out, and the wedding took place during a one-day suspension of mourning on November 14, 1894, a week after the funeral. Nicholas was gloriously happy. He wrote triumphantly in his diary on November 15, "So today I am a married man!"[86]

Alexandra's melancholy, vulnerability, and ethereal spiritual aura made her only more appealing to Nicholas. Both had a powerful distrust of society and both found public appearances burdensome and preferred their own company. No previous emperor and empress were so similar in their personalities. Nicholas I's cold and intimidating presence contrasted with the endearing figure of the empress Alexandra Fedorovna. Alexander II had been charming, sociable, and Germanophile; Maria Aleksandrovna withdrawn, religious, and nationalistic; Alexander III dour, menacing, and surly; Maria Fedorovna convivial and enchanting. The diverse personalities gave the imperial family a breadth of appeal, a flexibility in dealing with the broad range of personalities and situations taken on by the Russian monarchy. Nicholas and Alexandra on the other hand presented a common face to the outside world, one that was aloof and often both inscrutable and exasperating.

Nicholas and Alexandra entered into a union of two like people, in which each sought and found sustenance in the approval and love of the other and in the family. Alexander III had wanted his sons to grow up like normal and healthy children. He had sought what was normal and healthy in his own family life and regarded the crushing burden of autocratic power, which he bore daily, as abnormal and oppressive. The upbringing of his son succeeded to the extent that Nicholas found his happiness as an ordinary person in the family. But the Russian monarch was not supposed to be an ordinary person: He was a being whose extraordinary efforts distinguished him from other mortals and justified his autocratic prerogatives. With Nicholas II, the public obligations of the Russian sovereign faded into the background of scenes of marital happiness.

·

In the first years of Nicholas II's reign, home and children became the sacred center of the life of the imperial family. Zealous believers, the emperor and empress shared a cult of the family, more British than Orthodox, which may be one reason why their plight seems so familiar and touching to present-day sensibilities. Alexandra preoccupied herself with childbirth and the care

---

[86] B. V. Anan'ich and R. Sh. Ganelin, eds., *Nikolai Vtoroi: Vospominaniia, Dnevniki* (St. Petersburg, 1994), 34–35; B. V. Anan'ich, R. Sh. Ganelin, and V. M. Paneiakh, eds., *Vlast' i reformy: ot samoderzhavnoi k Sovetskoi Rossii*, (St. Petersburg, 1996), 395; *Dnevniki Nikolaia II* (Moscow, 1991), 48.

of the babies. On the birth of Olga in 1895, she followed the practice of late-nineteenth-century Victorian England and insisted on nursing the infant herself. The diaries of Nicholas and the grand duchesses describe the extraordinary scene of an empress breast-feeding her firstborn. Nicholas noted with pride that he had bathed his daughter. The births of Tatiana in 1897 and Marie in 1899 were followed by similar scenes of nursing and parental delight, all the while accompanied by a sense of unease that the empress had not produced a male heir to the throne.[87] The Fabergé egg that Nicholas presented to Alexandra at Easter in 1898 was an art nouveau apotheosis of the family (fig. 45). Dozens of pearls form trellises of lilies of the valley over the pink enamel of the egg and leaves enameled in green. The surprise is a trefoil of portraits framed in diamonds, of Nicholas himself, beneath a gold and diamond studded crown, Olga, and the infant Tatiana.[88]

The family became the focus of Alexandra's religious feelings. Her faith remained one based on personal conscience and private virtue, more akin to Protestantism than the Orthodoxy practiced in the court. She was a devotee of the type of feminized religion that made maternal obligation and fulfillment principal Christian virtues. She sought practical guidance for the life of a Christian wife and mother in the writings of Protestant clergymen. From 1896 to 1901 she transcribed hundreds of pages verbatim from such works, especially those of the American Presbyterian minister James Russell Miller—*The Gentle Life*, *Secrets of a Beautiful Life*, *Housemaking or the Ideal Christian Life*, and *Building of Character*.[89]

For Miller, gentleness was the most Christian of qualities and love the most Christian of feelings. "We are made for love—not only to love, but to be loved," Alexandra copied out and underlined. He described the type of personal suffering that she had endured as a special grace. Those who suffered were especially inclined to tenderness and gifted in love. She underlined: "A great sorrow always for the time at least softens hearts." Sorrow taught the lesson to live more earnestly for others, and the principal object of selflessness that Miller extolled was the home. "Home ought to be the best place in the world in which to grow into Christlikeness." Married life was "God's ideal of completeness." "As a relationship, it is the closest and most sacred on earth," she wrote and underlined. Marriage was the highest expression of Christian love. She underlined: "Each must forget self in devotion to the other."[90]

---

[87] Maylunas and Mironenko, *A Lifelong Passion*, 130–33, 164, 184–85.

[88] Pfeffer, *Fabergé Eggs*, 54–55.

[89] James Russell Miller, 1840–1912, was a leading organizer of the United Presbyterian Church, the founder and editor of the journal, *Forward*, and the author of numerous books (*Dictionary of American Biography* [New York, 1943], 12:627–28).

[90] "Zapisnaia knizhka Imp. Aleksandry Fedorovny s vypiskami iz knig religioznogo soderzhaniia, 1897–1901," GARF, 640-1-301, 1–2, 4, 5, 7, 29–30, 33, 48, 85–108.

45. *Lilies of the Valley Egg*, by Fabergé. 1898. Photograph
by Joe Coscia Jr. The FORBES Magazine Collection, New York.
© All rights reserved.

The flamboyant domesticity of Nicholas I had made the home the model of service to state and nation. Nicholas's and Alexandra's life in the home, on the contrary, represented a haven from the demands of rule. But unlike his father, for whom the family was also a haven, Nicholas II made his domestic virtues a public sign of his supreme humanity. From the beginning of his reign Nicholas cultivated the image of himself as an ideal family man who doted on his children. Popular pictures show him and Alexandra in warm scenes with beautiful cherubic children, as exemplars of family happiness. On the cover of a calendar for 1899 we see a typical example, published by the house of E. I. Konovalova (fig. 46). Nicholas and Alexandra appear close to each other, linked by bonds of love. In the midst of lush glowing flowers, Nicholas clasps Olga and Alexandra holds the infant Tatiana. It is as if we are peering through a window at parents and children in close and loving contact, unlike earlier family groups, in which members strike stiff formal poses appropriate to royalty viewed through a proscenium. Such scenes also appeared in popular periodicals abroad, winning sympathy for the Russian tsar as a model of paternal love.[91]

Unlike Alexander III, Nicholas and Alexandra were prepared to live part of the year in the Winter Palace. They had their chambers, formerly the apartments of Nicholas I and Alexandra Fedorovna, designed in neoclassical and eclectic styles under the guidance of the empress's sister, the grand duchess Elizabeth.[92] But the Alexander Palace at Tsarskoe Selo soon became their favorite residence, and, after disturbances began in St. Petersburg in 1904, they stayed in the Winter Palace only during the tercentenary events of 1913. If Gatchina afforded a protective haven for the imperial family under Alexander III, Nicholas and Alexandra made the Alexander Palace the picturesque setting of an affectionate family life. The layout and design of the rooms reflected the empress's personal attachments, with little mind to matters of aesthetic unity or harmony. Alexandra collected pictures and objects that evoked feelings or places close to her heart. "She liked a thing often more for its association than its beauty, for hers was a sentimental more than an aesthetic nature," her friend Sophie Buxhoeveden, wrote.[93] In this respect, she followed the example of her grandmother, Queen Victoria. Many of the

[91] See, for example, a sketch printed in *Harper's New Monthly Magazine* 96, no. 576 (May 1898). Nicholas bends over Olga, who sits on a couch being held by Alexandra kneeling at her side. It is entitled, "The Most Popular Picture in Russia." A number of these are held in the Print and Photographic Collection of the New York Public Library.

[92] On their chambers in the Winter Palace, with Karl Kubesh's photographs of the individual apartments, see T. A. Petrova and T. A. Malinina, "The Private Rooms of the Imperial Family in the Winter Palace," in *Nicholas and Alexandra: The Last Imperial Family of Tsarist Russia*, 22–26, 97; Vadim Nesin, *Zimnii Dvorets v tsarstvovanie poslednego imperatora Nikolaia II (1894–1917)* (St. Petersburg, 1999), 71, 124–57.

[93] Baroness Sophie Buxhoeveden, *The Life and Tragedy of Alexandra Feodorovna, Empress of Russia* (London, 1928), 51–52.

46. Nicholas II, Alexandra Fedorovna, and Grand Duchess Olga. Color lithograph,
1899. Russian National Library, St. Petersburg.

chambers were furnished in English taste and overstuffed with furniture, paintings, and bric-a-brac.[94]

But Victorian rooms were only one inspiration for the family's chambers.[95] The empress's brother, Prince Ernest of Hesse, was a patron of *Jugendstil*, and the most important family rooms on the first floor were redesigned by Roman Meltser in art nouveau style during the first decade of Nicholas's reign. The aesthetic floral eroticism of art nouveau gave expression to the intense personal relationship of the imperial couple. Nicholas and Alexandra were the first Russian emperor and empress to share a bed.[96] The master bedroom was the center of their family life. After Meltser completed the renovation, Alexandra decorated the room with bright English chintzes, with patterns of green wreaths and pink ribbons. The same motif appeared on the walls and furnitures. Nicholas found it "gay and cozy." After the turn of the century the room was hung with hundreds of icons, expressing the couple's search for a personal Orthodoxy that linked them to the Russian people (see chapter 11).

The master bedroom adjoined a small chapel and the Mauve Room. Meltser's Mauve Room, the empress's boudoir, had walls cheerfully decorated with mauve silk and a frieze of lilac blossoms: It was the scene of intimate family gatherings and the empress's favorite room in the palace. The Maple Room, used for large family gatherings, was filled with the overflow of paintings and art objects, including Easter eggs, which Alexandra could not fit appropriately in the other chambers. Reliefs of rose trellises on the pink walls ascended to the ceiling where they formed a wreath. The balcony also was decorated with intertwining trellises. Nicholas's "new" study, redesigned by Meltser in 1902, had an art nouveau paneled ceiling and a mezzanine with marble columns that connected to the Maple Room. The children's rooms were on the second floor, though often their toys found their way below.

The family rooms were cluttered and bright. They expressed what was most sacred to Nicholas and Alexandra: connubial and parental love, later combined with a worship of Russian saints, from the people, represented by

[94] Vladimir Veidlé expressed discomfort with Alexandra's disregard of the neoclassical interiors. He remarked on the imperial family's distempering of bronzes with bright colors, purchasing simple furniture, "covering up their chandeliers and removing their damask, tricking out their windows with neat cretonne curtains and decorations, their walls with picture postcards, stuck fanwise on priceless brocades" (Wladimir Weidlé, *Russia: Absent and Present* [New York, 1961], 84).

[95] The following description is based on that given in the World Monuments Fund publication, *The Alexander Palace, Tsarskoe Selo, Russia: Preliminary Report for Restoration and Adaptive Re-Use* (n.p., 1998), 27–36. Cynthia Coleman collected much of the data on these sections and has generously shared her knowledge with me about the design and furnishing of the apartment.

[96] For a photograph of the master bedroom in the Winter Palace with a double bed, see *Nicholas and Alexandra: The Last Imperial Family of Tsarist Russia*, 97.

the icons. They devoted less attention to the parade rooms, meant for official meetings. These were decorated with stately Louis XV and Louis XVI furniture, and contained rare busts of the empress Elizabeth, Paul I, and Alexander I. The Victorian, the art nouveau, and the neoclassical coexisted in a palace turned into a middle-class home meant to raise children in a setting accessible to, but separated from, the state and the court.

Accession and Coronation

Our grief cannot be expressed in words, but every Russian heart will understand it and We believe that there will no place in Our vast State where warm tears will not be shed for the Sovereign prematurely departing for eternity and leaving his native land, which He loved with all the force of His Russian soul and the well-being of which was the subject of all his thoughts, sparing neither His health nor His life. And not only in Russia, but far beyond its borders, the memory will never cease to be honored of a Tsar who personified implacable justice and peace, which was unbroken for the duration of his Reign. May the sacred will of the All-High strengthen our unshakeable faith in the wisdom of Heavenly Providence, may We be comforted by the consciousness that Our grief is the grief of all Our beloved people, and may [the people] not forget that the strength and firmness of holy Rus' lies in its unity with Us and in its limitless devotion to Us. And We, in this grievous but solemn hour of Our ascent to the Hereditary Throne of the Russian Empire, and the Kingdom of Poland and the Grand Duchy of Finland, which are indivisible from it, recall the behest of Our deceased Father, and imbued with it, We take the sacred vow before the All-High to have as Our constant goal the peaceful success, might, and glory of dear Russia and the organization of the happiness of all Our loyal subjects. May all-powerful God, who has seen fit to summon us to this great service, give us help.

—Accession Manifesto of Emperor Nicholas II,
October 20, 1894[1]

ACCESSION

Nicholas's accession manifesto, probably written by Pobedonostsev, stated the fundamental themes of the new national myth introduced during the previous reign. For the first time the deceased monarch spoke of every Russian heart understanding the monarch's grief, of the late tsar's "Russian soul" with which he loved the Russian land. For the first time, an accession

---

[1] *PSZ*, series 3, 11014.

manifesto referred to "holy Rus' " as well as Russia (*Rossiia*) and attributed its strength to the "unity" of the people with the monarch. Nicholas ascended to the throne believing in the chronotope of Moscow, a scene and a time of divinely and popularly sanctioned personal rule.

The synchronic grounding of the national myth bestowed the nation's spirit on the new monarch, regardless of his own achievements. It expressed an underlying continuity embodied in the monarchy and exemplified in his father. But the myth did require evidence of the emperor's national character—to show that the dynasty, by blood nearly entirely German, had nonetheless preserved its Russian spirit. The Russian party had constructed a national scenario for Alexander III. Alexander's size, personality traits, and simple tastes had enabled him to appear as Russian Tsar, without abandoning the role of All-Russian Emperor. Nicholas cherished and believed the imagery of the national myth, but his mannerisms, features, and height did not conform to the image of a Russian tsar.

From the start he felt unequal to his father's example. His upbringing had not encouraged him to develop a sense of his own scenario or even an understanding that it was necessary for the divinely appointed monarch to have his own political persona for his subjects to revere. Memoirs of the first two years of Nicholas's reign comment on the discomfort of a young man who had not been prepared for the throne and felt himself awkward in the office. He pleaded with Foreign Minister Giers to remain in his position, "I don't know anything. The late tsar did not foresee his death and did not let me into anything."[2] He told Grand Duke Alexander Mikhailovich, "I am not prepared to be a Tsar. I never wanted to become one. I know nothing of the business of ruling. I even have no idea how to talk to the ministers."[3] Only after the turn of the century did Nicholas begin to define his own role in the myth and to present his own scenario.

In the first years of Nicholas's reign he adhered to his father's policies and retained most of his father's ministers. He relied particularly on Sergei Witte, who had carefully cultivated him as tsarevich. But at the same time Nicholas revealed a manner of rule and a conception of the office of tsar quite different from Alexander III's. Alexander strove for an administration free of the encumbrances of the institutions and legal principles of the reform era, which he saw as alien intrusions in a monarchical system. He placed his trust in "true Russians," officials in principle ethnically Russian but above all devoted to energetic, authoritarian rule. Nicholas II regarded the entire formal apparatus of administration as alien and anti-monarchical. He distrusted nearly all officials, and especially dynamic, gifted ones, as threats to his personal authority.

Nicholas did not seek a group of officials with views similar to his or friends who could give him council. He disliked any opinion contrary to his

---

[2] The conversation is reported by Lamzdorf, *Dnevnik, 1894–1896*, 85.
[3] Alexander Mikhailovich, *Once a Grand Duke*, 169.

own, as indicated by his initial clash with Vorontsov-Dashkov on the timing of the wedding. He believed that the national sanction for his power entitled him to exert authority as he wished, regardless of constraints, either of institutions or reality. From this faith arose a capriciousness of judgment, a contempt for rule and consistency that exasperated his ministers and admirers. They were troubled by his hasty judgments, his unwillingness to heed contrary opinions, and his opaque manner. A disarming if reserved cordiality replaced the distance conferred by majesty.[4]

If Alexander's suspicion of the bureaucracy became with Nicholas general and indiscriminate, Alexander's growing reliance on members of the imperial family accorded them a special status in his eyes. He believed implicitly that political power was the private possession of the imperial family. Such power was not to be challenged by outsiders, whether officials or members of educated society. His uncles, the grand dukes, exerted considerable influence on him, especially in the first years of his reign. They intimidated him and took advantage of his lack of experience. They were able to do so because the imperial family, including his mother and later his wife as well as the grand dukes, constituted the single circle of trust in his eyes.

His trust in the family was accompanied by an aversion to the imperial court. Alexander III had relegated the court to the empress, who maintained its vitality without according it especial significance. Both Nicholas and Alexandra regarded the social occasions of the court as impositions on their private happiness and spiritual peace. Alexandra was loathe to adopt the pretense of a public role and did little to disguise her discomfort at court presentations. "The theatrical instinct is so deep in Russian nature that one feels the Russians act their lives rather than live them," Sydney Gibbs, the English teacher to the tsarevich Alexei, later observed. "This was entirely foreign to the Empress's thought, shaped mostly under the tutelage of her Grandmother Queen Victoria."[5]

Nicholas tried to carry on court functions after the end of the period of mourning. But the spirit was dampened by the cold and forbidding figure the empress presented at the balls and receptions she had to arrange. Alexandra could not compete with the dowager, who, only forty-seven years old at her husband's death, remained vivacious and charming. Ill-at-ease, a poor dancer and conversationalist, Alexandra made clear that she found high society frivolous. Her shyness looked like anger, and, when she was nervous, red blotches appeared on her face.[6] Her poor Russian identified her as a foreigner. Indeed, the favored language between the emperor and empress was English. Her British earnestness and interest in voluntary charity work also

---

[4] See, for example, Anan'ich et al., *Nikolai Vtoroi*, 34–35; and S. Iu. Witte, *Vospominaniia*, 2:8–15.

[5] Cited in Lieven, *Nicholas II*, 55.

[6] Ibid., 54–56.

seemed inappropriate in the sophisticated spheres of Russian high society. A charity bazaar she organized in the Winter Palace and sewing circles for aristocratic women provoked anger and contempt.

The relationship between both emperor and administration, and emperor and court, became strained in the first years of his reign. From the start Nicholas's attitude toward educated society and the estates was openly antagonistic. His initial confrontation with the constitutional movement set the tone for his relationship with society during his entire reign. The Tver *zemstvo* had issued an address to the tsar requesting strict observance of the laws and the right of public institutions to declare their views "so that an expression of the requirements and thoughts of the representatives of the Russian people, and not only of the administration, may reach the heights of the throne." The address drew a swift response. F. I. Rodichev, who had presented the address to the Tver *zemstvo*, was deprived of all civil rights, including the right to participate in public assemblies. Then, at a belated wedding reception held on January 17, 1895, Nicholas met members of various estates—the nobility, the merchantry, the Cossacks, and foreign dignitaries—who brought him and the empress congratulations. Nicholas delivered a curt statement dismissing constitutional projects as "senseless dreams" and vowed "to maintain the principle of autocracy just as firmly and unflinchingly as my unforgettable father." One of the deputies described the impression.

> A little officer boy came out, in his hat there was a slip of paper. He started to mumble something looking at the paper and then suddenly shrieked "senseless dreams." We understood that we were being scolded for something. But what was there to snarl about?[7]

The speech gave open expression to the emperor's hostility, not only to the constitutional opposition but to those conservative pillars of the regime, noblemen, merchants, and officials who had to listen to a rebuke in the midst of a ceremony staged to extend good wishes. The words were published in all newspapers, in some with brief, ironic commentary.[8] They "reverberated through Russia," Princess Radziwill wrote. "Loyal Russians felt not only aggrieved but ashamed that such a reproof should have been administered to them before foreigners, such as Poles and Germans, of whom there were many in the various delegations."[9]

[7] V. N. Lamzdorf, "Dnevnik," *Krasnyi Arkhiv* 46 (1931): 26; L. G. Zakharova, "Krizis samoderzhaviia nakanune revoliutsii 1905 goda," 120.

[8] For example, *NV*, January 18, 1895, 1. The words were followed with a comment, perhaps meant sardonically, on the firmness (*tverdost'*) of the speech and suggesting that the autocracy never excluded opinions that indicated the people's needs. For the response of liberal periodicals, see S. S. Ol'denburg, *Tsarstvovanie Imperatora Nikolaia II* (Washington, D.C., 1981), 47.

[9] Radziwill, *Behind the Veil*, 255–56.

THE CORONATION: PREPARATIONS

In the framework of the national myth, the coronation assumed a distinctive meaning. Lev Tikhomirov's book, *The Monarchical State Spirit*, emphasized the exclusive importance of the coronation ceremony. Tikhomirov cited a statement of the metropolitan Filaret of Moscow that the rites expressed "the sacred character of authority and the union of love between tsar and people." Nicholas I's coronation in 1826 had been the first to be presented as a national celebration of the monarchy as the incarnation of the nation. Since then, imperial coronations consecrated not only the tsar's power but the bond with the people as well and gave religious sanction to the monarchical nation.[10]

In 1881 the national myth shifted focus from the consecration of the monarchy to a consecration of autocratic power as a sacrosanct as well as historical Russian tradition. Nicholas II's reign took this a step further: The coronation bestowed consecration not on the monarchy but on the monarch himself as the chosen of the Lord. According to the assistant minister of the court General Mosolov, Nicholas believed that "his calling came from God. He answered for his acts only before his conscience and the Almighty."[11] Nicholas dedicated himself to this calling after the crowning, when the tsar knelt, in full regalia, and pronounced the supplication asking God's help to enlighten him and guide him "in the great service" of ruling for the good of his people. Official literature in Nicholas's reign cited this prayer as a declaration of the union of tsar and people. Lt. D. N. Loman wrote in his popular account of the coronation: "On this day the hearts of the whole people merge in one general prayer," to help the tsar. The tsar prayed to the Lord, he wrote, citing the prayer, "to teach, to direct, and to enlighten Him in the great deed of service to his people."[12] Empress Alexandra told Sophie Buxhoeveden that at the coronation Nicholas "felt he was solemnly consecrating his life to his country's service."[13]

The official literature on the coronation stressed the human character of the Russian monarch. The extended history of the coronation that opened

---

[10] L. A. Tikhomirov, *Monarkhicheskaia gosudarstvennost'* (Buenos Aires, 1968), 248–49, 356–58. On Nicholas I's coronation, see Volume 1: 279–95.

[11] Mosolov, *Pri dvore poslednego Rossiiskogo imperatora*, 22. For a perceptive discussion of Nicholas's attitudes toward religion, see Mark Steinberg, "Nicholas and Alexandra: An Intellectual Portrait," in Mark Steinberg and Vladimir M. Khrustalev, eds., *The Fall of the Romanovs: Political Dreams and Personal Struggles in a Time of Revolution* (New Haven, 1995), 10–12.

[12] D. N. Loman, *Ko dniu sviashchennogo koronovaniia i muromazaniia Ikh Imperatorskikh Velichestv* (St. Petersburg, 1896), 5–6. See also, in chapter 14 of this work, the discussion of the central role of this prayer in Elchaninov's popular biography of Nicholas.

[13] Sophie Buxhoeveden, *Before the Storm* (London, 1938), 151. Buxhoeveden's father, who was present at the ceremony, thought that this moment was the most impressive of the ceremony. "There was intense feeling in the voice of Nicholas II as he read out the solemn words."

the coronation album repeated the distinction drawn in the album of 1883 between Byzantine and Russian conceptions of monarchy but now elaborated it into a variant of the doctrine of Moscow, the Third Rome. Byzantium rejected the Roman conception of the emperor as man-god and propounded the doctrine that the emperor was only the most holy of mortals. "But Byzantium, creating the idea of Christian Autocrat, could not embody it in its history." Its way of life "was still deeply imbued with pagan traditions of the Roman state spirit." It was left to Russia to realize the idea of Christian autocrat. After the Council of Florence of 1439, when Byzantium, threatened by the Turks, agreed to a union with Rome, Russia became the true empire. The office of Emperor, "created by the political life of the rulers of the world, the Romans, now became the property of the Russian Orthodox Autocracy alone."[14]

Other accounts asserted the distinctively Russian character of the direct bond between God and tsar and tsar and people. *Moskovskie Vedomosti* contended that it was the idea of divine sanction that had freed Russian government from the written contracts and endless compromises of governments elsewhere. The prayers of the people created the unity that allowed the tsar to achieve his great heroic deed (*podvig*) and avoid the ills of the West.[15] A popular coronation album, printed at the press of the illustrated weekly *Zhivopisnoe Obozrenie*, expressed the sense of religious union of church and people. "The coronation sealed the unbreakable union of the Russian Autocrat with the Orthodox Church. In the person of the crowned Sovereign, the people, hundreds of million strong, joined in this Grace, for the Russian people are inseparable from their tsar!"[16]

The coronation celebrations were to be a demonstration of the vitality of a monarchy with mass democratic support. Although security measures were extensive and conspicuous, the coronation lacked the sense of constraint surrounding the 1883 events. It assumed a grander scale in many respects— more spectators, more foreign guests, and more extensive newspaper coverage. Nicholas II's inspiration might be personal and private, Russia might be holy and unaffected by Western materialism, but the celebrations of his consecration as tsar would show the monarchy adapting to contemporary forms of mass publicity and consumption as well as presenting Russia as a center of Western high society.

The contradictory influences were made vivid in the coronation album. As its title, *Coronation Collection* (*Koronatsionnyi Sbornik*) suggests, the album is a book of souvenirs as much as a description. The improved technical capacities of the Office for the Production of State Papers (*Ekpeditsiia*

---

[14] *Koronatsionnyi Sbornik: Koronovanie v Moskve; 14 maia 1896* (St. Petersburg, 1899), 1:5–8.

[15] *MV*, May 6, 1896, 2.

[16] *Koronatsionnyi al'bom v pamiat' sviashchennoi koronovaniia ikh Imperatorskikh Velichestv 14 maia 1896* (St. Petersburg, 1896).

Zagotovleniia Gosudarstvennykh Bumag) permitted the inclusion of new types of color reproductions, illustrative materials, and, most notably, photographs. The historical text and format of the volume strove to emphasize the national character of the event.[17] The opening 132 pages of the first volume are devoted to an illustrated history of coronation ceremonies emphasizing its Muscovite roots. Slavonicized lettering is used for chapter titles throughout the album. On the title page, by Victor Vasnetsov, the letters are entwined in old-Russian floral motifs. A. Riabushkin's program for the gala performance of *A Life for the Tsar* was decorated with old-Russian letters and an inset portrait of Tsar Mikhail Fedorovich. The elaborate, flamboyant lettering and the design on the menu executed by Victor Vasnetsov for the coronation feast, *Moskovskie Vedomosti* pointed out, came from the seventeenth-century album *Votsarenie Mikhaila Fedorovicha*.[18]

At the same time, the album employed the methods and appeals of the contemporary press to popularize the image of the imperial family as human beings. A remarkable page of photographs introduces the imperial family early in the coronation description (fig. 47).[19] A photograph of Empress Maria Aleksandrovna, the spiritual exemplar of the monarchy, is at the head of the page; Alexander's II's portrait is noticeably absent. Beneath are the parents of the imperial couple, to the right Alexander III as heir and Maria Fedorovna as grand duchess, to the left Prince Ludwig and Princess Alice of Hesse. In the center of the page are photographs of Nicholas and Alexandra, and, beneath, snapshots of them as infants. The coronation album has become a family album. Volume 1 also contains portraits and photographs of the leading court officials in uniform and court ladies, wearing the *kokoshniki*, the tiara headpieces studded with pearls and gems that was required at formal court events.[20]

The albums were printed on glossy paper and issued in the largest edition for a coronation album: at least 1,300 copies in Russian and 350 in French.[21] The coronation rubles also were intended to reach a broad public: 190,845 were minted, or three times the number issued for Alexander III's coronation. The silver coins were distributed principally to estate representatives,

---

[17] The official memorandum on the album recommended that it "have a solemn and elevated style with gallicisms avoided as much as possible" ("Koronatsionnyi sbornik i khudozhestvennyi al'bom," RGIA, 472-65-113, 2).

[18] *MV*, May 15, 1896, 4.

[19] *Koronatsionnyi Sbornik*, opposite 160.

[20] Most of the second volume is devoted to photographs of all the delegations, foreign and Russian, who attended. It also contains facsimiles of menus and programs of the gala performance and peoples feast.

[21] An additional 2,100 volumes were planned with paper covers, but I have no evidence that they were published. The production costs for publication were 165,905 rubles, or 77 percent above the 93,472 rubles for the 1883 album ("Koronatsionnyi sbornik i khudozhestvennyi al'bom," 31; "Sostavlenie obshchikh schetov i denezhnogo otcheta i 'Ocherka deiatel'nosti Ministerstva Imperatorskogo Dvora po prigotovleniiam k koronatsii," RGIA, 422-65-100a, 204).

47. Family photomontage. Nicholas II coronation album, *Koronatsionnyi Sbornik*. Slavic and Baltic Division, New York Public Library. Astor, Lenox, and Tilden Foundations.

officers of the suite, the coronation guards, and court and government officials.[22] The design, at Nicholas's insistence, followed the model of his father's coronation ruble. Nicholas's profile faced left, with the words: "By the Grace of God Nicholas II Emperor and Autocrat of All the Russias / Coronation in Moscow 1896." The reverse carried the coronation regalia surrounded by a wreath.[23]

Press coverage was more extensive than at Alexander III's coronation. In addition to the daily reports, Russian newspapers provided coronation supplements with photographs of the events and figures from the court and abroad. Foreign coverage was also far more extensive than in 1883, to which forty-nine correspondents had received special invitations from the government, and about eighty attended. In 1896 more than three-hundred foreign correspondents, artists, and photographers arrived in Moscow for what was to be a major event, giving cachet to the standing of each country's press.[24] The Ministry of the Court made every effort to assist the unaccustomed number of foreign journalists eager to see all the events. V. S. Krivenko, the head of Minister Vorontsov-Dashkov's chancellery, believed that the more easily foreign correspondents could see the spectacles, the more accurate and the more favorable would be their accounts. Krivenko set up a press bureau that provided them access to telegraph lines, helped them gain access to closed events, and served as a meeting place where they could exchange impressions over coffee, sandwiches, and cookies. The number of correspondents admitted to the narrow confines of the Assumption Cathedral rose from twelve, in 1883, to twenty, in 1896, ten of whom were from abroad.[25]

The American journalist Richard Harding Davis described the coronation as "a play at the royal boxes of Europe and the grandstands of the world."[26] The "royal boxes of Europe," indeed, were well represented. The number of royal personages and their entourages nearly tripled from 144 at the previ-

[22] *Ocherk deiatel'nosti Ministerstva Imperatorskogo Dvora po prigotovleniiam i ustroistvu torzhestva sviashchennogo koronovaniia ikh Imperatorskikh Velichestv v 1896 godu* (St. Petersburg, 1896), 2:213–15.

[23] See Robert Papp, "The Road to Chervonets: The Representation of National Identity on Russian Money, 1896–1924," unpublished ms., 1996, 10; *Ocherk deiatel'nosti Ministerstva Imperatorskogo Dvora*, 2:195–215.

[24] For example, an editorial in the Athens newspaper *Acropolis* announced, "The stunning wealth, beauty, and majesty of the festivities of the Jerusalem of the North, as our special correspondent characterizes, will be described in his dispatches from the direct experience of events, and we can justly take pride that a Greek correspondent, too, is among the representatives of the European press" (I. P. Medvedev, "Koronatsiia Nikolaia II glazami grecheskogo zhurnalista," in A. A. Fursenko, ed., *Rossiia v XIX-XXvv.: sbornik statei k 70-letiiu so dnia rozhdeniia Rafaila Sholomonovicha Ganelina* [St. Petersburg, 1998], 91).

[25] Krivenko, "V ministerstve imperatorskogo dvora," 212–14; V. I. Nemirovich-Danchenko, "Moskva v mae 1896 goda; pis'ma o koronatsii," *Niva*, May 10, 1896, 527; Krivenko, *Ocherk deiatel'nosti Ministerstva Imperatorskogo Dvora*, 1:138–39.

[26] Richard Harding Davis, *A Year from a Reporter's Notebook* (New York, 1898), 40, 69–70; Kate Koon Bovey, *Russian Coronation, 1896* (Minneapolis, 1896), ix, 7–8.

ous coronation to 412.[27] The high society of France and the United States also took the opportunity to appear at what was a major social occasion. Vasilii Nemirovich-Danchenko, the war correspondent and travel writer, described the scene in a series of vivid "letters on the coronation," for *Niva*. The large number of Western guests, he wrote, "signifies the high international position of Russia." He observed that "more and more often one hears foreign languages and not the Great Russian dialect."[28]

The coronation made clear the return to favor of the guards and the resumption of military pageants as a central ceremony of monarchy.[29] The arrival in Moscow of Petersburg guards' regiments changed the appearance of the city. On April 28 Grand Duke Constantine Konstantinovich, chief of the Preobrazhenskii Regiment, noted in his diary his great pleasure as he rode at the head of two battalions into Moscow along Tver Boulevard to the march from *Life for the Tsar*. At the building of the City Duma, they rested arms. Then he led them to the Iberian Chapel where they paid homage to the Moscow icon. They entered the Kremlin through the Spasskii Gates followed by shouting people. "The music stopped, we bared our heads and entered the Kremlin—the heart of Russia. What rapture. I heard afterward from the officers that many shed tears." Each day he saw more and more military men, "dressed spiffily in full uniform. My Preobrazhentsy make my heart rejoice. They have such a holiday look."[30]

Such a transformation accompanied each coronation, but the extent appeared to have been greater, and the official literature's emphasis on the Muscovite character of the coronation seems to have only made observers more aware of the disparity between the Western court and the old capital. The scope and visibility of the 1896 coronation and the effort to attract leading journalists and artistic talents multiplied the voices interpreting the event. They introduced judgments, styles, and sensibilities that competed with the national myth and broke the monologic unity of the celebration.

Nemirovich-Danchenko observed that military uniforms, usually not a prominent feature of the Moscow scene, now flashed everywhere. Petersburg had resettled in Moscow. "It is beginning to teach the old lady at least some genteel conduct." The court, the foreign princes, the State Council, all stunned the spectators "with their wealth, refinement, and lightness." Some foreigners understood the celebrations as a re-creation of a European not a Russian past. The model was "Versailles relived," recalling the grandeur of European absolutism rather than the spiritual depths of old Moscow.[31]

[27] RGIA, 422-65-100a, 1, 178, 203).

[28] Nemirovich-Danchenko, "Moskva v mae 1896 goda," *Niva*, April 27, 1896, 451; April 29, 1896, 505; May 10, 1896, 21:527.

[29] See the article marking the parade in *Niva*, May 4, 1896, 426, with illustrations on 425, 428, 429.

[30] Vel. Kn. Constantine Konstantinovich, "Dnevnik, 1896 g.," GARF, 660-1-43, 49–54.

[31] Nemirovich-Danchenko, "Moskva v mae 1896 goda," *Niva*, April 27, 1896, 451; April 29, 1896, 505; Carl Graf Moy, *Als Diplomat am Zarenhof* (Munich, 1971), 16; Henry La-

The elaborate decorations transformed Moscow's appearance. Following traditional practice, triumphal arches, flags, tribunes, pavilions, and obelisks ornamented the city. Pictures were placed before buildings, and colored flags and cloths, many of them in the national colors, white, red, and blue, hung along the streets. Electric lights were installed, and special illumination was provided for the Kremlin.[32] The correspondents sensed an artistic incoherence and inappropriateness in the decorations that ill suited the unkempt Moscow scene. Nemirovich-Danchenko wrote with Petersburg hauteur about the problems of beautifying Moscow's inelegant and asymmetrical spaces. While Kiev and Odessa had introduced electric lights along the streets years before, electric lighting could be found in only a few places in Moscow and seemed not to fit the jumbled medieval landscape. "Cumbersomeness is a characteristic of all Russian nature. And it cannot be submerged by contrivances of American genius."[33]

Huge illuminated fountains, which had delighted Muscovites during a French exhibition of 1890, now embellished the Moscow scene. Pavilions were erected around the city. The Smolensk Railway Station had one in Russian style, while the Brest station's pavilion displayed French furniture and paintings by Vladimir Makovskii.[34] The tent-style masts over the bridges, the Monomakh cap over the Tver Gate, appeared more as ornaments than historical evocations. Fedor Shekhtel's pavilion for the welcome of the tsar used the neo-Russian style to create a national fantasy. As in the coronation album, the decorative imagination took precedence; stylistic variety and effervescence vied with the historical message of the event.[35]

The extent and expense of the preparations prompted misgivings among officials and members of the court, especially in the light of the mass starvation of previous years. After seeing the poor throw their kopeks on the collection plate in St. Isaacs, on May 2, Count Vladimir Lamzdorf noted in his diary, "Sad thoughts come to mind about the sumptuous magnificence that we soon intend to put on display in Moscow. In the background of the glitter that puts your teeth on edge, poverty acquires an exalted halo of true dignity and majesty."[36] Grand Duke Constantine lamented the huge expense for the silver and gold plates to be used for the bread and salt to welcome the tsar. "What an unproductive expense! How much good would be and could be done with such money!"[37] The English Tolstoyan Aylmer Maude derided the

Pauze, *De Paris au Volga* (Paris, 1896), 77–78. Also see the description by the worker Semen Kanatchikov (Reginald Zelnik, *A Radical Worker in Tsarist Russia: The Autobiography of Semën Ivanovich Kanatchikov* [Stanford, Calif., 1986], 39–40).

[32] *Stroitel'* 10–12 (1896): 398–438; O. V. Nemiro, "Iz istorii organizatsii i dekorirovaniia krupneischikh torzhestv goma romanovykh: 1896 i 1913gg.," in *Dom Romanovykh v istorii Rossii*, 252–54.

[33] Nemirovich-Danchenko, "Moskva v mae 1896 goda, *Niva* 19 (1896): 448.

[34] Ibid., 448, 450; 20 (1896): 502–3.

[35] *Stroitel'* 10–12 (1896): 422–24.

[36] Lamzdorf, *Dnevnik, 1894–1896*, 380.

[37] Constantine Konstantinovich, "Dnevnik, 1896g.," 62–63.

show of splendor, "this childish pomp," when the Moscow population was living four to a room and many were starving. "If the government existed to compete with the circuses in giving shows to the people at the people's expense, it would all be easier to understand."[38]

THE IMPERIAL ENTRY AND THE CORONATION CEREMONIES

The tsar's entry into Moscow on May 9 again opened with a veritable cavalcade of empire, parading the triumphs of Russian expansion over the previous century. After a detachment of gendarmes, the procession again began with the Cossacks from the emperor's own convoy. The coronation album described these "daring swarthy horsemen" in red Circassian coats and fur hats, brandishing their swords. "At their appearance," the *New York Times* correspondent wrote, "the crowd's admiration burst forth into hurrahs and shouts of pleasure." They were followed by a company of Cossacks of the Guard. The album described them as "handsome fellows, their fur caps (*papakhi*) cocked to the side, holding frightening lances in their hands like feathers and merrily looking out at God's world." Then followed forty-one "Asiatics," the cynosure of all eyes, according to the album, led by the khan of Khiva and the emir of Bukhara. The report in *Novoe Vremia* marveled over the "proud representatives of our Asia." The procession, the original costumes, "carried the spectator to the hot steppes of Asia, to the Ural Mountains, to the canyons of Dagestan, to the expanses of Bukhara."[39]

Then followed deputies from the nobility, members of the court, and the carriages of the ministers. Later came deputies from the Caucasus and Central Asia, horsemen bearing standards of the various provinces, and officials with the shields of the towns and the realms that made up the empire. Finally, after deputations from provincial institutions and other officials, and a detachment of Cavalier Guards, came the tsar "on a pure white horse." "He sat erect and looked every inch the Caesar he is," the *New York Times* correspondent wrote. Saluting to the crowd, the tsar was greeted with "the shout peculiar to Russians, which is a prolonged roar. This was taken up on all sides and swelled into a perfect hurricane of sound." The two empresses followed, riding in the traditional coronation carriages of the eighteenth century. Maria Fedorovna rode in one decorated with a large gold and silver crown. Alexandra's gilded carriage followed, escorted by two esquires and two Cossacks. Other carriages followed with the Queen of Greece, officials, and ladies of the court.[40]

[38] Aylmer Maude, [De Monte Alto], *The Tsar's Coronation* (London, 1896), 10–15, 23, 38–39.

[39] *Koronatsionnyi Sbornik* 1: 209–10; *New York Times*, May 22, 1896, 7; *Novoe Vremia*, May 11, 1896, 1.

[40] *New York Times*, May 22, 1896, 7; Constantine Konstantinovich, "Dnevnik, 1896g.," 58.

The procession stopped for the imperial family's traditional prayers at the Iberian Mother of God. Then they proceeded on foot to the Kremlin cathedrals. The size of the turnout, the thunderous enthusiasm, again were taken as measures of the extent and internal cohesion of the empire. The large number of representatives from within Russia, the *Niva* correspondent wrote, showed "the immense breadth of power of the state authority that the young tsar possesses."[41] Foreign correspondents considered the response to the procession a sign of acclaim and power. The French journalist La Pauze, stirred by the hats thrown into the air and the people's wild enthusiasm, fixed his attention on Nicholas. With the entry, the emperor had "taken possession of the capital."

Foreign correspondents understood the variety of national types in the entry as a demonstration of their devotion to the Russian throne. Richard Harding Davis marveled at the variety of costumes and national groups in a procession that included "the representatives of what had once been eighteen separate governments, each of which now bowed in allegiance to the Russian Emperor." Each of these representatives, he wrote, "bore himself as though his chief pride was that he owed allegiance to a young man twenty-eight years old, a young man who never would be seen by his countrymen in the distant provinces from which he came, to whom the Tsar was but a name and a symbol, but a symbol to which they prayed and for which they were prepared to give up their lives." An eyewitness, B. A. Engel'gardt, inspired by the rousing acclaim that met the tsar's bows from the Red Staircase, later wrote, "I looked over the shoulders of the empress at this tumultuous sea of human heads, and I thought that there was nothing equal on earth to the might of the Russian Monarch."[42]

Deprived of the spectacle, and without his equestrian grace and stature, Nicholas made a less favorable impression. The American society lady, Kate Bovey, so taken by the sight of the Russian guardsmen, expressed a general sense of disappointment. "The more I saw of him, the less he impressed me. He is not at all kingly, for he is rather short and lacks the carriage that [the empress has] though he seems thoroughly natural in his movements."[43] The grand duke Constantine observed Nicholas's first missteps. The tsar had neglected to greet the guards' regiments as was required and had passed by the Annunciation Cathedral on his procession to the Red Porch, leaving the metropolitan trailing behind him. Nonetheless he found Nicholas's bowing to the people "a wonderful spectacle."[44]

Riding to the Kremlin, Nicholas felt the elation of being in Moscow. "About the welcome there is nothing to say but that it was joyous and festive,

[41] Nemirovich-Danchenko, *Niva* 20 (1896): 505.

[42] LaPauze, *De Paris au Volga*, 79, 85; Davis, *A Year from a Reporter's Notebook*, 28–34; B. A. Engel'gardt, "Torzhestvennyi v"ezd v Moskvu gosudaria Imperatora Nikolaia II," in Sergei Zavalishin, *Gosudar' Imperator Nikolai II Aleksandrovich* (New York, 1968), 23–24.

[43] *New York Times*, May 24, 1896, 1; Bovey, *Russian Coronation, 1896*, 42.

[44] Constantine Konstantinovich, "Dnevnik, 1896g.," 57–58.

as it can be only in Moscow," he wrote in his diary. However, he awaited the long and arduous coronation ceremonies on May 14 with considerable apprehension. According to Sophie Buxhoeveden, he asked to be crowned with the Monomakh cap, which, aside from its historical associations, was considerably lighter than the diamond studded imperial crown of Catherine, nearly five pounds in weight. On the eve of the coronation, he wrote in his diary; "May the merciful Lord give us strength tomorrow! May he bless us for a peaceful working life!!!" and he sketched a cross after his words.[45]

On the day of the coronation Nicholas wore the uniform of the Preobrazhenskii Guards Regiment, and Alexandra a silver brocade gown with an old-Russian design, the work of nuns from the Ivanovskii Convent. The procession from the palace to the cathedral was long because of the large numbers of delegates from *zemstva* and estates as well as foreigners.[46] This time the coronation album made no mention of the peasant deputies, who, as in 1883, marched at the beginning of the procession.[47]

The speech of the Moscow metropolitan Sergii at the portal of the cathedral indicated the new importance the church hierarchy attributed to the rite of anointment at the coronation. The metropolitan declared that the tsar had come to Moscow to crown himself and to be anointed. The hereditary throne belonged to Nicholas himself "as Monocratic Tsar" (*Tsar-Edinoderzhavnyi*). His first anointment at christening made him like all other Orthodox Christians and was not to be repeated. Sergii stated the reason for the second baptism, the second anointment. "There is nothing higher, there is nothing more difficult on earth than imperial power. There is no burden heavier than imperial service (*sluzhenie*). Therefore, to bear it, the Holy Church from ancient times recognized the necessity for an extraordinary, mysterious, expression of grace."[48] The speech expressed the sense in the Orthodox hierarchy of the need to elevate the tsar's ecclesiastical role. Unlike his predecessors, Nicholas would take communion behind closed doors like members of the clergy and the tsars at the end of the seventeenth century.[49]

The emperor was invested in the mantle and the chain of St. Andrew, which broke and fell to the ground while the mantle was being adjusted.[50] Then Nicholas crowned himself and sat on his throne in full regalia. The crowning was made known by the thunder of cannon, the tolling of the bells

[45] *Dnevniki Nikolai II*, 143–44.

[46] For complete numbers of the representatives of the estates participating in this and other coronation events, see *Ocherk deiatel'nosti Ministerstva Imperatorskogo Dvora*, 2:80–110.

[47] *Koronatsionnyi sbornik*, 1:250–52; Constantine Konstantinovich, "Dnevnik, 1896g.," 60.

[48] *Koronatsionnyi sbornik*, 1:253.

[49] Uspenskii, *Tsar' i patriarkh*, 185–86. The change was significant, but there is no evidence that those present took note of it at the time.

[50] A. Suvorin, *Dnevnik* (Moscow, 1992), 124. Nicholas apparently took this as an ill omen. Iswolsky, in *Recollections of a Foreign Minister*, claims that it happened later in the ceremony when Nicholas made his way to the anointment (273–74).

of the capital, and the playing of "God Save the Tsar." The empress knelt before him, and he placed the small crown on her head. She then ascended the steps of the throne to him, and, before they received congratulations, they kissed. The touching moment of the young emperor and empress, both in crowns, kissing was illustrated in the coronation album (fig. 48).[51] Nicholas fell to his knees, while the entire congregation stood, and he pronounced the prayer of Solomon, vowing before God to embark on the "great service" of rule. "The tsar's voice was strong and assured," the correspondent of *Le temps* wrote, but Suvorin claimed that the tsar's voice was faltering and that the prayer had been abbreviated to reduce the time Nicholas would have to spend on his knees. According to the coronation album, his words "were eagerly caught by his subjects who repeated them to themselves, with a prayer to the Creator to send the strength to the Tsar for the great and laborious service of his native land."[52]

The coronation ceremonies took place before about a thousand representatives of the Russian and European elite and the press in the close confines of the Assumption Cathedral. Again it was the popular demonstrations of support outside the church, in the Kremlin and outside its walls, that gave the ceremony its public amplitude and meanings. Shouts from the crowds greeted the emperor and empress as they made their way from the Assumption Cathedral to the Archangel and Annunciation cathedrals. The enthusiasm reached its height when Nicholas performed the "ancient tradition" of the triple bow from the Red Staircase.[53]

Those present perceived this as an ecstatic moment of reconquest and union of tsar and people. The French journalist LaPauze, astonished at the acclaim at the Red Staircase, once again described the coronation as a "taking possession." *Moskovskie Vedomosti* proclaimed that the roar from the Kremlin "echoed everywhere across the extent of great Russia." The author described the inspired feelings of the crowd: "No one lived his own personal life. Everything fused into one whole, into one soul, pulsing with life, sensing and aware that it was the Russian people. Tsar and people created a great historical deed and, as long as this unity of people and Tsar exists, Rus' will be great and invincible, unfearing of external and internal enemies."[54]

Like Alexander III's coronation, Nicholas II's was presented as a fusion of kindred spirits rather than of opposites. The coronation album empha-

---

[51] *Koronatsionnyi Sbornik*, 1:264.

[52] *Le temps*, May 28, 1896, 1; *Koronatsionnyi Sbornik*, 1:262; Suvorin, *Dnevnik*, 123–24. Buxhoeveden recalled that her father told her that everyone was impressed with "how deeply he felt every word. His voice was tense with emotion" (Buxhoeveden, *Before the Storm*, 150–51).

[53] *Koronatsionnyi Sbornik*, 1:271; *Koronatsionnyi Al'bom*, 55; Grand Duke Alexander Mikhailovich, *Once a Grand Duke*, 74; Engel'gardt, "Torzhestvennyi v"ezd v Moskvu gosudaria Imperatora Nikolaia II," 23–24; Moy, *Als Diplomat am Zarenhof*, 160–63; Epanchin, *Na sluzhbe trekh imperatorov*, 232.

[54] LaPauze, *De Paris au Volga*, 111; *MV*, May 15, 1896, 2–4.

48. Embrace of Emperor and Empress. Nicholas II coronation album,
Koronatsionnyi Sbornik. Slavic and Baltic Division, New York Public Library.
Astor, Lenox, and Tilden Foundations.

sized this theme by describing an unprecedented appearance of Nicholas and
Alexandra on the Kremlin balcony overlooking the Moscow River after the
procession. According to the album, the emperor and empress emerged in
full regalia and repeated the triple bow to the city of Moscow and the Russian people. This was meant to reproduce one of the "distinctive touching

means of contact of the tsar with the masses of the people during coronation festivities" in old Moscow.

> A marvelous view opened from the balcony onto the Moscow River, and into the limitless expanses beyond. . . . The Tsar's bow greeted not only Moscow, but all of Russia spread out before him, which, from the lips of its immemorial representatives, the Muscovites, who covered both banks of the river, answered their Sovereign Ruler with an enthusiastic spontaneous "Hoorah!"[55]

The vast expanse of the emperor's land and Russia's imperial destiny were the themes of the cantata performed at the banquet, a work written by Alexander Glazunov and the popular playwright and chief of repertoire of the imperial theaters of St. Petersburg Victor Krylov. The singers gave voice to the joy of all parts of the empire, North, South, East, and West, at the coronation of its sovereign. "Russia is united in a single feeling," the chorus sang. The mezzo-soprano, in the role of the South, sang of their forefathers' defeat of the Tatars. The basso, as the North, told how nature fell silent "before the great celebration." The East, a soprano, announced that Russia was awakening Eastern nations, and the West, again the mezzo-soprano, told how Europe had shared enlightenment with Russia. Russia was the force of progress in the East.

> The Kamchatkian, the Kalmyk, and the Sarmat,
> Leave their wretched hovels,
> And they greet the softening influence of morals,
> The mercy and kind impulses,
> Like sons, with open arms.

Then Russia, "conscious of its strength," turns in friendship to the West, "in mutual love and accord," a reference to the image of Russian tsar as bringer of peace. The cantata ended with the chorus's apostrophe to Moscow.

> Moscow of the golden cupolas.
> In your walls was born the start,
> Of all these sovereign labors.[56]

In the evening the city was brilliantly lit. No account of the coronation failed to mention the cascades of lights against the Kremlin. The metaphor in every account was of gems; the image obscuring the historical and geographical reality, evoking incandescence and glitter. Nemirovich-Danchenko wrote in *Niva*, "The lights played like diamonds, rubies, and emeralds on black velvet. . . . The Bell Tower of Ivan the Great stood out as if drawn in diamonds." The English Tolstoyan Aylmer Maude was so stunned that, he wrote, "I was for a moment half inclined to forget what injury to human

---

[55] *Koronatsionnyi Sbornik*, 1:275.
[56] Ibid., 1:280–83.

life and limb and what tremendous cost and labour had been needed to prepare it all."[57]

The art in the coronation album introduced a sensibility sometimes at odds with the solemn spirituality of the ceremonies. The watercolors, reproduced in chromolithography, dissolved the masses of the Kremlin buildings into iridescent and translucent forms caught in a play of light, expressing the pictorial brilliance rather than the gravity of the occasion. V. A. Serov turns the anointment ceremony into a study of color and form—the white robes of the tsar and the blue of the courtiers, the yellow of the clergy, with patches of red visible from the rear of the cathedral. The flattening of perspective and the glitter of the candelabra produce an effect of the airiness and bustle of a French music hall more than a Russian cathedral. A. Riabushkin's painting of the greeting from the Red Staircase becomes an interplay between the pink of the palace, the white of the Assumption Cathedral, the blue of the sky, the white and red of the uniforms, and the black mass of the crowd in the square beneath. Albert Benois's watercolor of the illumination turns Moscow into a fantasy of yellows, whites, and blues against a somber background. The artists transformed the event into personal visual statements that betray the influence of contemporary Paris more than that of seventeenth-century Moscow, form warring against content.

The sense of anomaly was most apparent at the gala performance at the Bolshoi Theater. The program again consisted of two acts of *Life for the Tsar* and a one-act ballet, this time *The Splendid Pearl*, choreographed by Marius Petipa to music by Riccardo Drigo, director of the Mariinskii Ballet Orchestra. But the uniforms and medals, and the stiff official character of the event, conflicted with the spontaneous shows of emotion outside and prompted chiding from the press and observers. The *Niva* correspondent wrote, "A more pompous show could hardly be imagined." The orchestra continued to be reserved for men, civil and military generals, "with stars and ribbons, brilliant epaulets, and uniforms shining with gold," except for the artists Vladimir Makovskii and Ilia Repin, who wore tuxedos. Women sat in the mezzanine and the balcony, along with many guards' officers and kammer-junkers in court uniform.[58]

The gala performance was a mélange of diverse themes and styles of the coronation events. The audience first witnessed the scenes of old Moscow in Glinka's opera, culminating in the great procession to the Kremlin and the *Glory* chorus. Then they saw the ballet, *The Splendid Pearl*, a fairy tale set on the floor of the ocean, in a grotto of pearls. A ray of light illuminated the pearls of various colors, the ballerinas. Into the grotto ventured a genie,

[57] Nemirovich-Danchenko, *Niva*, May 17, 1896, 562–63; Gerua, *Vospominaniia o moei zhizni*, 102–3; LaPauze, *De Paris au Volga*, 115–16; Bovey, *Russian Coronation, 1896*, 33; Maude, *The Tsar's Coronation*, 65.

[58] Nemirovich-Danchenko, *Niva*, May 17, 1896, 564; LaPauze, *De Paris au Volga*, 124–25; Maude, *The Tsar's Coronation*, 71–72.

frightening all the pearls to flight but one, the white pearl, who slept. When she awoke, the Genie, enamored, entreated her to stay with him. But the king of the corals, angered, gathered his forces and attacked the Genie, who in fact was the king of the metals—gold, silver, and iron. The king of the metals triumphed but wanted only "the magnificent pearl" for the best ornament of the throne. The ballet concluded with an Apotheosis of Triton and Amphitrite reigning over the denizens of the deep.[59]

The fairy tale motif carried varied associations of the moment. The handsome prince won not by his beauty or magic but by power conferred by the force of modernity, symbolized by the metals. Power conferred love. The pearl, it was rumored, was supposed to represent the empress Alexandra, and the ballet can be understood as an allegory of total dedication of the irresistible, flawless object of love. The illustration of the official program, reproduced in the coronation album, renders the ballet in the erotic idiom of art nouveau. E. Samokish-Sudkovskaia's pearls are shapely maidens, wearing diaphanous skirts, their breasts and nipples bared. The apotheosis is a scene of semi-nude sea nymphs and sirens, looking out languorously as they bathe before an Adonis-like Triton. The king of metals stands in the rear, his arm around a voluptuous "magnificent pearl" (fig. 49).[60]

KHODYNKA

The most potent historical memory left by the coronation of Nicholas II was not glorious ceremonies and celebrations, prepared with such great cost and effort, but the massacre of more than one thousand Russians on Khodynskoe Field, gathered for the great popular feast in honor of the tsar. Coronation events, it has been contended throughout this work, announced the beginning of a reign, presenting the new tsar's idealized image in the role of autocrat for the coming reign. They celebrated a monarchy reborn and transformed. Khodynka became the immediate association of Nicholas II's coronation for posterity. The massacre disclosed a regime bereft of control, born under the omen of disastrous tragedy, a tsar barely consecrated who could not make proper amends. The message was trumpeted to the world by the mass of horrified journalists, whom the tsarist state had itself assembled to make known the glory of the monarchy.

Khodynka was made possible by two presumptions held by the less critical adepts of the national myth—first, that the people absolutely were devoted and trusting in the authorities, and, second, that the authorities could easily cope with mass gatherings. The people's feast had grown larger at each coronation, and, as we have seen, the order observed at the Khodynskoe Field celebration in 1883 was a matter of especial pride in official publications.

---

[59] *Koronatsionnyi sbornik*, 1:318–19. The name of the ballet is now *The Pearl*.
[60] *Koronatsionnyi sbornik* 2.

49. Program for gala performance of "The Magnificent Pearl," by Samokish-Sudkovskaia. Nicholas II coronation album, *Koronatsionnyi Sbornik*. Slavic and Baltic Division, New York Public Library. Astor, Lenox, and Tilden Foundations.

The 1896 celebration was to repeat the elaborate 1883 event with plays, games, beer, packets of food, and souvenirs. The crowds at this coronation seemed to be larger than in 1883, and the number of booths on Khodynskoe Field had been increased from 100 to 150.[61] The problem of crowd control had arisen in the first days of the celebration when several episodes had been reported in the press. During the ceremonial promulgation of the date of the coronation, eighteen were killed in a scramble for the souvenir announcements. At one point during Nicholas's entry, the crowds broke the cordon, wrecking a carriage.[62]

Yet the authorities failed to take measures to ensure the safety of the crowds at the feast. Grand Duke Sergei, the governor-general of Moscow, believed that the exemplary order shown in 1883 and at Alexander's funeral observances in 1894, proved the peasants' devotion and submissiveness. He therefore avoided the concentration of troops that had controlled the crowds in 1883. He limited the security forces to a few dozen Cossacks and guards, who were responsible for containing more than half a million people. Four hundred infantrymen were deployed on the field, but they received instructions not to touch the people. Most of the units were reserved for the moment of the tsar's arrival. The field was broken by ditches and pits that had not been filled; these presumably would discourage the crowds from descending suddenly on the fairground area. They served instead as death traps.[63]

The peasants converging on Moscow from the surrounding region slept on the ground in the area and awakened early in the morning, though the booths were scheduled to open only at ten. At six, the crowd began to surge forward, and the officers in charge of the Cossacks gave the order to begin the festivities. Many fell underfoot and were trampled; others tumbled into ravines and wells. The panic lasted only ten or fifteen minutes, but by that time the field was covered with injured and dead, 1,350 fatalities by official count, by others as many as 2,000.

The foreigners invited to attest to the grandeur and might of the Russian emperor witnessed carts winding along the streets of Moscow, carrying

[61] Estimates vary on the size of the crowds. The number appears to have been about the same as in 1883, more than half a million, though they perhaps were as high as seven hundred thousand or eight hundred thousand.

[62] Suvorin, *Dnevnik*, 124; Maude, *The Tsar's Coronation*, 44.

[63] Suvorin, *Dnevnik*, 133–34, 140–41; *NV*, May 22, 1896, 2; A. Suvorin, "Malen'kie pis'ma," *NV*, May 24, 1896, 1. The security arrangements had also become embroiled in a jurisdictional dispute between the Ministry of the Court, still headed by Vorontsov-Dashkov, and the Moscow authorities. The organization of the feast had been formally assigned to officials in the Ministry of the Court, which had failed to show initiative. In any event, both the ministry and the governor-general were strikingly complacent about organization and security, two matters of central concern at all previous coronations. The jurisdictional dispute permitted both to deny responsibility for maintaining order (Lieven, *Nicholas II*, 66–67; V. F. Dzhunkovskii, "Vospominaniia, 1893–1897," GARF, 826-1-43, 226–27; Anan'ich et al., *Nikolai Vtoroi*, 46). For the eyewitness account of the Greek correspondent, who himself fell into the melee, see Medvedev, "Koronatsiia Nikolaia II glazami grecheskogo zhurnalista," 93–95.

corpses emitting the smell of rotting flesh. The publicity courted by the regime now spread the news of its incompetence and inhumanity to the world. It became known that the authorities ignored the desperate calls for help from the officers in charge. The many accounts in the Russian press made known the extent and horror of the disaster.[64] V. A. Giliarovskii wrote in *Russkie Vedomosti*:

> Horrible heart-rending groans and howls sounded in the air. . . The crowd pressing back threw thousands of people down into the ditch; those caught in pits were trampled . . . The few dozen Cossacks and guards at the booths were crushed and hurled into the field, while those who had gotten into the field from the other side crawled behind the exits, not permitting those who had entered to leave, and the surging crowd pressed people up against the booths and crushed them. This continued no longer than ten excruciating minutes.[65]

It was at this point, at a moment of national mourning, that the tsar could have shown his solidarity with the people. Nicholas, undoubtedly deeply aggrieved by the catastrophe, made the necessary public statements of regret.[66] He promised financial assistance to the victims, and he and the empress spent the day visiting hospitals. He also established a commission to look into the causes of the catastrophe. But his immediate response seemed perfunctory. The people's feast went on as if nothing had taken place, indeed before all the corpses had been cleared from the field. Nicholas appeared at the pavilion and bowed to the cries of the people. F. A. Golovin wrote, "Rather than a prayer for the peace of the thousand perishing at the people's festival as a result of the inefficiency and inaction of the tsar's servants, the Orthodox tsar marked the catastrophe with the idiocy of balagan barkers, songs, and dances of the *skomorokhi* (minstrels and buffoons)."[67]

Most scandalous was his appearance at the ball at the French ambassador's residence, which took place as scheduled that evening. Many urged Nicholas to send his regrets, but his ministers pressed him to attend, pointing to the elaborate preparations made by Russia's only ally for the event.[68] Grand Duke Sergei also importuned him to appear. Nicholas had intended to follow his mother's advice, which was to attend but to retire before supper. But when supper was served, his uncles, Sergei, Vladimir, and Alexei, prevailed upon him to remain. Composure and imperturbability were now

---

[64] See the review of Moscow newspapers in *NV*, May 22, 1896, 2–3.

[65] Ibid., 2.

[66] Nicholas wrote in his diary: "Today a great sin occurred. The mob, spending the night on Khodynskoe Field, in expectation of the distribution of food and [souvenir] mugs, pressed on the structure and there was a terrible crush, and it is horrible to add, nearly thirteen hundred were trampled!!" (*Dnevniki Nikolaia II*, 145–46).

[67] Suvorin, *Dnevnik*, 126–27; F. A. Golovin, "Zapiski," *Krasnyi Arkhiv* no. 6 (1926): 114. Kuropatkin, in his diary, also remarked on the need for a solemn state funeral (Anan'ich et al., *Nikolai Vtoroi*, 47).

[68] Lieven, *Nicholas II*, 66.

the signs of power. To leave, they insisted, would be "sentimentalizing" (*santimental'nichan'e*).[69]

The remarks of the grand dukes spread through the officialdom and society. Suvorin heard that they had claimed that leaving the ball would show sentimentality, that this was the time to show autocratic power, that four thousand had presumably perished in London at Victoria's fiftieth jubilee and that no one there had shown concern.[70] The callous derision and Nicholas's response indicated that any display of sympathy or feeling evoked the discredited scenario of Alexander II and would be understood, in the framework of the national myth, as a sign of weakness. The national myth had separated the attribute of compassion from the office of Russian emperor, affronting the belief in Russia and abroad that a modern ruler should display features of a sympathetic human being.

The tsar's response shook the faith even of convinced monarchists.[71] Grand Duke Constantine, who retained the humanitarian sensibility of an earlier era, wrote in his diary, "Everything bright and joyous, everything that was touching and tender experienced these days has been darkened and spoiled by the Khodynskoe catastrophe. And not so much the catastrophe, which represented God's will, as much as the attitude of responsible figures toward it." Nine days after the tragedy, he sent a note to Nicholas suggesting that the tsar arrange and attend a memorial service for the dead. "What a calming impression it would make!" But Nicholas did not reply.[72] For Gen. Alexei Kuropatkin, the event proved the emptiness of the popular demonstrations for the tsar. He wrote in his diary, "From this the view follows that the people's feast is organized not for the people, that the people should present only a majestic living decoration, and that this decoration at the appropriate moment must cry 'Hoorah' and throw their hats into the air."[73]

The news of Nicholas's appearance at the ball reached Europe quickly, giving substance to the notion that the emperor was a man who lived idly and lavishly at the expense of his suffering subjects. The term *massacre*, suggesting intentionally inflicted violence, became attached to the catastrophe. Aylmer Maude wrote, "Nero fiddled while Rome was burning, and Nicholas II danced at the French ball on the night of the Khodynskoe

[69] Constantine Konstantinovich, "Dnevnik, 1896g.," 66.

[70] Suvorin, *Dnevnik*, 134; The source of the tale seems to have been the Duke of Edinburgh, who, the grand duke Vladimir informed Kuropatkin, had told him that twenty-five hundred had perished at the Victoria's Golden Jubilee in 1887 (Anan'ich et al., *Nikolai Vtoroi*, 48). The grand duke Sergei and the grand duchess Elizabeth Fedorovna had represented the Russian imperial family at the Golden Jubilee, and Alexandra came from Darmstadt to ride in the procession. The basis of this story is unclear and may indeed have been concocted by the duke, since the jubilee took place without incident. See Jeffrey L. Lant, *Insubstantial Pageant: Ceremony and Confusion at Queen Victoria's Court* (London, 1979), 1–15, 92.

[71] See Golovin, "Zapiski," 114.

[72] Constantine Konstantinovich, "Dnevnik, 1896g.," 69–71.

[73] Cited in Anan'ich et al., *Nikolai Vtoroi*, 51.

massacre."[74] Russian newspapers juxtaposed the account of the disaster with descriptions of the magnificent celebrations of the previous week. The May 21 issue of *Novoe Vremia* set Khodynskoe against an account of the ball at the French ambassador's residence. "A kaleidoscope of guests, a kaleidoscope of beauty, youth, elegant toilets, and glittering uniforms" appeared in a mansion decorated with priceless tapestries brought from France, works of Watteau and Froment. The emperor and empress arrived at ten. The tsar and grand dukes wore ribbons of the Legion of Honor. They drank champagne and punch with a fine supper. "The tables in the Tsar's room were particularly grand—aromatic flowers lay in mountains literally in the midst of the sumptuous silver." The next paragraph opens without a subheading with the words found in most newspapers in these days; "A great misfortune has darkened the joyous course of the celebrations." The following day the editors placed the report of the memorial service and burial of the dead above the description of the elegant ball at Grand Duke Sergei's mansion, which they called "one of the outstanding celebrations of the coronation."[75]

The effect of the event on the people of Moscow is difficult to assess, but Khodynka clearly heightened the distrust of the government. Semen Kanatchikov and his fellow workers arrived after the crush and heard shouts about people falling into wells and saw carts piled with corpses. They were outraged at the low official estimates and the inability to find "the guilty party." "What aroused people's indignation most of all was the irresponsibility, the impunity, of the authorities who had destroyed thousands of lives."[76] Peasant deputations returning to the village brought news of the catastrophe, and, Princess Radziwill claimed, were disappointed that the tragedy, rather than providing an occasion for a display of common mourning, had been met with "indifference and icy impassiveness."[77]

Nicholas's speech at the dinner of peasant elders (*starshiny*) at the Petrovskii Dvorets took place later in the day of his appearance at the people's feast. Assuring the elders of his constant care for their well-being, he reminded them about Alexander III's words at the 1883 coronation, warning the peasants to follow the advice of their marshals of the nobility and not to believe rumors about a redistribution of the land. "Among you are many who heard them yourselves," he said, revealing that these were an especially chosen group of peasant leaders. "I want these words always to serve as your firm guide." Repin's watercolor in the coronation album captured the strain of the moment. We see the peasants forming a line, their dark caftans contrasting with the gold embroidered uniform of the suite. Nicholas stands, awkward and slight, looking away from them, as if trying to avoid their

---

[74] Maude, *The Tsar's Coronation*, 73–100.
[75] *Novoe Vremia*, May 21, 1896, 2; May 21, 1896, 1.
[76] Zelnik, *A Radical Worker in Tsarist Russia*, 45.
[77] Radziwill, *Behind the Veil*, 278.

gaze. Alexandra, dressed in a flowing white dress, holds a bouquet of flowers in her hands.[78]

On May 22 Nicholas made the traditional visit to the Trinity Monastery, where he suffered through the numerous offerings of refreshments and the terrible heat. The last day of his stay, May 26, was the occasion of a large parade near the Petrovskii Palace. "The parade was brilliant in every respect, and I was delighted that all the troops appeared at their best (*molodtsami*) before the foreigners." He was even more delighted to reach Sergei's estate, Ilinskoe, a word he underlined in his diary. "It was an indescribable joy to reach this fine and quiet place! And the chief consolation is knowing that all these celebrations and ceremonies are over!"[79]

At Ilinskoe, Nicholas and Alexandra spent three tranquil weeks with members of the imperial family. Sergei remained imperturbable and announced that he was concerned only to protect his young nephew from "annoyances" (*nepriiatnosti*) during his stay. Nicholas amused himself with the sports and outdoor activities he loved—horseback riding, lawn tennis, even water skiing.[80] With a newly acquired camera, he began photographing himself and the imperial family at play. In 1896 he also began placing snapshots of family members in his diaries and compiled his first photo album. Later, his daughters took up his interest and carefully glued their snapshots into numerous albums, which they enjoyed with friends and relatives. The fascination with photography reflected the preoccupation of the members of the imperial family with their own activities—the focus of their admiration and interest.[81]

---

[78] *Koronatsionnyi Sbornik*, 1:327–28.

[79] *Dnevniki Nikolaia II*, 147–48.

[80] Ibid., 148–52; Constantine Konstantinovich, "Dnevnik, 1896g.," 74.

[81] On Nicholas's passion for photographs of himself and his family, see Alia Barkovets, "Photographs in the State Archive of the Russian Federation of the Last Russian Emperor and His Family," in *Nicholas and Alexandra: The Last Imperial Family of Tsarist Russia*, 230–38. Barkovets mentions two of Nicholas's albums and thirty-three of the grand duchesses held at GARF. The Beinecke Library at Yale University has seven more albums of photographs of the imperial family.

CHAPTER ELEVEN

Demonstrations of Godliness

And our Sovereigns appear not only in name but in fact truly the most
pious ones, giving their people a great example of observance of church
laws and reverential respect for the representatives of Church Authority.
And how much the Russian people cherish this example! The people are
filled with tender feelings seeing how strictly the Tsar and Tsaritsa observe
all the rites of the Orthodox Church. One had to witness on March 30
those radiant faces washed with tears of joy of the people who were surrounding the Iberian Chapel as the Imperial couple so simply and reveren-
tially approached for the blessing of the Archpriest, as all Orthodox Christians do without distinction of age, estate, and wealth! One must observe
the tender feelings (*umilenie*) of our people when now they read every day
about how the Tsar and Tsaritsa zealously worship, attending all services
required by the Church for Holy Week.

—Moskovskie Vedomosti, *on the visit of the Imperial family to Moscow,
March–April 1903*[1]

EASTER VISITS TO MOSCOW

In the opening years of their reigns, Alexander I, Nicholas I, Alexander II,
and Alexander III all assumed larger-than-life roles that gave their rule the
grandeur of myth. Nicholas II, however, began to present his scenario of
power only after 1900, when the opposition began to gain force and embraced broader circles of society, including the *zemstva*, educated society,
students, peasants, and eventually workers. Nicholas regarded these movements, from the vantage of the national myth, as challenges to the historical
bond between tsar and people to be countered by shows of popular devotion
and efficacious repression.

Nicholas II remained true to the national myth, but his scenario was very
different from his father's. In Alexander III's reign, the tsar was united with
the Russian people through the Orthodox Church, a revitalized administration, and the system of estates—the foundations persisting from the distant
past. In Nicholas II's scenario, institutions, of both church and government,

---

[1] *MV*, April 2, 1903, 2.

receded into the background. Nicholas claimed a direct though unspoken and invisible spiritual bond with the people—a shared sense of piety he believed had persisted from ancient Russia. At the beginning of the century he began to appear before and among the people to display this bond and to compete with opposition movements for popular support. In public demonstrations of godliness he felt himself communing with the people, as they prayed together.

At such moments he was moved by an almost mystical spiritual exaltation, a bond that united him at once with the people, God, and history. This type of personal rapport with the common people was more akin to Russian populism than to the liturgical collectivism of the Slavophiles and Pobedonostsev. The feeling of exaltation arose as he began to play varied ceremonial roles that would endow him with the national image demanded by the myth. He appeared as Muscovite tsar, as pilgrim, as everyman, and later, after the revolution of 1905, as heir to the mantles of great national leaders exemplified by Peter the Great and Alexander I. The disjunctures between his roles and his private life, and between the successive roles themselves, lent his scenario an aspect of fantasy and make-believe. But Nicholas clearly believed that the roles reflected his national self, and he came away from these appearances with a heightened sense of mission and determination to restore pure autocracy. As a result, in the opening years of the twentieth century we witness the collision of two violently opposed insurgent forces, a Russia awakening politically and demanding to be heard and a monarch seeking to create a pure autocracy where a tsar drew personal authority from God and the people, unencumbered by institutions of state.

Confirmation for his role in the national myth had come with the deceptively easy success Russia registered with the occupation of Port Arthur in 1897 and 1898. Nicholas's dreams of Far Eastern expansion had been encouraged by Witte and P. A. Badmaev in 1895 and 1896. In 1897 Nicholas abandoned his father's caution, and backed the recommendation of Foreign Minister M. N. Murav'ev to occupy Port Arthur in response to the German seizure of Kiaochow. He overruled recommendations of restraint by Witte, the war minister Alexei Vannovskii, and the minister of the navy Pavel Tyrtov. On December 4, 1898, three Russian warships were welcomed in Port Arthur Harbor and on March 15, 1898, China signed an agreement leasing the city and Dalien to Russia.[2] Nicholas was delighted. He wrote to his brother, George, on March 29, "Yes, one has to look sharp; there on the Pacific ocean lies the whole future of the development of Russia and at last we have a fully open warm-water port; while the railway will strengthen our position there further."[3]

---

[2] Schimmelpenninck Van Der Oye, *Ex Oriente Lux*, 249–54.
[3] Maylunas and Mironenko, *A Lifelong Passion*, 171. The original is in "Pis'ma Nikolaia II bratu Georgiiu," GARF, 675-1-56, 51.

The Russian conquest of Port Arthur became a demonstration of the truth of the national myth. Following Alexander III's example, an Orthodox Church in old-Russian style, set on the highest promontory overlooking the city and the sea, would be built to attest to the fact that Port Arthur was Russian land. The tsar approved of this "good deed," proposed by Admiral Fedor Dubasov, the commander of the Pacific fleet and chief director of the Liaotung Peninsula. Alexander Gogen designed the cathedral to be "purely Muscovite, without admixture of Byzantine or other style." Gogen gave the cathedral the form of a ship, with seven gilded cupolas and a tall tent-shaped bell tower (fig. 50).[4]

The setting for Nicholas's first displays of public devotion was Moscow—the locus of nation and miracle at the close of his father's reign. There he could worship together with his uncle, Sergei, a true believer in the national myth, who continued to exercise a dominating influence on him after the coronation. The visits to Moscow took place in the aftermath of increasing troubles in Petersburg. In 1896 and 1897 the capital was paralyzed by a general strike, which ended in concessions from the owners and the government, including the eleven and one-half hour day.[5] The workers' strikes were followed, in February 1899, by a student strike in Petersburg prompted by incidents of police brutality that quickly spread to other cities, including Moscow, Kiev, and Kharkov.[6]

At the end of March 1900 Nicholas and Alexandra traveled to Moscow, to celebrate Easter among the shrines and relics of Moscow with the grand duke Sergei and the grand duchess Elizabeth.[7] It was the first visit of a Russian tsar to the city for Easter since Nicholas I's visit in 1849. Merely leaving Petersburg improved Nicholas's spirits. He wrote in his diary on March 31, "It is pleasant to be in the railroad car beyond the reach of all those ministers!" On April 2 he described his feelings as he bowed from the Red Staircase: "I found the minutes of the bow deeply touching and spiritually exalting (*vozvyshaiushchee*)."[8]

The tsar's arrival and the Easter services were surrounded by great publicity. Besides newspaper communiqués for the press, the government published an account that was sent free of charge to the 110,000 subscribers to *Sel'skii*

---

[4] *Zodchii*, no. 5 (1898): 40; *Stroitel'* (1900): 536; Nichols, "The Friends of God," 227.

[5] On the 1896 textile workers' strike in St. Petersburg, see Allan K. Wildman, *The Making of a Workers' Revolution: Russian Social Democracy, 1891–1903* (Chicago, 1967), 23–24, 73–78; Richard Pipes, *Social Democracy and the St. Petersburg Labor Movement, 1885–1897* (Cambridge, Mass., 1963), 102–9; Suvorin, *Dnevnik*, 136.

[6] Kassow, *Students, Professors, and the State in Tsarist Russia*, 88–116.

[7] Robert Nichols has suggested the importance of Grand Duke Sergei in shaping Nicholas's religious attitudes. Sergei believed in the cult of the saints and wore a golden panagia, containing a relic of the fourteenth-century ascetic St. Arsenii, though Sergei's way of life can hardly be described as ascetic (Nichols, "The Friends of God," 216–17).

[8] Nicholas II, "Dnevnik, December 1, 1899–July 27," 1900, GARF, 601-1-241, 92–93.

50. Orthodox Church at Port Arthur. Architect, Alexander Gogen. Stroitel', 1902.

Vestnik. The brochure made explicit the parallels between Nicholas and the pious tsars of Muscovy. Nicholas had come to Moscow, "by sacred precept of our native ancient times" to spend Easter "in close union with the faithful Orthodox people, as if in sacred communion with the distant past . . . with that past when Moscow was 'the capital town,' when the tsar and Moscow Patriarch lived there, when the life of the first capital was an uninterrupted and undeviating observance of the Church Statutes, and the example of such a life was the Moscow Tsar himself." The brochure related the ceremonies and processions of the Lenten and Easter seasons in old Moscow, along with Nicholas's and Alexandra's devotions. A lengthy section described the ritual preparation of holy oil in the Kremlin, which the emperor and empress witnessed. Photographs showed crowds of people watching the procession to the Chudov Monastery and to the Assumption Cathedral.[9]

The climax was the great Easter Night procession to the Church of the Savior. At midnight Nicholas, in the uniform of the Preobrazhenskii Regiment, and the empress, in a white dress and wearing a *kokoshnik* studded with gems and pearls, followed the leading court ranks from the Kremlin Palace to the church. Behind them were members of the tsar's suite, court officials, and ladies of leading Moscow families. The city was brilliantly lit. Worshipers crowded into the Kremlin cathedrals. The clock on the Savior Gate struck midnight. A cannon salvo burst from the Tainitskii Tower. The Bell Tower of Ivan the Great began to ring and was echoed by the "forty times forty" bells of the churches of Moscow.[10]

Nicholas's rescript to Grand Duke Sergei declared the attainment of his "intense wish" to spend Holy Week in Moscow, "among the greatest national shrines, under the canopy of the centuries-old Kremlin." He declared that he had found his communion with his people, "with the true children of our beloved Church, pouring into the cathedrals," and a "quiet joy" filled his soul. Sharing the Easter holiday with the worshipers gave him a spiritual mandate. "In the unity in prayer with My people, I draw new strength for serving Russia, for her well-being and glory."[11]

On April 5 he wrote to his mother, describing how he and Alexandra had spent their days visiting the sights and reading about Muscovite history. "I never knew I was able to attain such *religious ecstasy* as I experienced during this Passion Week. This feeling is now much stronger than it was in 1896, which is understandable. This time my soul is so calm, everything here makes for the peace of prayer and the spirit." On April 6 he noted in his diary: "It was gratifying to receive communion here in the Kremlin close to all its shrines. I worked on tiresome papers brought this morning by the Feld-Jaeger."[12]

In 1901 and 1902 Nicholas and Alexandra took an active interest in the work on the iconostasis for the Port Arthur church. Admiral Dubasov had been reassigned to St. Petersburg, and his wife was supervising the design and crafting of the iconostasis in the Admiralty Building in the capital. Nicholas donated three thousand rubles. Alexandra worked on three frames of the iconostasis herself. In 1902 the journal *Tserkovnye Vedomosti* described the project and connected the activity of the empress to early-Russian traditions: "Her August Majesty thus continues the custom coming down from our ancient tsaritsas and Grand Princesses. Russia's monasteries and cathedrals

[9] *Tsarskoe prebyvanie v Moskve v aprele 1900 goda* (St. Petersburg, 1900), 15, 23–24, 27–33.

[10] Ibid., 53–55.

[11] Ibid., 56.

[12] Nicholas II, "Dnevnik, December 1, 1899–July 27, 1900," 95–99; "Pis'ma imp. Nikolaia II imp. Marii Fedorovne, 23 ianv. 1899–22 dekabria 1900," GARF, 642-1-2326, 56–57.

preserve in shrouds and icons numerous works by royal hands. The Christian devotion of wives and daughters of our sovereigns is incarnate in the holy succession from ancient days and in the Far East appears as an example of this spiritual continuity."[13]

•

From 1896 to 1903 Moscow was the scene of a curious experiment in state-sponsored social action described under the rubric of "police socialism" and connected with the name of its founder, Sergei Zubatov, the head of the Security Division (*Okhrana*) of the Moscow police. Zubatov believed in "pure monarchy," a system that would defend the downtrodden and work for the common good. The Russian monarchy, "owing to its complete independence from governmental and public parties," realized such an ideal.[14]

In 1896, at Zubatov's prompting, the Moscow police began to convince or compel factory directors to correct abuses. The Moscow police promoted mutual funds and self-help organizations that provided benefits to workers in case of sickness, death, or unemployment. The Moscow *Okhrana* offices remained open on Sundays to receive worker complaints, inform workers of their rights, and help them with material assistance and even intervention in the plants. Finally, the police began to organize unions in the industries of Moscow. They arranged for elective district assemblies, and a workers council (*soviet*) for the entire city of Moscow.[15] In the first years of the twentieth century the experiment of police socialism spread to other cities. Thus the tsarist administration, in resisting the appeal of revolutionary groups among the urban proletariat, sanctioned workers' grievances and gave them their first lessons in political participation.

This strange movement frightened many of the bureaucrats in Petersburg, among them such influential figures as Viacheslav Plehve and Sergei Witte. But it is clear that it represented another attempt to enact the national myth, and one that enjoyed Nicholas's sympathy. Zubatov's success owed largely to his protection by the grand duke Sergei, who was impressed by his ideas and looked upon the workers, like many conservative officials, as peasants relocated to the cities. Moscow, the symbol of the union between tsar and people, would become the scene of an alliance of police and workers demonstrating the popular basis of the national monarchy. Sergei endorsed a proposal to stage a massive demonstration on February 19, 1902, the anniversary of the emancipation, a date cherished and marked by liberal opponents of the regime. The initiative presumably came from the members of the *soviet*. At an audience with a deputation of workers from the *soviet*, one of

---

[13] Nichols, "The Friends of God," 227; *Zodchii* no. 5 (1898): 40.

[14] Jeremiah Schneiderman, *Sergei Zubatov and Revolutionary Marxism: The Struggle for the Working Class in Tsarist Russia* (Ithaca, N.Y., 1976), 56–57.

[15] Ibid., 84, 99–117; D. N. Liubimov, "Otryvki iz vospominanii," *Istoricheskii Arkhiv* (November–December 1962): 76.

the deputies, Fedor Slepov, delivered a speech and a poem that deeply moved the grand duke. Sergei told the Moscow police chief Dmitrii Trepov that he wanted to continue the conversation "since he had never felt so good as when talking with them." Trepov reluctantly agreed to the demonstration, though the workers were not permitted to march through the city as had been originally proposed. The Petersburg authorities acquiesced only because they learned of it too late to halt preparations.[16]

More than forty thousand workers streamed into the Kremlin in the early morning hours of February 19, 1902, and assembled on either side of the Alexander II Monument. The police remained outside, admitting only workers, and the workers' own patrols maintained order. The ceremony began at 8:00 A.M. with a memorial service in the Chudov Monastery held before a delegation of workers, city and state officials, and members of the imperial suite. Grand Duke Sergei arrived at the close of the service to join a procession of the cross to the Alexander II statue. After the bishop conducted a requiem mass, worker deputies laid two wreaths, one of them of silver and costing fourteen hundred rubles, before the statue. A band made up of workers from the Riazan Railway then played the hymn "Kol' Slaven." Prayers of thanksgiving and for the health of the tsar and the imperial house were followed by a rendition of "God Save the Tsar" that ended with shouts of "Hoorah!" and caps flying into the air. Sergei then delivered a brief speech. He told the workers how happy he was to pray with them for the memory of his father and for the health of the tsar, and he thanked them for the wreaths. The workers marched past the statue, before Sergei and his suite, Zubatov, and the director of secret police operations abroad, P. I. Rachkovskii. The demonstration was followed by a service for the health of Nicholas II at the Cathedral of Christ the Redeemer.

The event was considered a great triumph for Zubatov and the grand duke. Rachkovskii said that he could not believe his eyes at such a demonstration occurring only a few weeks after student disturbances had brought the intervention of armed forces in Moscow.[17] The official press responded with enthusiasm, hailing the event as proof that the Russian people, even the workers, remained monarchist at heart. The next day an editorial, "Russian National Feeling," in *Moskovskie Vedomosti* asserted that the demonstration showed that "the Russian person cannot think of himself and his happi-

[16] Schneiderman, *Sergei Zubatov and Revolutionary Marxism*, 129–31; N. Bukhbinder, "Zubatovshchina v Moskve," *Katorga i Ssylka*, vol. 14 (Moscow, 1925), 114–15. Sergei wrote to his brother Paul of the occasion: "All the people are young and mature, a benign element. They came to thank me for help. One of them read verses. Then I said a few heartfelt words and talked with each of them" (cited in A. N. Bokhanov, "Velikii Kniaz' Sergei Aleksandrovich," in *Rossiiskie konservatory*, 360).

[17] Schneiderman, *Sergei Zubatov and Revolutionary Marxism*, 131–32; B. V. Anan'ich et al., eds., *Krizis samoderzhaviia v Rossii, 1895–1917* (Leningrad, 1984), 84; Bukhbinder, "Zubatovshchina v Moskve," 103; Liubimov, "Otryvki," 76; *MV*, February 20, 1902, 2; *NV*, February 21, 1902, 2.

ness without the Tsar, the people's Father. He knows no solemn manifestation of his feelings without the closest bond with prayer to the Lord God, without the auspices of his native Orthodox Church." Moving to the city had not changed the simple Russian man, who always remained the same. The celebration was a "true Russian holiday," because it took the form of a requiem service."[18] A brochure, written by Lev Tikhomirov at Zubatov's request, described the ceremony as a coming-of-age ceremony for the Russian people, who at last had begun to act on their own and free themselves from bondage to the intelligentsia. The workers expressed their "limitless love for the Tsar," while remaining "one with their fathers and grandfathers and with all the Russian people, that is, keeping a close bond with their native faith."[19]

But other newspapers interpreted the demonstration as a sign of the political awakening of the Russian people. An article in *Sankt-Peterburgskie Vedomosti* announced: "A holiday of the intelligentsia, February 19, was finally turned into a holiday of the people. Without doubt, this is a step on the road to declaring the great day a national holiday." A few took the demonstration as a sign of the birth of a proletariat in Russia, which contradicted the official view that workers were peasants and that a working class could not develop in Russia. *Birzhevye Vedomosti* praised "the trust of the authorities in the social aspirations of the masses." Such statements alarmed Petersburg officials, whose concept of the national monarchy did not allow for mass gatherings of workers. The minister of the interior Dmitrii Sipiagin asked the tsar to allow him to bring the newspapers' speculation about the significance of the event to an end. The director of the Chief Bureau of the Press, N. V. Shakhovskoi, sent out a circular forbidding newspapers to explain the event as "an expression of the awakening social consciousness of the working masses and as an indication of the official recognition of a special class of workers among us."[20]

In subsequent months the clergy and religious organizations increasingly assumed leadership of the lecture series and discussion meetings of the Zubatov organizations in Moscow. At an inaugural meeting of the lecture program, members of the clergy, among them the metropolitan of Moscow, sat on the dais and held their miracle icons before the workers. The lectures took place in the Historical Museum and were supported by special funds assigned by the grand duke Sergei. The first half of each evening was devoted to religious subjects. Worker choruses sang hymns and "God Save the Tsar." Nicholas himself wished success to the lecture program.[21]

[18] *MV*, February 20, 1902, 2.
[19] The brochure was reprinted in L. Tikhomirov, "Znachenie 19 fevralia 1902 goda dlia moskovskikh rabochikh," *Byloe*, no. 12 (1912): 81–88.
[20] Schneiderman, *Sergei Zubatov and Revolutionary Marxism*, 134–35; Anan'ich et al., *Krizis samoderzhaviia v Rossii*, 84–85.
[21] Schneiderman, *Sergei Zubatov and Revolutionary Marxism*, 135–38.

Nicholas's second and last Easter visit to Moscow, in April 1903, occurred during the revival of the constitutional demands and after the outbreak of peasant insurrections in the southern black-soil provinces. Moscow and the Zubatov organization provided reassuring signs of popular support for the monarchy. As in 1900, Nicholas felt a spiritual uplift. "The procession to the Red Staircase, as always, made a tremendous impression on me," he wrote in his diary on March 30, and when he left on April 16 he expressed his regrets about leaving "nice Moscow."[22] The worship and the visit to the shrines repeated the schedule of Easter 1900 but now also brought him into direct contact with workers from the Zubatov organizations. On the second day Nicholas held a warm meeting in the Kremlin with a delegation of button makers, confectioners, perfumers, and tobacco workers.

The worker Slepov, who described the scene in *Moskovskie Vedomosti*, added that "the tsar knows about our organization" and that the workers would earn his favor "if we ourselves take the peaceful road." Slepov's articles in *Moskovskie Vedomosti*, reprinted in a pamphlet of 1909, conveyed the sense of his comrades' delirious joy at the sight of their tsar. The workers asked why the tsar did not come to live in Moscow. The tsar was happy, like a "father, finding himself among his children, seeing them after a long absence."[23] The editors of *Moskovskie Vedomosti* also expressed regret that the tsar did not remain in Moscow. Petersburg, they wrote, could not provide "the tranquil, clear, national setting for governmental work that exists here in old Moscow, with the walls of the sacred Kremlin, in the center of native Russia, which can conceive only of age-old Russian foundations (*ustoi*)."[24] In response, the Petersburg daily, *Novoe Vremia*, dismissed these claims as another futile appeal to "reduce the work of Peter the Great to nothing." The author confidently asserted that "the Petersburg period of Russian history has already lasted for two hundred years."

As the epigraph to this chapter indicates, Nicholas was now being presented as the religious exemplar for his people. In their common worship, *Moskovskie Vedomosti* wrote, the people demonstrated their unity with the tsar, in contrast to the dissension of Petersburg. An editorial asserted that the tsar encountered not the destructive spirit but the constructive force "with which Moscow created Russia." The Kremlin recalled Moscow's national mission: "Here, among the national shrines of the Kremlin, one's lips involuntarily whisper, 'This is the Third Rome. There will be no fourth.' "[25]

By Easter time, 1904, the disasters of the Russo-Japanese War had already begun, and the imperial family remained in Petersburg. Nicholas gave Alex-

---

[22] GARF, 601-1-245, "Dnevnik Nikolaia II, September 17, 1902–May 18, 1903," 146, 166–67.

[23] Schneiderman, *Sergei Zubatov and Revolutionary Marxism*, 184; MV, March 29, 1903, 1; April 1, 1903, 2–3; *Russkii tsar' s tsaritseiu na poklonenii Moskovskim sviatynam* (St. Petersburg, 1909), 25–26.

[24] MV, April 16, 1903, 1; NV, April 18, 1903, 3.

[25] MV, March 30, 1903, 1.

andra a present of a Fabergé egg in the form of the Assumption Cathedral in Moscow. A single golden cupola of the church rises from an elaborate rendering of the gates and staircases of the Kremlin in multicolored gold. Through the window of the cupola a replica of the cathedral's interior is visible, including altar and icons. A music box inside plays the "Cherubimic Hymn."[26]

NICHOLAS IN PETERSBURG: *LE BAL D'HIVER*

After 1900 Nicholas increasingly disregarded the advice of his ministers and formal channels of government. He ignored the pleas for caution from the foreign minister Vladimir Lamzdorf and the war minister Alexei Kuropatkin regarding the aggressive pursuit of Russian interests in the Far East. He rejected the majority opinion of the State Council and supported the ruthless imposition of the Russian legal code by Nicholas Bobrikov in Finland, which revolutionized the previously quiescent Finnish population. In July 1901 A. A. Polovtsov, state-secretary (*gosudarstvennyi sekretar'*) under Alexander III and now a member of the State Council, wrote of the tsar's contempt for "the organs of his own power" and his belief in "the beneficial power of his own autocracy." Polovtsov, who had been reading N. K. Shilder's biography of Paul I, was struck by the similarities between the two emperors.[27] The personal and capricious character of rule, the contempt for subordinates, indeed recalled Paul. Nicholas, however, displayed none of the harshness and open despotism of his forbear.

At the same time, Nicholas openly disclosed his preference for Muscovite cultural forms—art, dress, and ritual. He shared the belief, gaining widespread acceptance among the public, that ancient icons represented a true Russian art form, uncorrupted by the Western spirit, and revealed the spiritual reality of God's grace to Russia and the Russian people. In 1901 he established a Trusteeship for Icon Painting, whose purpose was to create "active bonds" of national painting "with religious painting in general and church painting in particular." The chairman, the Slavophile nobleman S. D. Sheremet'ev, wrote that the trusteeship represented the rebirth of "imperial patronage that appeared with particular strength under Tsar Alexei Mikhailovich."[28]

Nicholas found a common language and conception of power with Dmitrii Sipiagin, his minister of the interior from 1900 to 1902. Sipiagin, a wealthy landowner, had served as provincial marshal of the Moscow nobility in 1894. He rose through the Ministry of the Interior and served as vice-

[26] Snowman, *Carl Fabergé*, 92, 103; Pfeffer, *Fabergé Eggs*, 82–83; Lopato, "Fresh Light on Carl Fabergé," 48–49.

[27] A. A. Polovtsov, "Dnevnik," *Krasnyi Arkhiv* (1923), 3:99.

[28] Tarasov, *Ikona i blagochestie*, 236–39, 243.

governor of Kharkov, governor of Kurland and then of Moscow province. Sipiagin envisioned the Russian state as a patriarchal organization inherited from Muscovite Russia by benevolent landlord-administrators advancing the well-being of the peasants who worked for them.[29] He viewed petitions to the tsar as a way to overcome the shortcomings of the administration and to establish a patriarchal justice resembling the petitions (*chelobitiia*) of Muscovite Rus'.[30] Such ideas appealed to Nicholas. In the census of 1897 the tsar categorized himself as "landowner" (*zemlevladelets*) and as "proprietor" or "master of the Russian land" (*khoziain russkoi zemli*). The term *khoziain* had been used to describe the first Russian tsars.[31]

Sipiagin's political ideas were inspired by feelings rather than thought or calculation, and his strongest feeling was devotion to his sovereign. He hardly resembled an official and for that reason enjoyed Nicholas's trust. He encouraged Nicholas's belief in himself as Muscovite tsar who ruled by divine inspiration and could re-create a national Russia. As minister of the interior, he plied Nicholas with memorandums on the restoration of the power of the state, the elimination of non-Orthodox religions, and the Russification of nationalities. He acted to curtail the privileges of the *zemstva*, and in 1900 he issued an order to draft students involved in the student movement into the army. The assassination of the minister of education N. P. Bogolepov was followed by a wave of protests by student and intellectuals across Russia, culminating in the great demonstration on Kazan Square in St. Petersburg on March 4, 1901.[32]

On March 4 Sipiagin dispatched Cossacks and mounted police to the square to disperse the demonstrators, and the resulting mêlée caused outrage both in educated society and among the officialdom. The Cossacks beat many participants, and fifteen hundred of them, including Ivanov-Razumnik, Peter Struve, and M. I. Tugan-Baranovskii, were arrested. When the St. Petersburg Writers' Union met a week later to protest the government's reaction, Sipiagin promptly had it closed. A wealthy, aristocratic member of the State Council, Prince Leonid Viazemskii, who happened on the demonstration, admonished the police for violence administered to ladies, for which he was reprimanded and ordered out of the capital. At a meeting of the State Council held on March 5, many of Viazemskii's fellow council members welcomed him as a hero.[33]

[29] Witte, *Vospominaniia*, 2:30.

[30] A. M. Lebov, "Odin iz ubitykh ministrov," *Istoricheskii Vestnik* 107 (February 1907): 485.

[31] Anan'ich, "The Economic Policy of the Tsarist Government," 136–37. The Russian terms are cited from the original manuscript version, "Ekonomicheskaia politika i predprinimatel'stvo v Rossii v kontse XIX–nachale XX veka," 21.

[32] On the rise of the student movement, see Kassow, *Students, Professors, and the State in Tsarist Russia*, 88–140.

[33] Shmuel Galai, *The Liberation Movement in Russia, 1900–1905* (Cambridge, 1973), 113–14.

Ill at ease in Petersburg, Sipiagin acted out the return to the past by wearing seventeenth-century attire and, when he visited the tsar, observing seventeenth-century forms of address.[34] He had the dining hall in his neoclassical mansion redesigned with vaults to resemble the Hall of Facets in the Kremlin. The walls and ceilings were painted with gold patterns on a crimson background, the Sipiagin family coat-of-arms, and a mural of the summoning of Tsar Mikhail Fedorovich in 1613. An inscription in Slavonic script at the edge of the paneling read: "The Boyar Dmitrii Sergeevich Sipiagin and his *Boyarinia* Alexandra Pavlovna Sipiagin built this dining hall (*palata*)"[35]

Sipiagin, an amicable and magnanimous nobleman of the old type, loved to indulge his Russian largesse (*razmakh*) by giving lavish feasts for his friends, which, his physician N. A. Vel'iaminov wrote, he regarded as "a sacred ritual that he performed artfully." He treated his guests to great portions of the Moscow Russian dishes he loved, especially suckling pig. He dreamed of receiving the tsar in his "dining hall" with Muscovite ritual and hospitality. When Nicholas accepted his invitation, he ordered an elaborate Russian supper with a Gypsy orchestra brought from Moscow. But the day before the occasion was to take place, on April 2, 1902, the minister of the interior was felled by an assassin's bullet. Vel'iaminov concluded, "Russia lost little in Sipiagin, but Nicholas lost much—a sincere, faithful, and truly devoted servant."[36]

The political events during Sipiagin's tenure and the sympathy shown for Prince Viazemskii by members of the State Council only confirmed and strengthened the tsar's distrust of high officials. On the occasion of the centenary celebrations of central state institutions—the ministries, the Committee of Ministers, the State Council—Nicholas openly distanced himself from the system of the previous century. Alexander I had established these bodies to ensure regularity and legality in the operation of the administration. To be sure, the system never functioned as intended, and personal influence and arbitrariness, wielded through direct contact with the tsar, persisted. But the institutions did pose requirements for compliance with rules that were observed on most state matters. Although Nicholas participated in the jubilee ceremonies and sat for Ilia Repin's famous painting of the State Council at its formal, centenary meeting on May 7, 1901, there was neither enthusiasm nor warmth in his fulfillment of these obligations. At the jubilee of the ministries and the conferring of a commemorative charter on the Committee of Ministers, in 1902, Polovtsov observed that "none of those present heard

[34] On Sipiagin, see Polovtsov, "Dnevnik," *Krasnyi Arkhiv* (1923), 3:99–100; Zakharova, "Krizis," 130–32; S. E. Kryzhanovskii, *Vospominaniia* (Berlin, n.d.), 192–93, 206–8; Gurko, *Features and Figures of the Russian Past*, 87; Iswolsky, *Recollections of a Foreign Minister*, 272–73; Lebov, "Odin iz ubitykh ministrov," 483.

[35] Kirichenko, *Russkii stil'*, 208.

[36] N. A. Vel'iaminov, "Vospominaniia N. A. Vel'iaminova o D. S. Sipiagine," *Rossiiskii Arkhiv* (1995), 6:391.

a single word of favor from the tsar." Neither celebration prompted special bonuses or awards to the officials. Yet, unlike his father, whose gruff aloofness met all servitors equally, Nicholas made demonstrative and invidious shows of his attachment to the elite world of the military. On the anniversary of the Page Corps—the training school for most of the officers of the guards—he bestowed numerous awards on officials connected to the corps, held gala receptions, and allowed all those who had received training in the Page Corps to wear the Maltese Cross, the legacy of tsar Paul.[37]

•

The most spectacular evocation of Muscovy took place at the celebrated "*bals d'hiver*" of February 7 and February 11, 1903. The court received instructions to appear in seventeenth-century dress. Museums were searched for pictures, and artists and couturiers hired to design and make costumes at enormous cost. Courtiers came dressed as boyars, *okol'nichie* (the rank below boyar), and other servitors of seventeenth-century Muscovy. Their wives were bedecked in robes patterned on those of the seventeenth century and studded with ancestral jewels. The guards were in uniforms of the *strel'-tsy*, the musketeers of old Russia. Nicholas wore the gold-brocaded processional robe and the crown of tsar Alexei Mikhailovich, while Alexandra came as the first of Alexei's wives, Maria Miloslavskaia, and wore a specially designed gown, brocaded in silver, and a miter set with a huge emerald pendant surrounded by diamonds.

On February 7 the ball in the Hermitage Theater opened with a Russian dance choreographed for the occasion, and then the couples proceeded to dance a waltz. The tsar wrote in his diary that "the court looked very pretty filled with ancient Russian people." Others present were also enchanted by the evening. Grand Duke Constantine Konstantinovich wore the red uniform of the chief of the *strel'tsy* of 1674, with gold embroidery and ermine collar. He found the gathering "astonishingly beautiful." The grand duchess Maria Georgievna recalled that "some mysterious magic seemed to have changed all these familiar figures into splendid visions of Russia's oriental past." V. N. Voeikov, a member of the tsar's suite, wrote that "the imagination was transported back several centuries . . . it gave the impression of a living dream." Fedor Chaliapin played the lead in a performance of the second act of *Boris Godunov*. The event was repeated two days later in the Concert Hall on a larger scale for the dowager, who had been abroad, and for members of the diplomatic corps who came in their usual evening dress. The guests came in pairs to bow before the imperial family, and again there was a Russian dance. A concert of Russian songs entertained the guests at the supper in the Nicholas Hall. The chorus and soloists sang *byliny*, "Matushka

[37] Polovtsov, "Dnevnik," *Krasnyi Arkhiv* (1923), 3:162–65.

Golubushka," songs by Alexander Dargomyzhskii and Tchaikovsky, as well as the "Song of the Volga Boatmen."[38]

The balls received considerable publicity. A deluxe three-volume album of photographs presented all the guests in their costumes, with indications of the twentieth- and seventeenth-century ranks.[39] The newspaper *Sankt-Peterburgskie Vedomosti* published three articles on the occasions. The accounts described the costumes in detail, noting their seventeenth-century provenance and the sumptuous jewels, particularly those worn by the imperial family. "The magnificent sarafans of brocade and silver, the silk of the ladies, and the variety of costumes of the time of Alexei Mikhailovich carried the imagination back to the pre-Petrine period."[40]

What did the ball mean? Members of the court thought of it as a masquerade, a diverting evocation of a distant exotic moment in the national past. Alexander Mosolov, the head of the Chancellery of the Ministry of the Court, wrote that Nicholas regarded the event as a first step to restoring Muscovite court ritual and dress, and had the designs drawn up but was dissuaded by the high costs.[41] Nicholas and Alexandra did not again appear in public in seventeenth-century dress. But portraits of him and the empress in their costumes were published frequently during the next decade, keeping alive the association between the monarch and his Muscovite forebears (fig. 51). Such portraits mark a break in the iconography of the Russian monarch. Russian emperors in the nineteenth century did not wear masquerade dress, as the scene of Alexander III at the 1884 costume ball indicates (see chapter 8). But Nicholas II clearly regarded seventeenth-century robes as something more than a costume. They were a challenge to the norms of the Western imperial court. They set the tsar and tsaritsa in a different time-space continuum, a cultural and aesthetic universe distant from Petersburg society.

In subsequent months Nicholas's made his aversion to ceremonies in the capital more evident. He showed indifference to the two-hundredth anniversary celebration of the founding of Petersburg, celebrated on May 3, 1903. His diary entry details a review he attended but says nothing about the anniversary. When Mosolov referred to the occasion and remarked on Peter's achievements, Nicholas indicated that he liked Peter less than his other forbears because of his "infatuation with Western culture and destruction of all purely Russian customs."[42] By 1903 Nicholas's disregard for court cere-

---

[38] "Dnevnik Nikolaia II, September 17, 1902–May 18, 1903," GARF, 601-1-245, 113; Zakharova, "Krizis," 131; Vel. Kn. Constantine Konstantinovich, "Dnevnik, 1903g.," GARF, 660-1-51, 20–21; Grand Duchess Maria Georgievna, *Memoirs* (Personal Collection of David Chavchavadze), 129–32; V. N. Voeikov, *S tsarem i bez tsaria* (Helsinki, 1936), 38–40.

[39] *Al'bom kostiumirovovannogo bala v Zimnem Dvortse v fevrale 1903g.* (St. Petersburg, 1904).

[40] *Sankt-Peterburgskie Vedomosti*, February 9, 1903, 4; February 15, 1903, 3; February 13, 1903; 3.

[41] Mosolov, *Pri dvore poslednego Rossiiskogo imperatora*, 29.

[42] Nicholas II, "Dnevnik, September 17, 1902–May 18, 1903," GARF, 601-1-245, 179–81; Mosolov, *Pri dvore poslednego Rossiiskogo imperatora*, 26–27.

monies had spread to governmental officials. The Blessing of the Waters ceremony on January, 6, 1903, was sparsely attended. Polovtsov had expected
to bow to the procession and leave but found so few fellow members of the
State Council that he felt obliged to remain.[43]

THE TSAR AS PILGRIM

The assassination of Dmitrii Sipiagin in April 1902 marks the beginning of
a new stage of social unrest and political organization. That same month,
peasant unrest swept through Kharkov and Poltava provinces where crop
failure had struck the previous year. Large-scale peasant disturbances
gripped entire provinces with the seizures of noble estates, looting, and burning. The constitutional opposition now began to reach beyond the *zemstvo*
constitutionalists, who had been organizing congresses and preparing addresses since 1900. The professional intelligentsia organized a network of
groups in the *zemstva* and the cities to unite all liberal opinion in the effort
to secure a constitution. The movement, Liberation (*Osvobozhdenie*), began
publishing a journal by that name in Stuttgart in the summer of 1902. Its
initial programmatic statement announced the intention of uniting "diverse
groups" with the aim of forming a constitutional party. The political scene
that led them to these measures gave a good picture of the turmoil in Russia.
It described

> ceaseless disorders in the institutions of higher education, the widespread work
> ing-class movement, agrarian disturbances by peasants, the extraordinarily
> widespread distribution of revolutionary publications among the lower orders
> of the population, and new outbreaks of terrorism, as manifested in the killing
> of two ministers in the space of a single year.[44]

This was the scene facing Sipiagin's successor as minister of the interior,
Viacheslav Plehve. Plehve had risen in the hierarchy of the ministry during
the 1880s, where he distinguished himself as an able and ruthless official
and a spokesman of administrative centralization and Russification. In 1882
he wrote a memorandum arguing that the state confronted an enemy not of
"flesh and blood" but of ideas. Like Pobedonostsev, he regarded the autocracy, in the person of the emperor, as a spiritual force. A memorandum to
Dmitrii Tolstoi in 1883 pointed to ideas as the state's chief foe that had to
be countered with the "religious-moral retraining of our intelligentsia." In
1899 he wrote that the government should accentuate this spiritual side of

---

[43] He was shocked to see the grand dukes Aleksei Aleksandrovich and Nikolai Nikolaevich
taking a smoke rather than attending service, the first time he had seen "such a public violation
of elementary Grand-Ducal obligations" (A. A. Polovtsov, "Dnevnik," *Krasnyi Arkhiv* [1923],
3:170).

[44] Cited in Terence Emmons, *The Formation of Political Parties and the First National Elections in Russia* (Cambridge, Mass., 1983), 23.

51. Nicholas II in Robes of Tsar Alexei Mikhailovich. Portrait in M. S. Putiatin, ed., *Letopisnyi i Litsevoi Izbornik*, 1913. Slavic and Baltic Division, New York Public Library. Astor, Lenox, and Tilden Foundations.

autocracy and emphasize "its service . . . to the good of the people." He also shared Pobedonostsev's belief that the masses were more devoted to the monarchy than were the elite.[45]

Plehve showed his devotion to the national myth by spending three days at the Trinity Monastery, where he engaged in a public display of his piety. The archimandrite Nikon presented him with an icon and referred to his appointment as "a new holy penance imposed on you by our devout sovereign." The archimandrite's sermon, reported in the press, described Saint Sergei, the founder of the monastery and the patron saint of Russia, as a "Russian in his soul" and "the helping hand of the Autocracy of our Tsars." It was most appropriate, Nikon continued, to seek the saint's blessing for his "new great deed of service," for Sergei's "holy signature" sealed the testament of Dmitrii Donskoi, "from which, one may say, Russian Autocracy organically grew." Officials like the war minister Alexei Kuropatkin and General Alexander Kireev urged Plehve to win the trust of society to fight the revolutionary movement. But he insisted instead on measures that would "restore the church's influence over the population."[46] Plehve visited the areas of disturbance and then sought ways to strengthen the authority of the provincial governors. Despite Kuropatkin's objections, he made extensive use of the army, not only in defense of the landlords but in punitive expeditions to discourage further disturbances.[47]

The most influential figure persuading the tsar to seek broader support for his rule of this time was Prince Vladimir Meshcherskii, who had been in disfavor since Nicholas's accession. In the editorial pages of Grazhdanin and in diaries that he sent to Nicholas, Meshcherskii appealed to the memory of Alexander III and likened the period of trouble after Sipiagin's death to the months following Alexander II's assassination. He called upon the tsar to issue a manifesto indicating his resolve to maintain autocratic powers but also to grant certain concessions, namely, freedom of speech and religion. He also urged Nicholas to unite with the "best parts of the population" in the struggle against the revolution.[48]

Nicholas's display of unity once more assumed the form of ceremony. In August 1902 Plehve arranged a well-publicized visit to the town of Kursk, during maneuvers the tsar was attending nearby. The visit provided an occa-

---

[45] Wcislo, Reforming Rural Russia, 141, 144; Lieven, Nicholas II, 133; M. S. Simonova, "Viacheslav Konstantinovich Pleve," in Rossiiskie konservatory (Moscow, 1997), 298.

[46] Edward H. Judge, Plehve: Repression and Reform in Imperial Russia, 1902–1904 (Syracuse, N.Y., 1983), 40; MV, April 16, 1902, 3; Iu. B. Solov'ev, Samoderzhavie i dvorianstvo v 1902–1907gg. (Leningrad, 1981), 74.

[47] The Kharkov governor, I. M. Obolenskii, stemmed the uprisings by calling in Cossacks and the army and having the peasants flogged. Plehve rewarded him with an order while the governor of Poltava Province, who had taken weaker measures, was dismissed (Anan'ich et al., Krizis samoderzhaviia v Rossii, 137; Judge, Plehve, 40–41; Simonova, "Viacheslav Konstantinovich Pleve," 309).

[48] Vinogradoff, "Some Russian Imperial Letters to Prince Meshcherskii," 123–32; Anan'ich et al., Krizis samoderzhaviia v Rossii, 134.

sion for a show of force in a region that bordered on the two troubled provinces of Poltava and Kharkov and for a display of the tsar's authority before the heads of the local administration and estates. The tsar met with the governors of Kursk and the adjacent provinces. The warmest meetings took place with the nobility. At the unveiling of a monument to Alexander III in the Noble Assembly, Nicholas praised the nobles for their role in administering the peasants and promised to involve representatives of the local nobility and the *zemstva* in the reform of laws governing the peasantry. The speech seemed to mark a change in direction from the refusal to consider any participation of society in the consideration of reform.[49]

The most significant aspect of the Kursk sojourn was the prominence given to the tsar's meetings with peasant elders from Kursk and six other provinces, including Kharkov and Poltava. When Nicholas arrived, a delegation of eighty-seven *volost'* elders greeted him with bread and salt. With Plehve at his side, Nicholas threatened punishment for those who disobeyed, but he promised his own attention to the peasants' well-being and recalled the words of admonition to obey the marshals of the nobility and the demand to ignore "foolish rumors," which Alexander III had addressed to the peasant elders at his coronation.[50]

The Kursk meetings marked a return to the practice of Alexander II—the use of ceremonial gatherings in the provinces to seek and display popular support. But Nicholas understood these meetings, in terms of his scenario, as expressions of his particular personal and spiritual bond with the peasants, not as manifestations of their love for their sovereign. In a letter to Alexandra of September 1, 1902, he described the Kursk events, mentioning a visit to the Znamenskii Monastery, where he kissed the Virgin's image; then he wrote that the speech to the peasants went off well "because it is much easier to talk to simple people."[51] On October 20 he wrote to Meshcherskii that he had returned from Kursk "in a very elevated and cheerful frame of mind." "We ourselves have constantly wanted to go to the interior of our Native Land but circumstances have prevented it. In the future, I hope that such trips will follow one after another."[52]

The feeling of communion with the people reassured Nicholas and dispelled the idea of making concessions to society. Plehve, with Meshcherskii's advice, worked on the manifesto, reducing the reforms to a minimum. The manifesto, issued on February 26, 1903, employed the historical idiom of the national myth. Nicholas alluded to involving "true patriots" in the work of the state. But he also declared that he recognized the need for the "greater

[49] Anan'ich et al., *Krizis samoderzhaviia v Rossii*, 136; Wcislo, *Reforming Rural Russia*, 144–45.

[50] Wcislo, *Reforming Rural Russia*, 145–46.

[51] Maylunas and Mironenko, *A Lifelong Passion*, 221–22.

[52] Vinogradoff, "Some Russian Imperial Letters to Prince Meshcherskii," 134.

strengthening and development of the basic foundations (*ustoi*) of Russian rural life—the landed nobility and the peasantry." The "foundations" referred to the estate principle (*soslovnost'*), which, the document maintained, had weakened since 1861.[53]

The manifesto announced few specific changes. It promised attention to rural needs and an increased role of "local people" in this process, which would take place under the guidance of a "strong and rational" authority. Plehve meanwhile drafted projects to give provincial governors powers over local institutions, particularly over the factory inspectors, who were under the authority of the Ministry of Finance.[54] The change in the tenor of the document, Boris Anan'ich has shown, resulted from Nicholas's own final review of the projects. He approved of Plehve's reform of local administration and entered the word *master* (*khoziain*) next to the word *chief* (*nachal'-nik*) as a term for governor, suggesting personal power, in the image of the tsar, without legal restraint. He removed any mention of freedom of religion and of the press and inserted instead a statement confirming the dominant role of the Orthodox Church.[55]

•

In 1902 and 1903 Nicholas and Alexandra began to look to the Russian people for examples of piety and sources of religious inspiration. They sought not the mediated faith of the church, ministered through sacraments and prayers practiced through the ages, but direct expressions of the will of God in charismatic holy men from the people. Their quest for a personal mystical faith was in part a result of their longing for the birth of a son, in part a response to Alexandra's reading of mystical texts and the lives of Russian saints in these years.[56] They were particularly inspired, Robert Nichols has shown, by recent literature from the West, particularly August Jundt's *Les amis de Dieu*. Jundt portrayed a group of fourteenth-century mystic reformers whose example influenced other prophetic religious figures in later centuries. Nicholas and Alexandra began to seek their own friends of God among the Russian people. These were not ordained priests, like Ioann of Kronstadt, but simple people with a special grace who felt and expressed God's spirit.[57]

[53] *PSZ* 3, no. 22581 (February 26, 1903).

[54] Vinogradoff, "Some Russian Imperial Letters to Prince Meshcherskii," 146; Anan'ich et al., *Krizis samoderzhaviia v Rossii*, 135–38. This section of the book is the work of Anan'ich.

[55] Anan'ich et al., *Krizis samoderzhaviia v Rossii*, 138–40.

[56] Her notebook from 1901 to 1905 includes citations from the German mystical and pietist writers Meister Eckhardt and Jacob Boehme, French religious philosophy, and even the Bhagavad-Gita. The last sections contain lengthy quotes from the patericons of the Orthodox Church and Serafim of Sarov ("Zapisnaia knizhka Imp. Aleksandry Fedorovny s stikhami, vypiskami iz filosofskikh i religioznykh sochinenii, 1901–1905," GARF, 640-1-304, passim).

[57] Nichols, "The Friends of God," 218–19; Steinberg and Khrustalev, *The Fall of the Romanovs*, 32–33.

Their new form of devotion showed Nicholas and Alexandra as one with the Russian people, sharing their religious feelings and taking on their humility and holiness. They adopted the cult of the elder (*starchestvo*), gaining adherents in educated society during these years—the idealization of monastic ascetics who broke with the usual monastic rule and became teachers and healers for the laity.[58] Holy Russia meant not only a Russian population devoutly observing the rites of the Orthodox Church but a nation where Christianity in its earliest sense had been reborn. It was a literal return to ascetic Christianity, a sense that Russia was the actual site of Christ's rebirth. This sense was vividly expressed in Michael Nesterov's 1905 painting, *Holy Rus'*, which showed Christ appearing among the people in a landscape of rural Russia.[59]

Mystical experiences and apparitions of the Virgin had been accepted by the Roman Catholic Church in the second half of the nineteenth century in answer to the appeals of liberalism, socialism, and positivism.[60] In Russia the Orthodox Church remained wary of individual mystical experience, and it was the tsar who turned to charismatic religious figures to prove the sanctity and national character of imperial authority. Nicholas and Alexandra may have learned of such potentialities for popular religion from "Monsieur Philippe," Philippe Nizer-Vachot of Lyon. Phillippe, a French hypnotist and medium, claimed to have the power to induce pregnancy and even to determine the sex of the child. He was summoned by Alexandra in 1902, at the suggestion of her Montenegrin cousins.[61] An active figure in conservative nationalist circles in France, and a champion of the canonization of Joan of Arc, "Philippe" brought the example of French religious nationalism to the attention of the imperial family. At the home of Nicholas's great-uncle, the grand duke Peter Nikolaevich, he suggested the canonization of Serafim of Sarov as a Russian national saint.[62]

Serafim, the abbot of the monastery at Sarov in Tambov Province, was an early-nineteenth-century elder (*starets*), known for his holy life, his visions, and his powers of curing and prophesy. It was said that he foretold a long

---

[58] Nicholas Berdiaev, *Dream and Reality: An Essay in Autobiography* (New York, 1962), 185–86.

[59] I. Nikonova, *M. V. Nesterov* (Moscow, 1984), 88–91; A. A. Rusakova, *Mikhail Nesterov* (Leningrad, 1990), 15–17.

[60] Marian apparitions were "among the great collective dramas of the nineteenth century." The most famous authenticated sites, La Sallette and Lourdes, attracted thousands of pilgrims who came to worship or to be cured. The phenomenon of apparitions spread across Europe, France, Germany, Spain, Italy, and Poland. See David Blackbourn, *Marpingen: Apparitions of the Virgin in Nineteenth-Century Germany* (New York, 1994), esp. chap. 1; Pope, "Immaculate and Powerful," 173–99; Victor and Edith Turner, *Image and Pilgrimage in Christian Culture* (New York, 1978), 208–11, 231–32, 236.

[61] Maylunas and Mironenko, *A Lifelong Passion*, 217–20; Polovtsov, "Dnevnik," *Krasnyi Arkhiv* (1923), 3:152–53, 158.

[62] Nichols, "The Friends of God," 214–15.

and glorious reign following a period of troubles at the beginning of the twentieth century. In the 1890s a movement began in the church for his canonization, but it encountered resistance from the church hierarchy and the Synod. Whether the church's opposition resulted from the modesty of Serafim's achievements or the usual skepticism of the institution toward popular saints is a matter of historical dispute.[63]

It is clear that the order for canonization came from the throne. In July 1902 Alexandra told Pobedonostsev that she wanted Serafim canonized within six days. The chief-procurator resisted her demands but yielded when Nicholas insisted that the elder's canonization take place the following year.[64] The fact that Serafim's remains had decayed threw some doubt on the canonization, but the metropolitan of St. Petersburg insisted that it proceed.[65] The Serafim cult became a Russian counterpart to the Marian revival in the Catholic church—an evocation of miracle to provide a form of emotional, participatory, collective religion with a mass following. Sarov, the scene of miracles, would become a center of pilgrimage for those in need of cure or succor, a Russian Lourdes.

The life of Serafim of Sarov was a unique example of a Russian *starets*, who propagated a cult of virginity, unusual in Russian Orthodoxy. The nuns in the Diveevo Convent near Sarov became Serafim's confidantes and followers. He witnessed numerous visions of the Virgin Mary; in one, she confronted him with twelve Virgin saints.[66] He insisted that the virgins live sepa-

---

[63] Ibid., passim. For a critical view of the canonization and this question, see the discussion in Gregory Freeze, "Subversive Piety: Religion and the Political Crisis in Late Imperial Russia," *The Journal of Modern History* 68 (June 1996): 312–29.

[64] Witte, *Vospominaniia*, 2:242–43; Nichols, "The Friends of God," 214–15. Nichols is skeptical of Witte's account, but it seems completely consistent with the procurator's attitude to all innovation, including new canonizations. Polovtsov also reports Pobedonostsev's indignation at the order to canonize Serafim (Polovtsov, "Dnevnik," *Krasnyi Arkhiv* [1923], 3:170).

[65] When Serafim's remains were exhumed, it turned out that they had decayed. The common people and clearly many clerics believed that the remains of a saint must be imperishable, though there was no church law to that effect. Neither the Tambov bishop Dmitrii nor the Petersburg metropolitan confirmed that they were imperishable, and when Dmitrii refused to sign the act of canonization, he was removed from his position. The debate within the Synodal commission became known through an antireligious pamphlet calling into doubt Serafim's sanctitude. The Petersburg metropolitan was forced to issue a statement of the contents of the coffin, declaring that the body had perished but that the bones and hair had been preserved and that the canonization would proceed (Gregory Freeze [G. Friz], "Tserkov', religiia, i politicheskaia kul'tura na zakate starogo rezhima," in *Reformy ili revoliutsiia: Rossiia, 1861–1917* [St. Petersburg, 1992], 34; *MV*, July 27, 1903, 2).

[66] The veneration of the Virgin, George Fedotov observed, was not characteristic of Russian orthodoxy. It was a Western symbol that combined the opposites of celibacy and maternity, of purity from sin and childbirth. Russians venerated miracle icons of the Mother of God that accompanied Russian troops into battle, ensured victory, and saved cities. The popular movement in the church had promoted the painting of Mother of God icons that could promise alleviation of suffering and a better life. But the Mother of God remained a symbol of the church, whose intercession came from prayer and sacrament, not from her virginity or visions

rately from the widows. Serafim attained, one biographer remarks, "an astounding intimacy with the Mother of God," who brought him "mysterious fruits of strange flavor." The nuns at Diveevo also claimed to have received visits from "a beautiful lady" in their church.[67]

Earlier in the nineteenth century Russian empresses were the principal adepts of the Serafim cult. They found his teaching of the virgin congenial to their Western concept of the Mother of God. Alexandra Fedorovna, the wife of Nicholas I, had surrounded herself with artistic representations of the Virgin. Tradition said that she died wrapped in Serafim's cloak, declaring, "I am sure that this little old man will help me to die well." Anna Tiutcheva wrote that she gave the empress Maria Aleksandrovna an icon of Serafim on New Year's Day, 1856, and cited his prophesies that Maria would be a mother who brought grace both to Russia and the Orthodox Church.[68] In Serafim these Russian empresses found a Russian monk who reflected their own conceptions of feminine purity and devotion. Alexandra Fedorovna now had the religious conviction and will to make Serafim a Russian saint.

The decision to turn the canonization ceremony into a great public celebration seems to have been made in the Ministry of the Interior. Plehve organized the event as an immense display of the "union of tsar and people."[69] In July 1903 nearly 150,000 worshipers converged at the Sarov Monastery, many of them sleeping in barracks or the open air. They came by train, on horseback, or on foot from different areas—Russian, Ukrainian, Mordvinian peasants. Most of them, judging from the pictures, were women.

Representatives of the church also arrived in great numbers—among them the Synodal choir from Petersburg for the cathedral services, sixty priests from neighboring areas to hold services in churches and chapels for those who could not gain admittance to the cathedral, and nearly one thousand gonfalon bearers to participate in numerous processions of the cross. The ceremonies began on July 17, 1903. A massive procession of the cross, made up of clergy and worshipers from many monasteries and villages, moved from the Diveevo Convent to the edge of the Sarov grounds, where it was met by a procession coming from the monastery. The two joined to proceed to the Assumption Cathedral. "The brilliant multicolored chasubles of the clergy, the black habits of the monks and the nuns, the blue and dark caftans of the banner bearers, and streams of the mass of people coming . . . from all ends of Russia made up a wonderful picture before the pilgrims." After the morning service another procession moved out from the Assumption Cathedral to the site of the remains of the Saint. The "gonfalon bearers" carried the treasures of the monastery: altar crosses, icons, vestments, icon

of her on Russian soil (G. P. Fedotov, *A Treasury of Russian Spirituality* [New York, 1965], 244; Marina Warner, *Alone of All Her Sex: The Myth and Cult of the Virgin Mary* [New York, 1976], 236–39).

[67] Valentine Zander, *St. Seraphim of Sarov* (Crestwood, N.Y., 1975), 81.

[68] Ibid., 35; Tiutcheva, *Pri dvore dvukh imperatorov*, 2:92–93.

[69] Solov'ev, *Samoderzhavie i dvorianstvo v 1902–1907gg.*, 75.

lamps. They were followed by nuns with a miracle icon of the Mother of God, the chorus of monks of Sarov, members of the clergy, and then an icon of the Mother of God of Loving Tenderness.[70]

The emperor and empress arrived at Sarov later the same day. They were accompanied by Maria Fedorovna; the grand dukes Sergei Aleksandrovich, Nicholas Nikolaevich, and Peter Nikolaevich; the grand duchesses Olga Aleksandrovna, Elizabeth Fedorovna, and Militsia Fedorovna; and other members of the imperial family. Court ladies and the leading ranks of the court attended, as did the minister of the interior Plehve and the minister of communications Prince Michael Khilkov.[71]

The ceremony of canonization presented a spiritual and symbolic union of three elements—the "people," represented by the pilgrims; the church, symbolized by the participating clergy and the volunteer gonfalon-bearers; and the monarch, with his family and entourage. They were united in a great procession of the cross, which, on the evening of July 18, started out from the Assumption Cathedral, led by the metropolitan of St. Petersburg Antonii, to the Church of Saints Zosima and Savvatii where Serafim had held his last service and taken communion for the last time and where his coffin had been placed after the disinterment. Nicholas and the grand dukes—the "August Pilgrims"—lifted Serafim's coffin and carried it in procession into the square before the hushed crowd. The tsar and the grand dukes carried the remains around the Assumption Cathedral, with prayers uttered at each side, then brought the coffin into the cathedral in a procession of the cross, followed by the metropolitan, the bishops, and members of the imperial family. When the coffin approached, many fell to their knees and wept.

In the background was a great crowd of people, holding candles and in prayer. The newly appointed Bishop of Tambov, Inokentii, delivered a sermon that extolled the canonization as an indication of Russia's holiness and destiny. "These holy remains are a new sign of the mercy and grace to the Russian people and the Orthodox Church, for in the unfolding of the heavens a new man of prayer, a new intermediary and intercessor for us unworthy ones, stands at the altar of the Lord." The metropolitan opened the coffin exposing Serafim's remains, and the choir sang a hymn to Serafim's glorification as a saint.[72]

Despite her poor health, the empress stood for the entire four and one-half hours of the canonization service. "During the entire procession," Nicholas wrote in his diary, "we carried the coffin on a stretcher. The impression was tremendous to see how the people, and especially sick cripples and the unfortunate, regarded the procession of the cross. The moment when the beatification began and then the kissing of the remains was most solemn." The scene overwhelmed the Slavophile writer and confidant of the empress Gen-

[70] *NV*, July 20, 1903, 3.
[71] Ibid., July 16, 1903, 2; July 20, 1903, 3; July 21, 1903, 3.
[72] Nichols, "The Friends of God," 209–11; *NV*, July 20, 1903, 2.

eral A. A. Kireev as well. "It was touching and exalting to see the tsar and the tsaritsa kneeling with hundreds of thousands of their subjects."[73]

The canonization was made known in a special service, performed on July 19, in all Russian Orthodox Churches. On that day, the imperial family and their entourage participated in a morning service at the Assumption Cathedral. Serafim's coffin was moved from the altar to a special shrine donated by the emperor and empress. The shrine was designed to resemble a flamboyant old-Russian chapel with a tent canopy and small cupola. The tsar and the grand dukes again bore the coffin in a procession of the cross around the monastery grounds, now with the sacred remains open. Nicholas wrote, "How touching (*umilitelen*) the procession of the cross was yesterday, but with the coffin open. The elevation of the spirit (*pod"em dukha*) was enormous." On July 20, before their departure, the imperial family rode in carriages to the Diveevo Convent. Along the way they were greeted by peasants, who showed them their handiwork, and by the provincial marshal of the nobility and chamberlain. A procession of the cross from the convent greeted them. At the convent cathedral the emperor and empress kissed the miracle icons and received icons as gifts from the nuns, then toured the convent buildings and grounds.[74]

The canonization and the presence of the imperial family was widely publicized. Newspapers and church journals described the ceremonies in detail. *Novoe Vremia* and *Niva* carried photographs of the processions and the imperial family at various sites. A photograph of the tsar and grand dukes carrying the bier was circulated in large numbers; it was painted on the Easter egg Fabergé made to celebrate the fifteenth anniversary of Nicholas's reign in 1911.[75] Copies of icons of the bent "wretched Serafim" as the symbol of innocent suffering were reproduced in large numbers for the church's campaign of moral edification.[76]

The *Novoe Vremia* correspondent V. Prokov'ev described the deep impression made by the emperor's and empress's appearance. "The people saw Them—those whom they love and worship with their simple and tender hearts—in their midst, in the hallowed places dear to their religious feeling, and in the cathedral itself together as worshipers."[77] It was a demonstration of the unity of the realm, *Moskovskie Vedomosti* reported, uniting the various estates before "an ideal of holiness." The article made the political pur-

---

[73] Anatolii Timofievich, *Prepodobnyi Serafim Sarovskii* (Spring Valley, N.Y., 1953), 110–11; Mosolov, *Pri dvore poslednego Rossiiskogo imperatora*, 117–19; MV, July 27, 1903, 2; "Dnevnik Nikolaia II, May 19–December 31, 1903," GARF, 601-1-246, 42–45; Zakharova, "Krizis," 127–28; Solov'ev, *Samoderzhavie i dvorianstvo v 1902–1907gg.*, 75 n.

[74] NV, July 24, 1903, 2–3; "Dnevnik Nikolaia II, May 19–December 31, 1903," 46–47. There is a photograph of the shrine in MV, July 30, 1903, 9.

[75] The photograph is reproduced in Major-General A. Elchaninov, *The Tsar and His People* (London, 1914), opp. 68; A. Elchaninov, *Tsarstvovanie Gosudaria Imperatora Nikolaia Aleksandrovicha* (St. Petersburg-Moscow, 1913), 66; *Niva*, August 3, 1903, 626.

[76] Stephen Graham, *The Ways of Martha and the Way of Mary* (London, 1916), 122; Tarasov, *Ikona i blagochestie*, 52.

[77] MV, July 24, 1903, 3.

pose of the event absolutely explicit. "Around the holy remains of the Most Saintly, one can say that the entire Russian land has gathered. This is a type of representation that is so inspiring that all possible national elections fade before it."[78]

Sarov, like the sites of European pilgrimage, provided the demonstrations of miracles that could answer the challenges of skeptics and unbelievers.[79] Articles in *Niva, Moskovskie Vedomosti,* and *Novoe Vremia* described the many cures of those who bathed in these days in the Sarov stream. *Moskovskie Vedomosti* mentioned fifty letters reporting healing after prayers to Serafim. The canonization, the newspaper claimed, refuted the doubts of unbelievers "with such miraculous signs of Faith and majestic grandeur, which transcend the ordinary according to the will of the Orthodox Tsar."[80]

The extensive publicity also revealed the distance between the tsar and the people. *Novoe Vremia,* while acclaiming the religious significance of the event, carried descriptions of the tsar and his entourage arriving in sumptuous carriages, and the poor, the lame, and the sick reaching Sarov—forty miles from the nearest railway station—on foot. Many had to sleep in the open air. Food was in short supply. "Nowhere can you buy bread. Everyone begs for bread, not money. Neither the monastery nor the surrounding area has stores of bread." Security measures ensured that the masses did not approach the tsar. Most of the pilgrims did not receive tickets but waited crowded outside the monastery walls; only a chosen few could see the services within the church. "Many, not reaching the 'saint of God,' did not see the church services and, with sorrow in their souls, returned home or went to other monasteries." An editorial in *Sankt-Peterburgskie Vedomosti* used the occasion to hint that the tsar should be concerned for the more practical needs of the people.[81]

Nicholas took the canonization as proof of the divine presence in Russia. He noted in his diary the reports of cures, one of which presumably occurred while the remains were being carried around the altar. "Wondrous is God in all His saints. Great is His ineffable mercy to dear Russia; indescribably consoling is the obvious new manifestation of the Lord's grace toward all of us."[82] The empress, along with her sister, the grand duchess Elizabeth Fedorovna, and her sister-in-law, the grand duchess Olga Alexandra, also bathed in the brook.[83]

When, in 1904, Alexandra finally gave birth to a son, she believed it was the work of Serafim, effected by the waters of Sarov. Thereafter, the cult became a focus of the life of the imperial family. Nicholas hung the icon of

---

[78] Ibid., July 19, 1903, 1.

[79] On the Catholic Church's acceptance of vision in response to the challenges of science and rationalism, see Victor and Edith Turner, *Image and Pilgrimage in Christian Culture,* 210–11.

[80] *Niva,* August 2, 1903, 624–28; *MV,* July 20, 1903, 1; July 26, 1903, 2.

[81] Freeze, "Subversive Piety," 324–26; *MV,* July 20, 1903, 2–3; July 29, 1903, 2–3. The citation from *Sankt-Peterburgskie Vedomosti* is cited in *MV,* July 19, 1903, 1.

[82] GARF, "Dnevnik Nikolaia II, May 19–December 31 1903," GARF, 601-1-246, 47.

[83] Zakharova, "Krizis," 128; Timofievich, *Prepodobnyi Serafim Sarovskii,* 111–18.

Serafim in his study; Alexandra later placed his relics in the Fedorov Cathedral at Tsarskoe Selo.[84] They named the child Alexei, after Tsar Alexei Mikhailovich. He was the first heir to the throne to receive the name since the death of Peter the Great's firstborn son in 1718.

For Nicholas, Sarov and the birth of Alexei confirmed his sense of divine communion, shared by tsar and people. A painting of 1904, *Nicholas II and Alexandra at the Bed of the Newborn Heir*, shows the couple in their coronation mantles, bending over Alexei in the cradle; an angel watches above, wings open, sheltering the family. Beneath, peasants crowd forward, looking raptly upward, extending their arms and crossing themselves.[85] After Sarov, A. A. Mosolov recalled, the words *tsar* and *people* followed each other directly in many of the tsar's statements, and Nicholas increasingly looked upon the people as "grown children." He felt a desire to come close to them, to "show physical affection to the people he loved," but he was prevented by the size of the crowds and fears of another Khodynka.[86] For Nicholas, this was a spiritual bond between likes, rather than an attraction of opposites. It expressed the sense that peasants shared a faith like his own, exemplified in the veneration of Serafim.

•

In 1903 Nicholas increasingly identified his religious mission with Russia's advance into the Far East. The minister of war General A. N. Kuropatkin wrote in his diary early in 1903 about the "grandiose plans" Nicholas had for Russia in the Far East. Nicholas wanted "to absorb Manchuria into Russia, to begin the annexation of Korea. He also dreams of taking Tibet under his orb. He wants to rule Persia, to seize both the Bosphorus and the Dardanelles."[87] The pilgrimage to Sarov confirmed Nicholas's vision of a holy mission in the East. Robert Nichols has shown that many of the clergy at Sarov who had participated in the movement to canonize Serafim were also involved in missionary work in the Far East. A fortnight after the canonization Nicholas issued a decree, without consulting his ministers, establishing a Vice-Royalty of the "Amur region," and he appointed as viceroy A. E. Alekseev, an advocate of vigorous Russian expansion in the Far East. Alekseev reported directly to the tsar and exercised virtually unlimited power over the region. Two weeks later Witte, who continued to urge restraint, was dismissed.[88]

---

[84] Zakharova, "Krizis," 128; Timofievich, *Prepodobnyi Serafim Sarovskii*, 111–18.

[85] Reproduced in Mikhail Iroshnikov et al., *Nikolai II* (St. Petersburg, 1992), 312.

[86] Mosolov, *Pri dvore poslednego Rossiiskogo imperatora*, 119–21.

[87] Schimmelpenninck Van Der Oye, *Ex Oriente Lux*, 55.

[88] Nichols, "The Friends of God," 213–14, 223–25. Judge argues the connection persuasively between the canonization and the decision to embark on the war (*Plehve*, 166–67). The advocates of Eastern missionaries also were participants in the movement to bring religion closer to the people. For example, Father Leonid Chichagov, a former army officer, influenced by John of Kronstadt, had become an army priest. Leonid had published memoirs about Serafim

In July 1903 Nicholas allowed two young aristocrats who were officers in the Cavalier-Guards, A. M. Bezobrazov and V. M. Vonliarliarskii, to develop a timber concession they had been seeking on the Yalu River. Bezobrazov and Vonliarliarskii were less interested in producing timber than establishing a Russian presence in Northern Korea. Their contempt for formalities and their determination to show Russia's superiority to Orientals won Nicholas's admiration.[89] The growing Russian presence in Korea, as Witte had feared, antagonized the Japanese, who now demanded Russian recognition of Japanese dominance in Korea.

In late 1903 Nicholas faced the dilemma of how to respond. On the one hand, he informed Alekseev that he did not want a war. On the other, he recalled that the Japanese had given in after the seizure of Port Arthur, and he described Japan as "a barbarian country."[90] On January 27, 1904, Japan launched a surprise attack on Port Arthur. Nicholas dismissed the move as "a flea bite." At the outset, the government presented the war as a religious struggle, with Serafim as its patron saint. Officers setting out for the front made pilgrimages to Sarov, and parents of soldiers traveled to Sarov to beg Serafim's protection. Priests blessed the troops with his icon. The grand duchess Elizabeth Fedorovna carried the relics of Serafim with her when she attended to the war casualties in Moscow's military hospitals. Serafim's portrait was placed next to those of St. Sergei of Radonezh, the patron saint of Moscow, and the Archangel Michael, in a silver triptych presented to the minister of war Kuropatkin, to protect the Russian armies.[91] But the grand duke Alexander Mikhailovich recalled that the soldiers did not recognize the new saint on the icon and felt confused and distressed.[92]

---

and worked within the church to have him canonized. Archpriest Filosov Ornatskii, the energetic leader of the Society for the Spread of Religious and Moral Enlightenment, had served in the Russian Orthodox Mission to Japan and published a book on his experience that called upon Holy Rus' to enlighten "the still benighted peoples of the Far East." Ornatskii reported on the Sarov celebrations to the Varlaam Monastery, which had grown rapidly at the beginning of the century and had been associated with missionary work in the Far East.

[89] Lieven, *Nicholas II*, 97–99; S. Iu. Witte, *Vospominaniia*, 2:165. For a critique of Witte's account of the coming of the Russo-Japanese War, see B. V. Anan'ich and R. Sh. Ganelin, *S. Iu. Vitte—Memuarist* (St. Petersburg, 1994), 16–40.

[90] Lieven, *Nicholas II*, 99.

[91] Nichols, "The Friends of God," 217, 222–23.

[92] "It came to a point toward the end of the Russo-Japanese War that I began to loathe the very name of Seraphim Sarovskii. He may have led an exemplary life, but as an inspiration for the troops he had proved a total failure" (Alexander Mikhailovich, *Once a Grand Duke*, 218).

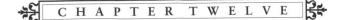

The 1905 Revolution and
the Jubilee Celebrations

I have experienced the last two days with deep emotion, and you and I
probably felt the same feelings together on the same fields of Poltava
where two hundred years ago the fate of our fatherland was decided.
Through the will of the Lord God, through the genius of Peter and the
tranquillity of the Russian people, a victory was won that gave Russia
greatness. Russia has just now lived through a time of adversity. I believe
that now she will enter onto a path of development and prosperity and
that the future generation will find it easier to live and to serve its native
land. But for this, all my loyal subjects must help their Sovereign (*Gosudar'*); they must show faith in the power of their fatherland and love for
their past. I drink with the hope that Russia will develop in the spirit of
the unity of Tsar with the people, and in the close bond of the entire population of our native land with their Sovereign. I drink to the descendants
of the glorious heroes who fought where today the brilliant sight of the
combined detachments filled Me with such joy. I drink to their health, to
the entire army, and to our great mother Russia.

—*Nicholas II, Speech on the Two-hundredth Anniversary
of the Battle of Poltava, July 16, 1909*[1]

THE NATIONAL MYTH DURING THE REVOLUTION

While Nicholas conceived of a triumphal national monarchy, expanding into
the Far East, a new conception of the nation was spreading through Russian
society. In June 1902 Peter Struve, the editor of *Osvobozhdenie*, announced
the goal of enlisting the whole nation in the struggle for political freedoms
and national autonomy. Over the next two years the leaders of this struggle,
among them the historian Paul Miliukov and the *zemstvo* liberal Ivan Petrunkevich, set about organizing all those engaged in the struggle for freedom and representative government into a single movement. The movement
embraced the national goals of freedom, civil rights, and equality, and by

[1] *Rossiia*, June 28, 1909, 3.

the end of 1904 comprised a broad front, extending from the Social Revolutionaries on the Left to *zemstvo* constitutionalists on the Right.

The beginning of the war in January 1904 brought an outpouring of patriotic enthusiasm from educated society. But the news of the failure of Russian arms dispelled the hopes of an easy victory. By the end of the year it became evident that Russia was facing defeat at the hands of a people that the government and many in educated society regarded as Russia's inferiors. But the war situation did not weaken Nicholas's or the tsar's resolve to struggle against those who worked toward increased participation in government. The *zemstvo* movement offered its "unlimited support" and formed a general *zemstvo* organization to conduct war relief, but Plehve saw it as a challenge to state authority and restricted its operations.

Both the tsar and Plehve viewed the "public men" in the *zemstvo*, like Dmitrii Shipov, who wished to gain a consultative role in government, as the most immediate and dangerous enemies. Plehve regarded them as a cover for radicals who served in the *zemstvo* administration—the "third-element" types like doctors, statisticians, agronomists, and schoolteachers. During 1904 Plehve launched an offensive against the *zemstva*, removing heads of the *zemstva* boards, prohibiting debates on certain subjects, and refusing to confirm leading *zemstva* moderates, like Shipov, in office.[2] The autocracy in this way eliminated the moderate option and encouraged the more radical leaders of Liberation and the revolutionary movement to engage in direct struggle. On June 4 the governor-general Nicholas Bobrikov, who had been ruthlessly enforcing Russification policies in Finland, was assassinated. On July 15, 1904 a Socialist Revolutionary E. S. Sazonov hurled a bomb at Plehve's carriage and blew him to bits. The murder was met by general indifference and in some quarters, among them the upper echelons of the government, rejoicing at the fall of a hated, rigid bureaucrat.[3]

The assassination of Plehve marks the beginning of the revolutionary events of 1904 and 1905. To replace Plehve, Nicholas appointed Dmitrii Sviatopolk-Mirskii, a liberal member of his suite and a protégé of the dowager empress. With Mirskii's appointment, Nicholas embarked on an uncertain course of promised concessions alternating with repression, ongoing vacillation that exasperated his ministers and convinced Russians of all classes that the government was out of control. The usual interpretations attribute Nicholas's course of action to his weakness or ignorance of Russia. But Andrew M. Verner's painstaking unraveling and astute analysis of the internal discussions from July 1904 through the spring of 1906 allow us to gain a clearer sense of the tsar's thinking.[4]

[2] Thomas Fallows, "The *Zemstvo* and the Bureaucracy," in Terence Emmons and Wayne Vucinich, eds., *The Zemstvo in Russia* (Princeton, N.J., 1982), 67.

[3] Abraham Ascher, *The Revolution of 1905: Russia in Disarray* (Stanford, 1988), 53–55.

[4] Verner, *The Crisis of Russian Autocracy*, esp. 104–280.

Verner makes it clear that Nicholas held to his belief in his own autocratic power throughout the various negotiations of the revolutionary period. Under pressure of the revolutionary events and the insistent advice of officials and members of the imperial families, he accepted concessions when absolutely necessary. But he was able to accommodate these concessions to the persistence and triumph of the national myth. At all times he regarded himself as the source of order and authority, and throughout the demonstrations, strikes, mutinies, and violent peasant insurrections he never wavered in his view that the Russian people remained united with their tsar. He knew exactly what was occurring in Russia but, comprehending the events in terms of myth, he regarded them as the work of foreign revolutionaries, Jews, and intelligentsia, whom incompetent ministers had left free to wreak havoc. Underlying this was the persistent Katkovian faith in the invincible punitive capacities of Russian autocracy. As shrewd an observer as Sergei Witte shared this view. Meeting with two leaders of Liberation, I. I. Petrunkevich and I. V. Gessen, in October 1904, Witte, at this point chairman of the Committee of Ministers, emphasized that society was too weak and reaffirmed his belief that the autocracy "rests on three hundred years of history" and that "the interests of the people are closely linked to the interests of the autocracy."[5]

In his first meeting with the tsar on August 25, 1904, Sviatopolk-Mirskii aptly described the situation: "The condition of things has become so aggravated that one may consider the government to be in a state of enmity with Russia. It is necessary to make peace." Mirskii accepted the position of minister of the interior on the condition that the tsar announce a program of reforms, including civil liberties and a limited degree of participation.[6] He argued for the need to win the support of society (*obshchestvo*), which had been developing since the era of the Great Reforms. He tried to show that the participation of elective representatives from *zemstvo* and major city Dumas in governmental decisions was compatible with autocracy. The tsar would retain the right to change the administrative order. The representatives would help the government formulate plans to increase legality in the Senate and other state institutions, and to reform and democratize the *zemstva*.[7]

Nicholas promised him full support. But this generosity of spirit soon passed. He detected the influence of the intelligentsia in all requests for participation, even those from the highly conservative provincial marshals of the nobility. The request of the *zemstvo* members to participate he viewed as "an egotistical desire to obtain rights and a contempt for the needs of the

---

[5] Ascher, *The Revolution of 1905: Russia in Disarray,* 59.

[6] The account comes from the diary of Sviatopolk-Mirskaia, who kept an exact record of the events in order to protect what she feared was her husband's endangered reputation (Verner, *The Crisis of Russian Autocracy,* 109–10).

[7] Ibid., 124–29.

people."[8] Mirskii's program of uniting with society and increasing legality in government was alien to Nicholas's entire conception of autocracy, which embraced more than the unlimited power of the tsar. At one point in the conversations Nicholas proposed an Assembly of the Land, which could express his direct bond with the people and circumvent "society," which from 1881 had been excluded from the conception of Russia expressed in the national myth.

Nonetheless Nicholas kept his promise to move forward, despite pressure from the court and from his uncle, the grand duke Sergei, who resigned in protest in November 1904. In December a conference of leading state officials considered Mirskii's reforms and approved a program that included a provision for elected officials to consider measures in a separate chamber from the State Council. Nicholas now wavered, pressed by Grand Duke Sergei and, most important, Witte. In a conversation with the tsar, while the grand duke was present, Witte suggested that allowing elective representatives would amount to Russia's following universal trends, that is, the path to constitutionalism. This violated the conception of the unique character of Russian autocracy intrinsic to the national myth, and Nicholas refused to approve the recommendation. The decree of December 12, 1904, listed proposed reforms without public participation. After the removal of the provision, Mirskii remarked: "Everything has failed. Let us build jails."[9]

The increased freedom of Mirskii's rule, however, allowed the oppositional movement to spread. A *zemstvo* congress, which he permitted to take place in Petersburg in November 1904, was taken over by constitutionalists, who rejected Shipov's moderate plans for participation. A banquet campaign, following the example of the revolution of 1848 in Paris, spread to twenty-six Russian cities. Many banquets agreed on calls for participation in government, others for a constituent assembly, all for the granting of freedoms. They were reported in the press and appealed for support from other groups, students, and workers. The banquets continued into January.[10]

On January 9, 1905, a mass of workers led by Father Gapon, a figure active in police unions, marched peacefully to the Winter Palace to present demands for a representative assembly in addition to the rectification of their particular economic grievances. The massacre that ensued, when the troops protecting the palace fired on the workers, left hundreds dead. For many workers and peasants, it undermined the image of the tsar. The massacre unleashed strikes of workers and professional organizations and gave impetus to the formation of political parties that would demand a part in government. It desecrated the symbols of Russian monarchy. The Winter Palace was now marked as a symbol of despotism and Nicholas as the executioner of his own people. Moscow, the principal scene of the national

[8] Ibid., 134.
[9] Ibid., 137–39; Ascher, *The Revolution of 1905: Russia in Disarray*, 70–72.
[10] Ibid., 61–73.

myth was gripped by strikes after Bloody Sunday.[11] In February 1905 a member of the Socialist Revolutionary Party gained access to the Kremlin and hurled a bomb, killing the grand duke Sergei. At the same time, the authorities became concerned about the loyalty of the army. Disturbances among sailors on the Black Sea culminated in the mutiny of the crew of the battleship *Potemkin* and the temporary deactivation of the entire Black Sea fleet.

In the spring and summer of 1905 the revolution spread to the village. Peasants, particularly in the central Russian provinces where communal land tenure predominated, began to pillage, loot, and set fire to estates. Kursk, the town where Nicholas had cordially spoken with peasant deputies in February 1902, became the scene of the first significant agrarian disturbances of 1905, which brought extensive destruction of property and incited unrest in neighboring provinces. Tambov, the site of Nicholas's Sarov celebrations, witnessed some of the most violent disturbances of the year.[12] The 1905 revolution seemingly belied the fundamental premise of the national myth— the Russian people's unswerving devotion to the tsar, which had spared Russia the upheavals of the West.

Under the blows of Bloody Sunday, the concern about foreign loans, the lack of confidence in the loyalty of the army, Nicholas relented once more and accepted the principle of popular participation. The model that appealed to him remained the model of the Assembly of the Land. This would be a national assembly that represented the people without imposing institutional limitations or elevating the leaders of society. On January 31 the minister of agriculture Alexei Ermolov presented a report, written in early-Russian rhetoric, calling for a *zemskii sobor*. Nicholas had to hearken to the people's voice "before Rus' loses faith in its God-given Tsar, in his force and his might." He should summon elective representatives, "from all estates of the Russian land."[13]

On February 18, 1905, Nicholas issued a series of seemingly contradictory directives: a manifesto reaffirming the principles of autocracy and condemning "the malevolent leaders of the insurrectionary movement"; a decree to the Senate, directing the Committee of Ministers to receive opinions from the people—the basis for the receiving of petitions and letters; and, finally, a rescript to the new minister of the interior Alexander Bulygin an-

---

[11] On Moscow in 1905, see Laura Engelstein, *Moscow, 1905: Working Class Organization and Political Conflict* (Stanford, 1982).

[12] Kursk ranked third and Tambov fifth of European Russian provinces in total property damage inflicted during 1905 (Manning, *The Crisis of the Old Order in Russia*, 142–43; Maureen Perrie, *The Agrarian Policy of the Russian Socialist-Revolutionary Party from its Origins through the Revolution of 1905–1907* (Cambridge, 1976), 101; Gerold Tanquary Robinson, *Rural Russia under the Old Regime* (New York, 1961), 155–56; Ascher, *The Revolution of 1905: Russia in Disarray*, 267–68).

[13] Verner, *The Crisis of Russian Autocracy*, 170–73.

nouncing the tsar's wish to assemble "the worthiest people" to head a commission to draft plans for a representative institution.[14] These directives flowed from Nicholas's twin beliefs in his obligation to rule forcefully and in the bond between himself and the Russian people. He declared his beliefs before a delegation of fourteen *zemstvo* workers he received at Peterhof on June 6. Nicholas declared, "Let there be, as there was of old, that unity between Tsar and all *Rus'*, the meeting between me and the people of the land that forms the basis of the system resting on unique (*samobytnye*) Russian principles."[15]

In the complex formulation of an election law, Nicholas, the grand duke Vladimir, and even Pobedonostsev worked to ensure a substantial representation of the peasantry. The initial project, formulated under Bulygin and Sergei Kryzhanovskii utilized a system of separate curias used to elect the *zemstva*. The principle to be applied was suffrage based on property, except for the peasants, who would vote by communes. The scheme aimed to reproduce the *zemstvo*'s composition, with a dominant noble majority. But at a special conference to review the proposals, the grand dukes and Pobedonostsev raised questions about the nobles' loyalty, in view of the activity of the *zemstvo* constitutionalist movement. The conference introduced a provision guaranteeing the peasants at least fifty-one deputies. Another provision for the same reason eliminated a literacy requirement for Duma deputies.[16] This part of the Bulygin project would be carried over to the law of December 11, 1905, which governed the elections to the State Duma.

On the other hand, most of the urban population, including the entire working class, was left without franchise. Furthermore, the Duma would have only a consultative voice. It would pass on all legislation but the government could issue laws without its approval if it gained the consent of the State Council, which remained an entirely appointive body. Nicholas considered that the institutions, which would make known the needs of the people, did not conflict with the principle of autocratic power. In the manifesto of August 3 Nicholas expressed the hope that the deputies would justify his confidence and that they would "render to Us useful and zealous assistance in Our toils for the sake of Our common Mother Russia, to uphold the unity, security, and greatness of the State as well as national order and prosperity."[17] He clearly felt confident that the project did not jeopardize his absolute power. When several officers of the Preobrazhenskii Guards asked whether military men could serve as deputies, Nicholas replied, "Military men, mem-

[14] Ascher, *The Revolution of 1905: Russia in Disarray*, 180–81.

[15] *Polnoe sobranie rechei Imperatora Nikolaia II* (St. Petersburg, 1906), 57–58; Verner, *The Crisis of Russian Autocracy*, 195–96.

[16] The clearest and most succinct description of the elector system is given by Emmons, *The Formation of Political Parties*, 11–13; and Verner, *The Crisis of Russian Autocracy*, 205–14.

[17] Verner, *The Crisis of Russian Autocracy*, 213–14.

bers of the Duma? On the contrary, they must dissolve the Duma if this is required."[18]

The plan convinced the leaders of the Liberation movement that they could no longer count on major reforms by personal appeals to the tsar. They increasingly sought democratic support among urban workers and peasants.[19] The strike movement continued, culminating in the great general strike of October 1905. On October 9 Witte argued that to pacify the country the government had to ally with liberal and moderate elements against the revolutionary parties in building a civil order. But Nicholas saw no difference between moderates and revolutionaries. He continued to believe that it was the weakness and ineptitude of officials that caused the problems. On October 12 he ordered the Petersburg governor-general Dmitrii Trepov to end the unrest. Trepov sent out a directive to police chiefs "to act in the most drastic manner . . . not stopping at the application of force." But the directive was ignored. Nicholas then decided to appoint his cousin, Nicholas Nikolaevich, to serve as military dictator, but the grand duke refused to serve, threatening to shoot himself if the tsar did not agree to Witte's suggestion for representative government. By now, even Trepov was warning of a blood bath if a dictatorship was instituted.[20]

On October 17, 1905, Nicholas II issued the October Manifesto, drafted under the guidance of Sergei Witte, which promised the establishment of a State Duma, elected by all classes of the population, without whose agreement no law could go into effect. The manifesto also granted the basic civil liberties, personal inviolability, freedom of religion, speech, assembly, and association. On the same day Nicholas appointed a cabinet headed by Witte, Russia's first prime minister, who was responsible to the tsar. The manifesto brought general rejoicing at what society regarded as the end of absolute monarchy. Clearly, however, Nicholas believed that the very issuing of the manifesto was a confirmation of autocratic authority. His reasoning came out in a disagreement over the form the announcement of the concessions would take. Witte had urged Nicholas merely to declare that he had asked him, as prime minister, to formulate the projects and work out the details of the new institutions. In this way, he argued, the tsar would not bind himself with promises. But, Verner has persuasively argued, Nicholas believed that such a measure would make it seem that the reform came from state officials, representing a break from the old system of personal rule of the tsar himself. Nicholas insisted on a manifesto which clearly indicated that the reform was the tsar's grant for the benefit of the people. In this way he denied a break between the autocracy and the new order. He appeared as

[18] Epanchin, *Na sluzhbe trekh imperatorov*, 324–25.
[19] Ascher, *The Revolution of 1905: Russia in Disarray*, 180–82.
[20] Ibid., 222–28.

the founder of the new system and, having founded it, clearly felt himself entitled to change it when he saw fit.[21]

Indeed, the events after the manifesto seemed to confirm the tsar's misgivings. In a letter to his mother two days after it was issued, Nicholas lamented, "Nothing but strikes in educational institutions, pharmacies, etc., killings of townspeople, Cossacks, and soldiers, various disorders, riots, and mutinies. And the Messrs. Ministers, like chicken-hearts, assemble and discuss how to achieve unity of all ministers instead of acting decisively."[22] Disturbances continued through November and December.

Nicholas found, in Peter Durnovo, the person who would respond ruthlessly and energetically to the challenge. Nicholas distrusted Durnovo, who seemed to him a bureaucrat concerned for his own power, unlike Trepov, who had ties with the court and imperial family. But Witte recommended him strongly, and Nicholas appointed him minister of the interior. Durnovo was hated in educated society for his unscrupulous repression of the opposition. His appointment reinforced the suspicions of moderate leaders like Dmitrii Shipov and Alexander Guchkov, who now refused to consider participating in Witte's cabinet.[23]

Durnovo lived up to his reputation. With energy and unswerving determination, he reorganized the administration and sent governor-generals to provincial towns to quell the uprisings. Nicholas's correspondence indicated his approval of Durnovo's brutal and effective retribution. He exulted at the obliteration of insurgent groups and the execution of insurrectionary workers. In a letter to his mother about the bloody suppression of the Bolshevik armed uprising in December 1905, Nicholas expressed his relief and his expectation that the same tactic would be used elsewhere. "Terror must be answered by terror. Now, Witte himself has realized this."[24]

At the same time, Nicholas remained convinced that the majority of the people remained personally loyal to him. He had written to his mother on October 25, 1905, defending the pogroms. He claimed that "nine-tenths of the troublemakers are Jews" and that the people had turned against them violently for that reason. "But not only the kikes suffered; so did the Russian agitators, engineers, lawyers, and all kinds of other bad people."[25] Because of his hatred of Jews and any group opposed to the monarchy, he regarded the pogroms as an expression of the unity of tsar and people and sympathized with the extreme right anti-Semitic organization, the Union of Russian

[21] Verner, *The Crisis of Russian Autocracy*, 239–41.

[22] Ibid., 234.

[23] Ibid., 250–51. For a vivid characterization of Durnovo as man and minister, see Dominic Lieven, *Russia's Rulers under the Old Regime* (New Haven, 1989), 207–16.

[24] Verner, *The Crisis of Russian Autocracy*, 272–75.

[25] Ibid., 260.

People.[26] Nicholas approved all petitions for pardon submitted by members convicted for participation in pogroms.[27]

On December 23, 1905, a delegation of the Union of Russian People presented Nicholas with two badges of the Union, one for himself and one for the tsarevich. Not only was the tsar honored by this moment but apparently deemed it proper for a report about it to appear in the pages of the nationalist, monarchist newspaper *Moskovskie Vedomosti*. Nicholas accepted the badges with thanks, and then declared: "The burden of power placed on Me in the Moscow Kremlin I will bear Myself, and I am certain that the Russian people will help Me. I will be accountable for My authority before God." A member delivered a speech declaring that the tsar should not accept those put forward by Masons and others "who depend on foreigners." The Russian people had crossed themselves before the tsar, and the tsar should rely on "Russian people." "No gates of hell will overcome the Russian Tsar, surrounded by his people." The tsar replied, "Yes, I believe with your help, I and the Russian people will succeed in defeating the enemies of Russia."[28]

The election law of December 11, 1905, worked out by Witte and Kryzhanovskii, merely extended the systems of curiae, proposed for the Bulygin Duma, to the workers and urban population. The workers received their own curia, but no minimum of seats like the peasants. As a result, the workers occupied 2.5 percent of electors' seats in provincial elector assemblies compared to 43 percent for the peasants and 34 percent for rural landowners.[29] The peasants, though their representation was considerably less than their numerical weight in the population, would determine the complexion of the next Duma. Many officials, including Witte himself, and those close to the tsar thought this expedient, since they believed that the peasants remained devoted to the tsar.[30] The grand duke Constantine Konstantinovich also placed his hopes in the peasants. He wrote in his diary on October 26, 1905: "My companions and I all maintain our support for autocratic government and nurture the hope that if many peasant deputies are elected to the State Duma, then it may be possible to return to the autocratic model of government, which undoubtedly has the support of our peasant masses."[31] In February 1906 a new State Council was created, half elective from estates and institutions, half appointed by the emperor to act as a counterweight to the Duma.

In April 1906, shortly before the elections, deliberations began on new Fundamental Laws to formalize the reforms in the state system introduced

[26] On Nicholas's relations with the Union of the Russian People, during and after the 1905 revolution, see Heinz-Dietrich Löwe, *Antisemitismus und reaktionäre Utopie: Russischer Konservatismus im Kampf gegen den Wandel von Staat und Gesellschaft* (Hamburg, 1978), 96–100.

[27] A. S. Tager, *Tsarskaia Rossiia i delo Beilisa* (Moscow, 1933), 39–40.

[28] *MV*, January 15, 1906, 2.

[29] Emmons, *The Formation of Political Parties*, 12–14.

[30] Verner, *The Crisis of Russian Autocracy*, 288–91.

[31] "Dnevnik v. kn. Konstantin Konstantinovich, 10/8/05–11/6/06," GARF, 660-1-55, 90.

since October. The question arose regarding the definition of the monarch's power in Article 1 of the Fundamental Laws as "autocratic and unlimited" (*samoderzhavnyi i neogranichennyi*). Both adjectives had been removed in the draft of the Duma charter of February 20, 1906, but Nicholas had insisted on retaining the term *autocratic*. By the April conference Nicholas wanted the word *unlimited* restored as well. He had been convinced to return to the old terminology by the ebbing of the revolution and the campaign of letters and telegrams, organized by those opposed to the October Manifesto in the government and the far-right parties. He described "the touching feelings of loyal subjects, together with the plea not to limit My power." In fact, the telegrams wrote of the authors' desire to restore autocracy and said nothing about limitations, but, in their minds, that clearly meant the return of the tsar's unlimited prerogatives. Reproach, Nicholas declared at the conference, would come from "the so-called educated element, the proletarians, the third element. But I am certain that 80 percent of the Russian people will be with me."[32]

At the April conference, therefore, Nicholas insisted on the old definition of "unlimited and autocratic." In his mind the existence of the new representative institutions in no way constrained his right to dispense with them if he so wished. But the officials thought otherwise, observing that the new institutions did limit the tsar's power in some ways. Nicholas relented on the term *unlimited*, but *autocratic* remained in the Fundamental Laws issued on April 23, 1906. However, *autocratic* had one meaning for the leading state officials, another for the tsar. For the officials, it meant that the tsar received his power from God and his forbears.[33] For the tsar himself, it meant that he remained sovereign, that he retained the primary legislative authority that allowed him to issue the October Manifesto, that he was the creator of the new institutions, and that he alone could change them.[34] It was this conviction—that the Duma was an extension of the tsar's autocratic will and that its deputies were obliged to earn his confidence—that he expressed in his speech to the first Duma on April 27, 1906.

THE MONARCHY AND THE DUMAS

The results of the elections to the first State Duma immediately dispelled the illusions of a conservative, monarchist peasantry. The peasants voted heavily for the opposition parties, the Constitutional Democrats (Kadets) and the Laborer (*Trudovik*) Party, which promised expropriation of noble estates. Nicholas used the official reception of Duma deputies to make clear that he remained sovereign. His moderate advisers urged him to appear at the Taur-

---

[32] Verner, *The Crisis of Russian Autocracy*, 299–300.
[33] Ibid., 299.
[34] Emmons makes this point well in *The Formation of Political Parties*, 16–17.

ide Palace, in the precinct of the Duma, as a gesture of conciliation. He chose instead to follow the German example for the opening of the Reichstag, namely, to address the deputies in sovereign precincts amid sovereign symbols.[35] The reception took place in the throne room of the Winter Palace.

The ceremony impressed the deputies and the world with the apparent distance between the autocracy—that is, the emperor, the imperial family, the members of the court, and the officials in the State Council—and the elected deputies of the Duma.[36] On the right side of the hall stood the members of the State Council, courtiers and generals, wearing braided uniforms decorated with medals, and the ladies of the court in the decolleté "Russian dress" and *kokoshnik* tiaras worn at the highest state occasions. The women of the imperial family were bedecked in jewels, Assistant Minister of the Interior V. I. Gurko wrote, "naively believing that the people's representatives, many of whom were peasants, would be awed by the splendor of the Imperial court."[37]

Whereas the right side was harmonious in its uniformity, the Duma deputies standing on the left presented a motley picture, revealing the political and national diversity of the empire. Some of the liberal deputies dressed simply to demonstrate their identification with the common people. The American ambassador George L. Meyer wrote: "The contrast between those on the left and those on the right was the greatest that one could imagine, one being a real representation of different classes of this great Empire, the other of what the autocracy and bureaucracy has been."[38] Alexander Izvol'skii, who marched in the cortège as a chamberlain, remarked that among the deputies the dress that "predominated was not even the simple dress of the bourgeois, but rather the long *caftan* of the peasant or the factory workman's blouse. . . . The faces of the deputies, as they passed, were lighted by triumph in some cases and in others distorted by hatred, making altogether a spectacle intensely dramatic and symbolic."[39] The English journalist Henry Nevinson described a microcosm of the empire:

> Sturdy peasants in homespun cloth, one Little Russian in brilliant purple with broad blue breeches, one Lithuanian Catholic bishop in violet robes, three Tatar Mullahs with turbans and long gray cassocks, a Balkan peasant in white embroidered coat, four Orthodox monks with shaggy hair, a few ordinary gentlemen in evening dress, and the vast body of the elected in the clothes of every day.[40]

[35] Ascher, *The Revolution of 1905: Authority Restored*, (Stanford, 1992), 82; Izvolsky, *Recollections of a Foreign Minister*, 74.

[36] Ascher, *The Revolution of 1905: Authority Restored*, 82–84; Henry W. Nevinson, *The Dawn in Russia; or, Scenes in the Russian Revolution* (New York, 1906), 320–26; Epanchin, *Na sluzhbe trekh imperatorov*, 351.

[37] Ascher, *The Revolution of 1905: Authority Restored*, 85.

[38] Ibid., 83–84.

[39] Izvolsky, *Recollections of a Foreign Minister*, 74–76.

[40] Nevinson, *The Dawn in Russia*, 322.

52. Nicholas II's Speech to Duma Deputies, April 17, 1906. From *L'Illustration*.
General Research Division, New York Public Library. Astor, Lenox,
and Tilden Foundations.

The tsar set himself apart from both groups by entering in a formal imperial procession to the strains of "God Save the Tsar." Masters of Ceremony led with their maces; behind them court officials carried the imperial regalia. Following them came twelve Palace Grenadiers, then the emperor, flanked by the two empresses and followed by the members of the imperial family. After entering, the tsar kissed the metropolitan of St. Petersburg, who then held a brief prayer service. He ascended the steps and sat on the throne, which had been draped with the imperial mantle, it was said by the empress herself, in artistic folds. The imperial crown and other items of regalia were visible on stools at his side. The scene was caught in photographs published in newspapers and leading periodicals and a large painting that was publicly exhibited (fig. 52).[41]

The reception was staged to place the regalia at the focal point of the hall. Brought from Moscow for the occasion, the regalia confirmed the sacred sources of Nicholas's authority. They demonstrated the tsar's abiding preeminence as spokesman of the nation. Speaking down to the Duma representatives from the steps of the throne, Nicholas declared that Providence had moved him "to summon elected deputies from the people to help in legislation." He expressed his trust in them both to clarify the needs of the peas-

---

[41] See Peter Kurth, *The Lost World of Nicholas and Alexandra: Tsar* (Boston, 1995).

antry and to advance the education and prosperity of the people. He admonished them that, for these goals, "not only is freedom necessary but so, too, is order on the basis of law." He declared his "intense desire to see my people happy and to bequeath my son an inheritance of a strong, well-ordered, and enlightened state." He called upon God to bless his labors, "in union with the State Council and State Duma," and asked that the day mark "the renewal of the moral face of the Russian Land, the day of the rebirth of its best forces." Nicholas concluded by exhorting the deputies to turn to their work with "reverence" (*blagogovenie*) and asked them to justify the trust of tsar and people.[42]

The speech received loud applause from the right of the hall and hostile silence from the left. Not only had Nicholas continued to speak of "my" people; he had failed to make a gesture of conciliation by issuing an amnesty for political prisoners. The deputies returned to the Tauride Palace where they drafted an indignant response. Later that day Nicholas wrote in his diary that he had worked for a long time, "but with a light heart after the successful completion of the ceremony."[43]

•

The meetings of the first Duma, from April to July 1906, witnessed a struggle between the government and the Duma leadership. Witte had resigned over a disagreement concerning the government's land policy and was replaced by Ivan Goremykin, a courtier completely amenable to the tsar. The Kadets and the *Trudovik* Party demanded expropriation of land for the benefit of the peasants and a cabinet responsible to the Duma, neither of which the tsar would accept. In the meantime, disturbances in the countryside and terrorist attacks on officials continued, leading to a perpetuation of siege conditions. On June 20, 1906, the government issued a warning not to believe the deputies' promises of land. On July 6 the Duma issued a statement vowing to pass a law of expropriation. On July 9 Nicholas dissolved the first Duma, which had met for less than three months, and appointed the minister of the interior Peter Stolypin as prime minister, to bring the crisis to an end.

Stolypin had distinguished himself as governor of Saratov Province, where he had won the tsar's admiration by his courageous and decisive use of force to pacify widespread insurrections among the peasants and the military. As prime minister, he combined a policy of ruthless repression of insurrection with conciliatory gestures toward moderate society. He set before himself the task of restoration of order, using force if necessary, but at the same time insisting on the observation of strict legal norms. After his appointment he sent a circular to all provincial governors, declaring that "the struggle is

[42] *NV*, April 28, 1906, 1.

[43] Izvolsky, *Recollections of a Foreign Minister*, 77–78. But Izvolskii recalled erroneously that the tsar pronounced the word *constitution* in his speech; *Dnevniki Imperatora Nikolaia II*, 312.

being waged not against society but against the enemies of society. Therefore indiscriminate repression cannot be approved. Unconsidered and illegal actions, which generate resentment rather than pacification, are intolerable."[44]

Nicholas continued to consider force as the means to defend authority.[45] On August 12, 1906, when a bomb planted by Socialist Revolutionaries in Stolypin's suburban villa left twenty-six dead and Stolypin's son and daughter seriously injured, Nicholas demanded that the prime minister find ways to realize his "inexorable will to eradicate sedition and restore order." Fearing that the tsar might choose to establish a dictatorship, Stolypin submitted a proposal for field court-martials to counter terrorism. It was issued on August 19, 1906, as an emergency decree, under Article 87 of the Fundamental Laws.

The decree assigned governor-generals the power to bring revolutionaries before military courts, which could issue summary sentences, including death. While court-martials had been included in the emergency provisions governing most of Russia during the revolution, they did not forego rules of legal procedure and could be appealed. The law of August 19, 1906, dispensed even with an investigation when guilt was "so obvious" that one was not necessary. Only Stolypin and the minister of justice Ivan Shcheglovitov opposed. The decree turned the countryside into a battlefield. Between 1906 and 1909 the field court-martials sentenced nearly twenty-seven hundred people to execution. In these three years more people lost their lives for political crimes than during the entire nineteenth century. In addition, more than twenty-two thousand were sent into administrative exile.[46]

While Stolypin defended and supported the field court-martials, his goal was the creation of a new political nation made up of property owners who would have a stake in defending the state and the monarchy. This grew out of the view embraced by Witte and others in the bureaucracy that the government could lead society. But it also involved a transformation of the peasantry, by dissolving the commune. Provinces with communal land tenure were the site of the most frequent and violent insurrections, convincing many officials and noblemen that the commune, rather than a bulwark of order, had become a hotbed of peasant rage.[47] The landed nobility supported Stolypin's program of the protection of property and the dissolution of the peasant commune while calling for a narrowing of the electorate for the Duma.[48]

---

[44] Geoffrey A. Hosking, *The Russian Constitutional Experiment: Government and Duma, 1907–1914* (Cambridge, 1973), 23–24.

[45] On Nicholas's "unflinching determination to use force against opponents," see Steinberg, "Nicholas and Alexandra," 25.

[46] See the illuminating analyses of these court-martials in Ascher, *The Revolution of 1905: Authority Restored*, 244–49; William C. Fuller Jr., *Civil-Military Conflict in Imperial Russia, 1881–1914* (Princeton, N.J., 1985), 173–74.

[47] Macey, *Government and Peasant in Russia*, 34.

[48] For a thorough analysis of the nobility's shift to the Right after the revolution, see Manning, *The Crisis of the Old Order in Russia*, 131–321.

In November 1906, under Article 87, Stolypin began issuing the laws that would permit the breakup of peasant communes and the establishment of separate farms, which would be held with individual property rights. Article 87 required that the Duma confirm the decrees when the next assembly resumed sessions. But the elections to the second Duma, which convened in March 1907, increased the strength of the Left. The majority of deputies continued to demand expropriation of land and refused to approve the laws. On June 3, 1907, Nicholas issued a manifesto announcing the dissolution of the second Duma. A new electoral law was introduced under Article 87. This violated the Fundamental Laws, which specifically barred the use of the emergency provisions to change the electoral law.[49]

The manifesto of June 3, 1907, is usually referred to as the Stolypin "coup d'état." But the prime minister once more had acted only under the emperor's insistent prodding. On June 2, when Nicholas signed the law, he wrote to Stolypin that delay in dissolving the Duma was "intolerable." "It is necessary to display decisiveness and firmness to Russia. . . . There must be no delay, not one minute of hesitation! God favors the bold!" In the decree of June 3, announcing the dissolution of the Duma, Nicholas declared that he would continue to honor the rights granted by the October Manifesto but would change only "the means of summoning deputies from the people" to the Duma. He insisted that the Duma, "created for the strengthening of the Russian state (*gosudarstvo rossiiskoe*), must be Russian (*russkii*) in spirit as well," and although other nationalities should have deputies, they should not be allowed to decide "purely Russian" questions. These problems could not be decided by legislative means but only by the authority giving the first law—"the historical Power of the Russian Tsar." He emphasized, "It is from the Lord, God, that imperial power over our people is entrusted to us. Before His throne we will answer for the fate of the Russian state."[50]

The call for a legislature "Russian in spirit" meant, in practice, a sharp reduction in the representation of other nationalities such as Poles, Tatars, and Armenians and the exclusion of deputies from Eastern borderlands such as the Steppe and Turkestan regions.[51] It also reflected the central theme of the national myth that identified all those who resisted the monarch's power as not truly Russian, as enemies of the state. Nicholas's telegram to the Union of the Russian People, which had campaigned for the Duma's dissolution and for a restoration of true autocracy, gives a sense of the future reality he envisioned for Russia: "I am confident that now all the truly faithful and affectionate sons of the Russian homeland will unite still more closely, and as they continually increase their numbers they will assist Me in bringing

[49] Ascher, *The Revolution of 1905: Authority Restored*, 351–57.

[50] *Ibid.*, 351; PSZ 3, no. 29240 (June 3, 1907).

[51] Ascher, *The Revolution of 1905: Authority Restored*, 354.

about a peaceful renewal of our great and holy Russia and in improving the goodly way of life of her people."[52]

Stolypin also desired a legislature "Russian in spirit," but his concept of the Russian nation differed sharply from Nicholas's belief in a unity between tsar and people. Stolypin strove to make the state the focus of national unity. The state would unite landholders of all classes, including peasant proprietors and merchant and industrial capitalists. Property would ensure a widespread interest in order and legality that would break down estate barriers; it would inspire a state spirit (*gosudarstvennost'*) among all groups in Russia who would find in it a champion of Russian domination in the empire and abroad.

Stolypin appealed to the patriotic feelings of the peasants through the ministry's organ, *Sel'skii Vestnik*, which the government, after 1905, had sought to make more accessible and appealing. He sent memorandums to other ministries urging them to circulate the newspaper through their agencies. To the minister of war he emphasized that the newspaper would keep alive the soldiers' national sense, so they "would remember with pleasure and love the native surroundings from which they have just departed."[53]

The prime minister looked to England as a model of national imperialism. He wanted to continue the efforts to subordinate Finnish legislation to the laws of the empire, but with the popular support of all Russians expressed through the Duma. He shared the sense of Russian supremacy widespread in the state administration, which increasingly regarded other nationalities not as participants in the empire but as subject people.[54] Their attitudes were reflected in the broadening of the meaning of the word *aliens* (*inorodtsy*), beyond its original significance of Jews and nomadic people, to include all non-Russian nationalities, in some cases even Ukrainians.[55] During Stolypin's tenure, the policy of Russification, suspended during the revolution, was revived, with the support of nationalists in the Duma, particularly in Finland and Poland, Ukraine, and the Baltic and Western provinces.[56]

---

[52] The telegram was immediately printed in the party newspaper *Russoe Znamia* (Ascher, *The Revolution of 1905: Authority Restored*, 357–58).

[53] See the excellent and important discussion of these tendencies in Krukones, *To the People*, 191–212.

[54] In the prime minister's speech to the Duma on May 5, 1908, he called on the deputies to assist the tsar, who was "trying to gather the scattered pieces of the edifice of Russian national feeling." He invoked the memory of Peter the Great and then warned them that "peoples sometimes forget their national problems, but those people perish, they turn into dung, into fertilizer, from which other stronger people rise and grow strong" (P. A. Stolypin, *Rechi v Gosudarstvennoi dume i Gosudarstvennom sovete, 1906–1911* [New York, 1990], 122–23). On the appearance of a feeling of national supremacy among tsarist administrators, see Weeks, *Nation and State in Late Imperial Russia*, 68–69.

[55] John W. Slocum, "Who, and When, Were the *Inorodtsy*? The Evolution of the Category of 'Aliens' in Imperial Russia," *The Russian Review* 57 (April 1998): 173–90.

[56] Hugh Seton-Watson, *The Decline of Imperial Russia, 1855–1914* (New York, 1964), 303–13.

Stolypin's state nationalism presumed the development of a cultural and historical sense that united a nation apart from the tsar. This type of thinking is evidenced in a memorandum written by one of Stolypin's subordinates in the Ministry of the Interior, P. M. Koshkin. Koshkin argued for the building of "Romanov houses" for the people throughout the empire. He emphasized the need to develop patriotism through education, which would be carried on by priests and teachers, from "the precepts of our ancient native traditions."[57] These precepts would not be found in the tsar or the dynasty, but in monuments of ancient Russia. Koshkin elaborated a program of trips through the empire to acquaint pupils with historical sites. Monuments scattered through the Russian land would nurture national feeling. Russia, he indicated, should follow the example of such trips in Germany, which he thought were a cause of the surge of German patriotism in the previous century. The scenes of the Russian past and artifacts collected in museums like the Romanov houses would turn abstract concepts into a living emotional sense of the land.[58] Decorated with shields and portraits of the tsars, these buildings would hold both historical museums and archives and present "a kind of pantheon, a depository of Russian traditions," which would promote the "patriotic mood of the visitors."[59]

The new electoral law attained Stolypin's goal of strengthening the conservative and nationalist forces in the third Duma, which served its full term from 1907 to 1912. The Octobrist Party, the party of landholders and industrialists, held a plurality, and at least for a while the prime minister was able to develop a working relationship with their leader, the Old-Believer industrialist Alexander Guchkov. The Duma approved of Stolypin's land laws, providing for the dissolution of the peasant commune. The Octobrist leadership cooperated with Stolypin to introduce reforms of the army and navy and laws for the development of universal primary education.

But the coalition with Guchkov and the conservative group was precarious. Stolypin's vision included an "all-class *zemstvo*," which had been discussed in the bureaucracy since the Kakhanov commission in the early 1880s. The conservative landed nobility, however, now organized to defeat such proposals. His attempt to introduce *zemstvo* institutions in the Western provinces that would favor Russian peasants against Polish and Lithuanian landlords, also encountered stiff resistance among conservative nobles, both

---

[57] The memorandum was presented in November 1910 to the Tercentenary Committee, which refused to adopt Koshkin's recommendations (*ZKT*, 20–21).

[58] Ibid., 21. Koshkin thus tried to evoke the sense of a *Heimat* (homeland) through what Anthony D. Smith described as the "sacred sites, buildings, and natural features that 'locate' a community in a landscape." On the *Heimat* movement in Germany, see Alon Confino, "The Nation as a Local Metaphor: Heimat, National Memory, and the German Empire, 1871–1918," *History and Memory* 5, no. 1 (1993): 42–85; Anthony D. Smith, *The Ethnic Origins of Nations* (Oxford, 1986), 188. For a different localized conception of the term, see Celia Applegate, *A Nation of Provincials: The German Idea of Heimat* (Berkeley, 1990).

[59] *ZKT*, 21.

inside and outside the Duma. Although Stolypin remained in power until his assassination on September 1, 1911, he no longer commanded the support of a moderate bloc that could allow him to speak for the nation. Octobrists and Kadets objected to his use of Article 87 and the government's continued abridgement of freedoms. Conservatives were alienated by projects that threatened the interests of the landed nobility.

BONDS WITH THE PEOPLE

Nicholas had little sympathy for Stolypin's vision of a state nationalism, united by a feeling of ownership and sentimental attachment to the land. His bonds with the people were personal, displayed in fervent expressions of spiritual kinship and mutual devotion, inspiring an almost mystical sense of exaltation. His family life at Tsarskoe Selo became the principal site of his communion with the people. There he gathered around him those who shared his views, his symbolic elite, now shrunk to those hostile to the institutions of state. Nicholas felt closest to the heads of his security corps, the guards officers he knew—the minister of the court Count Fredericks, the palace commandants Vladimir Dediulin and Vladimir Voeikov, and the chief of the palace administration Michael Putiatin—who avoided expressing opinions that might contradict the emperor's.[60]

In addition, Nicholas continued to be susceptible to figures outside the bureaucracy who played on his distrust of his ministers. One such individual was Michael Andronikov, a person associated with Meshcherskii, Rasputin, and the police. Andronikov traded in rumors and intrigue against government officials. He circulated passionate critiques of Stolypin that were apparently intended for the eyes of the tsar. A memorandum of 1910 accused Stolypin of seeking to usurp the tsar's power, impoverishing the peasantry, and creating a destitute, landless proletariat. Andronikov also charged the other ministers with trying to thwart the tsar's will.[61]

The one person who enjoyed Nicholas's complete trust was the empress. Mark Steinberg has made clear that Alexandra's political views were identical to her husband's on all significant issues—the importance of the assertion of autocratic power, its divine sources, and the devotion of the people to the throne. Alexandra brought the Victorian conception of the wife as strong and supportive helpmeet into the Russian imperial household. Her impassioned advocacy of these views before the tsar reinforced Nicholas's beliefs and gave him the reassurance that he sought among all he trusted.[62]

---

[60] Mosolov, *Pri dvore poslednego Rossiiskogo imperatora*, 113–14.

[61] Sir Bernard Pares, *The Fall of the Russian Monarchy* (New York, 1961), 283–84; Iu. B. Solov'ev, "Politicheskaia smert' P. A. Stolypina," in *Gosudarstvennaia deiatel'nost' P. A. Stolypina: sbornik statei*, (Moscow, 1994), 137–53.

[62] For an analysis of Alexandra's ideas and their relationship to Nicholas's, see Steinberg, "Nicholas and Alexandra," 34–36.

They found further support for their views in the "men of God," who congregated in their chambers at Tsarskoe Selo. Nicholas and Alexandra met Rasputin on November 1, 1905, shortly after the issuing of the October Manifesto, and thought him a man of the people, absolutely devoted to his tsar.[63] In addition to his seemingly miraculous power to stop the tsarevich's bleeding, Rasputin shared the imperial couple's distrust of educated and aristocratic society. He described both the emperor and empress as defenders of the people and religion against the enemies of God. Rasputin addressed Alexandra almost as a saint. She wrote in her notebook a remark he uttered in 1907: "She is the ascetic (*podvizhnitsa*), who, with experience and intelligence, struggles in a holy manner and with skill."[64]

Nicholas was also impressed by Rasputin. His concern for the tsarevich was as great as Alexandra's and grew as he began to present his son as the hope for Russia's future. He wrote to Stolypin in October 1906: "He [Rasputin] made a remarkably strong impression both on her Majesty and myself, so that instead of five minutes our conversation went on for more than an hour." He told General Dediulin that Rasputin was "just a good, religious, simple-minded Russian. When in trouble or assailed by doubts, I like to have a talk with him and invariably feel at peace with myself afterward." Nicholas's diaries mention numerous long conversations with Rasputin, without however suggesting their content. Stolypin warned Nicholas about having Rasputin close to him and, in 1911, banished him from the capital. This step only confirmed Nicholas's beliefs. That same year he sent Rasputin as a personal emissary to Nizhnii-Novgorod to determine the qualifications of the governor of the province, A. N. Khvostov, to serve as Stolypin's replacement as minister of the interior.[65]

At Tsarskoe Selo Nicholas and Alexandra created their own replica of an early-Russian town, the *Feodorovskii gorodok*, built for the tsar's personal convoy and for his Majesty's Rifles. The centerpiece was the Feodorov Cathedral (1908–12), dedicated to the Feodorov Mother of God—the protectress of the dynasty. The official name of the church, *Feodorovskii Gosudarev Sobor* (the Sovereigns' Feodorov Cathedral), made it clear that it was the domain of the tsar and tsaritsa. The sums for the church came from the tsar's cabinet and from his personal funds.[66]

---

[63] *Dnevniki Imperatora Nikolaia II*, 287.

[64] "Zapisnaia knizhka imp. Aleksandry Fedorovny s vyskazyvaniiami Grigoriia Rasputina (1907–1916) s darstvennoi nadpis'iu Rasputina," GARF, 640-1-309, 38–39, 52–54.

[65] Maylunas and Mironenko, *A Lifelong Passion*, 296–97, 314, 320–22, 328–30, 341, 343, 350–74, 376; M. V. Rodzianko, *The Reign of Rasputin: An Empire's Collapse* (London, 1927), 11; Pares, *The Fall of the Russian Monarchy*, 143; A. Ia. Avrekh, *Tsarizm i IV Duma* (Moscow, 1981), 255.

[66] Kirichenko, *Russkii stil'*, 367, 372; Ekaterina Abrosova, "Arkhitektor Vysochaishego Dvora Vladimir Aleksandrovich Pokrovskii," *Tsar'ino: Pravoslavnyi istoriko-kraevedcheskii almanakh* 4 (1998): 56.

The architect Vladimir Pokrovskii designed the cathedral in the spirit of the neo-Russian school, which sought sources of inspiration for a reborn national architecture in all periods of early-Russian architecture.[67] Pokrovskii took the model of the fifteenth-century Annunciation Cathedral in the Kremlin, which had served as private chapel of the Moscow tsar's family, but attached tent-shaped roofs over the main entrance and the covered vestibules, adding seventeenth-century elements. He also drew on Novgorod motifs for the bell tower. In this respect, the church presented its own amalgam that erased the historical and stylistic distinctions of early-Russian architecture and strove for a contemporary aesthetic true to the past rooted in a popular spirit. Pokrovskii's Railroad Station at Tsarskoe Selo (1910–11) used seventeenth-century *kokoshniki*, tent roofs, and painted vaulted chambers, recalling early-Russian palaces.[68]

The cathedral was intended as a museum of early-Russian religious art that would attest to the rebirth of a national religious tradition.[69] Mosaics in old-Russian style, early-Russian religious items, gold and gems, and icons—among them a copy of the Feodorov Mother of God donated by inhabitants of Kostroma—decorated the interior of the church. For Alexandra, Pokrovskii's assistant, Vladimir Maksimov, constructed a "cave church" in honor of Serafim Sarov below the cathedral, where the imperial family could worship before communion.[70] The walls were painted with motifs from the *terem*, the chamber where women had been kept sequestered in old Russia. The vestibules were decorated with scenes of Hell and Paradise and, above, the fortress of Heaven. The chapel held a pitcher of water from the stream at Sarov, in which the imperial family had bathed, an icon of Serafim, a box with a relic, and a copy of the "Tenderness" icon, which Serafim had kept

[67] On the neo-Russian style, see William Craft Brumfield, "The 'New Style' and the Revival of Orthodox Church Architecture, 1900–1914," in William C. Brumfield and Milos M. Velimirovic, *Christianity and the Arts in Russia* (Cambridge, 1991), 105–23; William Craft Brumfield, *The Origins of Modernism in Russian Architecture* (Berkeley, 1991), esp. chaps. 4 and 6; and Kirichenko, *Russkii stil'*, 305–6.

[68] Kirichenko, *Russkii stil'*, 305–8, 310–11, 366–68.

[69] Abrosova, "Arkhitektor Vysochaishego Dvora Vladimir Aleksandrovich Pokrovskii," 55–56. One of the principal sponsors of the church was the chief of the Tsarskoe Selo Palace Administration Michael Putiatin, a former officer of the Preobrazhenskii Guards and Marshal of the Court. Putiatin was a lover of Russian antiquities, who had helped organize the tsar's visit to Sarov and had designed the shrine for the saint's remains. He closely supervised the decoration of the church and insisted that the iconostasis be in old-Russian style. The church warden was Captain N. Loman, the author of the popular account of the coronation and a popular biography of Alexander II, and an associate of Rasputin (Général Alexandre Spiridovitch, *Les dernières années de la cour de Tsarskoe-Selo* [Paris, 1928–29], 1:352; 2:253–62; Mosolov, *Pri dvore poslednego Rossiiskogo imperatora*, 28, 118).

[70] On Maksimov, his buildings, and his tragic fate under Stalin, see Arkadii Krasheninnikov, "Russkii zodchii Vladimir Nikolaevich Maksimov (1882–1942)," *Tsar'ino: Pravoslavnyi istoriko-kraevedcheskii almanakh* 4 (1998): 63–83.

in his cell, and his pectoral cross.[71] The cathedral thus incorporated the symbols of modern charismatic religion into the artistic motifs of early Russia.

The town was to represent a spiritual model of a reborn nation taken from Russia's distant past. Stepan Krichinskii designed a Kremlin with walls and towers of elaborately decorated white Staritskii limestone.[72] Krichinskii and other neo-Russian architects favored the form of Kremlin walls that emphasized the separation of the church and the town from the outside world. If the models for Alexander III's official Russian style were urban churches in popular style like Vasilii the Blessed and Moscow-Iaroslavl churches, the models for the neo-Russian architects were often old-Russian monasteries, sequestered by walls from the intrusions of the outside world. Their purpose was not admonitory but exemplary, showing the survival and revival of old-Russian piety among those foreswearing the contestation and distractions of contemporary society.[73]

The officers and soldiers of the convoy and His Majesty's Rifles worshiped in the church and lived in the old-Russian-style barracks. They joined in a reenactment of an imagined seventeenth century, on a stage set in early Russia, to set the military-religious entourage of the imperial family apart from the court, state, and Orthodox Church. A contemporary wrote: "As if by magic you were transported to the era of the first Romanov. Your feet sank into thick carpets. You were met by soldiers dressed in the Russian costumes of the time of Michael Fedorovich." The costumes were designed by Victor Vasnetsov. The empress often worshiped not with the congregation but, like seventeenth-century tsaritsas, followed the service from a cell on the side. The cell was dimly lit, the faces of saints peering out, while the brilliant decorations of the altar could be seen through the doors. "From there the service seemed unearthly, the unseen capella sounded like a chorus of angels." The heir, at this and other services, wore national dress—a Russian shirt (*rubashka*), wide trousers (*sharovary*), and high boots—and later a Ukrainian costume and a sailor hat.[74]

---

[71] *Feodorovskii gosudarev sobor v Tsarskom Sele: Vyp. I, Peshchernyi Khram vo imia prepodobnogo Serafima sarovskogo* (Moscow, 1915); *Rodina*, September 16, 1912, 538; Spiridovitch, *Les dernières années de la cour de Tsarskoe-Selo*, 2:253–60; Maurice Paléologue, *Alexandra-Féodorowna, impératrice de Russie* (Paris, n.d.), 51–52; A. N. Naumov, *Iz utselevshikh vospominanii, 1868–1917* (New York, 1954–55), 2:226.

[72] *Pamiatniki arkhitektury prigorodov Leningrada* (Leningrad, 1983), 126–29.

[73] Pokrovskii's unrealized project for a Military-Historical Museum in St. Petersburg is an example of this (Abrosova, "Arkhitektor Vysochaishego Dvora Vladimir Aleksandrovich Pokrovskii," 44–46). See also Maksimov's unrealized projects for the building complex of the Railroad Guards' Regiment and a hotel complex at Tsarskoe Selo (Krasheninnikov, "Russkii zodchii Vladimir Nikolaevich Maksimov," 74).

[74] S. Ia. Ofromisova, "Tsarkaia sem'ia, (iz detskikh vospominanii)," *Russkaia Letopis'* (Paris, 1925), 7:240–41; I. M. Shadrin, "Pridvornaia Pevcheskaia Kapella i Imperatorskii Dvor do Velikoi Voiny 1914–1917gg.," BAR, Shadrin Collection, 55. On the theatricalization of church architecture in the neo-Russian style and particularly in Pokrovskii's Fedorov Sobor, see A. V. Ikonnikov, *Istorizm v arkhitekture* (Moscow, 1997), 304, 310.

The soldiers represented the Russian army and the Russian people united in worship in close union with the emperor and empress. An illustrated luxury album on the lower church, published in 1915 with Church-Slavonic lettering and pagination, described the importance of church buildings for the spirit and moral edification of young soldiers: "The ceaseless blessed effect of the temple of God and church shrines is particularly valuable in our time of upheavals and seductions." The edifices and images of the Orthodox Church had taken on a greater role than the church hierarchy itself. "Before the holy icons of the regimental church, in fervent prayer, and with dear memories of the church in his distant village, the young soldier's spirit is strengthened and gains the strength to fight all temptation." Worshiping in the church the tsar entered into a "a communion of prayer with those soldiers of His army coming out of the depths of the people."[75]

•

With the ebbing of the revolution, Nicholas reaffirmed his bonds both with officers and the rank and file. The use of guards' regiments to suppress the revolution made clear his dependence on elite officers, and this ensured the continued aristocratic domination of the military. After the revolution Nicholas resisted the campaign to professionalize the army, led by the Octobrists in the Duma, which would have shifted authority from status to ability and destroyed the world of military show that elevated his power. He fought the initiative of Guchkov, supported by Stolypin and the war minister A. F. Rediger, to oust the grand dukes from their high positions. In 1908 he announced, "I intend to take military affairs into my own hands."[76]

Rediger, a Swedish-Finn, was particularly odious to Nicholas and the far-right deputies. On February 23, 1909, Rediger responded sympathetically to a speech Guchkov gave decrying the slowness of military reform. Rediger declared that the problem was to find qualified candidates for high command positions and that this demanded time. That sealed Rediger's fate. In March Nicholas replaced him with V. A. Sukhomlinov, a figure who shared the tsar's love of uniforms and parade grounds and did his bidding. Sukhomlinov, William Fuller observed, continued to implement the reforms begun under Rediger, though Nicholas did what he could to slow the process.[77] But on the eve of World War I guardsmen and those with connections in the court occupied the principal command positions. The vast distance between elite and the lower ranks prevented the emergence of the sense of a nation in arms.[78] The social cleavage reflected Nicholas's determination to defend

[75] *Feodorovskii gosudarev sobor*, 3–6, 92–93.

[76] Zaionchkovskii, "Vyshee voennoe upravlenie," 78–83; Fuller, *Civil Military Conflict*, 220–32.

[77] Ibid., 232–37.

[78] See Allan K. Wildman, *The End of the Russian Imperial Army: The Old Army and the Soldiers' Revolt (March–April 1917)* (Princeton, N.J., 1980), 3–40, for a good summary of the social constituency and relationships in the Russian army. On the officer corps, see P. A.

414 • CHAPTER TWELVE •

the monarchical nation against the appeals of a nation of citizens fighting
for their own land rather than for the monarch.

Nicholas endeavored to appear as the embodiment of both elite and com-
moners and to show his rapport with both. For the elite, he restored the
glitter of the parade ground that they craved, which had been lost during his
father's reign, and he greatly enlarged the imperial suite.[79] He shared the
guards' officers' passions for military dress and parades. In 1907 and 1908
he introduced new designs for uniforms that returned to the dashing styles
of the nineteenth century. *Shakos*, like those worn by Russian officers in
1812, replaced the Russian hats, and stylish gilt braiding and the tsar's initials decorated officers' jackets. He restored the Hussar and Uhlan regiments,
which Alexander III had dissolved and incorporated with the Dragoons, and
provided them with elaborate and colorful uniforms, though they continued
to be combined during military operations.[80]

Unlike Nicholas I, who struck an intimidating paternal image, Nicholas
II presented himself as comrade-in-arms, both to elite officers of the guards
and the suite and to the rank and file. He revealed this simple manner at
regimental banquets, which he attended regularly. These gatherings "were
to have a strictly family character. The tsar in the camp of his regiment,"
B. V. Gerua wrote. Singers and balalaika bands performed, wine flowed, and
the mood was one of joyous camaraderie. Nicholas allowed soldiers to join
the officers in hoisting him into the air. Many in high society found such
conduct unbecoming to an emperor.[81]

Nicholas also embarrassed the military elite by publicly displaying his
rank of colonel in the Preobrazhenskii Guards' Regiment. The celebration
of the twenty-fifth anniversary of his service in the Preobrazhenskii Regiment
took place on June 12, 1912, at Peterhof, with the fountains playing and the
park decorated. At the parade before the palace Nicholas told the commander of the regiment, General Gulevich, that he would serve, as he had
before 1894, as battalion commander, and therefore the tsar marched behind
the general. In his memoirs A. F. Giers described his amazement at the scene:
"For the entire history of Russian armies there has been no example of a
Sovereign Leader placing himself under a regimental commander."[82]

Zaionchkovskii, "Russkii ofitserskii korpus nakanune Pervoi mirovoi voiny," in Zakharova et
al., *P. A. Zaionchkovskii*, 24–69.

[79] In 1914 the total number of suite adjutants was 171 compared to 105 at the end of Alexander III's reign (Shepelev, *Otmenennye istorrei*, 45). A list of adjutant-generals and major-gener-
als in the suite for 1915 can be found in Mosolov, *Pri dvore poslednego Rossiiskogo imperatora*, 280–83. See also Grand Duke Gavriil Konstantinovich, *V mramornom dvortse* (New
York, 1955), 80.

[80] Glinka, *Russkii voennyi kostium*, 89–94; Zaionchkovskii, "Vyshee voennoe upravlenie,"
87–89.

[81] Gerua, *Vospominaniia o moei zhizni*, 1:114; Spiridovitch, *Les dernières années de la cour
de Tsarskoe-Selo*, 1:145–46.

[82] Spiridovitch, *Les dernières années de la cour de Tsarskoe-Selo*, 2:239–40; A. F. Girs,
"Vospominaniia byvshego ofitsera Lb.-Gv. Preobrazhenskogo Polka i Minskogo Gubernatora,

The navy also figured in Nicholas's presentation of himself as a monarch who enjoyed close rapport with the nation's military. Between 1908 and 1913 he encouraged a rapid and costly rebuilding of the Russian fleet.[83] Public ceremonies restored the symbolic bond between him and his navy that had been destroyed by the mutinies of 1905. On his way to Livadia, at the end of August 1909, Nicholas reviewed the Black Sea Fleet at Sevastopol and found the national spirit reborn in the sailors' response. He tried to be "cold and dry" with them, he wrote in his diary, so that they would sense that "the abominations of 1905 are not soon forgotten." But his mood changed the moment he saw "their efforts to merit forgiveness, their desire to work with all their forces to attain good results, particularly in relation to combat. . . . I was moved by the shouts of "Hoorah!" that the crews gave every time they passed the yacht and particularly when they saw Alexei and his sisters." The display concluded on August 30, 1909, with a race, after which Nicholas conferred the prizes. "When the awards concluded I went out onto the gangplank to bid farewell to everyone, and a great "Hoorah!" resounded that can be compared with the one in Moscow on the Red Staircase, and it was a long time before we could stop these shouts."[84] Thereafter naval ceremonies became a frequent subject of publicity. Scenes in photographs and films showed the tsar in his smart, white naval uniform on the imperial yacht, the *Standard*, with the tsarevich in his sailor suit, and the tsar tasting the sailors' rations on the yacht (fig. 53).[85]

•

Nicholas increasingly advanced his son Alexei as the symbol of recrudescence of the Russian military under the leadership of a Russian tsar. Alexei, wearing a sailor suit, also became the centerpiece of the idyllic family scenes released to the public (fig. 54). He made Alexei the focus of a new youth organization, "*Poteshnye*" (Play Regiments), named after youthful army de-

---

A. F. Girsa o svoikh vstrechakh s Gosudarem Imperatorom Nikolaem II," Giers collection, BAR, 16.

[83] Naval rearmament was in part a response to his cousin Wilhelm's enthusiasm for building the German navy, even if Nicholas's military objectives were difficult to fathom. See Peter Gatrell, *Government, Industry, and Rearmament in Russia, 1900–1914: The Last Argument of Tsarism* (Cambridge, 1994), 138, 160, 300, 327.

[84] Kalinin and Zemliachenko, *Romanovy i Krym*, 78; Spiridovitch, *Les dernières années de la cour de Tsarskoe-selo*, 1:368–71.

[85] The crew of the *Standard* protected and befriended the children, some dined at the imperial table, and many observers considered them more akin to court servants than to sailors of the navy. The emperor regarded the *Standard* as his "floating palace," where he held reviews of the crew, gave large dinners, and traveled to other naval ceremonies (Spiridovitch, *Les dernières années de la cour de Tsarskoe-Selo*, 1:187–91; Mosolov, *Pri dvore poslednego Rossiiskogo imperatora*, 174; Major-General A. Elchaninov, *The Tsar and His people* [London: 1914], opp. 56, 86; Prof. A. Elchaninov, *Tsarstvovanie Gosudaria Imperatora Nikolaia Aleksandrovicha* [St. Petersburg-Moscow, 1913], 46, 47, 61; *Rodina*, April 17, 1911, "Vsemirnoe Obozrenie," 1).

53. Nicholas Tastes Sailors Rations on the Yacht, *The Standard*.
From A. Elchaninov, *The Tsar and His People*, 1914.

tachments formed by Peter the Great. Alexei participated in his own Play
Regiments and stood at his father's side during springtime reviews of the
Play Regiments of Mars Field. These were great events covered in the press
and the newsreels.[86]

The idea for *Poteshnye* came from an inspector of schools in Odessa,
A. A. Lutskevich, who had founded a boys' regiment. In 1908 Nicholas
handed the minister of war a sheet of his notebook indicating his intention
to introduce instruction in drill and calisthenics in Russian schools through-

[86] See *Sel'skii Vestnik*, July 28, 1911; July 29, 1911; and August 4, 1911; *Niva*, August 13,
1912; *Rodina*, July 31, 1911; and August 5, 1911. Permission to film the *Poteshnye* was granted
to Pathé by the Ministry of the Court, but with the provision that the filming should be under
particularly attentive observation of the managing cinematographer ("Po voprosu tsenzury kinematograficheskikh snimkov s izobrazheniem Vysochaishikh Osob," RGIA, 472-49-988, 1).

54. Tsarevich Alexei with Alexandra and Nicholas. Chromolithograph.
House of Konovalova. About 1907. Print Division, Russian National Library,
St. Petersburg.

out the empire, to be led "by retired reserve noncommissioned officers for low pay."[87] Despite the opposition of the minister of education, Play Regiments began to form at schools, churches, and under the auspices of various military units. The boys learned to parade with wooden rifles and do calisthenics and gymnastics. They heard speeches praising the church and autocracy and sang patriotic songs.[88]

The periodical of the Play Regiments, *Poteshnyi*, began publication in 1910. The first issue described a review, before the tsar and tsarevich, of Lutskevich's company, now named "The Heir Tsarevich Alexei Nikolaevich's First National Class of Military Drill and Calisthenics." A photograph shows Nicholas and Alexei reviewing the boys standing stiffly at attention in military uniform, holding wooden rifles.[89] The next year the magazine carried an account of the imperial review of sixty-five hundred boys on the Field of Mars. After the parade the boys were taken to a "People's House," where they were entertained by jugglers, gymnasts, singers, and players of the ancient Russian musical instrument, *gusli*. An article, "The Tsar and Children," told of one of their number, sent to Petersburg by his father. "When you see the Tsar you should pray!" When the boy saw Nicholas, he wept from joy. These boys, the article explained, would share their memories with their brothers, sisters, and friends, feeding the devotion of the young generation to their tsar.[90] A review of *Poteshnye* took place in the Moscow Kremlin on August 29, 1912, in the midst of the Borodino festivities.[91]

The magazine published historical articles that presented Peter's forming of his *Poteshnye* in the late seventeenth century and presented it as an act of renewal undertaken from the throne. The cover for the first issue of the journal was in old-Russian style, decorated with elaborate floral patterns. In the center Peter the Great is shown learning fortification from a bearded instructor in the Kremlin. An illustration on the editorial page—"Tsarevich Peter Alekseevich and his 'Play Regiments': The Storm of the Fortress"—sets the motif of military change in a seventeenth-century religious landscape

[87] *Poteshnyi: zhurnal russkikh detei*, no. 1 (1910): 6; *MV*, August 29, 1912, 2.

[88] The Minister of Education A. N. Shvarts was angered that Lutskevich, a person he regarded as incompetent and disreputable, had bypassed him and regular administrative procedures to reach the tsar. Nicholas, who despised the administration and administrative procedures, listened respectfully to Shvarts's remonstrations but went ahead with his plans (A. N. Shvarts, *Moia perepiska so Stolypinym; Moi vospominaniia o Gosudare* [Moscow, 1994], 61–64); Andronikov's 1910 memorandum accused the minister of obstructing the tsar's intentions for the *Poteshnye* and trying "to paralyze the Imperial will" (Solov'ev, "Politicheskaia smert' P. A. Stolypina," 146; Lieven, *Nicholas II*, 174; *Poteshnyi*, no. 1 [1910]: 6–7).

[89] *Poteshnyi*, no. 1 (1910): 1, 6–8.

[90] Ibid., no. 19 (1911): n.p.

[91] An article that appeared in *Moskovskie Vedomosti*, in preparation for the review, connected the *Poteshnye* with both the English Boy Scouts and examples of earlier Russian military training from boys in the reign of Peter the Great, Nicholas I, and Alexander II (*MV*, August 29, 1912, 1).

55. *Tsarevich Peter and His Play Regiments Storm a Fortress. Poteshnyi,*
no. 1 (1910).

(fig. 55). Two boiars dominate the foreground and cupolas of early-Russian
churches appear in the rear of a scene of Peter and his young soldiers preparing to capture the hill.[92] By 1911 the cover of the journal had changed, creating a new composite of past and present. The name remained in old letters,
but the picture was in modern format. A boy in sailor suit holds a rifle in a
medallion on the upper left. To his right is a scene of the Moscow Kremlin
and, beneath an inset, of the Kiev Monastery of the Caves.

The Play Regiments were clearly influenced by the example of Robert
Baden-Powell's Boy Scouts, though they were founded in the same year. The
Boy Scouts inculcated patriotism, Christian idealism, and loyalty to the
throne, and in the years before World War I trained their members in military
exercises. Most English scout groups were led by retired officers. Boy Scouts
served as altar boys at George V's coronation in 1911, and in 1912 the
organization was incorporated by Royal Charter. But the English monarchy
neither founded nor administered the Boy Scouts, whose fundamental myth,
moreover, was more imperial than military. Venturesome explorers were the
models for the boys, who read tales of the exploits of Sir Walter Raleigh and
Captain John Smith and wore the round hats and short pants of a scout in
the tropics. Inspired by a myth of empire and frontier, the organization

[92] *Poteshnyi*, no. 1 (1910): 6.

taught skills of survival in the wild—bushwacking, tying knots, building fires—instilling pluck and resourcefulness in addition to discipline.[93]

The Play Regiments, in contrast, wore army and navy uniforms as if they were military units. They strove above all to inspire devotion and obedience to the tsar. The monarchy that the journal described took its origin from the seventeenth century and had little to do with governmental changes since that time. An article, "Tsarist Autocracy," in 1911, told the story of the Moscow tsars' unification of Rus'. As "truly Orthodox" people, the tsars looked upon their office, "before the face of the Lord, as a great service and on their power as a God given means to realize everything for the secular and spiritual benefit of the people." The boys were to look back to the origins of the Russian state for the model of their current government. "Tsarist Autocracy is the dearest child of Holy Rus'. [Holy Rus'] conceived, nurtured, and brought it up. As a person cannot stop loving and cannot abandon his own mother, so Rus' cannot renounce Autocracy."[94] The boys expressed their devotion to Orthodoxy, Rus', and the imperial family in opening stanzas of the "Song of the Play Regiments."

> Our young unit is a young eagle,
> And it rises like a burning flame,
> For Faith, Church, and the Throne
> Of the Sovereign Tsar!
>
> For Good, the honor of our native land,
> For our Rus', our Holy Mother,
> We would love to go into battle,
> Into battle to die!
>
> May the Tsesarevich Alexei,
> Lead us forever:
> He is Our Angel,
> The hope, the bulwark of all Russia![95]

The vision inspiring the Play Regiments was of the formation of a rejuvenated army, like the army Peter the Great had created for a transformed Russia. A 1911 article in *Rodina* claimed that the young members of the regiments would be inspired by religious national sentiments and military virtues. They would grow into a new kind of citizen, "penetrated by conscious love for the native land, people with sound national feeling."[96] *Sel'skii Vestnik* called upon its peasant readers to support the Play Regiments in raising their children as citizen-subjects of an autocratic monarchy.

[93] On the English Boy Scouts, see Robert H. MacDonald, *Sons of the Empire: The Frontier and the Boy Scout Movement, 1890–1918* (Toronto, 1993).

[94] *Poteshnyi*, no. 19 (1911): n.p.

[95] Ibid., no. 21–22 (1911): 8.

[96] *Rodina*, July 31, 1911, 2–4.

All us subjects of the Beloved Tsar, who fulfill his will, each in his little deed, should do the Sovereign's work, devote our labor to the good of the future generation, and its upbringing, which seeks two goals—first, to develop one's love of God, Tsar, and Native Land, and the ability to sacrifice oneself in fulfilling the duty of the citizen and soldier; and, second, to increase our children's knowledge.[97]

THE POLTAVA JUBILEE

The great historical jubilee celebrations from 1909 to 1913 generalized the bond Nicholas felt between himself and the people. They sought to evoke a broad popular response that would confirm him as the embodiment of the national myth. The celebrations of the anniversaries of the Battle of Poltava in 1709, the Battle of Borodino in 1812, and the election of the first Romanov tsar in 1613 represented something new in their scale and publicity. They were accompanied by the mass publication of historical works, under both governmental and private auspices. The publisher I. V. Sytin claimed that his house alone printed and issued 350,000 copies of books and pamphlets for the Borodino centenary. The government tried to mobilize the feelings of national pride among the growing number of readers of popular brochures and literature.[98] The new medium of film also became part of the publicity of the celebrations. Alexander Khanzhonkov's battle spectacle,*1812,* opened simultaneously in movie theaters throughout the empire on the anniversary of Borodino and was reviewed in many newspapers.[99]

The celebrations emulated the spectacular arrays and mass appeals of the jubilees of Queen Victoria in 1887 and 1897, Franz Josef in 1908, and Kaiser Wilhelm in 1912. Jubilees brought monarchs out of the palace and made them objects of mass popular love and acclaim, attracting attention to their *persons* rather than the office of sovereign, and connecting the monarchy with a national, popular past. Their principal model was England, where, in 1887, Victoria left her seclusion and appeared in public as a symbol of love of nation and home. Her figure kept the royal dignity of the office, now representing the virtues of the nation as a whole.[100] Queen Victoria was "no longer the head of society, but the head of the nation as well," David Can-

---

[97] *Sel'skii Vestnik*, July 26, 1911, 2.

[98] Brooks, *When Russia Learned to Read*, 112–15, 167, 244–55, 314–15.

[99] Jerzy Toeplitz, *Geschichte des Films*, vol. 1 (Berlin, 1992), 92–95; Jay Leyda, *Kino: A History of the Russian and Soviet Film* (Princeton, N.J., 1983), 53, 60.

[100] Thomas Richards, *The Commodity Culture of Victorian England: Advertising and Spectacle, 1851–1914* (Stanford, 1990), 82–83, 76–82; Arno Mayer, *The Persistence of the Old Regime: Europe to the Great War* (New York, 1981), 135–46.

nadine has written. The jubilee presented the monarch "as a symbol of consensus and continuity to which all might defer."[101]

Stolypin looked to these celebrations as expressions of a national consensus, led by the monarch, as in Europe. Nicholas, however, used them as a partisan device to compete with the Duma and to show himself as sole focus of national sentiment. By appearing at the sacred sites of great national battles, he drew precedents for the resurgence of Russian monarchy from his forbears' triumphs at moments of crisis. The anniversaries of the Great Reforms, however, carried a different message and received perfunctory observance from the monarchy. In 1911 the Ministry of the Interior forbade the showing of two films issued to commemorate the fiftieth anniversary of the emancipation.[102] Only pressure from the Duma brought about a prayer service at Kazan Cathedral and official recognition of the jubilee on February 19, 1911. Nicholas used the opportunity to meet with a gathering of 126 elders from Petersburg Province and 51 peasant deputies from the Duma, who informed him of their proposal to place a bust of Alexander II in the Duma's chambers.[103]

At the end of June 1909 Nicholas II traveled to the battlefield at Poltava to commemorate Peter the Great's defeat of Charles XII of Sweden, the victory that marked Russia's emergence as a major European power. He showed his connection with Peter by reaffirming his bonds with the Preobrazhenskii Regiment, the first regiment Peter established. On the evening of June 25, wearing the Preobrazhenskii uniform, he met the regiment at their bivouac for a dinner. He mingled with the officers as one of them. He heard stories of the Battle of Poltava that recalled an illustrious moment in their history, when Peter, protected by God, escaped unharmed though three bullets had passed through his clothing. After dinner, a chorus performed the folk song "Three Bullets" about the episode and Peter's heroism. The grand duke Constantine Konstantinovich, who commanded the regiment, wrote in his diary that the song "sung by the descendants of Petrine heroes, on the very site where their forbears were 'crowned with blood' two-hundred years ago, penetrated to the soul." The next day the tsar arrived in his Preobrazhenskii uniform and reviewed the troops spread out on the fields. Then, at a special service, he laid a wreath on the grave of Colonel Alexei Kelin, the commander of the Poltava fortress, who had perished dur-

[101] David Cannadine, "Splendor out of Court: Royal Spectacle and Pageantry in Modern Britain, c. 1820–1977," in Sean Wilentz, ed., *Rites of Power: Symbolism, Ritual, and Politics since the Middle Ages* (Philadelphia, 1985), 218–21; Eric Hobsbawm, "Mass Producing Traditions: Europe, 1870–1914," in Eric Hobsbawm and Terence Ranger, eds., *The Invention of Tradition* (Cambridge, 1983), 281–83.

[102] The films were *On the Eve of the Manifesto of February 19*, directed by P. Chardynin, and *Cross Yourselves, Orthodox, Russian People!*, directed by W. Karin (Toeplitz, *Geschichte des Films*, 1:96).

[103] *Rodina*, February 18, 1911, 2.

ing the battle.[104] During the festivities Nicholas was attended by three offi-cers—Victor Kochubei, Alexander Sheremet'ev, and Paul Skoropadskii—who were direct descendants of military men at Peter's side at Poltava. At the parade Nicholas honored Kochubei and Sheremet'ev with appointments as adjutant-generals, a rank, he remarked, that he himself had not at-tained.[105]

On the afternoon of June 26 Nicholas showed his rapport with those he regarded as Russian peasants.[106] More than two thousand peasants stood in a circle grouped by districts (*uezdy*) around Nicholas and Stolypin. Nicholas was relaxed and chatted amicably with ordinary peasants as well as the el-ders. The peasants felt, wrote Alexander Spiridovich, the chief of Palace Se-curity, that "one could tell the tsar everything, as at confession." Nicholas spent more than three hours in animated conversations; he burst into laugh-ter at the peasants' good-humored and apt replies. Delighted with the meet-ings, Nicholas asked that the people be allowed to approach him when he visited Kiev after the Poltava celebration. At the conclusion, he said "thank you for your love and devotion, little brothers" to shouts of "Hoorah!" from the crowd. "It was deeply touching and significant," Grand Duke Con-stantine Konstantinovich wrote in his diary. Stolypin asked the peasants questions about their allotments of land in the new individual homesteads created on the basis of his reform.[107]

The French military attaché also was impressed with the warm reception Nicholas received from the crowd. Nicholas told him, he wrote, that they "were no longer in Petersburg and that one could not say that the Russian people did not love their Emperor . . . He is certain that the landowners, the nobility, and the army remain loyal to the Tsar" and that these were the elements represented at Poltava. Nicholas believed that the revolutionaries were "composed above all of Jews, students, landless peasants, and some workers"—elements he identified with Petersburg.[108]

The next day, June 27, at a luncheon for the cadets and officers attending the celebration, Nicholas delivered an impassioned speech, intended for mass circulation, on the contemporary significance of the celebration. The speech, cited in the epigraph, reaffirmed the personal character of his rule

[104] A. Girs, "Svetlye i chernye dni," *Chasovoi* (March 1953): 9–10; April 1953): 9; Spirido-vitch, *Les dernières années de la cour de Tsarskoe-Selo*, 1:328–29; "Dnevnik Konstantina Kon-stantinovicha, 5 marta–12 dekabria 1909 goda," GARF, 660-1-61, 65–68.

[105] "Dnevnik Konstantina Konstantinovicha, 5 marta–12 dekabria 1909 goda," 68–69; Spi-ridovitch, *Les dernières années de la cour de Tsarskoe-Selo*, 1:324–26, 329–30.

[106] The population of Poltava Province was only 2.6 percent Great Russian (Emmons, *The Formation of Political Parties*, 176). But Nicholas, like his predecessors, regarded Ukrainians as Russians, not as a distinct nationality.

[107] A. Girs, "Svetlye i chernye dni," *Chasovoi* (April 1953), 9; Spiridovitch, *Les dernières années de la cour de Tsarskoe-Selo*, 1:326–27; *MV*, June 30, 1909, "Dnevnik Konstantina Konstantinovicha, 5 marta–12 dekabria 1909g.," 67.

[108] Cited in Lieven, *Nicholas II*, 167.

and called on his subjects to show their devotion to the throne. Omitting all mention of the government and the state, he looked forward to the re-affirmation of the unity of "the tsar with the people" and the "close bond of the entire population of Our native land with their Sovereign." Grand Duke Constantine wrote in his diary, "In the shouts of 'Hoorah' drowning out the Tsar's words, you could detect the extraordinary spiritual elevation they prompted—a feeling that we had not experienced for a long time." When the tsar left, he was greeted with enthusiastic shouts from the officers on the staircase, then from the brigades waiting downstairs, and another rendition of the anthem. Stolypin commented, "This marks the end of the revolution."[109]

The reports in *Rossiia*, the organ of the Ministry of the Interior, described popular support for the celebration and tried to minimize the presence of the Union of the Russian People.[110] The correspondent N. Sarmatov focused first on the procession of the cross that moved from the town of Poltava out to the St. Sampson Church on the field of battle on June 26. Following the clergy were members of the Union of Russian People, though "not many," fewer than one hundred, then a mass of townspeople, moving to the sound of church bells and military music. Once the procession left the town, its numbers swelled with rural folk. "Great is the power of faith among the people," Sarmatov concluded.[111] He reported the peasants' talk about the tsar. They said that though a tsar was supposed to be frightening (*groznyi*) Nicholas seemed to them kind and to love the peasant ("*U nas Tsar dobryi. On muzhika liubit*"). The older members of the *zemstva* also were enchanted by Nicholas. One observed that he displayed "a purely human charm." "Kind eyes, a tender manner in his contact with everyone from the highest to the lowest with whom he chatted." Another was convinced that "the best system of internal politics would be that we see the Tsar more often." The author concluded, "We are apparently monarchist by our blood, our race. We need a Tsar, for we have a need in us to give our love . . . to one person, standing above parties, above all our material and political interests."[112] The reception in Kiev was equally enthusiastic.

The success of the celebrations produced a sense of euphoria in the imperial party, whose members took the response as proof that the social revolution was over and that the nation had rallied around the tsar. At the train station, Stolypin remarked, "Two years have elapsed since the revolution

[109] "Dnevnik Konstantina Konstantinovicha, 5 marta–12 dekabria 1909 goda," 70–71.

[110] The German ambassador, Friedrich von Pourtales, reported to Berlin on June 26, 1909, that Stolypin had succeeded in preventing a large-scale reactionary demonstration on the occasion of the Poltava celebration (Politisches Archiv des Auswärtigen Amts, Abteilung A, Russland. Bonn). I am grateful to Professor Abraham Ascher for this citation.

[111] *Rossiia*, June 30, 1909, 2–3.

[112] Ibid., July 1, 1909, 1; ellipses mine.

and it has left no trace. Everything is forgotten, everything has changed."[113] Nicholas wrote on June 27 that he was leaving Poltava, with "the very best impression of the days we have spent here and of the moving reception by the population of Poltava Province." The Poltava celebration provided a model for meetings with peasantry, staged by the Ministry of Interior, at Kharkov and Chernigov in 1911 and at Belovezh in 1912.[114]

Nicholas's speech before the cadets indicated his increasing identification with forbears and inspiration with their achievements as a leader of the nation at moments of crisis. To commemorate the anniversary of the Battle of Poltava, he donated two statues of Peter that were placed opposite the Admiralty Building in St. Petersburg. One showed Peter saving drowning sailors at Lakhta, the other Peter building a boat. Both presented the emperor as descending from his throne and sharing the lives of his subjects.[115] Nicholas now was beginning to see himself as military leader in the image of Peter and Alexander I. The war minister General Vladimir Sukhomlinov recalled that at this time the tsar constantly remarked that in the event of war he would take on the role of commander-in-chief. At the beginning of 1911 Sukhomlinov even summoned his commanding generals to Petersburg to conduct war games, with maps and plans, in the Winter Palace, with Nicholas in charge, so that "the tsar could become acquainted with the generals who would lead the army." Nicholas liked the idea and helped work out the details, but the grand duke Nicholas Nikolaevich intervened at the last moment to convince him to cancel what could have been an embarrassing exercise.[116]

•

The enthusiasm generated by the Poltava celebrations only drew the lines more sharply between the monarch and the new political nation. Sergei Iablonovskii, writing in *Russkoe Slovo*, asked whether the Poltava events could prompt true national enthusiasm. He recalled that "long ago, when we were still weak and ignorant, we won a glorious victory." Yet only recently, "when we already thought ourselves both strong and enlightened, a people who not long ago were weak and from the point of view of European culture, ignorant, won a glorious victory over us." He asked how Russia could joyously recall past progress "in the days of the wreck of all our proud

[113] Spiridovitch, *Les dernières années de la cour de Tsarskoe-Selo*, 1:332–33; "Dnevnik Nikolaia II, 1909," GARF, 601-1-254, 55–56, 58.

[114] Elchaninov, *The Tsar and His People*, 82–86; *Tsarstvovanie Gosudaria Imperatora Nikolaia Aleksandrovicha*, 82–86.

[115] Grigorii Moskvich, *Petrograd i ego okresnosti* (Petrograd, 1915), 104; Nesin, *Zimnii Dvorets*, 56.

[116] V. Sukhomlinov, *Vospominaniia Sukhomlinova* (Moscow-Leningrad, 1926), 191–92; see the comments on the episode in Wildman, *The End of the Russian Imperial Army*, 1:71.

ideals and bright hopes?" The Poltava holiday "will not turn out to be a national holiday, for all of Russia will not fuse with it as a single person."[117]

The mutual incomprehension between the monarchy and educated society was vividly revealed by the reception of Paolo Trubetskoi's equestrian statue of Alexander III in St. Petersburg, which was dedicated on May 23, 1909. The statue was the choice of the imperial family, despite the misgivings expressed by several of its members. The dowager empress and the grand duke Vladimir Aleksandrovich approved a model of the statue. In 1910 Nicholas thought enough of the statue to give his mother a rock crystal Fabergé egg containing a miniature replica of it set on a lapis-lazuli base edged with diamonds. The statue was placed on Znamenskaia Square before the Nicholas Railway Station—the starting point of the Trans-Siberian Railroad, which Alexander III had initiated.[118]

Trubetskoi faced the problem of creating the semblance of a national Russian tsar in the medium of statuary, which had previously been dedicated to glorifying the Russian monarch in a Western neoclassical idiom. His solution was original but inscrutable, and from the moment of its dedication, the statue became a center of controversy. The sculptor abandoned the grace and majesty of classical equestrian monarchs and presented Alexander III in his national military uniform, swollen and ungainly, on a small, heavy, bob-tailed horse, its head lowered as if balking (fig. 56). Trubetskoi gave Alexander the massive bearlike form of the *bogatyr'*, the medieval Russian knight, which had become a popular motif in official rhetoric about the tsar and in recent art, particularly in the paintings of Michael Vrubel' and Victor Vasnetsov.[119]

That the statue sought to place Alexander III in the context of the national myth was a point made forcefully in an article by the monarchist literary critic and philosopher Vasilii Rozanov. Rozanov praised the work as a tribute to the autocracy and the Russian people. The statue, he claimed, was an answer to Falconet's statue of Peter the Great, which he described as "an opera, a fairy tale"; Trubetskoi's was "something kindred, 'mine,' 'ours,' 'all-Russian.' " That it did not resemble a horse, or in any event an elegant horse, seemed completely appropriate to Russia. "What kind of stallion is Russia; Russia is a pig, not a stallion."[120] Rozanov perceived Trubetskoi's statue as a repudiation of the imperial tradition of magnificence. He wrote that Kaiser William II should build magnificent statues; Russian statues were not supposed to be magnificent. "Our mother-natures are ugly. They are old and ill and naked, but we won't trade them for anything."

Rozanov saw in the statue a symbol of the relationship between the tsar and Russian society. "The horse is a horrid liberal. He doesn't know whether

---

[117] *Russkoe Slovo*, June 25, 1909, 2.

[118] Witte, *Vospominaniia*, 1:455–63; Pfeffer, *Fabergé Eggs*, 90–91.

[119] This interpretation is developed in an interesting article by Donald C. Carlisle, "V poiskakh propavshego 'mednogo vsadnika,' " *Obozrenie*, no. 9 (April 1984): 27–29.

[120] V. V. Rozanov, *Sredi khudozhnikov* (St. Petersburg, 1914), 310, 313–14.

56. Alexander III Statue, St. Petersburg. Sculptor, Paolo Trubetskoi. Niva, 1909.

his head is on his front, back, or side." The horse was refusing to move. There was a misunderstanding between the two: The horse does not understand the benevolent horseman, and suspects him of evil intentions, to ride him into an abyss. "The horse is so dumb that he does not see that he will fly with the horseman and that the horseman can have no 'evil intention.' "[121]

Most responses from the conservative press, however, condemned the statue, their criticisms revealing the loss of a common artistic language among the sympathizers of the monarchy. M. Menshikov, writing in *Novoe Vremia*, called the monument "an event in Russian life and, sad to say, another unhappy event, it is such a failure." The absence of a tail on the horse was the source of much concern and mirth. *Moskovskie Vedomosti* re-

[121] Ibid., 314–17.

marked that the statue "leaves an impression of preposterousness. The simple people say that such a workhorse (*bitiug*) should have a tail that's a tail." They joked that the tail had been cut off for economy's sake and talked of starting up a collection to make a new one.[122] Most of the statue's admirers, unlike Rozanov, were liberals and radicals, who understood it as a caricature of the tsarist regime. Alexander Benois, who had served on the commission supervising the construction, called it "a reactionary monster in soldier's dress." Ilia Repin praised the courage of an artist who issued "a cruel sentence on the Tsar-Peacemaker."[123]

In the eyes of modernist poets, the statue symbolized a terrifying sense that Russian monarchy was empty of meaning. In Valerii Briusov's poem "Three Idols" (1913), the statue completes the decline begun by the Nicholas I statue.

> With frenzy the Bronze Horseman gallops,
> The other stallion rides not too fast,
> And severely, with all inherited might,
> The third cavalryman stands frozen over the crowd.[124]

The ominous cadences of Velimir Khlebnikov's poem, "Monument," tell of the mounted figure of Alexander III leaving its pedestal to appear mysteriously before the doomed Russian fleet in the Pacific during the Russo-Japanese War. The statue descends to the depths among the corpses of Russian sailors. The disappearance is noted, and a prophetic voice makes known that this is an apparition of evil. The rider reappears in St. Petersburg. The police interrogate him and order him to resume his position on his pedestal. The "prisoner" feels "close and cramped on the square." The crowd stirs "like the fur of a beast." People are speaking French, and a loud laugh is heard.[125]

THE RETURN TO MOSCOW AND THE BORODINO CELEBRATIONS

The assassination of Prime Minister Peter Stolypin in September 1911 created circumstances for renewed conflict between the tsar and the Duma. The success of the Poltava celebrations confirmed Nicholas's belief in the resurgence of autocracy and its national destiny. Now he was rid of the figure he saw as threatening his power. But he still had to contend with the Duma, which, though overwhelmingly conservative in makeup, continued to represent for him an illegitimate encumbrance on his rule. Relations became particularly strained when the deputies, led by the successive Octobrist presidents of the assembly, Alexander Guchkov and Michael Rodzianko,

[122] *NV*, May 28, 1909; *MV*, May 28, 1909.
[123] Carlisle, "V poiskakh propavshego 'mednogo vsadnika,' " 26.
[124] V. Briusov, *Izbrannye sochineniia v dvukh tomakh* (Moscow, 1955), 1:362–63.
[125] Velimir Khlebnikov, *Sobranie proizvedenii* (Leningrad, 1930), 85–88.

openly condemned Rasputin's influence on the imperial family. Copies of letters from the empress and the children to Rasputin expressing their warm feelings circulated in society. Nicholas also had to cope with the press, which, in the major cities, had been given freedom from preliminary censorship by the laws of 1906, even if censorship continued to operate under various criminal regulations.[126] On January 24, 1912, Guchkov's *Golos Moskvy* printed an article condemning Rasputin, which was cited in its entirety during the Duma debate and then carried widely in other newspapers. Guchkov gave a rousing speech stating that "dark phantoms from medieval times trouble our state." At Nicholas's instance, an order forbade the mention of Rasputin's name in the press, a measure contrary to the censorship law of 1906.[127]

The president of the Duma who succeeded Guchkov, Michael Rodzianko, narrowly averted an open debate on Rasputin, but with the assistance of the police, he opened an investigation into the holy man. At an audience with the tsar, Rodzianko informed Nicholas of his apprehensions about Rasputin's growing influence in the court, police, and especially the Orthodox Church. He described Rasputin as "an instrument for undermining the Church and the Monarchy itself." These accusations only confirmed Nicholas's conviction that Rasputin was a man of the people calumniated by deputies and officials. In 1911 and 1912 the tsar urged his ministers to limit the press and considered plans to curtail the powers of the Duma.[128]

It was during 1911 and 1912 that the central government, with Nicholas's tacit approval, became involved in the ritual murder case of Mendel Beilis in Kiev. The trial had been pressed by the Kiev organization of the Union of Russian People and by right-wing deputies of the Duma, when the Duma had begun considering proposals to eliminate the Pale of Settlement and to extend equal rights to Jews. Despite the absence of evidence of ritual murder in the autopsy, or any other proof, local authorities, supported by the minister of justice Ivan Shcheglovitov, decided to prosecute Beilis. Although there is no indication that Nicholas played a role in the case, he received numerous reports on its progress and did nothing to stop it. Most important, he continued to regard the extreme Right as true Russians, who deserved his support. The prosecution was a clear example of action meant to sustain Nicholas's scenario of national tsar, acting in accordance with what he understood to be the instincts of the Russian people. Hans Rogger concludes that Shcheglovitov acted "because he had come to accept and to share the imperial self-image." By the summer of 1912 the case had become a symbol of

---

[126] On the press laws and governmental policy after 1905, see Ruud, *Fighting Words*, 207–26; and Ferenczi, "Freedom of the Press under the Old Regime, 1905–1914," 191–205.

[127] Rodzianko, *The Reign of Rasputin*, 23–40; Pares, *The Fall of the Russian Monarchy*, 142–48; Ben-Cion Pinchuk, *The Octobrists in the Third Duma, 1907–1912* (Seattle, 1974), 185–89.

[128] Rodzianko, *The Reign of Rasputin*, 40–56; Pares, *The Fall of the Russian Monarchy*, 148–52.

the monarchy's backwardness and obscurantism, and prompted outraged condemnation from educated society. Leftist deputies asked the government to investigate the case just before the Third Duma terminated its sessions in June 1912. The case had also begun to prompt censure from newspapers abroad.[129]

The months before the Borodino celebration also witnessed the revival of the strike movement. On April 4, 1912, at the Lena gold fields in Siberia, soldiers fired on workers peacefully gathering to submit demands to the authorities, leaving nearly two hundred dead. This repetition of Bloody Sunday unleashed a wave of strikes and protests. In the month following the massacre, twice as many workers walked out as in the previous four years. Over the course of the year three-quarters of a million workers would strike, more than any year except 1905 and 1906.[130] Newspapers were filled with articles reporting investigations of the causes of the massacre. The event brought forth condemnations from the increasingly oppositional Moscow industrialists, who saw the strike as proof of the danger posed by the "police perspective" on Russian industrial development.[131]

In May 1912 Nicholas set out to reclaim Moscow as the principal sacred site of the myth. The occasions for his first visit to the city since 1903 were the dedication of the statue of Alexander III before the Cathedral of Christ the Redeemer and the opening of the Alexander III Museum of Fine Arts. Fearing trouble, the authorities tightened security measures and increased arrests. The police interrogated the entire consular corps about foreigners in Moscow. The guards' regiments entering the city were met with cries of "butchers, Praetorians, tsarists," in reference to the bloody suppression of the Moscow insurrection of December 1905. Even the meeting with peasant elders was strained. The empress was particularly inaccessible and failed to appear at the opening of the museum, offending Moscow society.[132]

The dedication ceremony of the statue on May 30 gave an imposing display of Nicholas's homage to his father. A procession of the cross circled the monument, joined by the tsar and the two empresses. Then after the metropolitan Vladimir blessed the statue, the choir, dressed in seventeenth-century-style vestments, intoned hymns and the cloth fell from it. Nicholas

---

[129] Hans Rogger, "The Beilis Case: Anti-Semitism and Politics in the Reign of Nicholas II," *Slavic Review* 25, no. 4 (December 1966): 615–29; Tager, 46–47, 88, 144, 155–62; Löwe, *Antisemitismus und reaktionäre Utopie*, 137–39.

[130] Leopold Haimson, "The Problem of Social Stability in Urban Russia, 1905–1917," in Michael Cherniavsky, ed., *The Structure of Russian History: Interpretive Essays* (New York, 1970), 347; Victoria E. Bonnell, *Roots of Rebellion: Workers' Politics and Organizations in St. Petersburg and Moscow, 1900–1914* (Berkeley, 1983), 353–54.

[131] Lewis H. Siegelbaum, *The Politics of Industrial Mobilization in Russia, 1914–1917: A Study of the War Industrial Committees* (Oxford, 1983), 17.

[132] Spiridovitch, *Les dernières années de la cour de Tsarskoe-Selo*, 2:230–31; R. H. Bruce Lockhart, *British Agent* (New York, 1933), 73; Bogdanovitch, *Tri poslednikh samoderzhtsa*, 501.

led a ceremonial march of the regiments past his father's figure and, with his saber bared, saluted him.[133]

The statue, by Alexander Opekushin, was placed at a relatively secluded inconspicuous site, where, in order to face the Kremlin, the figure of the tsar had his back to the cathedral. If Trubetskoi's statue baffled by its strangeness, Opekushin's seemed to present the tsar without a discernible persona (fig. 57). Those close to the imperial family could find nothing recognizable or inspiring in the monument. A. N. Naumov, a staunch monarchist and provincial marshal of the nobility from Samara Province, remarked on the unnatural pose of Alexander sitting tensely on the throne. Grand Duke Gavriil Konstantinovich wrote that it failed completely to capture the sense Alexander had given of a consciousness of his majesty when he sat on his coronation throne. Its impassivity gave the statue the appearance of an idol.[134] Alexander III sat stolid and immobile on his coronation throne, in full regalia. He was defined entirely by the insignia of power, which expressed a purely sacramental notion of the office of tsar. In this way, it reflected Nicholas's II's own belief that the tsar's divine designation conferred at the coronation was the exclusive source of autocratic power.

•

The Borodino celebrations in the last days of August 1912 focused the memories of the heroic battle on the monarchy and, more particularly, on Nicholas himself. On August 25 the tsar, with the tsarevich at his side, reviewed the units whose forebears had fought in the battle. Nicholas chatted with several old men who, he had been told, had been present at Borodino. One of them, Sergeant-Major Voitiniuk, claimed to be 122 years of age, and he astonished the tsar by recounting the exact details of the battle. Nicholas wrote to his mother: "Just imagine, to be able to speak to a man who remembers everything, describes details of the action, indicates the place where he was wounded, etc., etc.! I told them to stand next to us at the tent during the prayer service and watched them. They all were able to kneel with the help of their canes and then stood up!"[135] That the old soldiers were well-rehearsed seems to have been known to all but the tsar himself.[136] Photo-

---

[133] NV, May 31, 1912, 3; V. F. Dzhunkovskii, Vospominaniia (Moscow, 1997), 1:660–67; Grand Duke Gavriil Konstantinovich, V mramornom dvortse, 159.

[134] Naumov, Iz utselevshikh vospominanii, 2:221; Grand Duke Gavriil Konstantinovich, V mramornom dvortse, 159. Spiridovitch described its impression as "strong and bizarre. There was something pagan about it" (Les dernières années de la cour de Tsarskoe-Selo, 1:231).

[135] Bing, The Secret Letters of the Last Tsar, 271; "Pis'ma imp. Nikolaia II imp. Marii Fedorovne, 6 aprelia 1912–20 iiulia 1916," GARF, 642-1-2332, 14–15. To his cousin, the grand duke Constantine, he was no less contained. "And then to meet and talk with a survivor of the battle—a 122-year-old former sergeant-major! I felt as I would in the presence of the greatest relics!" (Maylunas and Mironenko, A Lifelong Passion, 353–54); Grand Duke Gavriil Konstantinovich, V mramornom dvortse, 163.

[136] Dzhunkovskii described meeting with the old soldiers on August 22 and recalled that they remembered little about the battle but were accorded special treatment. They rode about in

57. Alexander III Statue, Moscow. Sculptor, A. M. Opekushin.
Niva, 1912.

graphs of them, identified as veterans of the Napoleonic Wars, appeared in
L'Illustration, Niva, and again in Andrei Elchaninov's 1913 biography of
Nicholas II.[137]

The procession of the cross bearing the miracle icon of the Smolensk
Mother of God, which had blessed Field Marshal Kutuzov's armies before
the battle, was the principal ceremony of the celebration. The procession
had brought the icon all the way from Smolensk to Borodino, a distance of
more than 140 miles. On August 25 several soldiers bore it on poles across
the field toward the emperor, who wore the uniform of the Horse-Guards,
a unit that had distinguished itself at Borodino. Vladimir Dzhunkovskii, the
governor of Moscow, had introduced new security arrangements that permitted the crowd to view the procession close-up. The clergy, wearing crimson chasubles with gold embroidery, moved slowly and with great dignity.

carriages and received the best accommodations and places at the ceremony. One even described
Napoleon as a "fine fellow" with a "beard down to his waist" (Dzhunkovskii, *Vospominaniia,*
2:19–19).

[137] *L'Illustration,* May 19, 1906, 156, 424–25; *Niva,* September 8, 1912; Elchaninov, *The
Tsar and His People,* opp. 122; *Tsarstvovanie Gosudaria Imperatora Nikolaia Aleksandrovicha,* 114.

58. Nicholas II marches in icon procession at Borodino, August 28, 1912.
From *L'Illustration*.

Dzhunkovskii recalled, "The moment was touching and solemn. Great excitement was on every face."[138]

To the strains of the hymn, *Kol' slaven*, Nicholas met the procession and moved with it to the Campaign Chapel of Alexander I for a prayer service. This was followed by the solemn bearing of the icon before troops whose units had fought at Borodino, reenacting the ceremony of 1812. Accompanying the icon, the emperor and his suite passed by three lines of troops that extended nearly three miles (fig. 58). Arms were held at prayer position, while the bands once again played *Kol' slaven*. "The movement of the Sovereign with his brilliant Suite behind the icon along the line of troops left an extraordinarily solemn impression," Dzhunkovskii wrote in his memoirs.[139] A. N. Naumov remarked to the minister of foreign affairs S. D. Sazonov, "Look at these armies! Isn't this might?" He was surprised to hear Sazonov reply that everything was superficial and that the Russian armies were not ready.[140]

Nicholas wrote to his mother: "A common feeling of deep reverence for our forebears seized us all there. No description of the battle can ever pro-

[138] Dzhunkovskii maintained the faith in the loyalty of the Russian people held by the grand duke Sergei, whom he had served under (Dhzunkovskii, *Vospominaniia*, 2:12–13, 26; Grand Duke Gavriil Konstantinovich, *V mramornom dvortse*, 162).

[139] Dzhunkovskii, *Vospominaniia*, 2:27–28; *Niva*, September 1912, 722–23; *MV*, August 28, 1912, 3.

[140] Naumov was referring to the crises in the Balkans where Russia's allies were mobilizing for war against Turkey (Naumov, *Iz utselevshikh vospominanii*, 2:224).

duce an impression comparable at all to the one that penetrates to the heart on setting foot on the soil where the blood was shed of fifty-eight thousand of our heroes, dead and wounded in the days of the battle of Borodino." He mentioned the presence of the icon at the Te Deum services, "the same that had been at the battle a hundred years ago, the carrying of it along the front of the massed troops, these were moments one rarely experiences in our own days."[141]

August 26, the day of the battle itself, combined the three ceremonies—procession of the cross, parade, and meeting with peasants. After a mass in the Spaso-Borodinskii Monastery, a procession of the cross accompanied the Smolensk Mother of God to the Borodino Monument. Peasants were lined up along the road. Nicholas rode on horseback past the lines of the regiments, then they passed by him in ceremonial march. "The parade was very pretty," he noted in his diary, "because of the uniforms' variety of colors." After lunch Nicholas rode through the fields, halting at the various monuments to the regiments that had participated in 1812 and for a ceremony of dedication to the French who perished on the field.

Along the way he stopped at the peasant bivouac and was greeted by 4,550 peasant elders. He spoke to them of the battle "where your grandfathers and great-grandfathers fought against the courageous foe and defended the native land with the help of faith in God, devotion to the Tsar, and love for the native land." To the tsar, his trusted officials, and nationalist newspapers, the peasants on the field represented the Russian peasantry as a whole. *Moskovskie Vedomosti*, relating the joyous response of the peasant elders, asserted that each of them "carried in his soul bright and exalted memories of visiting the camp of Little Father-Tsar, and the words of the Tsar, undoubtedly, will meet a warm response in all villages and hamlets where they will be transmitted by the fortunate participants in the Borodino festivities."[142]

An imperial decree, declaimed to the troops at the parade, made clear the monarchical message of the event.[143] Nicholas recalled the day one hundred years before when the Russian army, under the command of its "Supreme Leader" (*Verkhovnyi Vozhd'*), was called on to defend "the dignity of great Russia and the inviolability of the Fatherland."[144] The Russian people, with

---

[141] "Dnevnik Nikolaia II, August 25, 1912–May 6, 1913," GARF, 601-1-259, 2; "Pis'ma imp. Nikolaia II imp. Marii Fedorovne, 6 aprelia 1912–20 iiulia 1916," 14; Bing, *The Secret Letters of the Last Tsar*, 270–71; Spiridovitch, *Les dernières années de la cour de Tsarskoe-Selo*, 1:324–31.

[142] "Dnevnik Nikolaia II, August 25, 1912–May 6, 1913," GARF, 601-1-259, 3–4; Dzhunkovskii, *Vospominaniia*, 2:35–36; *Niva*, September 8, 1912, 722–23; *MV*, September 8, 1912, 2.

[143] *Niva*, September 8, 1912, 722–23.

[144] Alexander, to his own chagrin, proved unable to command on the battlefield in the struggle against Napoleon (see Volume 1: 205, 217–19).

faith in God and "complete unity with its Sovereign," showed "obedience before the many difficult tests" and saved the Fatherland.

Another sense of the meaning of 1812 was set forth in the popular literature of the time. An article written by an Ufa school teacher, V. Efremov, entitled "Why is the War of 1812 Called the War for the Fatherland," appeared in a brochure, *Love for the Fatherland: The Source of National Strength.* For Efremov, the united people and the fatherland were the two main components of Russian nationality; Alexander was in the background. It was "the people who defended the freedom, independence, and unity of their land; then the entire people in the true sense of the word (not only the army) came to the defense of the fatherland." At this time "the native inhabitants of the Russian state felt immediately that they are Russian, that they formed one people, who were ready to sacrifice anything for the good of their fatherland." The union was not only between tsar and people but "the close union of all estates with one another" for the purpose of attaining the general good.[145]

•

The Moscow celebrations in the next few days maintained the heightened religious tone of the celebration. Nicholas was greeted by enthusiastic crowds when he visited the Iberian Mother of God and bowed to the people in the Kremlin. The partisan message of the celebration was voiced strongly at the reception that the Moscow nobility gave for the emperor and empress. After the singing of "God Save the Tsar" and a performance of Tchaikovsky's *1812 Overture*, a group of marshals of the nobility entered in pairs, led by A. D. Samarin of Moscow and I. N. Saltykov from Petersburg. They formed a semicircle before the tsar, who stood on the stage. Samarin presented a banner designed on an early Russian pattern as an emblem of the unity of nobility and crown. He then delivered an impassioned speech in the name of the Russian nobility of the entire empire, vowing that they would sacrifice their lives for the tsar, the "Sovereign Leader," and native land as they had one hundred years before. The banner would be a reminder of "that glorious year, when all the might of the Russian land told in the union of Tsar and people." The speech ended with lines of "God Save the Tsar" and then all joined in singing the anthem to their sovereign.

At the insistence of the monarchist noblemen, the final version of the speech referred to the tsar as an autocratic monarch. According to Spiridovich, the address was regarded at the time as the most significant political moment of the Borodino celebrations, attesting to the conservative nobility's determination to stand by their tsar. Alexandra and Nicholas were moved

---

[145] V. Efremov, "Otchego voina 1812 goda nazyvaetsia 'Otechestvennoi'?" in V. Efremov and P. D. Zhukov, *Liubov' k otechestvu: istochnik sily narodnoi* (Ufa, 1912), 11, 20–21. I thank Charles Steinwedel for providing me with a copy of this brochure.

to tears and cherished the banner, which they kept in their recently built Feodorovskii Cathedral.[146]

The Moscow celebration concluded on August 30, the day of the patron saint of Alexander I, Alexander Nevskii, with a massive prayer service on Red Square in memory of Alexander I.[147] Nicholas followed a procession of the cross from the Assumption Cathedral to Red Square, reversing the usual direction of movement to the church from the square. An immense number of churchmen, nearly two hundred sextons alone, led the procession, bearing embroidered gonfalons, reliquary crosses, and a large number of miracle icons, among them the Smolensk, the Georgian, and the Vladimir Mothers of God. Followed by members of the court and the imperial family, they led the way past lines of troops of the Moscow garrison out of the Kremlin and along the Kremlin Wall.

Nicholas and Alexandra then ascended a dais, constructed in old-Russian style with a tent roof, near the monument to Minin and Pozharskii. "The crowd in the square was enormous, a sea of heads, and stood in perfect order and quiet," Nicholas wrote to his mother. A protodeacon declaimed the manifesto commemorating the battle. This was followed by a prayer service conducted by the metropolitan, joined by the Synodal Choir, and a People's Choir of more than three thousand. The emperor and empress and the immense crowd then fell to their knees as the choirs intoned a prayer in memory of Alexander I. The ceremony ended with a triple salvo from the troops on the square and the tolling of bells of the churches of Moscow, as the metropolitan made the sign of the cross with the icon of the Moscow miracle workers—the metropolitans Peter, Alexei, Iona, and Phillip.[148]

Moskovskie Vedomosti hailed the festivities for "dealing the final blow to the harmful legend of the so-called revolutionary character of Moscow." According to the editorial, the revolutionary events in Moscow were the result of outside insurgent bands, which were clumsily suppressed by officers sent from outside Moscow.[149] But in exalting the heroism of the monarchy, the Borodino celebrations demonstratively offended the members of the conservative Duma that Stolypin had designed to support the monarchy. Only the chairmen of the Duma and the State Council had been invited to the

---

[146] NV, August 28, 1912, 2; Spiridovitch, *Les dernières années de la cour de Tsarskoe-Selo*, 2:266; Naumov, *Iz utselevshikh vospominanii*, 2:225–26.

[147] On the last day, August 30, the day of Alexander Nevskii, Nicholas presumably was to visit an exhibition of products from cottage industry arranged by the Ministry of the Court. However, he was persuaded by the archpriest Anastasii and the grand duchess Elizabeth Fedorovna, who had taken vows and now was the abbess of the Convent of Mary and Martha, to participate instead in a thanksgiving ceremony on Red Square (Liubov' Miller, *Sviataia muchenitsa Rossiiskaia Velikaia Kniaginia Elizaveta Fedorovna* [Frankfort-am-Main, 1988], 190–91). Miller cites Archpriest Anastasii, who was a member of the commission planning the Moscow events, about the change of plans for August 30.

[148] MV, August 31, 1912, 1–2; Dzhunkovskii, *Vospominaniia*, 2:59–61; Bing, *The Secret Letters of the Last Tsar*, 272–73; Lockhart, *British Agent*, 73.

[149] MV, September 8, 1912, 1–2.

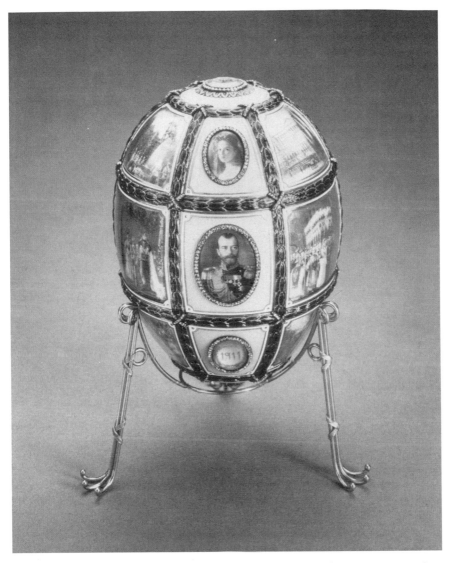

59. *Imperial Fifteenth Anniversary Egg*, by Fabergé. 1911. The FORBES Magazine
Collection, New York. © All rights reserved.

observances on the field of battle. "For the evident reason, the *Novoe Vremia*
columnist sardonically observed, "that in the midst of the enormous gathering of the people no room could be found for several hundred on the Borodino field." To deepen the insult, members of the half-appointive State Council received invitations to the Moscow events, but not the Duma deputies.
This act led Michael Rodzianko, the president of the Duma and a chamberlain of His Majesty's Court, to boycott the Moscow celebration. Rodzianko

threatened to write a protest about the absence of the people's representatives. *Novoe Vremia* also condemned this as a sign of "disrespect for the people," but it blamed the mistake on the officials of the Ministry of the Court.[150] The officials of the ministry, however, were merely heeding the wishes of the tsar, whom the newspaper could not openly criticize.

Nicholas regarded the jubilees as personal celebrations of the tsar as representative of the Russian people and of the Romanov dynasty. Such a ceremonial mentality was shared not only by the imperial family and the tsar's entourage, but also by many the foreign observers and journalists who took mass demonstrations of approval, however orchestrated, as signs of popular consent and admiration. For Nicholas and Alexandra the memories of such ceremonies were enshrined as personal triumphs in Fabergé eggs, which, like all Victorian household "kitsch," turned events into household ornaments and transformed the monumental into the domestic.

The use of domestic memorials to celebrate the tsar's ceremonial triumphs is exemplified by "the fifteenth-anniversary egg," Nicholas's gift to Alexandra on the anniversary of his coronation in 1911. "The fifteenth-anniversary egg" memorialized nine outstanding moments of Nicholas's reign in delicate ivory panels painted by Vasilii Zuev from photographs and drawings (fig. 59). Six of the events were ceremonial. Two miniatures depict the coronation—the tsar and the empress in the procession to the cathedral and Nicholas placing the crown on his head. One is a copy of the photograph of Nicholas carrying the bier at Sarov, and others show him before the throne at the reception of the Duma, descending the steps from the monument at Poltava, and at the unveiling of a statue to Peter the Great in Riga.[151] Similarly, he gave his mother a green enamel egg commemorating the Battle of Borodino in 1912. It encloses a screen with panels depicting officers from the regiments for which she was honorary chief. They are wearing the fancy uniforms of 1812 that Nicholas had restored for his army.[152]

---

[150] *NV*, September 1, 1912, 3. Rodzianko explained his absence to the minister of the interior Kokovtsev and to the master of ceremony Baron Korff. According to Rodzianko, the latter replied, "Members of the Duma do not enjoy the right of access to the Court." Rodzianko retorted, "This is not a Court, but a national celebration. Besides, Russia was saved not by masters of ceremony but by her people" (Rodzianko, *The Reign of Rasputin*, 65–66); *Russkoe Slovo*, however, expressed the liberals' contempt for Rodzianko's effort to mediate between court and people, and dismissed the possibility that Rodzianko would write such a protest. "Like every Octobrist, like Mr. Guchkov, Mr. Rodzianko 'boils heavily, but quickly cools down.'" (*Russkoe Slovo*, September 4, 1912, 2).

[151] The remaining three miniatures depicted the Huis ten Bosch in the Hague, which was the site of the Peace Conference; the Alexander III bridge in Paris; and the Alexander III Art Museum, which had recently opened in St. Petersburg; Marilyn Pfeifer Swezey, "The Imperial Easter Egg of 1911: Russia during the Reign of Nicholas II," in von Solodkoff, *Masterpieces from the House of Fabergé*, 111–22; Pfeffer, *Fabergé Eggs*, 92–95.

[152] Pfeffer, *Fabergé Eggs*, 100–101.

The Tercentenary Celebrations of 1913

With the combined labors of Our crowned predecessors on the Russian
throne and of all the true sons of Russia, the Russian State formed and
grew strong. Our Fatherland repeatedly became subject to trial, but the
Russian people, firm in their Orthodox faith, strong in their warm love
for the Fatherland and the self-sacrificing devotion to its Sovereigns, overcame misfortune and emerged renewed and strengthened. The close
boundaries of Muscovite Rus' expanded and the Great Russian Empire
now stood in the ranks of the first powers of the world.
In constant union with our beloved people, we hope to lead the State
in peaceful building of our national life.

—*From Nicholas II's Tercentenary Manifesto, February 21, 1913*[1]

CROSSING NARRATIVES: THE HISTORICAL MEANINGS
OF THE TERCENTENARY

The anniversary of the coming to the throne of the first Romanov tsar in
1613 assumed a far greater scope than previous jubilees. The opening celebrations, marking the election of Michael by the Assembly of the Land, took
place in Petersburg in February 1913. In May the imperial family journeyed
to the Volga towns including Kostroma, the ancient Romanov patrimony
where Michael Fedorovich at the Ipat'ev Monastery received the invitation
to rule from the Great Embassy of the assembly of 1613. They then proceeded to Moscow to commemorate Michael's gala entry into the city and
coronation.

The celebration was accompanied by an unprecedented outpouring of historical literature, as well as lectures, plays, operas, and films on the subject
of 1613 and its historical consequences. The Poltava and Borodino jubilees
had commemorated great victories in which the emperors had played the
central role. In 1613 there had been no tsar, and all social groups had participated in the rebirth of the Russian state. The anniversary of 1613 raised the
question of the meaning of the word *nation* and its relationship to monarch
and state. Rather than provide an occasion for consensus, the celebration

[1] *MV,* February 23, 1913, 1.

became a focus of contention between diverse understandings of nation—liberal, statist, monarchical, and clerical.

It was in the final decades of the nineteenth century that the seventeenth century replaced the reign of Peter the Great as the founding period of modern Russia and educated society, like the monarchy, began a search for a national culture and institutions in the pre-Petrine past. Vasilii Kliuchevskii's popular *Course of Russian History* located the beginning of modern Russia at 1613 rather than at the reign of Peter the Great. However sordid the details, Kliuchevskii argued, the election of Michael Romanov by the Assembly of the Land reflected an inchoate idea of a nation-state. "The idea shone through the personages, and this idea of state (*gosudarstvo*), separate from the idea of sovereign (*gosudar'*), began to fuse with the idea of nation (*narod*)."[2]

To moderate society, 1613 offered a model for an alliance between society, state, and tsar. The election of Michael provided an example of tsar and representative institutions working together. It served as a metaphor for a renovated national monarchy, one that appealed to those who sought to strengthen the state and empire.[3] The Kadet leader Peter Struve expressed this sense in his famous article of 1909, published in the collection *Vekhi*, which gave an enthusiastic description of the restoration of monarchical authority after the election of 1613. "In the events of the troubles of the early seventeenth century," he asserted, "the immeasurable significance of the state and national principles (*gosudarstvennost' i natsional'nost'*) rises before us with startling power and clarity."[4]

This focus reflected a broader consciousness of a great national cultural and artistic tradition to be discovered beyond the Petrine divide. In the years after 1905 early-Russian icons began to gain recognition as a form of artistic as well as religious expression.[5] The first public exhibition of Russian icons, which opened in February 1913, was a great revelation to the large numbers who attended. P. Muratov wrote in *Starye Gody*, "For many, perhaps for everyone, these impressions were completely unanticipated. Suddenly there opened before us a vast new sphere of art, or, more exactly, there opened a completely new art."[6] Modest Moussorgskii's operas *Boris Godunov* and *Khovanshchina*, which had been virtually ignored during previous decades, became great popular successes. *Khovanshchina*, the tale of the destruction

---

[2] V. O. Kliuchevskii, *Sochineniia* (Moscow, 1957), 3:62–65. Kliuchevskii's *Kurs* was published only beginning in 1904, but his ideas were widely known from his lectures, beginning in the 1880s, and lithographed and handwritten notes that were widely circulated.

[3] See Pinchuk, *The Octobrists in the Third Duma*, 13–15, on the mix of ideas among the members of the Octobrist Party.

[4] P. V. Struve, "Intelligentsiia i revoliutsiia," *Vekhi* (Moscow, 1909), 156–57.

[5] A. Grishchenko, *Russkaia ikona kak iskusstvo zhivopisi* (Moscow, 1917), 30–31.

[6] P. Muratov, "Vystavka drevne-russkogo iskusstva v Moskve," *Starye Gody* (April 1913), 31; see also Muratov's assessment of the event in Imperatorskii Moskovskii Arkheologicheskii Institut imeni Nikolaia II, *Vystavka drevne-russkogo iskusstva* (Moscow, 1913), 3.

of old Russia and the Old Believers, received its first professional productions at the Mariinskii and Bolshoi theaters in 1911 and 1912. In 1913 it was performed more frequently than any Russian opera except Tchaikovsky's *The Queen of Spades*.[7]

The seventeenth-century myth, the chronotope of Moscow, became a metaphor for the long-sought merger of educated Russians, eager to find a stable, conservative state, resting on foundations of law with the monarchy. The Muscovite past provided a template for the emergence of a unified "nation-state," recovered after the divisive effects of Westernization and revolution. The approach of 1913 inspired anticipation and preparations among the landholding nobility. In 1910 a gathering of noble marshals and deputies in Moscow Province issued a statement that it is in the present era, "when true patriotism is often condemned and ridiculed, when many regard the church and faith with indifference," that such a celebration would be the most significant of historical events."[8]

The tercentenary brought forth a spate of history books and newspaper articles, many of which treated the election as a model for reconciliation of differences and the national unity of Russia.[9] Sergei Platonov, perhaps the most distinguished living Russian historian in 1913 and a monarchist in his political views, connected the first monarchs' authority with a patriotic upsurge manifested in the election. His article, "The Whole Land," was published in a collection entitled *The Beginning of the Romanov Dynasty*, under the auspices of the Tercentenary Committee. Platonov portrayed the election as a fusion of people, state, and tsar: "The unanimous election by 'the whole land' was the pure and noble source of the Romanovs' authority. Such an election elevated Muscovite authority, previously proprietorial, to the significance of a national state (*narodno-gosudarstvennyi*) and gave it extraordinary strength and popularity." Platonov presented the first Romanovs as selfless servants of the nation who enjoyed extraordinary popularity. "From the 'tsar's little father,' Filaret Nikitich, to his great (*velikii*), great-grandson, Peter, all of the first representatives of the Romanov dynasty were equally inspired with dedication to the good of the state and the nation."[10]

[7] *Ezhegodnik imperatorskikh teatrov* (1913), 4:126; 5:103.

[8] O. V. Nemiro, "Iz istorii organizatsii i dekorirovaniia krupneishikh torzhestv Doma Romanovykh: 1896–1917gg.," in *Dom romanovykh v Rossii* (St. Petersburg, 1995), 255–56.

[9] For a partial listing of the literature, see "Romanovskie iubileinye dni," *Istoricheskii Vestnik* (March 1913): 3–6.

[10] Previously Platonov had shared Kliuchevskii's view that an incipient national idea had awakened at the 1613 Assembly of the Land, but he claimed that that idea had not manifested itself in noble acts of patriotism or a strong sense of unity at the time. In 1913 he became less restrained in his depiction of the period (S. F. Platonov, " 'Vsia zemlia,' " in P. G. Vasenko et al., eds., *Nachalo dinastii Romanovykh* (St. Petersburg, 1912), 233–34. The same argument was presented by Platonov's student, A. E. Presniakov, in the jubilee collection *Tri veka*. "The idea of a national state (*natsional'noe gosudarstvo*) was freed from the patrimonial-proprietorial form that arose among the Daniilovichi. 'The sovereign's cause' (*gosudarevo delo*) became 'the cause of the land' (*zemskoe delo*), which was assigned to the hereditary bearer of authority

Platonov delivered his views before numerous crowded lecture halls in 1913. Other historians lectured to audiences outside St. Petersburg. Professor I. I. Lappo declared at Iur'ev University that Michael had been chosen by the "whole land" and that the election transformed the patrimony of Kalita into "the all-Russian state." He asserted (incorrectly) that the first Romanovs traced the origins of their authority not to Augustus but to the election.[11] The same theme was set forth in the press. An editorial in the moderate conservative *Niva* explained that the election of 1613 had endowed the Russian state with the trust of the people, enabling the tsars to rise above class interest. Russia had progressed not in response to social strife—as had occurred in the West—"but exclusively as a result of the monarchs' comprehension of the demands, needs, and requirements of the Russian land." This comprehension had led to reforms such as the emancipation of the serfs. The "state idea" (*gosudarstvennost'*) served by the Romanovs was the source of Russia's greatness.[12]

The ideals expressed in moderate periodicals and books corresponded to those set forth in many official, state publications. The latter presented a statist view of Russian past development, describing the evolution of a union of state and society, led by Romanov monarchs, to attain the general good. Most of the popular tercentenary histories drew a connection between the achievements of the autocracy and the national mandate of 1613, making the assembly a predecessor of contemporary representative institutions. I. N. Bozherianov's richly illustrated *Three Hundred Years of the Romanov House* presented the Duma as the expression of the "eternal foundations" of the Russian past, citing Ivan Aksakov's dream of a union between the land and a national monarchy.[13] The same theme ran through the brochure, *Russia under the Scepter of the Romanovs*, sponsored by the Tercentenary Committee and distributed to schools and to lower ranks of the army and administration. Michael was elected not only because of the ties of the Romanov clan to the old ruling house but because the Romanovs in general, and Michael in particular, were beloved by the people. From this point commenced "the gradual development and growth of the Russian state under

---

by God" (V. V. Kallash, ed., *Tri veka; Rossiia ot smuty do nashego vremeni* [Moscow, 1912], 1:2, 28, 45).

[11] Professor I. I. Lappo, *Rech' proiznesennaia 21 fevralia 1913 goda* (Iur'ev, 1913), 21–22. On the continued allusions to the myth of Prus in the seventeenth century, see Volume 1: 32.

[12] "Reading history, one must believe in the limitless moral power and legendary vitality of Russia. Making its way along a thorny path under the leadership of its tsars of the Romanov House, it came out on the wide road to a glorious future, illumined as if by the rays of the sun, by the great and radiant Russian state idea, at the basis of which lies the unshakeable national faith in the justice and unconditional moral authority of state power. The preservation of this faith in the hearts of the people represents the greatest duty and the greatest merit of our rulers" (*Niva*, February 16, 1913, 138–40); see also the descriptions of 1613 as a popular national awakening in *Rech'*, February 21, 1913, 5; and *Utro Rossii*, February 21, 1913, 1, 3.

[13] I. N. Bozherianov, *Trista let tsarstvovaniia doma Romanovykh* (St. Petersburg, 1912), 165–70.

the scepter of the tsars of the Romanov house." Religion and the church were mentioned only in passing. The concluding sections on Nicholas II emphasized the summoning of the Duma and the State Council as an indication of his unity with the people.[14]

The historical literature expressing Nicholas II's scenario laid out a completely different narrative of 1613. This narrative, which I will call the "monarchical narrative," could be found along with the statist narrative in official publications. It made the tsar and his family the dominating actors, reducing the other participants to secondary figures. The monarchical narrative portrayed the events of 1613 as a foundation tale of a monarchy whose members themselves embodied the nation. It presented the assembly's election of Michael not as the birth of a political nation but as a divine designation of Michael Romanov and his descendants. It evoked the seventeenth century of the national myth, of Russians personally devoted to their tsar, as a synchronic paradigm for a restored absolute monarchy. The statist and the monarchical narratives, both meant to elevate the dynasty, crossed and, as it were, canceled each other, revealing the divisions in the Russian body politic.

While the state narrative of Kliuchevskii, Platonov, and the moderate monarchists emphasized the emergence of a concept of nation, *apart from* the personal figure of the monarch, the monarchical narrative extolled the indivisibility of the two. It evoked a personal and organic bond between tsar and people, expressed in dramatic acts of individual sacrifice. The emblematic event of 1613 was not the election of Michael but his acceptance of the throne from the delegation of boyars and clergy who made their way from Moscow to the Ipat'ev Monastery in the Romanov patrimony of Kostroma. According to various charters of 1613, Michael, a boy of sixteen, and his mother, Martha, agreed to the invitation only after long and tearful exhortation in the Trinity Cathedral of the monastery. It was the invocation of the "righteous and inscrutable judgment of God" that forced them to relent. Michael's acceptance, Martha announced, "was not at all my or my son's desire."[15] According to tradition, Martha then blessed Michael with the Feodorov Mother of God, the Kostroma miracle icon.

[14] *Rossiia pod skipetrom Romanovykh* (St. Petersburg, 1913), 3–4, 11–12, 31. The volume appears to have been written by two schoolteachers, A. D. Muretov and A. V. Korolev, though they are not mentioned in the text. It was published in an edition of 1,000,550 copies, of which nearly 900,000 were distributed, about one-third free of charge ("Ob izdanii populiarnoi istorii Rossii za vremia tsarstvovaniia Doma Romanovykh," RGIA, 1320-1-31, 66, 245–46; Ingeborg Kaufmann, "Das dreihundertjährige Thronjubiläum des Hauses Romanov: Russland 1913," masters thesis, Humboldt University, Berlin, 1996, 140–41.

[15] *Sobranie gosudarstvennykh gramot i dogovorov* (Moscow, 1822), 3:44–54. The description in the charters may have been copied from Godunov's acceptance of the invitation to rule in 1598 (S. F. Platonov, *Lektsii po russkoi istorii* [St. Petersburg, 1901], 253; D. Ilovaiskii, *Smutnoe vremia Moskovskogo gosudarstva* [Moscow, 1894], 255). See the descriptions in I. M. Pokrovskii, "Russkoe dukhovenstvo, ego patriotizm i deiatel'nost' v zashchite Pravoslaviia i zakonnoi natsional'noi tsarskoi vlasti v smutnoe vremia i pri izbranii na russkii tsarskii prestol

The monarchical narrative turned the reluctant acceptance of the throne into an exemplary act of personal sacrifice expressing the subordination of the tsar's personal advantage to the public good.[16] The image of the tsar as a Christlike figure appeared in many commemorative histories issued in 1913. The most explicit statement was in Captain S. A. Toluzakov's *The Heroic Feat (Podvig) of the Three-Hundred-Year Service to Russia of the Tsars of the Romanov House.* Toluzakov described the Russian tsars' propensity for self-sacrifice as the chief causal factor in Russian history. They had worn a "crown of thorns." Michael had accepted the throne to save Russia from ruin, and since then all the tsars had displayed only one desire— "the well-being of their native land." Motivated by "a consciousness of infinite responsibility," they had "limited their personal lives in every respect." "They even often sacrificed the right accessible to the humblest of their subjects to marry for love, in behalf of political considerations advantageous to Russia." As a result, their will had become subject to the will of the people, erasing the distinction between ruler and subjects. "The thought of the people is expressed in the will of the tsar, and the will of the people becomes the thought of the tsar."[17]

These accounts detached the service ethos from the rationalistic, utilitarian principles that had underlain it since the eighteenth century and, instead, associated service to the people with a saintly image of self-denial. The tsar, rather than dedicating himself personally to serve the state, responded to a divine injunction to devote himself to his people. The 1613 tale of foundation brought the sovereign down from a distant Olympus and presented him as an ordinary person with human features, but one who spent his life working for their well-being. It showed that the tsar shared a common humanity with his people and allowed him to speak for the nation, in spite of the apparent differences in dress and lifestyle. *Moskovskie Vedomosti*, in May 1913, asserted that the seventeenth-century tsars had developed the state spirit (*gosudarstvennost'*) and built Russian institutions. They, not the people, had created a national consciousness. Few other dynasties had produced so many able rulers. This was not an accident but the result of "the tsarist principle" that "the tsar lives not for himself but for the people, does not his work, but the people's."[18]

---

boiarina Mikhaila Feodorovicha Romanova," *Pravoslavnyi Sobesednik* (March 1913): 412–13; N. V. Pokrovskii, "Kostromskii Ipat'evskii Monastyr'—kolybel' tsarstvuiushchego doma," in M. S. Putiatin, ed., *Letopisnyi i Litsevoi Izbornik Doma Romanovykh: Iubileinoe izdanie v oznamenovanie 300-letiia tsarstvovaniia* (Moscow, 1913), 1:53–54.

[16] See, for example, I. Bazhenov, "Prizvanie Mikhaila Feodorovicha k prestolu," *Iubileinyi sbornik kostromskogo tserkovno-istoricheskogo obshchestva* (Kostroma, 1913), 58–59; MV, February 22, 1913, 3; P. G. Vasenko, ed., *Boiare Romanovy i votsarenie Mikhaila Feodorovicha* (St. Petersburg, 1913), 142–52.

[17] S. A. Toluzakov, *Podvig 300-letiia sluzheniia Rossii gosudarei doma Romanovykh* (St. Petersburg, 1913), 3–4, 312.

[18] *MV*, May 26, 1913, 1. Official publications of the Orthodox Church and the government set forth similar views. Sermons attributed Russia's power, size, and economic development

The emperor and empress, as the Feodorovskii Cathedral and village suggest, felt themselves in direct contact with the spirit of the nation as it had been revealed in the seventeenth century. They expressed this spirit in a lavish two-volume collection, published under their patronage in old-Russian style, to mark the tercentenary.[19] The collection was entitled *Izbornik*, the name of popular early-Russian collections of texts and was rendered with lavish pseudo-medieval illustrations as if it were an illuminated manuscript. It contained paintings and ornamentation by such accomplished artists as S. I. Iaguzhinskii, Nicholas Rerikh, and Victor Vasnetsov. The album, published as the works of "the First All-Russian Congress of the members of the Nicholas II Imperial Archaeological Institute," contained historical studies of the Romanov past.

The two volumes open with water-colored portraits by A. F. Maksimov of Nicholas and Alexandra facing their seventeenth-century predecessors. The portraits are framed by designs resembling the silhouettes of old Russian churches and surrounded with floral motifs by S. I. Iaguzhinskii (figs. 51 and 60). Volume 1 juxtaposes Michael with Nicholas. The portrait of Michael, a copy from the archive of the Ministry of Foreign Affairs, shows him in full regalia. Opposite Michael, Nicholas appears in seventeenth-century robe and crown, holding the scepter, a copy of a 1903 portrait, probably from the costume ball of that year. Volume 2 opens with a similar pairing: Maksimov's portrait of Empress Alexandra in seventeenth-century headdress and robe faces a portrait of the tsaritsa Evdokiia Luk'ianovna, the second wife of Tsar Michael.

These juxtapositions carried more than a decorative and celebratory meaning: They substantiated a mystical organic bond linking the imperial couple with their seventeenth-century forebears. A curious study by Baron A. Taube disclosed "a remarkable coincidence": contacts in the seventeenth century between the forbears of the house of Hesse-Darmstadt and the Romanovs. Apparently two Saxon princesses were considered as brides for Tsar Michael. This did not come to pass, and instead they wed princes of Hesse-Darmstadt. Taube traced the genealogical lines and concluded that the two Saxon princesses, through their Hessian progeny, became "great-

---

to the dedication of the Romanov tsars. One archpriest asserted that "Russian might grew over the previous three hundred years, its population increased, and riches multiplied." "Who, Russians, gave the impetus to your great work, who is your mainspring, who commands the march of the Russian land? It is your Tsar and Sovereign." Peter the Great had provided an example of ceaseless, stubborn labor. Alexander II had freed them. Nicholas II had given them land in full possession. The Russian people should say thanks to God, who had given "peace to our land and wise tsars" (Protoierei Mikhail Lisitsyn, "Pouchenie k narodu na den' trekhsotletiia tsarstvovaniia doma Romanovykh," *Tserkovnye Vedomosti*, February 9, 1913, 272).

[19] *Letopisnyi i Litsevoi Izbornik* was edited by Prince Michael Putiatin, a member of the imperial suite and a student of Russian antiquities, who shared and probably encouraged Nicholas's passion for early Russia and advised in the decoration of the Feodoroff Cathedral.

60. Portrait of Empress Alexandra in seventeenth-century robes. M. S. Putiatin, ed., *Letopisnyi i Litsevoi Izbornik*, 1913. Slavic and Baltic Division, New York Public Library, Astor, Lenox, and Tilden Foundations.

grandmothers of the entire Romanov imperial house and of Nicholas and Alexandra."[20]

The book also demonstrated the artistic rebirth of national Russian art now exemplified in the Feodorov village. There were illustrations of an old-Russian goblet and a ladle, shown in photographs, and icons of the Feodorov Mother of God. A color photo-reproduction of the icon was placed prominently after the introduction. Pictures of copies of the icon in the Moscow and Kostroma Assumption Cathedral and of the original in the Trinity Cathedral in the Ipat'ev Monastery accompanied a historical and analytical essay by the eminent medievalist N. V. Pokrovskii. Illuminations by Victor Vasnetsov of Patriarch Hermogen and by Nicholas Rerikh of scenes from the early history of the Romanov family reproduced the style of early-Russian manuscripts, but with a brightness of color and draftsmanlike skill alien to early-Russian art.

The brief preface declared the political and religious significance of 1613. "In the election of Michael Romanov as tsar, the people saw the manifestation not of their personal will but of the will and grace of God. The chronicle says, 'Not the people but God made him Tsar; the people only fulfill the divine will.' " The same feeling lived on into the present. "The image of the Autocratic tsar has not died in the national heart even during the murderous years of breakdown." The anonymous author called upon God "to instill unity of thought (*edinomyshlenie*) in our hearts, as He did three hundred years ago."

An article by the Bishop Nikon, entitled "The Inscrutable Fates of Divine Providence in the Election of Michael Romanov," described how "the most pious Mother took her son's hand and reverently knelt with him before the blessed Feodorov icon." The people, the Bishop wrote, understood the "calling" of Michael Romanov to rule as a "clearly divine indication," as attested by Ivan Susanin's martyrdom in the cause of saving the Tsar's life.[21] Words and music to a "Romanov Anthem" closed the book with a prayer to God for a return to early Russia, when the tsar ruled untrammeled.

> Under Your blessing,
> Our great Sovereign (*velikii Gosudar'*),
> With Divine Blessing, is a mighty autocrat.
> As in Olden Days.[22]

The monarchical narrative took up the theme of the close bond between the new dynasty and the people. The soldiers' newspaper *Vitiaz'* proclaimed, "The Russian people were very clearly aware that it was as impossible to live without a tsar as to live without a head." The government newspaper *Pravitel'stvennyi vestnik* used a different metaphor: "Elected by the voice of

[20] *Letopisnyi i Litsevoi Izbornik*, 2:11–24.

[21] Ibid., 1:12, 30–31.

[22] Ibid, 2:115. N. N. Bronevetskii wrote the music and Prince D. N. Golitsyn-Muravlin the words.

the popular masses, the service class, and the clergy, the new tsar, the progenitor of the Romanov house, grew, as if out of the womb of the people, and became strong defended by them."[23]

The monarchical narrative emphasized that the tsar's self-abnegation was complemented by the self-abnegation of the people, personified in the figure of Ivan Susanin, who, the tale went, had given his life to lead the Poles astray and save his lord, Michael Feodorovich. Susanin's heroism, the theme of Glinka's opera *A Life for the Tsar*, complemented Michael's.[24] His absolute devotion to Michael united tsar and people in acts of personal sacrifice. *Pravitelstvennyi vestnik* declared, "Ivan Susanin splendidly symbolizes the bond between the new monarch and the masses of the people." Susanin's image became ubiquitous during the celebrations. Newspapers, popular books, and priests in their sermons recounted the familiar story. Soldiers and officers dressed in peasant clothing for regimental productions of Glinka's opera, and high school students performed it for local officials and schoolchildren.[25]

The sermons of 1913 presented Susanin's heroism as an irrevocable relinquishment of power by the people to the tsar. The people had merged with the sovereign and had lost all separate identity. As a result, the tsar had no reason to do harm to them, any more than he would want to do harm to himself. The people and the tsar were "the closest of the close," wrote Archpriest Ioann Vostorgov, a leader of the Union of the Russian People.[26] The bond went beyond obedience: Tsar and people shared common goals and values.

The narrative of a national monarchy shifted the historical focus from the governmental system to historical personages. It reduced the abstractions of state and power to personal representations of authority and subordination. The institutions of the bureaucracy in this framework were portrayed as a mere encumbrance, "a dividing wall" (*sredostenie*), between tsar and people. Nicholas II believed that he had succeeded in breaching this wall.[27] The Slavophile vision of a harmonious unity between tsar and people appeared in this narrative not as an assembly where all classes could meet their sovereign but as a mystic bond transcending all institutions.

•

Many of the accounts of 1613 in church organs contested both state and monarchical narratives. Preaching devotion to the tsar, these articles emphasized the role of the Orthodox clergy in Russian history. In a sermon written "for the people," Archpriest Lisitsyn declared that it was the Orthodox faith

---

[23] *Vitiaz'*, February 21, 1913, 138–39; *Pravitel'stvennyi Vestnik*, February 21, 1913, 4–5.

[24] On the Susanin theme in Nicholas I's reign, see Volume 1: 390–95.

[25] *Vitiaz'*, January 17, 1913, 51; V. A. Kamenskii, "Memoirs," 24, Bakhmeteff Archive, Columbia University; *Ezhegodnik imperatorskikh teatrov* 4 (1913): 120; *Russkoe Slovo*, February 23, 1913, 3; *Vestnik Orenburgskogo Uchebnogo Okruga*, no. 2 (1913): 113–18; no. 3 (1913): 181.

[26] Protoierei Ioann Vostorgov, "Ideinye zavety iubileiia," *Tserkovnye Vedomosti*, February 9, 1913, 271.

[27] See, for example, Mosolov, *Pri dvore poslednego Rossiiskogo imperatora*, 115–16.

that had provided the salvation of Russia three hundred years before, giving the nation the strength to unite and resist the enemy. The Kazan Mother of God had saved Russia by enabling the troops to take Moscow in 1612. In recent years the church had delivered Russia from the misfortunes that wicked people had brought upon the country. The Russian people owed their survival to "the remnants of our fathers' faith, to the prayers of the sacred humble before God (*ugodniki*), Serafim of Sarov and John of Kronstadt." Lisitsyn concluded with an exhortation to love and maintain faith in the tsar. The lesson of history was simple: "Remember, if there is a Tsar, then there is order. While the Tsar lives, there is peace in our land!"[28]

Archpriest Ivan Vostorgov, concluded in his article that "the election of the Romanovs was directly and exclusively the work of the church."[29] The central figure in the narrative of the national church was Patriarch Hermogen, who had refused to recognize a Roman Catholic, a Pole, as tsar of Russia and summoned the nation to unite. Hermogen's writings, republished in preparation for the canonization, contained descriptions of his efforts to subdue Tatar regions and to convert the population to Orthodoxy.[30] The church extolled Hermogen as "the most typical Russian person," as the leader of the national struggle.[31] The sermons published in 1913 described Hermogen's preparation of new cadres of priests to organize the nation. The Trinity Monastery at Radonezh became the center of the national movement. The prelates at the Assembly in Moscow, particularly the Kazan metropolitan Efrem, had insisted on Michael's election. Avramii Palitsyn, the cellar-keeper of the Trinity Monastery, was an influential adviser to Michael's supporters and had worked to organize the election and the acclamation for him. The first thirty-two signatures on the election charter belonged to members of the clergy.[32]

Beginning in 1910 the church took up the cause of Hermogen's canonization, presenting his death for the nation as religious martyrdom. This represented a shift to a more assertive role by the hierarchy for previously, as one article remarked, Hermogen had been regarded "not so much as an ascetic saint, the isolated monk, but as a strong public figure, ready for any sacrifice."[33] Immediately before the canonization, Hermogen's resting place in the Assumption Cathedral became a center of activity and attention. Pilgrims, the lame, the blind, and the demented gathered to pray and be

---

[28] Lisitsyn, "Pouchenie k narodu," 74.

[29] Protoierei Ioann Vostorgov, "Uchastie tserkvi i dukhovenstva v velikikh sobytiiakh trista let tomu nazad," *Tserkovnye Vedomosti*, February 21, 1913, appendix, 329–32.

[30] *Tvoreniia Sviateishego Germogena; Patriarkha Moskovskogo i vseia Rossii* (Moscow, 1912), 17–24, 34.

[31] Freeze, "Subversive Piety," 330–31.

[32] I. M. Pokrovskii, "Russkoe dukhovenstvo," 371–416; Sviashchennik T. I. Liashchenko, "Slovo v den' trekhsotletiia votsareniia Tsaria Romanovykh; Tserkov' Pravoslavnaia opora Prestola i Tsarstva Vserossiiskogo," *Trudy Imperatorskoi Kievskoi Dukhovnoi Akademii* (February 1913): i–x.

[33] *Tserkovno-Obshchestvennyi Vestnik*, May 23, 1913, 7.

healed.[34] Canonization took place on May 12, 1913, at the Assumption Cathedral in the Moscow Kremlin. The metropolitan of Vladimir officiated, and the patriarch of Antioch participated in the service. After the ceremony, both joined the procession of the cross into Red Square. Thousands witnessed the spectacle, which was vividly described in *Novoe Vremia*. The backdrop of the Kremlin walls and Vasilii the Blessed formed "a grandiose frame" for the event. The procession filed through cordons of grenadiers "like an endless ball of silver thread." The silver of the priests' vestments and the gold of the gonfalons flashed in the sunlight. Above the crowd could be seen the Kazan Mother of God, bordered by flowers and beneath it a cross of roses. Victor Vasnetsov's large icon of Hermogen "floated over the heads of the thousands, as if living, and blessed them."[35]

Nicholas and Alexandra, however, did not appear among the pilgrims as they had at Sarov, a canonization undertaken at their own initiative. Serafim was an elder, a man of the people, whereas Hermogen represented the church hierarchy. The emperor and empress instead attended the wedding of the Kaiser's daughter in Berlin, which was certainly a royal obligation. However, they ignored a proposal advanced by the Synod commission on the canonization to postpone the ceremony until the May celebration of the tercentenary.[36] Exalting Patriarch Hermogen during the May events of the tercentenary would have given the church even more prominence and created a symbol to rival the patriarch Filaret, the progenitor of the dynasty. The imperial family was represented at the canonization by the grand duchess Elizabeth Feodorovna—Alexandra's sister and now Mother Superior of the Convent of Martha and Maria—and the twenty-seven-year-old grand duke Ioann Konstantinovich, a cousin of the tsar.

TERCENTENARY MONUMENTS

The clash between the statist and monarchical views of the celebration was exemplified in the planning of the two tercentenary monuments—the Tercentenary Cathedral near the Nicholas (Now Moscow) Railway Station in St. Petersburg and the Romanov Monument in Kostroma—both of which were under construction at the time of the festivities. Both monuments failed to receive the endorsements of the committee established to organize the Tercentenary.[37] The committee preferred to decline proposals that had a partisan

---

[34] See *Narodnaia vera v sviatosti Patriarkha Germogena i plody etoi very, chudesa, sovershaiushchiiasia po ego molitvam* (Moscow, 1914), 9. The text stressed Hermogen's national role. "Hermogen alone stood for the defense of the fatherland, the orthodox faith, and Russia's uniqueness. He saved the faith from profanation and the fatherland from enslavement."

[35] NV, May 12, 1913, 3; May 13, 1913, 3.

[36] Freeze, "Subversive Piety," 336.

[37] Its full name was the Committee on the Organization of the Celebration of the Tercentenary of the Romanov Dynasty (*Komitet dlia ustroistva prazdnovaniia trekhsotletiia Doma Ro-*

character, even those that had the blessings of the imperial family, but in the end it was powerless to stop either project.

The initiative for the Tercentenary Church came from the Feodorovskii Gorodetskii Monastery in Nizhegorodskii Province and gained the backing of the imperial family. The monastery, in fact, had little to do with the Feodorov icon or the events in 1613. But the hegumen, the archimandrite Aleksii, had worked actively to turn the monastery's small chapel in the Nicholas Railway Station into a church. The Tercentenary Committee refused to fund the building of the church, pointing out that the monastery had been connected with the name of Alexander Nevskii, who had been tonsured and had died there, rather than with the Romanovs or the year 1613. But Aleksii succeeded in gaining the patronage of Alexander III shortly before his death and, later, of the grand duke Michael Aleksandrovich. The building of such a church was also backed by the leadership of the Union of Russian People. Nicholas himself opened a national subscription for the church with a large donation. Other funds came from the St. Petersburg City Duma and Church and governmental institutions.[38]

The Tercentenary Church presented the dynasty and Nicholas's family as the embodiment of the nation. The Feodorov Mother of God was the central motif of the building. A large majolica copy of the icon, based on Iaroslavl frescoes, was placed on the cathedral's north wall in the center of a genealogical tree of the Romanov house. The bells carried relief portraits of each member of Nicholas's family and their patron saints.

The cathedral's design was a copy of Rostov wall churches of the seventeenth century, particularly those from the Rostov Kremlin, which, the architect Stepan Krichinskii asserted, exemplified the true Russian style. Constructed from reinforced concrete, it was considerably larger than its prototypes—nearly as high as the Kazan Cathedral—and accommodated more than four thousand worshipers (fig. 61). Like the *Feodorovskii* village it was to be separated from the profane reality of its Western surroundings. "The idea was to create an entire corner of the seventeenth century," Krichinskii wrote. A Kremlin was planned to surround the church, with one of the towers devoted to a museum of the early seventeenth century. The complex would transplant a bit of Muscovy to St. Petersburg where many, like the art critic George Lukomskii, believed it did not belong.[39]

---

manovykh). Its membership consisted of representatives of most of the ministries and of the Holy Synod. For a more extensive discussion of the committee's activities, see Kaufmann, "Das dreihundertjährige Thronjubiläum des Hauses Romanov."

[38] *Istoriia Feodorovskogo Gorodetskogo monastyria (Nizhegorodskaia guberniia) i postroenie v S-Peterburge khrama v pamiat' 300 iubileiia tsarstvovaniia imperatorskogo Doma Romanovykh* (St. Petersburg, 1913), 113–24; *ZKT*, 5–6, 43–45.

[39] S. Krichinskii, "Khram v pamiat' 300-letiia doma Romanovykh," *Zodchii* (1914): 122–23; *Niva*, no. 5 (1914): 97; "Snimki vidov tserkvi postroennoi v pamiat' 300-letiia tsarstvovaniia Romanovykh," GARF, 601-1-1841; Georgii Lukomskii, "Khram v pamiat' 300-letiia tsarstvovaniia doma Romanovykh," *Apollon*, no. 5 (1914): 47–49; Kirichenko, *Russkii stil'*, 309–10, 316–17.

61. Tercentenary Church. Architect, Stepan Krichinskii.
1911–1915. GARF.

The idea for a Romanov Monument in Kostroma originated among the local Kostroma nobility in 1910. A Kostroma committee, consisting of the governor of the province and the provincial and district marshals of the nobility, approved a project submitted by A. I. Adamson and opened a public subscription. Adamson's initial project took the form of a tent-shaped chapel and emphasized Russian subjugation of the various nationalities of the empire. Groups of Poles, Lithuanians, Tatars, Central Asians, and other nationalities occupied the pedestal around a central figure of "a shepherd of Great Russian nationality." A Little Russian was also shown shaking hands with a Great Russian behind a shield of Kostroma.[40]

Adamson submitted this project, and later a revised version, to the competition for a Romanov Monument judged by a committee of the Academy of Arts in St. Petersburg. The academy committee did not share the Kostroma committee's enthusiasm and concluded that the projects were not worthy of execution. On March 1, 1912, the Tercentenary Committee accepted the judgment of the experts from the academy, finding the form of the chapel and the various groups on the statue unsuitable. It also determined that the funds collected were inadequate for a proper monument.[41] The Kostroma Committee appealed to the minister of the interior, but he refused to intervene. Work on the statue nonetheless went forward, suggesting that authorization came from the tsar himself.

The final project retained the form of a tent-shaped chapel, but without the scenes of subjugated national groups. The monument rose in layers of *kokoshniki* following a tent silhouette to a small onion-shaped cupola.[42] Figures of sixteen Romanov monarchs appeared in tiers, striking dramatic classical or realistic poses characterizing their reign. For example, Alexei Mikhailovich holds the Law Code of 1649; Peter the Great is shown with Archbishop Feofan Prokopovich and Field-Marshal B. P. Sheremet'ev; and Elizabeth Petrovna, with emblems of the Academy of Sciences and Moscow University, which she founded. Alexander II holds the emancipation manifesto.

The center of attention is Tsar Michael, sitting on his throne, his hand resting on a map of Muscovite Rus'. Michael's father, the patriarch Filaret, and his mother, the nun Martha, stand at his side. Beneath are the figures of Minin and Pozharskii, leaders of the national militia. At the base of the statue, Ivan Susanin kneels before an allegorical female figure of Russia in armor and holding a sword. Her dress was designed according to seventeenth-century models, and some of the details were taken from photographs of the empress Alexandra. Susanin, the description in the Kostroma jubilee volume asserted, was close to Martha and served as a steward of the Romanov estates. He appeared as a confident, well-to-do peasant and was dressed in an ample sheepskin coat as a symbol of the rich peasants who represented the hope of the Stolypin land reform (fig. 62).

The monument was completely devoted to acts of members of the dynasty and, unlike the Millennium Monument, did not include representatives of

[40] "Po torzhestvam v Kostrome," RGIA, 1320-1-4, 29, 33.

[41] *ZKT*, 71–74.

[42] My discussion is based on the description and the picture of the model in *Prazdnovanie trekhsotletiia tsarstvovaniia Doma Romanovykh v Kostromskoi gubernii 19–20 maia 1913* (Kostroma, 1913), 117–19; *Niva*, February 16, 1913, 138.

62. Ivan Susanin and Allegory of Russia, Romanov Statue, Kostroma.
Sculptor, A. I. Adamson. Niva, 1913.

Russian culture. The bas-reliefs depicted the beginnings and achievements of the dynasty—the prophesy of St. Gennadii of Kostroma of the elevation of the Romanov's to the throne, the summoning of Michael, and the emancipation of the serfs—and three depict the battles of Poltava and Borodino and the siege of Sevastopol. On the reverse side of Michael's statue, Nicholas II is shown on a bas-relief holding a map of the Russian empire in 1913, before his son, Alexei. In the initial projects, the two figures were also supposed to appear as statues, but two members of the Tercentenary Committee raised doubts about the permissibility of presenting the tsar and tsarevich on a monument.[43]

The bas-relief was clearly a compromise but still a significant departure, marking the first representation of a reigning sovereign on a public monument. The history of the dynasty reached its final and highest embodiment in the tsar's family in 1913. The description pointed out the equivalence between the figures of Michael at the center of the monument and Nicholas and Michael beneath, suggesting a direct bond between the two. The maps held by Michael and Nicholas showed the progress of three centuries, the former displaying "the small number of regions of the Moscow State" in 1613 and the latter "the extent that Muscovite Rus' of the seventeenth century attained after three centuries of the Reign of the Romanov House." It "had grown into the mighty contemporary European and Asian Russian Empire (*Rossiiskaia Imperiia*)."[44]

The monument thus presents the theme of empire not in terms of the subjects' acceptance of Russian domination, but through simple evidence of immense territorial expansion. The same theme was affirmed in the Tercentenary Manifesto and in the form of Fabergé's Tercentenary Egg, which decorated the imperial family's home. The egg's shell combines symbols of Muscovite and imperial Russia—Monomakh caps, golden eagles, and imperial crowns, as well as miniature portraits of eighteen Romanov rulers from Michael to Nicholas. The surprise inside is a globe, one-half showing Russia with the boundaries of 1613, the other the vast reaches of the empire in 1913.[45]

PREPARATIONS FOR THE CELEBRATION

The planning of the festivities, supervised by the Tercentenary Committee, ensured that the events would celebrate the monarchical narrative and focus on the tsar and his forbears. But the figure of the monarch could not so easily be detached from the physical and institutional setting of the monarchy— the city, the state, the court, the Duma, and the modern press that communicated the events to the population. These elements contributed to a symbolic dissonance and a sense of underlying conflict throughout the celebrations.

The first significant decision of the Tercentenary Committee was to make February 21, the anniversary of Michael's election, the principal date of the celebration. The committee rejected a proposal of the representatives of the Holy Synod to celebrate July 11, the anniversary of Michael's coronation. The committee's journal bluntly stated that the "autocratic power of the

[43] "Po torzhestvam v Kostrome," 47–48.
[44] *Prazdnovanie trekhsotletiia tsarstvovaniia Doma Romanovykh*, 119.
[45] Snowman, *Carl Fabergé*, 114; Pfeffer, *Fabergé Eggs*, 102–3.

Russian Tsar" did not have "an ecclesiastical origin, like some Western countries where kings depended on the papal throne." It was Michael's election that gave the dynasty its popular mandate. February 21 was the day, the chair of the committee and former minister of the interior Alexander Bulygin declared, that that would have "the broadest, truly state and all-Russian character."[46]

The committee defended the election as the beginning of the dynasty, while rejecting the doctrine of popular sovereignty. The election was unconditional, implying no constraints on the monarch's power: "The autocratic power of the Russian Tsar has never rested on any contractual legal basis." Bulygin invoked the organic rhetoric of the monarchical narrative. He shifted the focus from the electoral body to the consciousness of the whole people—the "national soul" and "the historical habit never to separate the sacred image of the Tsar from the image of the native land (*rodina*), which is equally sacred to the Russian heart." The deputies merely expressed the promptings of the national soul. When the first Romanov tsar arrived in Moscow, the people, "like a single person, cried that they wanted Tsar Michael Feodorovich. . . . For His name alone people were ready to die and went to their death. His reign began in the hearts of Russian people from this point."[47]

The committee also decided that the anniversary of the election should be celebrated in Petersburg. Petersburg, a city that represented a break with early Russia, now was supposed to demonstrate its origins in Moscow. The February events brought out the discontinuities rather than continuities of Russian history and gave a vivid display of the rift between the tsar and the state through which he ruled.

The clashes began with the decoration of the city, a responsibility assumed by the Petersburg city government, which refused to appropriate the sums of money requested by central government institutions. The motifs and colors selected by the artists directing the work reflected an aesthetic tradition of empire, whose inspiration came from the neoclassicism of the Westernizing monarchy. The artists chose yellow and orange for the flags to decorate the city, colors meant to imitate the decorations on St. Mark's Square in Venice, recalling the theme of Petersburg, "the Venice of the North." The masts for the flags before Kazan Cathedral were also patterned on those set before St. Mark's, and Alexandrine obelisks were placed on the squares.

Observers noted a striking absence of traditional Russian national motifs. Many of the busts and bas-reliefs ignored the theme of the ceremony and began not with Michael but with Peter, though on the Winter Palace Square the ensemble was Michael–Peter I–Nicholas II. Two historical narratives were presented simultaneously. The Petersburg governor-general protested

[46] "Po voprosu o dne vserossiiskogo prazdnovaniia 300-letiia Tsarstvennogo Doma Romanovykh," RGIA, 1320-1-20, 4–5.

[47] Ibid., 4.

the colors, but only after the flags were hung. On the day of the celebration, however, national flags, the Russian red, white, and blue, finally appeared on Nevskii Prospect, adding to the confusion of symbols. G. K. Lukomskii remarked on "the mechanical pasting together of disparate motifs."[48]

Conservative and monarchist newspapers judged the expenditures of the Petersburg city government niggardly and the decorations tawdry for such an occasion. In "Petersburg Letter," the *Moskovskie Vedomosti* reporter complained that the Petersburg city government had reduced its promised allocations for decorations so sharply "that it was impossible to put up anything artistic or splendid." A *Novoe Vremia* columnist lamented, "We were promised a spectacle, and we got nothing but sadness." The physiognomy of the city should have been transformed, vested in "a fantastic, legendary garb. Then the people would be in a gay mood, would for the moment shed their everyday cares and feast on the spectacle, which in our dull time is needed more than ever."[49]

The political mood in February was also antagonistic. In December 1912 Nicholas appointed Nicholas Maklakov acting minister of the interior, and in February he was confirmed in his position. Maklakov made it immediately clear that he, like Viacheslav Plehve ten years before, intended "to strengthen authority." He assigned new police authority to the governors and announced that he wanted changes in the press law.[50]

Liberals and moderate society, however, had hoped for a broad political amnesty.[51] *Zemstvo* and town assemblies, the Duma and the State Council, all called for a true amnesty. An article of January 27, 1913, in *Russkoe Slovo*, concluded, "Now when the 'Time of Troubles' has passed, by official announcement of the ministry, . . . the belief has been born in the public consciousness that a free and generous hand will bear a new cup of mercy." The newspaper called for a closing of accounts on conflicts of the revolutionary era, "a total oblivion of the past in the name of pacification and tranquillity." It was especially important to free those convicted of political crimes in the struggle for the very institutions that had been established. On February 17 an article in *Utro Rossii* affirmed that "Russia craves surcease. She strives for peace and reconciliation."[52]

---

[48] Katerina Clark, *Petersburg: Crucible of Revolution*, (Cambridge, Mass., 1995), 58; *NV*, February 20, 1913, 5; *Rech'*, February 20, 1913, 1; Nemiro, "Iz istorii organizatsii i dekorirovaniia krupneishikh torzhestv Doma Romanovykh," 257.

[49] *MV*, February 24, 1913, 2; *NV*, February 23, 1913, 14.

[50] V. S. Diakin, *Burzhuaziia, dvorianstvo i tsarizm v 1911–1914gg.: razlozhenie tret'eiun'-skoi sistemy* (Leningrad, 1988), 115.

[51] On January 12 the newspaper *Russkoe Slovo* expressed the view that "the people are waiting and hope that February 21, 1913, will prove as historical and unforgettable a day as February 21, 1613." The author adduced examples of amnesties in other countries (*Russkoe Slovo*, January 8, 1913, 4; January 10, 1913, 4; January 12, 1913, 1).

[52] Ibid., January 15, 1913, 4; January 18, 1913, 4; January 23–24 1913, 4; January 25, 1913, 3; January 27, 1913, 2–3, 5; *Utro Rossii*, February, 17, 1913, 2.

By Nicholas II's intention, the decree issued on the day of the celebration was not an amnesty but rather a carefully measured forgiveness designed to show his determination not to yield even in spirit to the entreaties from moderate society.[53] *Russkoe Slovo* pointed out that the amnesty was issued not as a *Vsemilostiveishii Manifest* (Most Gracious Manifesto), showing the tsar's feelings of generosity and sympathy with his subjects, but as a formal decree to the Senate. The crimes eligible for reduction or elimination of sentences were determined by the maximum sentence possible for each crime rather than the sentence actually given, a measure that put many political crimes with high maximum sentences outside the scope of the law. The reductions of sentences for those political crimes amounted to about one-third of the remaining term, rather than two-thirds as in the 1904 act of clemency. The law also left the question of whether years were to be calculated on the basis of time served or the original sentence to be determined by officials in the administration. The government was most generous in cases of press crimes. It halted prosecution of *Den'*, *Luch*, *Pravda*, and *Rech'*, and the editors of *Pravda* and *Luch* were released from prison. Writers such as Maxim Gorky, Constantine Balmont, and Nicholas Minskii were allowed to return to Russia.[54]

The Tercentenary Committee decided that February 21 would be marked by a solemn religious service in the Kazan Cathedral, officiated by the St. Petersburg metropolitan and including the dignitaries of the state and the church. The Kazan Cathedral was chosen, the committee's journal indicated, because of the great reverence inspired by the Kazan Mother of God. In addition to the religious service, the committee recommended staging processions of the cross "everywhere"—in villages, in schools, and on squares—so that the religious ceremony would reach out to the population beyond the walls of the church. "This ritual, as something unusual, would give greater meaning to the day of the ceremony and may arouse a general upsurge of patriotic sentiment in the people." The tsar, it was agreed, would ride to the Kazan Cathedral in a procession from the Winter Palace.[55]

Miracle icons of the Mother of God, the symbols unifying the religious ceremonies with the Russian people, combined the religious and the political messages of the celebration. Two of the principal icons in the service, the

---

[53] It was a long and intricate document covering a range of crimes. More than three hundred prisoners were released in Petersburg alone. Death sentences were commuted to twenty years. Authorities were given the discretion to allow students who had been exiled for participation in illegal meetings to return to their place of residence. The decree made some concessions to the peasantry: it forgave back payments on some of their loans and made additional funds available to peasant and noble banks as well as to peasant model farms. Some pensions were increased, and bonuses and orders were awarded (*MV*, February 22, 1913, 1).

[54] *Russkoe Slovo*, February 21, 1913, 2; February 27, 1913, 1; *Rech'*, February 22, 1913, 1; *Ezhegodnik Rechi za 1913*, 67–68; *Birzhevye Vedomosti*, February 21, 1913 (Morning ed.), 1; February 22, 1913 (Morning ed.), 6.

[55] *ZKT*, 58, 60; Dzhunkovskii, *Vospominaniia*, 2:145–46.

Kazan Mother of God and the Pochaev Mother of God, expressed the national, imperial mission of Russian Orthodoxy. The Kazan Mother of God had revealed the divine blessing over the extent of the empire's Eastern territories. It had been discovered in 1579, when Hermogen, serving as bishop in Kazan, began efforts to convert the Tatars in the city. The icon had accompanied Russian troops both in 1612 against the Poles and again, along with the Smolensk Mother of God, in 1812 against Napoleon. At the side of the Kazan icon was set the Pochaev Mother of God, from the Pochaev Monastery in Volynia, five miles from the Austrian border. The Pochaev Monastery had accepted the Uniate faith in the eighteenth century. In 1831 Nicholas I had placed it under the jurisdiction of the Orthodox Church, and from that time it had represented an outpost of Orthodoxy and the imperial national mission on the western frontier. The abbot Vitalii was a spokesman of the Union of the Russian People, and the monastery published *Pochaevskii Listok*, an anti-Duma, anti-Semitic organ of the Union. The Petersburg tradition would be represented by Peter the Great's beloved Icon-of-the-Savior, which he brought with him into battle and hung in a chapel near Peter's small house on the Neva.[56]

THE PETERSBURG CELEBRATIONS

On the evening of February 20, 1913, Nicholas and Alexandra arrived in Petersburg from Tsarskoe Selo. Nicholas wore the uniform of the Erevan Grenadiers Regiment, which had originated in a unit Michael formed in 1642, ostensibly the first to be organized as a standing detachment on a foreign model. The emperor and empress venerated the Icon of the Savior, then attended a memorial service at the Peter-Paul Fortress and paid their respects to the graves of Nicholas's forebears and the icon of the Feodorov Mother of God. Similar memorial services were held in the Assumption Cathedral in the Moscow Kremlin and in churches throughout Russia.[57]

On the eve of February 21 the mood in the capital was tense, for fear of actions organized by the part of the revolutionary parties. Rumors circulated that a bomb had been found at the place the tsar was to occupy in the Kazan cathedral.[58] The gendarmerie dispatched two officers to each church of the capital, after receiving reports that workers planned demonstrations during the solemn services on February 21, then to walk out of the churches, unfurl

[56] On Hermogen and the Kazan Mother of God, see *Tvoreniia Sviateishego Germogena; Patriarkha Moskovskogo i vseia Rossii*, 17–26; Leonid Ouspensky and Vladimir Lossky, *The Meaning of Icons* (Crestwood, N.Y., 1982), 88; John Curtiss, *Church and State in Russia: The Last Years of the Empire* (New York, 1940), 255; Avrekh, *Tsarizm i IV Duma*, 237–38.

[57] NV, February 21, 1913, 22; Spiridovitch, *Les dernières années de la cour de Tsarskoe-Selo*, 2:316; Dzhunkovskii, *Vospominaniia*, 2:148–49; Ivan Shadrin, "Prazdnovanie 300-letiia Imperatorskogo Doma Romanovykh," BAR, Shadrin Collection, 2–3.

[58] Shadrin, "Prazdnovanie 300-letiia Imperatorskogo Doma Romanovykh, 3.

red flags, and sing the Marseillaise.[59] Police and army units invested the entire city, while others remained in reserve. "The city was literally turned into an armed camp," wrote Vladimir Dzhunkovskii, the newly appointed chief of gendarmes and assistant minister of the interior. This, he remarked with dismay, could "make a bad impression not only on the inhabitants but on the soldiers themselves." There were no disorders during the centenary days, and could be none, he wrote, for "there has never been an antigovernment demonstration during days of patriotic upsurge."[60]

The celebration immediately assumed a partisan character. Despite the committee's objections to the involvement of right-wing political groups in the celebration, members of both the Union of the Russian People and the Union of the Archangel Michael were prominent participants in the religious processions on February 21. The evening before, the Sixth Congress of Monarchist Organizations of "Russian People," (*S"ezd russkikh liudei*) opened in the mansion of the chief-procurator of the Holy Synod, Vladimir Sabler. After prayers and hymns sung by the chorus of the Egerskii Regiment, the members of the Tercentenary Committee of Monarchist Organizations announced that a telegram had been sent to Nicholas, declaring: "We can say to the Tsar, 'Lead us boldly, the cross of Christ is above you and the Russian people and Russian land are with you, and no one is frightened now for *Rus'*.' "[61] Their presence and acceptance by the government immediately identified the celebration with the extremist right, anti-Semitic groups, whom Nicholas was protecting.

At eight in the morning on February 21 a salvo resounded from the Peter-Paul Fortress, and twenty-five processions of the cross began to wind through the streets of the capital to meet at seven cathedrals. The three principal processions converged at the Kazan Cathedral. The procession from the Nevskii Monastery bore an icon of Nevskii, that from the Synodal Center, the Pochaev Mother of God, and the third, from the Peter-Paul Cathedral, the Icon of the Savior. The clergy marched with icons, accompanied by phalanxes of monarchist organizations, the Union of the Archangel Michael and the Chief Council of the Union of Russian People, carrying their banners and national flags. The reporter in *Moskovskie Vedomosti* wrote, "Over the gigantic rectangle of flags rose crosses and banners, as well as the banners of monarchist organizations." They marched to the singing of the monks and members of the temperance society.

At the Anichkov Palace, they halted and joined in the chorus of a hymn, "Save, Lord, Your People" (*Spasi, Gospodi, Liudi Tvoia*") and a chorus of "God Save the Tsar." The three processions were greeted on the steps of the cathedral by the metropolitan of Vladimir and the icons were brought inside,

[59] Nemiro, "Iz istorii organizatsii i dekorirovaniia krupneishikh torzhestv Doma Romano-vykh," 259.

[60] Dzhunkovskii, *Vospominaniia*, 2: 147–48.

[61] *MV*, February 23, 1913, 3; *NV*, February 20, 1913, 5; *ZKT*, 5–6, 46–47.

the Pochaev icon being placed before the altar. The monarchists stood in a semicircle before the cathedral, holding their flags aloft during the entire service. Across Nevskii Prospect, members of the clergy held crosses and gonfalons.[62] The religious processions had taken on the aspect of a political demonstration in behalf of the tsar.

The elite of the Russian state, the State Duma, and the diplomatic corps, marshals of the nobility, representatives of the urban estate, and peasant elders made up a throng of four thousand, gathered in the neoclassical magnificence of the Kazan Cathedral. The scene, *Novoe Vremia* reported, was equal to the requirements of solemnity (*torzhestvennost'*)." "It was all brilliance, the brilliance of the ladies' diamonds, the brilliance of the medals and the stars, the brilliance of the gold and silver of the uniforms." In the rear of the cathedral stood representatives from Finland and "aliens" (*inorodtsy*). Peasant elders from villages across Russia were placed behind the columns and along the windows.[63] On the dais waited the court choir in crimson caftans and the metropolitan's choir in blue.

Political conflict intruded into the cathedral as well. Rodzianko's memoirs tell of an altercation over the placement of senators, who were supposed to stand in front of the Duma. Such an arrangement, he protested, made it appear that the deputies representing the people of Russia had been placed behind the appointive officials of an administrative institution. Rodzianko remonstrated with the master of ceremonies and convinced him to move the senators back. He defended their new position by posting the Duma's sergeants-at-arms. At this point Rasputin appeared in a crimson, silk tunic and stood before the space reserved for the Duma. After a confrontation with Rodzianko, he withdrew. The incident was reported in the press, but with no mention of Rasputin.[64]

As the patriarch of Antioch, a special guest for the occasion, conducted a memorial service in the cathedral, Nicholas left the Winter Palace to ride down Nevskii Prospect. Members of the Union of the Russian People and the Union of the Archangel Michael lined the avenue and stood before the cathedral. Phalanxes of guards and cadets from military schools guarded the avenue. Shutters along the way were closed (fig. 63). Convoy Cossacks in scarlet uniforms led the way. The tsar and the tsarevich followed in an open victoria, both wearing the uniforms of His Majesty's Rifles. The tsarevich,

---

[62] *MV*, February 22, 1913, 3; February 23, 1; *Birzhevye Vedomosti*, February 21, 1913 (Evening ed.), 3.

[63] *NV*, February 22, 1913, 3; *MV*, February 23, 1913, 1.

[64] Rodzianko, *The Reign of Rasputin*, 75–77; Kaufmann, "Das dreihundertjährige Thronjubiläum des Hauses Romanov," 87–88. Kaufmann's reference is to *Peterburgskaia Gazeta*, February 27, 1913, 3. On the other hand, there is no mention of the dispute in the above-mentioned issues of *NV* and *MV*; these describe the Duma placed before the Senate. The official ceremonial, while it does not give seating arrangements, lists the Duma before the Senate ("Vysochaishe utverzhdennyi Tseremonial torzhestvennogo prazdnovaniia 300-letiia tsarovaniia doma Romanovykh" unpublished printed circular, Library of Congress, Rare Book Room).

63. Procession to Kazan Cathedral, February 21, 1913. From *L'Illustration*.

a *London Times* correspondent wrote, "looked as well as any boy his age."
Behind them rode the two empresses in a gilded state carriage drawn by four
horses. Two large Cossacks stood on the rear platform. Another carriage
followed with the grand duchesses. A company of Convoy Cossacks brought
up the rear. As the procession approached, bands struck up "God Save the
Tsar" while the crowd and the guards shouted "Hoorah!"[65]

The imperial family was met by the Petersburg metropolitan on the cathedral steps. Followed by an honor guard from his suite, Nicholas proceeded
to the "tsar's place," a sumptuous marble throne located beneath the words,
"The Tsar Is in the Hands of God." A protodeacon declaimed the imperial
manifesto, written by the minister of agriculture A. V. Krivoshein, which
would be read from the pulpits of churches across Russia that day. The manifesto, cited in the epigraph to this chapter, attributed Russia's emergence
from the troubles and its subsequent expansion to the union between tsar
and people. *Moskovskaia Rus'* had grown into the *Rossiiskaia Imperiia*.

The tsar announced his intention to lead the state in union with his people
in building a "national life" (*zhizn' narodnaia*). But the phrase pointedly
omitted mention of the Duma. Nicholas had excised words in Krivoshein's
draft about the union "with deputies from the people . . . who have been
summoned to participate in the work of legislation."[66] Nicholas mentioned
no specific institutions. In the second part of the manifesto, he cited, "with
grateful emotion" (*s priznatel'nym umileniem*), those who had given great
service to Russia, referring to them as the tsars' "comrades-in-arms" (*spo-*

[65] Spiridovitch, *Les dernières années de la cour de Tsarskoe-Selo*, 1:315–16; *London Times*,
March 7, 1913, 7.

[66] Diakin, *Burzhuaziia, dvorianstvo i tsarizm*, 113–14.

dvizhniki): the clergy, the nobility, the military, serving people of all ranks, the practitioners of sciences, literature, and the arts, those working in industry and agriculture, and, finally, the tillers of the soil.

Those present heard whispered rumors that Rasputin was in the cathedral, and as the clergy intoned their prayers and the choruses lifted their voices in hymns, necks craned to catch a glimpse of him. Nicholas looked troubled and distracted. Alexandra was visibly nervous. When the congregation knelt in prayer, the tsar and tsarevich stared upward at two pigeons flying about in the dome.[67]

At the close of the service the Antioch patriarch recited a blessing. This was followed by readings of the Gospel, in Greek by the patriarch and in Church Slavonic by the metropolitan. The choirs intoned a hymn, the congregation knelt, as did the emperor and empress, and the metropolitan delivered a prayer of thanksgiving. After the prayer for the tsar's long life, the cannons of the Peter-Paul Fortress fired a salute, and the bells of the churches of the capital tolled in the background. The imperial family moved to the dais and kissed the miracle working icons which they believed had bestowed the grace of God on Russia.[68]

Receptions, balls, and theatrical presentations followed the service. On the afternoon of February 21 Nicholas received congratulations from the hierarchs of the church and the heads of state institutions in the Winter Palace. Presidents of the State Council and the Duma gave icons to Nicholas. Rodzianko, the president of the Duma, also presented an ancient tapestry depicting Tsar Michael welcoming his father, the patriarch Filaret, on his return from captivity. Then he insisted on delivering a speech of loyalty to the tsar.[69] In addition, Nicholas and Alexandra received representatives of the estates of the realm and the nationalities. He also met the descendants of the signers of the 1613 manifesto inviting Michael to be tsar, among them members of Russia's oldest aristocratic families—a Trubetskoi, a Golitsyn, a Lobanov-Rostovskii, and a Putiatin.[70]

These ceremonies, meant to display the solidarity between the monarch and his state, were performed with little spirit by the emperor and empress. Naumov and Spiridovich recalled Nicholas's striking disregard for the repre-

---

[67] Spiridovitch, *Les dernières années de la cour de Tsarskoe-Selo*, 2:316; A. A. Vyrubova, *Stranitsy iz moei zhizni* (New York, 1923), 46; Meriel Buchanan, *The Dissolution of an Empire* (London, 1932), 35–37.

[68] *MV*, February 23, 1913, 1; Spiridovitch, *Les dernières années de la cour de Tsarskoe-Selo*, 2: 316.

[69] V. I. Nazanskii, *Krushenie velikoi Rossii i doma Romanovykh* (Paris, 1930), 80–81; Rodzianko believed that only he, the president of the Duma, delivered an address, but the minister of justice, I. G. Shcheglovitov, also gave a speech in the Senate's behalf (Rodzianko, *The Reign of Rasputin*, 78; Nazanskii, *Krushenie velikoi Rossii*, 82–83). Nicholas reluctantly agreed to the participation of the Duma in the ceremony (Diakin, *Burzhuaziia, dvorianstvo i tsarizm*, 115).

[70] Naumov, *Iz utselevshikh vospominanii*, 2:233–34; Spiridovitch, *Les dernières années de la cour de Tsarskoe-Selo*, 2:316–17.

sentatives of the noble and merchant estates and even for the descendants of
the signers of the 1613 manifesto. Nicholas stood chatting with the adjutants
of his suite, leaving the estate representatives feeling perplexed and offended.
Men who had journeyed to the capital for perhaps their single opportunity
to meet the tsar were filed past rapidly, many of them unable even to glimpse
his face. The aristocratic scions of the illustrious figures of 1613 felt snubbed.
According to Naumov, one nobleman asked his friend, "Tell me, Alexander
Nikolaevich, when we passed by, was he there or not?"[71] Ivan Tolstoi, a
Hofmeister of the Imperial Court and former minister of education, wrote
in his diary:

> Two steps from the tsar stood the empress Maria Fedorovna openly and gra-
> ciously smiling, having a young look despite her sixty-five years, thanks to heavy
> makeup. Then somewhat apart, about ten to fifteen feet from the dowager, the
> young empress sat on an armchair, in a pose of exhaustion, all red, like a peony,
> with eyes that were almost mad. Next to her, also sitting on a chair, was the
> unmistakably weary heir in the uniform of the Rifles of the Imperial Family. The
> group had a most tragic look.[72]

Alexandra failed to appear at most of the receptions. She did attend the
gala performance of *Life for the Tsar* at the Mariinskii Theater. Meriel Buchanan, the daughter of the English ambassador, noticed how beautiful she
was in her diamond tiara and parure. But as she stood next to Nicholas
during the anthem, her eyes seemed "fixed on some secret, inward thought
that was certainly far removed from the crowded theater and the people who
acclaimed her. Not once did a smile break the immobile somberness of her
expression." In the midst of the opera, she was seized by a fit of nerves; her
fan trembled convulsively. "We could see how a dull unbecoming flush was
stealing over her pallor." She left after the first act. "A wave of resentment
rippled over the theater."[73] The chief of the chancellery of the Ministry of
the Court, A. A. Mosolov, found the evening dispiriting. He wrote to his
father on February 22, "I was at . . . 'the gala performance'. . . . I inserted
inverted commas because the performance was not at all gala. The singers
were vile and played without any enthusiasm. In general, no enthusiasm was
evident anywhere. We clearly live in those times when faith, and love for the
tsar and fatherland have died out."[74]

The empress was equally distant at the ball at the Noble Assembly the
next evening. It was the first appearance of the empress and emperor at a
ball since the 1903 masquerade pageant. The dress and jewels were brilliant,
recalling the era of Alexander III. But the empress looked haggard and left

[71] Naumov, *Iz utselevshikh vospominanii*, 2:234; Spiridovitch *Les dernières années de la cour de Tsarskoe-Selo*, 2:317.

[72] I. I. Tolstoi, *Dnevnik, 1906–1916* (St. Petersburg, 1997), 428; entry of February 21, 1913.

[73] Buchanan, *The Dissolution of an Empire*, 36–37; *Dnevniki Imperatora Nikolaia II*, 384.

[74] Avrekh, *Tsarizm i IV Duma*, 261.

early, inflicting more wounded feelings. Many also resented the emperor's and empress's failure to give their own court ball.[75]

The banquet held for the upper ranks of the state, the church, and marshals of the nobility was another divisive event. The imperial family dined at a lavishly decorated table in the throne room. During the dinner an orchestra and several military bands played Russian music. Members of the State Council were invited, but only the chairman and vice-chairman of the Duma. According to one account, Rodzianko was not given the honor of dining in the hall with the emperor, and he stormed out of the palace.

On the other hand, 1,320 members of monarchist organizations, the Union of Russian People, and the Union of the Archangel Michael enjoyed the privilege of standing in the halls to witness the Great Procession of the imperial family and the court from their apartments to the banquet tables. In each room the monarchists, many of them peasants, shouted "Hoorah!" and broke into a chorus of "God Save the Tsar!" They had been allowed a privilege not granted to other political groups.[76]

At the dinner for peasant elders, held on February 23, Nicholas showed his attention to the peasantry. The elders bowed to Nicholas, and he spoke informally with them. Then he greeted them as "the representatives of Great Mother Russia." He declared, "Our Russia grew strong from faith in God, and love of the tsar for the people, and the devotion of the Russian People to the Imperial throne." The oldest of the peasants, from Shlisselburg district of Petersburg Province, responded to the emperor with traditional words. He thanked the tsar for his kindness and prayed God to bless the tsar and tsarevich. "And believe, Sovereign, that our life is for You. Believe that at Your first summons we stand as a firm wall and give our lives for You, Tsar, like Ivan Susanin, for Your valuable life, for Your family, for the glory of the native land." Nicholas kissed him and left the room to shouts of "Hoorah!" and the strains of "God Save the Tsar!" played by the Preobrazhenskii Guards' Band. The elders were served *borshch*, *pirogi*, chicken and dessert.[77]

In planning the festivals for the people, the authorities sought to avoid large concentrations of people, which might encourage demonstrations. They organized subdued gatherings at six sites far from the center, where the people would be entertained with plays, panoramas, and magic lantern

[75] Ibid.; Princess Catherine Radziwill, *The Intimate Life of the Last Tsarina* (London, 1929), 74–75; Madame Marfa Mouchanow, *My Empress* (New York, 1938), 181; Naumov, *Iz utselevshikh vospominanii*, 2:236; Kaufmann, "Das dreihundertjährige Thronjubiläum des Hauses Romanov," 98.

[76] NV, February 25, 1913, 4; Naumov, *Iz utselevshikh vospominanii*, 2:236; Shadrin, "Prazdnovanie 300-letiia Imperatorskogo Doma Romanovykh," 8. According to Dzhunkovskii, Nicholas had unthinkingly agreed to Purishkevich's request for a special reception of the leaders of the organization where they would present bread and salt to the tsar. As a compromise, they were allowed to line the halls of the palace before the banquet. The tsar, realizing the awkwardness of the situation, winced when he appeared before them (Dzhunkovskii, *Vospominaniia*, 2:154–56).

[77] MV, February 24, 1913, 2.

pictures from the history of the Romanov dynasty with explanations. Bands played military music, and the celebrations ended with solemn singing of the hymn *"Kol' slaven"* as the halls were illuminated with Bengal lights and projectors. A battalion of infantry, a company of Cossacks and seventy police officers, provided security at each location.[78] The committee decided to refrain from public distribution of free food and souvenirs lest it lead to disorder as at the coronation. Instead, the organization of Sobriety Trusts served meals in people's cafeterias and tea with sugar in lodging houses. The people's entertainments proceeded without incident.[79]

Many newspaper and memoir accounts give the sense that the celebration remained an official one with little popular resonance. The progressive newspaper, *Utro Rossii*, commented in an article of February 21, "The idea that this is not only a government holiday, a celebration of authority, but also a holiday of the people is so far from us that we are not even surprised that on this day *Moscow has been forgotten.*"[80] Nicholas, however, was pleased. He wrote in his diary on February 21, "The mood was joyous, reminding me of the Coronation." After the end of the celebrations, he wrote "Thanks be given to the Lord, God, bestowing grace on Russia by allowing us to celebrate the days of the tercentenary of the accession of the Romanov dynasty in so worthy and radiant a manner."[81] Some accounts in the conservative press confirmed Nicholas's sense of the celebration. *Sankt-Peterburgskie Vedomosti* described a great lofty upsurge of the population who "united with the great experiences of 1613 and feelings of gratitude to the Anointed of God." Petersburg fused with all of Russia, "for it shared all its past with her."[82] The *London Times* and *L'Illustration* echoed the sense of solidarity between monarch and population and described a joyous popular response. The reporter for *L'Illustration* wrote, "The dynasty's holiday remains a national holiday . . . it is still and forever a life for the tsar that is playing on the great popular stage."[83]

THE MAY CELEBRATIONS

The May celebrations took Nicholas and Alexandra to the scenes of the events of 1613, the Volga towns, where Nicholas had not appeared since the summer of 1881, when he was thirteen years old. Alexandra had longed to

---

[78] "Zhurnal pri komitete dlia ustroistva prazdnovaniia trekhsotletiia . . . kommissii po ustroistve torzhestva prazdnovaniia," RGIA, 1320-1-114, 1, 7.

[79] Ibid., 2–3, 5, 16; Kaufmann, "Das dreihundertjährige Thronjubiläum des Hauses Romanov," 80–82, 94.

[80] *Utro Rossii*, February 21, 1913, 3.

[81] *Dnevniki Imperatora Nikolaia II*, 384–85.

[82] *Sankt-Peterburgskie Vedomosti*, February 27, 1913, 1.

[83] *The Times of London*, March 8, 1913, 5; *L'Illustration*, March 15, 1913, 223.

make the tour of the Volga region and to see the sites of the first Romanovs since her arrival in Russia in 1894.[84] The chief of Gendarmes, Dzhunkovskii, tried, as he had at Borodino, to make the security arrangements inconspicuous and to allow the people to come as close as possible to the events.[85]

Their trip began on May 16 in Vladimir. The imperial party traveled by train to Nizhnii-Novgorod, then boarded a steamship for a trip along the Volga, to Kostroma and Iaroslavl. They stopped in Rostov and Pereslavl on their way to Moscow, where they remained from May 24 to May 27. In each town they heard a service in the cathedral, received the dignitaries of the various estates, and gave dinners for the peasant *volost'* elders. They also visited historical sites and, at the empress's request, monasteries, ten of which are listed in the itinerary before they reached Moscow. In a book published at the time, Gen. E. E. Bogdanovich aptly described the trip as a "pilgrimage."[86]

Nicholas traveled in much the same company that surrounded him at the Alexander Palace and the other suburban palaces—his family, the security officials of Tsarskoe Selo, officials of the Ministry of the Court, and adjutants from his suite. For the Volga leg of the trip, the imperial party lived on a flotilla of four steamships that reproduced both the comfort and the opulence of the imperial palaces and eased the problem of security. Nicholas and Alexandra lived separately on the *Mezhen'*. The main ship, *Tsar Michael Foodorovich*, was outfitted for dinners and receptions for up to one hundred people. River travel also spared the tsar frequent contact with the ministers. Except for the prime minister Vladimir Kokovtsov and the ministers of the court and communications, the cabinet was not invited to join the river trip. Kokovtsov, to his chagrin, had to provide his own transportation to the point of embarkation in Nizhnii Novgorod.[87]

Kokovtsov recalled in memoirs that Nicholas kept his distance and showed his distrust during the entire trip. Nicholas, he observed, viewed the principal officials of state as a "dividing-wall" that hampered his direct bond with the people. Nicholas "became convinced more and more that the Sovereign could do everything by himself, because the people were with Him,

---

[84] Buxhoeveden, *The Life and Tragedy of Alexandra Feodorovna*, 70, 176.

[85] Dzhunkovskii, *Vospominaniia*, 2:191–206; Kaufmann, "Das dreihundertjährige Thronjubiläum des Hauses Romanov," 103–5.

[86] "Programma i marshrut puteshestviia Nikolaia II v sviazi s prazdnovaniem 300-letiia goma Romanovykh," GARF, 601-1-1840; E. E. Bogdanovich, *Istoricheskoe palomnichestvo nashego tsaria v 1913 godu* (St. Petersburg, 1914).

[87] Nicholas rejected a proposal for a single larger ship that could have carried his suite and court officials as well as his family. The rest of the imperial party lived on the *Tsar Michael Feodorovich* and the *Alexander the Blessed*. The fourth ship, the *Strezhen'*, accommodated several members of the suite and officials from the Ministry of Communications, who supervised the trip and the navigation (Spiridovitch *Les dernières années de la cour de Tsarskoe-Selo*, 2:334–35; *Utro Rossii*, May 8, 1913, 1; Kn. V. N. Shakhovskoi, "*Sic transit gloria mundi;*" *1893–1917* (Paris: 1952), 41; V. N. Kokovtsov, *Iz moego proshlogo* (Paris, 1933), 2:155).

knew and understood Him, and were blindly devoted to Him." He was impatient with the ministers, the Duma, everything boring him with the details of government, anything "diminishing the former prestige and darkening the aureole of 'the Muscovite Tsar,' ruling Russia as his patrimony."[88]

•

The May celebrations began in Vladimir, where Nicholas arrived by train on May 16, 1913. He proceeded by automobile through the town, then to Bogoliubova and to Suzdal, stopping along the way to visit the historical sites, the churches and icons of early Russia. Peasants flocked to see him, spreading out along the road. Dzhunkovskii wrote in his memoirs, "On the same road, we saw processions of the cross, pupils of village schools, and at crossroads, before their huts, peasant women laid tables with bread and salt in the old style." The tsar kissed the icons of the Vladimir Mother of God and the remains of the Prince Saints, George, Andrei, and Gleb. The visit was "a holiday for the entire Vladimir region."[89]

Dzhunkovskii described the trip as a festive and magical return of the tsar to the sources of the national spirit. He recalled great animation at Nizhnii-Novgorod, where they arrived on May 17—colorful decorations, flags, flowers, carpets, portraits of Michael and Nicholas. The whole town was on the streets "festively dressed and in a gala mood, shouting 'Hoorah.' "[90] *Moskovskie Vedomosti* evoked a similar feeling of exuberance. More than seventy thousand tickets had been given out for the events, and a People's Security Force was organized to keep order.[91] Others in the imperial party, however, did not feel the joyous spirit. Kokovtsov recalled "the absence of true enthusiasm and the relatively small gatherings of people." In Nizhnii-Novgorod the imperial cortege aroused only a "lackluster, weak manifestation of what was more curiosity than excitement in the mood of the crowds of people."[92] Nizhnii-Novgorod, the center of the movement of resistance to the Poles in 1612 and 1613, posed particular problems for the tsar's presentations. It was the home of Kuz'ma Minin, who, with Prince Pozharskii, had organized and led the militia in patriotic resistance to the foreign invader. The movement had ended with the restoration of the monarchy, but the liberation was hardly the work of Nicholas's forebears.

The celebrations shifted the focus of attention from the heroes of 1613 to the monarch. The bishop Ioakim met the emperor and empress at doors of the cathedral, then led them inside to Minin's grave. He gave a speech praising Minin's heroic deeds and declared that his descendants were also "selflessly devoted to their Sovereign-Leader." Minin's heroism was con-

[88] Kokovtsov, *Iz moego proshlogo*, 2:155–56; Kaufmann, "Das dreihundertjährige Thronjubiläum des Hauses Romanov," 102–3.

[89] Dzhunkovskii, *Vospominaniia*, 2:192.

[90] Ibid., 194.

[91] *MV*, May, 19, 1913, 1–2.

[92] Kokovtsov, *Iz moego proshlogo*, 2:168–69.

nected with his dedication to the monarch, cast in the role of leader.[93] This sense was conveyed by the term the bishop used, *Sovereign-Leader* (*Derzhavnyi Vozhd'*), a frequent one in the speeches and literature of the celebration, suggesting a monarch who was not only sovereign but one who had the capacity to lead and whose people were his followers.

After the service the emperor and empress joined a procession of the cross with more than five hundred banners to the Minin and Pozharskii Monument. The monument, from the description, resembled Martos's statues in Red Square. The reliefs on the base depicted Patriarch Hermogen's defiance of the Poles and the gathering of the militia. An *Utro Rossii* editorial observed that the plaque mentioned only the governor and the bishop of the town and said nothing about the population, though the statue had been built from public contributions. The tsar met with peasant elders, then dedicated the new building of the State Bank, constructed in old-Russian style.[94]

Despite shows of cordiality, a strain between the themes of imperial and governmental leadership and the participation of the population ran through the events. The officials of the Ministry of the Court tried to limit contact between the emperor and empress and local dignitaries, especially since the empress was ailing and had to absent herself from several functions. At the farewell celebrations, the members of the town government were to be allowed to greet their majesties only before they stepped on the wharf, without a formal reception. The mayor, angered at the arrangement, took the initiative of publishing his own ceremonial in a local newspaper. After discussions, Count Fredericks, the minister of the court, agreed to arrange a champagne reception with the imperial family and a gathering for the ladies of the town and the tsar's daughters.[95]

On the evening of May 18 the imperial party boarded the four steamships to travel down the river. The ceremony of departure submerged the tensions of the previous days. After the reception on the wharf, and a large formal dinner on the *Tsar Michael Feodorovich*, the grand duchesses appeared on deck and the other members of the family were visible through the windows of the ship. A chorus on the brightly lit docks along the shore sang the "Glory" chorus, "Down Mother Volga," and "God Save the Tsar." The account in *Moskovskie Vedomosti* described how people marveled at "the beautiful princesses." One woman asked to come closer to the tsar's boat and was permitted to get a glimpse of the tsar. Delighted, she said she would return to her village and tell how she saw the tsar. At eleven the flotilla lifted anchor. Priests, stevedores, townspeople, high school students all crowded the shore to bade the tsar farewell. Torches on the docks and shore

---

[93] *MV*, May, 19, 1913, 1–2.

[94] Ibid., May 21, 1913, 2; *Utro Rossii*, May 25, 1913, 2; Spiridovitch, *Les dernières années de la cour de Tsarskoe-Selo*, 2:333–34; Nazanskii, *Krushenie velikoi Rossii*, 88–89; *NV*, May 19, 1913, 2; May 21, 1913, 2.

[95] *Utro Rossii*, May 25, 1913, 2.

flickered in the water. "Enthusiastic and joyful responses to the imperial family" were heard, and the crowds lingered on the shore, some not dispersing until morning.[96]

The songs, Dzhunkovskii wrote, were taken up by the people, "hundreds of thousands of people, covering the banks of the Volga and not leaving until late at night. I will never forget the joyous excitement and patriotic exaltation that one had to feel." The shouts of "Hoorah" and the singing of the anthem continued as the boats moved off. Lights illuminated the entire town, showing the Kremlin, the Volga, and the fairgrounds. "On the fields along the Volga you saw the flicker of bonfires; barrels of tar were burning. At this hour of night Nizhnii presented a picture of rare and marvelous beauty."[97]

On the trip up the Volga to Kostroma, sailboats, covered with flags, went out to meet them. At the prompting of the Ministry of the Interior, scenes and ceremonies of welcome took place along the river banks. Villages put up triumphal arches decorated with plants and the words "God Save the Tsar." Peasants, gathered in camps, stood on the shore and even ventured into the river up to their waists to see the tsar. As the flotilla approached each town, church bells sounded, and priests led processions of the cross from their churches to banks, where they blessed the ships. Peasants knelt, crossing themselves, and shouted, many with tears, "God protect the little father, the tsar."[98]

Just before Kostroma the ships passed the village of Kinesha slowly to permit the tsar to be seen. The docks were decorated with an arch glowing with light bulbs spelling the words "God Save the Tsar" and the tsar's initials; these were donated by the local chapter of the Union of Russian People. Town and zemstvo officials stood on the dock, waiting to present the tsar with bread and salt. But the ships did not stop, and the presentation was carried back by the motor boat dispatched to collect official telegrams. The ships then passed the Konovalov cloth factory at Kostroma, adorned with national flags, greens, the imperial initials in electric lights, and the state coat-of-arms.[99] Passing by the town of Kostroma, they anchored opposite the nearby Ipat'ev Monastery, where the first ceremonies were to take place.

•

The visit to Kostroma was a return to the original Romanov patrimony and to the site where the original Feodorov Icon was kept. The Kostroma town government had been actively engaged in preparations for the anniversary. An elaborate luxury album contained detailed accounts and many photo-

[96] MV, May 21, 1913, 3.

[97] Ibid., 2; Dzhunkovskii, Vospominaniia, 2:195–96.

[98] Spiridovitch, Les dernières années de la cour de Tsarskoe-Selo, 2:335–36; Nazanskii, Krushenie velikoi Rossii, 92–93; Dzhunkovskii, Vospominaniia, 2:196. Kokovtsov claimed that the tsar never went out on deck and was not seen by the people (Iz moego proshlogo, 2:169).

[99] Kokovtsov, Iz moego proshlogo, 2:169; Prazdnovanie trekhsotletiia tsarstvovaniia Doma Romanovykh, 26–27.

graphs of the ceremonies.[100] The Kostroma Church–Historical Society published a collection of articles about the events of 1613 in Kostroma.[101] The Provincial *Zemstvo* organized an exhibition of the region's industrial and agricultural products. The Kostroma town government had completed the building of the new Romanov Museum in old-Russian style, but work on Adamson's Romanov Monument had begun just before the tsar's visit.

Kostroma, in 1913, was hardly a felicitous site for Nicholas's scenario. The region epitomized the rapid economic change and the social and political turbulence of contemporary Russia. Kostroma Province was a part of the Moscow industrial region, with numerous textile mills owned by Moscow entrepreneurs. In 1913 it had more than ninety thousand workers. The town of Kostroma had a population of forty-three thousand and twenty-one mills.[102] In a guide book of 1913 V. Ia. Lukomskii and G. Ia. Lukomskii remarked that the streets of Kostroma were more attractive than those of Iaroslavl or Pskov but that "the town would be even more congenial if there were no hulling mills, new factories, or power stations."[103]

In 1905 the workers of Kostroma had taken an active part in the strike movement under predominantly Bolshevik leadership.[104] In 1912 the region had remained quiet, but the police became concerned about efforts of the local intelligentsia to collect funds for the workers before the festivities. The police authorities dispatched a special official to reorganize the local apparatus, and the governor, Shidlovskii, was replaced by P. P. Stremoukhov, who had served as governor of Saratov and Suval Provinces under Stolypin. Stremoukhov fulfilled his duties effectively. The workers were unable to stage demonstrations on February 21 or on May Day, 1913, though they did succeed in distributing leaflets. A year later, however, a major strike movement erupted in the province, which continued even after the outbreak of the war.[105]

Kostroma was also a stronghold of noble liberalism and Kostroma nobles were among the most active and confrontational from 1905 to 1907. The Kostroma Noble Assembly voted to admit the noble signatories of the Vyborg Manifesto of July 1906 who had been expelled from their own local assemblies. This act brought forth condemnations from thirty-one noble assemblies. The town had elected many leftist and liberal deputies to the

---

[100] *Prazdnovanie trekhsotletiia tsarstvovaniia Doma Romanovykh.*

[101] *Iubileinyi sbornik kostromskogo tserkovno-istoricheskogo obshchestva v pamiat' 300-letiia tsarstvovaniia doma Romanovykh* (Kostroma, 1913).

[102] *Novyi Entsiklopedicheskii Slovar' Brokgauz-Efron* (Petrograd, n.d.), 22:931.

[103] V. Ia. Lukomskii and G. Ia. Lukomskii, *Kostroma* (St. Petersburg, 1913), 357.

[104] Ascher, *The Revolution of 1905: Russia in Disarray*, 149, 222.

[105] Figures on strikes are from the 1912, 1913, and 1914 editions of the *Svod otchetov fabrichnykh inspektorov*, published by the *Ministerstvo Torgovli i promyshlennosti; otdel promyshlennosti.* A former guards' officer, Stremoukhov, held the rank of chamberlain and had joined the tsar in a hunting expedition. See P. P. Stremoukhov, "Memoirs," Kamenskii Collection, BAR, 49–51.

Dumas, among them the Kostroma provincial marshal B. N. Zuzin, an out-spoken critic of the government and defender of constitutional rights. According to a later monarchist account, the alienation between society and administration in Kostroma was "complete."[106]

The Ipat'ev Monastery, where the Kostroma events were to begin, was in a sorry state in 1912. An article in *Russkoe Slovo* described it as "one of the most impoverished monasteries in Russia." The Duma had to vote special appropriations to provide the monks with vestments for the services. *Utro Rossii* reported that the monastery had frequently been vandalized in the previous decades. Of Nicholas II's predecessors, only Nicholas I had taken an interest in the monastery. His attempts at restoration had turned the buildings into replicas of early nineteenth-century imagination. In 1913, at a time when monasticism was flourishing elsewhere in Russia, there were only ten monks and twenty novices registered in the Ipat'ev Monastery. *Russkoe Slovo* indicated that the monks lived on the rents from nearby lands and that the novices were not leading lives of self-denial. Strains of phonograph music came from the cells, and in the evenings novices could be seen strolling in jackets and ties, with girls on their arms.[107]

The principal ceremonies on May 19 were a meeting with the peasants and a procession of the cross. At 9:45 A.M. the emperor and the empress disembarked onto a wharf, built especially for the occasion, to a salvo of cannons and band music. Nicholas appeared in the uniform of the Erevan Regiment; the empress and the grand duchesses wore billowing white dresses. The tsarevich was carried in the arms of a Cossack. Governor Stremoukhov welcomed them and delivered a report on the state of the province. Nicholas then descended to meet a delegation of peasants from the *volost'*. He stood on what had been part of the monastery lands in the seventeenth century. After a presentation of bread and salt, the elder gave a speech declaring that just as their predecessors had bowed to Michael before his departure they bowed to him in thanks for his and his ancestors' concern for the peasants.[108]

The words expressed a continuity and a common concern, but the photograph, published in the Kostroma album and in newspapers at the time, clearly illustrated the gulf and the strain between the tsar with his adjutants and the peasants (fig. 64). The peasants, led by their land captain, stand uneasily awaiting the tsar's gaze. Nicholas himself is stiff and formal. The members of his suite look about carelessly, with supercilious disinterest. The loose caftans of the peasants and the smart uniforms of the suite only

---

[106] Nazanskii, *Krushenie velikoi Rossii*, 110; Manning, *The Crisis of the Old Order*, 84–87, 118.

[107] *Russkoe Slovo*, January 27, 1913, 5; February 9, 1913, 2; *Utro Rossii*, May 15, 1913, 5.

[108] This description is based on *Prazdnovanie trekhsotletiia tsarstvovaniia Doma Romanovykh*, 35–70; Nazanskii, *Krushenie velikoi Rossii*, 92–99.

64. Nicholas II Converses with Peasants. Kostroma, 1913. GARF.

heighten the contrast between the two worlds. It was difficult for the camera to capture the exalted feelings evoked in official rhetoric.[109]

After the empress was greeted by the wives of town dignitaries, Nicholas reviewed his company of the Erevan Regiment sent for the occasion. He noted in his diary how happy he was to see them.[110] The emperor and empress rode, by carriage, to the gates of the monastery along a road laid for the occasion, lined by soldiers and peasants. The archimandrite Tikhon met the tsar with an icon and a lamp that had been a gift of Tsar Michael. He spoke of the great joy that had followed the election and declared that a contemporary chronicler would match that joy today.

After a greeting from Bulygin and a review of the local garrison, Nicholas entered the monastery through "the green tower." Inside the monastery he met descendants of the participants in the Great Embassy of 1613, including members of the Sheremet'ev and Golovin families, who held relics from the period. He toured the monastery grounds, inspected the candle factory, then met an assembly of town dignitaries. He kissed the monastery's copy of the Feodorov Mother-of-God icon, then left the grounds to meet a procession of the cross that had come from Kostroma.

Before the monastery walls Nicholas was blessed with the same Feodorov Mother-of-God icon that, in the hands of the abbess Martha, had blessed

[109] *Prazdnovanie trekhsotletiia tsarstvovaniia Doma Romanovykh*, 41.
[110] *Dnevniki Imperatora Nikolaia II*, 400.

65. Imperial Family before Assumption Cathedral, Kostroma. Niva, May 1913.

Michael in the Trinity Cathedral in 1613. The moment was the emotional climax of the morning's events. Crowds of peasants watched the scene. The tsar approached the archpriest Tikhon, then knelt and kissed the Feodorov icon. The correspondent from *Moskovskie Vedomosti* wrote, "Everyone crossed himself and wept from the deep feelings of love for the Sovereign-Leader. How gratifying it was to see tears glistening on the faces of grown people." People hugged one another ecstatically, and expressed warmth and joy as at Easter time.[111] Nicholas then returned to the monastery for a thanksgiving service. Members of the State Council, court officials, ministers, and the imperial suite assembled in the Trinity Cathedral, along with the nobility and officials of Kostroma and the descendants of the Great Embassy. Nicholas occupied the "tsar's place" that Michael had donated to the cathedral. The morning's ceremonies concluded with visits to the house of Michael Romanov to see the icons and gold and silver vessels in the collection. Photographs showed the emperor and empress, and the heir in the arms of the sailor Nagornyi (fig. 65).[112]

[111] *MV,* May 21, 1913, 1.
[112] *Prazdnovanie trekhsotletiia tsarstvovaniia Doma Romanovykh,* 49, 62–63.

In the afternoon, the flotilla sailed the short distance to the town of Kostroma. Nicholas was met at the wharf by the town fathers, then rode through the streets of the town before lines of schoolchildren and peasants. Peasants, in large numbers, had come from the surrounding countryside and stayed in camps built on the outskirts. The emperor and empress stopped at the new Romanov Museum where they viewed the museum's collection, including portraits of the members of the dynasty, historical objects connected with them, and a large painting of Ivan Susanin, donated by the owners of the Kostroma Flax Factory. Then they proceeded to the Noble Assembly receptions with local officials and noblemen.

It was in the Noble Assembly that the only mishap of the visit occurred. The marshal Zuzin welcomed the tsar with a provocative address that shocked the emperor and empress. The content of the speech was not made known, but it was clearly oppositional in spirit. The tsar responded with a curt, "Are you finished?" The ceremonies resumed with the presentation of bread and salt and an icon. But the atmosphere was strained. Alexandra conversed only with the governor's wife, snubbing Zuzin's, and remained aloof and troubled.[113]

In Kostroma, however, the spirit of celebration submerged the ill feeling. Even Kokovtsov was impressed by the response. "The Tsar and His family were surrounded by a massive crowd of people. Unaffected expressions of joy resounded and, as if from their own warmth, their hearts melted."[114] In the evening a gala dinner was held on the *Tsar Michael Feodorovich* for the imperial party, members of the government, local officials, and the nobility. The lighting of the town with electric bulbs gave it a "fairy-tale" quality, taking it out of the ordinary. The crowds on the shore, and the imperial family on their boat, witnessed a crescendo of fireworks concluding with a single great explosion of light. On the other side of town, popular entertainments included clowns, harmonium players, magicians, and games. A "Russian orchestra" played tunes from *A Life for the Tsar*, and a Petersburg dramatic troupe performed the story of Ivan Susanin at the Theater of the Sobriety Trusteeship. The Trusteeship also served food and tea, as it had in Petersburg.[115]

The second day was the high point of the Volga trip, and perhaps of the entire tercentenary celebration.[116] From morning to night enthusiastic crowds, shouting their acclaim for the tsar, filled the streets of Kostroma and covered the banks of the river, maintaining "exemplary order." The morning began with services in the Assumption Cathedral, during which the tsar was again blessed with the Feodorov icon. Then he followed a procession of

---

[113] Ibid., 87–90; Nazanskii, *Krushenie velikoi Rossii*, 102, 107; Spiridovitch, *Les dernières années de la cour de Tsarskoe-Selo*, 2:340.

[114] Kokovtsov, *Iz moego proshlogo*, 2:169.

[115] *Prazdnovanie trekhsotletiia tsarstvovaniia Doma Romanovykh*, 93, 96–99.

[116] Ibid., 103–64; Nazanskii, *Krushenie velikoi Rossii*, 110.

the cross through the town to the Romanov Monument.[117] The emperor and empress, to the singing of a chorus, placed bricks, sprinkled with holy water, on the monument's foundation. They proceeded to the town pavilion, which was decorated with state flags and the Romanov coat-of-arms. Nicholas was greeted with a thunderous "Hoorah" and an ovation from the crowd. The regimental band gave a show of marches to tunes from *A Life for the Tsar*. When the moment came to sing the tsarist anthem, the crowd sank to their knees.

As Nicholas stood above the thousands of kneeling peasants, his eyes moistened. Those present also felt moved, convinced that this was a significant show of popular devotion to the tsar. The duke of Mecklenburg-Schwerin, unable to contain his tears, exclaimed, "What joy it must be to be monarch of such a people!" A foreign attaché remarked to Naumov, "What power! What unity of national feeling! All our constitutions are nothing compared to what we are seeing." Among his entourage, only the grand duke Nicholas Mikhailovich, the tsar's cousin and an accomplished historian, sensed the dangers lurking in popular support. As the two cousins looked down upon the crowds, Nicholas Mikhailovich was heard saying, "They are just as they were in the seventeenth century when they chose Michael as Tsar, just the same; this is bad, what do you think?" The tsar remained silent.[118]

Another procession of the cross brought the tsar to the governor's house, where he received delegations from local institutions and organizations. A group of twelve peasants, who had separated their lands from the commune, brought bread and salt and thanked the tsar for the Stolypin land laws. They were accompanied by the minister of agriculture A. V. Krivoshein. The meeting was followed by a dinner for peasant elders of the provinces and the descendants of Ivan Susanin, who lived in the village of Domino. A photograph in the Kostroma album shows the tsar, next to the governor, standing before a crowd of more than three hundred peasants. After an exchange of toasts, an elder stepped forward to declare the loyal sentiments of the population. But he was struck dumb at the sight of the tsar and stood trembling and silent. Nicholas embraced the old man, and the peasants shouted in joy. They then sat down to a dinner of borshch and meat pie, chicken and dessert, served with wine. Placed before each setting was a box of chocolates with a portrait of the emperor, the empress, and the heir. During dinner a band and a children's choir performed the anthem and other patriotic songs.

Finally, Nicholas visited an elaborate industrial exhibition, which had been organized for the celebration by the *zemstvo* and was chaired by the

---

[117] Dzhunkovskii, *Vospominaniia*, 2:199.

[118] Nicholas Mikhailovich was the author of important works on Alexander I's reign. He was appointed president of the Imperial Russian Historical Society in 1910. His words were told to Gorky by Nicholas Mikhailovich's brother, Grand Duke Sergei Mikhailovich (Maxim

Moscow industrialist S. M. Tretiakov. In keeping with the event's national theme, the pavilions were built in old-Russian style and a stone statue of a *bogatyr'* stood in the center of the exhibition. A ceremonial volume described the items on view and the tsar's visit. Nicholas examined the fabrics and other manufactured goods. In the agricultural section he saw a display on the growth of trees, an insect collection, and a show of wooden folk art. He ended his visit at the cottage-industry pavilion. We see him in a photograph in the journal *Niva* standing next to a section of a three-hundred-year-old oak tree.[119] The departure in the evening again was dramatic. Officials in white uniforms and throngs of peasants stood on the shore. The crowds were asked to remain quiet lest they awaken the tsarevich. They waved their handkerchiefs as the ships moved up the Volga, the bells of the churches ringing farewell.[120]

•

The May celebrations reached their climax in Moscow. The festivities resembled those surrounding the coronation: the gala entry on horseback down Tver Boulevard to the Kremlin, the services at the cathedrals, visits to the graves of ancestors, the bowing to tumultuous acclaim from the "sea of heads" on the Kremlin square (fig. 66). Nicholas also held a meeting with peasant elders, receptions with the estates, gala balls, and dinners.

Again, the present intruded with reminders of social and political discord. The prime minister Kokovtsov could not persuade the tsar to admit Duma deputies to the imperial audience at the Kremlin Palace.[121] The authorities in the court and the Ministry of the Interior showed their displeasure with the leadership of the Moscow town government. The minister of the interior Nicholas Maklakov had refused to confirm the Moscow Duma's elected candidate for mayor, Prince G. E. L'vov, who then was excluded from several ceremonies, though he attended the Kremlin reception. The Town Bureau extended an invitation to the tsar to visit Moscow institutions, but it was not presented to him and a reception at the Town Duma was canceled without explanation.[122] The Moscow industrialists, the highest ranks of the merchantry, had more success. At the Kremlin they were expected to meet the tsar, as was traditional, with the merchantry and the lower middle class, the *meshchanstvo*, in Vladimir Hall, while the town counselors joined the nobility in the St. George Hall. Their representative, I. A. Krestovnikov, protested

Gorky, "On The Russian Peasantry," in R.E.F. Smith, ed., *The Russian Peasant, 1920 and 1984* (London, 1977), 16). The Russian original was published in Berlin in 1922.

[119] *Pamiat' milostivogo poseshcheniia gubernskoi zemskoi vystavki v oznamenovanii 300 letiia tsarstvovaniia Doma Romanovykh v Kostrome* (Kostroma, 1913).

[120] *Prazdnovanie trekhsotletiia tsarstvovaniia Doma Romanovykh*, 201–7.

[121] Diakin, *Burzhuaziia, dvorianstvo i tsarizm*, 115.

[122] *Utro Rossii*, May 28, 1913, 1. A. V. Bogdanovich wrote in her diary of "the grumbling and dissatisfaction" on the occasion of the tsar's visit to Moscow "which is in an unpatriotic mood" (Diakin, *Burzhuaziia, dvorianstvo i tsarizm*, 114).

66. "Sea of Heads" Moscow Kremlin, May 25, 1913. GARF.

to the minister of the court, Count Fredericks. "We are the masters (*khozi-aeva*) of Moscow. The second hall does not suit us." Fredericks finally yielded, permitting them to stand with the nobility in the George Hall.[123]

But these differences were overshadowed by the warmth of the reception by the Moscow nobility and merchantry and the exact scenes of the events of 1613 that gave the illusion of synchronicity, of being in Russia's national past. The usual spectacles amid the landmarks of the seventeenth century showed that Moscow's tradition of demonstrative hospitality to the Russian tsar lived on. The sense that the scenes of the celebration were those of 1613 produced a powerful effect on those present. The Kremlin had been "sanctified by centuries," Naumov wrote, and gave "special meaning to the celebration."[124] The response was exultant and contrasted with the apathy of the Petersburg celebrations. "The mass emotion this visit engendered was overwhelming," recalled Bruce Lockhart, then serving in the British Consulate in Moscow. Some observers found the response less spontaneous than that along the Volga, but E. E. Bogdanovich described it as "deeper and stronger." It was a "wonderful hymn of mutual love," which showed that it was "not the citizens of the white-stone city who were guilty of the disorders

[123] Lev Rabenek, "Moskva i eia khoziaeva," *Vozrozhdenie*, no. 105 (1960): 101–4. The official ceremonial, however, could not be changed and lists them as standing in the Vladimir Hall.
[124] Naumov *Iz utselevshikh vospominanii*, 2:236–37. Dzhunkovskii marveled that "the ancient Kremlin was the witness of everything occurring three hundred years ago . . . the same bells that rang at the entry of Tsar Michael Feodorovich rang also during the solemn entry of Nicholas II (*Vospominaniia*, 2:208).

of 1905." The receptions, balls, and dinners radiated a warm, cordial spirit. "There is good reason for Moscow to be called the heart of Russia."[125]

The celebrations also made known the tsarevich's poor health and the empress's frequent indispositions, which caused her to miss many of the functions. At the end of the gala entry to Moscow, when the tsar and the imperial family walked through the Spasskii Gate into the Kremlin, the crowd was shocked to see the tsarevich, a nine-year-old boy, carried in the arms of Nagornyi.[126] The ceremony of bowing to the people from the Red Staircase on May 25 was also marred by the sight of the tsarevich, held by Nagornyi, a scene captured in a photograph published in *L'Illustration* (fig. 67). Many were moved to exclamations of pity and grief. They shed tears and made the sign of the cross. The empress, too, looked sickly, and the blemishes on her face were plainly visible to those nearby.[127]

Nicholas and his entourage regarded the May celebrations as a great success. He expressed his own sense of the meaning of the trip in his speech of thanks to the marshals of the nobility for a scroll decorated with old-Russian motifs that they had given him to mark the event. The scroll reaffirmed the great Russian nobility's loyalty to the tsar, pledged further sacrifices, and concluded by entreating God to help the Russian land continue on the course set by her great and glorious past. Nicholas replied that his trip to the Volga and old Russian towns "has proved once more that the bond between Tsar and people that distinguished our Mother Russia in olden times exists indestructibly now as well." Russia owed its majesty to "that Love of the Tsar for the Native Land and the people and that limitless devotion of the people to their Tsar, and that warm cooperation which the true sons of Russia gave to their Tsar in the expansion of its borders."[128]

Nicholas returned to Tsarskoe Selo convinced that he had made contact with the Russian nation, both in his visits to the artifacts of early-Russian history and his appearance before the people of the Russian heartland. He wrote to his mother on May 29 of the forty-four churches that he and Alexandra had visited, "one more beautiful than the other. It is pure delight to see monuments of olden times that have been preserved." He wrote that the people "were as touching as always. On the Volga they left their villages and hamlets and stood all along the embankments on both sides." The visit to Moscow again recalled the coronation, "but the reception from the population seemed to me and to others even warmer. There were immense crowds of people on the streets and the order was remarkable."[129]

[125] R. H. Bruce Lockhart, "Preface," in Bing, *The Secret Letters of the Last Tsar,* 10; Bogdanovich, *Istoricheskoe palomnichestvo,* 163.

[126] Kokovtsov *Iz moego proshlogo,* 2:170.

[127] Dzhunkovskii, *Vospominaniia,* 2:215; Nazanskii, *Krushenie velikoi Rossii,* 126; Spiridovitch, *Les dernières années de la cour de Tsarskoe-Selo,* 2:353; Kokovtsov, *Iz moego proshlogo,* 2:169–70.

[128] *MV,* May 26, 1913, 2.

[129] "Pis'ma imperatora Nikolaia II Marii Feodorovne, 6 aprelia 1912–20 iiulia 1916," GARF, 642-1-2332, 33.

67. Nicholas, Alexandra, and Alexei on Red Staircase, May 25, 1913.
From *L'Illustration*.

On June 1, 1913, the leading ranks of the court and the Department of Appanages and the court clergy gathered at the Catherine Palace in Tsarskoe Selo to greet Nicholas and to mark the successful culmination of his journey. First, the clergy presented a large icon of the Feodorov Mother of God. Then the officials of the court unveiled a statue of the patriarch Filaret dressed in his vestments and holding a staff. The minister of the court Count Fredericks asked that the statue be placed in the tsar's chambers.[130] In Nicholas's home, the images of the protectress and the progenitor of the dynasty would recall that distant moment of history when God and the people seemed to speak in one voice for an Orthodox, Russian tsar.

[130] *MV*, June 4, 1913, 1; *Dnevniki Imperatora Nikolaia II*, 404.

CHAPTER FOURTEEN

Publicizing the Tsar

Thousands of invisible threads centre in the Tsar's heart which is, as in
the words of the Scripture, "in the hand of God"; and these threads
stretch to the huts of the poor and the palaces of the rich. And that is why
the Russian people always acclaims its Tsar with such fervent enthusiasm,
whether at St. Petersburg in the Marinski Theatre, at the opera "A Life
for the Tsar," or at the dedication of memorials to Russian glory at
Borodino, or on his way through towns or villages.

—*Major-General Andrei Georgievich Elchaninov*, The Reign of
the Sovereign Emperor Nicholas Aleksandrovich[1]

NEW MODES OF REPRESENTATION

The historical celebrations presented Nicholas as a democratic monarch, the
embodiment of the nation's past and the focus of the patriotic feelings of the
people. He claimed a direct rapport with the Russian people, who responded
to him personally at the meetings staged during the celebrations. Following
the example of Western monarchs, and especially Queen Victoria, Nicholas
began to seek popular support through mass publicity, which he used to
bring his image into everyday life, and to try to overshadow the divided and
faceless Duma. The government issued coins, stamps, souvenirs, and books
that gave broad dissemination to the tsar's image and acquainted the people
with his personal life. Films transmitted scenes of imperial ceremonies and
episodes from Russia's past to a mass audience.

The Russian monarchy entered the modern era of mass publicity to an
extent that has hardly been remarked on in the historical and biographical
literature. Nicholas II broke with traditional forms of representation and
made the image of the emperor available in the market place, participating
in the "commodity culture" that arose with the growth of commerce and
industry. Nicholas's likeness embellished the material items of the everyday,
associating him with the mundane. But such items, which helped enhance
what Thomas Richards calls Queen Victoria's "acquired charisma,"[2] weak-

[1] Andrei Georgievich Elchaninov, *Tsarstvovanie Gosudaria Imperatora Nikolaia Aleksandrovicha* (St. Petersburg-Moscow, 1913), 115; Elchaninov, *The Tsar and His People* (London, 1914), 121.

[2] Richards, *The Commodity Culture of Victorian England*, 82–83.

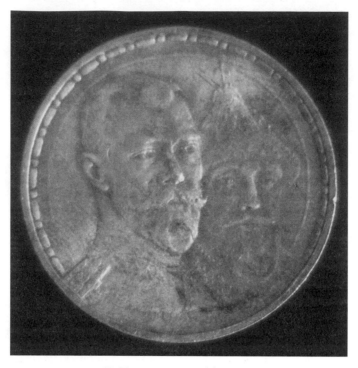

68. Tercentenary Ruble, 1913.

ened the charisma of a monarch who claimed to be the lofty embodiment of the Russian religion, state, and nation. Many of those who revered the tsar felt that the new forms of representation abased the imperial dignity, making him more like rulers and leaders of Western governments.

•

The magnitude of the break with the past is suggested by the great increase in the number of commemorative rubles issued to mark the tercentenary. Nicholas had begun to use commemorative rubles to reach a larger public at the time of his coronation in 1896, when the government circulated 190,845, far more than the numbers for previous coronations. As many as 1.5 million commemorative rubles were issued for the tercentenary celebration. The busts of Nicholas, bareheaded, dressed in the uniform of the imperial rifles, and Michael, wearing the Monomakh cap, decorated the obverse of the coin (fig. 68).[3]

The increased numbers sought brought the commemorative ruble to a broader public, beyond the court, the administration, and the armed forces.

[3] Robert G. Papp, "The Road to Chervonets: The Representation of National Identity in Russian Money, 1896–1924," unpublished paper for the American Numismatic Society Summer Seminar, 1996, 10, 16–17, 19.

But the rise in production was accompanied by a noticeable decline in quality. A breakdown of a die after the minting of the first 50,000 resulted in a flattening of the image of Michael, giving him a ghostly look. The jeweler F. P. Birnbaum wrote, "The layout of portraits is unsuccessful in both the decorative and sculptural relation," and a polemic in *Novoe Vremia* focused on who to blame for the failure. The numismatist S. I. Chizhov criticized the "market" production of the ruble, which was not, in his eyes, "a work of art." He pointed out that "the artist should not have placed a Greek decoration that has no relationship to the Romanov House on both sides of the ruble."[4] The tercentenary medal, which also bore images of Michael and Nicholas, prompted further dissatisfaction. A. I. Spiridovitch, chief of palace security, wrote that it was "as ugly as possible, and one asked, stupefied, how our mint could strike such a medal on the occasion of so memorable a jubilee."[5]

A more fundamental break with tradition occurred on January 1, 1913, when the Russian government circulated the first postage stamps carrying portraits of the Russian tsars. Although there is no evidence that Nicholas took part in this decision, it certainly could not have been made without his consent. As an ardent philatelist, he must have seen the faces of most European monarchs on postage stamps printed during the previous half-century. Nicholas's portrait appeared most frequently—on three stamps: the seven-kopek, the ten-kopek and the five-ruble. Since the seven- and ten-kopek stamps were used for single-weight letters sent in Russia and abroad, they gave his portrait the broadest possible dissemination. Peter the Great was shown on the one- and four-kopek stamps, Alexander II on the two-kopek, and Alexander III on the three-kopek. Of the pre-Petrine tsars, Alexei Mikhailovich appeared on the twenty-five-kopek stamp and Michael Fedorovich on the seventy-kopek.[6]

Stamps, unlike coins, had to be canceled, and the devout Orthodox and supporters of the monarchy indignantly condemned what they regarded as a desecration of the sacred image of the tsar. Bishop Nikon, writing in the official organ of the Holy Synod, deplored the number of kopeks printed beside the tsars' faces, which he believed demeaned the pious tsars worshiped by the people. Worse, "these portraits of the tsars must be soiled with a postmark, as if to profane us all the more." Nikon asked himself if he was still living in Russia, "or has the kike come and conquered our tsardom?"

---

[4] Ibid., 17; F. P. Birnbaum, "Iubileinyi rubl', medal'ernoe iskusstvo i Monetnyi Dvor," in T. F. Faberzhe, A. S. Gorynia, and V. V. Skurlov, eds., *Faberzhe i Peterburgskie iuveliry* (St. Petersburg, 1997), 357–60 (the article was originally printed in *Iuvelir'* in 1913); S. Chizhov, "Iubileinye rubli 1912 i 1913 godov," *Numismaticheskii Sbornik* (Moscow, 1915), 101–2.

[5] Spiridovitch, *Les Dernières années de la cour de Tsarskoe-Selo*, 2:357, 401.

[6] Michael Ercolini, "An Introduction to the Stamps of the 1913 Romanov Issue," *The Journal of the Rossica Society of Russian Philately*, no. 122 (April 1994): 11–14; *Niva*, January 5, 1913, 20. A. F. Giers refers to Nicholas and stamp collecting in "Vospominaniia byvshego ofitsera," 11.

The newspaper *Zemshchina*, an organ of the Union of Russian People, pointed out that the law specified sentences of penal servitude for those who defiled the imperial image. Many postmasters refused to desecrate the face of the tsar with postmarks and left stamps uncanceled. The government suspended the series in February 1913 but resumed printing it later that year.[7]

The tercentenary also became an occasion for the mass production of souvenirs with portraits of members of the imperial family. The number and variety of the "kitsch" of popular celebrations aroused the misgivings of officials in the Ministry of the Court but apparently did not concern the emperor or empress. The ministry received applications to produce a variety of household items carrying the portraits of members of the imperial family, among them trays, candy boxes, metal cases, china, and calendars. "The placing of the portraits of imperial personages on objects having a utilitarian character is usually not permitted," the official of the court censorship responded to one such application. All the requests, however, were approved, sometimes with restrictions, as in the case of a request to market scarves with the portrait of the tsar. The censor authorized this "as long as these are not of a size suitable for use as handkerchiefs."[8]

The effort to popularize the tsar's image in 1913 also led to the lifting of the ban on the presentation of Romanov tsars on the stage. A ruling issued by Nicholas I in 1837 forbade the presentation of Romanov tsars on the stage, though enforcement had been inconsistent.[9] The prohibition, however, had applied consistently to serious operatic productions, and particularly to *A Life for the Tsar.* At the end of Glinka's opera, a procession led the newly elected Michael Romanov into Moscow, but the curtain always fell before he appeared.

The emphasis of the monarchical narrative on the persons of Michael and Nicholas prompted the censors to lift the prohibition in February 1913. In the finale of the gala performance in February at Mariinskii Theater in Petersburg, Tsar Michael entered Moscow at the end of a procession of the principal historical figures of the period. Michael, played by Leonid Sobinov,

---

[7] Episkop Nikon, "Vera Khristova ne terpit dvoedushiia," *Tserkovnye Vedomosti*, February 9, 1913, 283–84.

[8] "Ob izdaniiakh kasaiushchiksia 300-letiia Doma Romanovykh," RGIA, 472-49-1083, 70, 134, and passim. The growth of the market, however, exceeded the capacity of the office of court censors, and some items, like a cheap jubilee medal produced by a private firm, had not even been submitted for approval (Kaufmann, "Das dreihundertjährige Thronjubiläum des Hauses Romanov," 68–69).

[9] In the early twentieth century, the censorship allowed three different performances showing Peter the Great, one of them a comic opera, and a portrayal of Catherine the Great. On the other hand, proposals to portray Michael Romanov, Fedor Romanov, and Alexander I in plays marking the anniversary of 1812 were refused ("Po povodu izgotovlennoi Lefortovskim Otdeleniem Damskogo Popechitel'stva o bednykh v Moskve kinematograficheskoi lenty s izobrazheniem sobytii za vremia 300-letiia tsarstvovaniia Doma Romanovykh," RGIA, 472-49-1252, 27).

rode in a gilded carriage led by companies of musketeers. With two boyars at his side, he received bread and salt from groups of boyars and a golden goblet from the oldest, Andrei Trubetskoi. Permission was also extended to the Malyi Theater in St. Petersburg, which presented Tsar Michael in a play by E. M Bezpiatov, *Oh, Quiet Light* (*Svete tikhii*), about the period of the election. The performance took place only after the censors' objections had been overridden by authorization from the throne.[10] The Ministry of the Court also permitted both the Moscow Malyi Theater and the Alexandrinskii Theater to present three excerpts from Nicholas Chaev's drama *The Election of Michael Romanov*, including the scene depicting the meeting of the Great Embassy with Martha and Michael in the Ipat'evskii Monastery. The performances ended with the cast singing "God Save the Tsar!" At the Alexandrinskii Theater, the voice of the actor Davydov, who played Michael Romanov, was heard above all the others. At the final "Hoorah!" he extended his arms to the audience and threw his hat into the air, to a loud "Hoorah!" from the crowd.[11]

The cinema offered the opportunity to disseminate the tsar's image to an even larger public. Moreover, Nicholas loved to be filmed. He had a private movie theater installed at Tsarskoe Selo where he reviewed films submitted for his approval.[12] The medium of film enabled Nicholas to establish direct visual contact with a mass audience without jeopardizing either his privacy or security. It also made his ceremonies and celebrations known to large numbers of his subjects, many of whom were illiterate or could not hope to witness them. Court censors freely gave permission to film imperial ceremonies with the tsar, even though the ban on *showing* films of the imperial family remained in force until 1910.[13] From 1911 to 1914 the censors approved more than one hundred requests to screen newsreels of the tsar submitted by such firms as Pathé, Khanzhonkov, Drankov, and Gaumont. These films gave the public glimpses of Nicholas at various ceremonial occasions, including the Borodino festivities, the tercentenary processions in Petersburg and Moscow, the Blessing of the Waters, military reviews, parades of the *poteshnye* regiments, the launching of ships, and receptions of foreign dignitaries.

---

[10] The procession at the conclusion of *A Life for the Tsar* reproduced the picture in the 1672 album, reprinted in 1856 (*Kniga ob izbranii na tsarstvo Velikago Gosudaria, Tsaria i Velikago Kniazia Mikhaila Fedorovicha* [Moscow, 1856]; *Russkoe Slovo*, January 18, 1913, 4; February 23, 1913, 3; and *Birzhevye Vedomosti*, February 22, 1913, 5).

[11] *MV*, February 23, 1913, 3; March 3, 1913, 2–3.

[12] The government elite cultivated the same taste. One Nicholas J. Bluman wrote in a letter from Moscow published in the April 19, 1913, issue of *Motion Picture World*, "I have often seen high officials in uniform sitting in the local theaters and I cannot say that of Germany or France" (Leyda, *Kino*, 67–69).

[13] Yuri Tsivian, *Early Cinema in Russia and Its Cultural Reception* (London, 1994), 126. On the censorship and the film, see Yuri Tsivian, "Censure Bans on Religious Subjects in Russian Films," in Roland Cosandey, André Gaudreault, and Tom Gunning, eds., *Une invention du diable? Cinéma des premiers temps et religion* (Sainte-Foy, 1992), 76–77.

Moviegoers also could see the emperor and his family attending ceremonies in the Crimea. A newsreel of his birthday celebration in 1911 showed Nicholas crossing himself continuously during the religious services. Others presented scenes of the empress at the "day of the White Flower" for the Red Cross in Yalta and the family's visit to the estate of Prince Lev Golitsyn, where the tsar examined the prince's vineyards and caves.[14]

The censors tried to ensure that the screening of these films took place with the appropriate dignity, and not in sequence with popular tales of romance and murder. They, in effect, understood the reception of early film programs, discussed by the film historian Iurii Tsivian, that the combination of short film subjects on a single program raised the possibility of associating one with the other. Audiences attended the theater to see an entire program, a show consisting of a series of short subjects, and "the impression made by one picture imposed itself involuntarily on the next." The proximity of images of the imperial family to scenes of bandits and lovers troubled the censors, and they took steps to break the association. Newsreels of the emperor and imperial family, they ruled, should be separated from the rest of the program, "not mixed up with the other pictures," and they should be shown without musical accompaniment. The curtain was to be lowered before and after the showing of the imperial family, and the films in which they appear were to be projected by hand, "at a speed that ensures that the movements and gait of those represented on the screen does not give rise to any comment."[15]

To publicize and associate himself with great accomplishments of the dynasty Nicholas also encouraged the production of historical films. He personally approved the release of two films to mark the tercentenary—Alexander Khanzhonkov's *The Enthronement of the Romanov House, 1613–1913*, and Alexander Drankov's *Three Centuries of the Ruling House of the Romanovs, 1613–1913: Historical Pictures*. Khanzhonkov's film depicted the last years of the Time of Troubles and Michael's election.[16] Only the first quarter of Drankov's footage was devoted to 1613; the remaining sections presented an overview of the principal events of the subsequent three centuries.[17] Both films consisted of a succession of tableaux vivants. Their format, like that of many other films of the time, conformed to the structure of the popular lubok literature: The actors struck conventional heroic poses from lubki to illustrate the particular historical event.[18]

---

[14] "Po voprosu tsenzury kinematograficheskikh snimkov s izobrazheniem Vysochaishikh Osob," RGIA, 472-49-988; Kalinin and Zemliachenko, *Romanovy*, 83.

[15] Tsivian, *Early Cinema in Russia*, 127.

[16] The film apparently concluded with a scene, which has not survived, of Michael's anointment ("Votsarenie Doma Romanovykh, 1613–1913," RGAK [Rossiiskii Gosudarstvennyi Arkhiv Kinofotodokumentov], I-12890).

[17] "Trekhsotletie tsarstvuiushchego Doma Romanovykh, 1613–1913: Istoricheskie Kartiny," RGAK, I-22645.

[18] Many of the authors of *lubok* tales in the penny newspapers became screenwriters at this time (S. Ginzburg, *Kinematografiia dorevoliutsionnoi Rossii* [Moscow, 1963], 114–18; Brooks, *When Russia Learned to Read*, 109).

These films, however, affronted conservative sensibilities. A Prince Kudashev wrote to *Moskovskie Vedomosti* that he found Khanzhonkov's presentation of the siege of the Trinity Monastery, which showed the portals as well as the icons painted on the walls, frightening and unusual. "A place, which as a shrine is dear to the people . . . has been turned into decoration for the picture to be performed." Kudashev not only deplored the showing of the pectoral cross but also was appalled that actors were dressed up as monks "*on this very spot*" and that one actually was permitted to play Patriarch Hermogen, whom the people worshiped as a saint.[19]

The censors accepted the dramatic portrayal of Michael Romanov on the screen, played by the actress S. Goloslavskaia in Khanzhonkov's production and by Michael Chekhov in Drankov's, as well as the presentation of eighteenth-century monarchs in pompous tableaux of eighteenth-century courts. The monarchs of the distant past could be portrayed in films as semi-legendary figures engaged in heroic exploits. More recent emperors, however, had to be presented with care and dignity, for their memory as persons had not faded, and they therefore could not properly be portrayed by actors. Drankov used busts to represent Alexander I and Nicholas I, and portraits for Alexander II and Alexander III. Their images alternated with tableaux of the great moments of their reigns, such as the struggle with Napoleon, the emancipation of the serfs, and the court reform of 1864.

Nicholas II, on the other hand, appeared as himself at the end of the film in a succession of clips of ceremonial occasions—the coronation, the dedication of the Petersburg Monument to Alexander III in 1909, and Nicholas with his troops and at the Borodino celebrations. Setting Nicholas in sequence with images of his predecessors associated him with their glory and achievement. Showing him at major celebrations recalled the moments of exaltation that confirmed the national backing of the monarchy.

"The Crowned Toiler"

The most important means to popularize the tsar and the monarchy during the celebrations was the printed word. At the end of 1905 the leaders of the government and Nicholas himself had resolved to create newspapers that could reach the people and argue the government's program against the opposition. The government dispensed large sums to support more than thirty newspapers across Russia. Under the aegis of the minister of the interior, the newspaper *Rossiia* was established as a private organ, supported by the government—what was called *ofitsioz*.[20] *Sel'skii Vestnik* was made an independent periodical, the change symbolized by the replacement of the former

---

[19] *MV*, March 3, 1913, 1.

[20] On the official press during and after the revolution of 1905, see Likhomanov, *Bor'ba samoderzhaviia*.

"manager" of the newspaper by an editor who was given leeway to make the newspaper more appealing to mass readership.[21] But, like the other government supported organs, neither of these attracted large numbers of readers.[22] The assistant minister of the interior, S. E. Kryzhanovskii, explained the failures of official organs by "the nearly complete absence of people prepared for publicistic activity. This is not surprising, since newspaper work was the province of oppositional circles that had at their disposal large staffs, mainly of Jewish origin."[23]

The official organs achieved far greater success in their publication of brochures and books sympathetic to the government. *Rossiia* and *Sel'skii Vestnik* circulated brochures in the millions.[24] The peasants, in particular, were unaccustomed to newspapers, but, as Jeffrey Brooks has shown, read chapbooks and popular journals eagerly. In the words of one student of peasant attitudes, S. A. Rappaport (An-skii), for the peasants, "printed means it is true, printed means it is just."[25] With Stolypin's help (see chapter 12), *Sel'skii Vestnik* acquired a printing press and storehouses. It published books on such practical matters as agriculture and law and also set up outlets at towns along the Trans-Siberian Railway. During the Borodino and tercentenary celebrations, the editors expanded their lists to include books on history and patriotic studies.[26]

These celebrations provided the occasion for a huge expansion of the distribution of monarchist literature in the countryside. In 1911 *Sel'skii Vestnik* entered into an agreement with the great house of Ivan Sytin, the publisher of the newspaper *Russkoe Slovo*. Sytin commanded a vast distribution network in the provinces. Books and pamphlets were also distributed through the Trusteeships of the People's Temperance, libraries, schools, the church, and the military. During the Borodino jubilees, the books and pamphlets published jointly by *Sel'skii Vestnik* and Sytin reached 2,860.000 copies. Portraits of the imperial family and war heroes numbered 700,000.[27] According to Sytin, his house published 3.8 copies of books and pamphlets for the tercentenary, and *Sel'skii Vestnik* reported 2.9 million books and 1.9 million portraits.[28]

---

[21] Krukones, *To the People*, 190–204.

[22] In 1906 the numbers of copies circulated of *Rossiia* ranged from 1,037 to 7,217 (Likhomanov, *Bor'ba samoderzhaviia*, 110–11). Circulation of *Sel'skii Vestnik* fell from more than 100,000 before 1905 to less than half this. By 1912 it had risen to only 47,500 and was increasing only slowly in 1913 (Krukones, *To the People*, 204). This compares to close to 4 million for *Novoe Vremia* in 1912 and close to 300,000 for *Russkoe Slovo* (McReynolds, *The News under Russia's Old Regime*, tables 5 and 8).

[23] S. E. Kryzhanovskii, *Vospominaniia* (Berlin, n.d.), 101–2.

[24] Likhomanov, *Bor'ba samoderzhaviia*, 112–13; Krukones, *To the People*, 209–10.

[25] Brooks, *When Russia Learned to Read*, 31–32.

[26] Krukones, *To the People*, 208–13.

[27] Ibid., 213.

[28] Brooks, *When Russia Learned to Read*, 314; "Ob izdanii redaktseiu Sel'skogo Vestnika knigi General-Maiora A. El'chaninova, *Tsarstvovanie Gosudaria Imperatora Nikolaia Aleksandrovicha*, i podnesenii eia Ego Imperatorskomu Velichestvu," RGIA, 472-49-1187, 56–57.

Sel'skii Vestnik also promoted and distributed the Tercentenary Icon, which the Synod had approved in December 1912. The icon was painted with pictures of saints whose names were borne by all Romanov tsars and empresses. It came in large versions suitable for churches, schools, and state and public institutions, as well as small ones for private use. The *kiot*, the icon case, could be of wood, marble, or silver.[29] The editor of *Sel'skii Vestnik*, P. P. Zubovskii, claimed that it was the most popular of those souvenirs sold for the tercentenary. Zubovskii wrote, "The Russian people know how to pray and enjoy praying for what they love."[30]

The very scope of official publications and other items connected with the ruling house confirmed the sense of the popularity of the monarchy. Such literature could make known the tsar's person and life, showing the qualities that would strengthen the bond between him and the people. This was the goal of an unprecedented biography of a living tsar, *The Reign of the Sovereign Emperor Nicholas Aleksandrovich*, published under the auspices of *Sel'skii Vestnik*. The author was a member of Nicholas's suite, Professor and Major-General Andrei Georgievich Elchaninov.[31] Elchaninov's book was released in early 1913, before the beginning of the February celebrations, and was carried in excerpts or installments in many major newspapers during and after the events.[32] French and English translations appeared in 1914.[33] Elchaninov presented Nicholas to the Russian people and to Russia's allies as a tsar expressing the needs and advancing the interests of his people—a democratic ruler on the Russian throne.

Elchaninov organized his text to permit the broadest possible dissemination in newspapers. The book comprises twelve brief chapters. The themes are set forth in the first chapter but are repeated throughout so each chapter can stand on its own. The prose is simple but elevated in tone like a panegyric. But it is realistic panegyric devoid of extended metaphor or allegory. The

---

[29] *Sel'skii Vestnik*, January 18, 1913, 4.

[30] Krukones, *To the People*, 214.

[31] Elchaninov, *Tsarstvovanie Gosudaria Imperatora Nikolaia Aleksandrovicha*; and *The Tsar and His People*. The intermediary between the editor and the tsar was Prince Michael Andronikov ("Ob izdanii redaktseiu Sel'skogo Vestnika knigi General-Maiora A. El'chaninova," passim). Elchaninov was a major-general in the tsar's suite and a professor of military art in the General Staff Academy. He had written specialized books on fortification and cavalry, a biography of the eighteenth-century military hero Alexander Suvorov, and a commemoration of the three-hundredth anniversary of the siege of the Trinity Monastery during the Time of Troubles (*Novyi Entsiklopedicheskii Slovar' Brokgauz-Efrona* [St. Petersburg, n.d.], 17:474).

[32] For example, *Novoe Vremia*, *Moskovskie Vedomosti*, *Russkoe Slovo*, *Grazhdanin*, *Kopeika*, and *Zemshchina* printed one or more excerpts from the book. An article in the *New York Tribune* summarized the sections on the tsar's family life and was headlined, "Intimate Details of the Czar's Daily Routine Given in a Book by a Well-Known Professor Reveal Him as a Kindly Man of Family" (April 13, 1913, 9).

[33] The French version is *Le règne de S. M. l'Empereur Nicholas II* (Paris, 1913); B. P. Semennikov, *Nikolai II i velikie kniazia* (Leningrad-Moscow, 1925), 58. Grand Duke Paul Aleksandrovich wrote to Nicholas on May 29, 1913, that his wife, Olga Pistolkors, had decided to translate the book into French "so that foreigners, and especially the French, had a correct idea of Russia and her tsar, a country that is a friend and ally."

author depicts Nicholas as a virtuous and exceptionally able and feeling human being on the basis of considerable detail from Nicholas's personal life and recent history. He gives his account a patina of verisimilitude, even if the idealization of his subject deprives the text of credibility. The mixture of panegyric and journalism clearly favors the former.

The book presents a unique statement of how Nicholas himself understood his office and wished himself to be perceived. Elchaninov gathered considerable material about Nicholas's personal life from observations and impressions of those close to the tsar, who clearly acted with Nicholas's consent.[34] The detail prompted the court censor to express misgivings about the book's "intimate character." "Similar publications have not been authorized until the present day," he observed. When Nicholas reviewed and corrected the page proofs in January 1913 he made one very significant change, which expressed his refusal to work with the Duma. He insisted that Elchaninov delete the sentence, "In his work, the Sovereign Emperor considers his closest assistants in legislative work the reformed State Council and the State Duma, which he has summoned to life."[35] He requested only a few changes in the account of his private life, removing sentences on prayers for the recovery of the heir, which might have placed undo emphasis on Alexei's recent illness.[36] The text therefore can be read as a verbal exposition of the scenario of a ruler not given to extended statements about his office and his relationship to the people.

The central theme of the biography is the tsar's absolute devotion to the people and they to him. The nation—Russia—here is identified with the people, the *narod*, and more specifically with the peasants.[37] The other estates, the state, and the church appear fleetingly. Nicholas's devotion to his people came not from philosophical principles but from his personal designation by God during his coronation. The book opens at the moment after his investiture when the tsar kneels before the congregation and God and begs God to help him "in his high service to order all for the good of his people and the glory of God." Nicholas's every word and deed, Elchaninov wrote, was occupied with this "mission, which cannot be compared to any obligation of our own."[38] Heeding his coronation vow, Nicholas was "the true father of his people," who thought and worked only for them. "He never lays down

---

[34] Elchaninov remarks in the last lines of chapter 1 that the reader should thank not "my humble and unworthy self" but "all those who, standing in close proximity to the throne, have honoured me with their confidence and enabled me to give to the world their observations and impressions" (*Tsarstvovanie Gosudaria*, 16; *The Tsar and His People*, 9).

[35] "Ob izdanii redaktseiu Sel'skogo Vestnika knigi General-Maiora A. El'chaninova," 8. The deleted sentence was on page 97 of the proofs.

[36] Ibid. These deleted passages were on pages 34 and 45 of the proofs.

[37] This theme is captured better in the English title, *The Tsar and His People*, than in the Russian.

[38] *Tsarstvovanie Gosudaria*, 7–8; *The Tsar and His People*, 1–2. The vow or supplication was introduced at the coronation of Anna Ioannovna in 1730 (see Volume 1: 101–2).

his work, on week days and weekends, resting only during his short period of sleep, offering in small things, as in great, a lofty example of 'loyalty in the performance of his duty.' "[39]

The conscientious, diligent, and able performance of his duty became the principal sign of the tsar's title to rule. His dedication set him apart from his subjects but also revealed him laboring like them: He was "the crowned toiler" (*ventsenosyni truzhenik*) who, "following the precept of the founder of the dynasty, Tsar Michael Fedorovich, ceaselessly devotes himself to serving his people."[40] Like the other authors expressing Nicholas's view of the tercentenary, Elchaninov makes Michael's self-sacrifice for his people the central act of 1613. The synchronic mode of the myth is reflected in the persistence of this ethos as the characteristic distinguishing all members of the dynasty.

The title of the first chapter, "The Sovereign Helmsman of the Russian Land" (*Derzhavnyi Kormchii Russkoi Zemli*), sets Nicholas on this timeless plane: Pushkin's image of Peter the Great as helmsman is juxtaposed with the initial designation of Russian unity in the chronicles "The Russian Land." Nicholas is endowed with Peter's traits of absolute control, will, and sense of direction. But he acts in behalf of the Russian land, the nation, a concept not present in the legislation or manifestos of Peter's time. Peter had directed his energies to the organization and strengthening of the Russian administration, the very institutions that now eluded Nicholas's influence and control.

Like Drankov's film, Elchaninov sets Nicholas in a historical frame with his illustrious forebears, associating him with their glories and heroism. At the conclusion he draws explicit parallels between the crisis of the early twentieth century and the troubles faced by Romanov tsars in the early seventeenth, eighteenth, and nineteenth centuries. Each had triumphed by uniting with the people. Michael had received his power from the people and then, "with a gentle but firm hand, in unity with his people, led his country back to the path of glory and greatness." Peter had brought Russia out of the chaos left by "the Empress Sophia." Russia was "raised to a greater height than ever before by 'the unity of the people with the Tsar.' " When Napoleon had taken Moscow, "the people with one accord offered their soul, full of love and devotion, to their Tsar, and by a united effort, with the aid of the army repulsed the terrible invasion and soon planted their standards on the walls of Paris." In all three cases, "as soon as the people responded to the Tsar's summons to unite with him, the sun once more shone on the Russian Land!"[41]

Elchaninov places Nicholas within the recurring motif of triumph of tsar and people. He shows Nicholas as leader of his people, taking initiative for the political, agrarian, and military reforms of his reign. He presents trage-

[39] *Tsarstvovanie Gosudaria*, 8; *The Tsar and His People*, 3.
[40] *Tsarstvovanie Gosudaria*, 16; *The Tsar and His People*, 9.
[41] *Tsarstvovanie Gosudaria*, 132–34; *The Tsar and His People*, 145–48.

dies and defeats as minor setbacks on the way to national unity and resurgence. The Khodynka massacre at Nicholas's coronation is mentioned only as an occasion for a show of Nicholas's pity and largesse to the suffering. The Russo-Japanese War is passed over with an assertion: "In spite of the unfortunate war with Japan, our country's international position is stronger than ever before, and all nations vie with one another in seeking to secure our friendship."[42]

•

Elchaninov's text focuses on two interlinked themes—the tsar's personal virtue and his direct, unmediated bond with the people. Chapters 2 and 3 are devoted to the person of the tsar and show his virtues at work and in his family. Chapter 2, "The Crowned Toiler," takes us through Nicholas's daily workday.[43] By 9:00 in the morning the tsar had finished his breakfast, "a simple frugal meal in keeping with his whole way of living," and was at work in his study. From 10:00 to 11:00 he might take a walk, alone or with the tsarevich, but usually forewent this to receive reports from high officials of the imperial court (who directed the imperial palaces and ceremonial functions), ministers, or other "less exalted personages." At 11:00 he tasted the soldiers' rations from His Own Infantry Regiment and the Imperial Escort, usually with the tsarevich. From 12:00 to 2:00 he took lunch, ample but simple, and then held audiences from 3:00 until 4:00. From 5:00 to 6:00 he had tea with the family, though sometimes this hour, too, was devoted to business. At free moments he would exercise—walking, bicycling, or canoeing—often with his children. He worked from 6:00 until dinner at 8:00, sometimes giving audiences to officials. At 9:30 he returned to work until he retired at 12:00 or 12:30, "and often much later." According to the author, the tsar spent ten to twelve hours working each day.

Following the image of helmsman, Elchaninov shows Nicholas taking charge of everything personally. Nicholas trusts no one to make decisions. He gathers information himself and reads all correspondence. He does not delegate responsibility and does not even allow a secretary to help him. Thus he remains true to the myth of all-competent absolute monarch, without concession to the complex demands of modern leadership. This section of the book makes clear Nicholas's complete independence from the institutions of state—the ministries and the Duma. In most cases the tsar thinks through a problem by himself, grasps its import, and composes the answer. When the tsar needs assistance, he turns not to government officials but to "heads of the various departments of the Palace," members of the imperial suite, and others." He attentively studies the bills submitted to him by the State Council—more than nine hundred from 1909 to 1911. The tsar annotates reports in his own hand, and the author cites several

---

[42] *Tsarstvovanie Gosudaria*, 14–16; *The Tsar and His People*, 6–9.
[43] *Tsarstvovanie Gosudaria*, 17–31; *The Tsar and His People*, 9–28.

of his notes. For example, "I am persuaded of the necessity of a complete reform of our law statutes to the end that real justice should at last reign in Russia."[44]

Much of the tsar's time is spent attending audiences, with ministers, ambassadors, officials, and private individuals. He held these frequently, sometimes receiving several hundred people in one day. "Courteous, attentive, and with a full and exact knowledge of every subject dealt with, the Tsar goes straight to the heart of the question, with a rare skill in anticipating a speaker's train of thought."[45] Private audiences lasted three to four minutes, those with ministers and ambassadors longer, but the tsar quickly understands the thread of all conversations and treats all according to their merits. All feel the tsar's proverbial charm. He gives pecuniary aid justly to supplicants, quickly understanding all their needs. He knows exactly what to say, speaks concisely, but always finds sympathetic things to say and is informed about the life and work of all those to whom he speaks. He makes no distinction according to status. "The humblest person is honored by the Tsar's knowledge of his past and services and by his inquiries after his family and relatives." In his work, the book shows, the tsar both displays his concern for his people and serves as a model for them. The chapter ends with Nicholas's own words, "I do the work of three men. Let every one learn to do the work of at least two."[46]

Three of the twelve chapters of the book are devoted to Nicholas's family life. The tsar is a model father. He has few friends. The family is Nicholas's favorite company. Elchaninov makes clear that Nicholas, the worker-tsar (*tsar'-rabotnik*) does not like "worldly pleasures" and "raises His Family in this spirit." "Entertainments at the Palace are comparatively rare. Great balls and processions are presented only when necessary, as a duty of service. A modest, frugal way of life is evident here, too."[47]

The imperial family is an enclosed sphere, completely separate from court and state. The members are united by love and a sense of the significance of every detail of their life, giving the sense of a domestic novel, much as Queen Victoria had been presented in the last decades of the nineteenth century.[48] In this respect, Nicholas II's elevation of the family was quite different from his grandfather's, Nicholas I. Nicholas I made his family the symbol of the state, the center of the court and the bureaucracy, whereas Nicholas II kept his family apart from these institutions.[49]

---

[44] *Tsarstvovanie Gosudaria*, 25, 31, 123–31; *The Tsar and His People*, 18–21, 28, 133, 141–44;

[45] *Tsarstvovanie Gosudaria*, 24; *The Tsar and His People*, 17.

[46] *Tsarstvovanie Gosudaria*, 31; *The Tsar and His People*, 28.

[47] *Tsarstvovanie Gosudaria*, 50, 54; *The Tsar and His People*, 47, 51. The word *tsar'-rabotnik* in the original is not translated directly in the English edition.

[48] Richards, in *The Commodity Culture of Victorian England*, 102–3, compares the life at the court of Victoria to a domestic novel.

[49] On Nicholas I's conception of the family, see Volume 1: 325–42.

One of the three chapters is devoted to the vigorous outdoor recreation preferred by the imperial family. They enjoy swimming, hunting, tennis, rowing, horseback riding, bicycling, motoring, and picking mushrooms and berries. The text dwells on their automobile rides in the Crimea and their walks and berry-collecting on the Finnish archipelagoes. The involvement of parents and children alike in their own family life is most strikingly reflected in their passion for photography. "All the Tsar's family have cameras and bring back from every visit numbers of excellent photographs." These are not pictures to be shown to the public but to themselves and to friends, snapshots that make them objects of their own delight. The imperial family shares the self-absorption of the middle-class family, one of the features that has made them so much more appealing to posterity than they were to their contemporaries.[50]

The recreations present Nicholas as an ordinary man, enjoying the pleasures of nature and sport. But the author cannot and, indeed, must not resist the urge to idealize, to make something better. Nicholas is an ordinary man, perhaps, but as a Romanov he must do things better than anyone else, something those favored by him knew to observe. In swimming "he has no equals among his suite; he is able to dive and remain under water for minutes together." Nicholas's hunting excursions received a particularly detailed description, including the order of each day and the types of quarry, illustrated by photographs in the book (fig. 69). Nicholas, the text emphasized, is a careful shot, not subjecting his baggers to danger. "Given his excellent marksmanship and his cool self-possession, it is not surprising that the Tsar should generally make the largest bag." He is also extremely proficient at billiards.[51]

Elchaninov describes Nicholas's cultural interests. Nicholas loves opera, particularly Russian opera, though also Wagner. His favorite newspapers are *Novoe Vremia*, the mass circulation conservative nationalist daily; *Russkii Invalid*, the military newspaper; and, among foreign periodicals, *Figaro* and *L'Illustration*. Nicholas's great love, however, is for history, which he believes is the source of Russia's greatness. "The Tsar brings to the consciousness of Russian society the sense that only that state is strong which respects the heritage of its past, and he himself is the first to honor that heritage. He . . . pays particular attention to the reign of the most tranquil tsar, Alexei Mikhailovich."[52] The tsar himself studies old manuscripts and follows the work of the Alexander III Historical Society. He recites to his children the

[50] *Tsarstvovanie Gosudaria*, 41–44; *The Tsar and His People*, 37–41.

[51] *Tsarstvovanie Gosudaria*, 36–38, 50–52, 54–55; *The Tsar and His People*, 33–34, 49, 52. Nicholas, from youth, prided himself on his triumphs in these sports and gladly heard flattery about his prowess. He wrote to his father on June 24, 1887, his first year on maneuvers at Krasnoe Selo, about his victories in billiards and boasted that he was considered the best player in his division ("Pis'ma V. Kn. Nikolaia Aleksandrovicha k Aleksandru III," GARF, 677–1-919, 110).

[52] *Tsarstvovanie Gosudaria*, 38; *The Tsar and His People*, 34, 52–53.

69. Nicholas in a Convoy Cossack Uniform, "after a shoot." Elchaninov,
The Tsar and His People, 1914.

old-Russian folk epics (*byliny*) and tells them tales of the exploits of heroes
like Suvorov. The breadth and precision of his knowledge is "astonishing."[53]

He has an equally great knowledge of Russian literature. His favorite writers, whose works he reads to his family, are Gogol and I. F. Gorbunov, a
theatrical monologist who delivered and published sketches from the life
of the people. In the evenings the family enjoys Cossack songs and dances
accompanied by balalaikas. The tsar is partial to Russian foods, particularly
borsch, kasha, pancakes, and the "monastery" kvas, the recipe for which
came from the Sarov Monastery. "Only Russian champagne is drunk in the
Palace."[54]

Such tastes associated the members of the imperial family with the Russian
people. Throughout the book Nicholas makes clear his special cultural and
spiritual bond with those of Russian nationality, who belong to the inhabitants of the Russian land, as distinguished from the empire. The palace servants are "for the most part Russians." Nicholas is "careful to notice and
support every unique Russian initiative, every manifestation of the Russian
national genius. Similarly he likes to have the country's affairs directed by
Russians."[55]

Orthodoxy also brought Nicholas closer to the Russian people. The chapter "The Orthodox Tsar" describes the imperial family's intense devotion,

[53] *Tsarstvovanie Gosudaria*, 34, 54; *The Tsar and His People*, 31, 51.
[54] *Tsarstvovanie Gosudaria*, 38, 55; *The Tsar and His People*, 34, 52–53.
[55] *Tsarstvovanie Gosudaria*, 26, 38; *The Tsar and His People*, 22, 34.

their attendance of all services and observances of fasts.[56] The tsar's rooms are hung with sacred icons. Nicholas loves the old chants and ceremonies, and when he meets priests he kisses their hands. But the church and clergy play a minor role in this chapter, an indication of Nicholas's belief in his direct relationship to God. "In all his work he seeks the instruction and support of God, from whom he derives his power as 'the Lord's anointed.' " Nicholas's religious observance expressed the bonds he felt between himself and God and between himself and the people, not between himself and the clergy. Almost half the chapter is dedicated to his appearance at the canonization of Serafim of Sarov. "The worshipers were deeply impressed by the sight of the emperor and empress in their midst as simple pilgrims, unattended by any suite or high officials." A photograph shows Nicholas carrying relics of Serafim at the Sarov observance. The tsarevich Alexei also loved to read the saints' lives, particularly Serafim's.[57]

Elchaninov briefly describes the warm and helping relationship between emperor and empress and their daughters' education and tastes. But it is the tsarevich who is at the center of the tsar's and author's attention. "The Tsar's relations with his son are extremely touching, their love for each other is extraordinarily deep and strong." Father and son idealize each other. Nicholas takes Alexei with him when he reviews the troops and, when possible, "spends three or four hours a day with him in healthy outdoor work."[58] To the emperor and empress, the tsarevich of course represented the continuation of the dynasty within the family. But Alexei also reflects Nicholas's conception of what the dynasty and the monarchy should become. He is a symbol of the rejuvenation of the Russian army and nation, "the future hope of the Russian people." Alexei is described as "thoroughly proficient in rifle exercises (with a wooden gun), skirmishing order, the elements of scouting, the rules and requirements of military discipline, and performs the exercises correctly and smartly." He "delights in gymnastics," and participates in the activities of the play regiments in the Crimea, made up of soldiers' sons.[59] Alexei appears in eleven of the forty-seven photographs in the volume, more than any member of the family except the tsar himself. We see him selling flowers in Yalta, standing in the ranks of his unit, the *poteshnye* (fig. 70), on the yacht *The Standard*, and held by his father, who is wearing "the full military outfit of a soldier of low rank" (fig. 71).[60]

[56] The chapter title is misleadingly translated "The Tsar and the Orthodox Church."

[57] *Tsarstvovanie Gosudaria*, 66–72; *The Tsar and His People*, 62–69.

[58] *Tsarstvovanie Gosudaria*, 36; *The Tsar and His People*, 31–32. *Tsesarevich* is the legal term for the heir, officially designating that he is next in line to the throne.

[59] *Tsarstvovanie Gosudaria*, 14, 16; *The Tsar and His People*, 7, 56–57. Another presentation of the heir to the throne as a model for the upbringing of Russian youth was the publication, on Alexei's tenth birthday, of a book on the childhood and upbringing of heirs to the Russian throne, I. N. Bozherianov, *Detstvo, vospitanie, i leta iunosti Russkikh Imperatorov* (St. Petersburg, 1914). The cover carries an inset of Alexei in Russian hat and early Russian costume. At the sides are griffons—from the Romanov coat-of-arms—holding shields.

[60] *Tsarstvovanie Gosudaria*, 46; *The Tsar and His People*, 38.

70. Tsarevich Alexei in the Ranks of Poteshnye. Elchaninov, *The Tsar and His People*, 1914.

•

Russian emperors were traditionally presented as paternalistic defenders of all estates of the realm, and Elchaninov does not fail to characterize Nicholas in this manner. But he devotes little space to the tsar's relations with the nobility and the merchantry, and the new classes of Russia--the professions and the industrial workers--are ignored. These groups, along with other nationalities, clearly do not fit his image as people's tsar. For Nicholas, the Russian peasants are the Russian nation. "The emperor devotes much attention and care to the welfare and moral improvement of the weakest of the estates in their economic condition, if also the most numerous--the peasantry," Elchaninov writes. To demonstrate this point, he describes Nicholas entering peasant huts "to see how they live and to partake of their milk and black bread."[61] He enumerates the agricultural reforms presumably initiated in their behalf by Nicholas—the abolition of mutual responsibility for taxes in 1903, of corporal punishment in 1904, of redemption payments and civil disabilities in 1906. The list concludes with statutes introduced by Stolypin to permit the dissolution of the peasant commune and to create a class of independent peasant proprietors, though there is no reference to Stolypin in this context. The tsar, Elchaninov emphasizes, is a "firm upholder of the new system of land tenure" and had introduced it on his Peterhof estate. A photograph shows Nicholas examining a new model of plough at Peterhof.[62]

[61] *Tsarstvovanie Gosudaria*, 76–80; *The Tsar and His People*, 73–78.
[62] *Tsarstvovanie Gosudaria*, 80–82; *The Tsar and His People*, 79–81.

71. Nicholas II soldier's uniform, holding Alexei. Elchaninov,
The Tsar and His People.

The lower ranks of the Russian armed forces were made up of peasants,
and Elchaninov emphasizes the tsar's personal rapport with the common
soldiers. Nicholas, he asserts, feels particularly close to the "Rifles of the
Imperial Family," which comprised peasants from the imperial estates, and
he preferred to wear their uniforms, particularly when traveling abroad.
Elchaninov also cites the details of a highly publicized episode of the tsar
hiking with the weight of the backpack of a rifleman of the Sixteenth Rifle
Regiment. He goes on to point out that Nicholas not only takes "every opportunity to see the army at close quarters," at reviews, and at maneuvers,
but also on such occasions "converses personally with the men, gives them
fatherly advice, thanks them for their service, praises them for their smart-

ness, and gives them monetary or other rewards." Nicholas displays the same concern for the lower ranks of the navy. In photographs he tastes sailors' rations (fig. 53) on *The Standard*, and he kisses, chats with, and decorates Sub-Ensign Shepel for bravery in the Russo-Japanese War.[63]

Through these descriptions Elchaninov endeavors to give Nicholas features of Peter the Great as he was presented in the popular literature—"as a Westernized gentleman, but also as a good comrade who does not recognize class distinctions."[64] Nicholas, like Peter, is portrayed as a military leader and reformer. The opening sentence of the chapter on the armed forces states that the tsar "personally directs all military affairs." Elchaninov attributes to him recent reforms of the military, among them increases in pay and pensions, the reform of the General Staff Academy, and other improvements in the recruitment and education of the rank and file. Nicholas, he claims, also promoted the production of airplanes, the construction of fortresses, and the rebuilding of the Baltic, Black Sea, and Pacific fleets.[65]

The lasting bond between tsar and people in Nicholas's scenario is revealed most fully at national celebrations, to which Elchaninov devotes an entire chapter and sections throughout the book. He describes Nicholas's conversations with peasants at Poltava, Chernigov, Grodno, and Borodino, and their tearful exclamations when they hear his simple and kind words. He cites their speeches of gratitude at length, as expressions of the feelings of the people as a whole. At Chernigov, a peasant from Liubech by the name of Protsko proclaims his devotion: "We have come to you our Father, not alone, but with our children *poteshnye*, future heroes and defenders of Tsar and country, and to bless your future exploits." Protsko then presents the tsar with an icon of "the first Russian monk," St. Antony of Pechera, who came from Liubech. He continues: "In Your reforms we see the prosperity of Russia. Follow bravely in the footsteps of your ancestors, the Tsar-Liberator, Alexander II of blessed memory, and the Tsar-Peacemaker, Alexander III, of blessed memory; fear no foe—God and Russia are with you."[66]

In meeting with the peasants Nicholas shows that he is one of them, sharing common Russian traits, as if their equal, and therefore their representative. They need no deputies to voice their point of view, for the tsar has a special, abiding rapport with them as a Russian. In the passage cited in the epigraph to this chapter, Elchaninov evokes the "invisible threads," the symbolic bonds that link people and tsar.

The bond with the people allows Elchaninov to minimize the importance of the State Council and the State Duma, which stand between tsar and people. The establishment of representative institutions he presents as the tsar's own initiative, and the institutions themselves as mere extensions of

---

[63] *Tsarstvovanie Gosudaria*, 92, 96–102; *The Tsar and His People*, 97–98, 103–8.
[64] Brooks, *When Russia Learned to Read*, 79.
[65] *Tsarstvovanie Gosudaria*, 87–92; *The Tsar and His People*, 91–97.
[66] *Tsarstvovanie Gosudaria*, 82–83; *The Tsar and His People*, 82–83.

the imperial will. As evidence of the tsar's constitutional intentions, he cites the evasive manifesto of February 26, 1903 (see pp. 382–83). In the spring of 1905, Nicholas decided that since the emancipation, "the Russian people had become educated and accustomed to dealing with public and political affairs." This conclusion moved Nicholas to "revive in all its original force the custom, practiced by the first Tsars of the Romanov dynasty, of allowing the people, through their representatives, to examine matters of state, and to investigate the needs of state." The revolutionary turmoil of 1905 apparently played no part in his decision.

Presenting the tsar as the creator of the Duma, Elchaninov describes Nicholas's reception of the deputies of the first Duma in the Winter Palace and cites his speech welcoming "the best people" of the land. But the ensuing "disorders" showed the tsar that the Duma deputies were not the best people and convinced him to change the electoral law on June 7, 1907. The new electoral system sharply curtailed the number of deputies of the nationalities, particularly in the outlying areas of the empire. "Aliens" (*inorodtsy*), Nicholas II declared, should not "settle questions that are purely Russian." Elchaninov does not indicate that the new law also reduced representation of the urban population, especially workers and professionals.[67] He emphasizes Nicholas's great concern for peasant deputies, without mentioning that many of them belong to oppositional parties. At his reception for the Duma deputies in December 1912, Elchaninov remarks, the peasants were placed in the rear, but Nicholas "marked them out for special attention, beyond the greeting he gave to all the members."[68]

•

Like all his forebears, Nicholas inhabited a realm of myth, validated by ceremonial performances of homage and adulation. As in the past, symbolic agency was invoked when the monarch's preeminence was challenged, and the devices of myth reshaped the appearances of reality to vindicate the tsar's self-image. But Russian institutions and society had changed drastically by 1913. The establishment of the Duma and the expansion of a mass circulation press, which, after 1905, thrived under relaxed censorship restrictions, had introduced new competitors for the attention of the Russian public. Nicholas, viewing himself as a democratic tsar, vied with the political parties through the media of publicity.

Alexander II had also claimed the love of the people, but his representations were directed principally to the elite and sought to elevate him above

---

[67] *Tsarstvovanie Gosudaria*, 116–22; *The Tsar and His People*, 123–32. On the expanded use of the term *inorodtsy* in this period, see John W. Slocum, "Who, and When, Were the Inorodtsy? The Evolution of the Category of 'Aliens' in Imperial Russia," *The Russian Review* 57 (April 1998): 186–90.

[68] *Tsarstvovanie Gosudaria*, 80; *The Tsar and His People*, 78.

his subjects by his supreme benevolence and beneficence. Nicholas addressed the masses directly. He vied with the Duma and in so doing relinquished the Olympian superiority to politics fundamental to the imperial myth. By bringing his life and rule into a public dialogue, he abandoned the monologic self-sufficiency characteristic of myth, which allowed no response but affirmation in elevating the absolute power of the Russian emperor.[69] At the same time, the resort to the display and kitsch of Western celebrations demeaned his image, associating him with the everyday and the cheap objects that carried his family's likenesses. Such items may have helped to popularize Victoria's homey grandmotherly character, but she was not a ruler seeking grounds to restore absolute monarchy. Nicholas lifted the prohibitions that could keep the figures of tsars off the stage and postage stamps, and thus affronted traditionalists who regarded the emperor as a demigod above such vulgarities. Elchaninov's characterization, with its excess of detail about Nicholas's daily life, could only further diminish the superhuman image of the Russian emperor. Indeed, the book revealed the intrinsic contradictions in the image of a national tsar. On the one hand, Nicholas's identity as "crowned toiler" is disclosed in anecdotes, showing him in contact with peasants and soldiers. On the other hand, he appears as the aficionado of tennis, yachting, and fancy automobiles, the recreations of Western high society.

The descriptions result not in an integral image of tsar, but a mélange of disparate characteristics. The contradictions are reflected in the book's uncertain genre. The author veers between panegyric and modern democratic propaganda. He employs grandiloquence and hyperbole while trying to paint the picture of a monarch who is an ordinary mortal. The resulting image is hardly convincing and so at variance with the known facts of Nicholas's reign that it could hardly have gained the credence of contemporary readers.

The main importance of *The Reign of the Sovereign Emperor Nicholas Aleksandrovich*, however, is not the effect the book had on the Russian public of the time but its effect on the tsar himself. The address of a life of a tsar to a mass audience, in Nicholas's scenario, presumed a positive response and showed his involvement with Russian people. The book sustained Nicholas's idealized conception of himself: It was a mirror, reflecting his belief in his virtues as father and Christian, and in his capacities as ruler of Russia's government and leader of its armies. It validated his sense of calling to rule Russia and to command the army, following the traditions of his ancestors, Michael, Peter the Great, and Alexander I. At the same time, it glorified him apart from the institutions of the Russian state, and this image distinguished him from all his predecessors, who identified their own supremacy, to greater

---

[69] See *Scenarios of Power* Volume 1: 7, on the epic and monologic character of the imperial myth.

or lesser degree, with the supremacy of the state. Elchaninov narrowed the mythical reality of the Russian sovereign to the personal world of the all-competent monarch, isolated from the institutional and social realities of Russia. The tercentenary celebrations convinced Nicholas that he had the support of the vast majority of the Russian people. Elchaninov's book confirmed his sense of prowess and destiny. In the fall of 1913 he turned to the task of restoring autocratic power with new conviction and resolve. In this respect, mass publicity insulated Nicholas from contrary views and sustained his determination to perform the mission enshrined in his scenario.

Epilogue: The Tsar, the Duma, and the Army

The Tsar with His deep Russian soul lives inseparably with the interests
of the people in this terrible time of war. At that particularly painful time,
in August 1915, when the foreign armies seized many of our native lands,
the Anointed of God Himself stood at the head of His armies, took the
sword, and halted the enemy invasion. . . .
The Lord has blessed the labors of the Russian Tsar: The foe was stopped,
we held him back. Our strength is growing, and the enemy is secretly falling into confusion, having seen what an invincible force the Russian army
has turned into under the leadership of the Sovereign Leader.
The Tsar has lived long months among His armies. He has been everywhere that his armies have been. The Tsar's soul, the Tsar's heart, beat
and feel together with the soul and heart of every soldier, officer, and general. The Tsar directs the war not from a distance of hundreds of versts.
He appears in the midst of battle. He feels the mood of the armies. He understands the soldier's soul. He knows what is said in the ranks, what the
troops do, and what they dream about.

—*Speech of Nicholas II, December 20, 1915*[1]

THE GREAT CELEBRATIONS substantiated Nicholas's own sense of the people's devotion. A. I. Savenko, a leader of the Nationalist Party, wrote his
wife on June 1, 1913, "The rapture with which the country met the tsar
during his trip has led [the tsar and the minister of the interior Nicholas
Maklakov] to the loyal conclusion that the country is to the Right of the
Duma. Oh, that is a bitter error. In reality, the country is far to the Left of
the Duma."[2]
By 1914 Nicholas's sense of reality was little more than a reflection of
his own self-image and sense of political destiny. Others, seeking his favor,
mirrored and enhanced his views, thus giving him the reinforcement he always needed. The aging Meshcherskii now made amends for his constitutional lapses of 1905 and 1906 in passionate restatements of Nicholas's
own views of himself. An editorial in *Grazhdanin* of February 21, 1913,

---

[1] Major General D. N. Dubenskii, *Ego Imperatorskoe Velichestvo Gosudar' Imperator Nikolai Aleksandrovich v Deistvuiushchii Armii*, 4 vols. (Petrograd, 1915–16), 4:232–33.
[2] Avrekh, *Tsarizm i IV Duma*, 261.

related Meshcherskii's boyhood feelings regarding 1613, when God had wrought "the most majestic miracle" and had chosen the Romanovs as "the path of salvation for Russia." Meshcherskii remembered the fear he felt while reading about the Time of Troubles. Appealing to Nicholas's mystical sensibility, he described his relief at "the unheard of Revelation that took place in the Russian land," which suddenly "illuminated the Russian land with the image of the elected youth." He expressed the great love inspired in him by the three tsars whom he had known personally. Taking up Elchaninov's theme, he wrote that he loved them because "every day they gave themselves selflessly to work dedicated to the state and the people, and without exaggeration one may say that of all the workers and laborers of Russia only one knows no rest. That is her tsar!"[3] Nicholas responded with a note expressing his "great satisfaction" with Meshcherskii's "splendid editorial that came from the heart. It is the symbol of faith, so to speak, of every honorably thinking Russian. You have rarely written something so deeply felt."[4]

Nicholas now went on the offensive to reclaim his autocratic prerogatives. Meshcherskii's protégé, the minister of the interior Nicholas Maklakov, made open statements echoing Nicholas's beliefs that politicians and officials in the capital did not express the mood of the country.[5] In April and May 1913 Maklakov gained the agreement of the Council of Ministers to a restriction of the Duma members' right of interpellation. Prime Minister Vladimir Kokovtsov, struggling to maintain a "unified government" of the ministers, drafted a plan to democratize suffrage in *zemstvo* institutions, in response to *zemstvo* and town activists. During September and October Meshcherskii conducted a campaign in the pages of *Grazhdanin* to drive the prime minister from office. He accused Kokovtsov of acting as a grand vizier and usurping the powers of the emperor by trying to introduce "parliamentarianism." Meshcherskii called for an end to these "West European innovations," including the abolition of the Council of Ministers, and demanded the restoration of a Committee of Ministers each of whom was directly responsible to the emperor.[6]

In October 1913, while Kokovtsov was away from the capital, Maklakov proposed that the tsar decree a state of extraordinary security and threaten the Duma with dissolution. The pretext was the restlessness of the workers and intelligentsia of the capital. Nicholas contemplated the more radical step of reducing the Duma's powers to the purely consultative right to submit majority and minority opinions—a change in the Fundamental Laws and an abrogation of the promises of the October Manifesto. He wrote Maklakov

[3] *Grazhdanin*, February 21, 1913, 11–13.

[4] Vinogradoff, "Some Russian Imperial Letters to Prince Meshcherskii," 127, 139, 150.

[5] "What stirs the figures high in government is not the concern of the majority of Russia," Maklakov asserted (Diakin, *Burzhuaziia, dvorianstvo i tsarizm*, 113).

[6] Ibid., 120, 155–58; Hosking, *The Russian Constitutional Experiment*, 201.

that such a measure would be "a good way of returning to the previous tranquil course of legislation;" it was "in the Russian spirit." But Maklakov encountered opposition and refrained from submitting Nicholas II's recommendation to the Council of Ministers.[7]

The ritual murder case of Mendel Beilis, which reached trial in Kiev in September 1913, gave an unequivocal demonstration of Nicholas's determination to rule according to principles remote from those of the Westernized educated society of his day. The belief in ritual murder was one that Nicholas could share with the masses, who, he believed, remained devoted to him. As far back as 1817 Alexander I had decreed that ritual murder could not be the basis of criminal charges in the empire, "in view of the fact that such accusations have previously been refuted by impartial investigations and royal charters."[8] But Nicholas regarded the legal experience of the West, which Alexander I had followed, as alien to the feelings of the Russian people. Nicholas saw all the reports of the prosecution and let the trial go forward. The members of the Union of the Russian People who concocted the charges and the government officials who encouraged them were among those he trusted as true Russians. The belief or nonbelief in ritual murder drew a clear line between those who shared his views and those who hoped to set Russian monarchy on a Western course.[9] The subversion of the court system, the most successful product of the great reforms, was a first step toward a reaffirmation of personal power.

Broad coverage of the trial in the press opened the government to widespread ridicule and condemnation. Reports and articles about the trial appeared in newspapers nearly every day in the fall of 1913. Nicholas's critics branded the trial a return to medieval justice based on prejudice and superstition. Vladimir Korolenko, in *Russkoe Bogatstvo*, wrote that the reader first looked for news of the trial.

> Evidently Russian citizens have understood finally that the Jewish question is a Russian question, that wrong and evil exposed at the Beilis trial are a Russian wrong and evil. They understood that one cannot be an indifferent spectator, that Russian nationalism is a threat to the entire Russian spirit. They understood what kind of arbitrary, savage, dark Russia is being created by nationalism for the Russians.[10]

The Beilis trial was the subject causing the greatest number of government actions against the press in 1913, resulting in 102 penalties including the arrest of three editors and the closing of three newspapers. Abroad, the press characterized the trial as another example of the backwardness and barba-

---

[7] Ibid. 201–2; Kokovtsov, *Iz moego proshlogo*, 2:156; Diakin, *Burzhuaziia, dvorianstvo i tsarizm*, 158–63; Avrekh, *Tsarizm i IV Duma*, 114–15, 261.

[8] Tager, *Tsarskaia Rossiia i delo Beilisa*, 17.

[9] Hans Rogger, "The Beilis Case: Anti-Semitism and Politics in the Reign of Nicholas II," *Slavic Review* 25, no. 4 (December 1966): 623–26.

[10] Tager, *Tsarskaia Rossiia i delo Beilisa*, 197–99.

rism of Russian autocracy. Appeals to end the trial came from Germany, France, England, and the United States. Even the anti-Semitic monarchist and editor of *Kievlianin*, Vasili Shulgin, wrote an outraged condemnation of the trial.[11]

The minister of justice Shcheglovitov crudely meddled in the trial ensuring that the majority of the jurors would be peasants and none would be intellectuals. "It is the fate of the simple Russian peasant to show the entire world the truth in this case," declared the Kiev monarchist newspaper *Dvuglavyi Orel*. But the jury voted to acquit. An officer of the police called the case a "police Tsushima, which never will be forgiven," comparing the trial to the great Russian naval disaster in the Russo-Japanese War. Maklakov and the tsar, however, claimed that although Beilis was innocent, ritual murder had taken place. A book, prepared under the auspices of the Ministry of the Interior, tried to demonstrate that the government had sufficient evidence of the ritual murder of Iushinskii. A portrait of Shcheglovitov was the frontispiece for the book, which appeared in 1917. On the eve of the war, the Ministry of Justice was preparing another ritual murder trial. The officials involved in the Beilis case were well rewarded. The presiding judge, F. A. Boldyrev, who presented a summation that strongly favored the prosecution, received a gold watch and a secret bonus and was promoted to the position of chairman of the Kiev Judicial Chamber—the chief of the magistracy of the entire South-Western Region. The prosecutor, G. G. Chaplinskii, who had been named procurator of the Kiev Judicial Chamber two days after the murder, was appointed to the Senate on January 1, 1914.[12]

As Nicholas made clear his hostility to the Duma and his contempt for the legal order, moderate leaders began to despair of finding a way to reconcile representative government and the monarchy. Kadets, Octobrists, and the industrialists in the Progressist Party feared the growing radicalism of the workers and the loss of faith in the authority of government, which was going back on its promises and discrediting the very possibility of consensual parliamentary government. The influential liberal wing of the Moscow industrialists now looked to the Left for support. Their leaders—A. I. Konovalov, S. M. Tretiakov, N. D. Morozov, and P. P. Riabushinskii—entered into negotiations with the Kadets, the Mensheviks, and even the Bolsheviks to coordinate opposition to the tsarist government.[13]

Nicholas remained convinced of the people's devotion. The countryside was relatively tranquil, for the combination of martial law and agricultural reform had quelled the urge to rebel. But the quiet was misleading. The majority of peasants still coveted the landlords' estates, which they believed

---

[11] Ibid., 201, 205–7; Maurice Samuel, *Blood Accusation: The Strange History of the Beilis Case* (Philadelphia, 1966), 164–65.

[12] Tager, *Tsarskaia Rossiia i delo Beilisa*, 221–23, 272; Rogger, "The Beilis Case," 628.

[13] Haimson, "The Problem of Social Stability in Urban Russia," 360–67; Siegelbaum, *The Politics of Industrial Mobilization in Russia*, 17–18.

to be rightfully theirs. They looked to the Duma and the government for a confiscation and redistribution of the landlords' estates, the "Black Partition." Complicated procedures for the elections to the fourth Duma allowed nobles and officials to exert considerable influence on the peasants' voting, and more than half the peasant deputies belonged to right-wing or conservative parties. But regardless of party affiliation, nearly all peasant deputies from estate provinces were concerned exclusively with the question of land and looked to the Black Partition, which Nicholas and all his ministers had disavowed.[14]

After a lull in 1913 the strike movement regained its momentum. During the first six months of 1914 factory inspectors reported 1,254,441 strikers, almost as many as for the entire year 1905.[15] To be sure, the number of strikes rose across Europe before the war, but they were neither as numerous nor as militant as those in Russia.[16] The Russian strikes were concentrated in or near the capital: Workers in Petersburg Province accounted for half the total. Bolshevik influence spread through the working class, which reacted to government restrictions on trade unions by heeding appeals for revolutionary political action.[17]

On the eve of the outbreak of war, in July 1914, St. Petersburg became the scene of a violent general strike. Barricades went up in the Vyborg district and Vasilievskii Island. Trams were overturned. Bands of strikers broke through the cordons of troops to enter the center of the city onto Nevskii Prospect. The English vicar M. Mansell Merry described a demonstration in his journal, "Great roaring, singing crowds sweep in City-wards from the outlying districts like a torrent in spate, and seem as if they must carry all before them by the sheer weight of their serried multitudes." They were driven back only by a charge of Cossacks at full gallop.[18]

To Nicholas, such an event pointed to the need for a reassertion of his autocratic prerogatives and curtailment of the Duma's powers. In January 1914 Prime Minister Kokovtsov resigned and was replaced by the aged and servile Ivan Goremykin. This represented the end of the principle of "united government"—a government headed by a prime minister to whom the individual ministers were responsible—and made the tsar, once more, the dominant figure in the government. Meshcherskii strengthened Nicholas's resolve

---

[14] Eugene D. Vinogradoff, "The Russian Peasantry and the Elections to the Fourth State Duma," in Leopold Haimson, ed., *The Politics of Rural Russia, 1905–1914* (Bloomington, Ind., 1979), 228–33.

[15] Haimson, "The Problem of Social Stability in Urban Russia," 348.

[16] In 1914, 5.4 times as many strikes took place in Russia as in France, 3.6 as many as in Britain, and nearly 3 times as many as in Germany, despite the fact that Russian industry was less developed than its Western counterparts (D.C.B. Lieven, *Russia and the Origins of the First World War* [London, 1983], 18).

[17] Bonnell, *Roots of Rebellion*, 390–438.

[18] M. Mansell Merry, *Two Months in Russia, July–September 1914* (Oxford, 1916), 57–59, 65.

to go further by sending him a political diary that contained such observations as: "*No matter how one kindles constitutionalism in Russia*, it is hampered in Russia by Russia itself, for the first day of the constitution is the beginning of the end of monocracy"; "As long as imperial power is not decorative and not dependent on party passions, the tsar is the defense of the people"; "The stronger the authority of any regime, the more helpless are the revolutionary elements."[19]

In an interview published in the February 4, 1914, issue of *Russkoe Slovo*, Meshcherskii declared that the government was "not obliged to submit to any bare principles or dead letters." The editors observed that the government, meaning Nicholas himself, intended to introduce restrictions on the Duma's authority gradually with the agreement of members of the State Council.[20] In June 18, 1914, three days after the assassination of the Archduke Ferdinand, Nicholas, frustrated over the Duma's refusal to pass the budget and changes in the press law, again sought to revoke the October Manifesto. He suggested a return to a consultative Duma, like that proposed in the Bulygin project of August 1905. Only Maklakov sided with the tsar. The other members of the Council of Ministers, including the usually amenable Prime Minister Goremykin, demurred.[21]

•

After the defeat in the Russo-Japanese War, the government was vulnerable to criticisms of its foreign policies, and the series of setbacks it suffered in the Balkans aroused especially pointed attacks. When Austria annexed Bosnia-Herzogovina in 1909, and Russia came away empty-handed from the negotiations, the Kadets, the Octobrists, and the Pan-Slavic press called the foreign office to task for failing to defend Russia's national interests. Paul Miliukov called the annexation a "diplomatic Tsushima."[22] In response to the Balkan wars, Pan-Slavic sentiment became widespread, with growing sympathy for intervention in behalf of Serbia and demands that Russia resume its role as a great power and take control of the straits.[23] The foreign minister Sergei Sazonov wrote in his memoirs that he advised Nicholas, in July 1914, that

---

[19] Avrekh, *Tsarizm i IV Duma*, 258.

[20] Diakin, *Burzhuaziia, dvorianstvo i tsarizm*, 189.

[21] Ibid., 196–97; Hosking, *The Russian Constitutional Experiment*, 204–5.

[22] See Caspar Ferenczi, *Aussenpolitik und Öffentlichkeit in Russland, 1906–1912* (Berlin, 1982), 150–243.

[23] When the Russian government intervened to stop Bulgaria from advancing into Turkey, the liberal, nationalistic press responded with outrage. The progressist newspaper *Utro Rossii* asserted, "The mood of society diverges with the views of the government: The government will expend all efforts to calm the Slavs, while society will send volunteers to them . . . The spirit of Slavdom and thus the spirit of Russia are for war." *Russkoe Slovo* wrote "For Count Bergholtz, the interests of Austro-Hungary stand in the first place, and then peace. For our governing bureaucracy, peace stands in first place, and then the interests of Russia." *Novoe Vremia* and *Golos Moskvy* expressed similar views (E. G. Kostrikova, *Russkaia pressa i diplomatiia nakanune pervoi mirovoi voiny, 1907–1914* [Moscow, 1997], 142).

"Russia would never forgive the tsar" if he capitulated and "heaped shame on the good name of the Russian people."[24]

The Balkan crisis challenged Nicholas's role as national leader and his effort to lay claim to the great military traditions of his forebears. On the other hand, he had been informed that Russian armies were not yet ready to confront Germany and Austro-Hungary. The conservative voices in the government feared that a war would bring a repetition of 1905—defeat and social revolution. The most eloquent statement of this viewpoint was the memorandum written at the beginning of 1914 by Peter Nikolaevich Durnovo, who had served as minister of the interior in 1905 and 1906. Durnovo prophesied a catastrophic end—a demoralized army, carried away with land hunger, no longer serving as "a bulwark of law and order. "The legislative institutions and the intellectual opposition parties, lacking real authority in the eyes of the people, will be powerless to stem the tide, aroused by themselves, and Russia will be flung into hopeless anarchy, the issue of which cannot be foreseen."[25]

Durnovo was arguing a common view in foreign-policy circles, advanced by, among others, V. F. Lamzdorf, Baron M. A. Taube, as well as by Meshcherskii and Rasputin. As prime minister, Kokovtsov, fearing for Russia's precarious financial situation, had also sought to preserve peace. But after his fall, David Mcdonald has suggested, Goremykin left the crucial issue of war in the hands of officials such as Foreign Minister S. D. Sazonov and Agriculture Minister A. V. Krivoshein, who wished to abandon the policy of restraint and take up a more assertive foreign policy.[26]

What McDonald describes as "official conservatism," expressed by Durnovo, clearly contradicted Nicholas's vision of the union of tsar and people. Nicholas did not dread "hopeless anarchy" because he believed that the people, despite appearances, remained devoted to their tsar. And although he had outgrown the reckless spirit of his earlier Eastern policy, he still believed, as Elchaninov wrote, that the emperors' leadership of the people, guided by Divine Providence, had wrought prodigies in the Russian past. Russian emperors had proved their destiny at moments of crisis, and he saw the coming conflict as his opportunity to restore the heroic role of autocrat, the leader of triumphal armies.[27]

[24] Geyer, *Russian Imperialism*, 314

[25] See F. Golder, ed., *Documents of Russian History, 1914–1917* (New York, 1927), 3–23.

[26] David M. McDonald, "The Durnovo Memorandum in Context: Official Conservatism and the Crisis of Autocracy," *Jahrbücher für Geschichte Osteuropas* 44, no. 4 (1996): 481–502. Taube listed other "pacifists" in addition to Meshcherskii—Witte; the justice minister I. G. Shcheglovitov, who was involved in the Beilis case; the education minister L. A. Kasso; Prince V. N. Orlov, head of the tsar's military chancellery; and Baron A. A. Rozen (see McDonald, "The Durnovo Memorandum," 496).

[27] See Goremykin's remark, cited below, about Nicholas's wish to serve as commander in chief at the beginning of the war (Michael Cherniavsky, ed., *Prologue to Revolution: Notes of A. N. Iakhontov on the Secret Meetings of the Council of Ministers, 1915* [Englewood Cliffs, N.J., 1967], 79).

On July 20, 1914, the day of the declaration of war, Nicholas appeared in Petersburg at the Winter Palace. He arrived along the Neva to deafening cheers and was rushed through the crowds to the palace. At the religious service he repeated Alexander I's vow that he could not make peace as long as one of the enemy remained on the soil of the fatherland. After a priest read the manifesto, Nicholas addressed the assembled officers as "the whole army, united in nation and spirit, strong as a granite wall" and received a wild roar of approval. Then he and the empress went out to the balcony to meet the crowds filling the vast palace square. The throng knelt and sang the national anthem. The tsar crossed himself and wept. "At this moment," the *Novoe Vremia* reporter wrote, "it seemed as if the Tsar and His people embraced each other strongly, and in this embrace stood before the great Native Land."[28] He returned to Peterhof at 6:00 P.M. on his yacht. Merry described him as "a solitary figure on the vessel's bridge, erect and rigid, his hand raised in unrelaxed salute to the peak of his naval cap, amid such a tumultuous demonstration of his people's reverence and love, as, surely, it has seldom fell to the lot of any ruler to receive."[29] On August 31 the name of the capital was changed to Petrograd.

The Petersburg ceremony, though stirring, was brief and fastidious. His appearance on August 5 in Moscow was more extended and the ceremonies more inclusive. He entered the city on the traditional route along Tver Boulevard, riding in an open carriage to popular acclaim. In the Kremlin Palace he received not only high officials but representatives of the estates. His speech was more inclusive than the Petersburg proclamation and evoked national and Pan-Slavic feelings. "In your persons, the people of the first capital, Moscow, I greet the Russian people, loyal to me. I greet them everywhere, in the provinces, the State Duma, the State Council, unanimously responding to rise amicably and cast aside discord for the defense of the native land and Slavdom."[30]

The scene of Nicholas bowing from the Red Porch to the frenzied crowd on the Kremlin square impressed foreign visitors with the power of Russian national sentiment. The English ambassador wrote, "The heart of Russia voiced the feelings of the whole nation." The ambassador's daughter felt she was no longer in the twentieth century. "This was the old Moscow of the Tsars. Little Mother Moscow, threatened and besieged over and over again, and yet always miraculously emerging from her smoking ruins!" The French ambassador also felt himself transported back beyond the eighteenth century and admired "the frantic enthusiasm of the Muscovite people for their Tsar." The tsarevich's tutor, Paul Gilliard, thought that the people of Moscow were

---

[28] Maurice Paléologue, *An Ambassadors' Memoirs* (New York, 1925), 1:50–52; NV, July 21, 1914, 4; Spiridovitch, *Les dernières années de la cour de Tsarskoe-Selo*, 2:482–83.

[29] Merry, *Two Months in Russia*, 85.

[30] MV, August 6, 1914, 2; Voeikov, *S tsarem i bez tsaria*, 104–5.

"so anxious to keep the tsar as long as possible that they mean to hold him here by manifest proofs of their affection."[31]

On subsequent days the tsar visited Moscow shrines, hospitals, and the stores of medical materials assembled by the Merchants Bureau and the *zemstva*. He met a gathering of the mayors of the principal towns. Finally, he visited the Trinity Monastery, where he was blessed by the Miracle Icon of the Visitation of the Virgin, which had accompanied Russian campaigns since 1654.[32]

Nicholas returned from Moscow inspired by the fervent reception. He believed that the country had united behind him and submerged political differences.[33] This sense was shared by liberal and moderate members of the Duma, who welcomed the war as a means to unite the nation for the defense of Slavdom. The Duma adjourned after one day, its president, Michael Rodzianko, declaring, "We shall only hinder you." Peter Struve hoped that the war would finally bring about the unity of holy Rus' with great Russia.[34]

The "embrace" of tsar and people evoked by the *Novoe Vremia* reporter expressed the patriotic exaltation of the first moments after the declaration of war. A new national flag was designed in order to symbolize the unity of tsar and people. The Russian tricolor, white, blue, and red, had become established as the national and state flag in the 1880s and 1890s. In the years before the war, monarchist groups had campaigned to introduce the imperial standard as the national flag—the black double-headed eagle on a gold background, with the crest of Moscow (St George and the Dragon) in white on its breast. The new flag represented a compromise. The imperial standard was placed in a canton on the Russian tricolor, uniting imperial and national symbols and colors on a single field.[35]

For the most part, the lower classes remained indifferent to the displays of enthusiasm. With the declaration of war, patriotic demonstrations, most of them organized by the police, advanced through the streets of the capital, challenging foreigners.[36] The peasants and the workers appear to have accepted the mobilization passively as their lot. Disturbances, however, marred the recruitment efforts, and in Mogilev and Kazan, mobilized reservists led groups of peasants in the burning and plundering of estates. These outbreaks could be contained, but their meaning was clear to provincial officials. One

---

[31] Sir George Buchanan, *My Mission to Russia* (Boston, 1923), 1:214–15; Buchanan, *The Dissolution of an Empire*, 103; Paléologue, *Memoirs*, 1:93, 95; Pierre Gilliard, *Thirteen Years at the Russian Court* (New York, 1970), 114.

[32] *MV*, August 9, 1914, 2; Voeikov, *S tsarem i bez tsaria*, 106.

[33] Gilliard, *Thirteen Years at the Russian Court*, 122.

[34] Hans Rogger, "Russia in 1914," *Journal of Contemporary History* 1, no. 4 (October 1966): 110–13.

[35] On the efforts to agree on a national flag, see *Gerb i flag Rossii, XI–XX veka* (Moscow, 1997), 451–61; and E. N. Voronets, *Chetyrkhsotletie Rossiiskogo Gosudarstvennogo Gerba* (Kharkov, 1898), 42–44.

[36] Merry, *Two Months in Russia*, 75.

governor phrased the thoughts of the mobilized soldiers: "The lords thought up this war" but the reckoning would take place after it was over.[37]

The defeats and colossal losses of the first months of the war dispelled the initial euphoria. In August and September Russian armies moved into East Prussia and Galicia. But the rout at the hands of the Germans at the Battles of Tannenberg and the Mansurian Lakes in East Prussia, stemmed their advance and made clear the problems of command and supply in the military. The provisioning of the troops and the cities became increasingly difficult. Prices soared, but grain prices lagged behind industrial products, and the peasants began holding back their crops. Each year a diminishing percentage of the harvest reached the cities, whose population was growing rapidly. By the spring of 1915 the strike movement had resumed as workers lost patience with the spiraling inflation and the bleak prospects in the war.

Shortages and disruptions of supply energized Russian society to independent action. The *zemstva* and the towns formed a national organization, Zemgor, to deal with these problems. The leading industrialists came together in a national network of War Industrial Committees to coordinate private production with government institutions. Overall, by 1916 these efforts coped with the problems of materiel, but the problem of manpower proved less tractable. The social and administrative problems of mass conscription exceeded the powers of the tsarist state. The Russian armed forces numbered only a little more than 14 million men for a population of about 180 million, only slightly larger than France's armies, though France had less than a quarter of Russia's population.[38]

From the beginning of the war Nicholas made clear that the leadership of the armed forces was to remain with the imperial family. According to Goremykin, at the outset he intended to appoint himself commander in chief.[39] He was dissuaded, however, and instead named his cousin, the popular Grand Duke Nicholas Nikolaevich. After the setbacks, the tsar frequently visited headquarters and appeared before the troops along the front. His direct and passionate involvement in the war became the theme of a four-volume book, *Tsar Emperor Nicholas Aleksandrovich with the Active Army*, composed by Major-General D. N. Dubenskii, the editor of the newspaper *Russkoe Chtenie* and a member of Nicholas's suite.[40]

Dubenskii's account elaborates the scenario set forth by Elchaninov. Although the work gives a sense of the scope, tragedy, and moment of the war, there are only two major actors—the people, now assuming the form of the army, and the tsar. The traditional meetings with estates take place as the tsar enters each town, but the Duma and the independent organizations are

[37] Wildman, *The End of the Russian Imperial Army*, 76–80.
[38] Norman Stone, *The Eastern Front, 1914–1917* (London, 1975), 208–15.
[39] Cherniavsky, *Prologue to Revolution*, 79.
[40] Dubenskii, *Ego Imperatorskoe Velichestvo Gosudar' Imperator Nikolai Aleksandrovich v Deistvuiushchei Armii.*

72. Nicholas II inspecting trenches on the "Western" front, 1914. Major General Dubenskii, *Ego Imperatorskoe Velichestvo Gosudar' Imperator Nikolai Aleksandrovich v Deistvuiushchii Armii*, vol. 1, 1915.

treated only in passing. According to Dubenskii, the news that the tsar was joining the army awakened rejoicing in Russia.[41]

Volume 1 of Dubenskii's book covers Nicholas's visits to headquarters and the front in September and October 1914. The author points out that although Nicholas Nikolaevich was commander in chief, the tsar watched closely over the conduct of war. The headquarters, he emphasizes, was called the "imperial" or "tsar's" headquarters (*tsarskaia stavka*). Nicholas is shown standing side by side with the grand duke, and sitting at a desk over a large battle map, presumably discussing strategy. He appears in a trench (fig. 72), reviewing guards' regiments dressed in combat attire, stopping at Kholm and Liuban', and inspecting churches destroyed by the enemy and fortresses that had been besieged. Cordons of soldiers cheer everywhere. At hospitals, he, like Nicholas I and Alexander II before him, stops at the beds to ask the soldiers about their injuries and to praise their service. The author, like Elchaninov, includes numerous excerpts of the tsar's conversations with soldiers and peasants he met along the way.[42] The March 28, 1915, issue of the journal *Niva* reviewed the first volume, reprinted several photographs, and cited some of the emperor's bedside conversations. "The Russian man, the simpler he is, the freer he talks with his Tsar," the editors observed.[43]

[41] Ibid., 1:iii.
[42] Ibid., 1:4–15, and passim.
[43] *Niva*, March 28, 1915, 246–48.

The first volume also presents the empress as an important figure in the family's leadership of the war. She takes charge of the care of the wounded. She presides over the Permanent Council for the Unification of Governmental, Public, and Private Activity for the Care of Families of War Casualties; the vice presidents are her sister, the grand duchess Elizabeth Fedorovna, and her sister-in-law, the grand duchess Olga Aleksandrovna. The Winter Palace, the book explains, had been turned into a gigantic workshop where women prepared linens and bandages for the war. The empress and the daughters worked as nurses in the Tsarskoe Selo Court Hospital, which now occupied the Great Catherine Palace, and often attended operations and bandaged wounds.[44] They also visited the wounded at other hospitals. The text is interspersed with many photographs of their visits and of the empress, her daughters, and other grand duchesses as nurses.

The second volume describes Nicholas's long journey from November 18 to December 19, 1914, through central Russia, the Caucuses, and ending in Moscow, with another display of national unity from the people and estates of Moscow. Nicholas began the trip with a visit to headquarters where he informed himself of the situation on Russia's western front. His mode of transport between towns was the railroad. Within towns, he traveled in large automobiles. Photographs show him arriving with his suite in his automobile at churches, hospitals, and government buildings. He chats with the artisans at the Tula Arms Factory. He speaks with peasants in Kursk and soldiers in Kharkov. The tsar meets with mountain people of the Caucuses, who had scored an important victory against Turkish troops in Armenia. He is received by the estates in Tbilisi. A brief summary appeared in *Niva*, with photographs of the tsar meeting troops in the Caucuses. In Voronezh he is joined by the empress and his daughters, who accompany him on stops at Tambov and Riazan on the way to Moscow.[45] In Riazan, Dubenskii notes the people's "moral attraction" (*nravstvennoe vlechenie*) to the tsar. The attraction was powerful because "they are aware and esteem the fact that in these difficult days the TSAR himself tours Russia and personally visits the injured, sees His armies Himself and in this way shows all of Russia how near he is to her, how dear her sorrow is to Him, her joy, her happiness."[46]

The account of the tsar's life in the army created a picture of reality that sustained and developed a sense that the tsar and the grand duke had inspired a unified national war effort. The third volume, devoted to the tsar's trip to Kiev, Ukrainian cities, and the Galician front from January to June 1915, opens with a statement declaring that after half a year of war all of Russia was rallying behind the war effort. In the text the people—both peas-

---

[44] Dubenskii, *Ego Imperatorskoe Velichestvo Gosudar' Imperator Nikolai Aleksandrovich v Deistvuiushchei Armii*, 1:xvi–xvii.

[45] Ibid., 2:13–14, 21, 23, 70, 127–31, 139–40, 169–71; *Niva*, July 4, 1915, 523–25.

[46] Dubenskii, *Ego Imperatorskoe Velichestvo Gosudar' Imperator Nikolai Aleksandrovich v Deistvuiushchei Armii*, 2:112.

ants and workers—are the constituents of the nation. The people, Dubenskii emphasized, were appreciating the commander in chief's "firm will" more and more. Workers and the peasants were showing "their sincere devotion to the TSAR, and never in the previous years has the SUPREME POWER, the autocracy of the TSAR, been so highly esteemed in the general awareness of the masses as in this difficult time in Rus'." His visits to the Galician front in April reaffirmed Russia's claims to this border region. According to *Armeiiskii Vestnik*, his appearance in L'vov reaffirmed Galicia's "historic ties" with Russia.[47]

The spring and summer of 1915 witnessed Russian armies in retreat before a powerful offensive of Austro-Hungarian and German armies. By August the enemy occupied all of Poland, Lithuania, and Courland and was threatening Belorussia. Leaders of the new national town and *zemstvo* organizations, such as Guchkov and Konovalov, voiced demands for increased participation and, particularly, a Council of Ministers responsible to the Duma. Nicholas responded by appointing several ministers who could work with the Duma and independent organizations—most notably, the minister of war, Alexei Polivanov; the minister of the interior, Nicholas Shcherbatov; and the minister of trade and industry, Vsevolod Shakhovskoi.

In July the Duma was reconvened. Political groups from the Nationalists on the Right to the Kadets on the Left united to form a "progressive bloc," supporting a call for a "Ministry of Confidence," all of whose members enjoyed the confidence of the nation.[48] In August 1915 the Moscow Town Council, at the instance of Konovalov, passed a resolution, soon to be endorsed by other town councils and *zemstva*, calling for a meeting with the tsar and a cabinet that could enjoy the support of the nation.[49]

Such a proposal clashed with Nicholas's belief that he was the historical embodiment of the nation and knew its interests better than representatives chosen from the educated classes. He refused to receive a delegation from the *zemstva* and the towns. Then, in September, he prorogued the Duma, which had met for only six weeks. Thus ended the effort to create a government of national unity like that created by other combatant powers, which would put aside political differences until the end of hostilities.

The national emergency emboldened Nicholas to perform his role of masterful and sympathetic commander who felt one with the people and the army. In August 1915 he declared, to the horror of nearly everyone, that he had decided to appoint himself commander in chief. Despite the setbacks, the grand duke enjoyed considerable popularity. He had cultivated good relations with the leaders of the Duma and other public institutions as well

---

[47] Ibid., 3:3–4, 91–93; Mark von Hagen, "Ukraine Between Empire and Union," forthcoming.

[48] On the progressive bloc, see Raymond Pearson, *The Moderates and the Crisis of Tsarism, 1914–1917* (London, 1977), 39–64.

[49] Pares, *The Fall of the Russian Monarchy*, 258–59.

as the press. Most of the ministers deplored the move. Prime Minister Goremykin demurred, but only because he thought it his duty to obey his sovereign under all circumstances. The ministers argued that by taking command the tsar would bear responsibility for a military setback. They also feared that he would be leaving government in the hands of the empress, increasing Rasputin's influence.[50]

Nicholas, Goremykin told the Council of Ministers, never forgave himself for failing to take command during the Russo-Japanese War. He went on,

> According to his own words, the duty of the Tsar, his function, dictates that the Monarch be with his troops in moments of danger, sharing both their joys and their sorrow. Many of you gentlemen probably remember the measures that were being prepared after the declaration of the present war and how difficult it was to dissuade the Emperor then. Now, when there is a virtual catastrophe at the front, His Majesty considers it the sacred duty of the Russian Tsar to be among the troops, to fight with them against the conqueror or perish. Considering such purely mystical feelings, you will not be able to dissuade the Emperor by any reasons from the step he has contemplated.[51]

Eight members of the Council of Ministers drafted a letter predicting dire consequences and pleading with the tsar to reverse his decision.[52] Such remonstrations merely confirmed Nicholas's belief that the ministers were out of touch with the people. On September 9, 1915, he wrote to Alexandra, "The people accepted this move as a natural thing and understood it as we did." He had received telegrams "with touching expressions" of support for him. This showed him that "the ministers, always living in town, know terribly little of what is happening in the country as a whole. Here I *can judge* correctly the real *mood* among the various classes of the people." The empress agreed that "the ministers are rotten," and in subsequent months most of those who objected were replaced, among them Polivanov and Shcherbatov, who had been appointed only in the spring of 1915.[53]

By the end of 1915 Nicholas had entered fully into his scenario of commander in chief leading his people in war. Since he lacked the training or capacity to deal with problems of command, his leadership was largely symbolic. He did, however, continue to promote aristocratic generals with courtly manners and little military talent to the highest command positions.[54] As the war progressed, the scenario of selfless patriotic leader in contact with his army and people became increasingly self-referential and remote from

---

[50] Cherniavsky, *Prologue to Revolution*, 77–83, 96–114, 158–67.

[51] Ibid., 79.

[52] Ibid., 166–67.

[53] Michael T. Florinsky, *The End of the Russian Empire* (New York, 1961), 84–87; Nicholas II, *The Letters of the Tsar to the Tsaritsa* (London, 1929), 85.

[54] Stone, *The Eastern Front*, 191–92. Figes gives a good sense of the demoralizing effects this had on the professionals in the army like Alexei Brusilov (Orlando Figes, *A People's Tragedy: The Russian Revolution, 1891–1924* [New York, 1998] 259–61).

military realities and public opinion. Aside from occasional portraits, the popular press and popular culture seem to have kept the image of the tsar in the background and emphasized the people's patriotic struggle for their native land (*rodina*).[55]

Nicholas expressed his sense of his role most poignantly in his "speech" of December 20, which was circulated on a broadside to the civilian population and the armies, and is cited in the epigraph to this chapter. In reply to rumors that the government was not prosecuting the war effectively and was seeking a separate peace, he declared that such rumors had been planted by German spies and, "like poison gas, cloud the mood of Russia." He answered the allegations by describing, in the third person, his sharing of the sacrifices of the struggle. He concluded with Alexander I's avowal that there would be no peace until the last enemy soldier was driven from Russia. These words written in large cursive script provided the heading for the speech. Nicholas's portrait in military uniform, decorated with the Cross of St. George, was placed beneath the scroll. Photographs in the corners showed him standing with the tsarevich at his side, reviewing troops, and meeting with a general.[56]

Volume 4 of Dubenskii's account covers the period between July 1915 and February 1916. It opens with a photograph of Nicholas sitting before a battle map, with the chief of Staff, M. V. Alekseev, and the quarter-master general, M. S. Pustovoitenko, standing at his side (fig. 73).[57] The description follows Elchaninov's format of trying to give a sense of the tsar's person by enumerating the details of his daily life. He lives in a Spartan manner in two simple rooms of the governor's house. Photographs show the spare furnishings of the room, focusing on his camp bed, the symbol of the self-denying sovereign as military leader, next to the heir, who arrived at headquarters on October 1, 1915. Like Elchaninov's text, Dubenskii's emphasizes Nicholas's

[55] For example, the multivolume luxury album *Velikaia Voina v obrazakh i kartinakh*, published in Moscow during the war, has little about Nicholas's whereabouts and activity, though it does contain many portraits of members of the imperial family. The few works published on war propaganda indicate that the tsar's image was not very prominent and was overshadowed by an effort to arouse feelings for the native land (*rodina*) (Louise McReynolds, "Mobilizing Petrograd's Lower Classes to Fight the Great War: Patriotism as a Counterweight to Working-Class Consciousness in *Gazeta Kopeika*," *Radical History Review* 57 [1993]: 160–80). Hubertus F. Jahn, in his work on popular culture, concludes that folk images and other personifications of military prowess attracted more attention than the ritualized mentions of the tsar. "While the figure of Wilhelm II personified the enemy for everyone, the tsar certainly did not embody Russia for everyone" (Hubertus F. Jahn, "For Tsar and Fatherland? Russian Popular Culture and the First World War," in Stephen P. Frank and Mark D. Steinberg, eds., *Cultures in Flux: Lower-Class Values, Practices, and Resistance in Late Imperial Russia* [Princeton, N.J., 1994], 143–44). Jahn focuses on popular culture in Petersburg in his *Patriotic Culture in Russia during World War I* (Ithaca, N.Y., 1995); he compares the great variety of *Fürstenpostkarten* of Wilhelm II to the small numbers of such official patriotic "fantasy cards" in Russia (41).

[56] Dubenskii, *Ego Imperatorskoe Velichestvo Gosudar' Imperator Nikolai Aleksandrovich v Deistvuiushchii Armii*, 4:232–33.

[57] The picture was also published in *Niva*, November 7, 1915, 818.

73. Nicholas II as commander-in-chief, with Chief of Staff M. V. Alexeev and Quarter-Master General Chief of Staff M. S. Pustovoitenko, 1915. Major General Dubenskii, *Ego Imperatorskoe Velichestvo Gosudar' Imperator Nikolai Aleksandrovich v Deistvuiushchii Armii*, vol. 4, 1916.

determination to learn things for himself. "The TSAR not only listens to the report of his chief of staff, but directly receives impressions of the actions of his army in telegrams."[58]

The book also singles out Nicholas's unswerving, self-sacrificing diligence. At 9:00 in the morning he walks to the General Staff where he receives reports from Pustovoitenko. At 12:30 he has a simple lunch with his allies' military attachés. Between 1:00 and 2:00 he returns to his study to work on reports. Later, at 3:30 or 4:00, he takes an automobile ride through the neighboring countryside. Then he, the "imperial toiler," returns to his desk

[58] Dubenskii, *Ego Imperatorskoe Velichestvo Gosudar' Imperator Nikolai Aleksandrovich v Deistvuiushchii Armii*, 4:58–60.

to labor over reports, while his mind and heart suffer everything that has occurred in his country. After dinner he toils deep into the night. Through all the troubling news, the tsar maintains calm. "No one has ever seen the TSAR lose self-control." The tsar's impassivity, which so exasperated the ministers, is presented here as a sign of his "strength of will," "restraint," and "clear understanding of circumstances," all of which are made possible only by faith in Divine Providence.[59]

Dubenskii, like Elchaninov, describes Alexei as a vigorous youth. The boy dashes about the headquarters and reads the war dispatches. He represents the revitalized army and monarchy. "The model of the Russian soldier, officer, general, that were admired with such enthusiasm in EMPEROR NICHOLAS II and His Son will not soon be forgotten." On October 17, 1915, Alexei received the Medal of St. George, fourth degree. A week later Nicholas himself was decorated with the coveted Cross of St. George, fourth degree. Exhilarated, Nicholas noted in his diary: "An unforgettable day for me when I received the Cross of St. George. . . . At 2:00 P.M. I received Tolia Bariatinskii, arriving by instruction of N. I. Ivanov, with a written petition of the Council of the Order of St. George of the Southwestern Front that I decorate myself with the dear white cross! The whole day I walked around as if intoxicated."[60]

The recommendation for the decoration appeared in the journal *Niva*, next to V. L. Borovikovskii's painting of the archangel Michael descending from the heavens holding a bolt of lightening and followed by helmeted goddesses.[61] The award placed Nicholas in the tradition of emperors courageously joining their army in wartime. A composite photograph in Volume 4 sets a portrait of Nicholas beneath vignettes of Alexander I, Alexander II, and Alexander III, all of whom had also received the order for bravery; Nicholas's picture is the largest (fig. 74). On October 27 the tsarevich joined Nicholas on a grueling month-long journey along the western front and down to Odessa and New Russia. The photographs in Dubenskii's volume show Alexei in the uniform of an ordinary soldier at the tsar's side, reviewing troops and meeting with soldiers.[62]

Absorbed by his mission to inspire his army, Nicholas became almost indifferent to the events on the home front. The ministers who reported to Nicholas at the headquarters at Mogilev were struck by his placid temperament when they posed critical problems of policy. Such deliberations

---

[59] Ibid., 4:62–63.

[60] Kashchenko and Rogulin, "Predstaviteli Doma Romanovykh," 263; *Dnevniki Imperatora Nikolaia II*, 553–54.

[61] The recommendation of the Council of the Order of St. George of the Southwestern Front was for inspiring "heroic exploits," strengthening morale among the armies, visiting positions that had come under fire, and serving as "an example of military valor and self-renunciation" (*Niva*, November 7, 1915, 817).

[62] Dubenskii, *Ego Imperatorskoe Velichestvo Gosudar' Imperator Nikolai Aleksandrovich v Deistvuiushchii Armii*, 4:48–50.

74. Composite of emperors awarded the Order of St. George, 1915. Major
General Dubenskii, *Ego Imperatorskoe Velichestvo Gosudar' Imperator Nikolai
Aleksandrovich v Deistvuiushchii Armii*, vol. 4, 1916.

prompted in Nicholas the same feelings of weariness that he had felt as heir when forced to attend to state matters. He wrote to Alexandra that ministers "persist in coming here nearly every day, and take up all my time." During the report of Minister of Agriculture A. M. Naumov in June 1916 on the mounting food-supply crisis, Nicholas constantly digressed into talk about children and flowers. He told Finance Minister Peter Bark how good he felt among his army and how unpleasant the atmosphere of the capital seemed to him when he returned to Tsarskoe Selo.[63] In 1916 the government seemed deprived of all direction. Three replacements of prime ministers occurred in less than a year, the so-called ministerial leapfrog. Alexandra and Rasputin were blamed, but the changes could hardly have been made without at least the tacit consent of the tsar.

In the fall of 1915 Russian armies repelled the enemy's offensive in the West. Dubenskii wrote, "The Russian EMPEROR, according to the ancient belief of the Orthodox people, the Anointed of God, the All-Russian Autocrat, taking the sword into His hands, halted the enemy invasion."[64] The Brusilov Offensive of 1916 penetrated Austria, and the Russian army moved forward elsewhere on the front. To Nicholas, these successes indicated divine intervention. He had the icon of the Vladimir Mother of God brought from Moscow to headquarters. "I am quite convinced that its blessing will be of great help to us." On May 28, 1916, the troops carried the icon along the streets of Mogilev, reminding him of Borodino. Then it would be taken to the front.[65]

But the tide soon turned, and the cost in lives again was enormous. Supplies in the cities dwindled, and rations were reduced for the army. Widespread dissatisfaction increasingly focused on the imperial family. Rumors circulated that the empress, her ministers, and Rasputin were themselves German spies. The rumors were ungrounded, but they expressed a growing distrust and belief that, contrary to the myth, members of the imperial family were betraying the Russian people, whom they had presumed to embody.

The officer corps to which Nicholas felt close had been decimated in the first two years of the war, and many officers were replaced by men of lesser birth and education, men who had little sympathy for the tsar or the monarchy. By 1916, 70 percent of the junior officers were of peasant background.[66] The enormous loss of men led to the massive recruiting of young soldiers, many of whom brought the dissatisfaction of the towns and villages into the army. When Petrograd erupted with strikes and bread riots at the end of

---

[63] Lieven, *Nicholas II*, 220–21; Nicholas II, *The Letters of the Tsar to the Tsaritsa*, 207.

[64] Dubenskii, *Ego Imperatorskoe Velichestvo Gosudar'*, 4:16–17.

[65] Nicholas II, *The Letters of the Tsar to the Tsaritsa*, 192–93; letters of May 28 and 29, 1916.

[66] Peter Kenez, "A Profile of the Pre-revolutionary Officer Corps," *California Slavic Studies* 7 (1973): 145–50.

February 1917, the 180,000 troops in the capital consisted largely of new recruits to the guards' reserve battalions.[67]

Nicholas was aware of the massive turnover.[68] He continued to believe, however, that the troops at the front remained loyal, and he urged that several regiments be dispatched to Petrograd to suppress the disturbances. The prime minister Nicholas Golitsyn pleaded with the tsar to appoint a new ministry acceptable to the Duma, but the tsar remained intransigent. In the midst of the crisis, on February 27, 1917, Nicholas decided to return to Tsarskoe Selo to be near his family. He started out, but the generals could not guarantee his safety in passing through the Petrograd region, and so he waited in Pskov. In the meantime, crowds in the capital demanded his abdication, and a soviet of workers' deputies took form.

At headquarters in Mogilev, Nicholas de Basily, the director of the Diplomatic Chancellery, drafted an abdication manifesto, which the leaders of the Russian army sent to the tsar.[69] According to the Fundamental Laws, de Basily reasoned, the tsar could only abdicate to the next in succession, Alexei, who at age twelve would not be able to rule until his majority, at age sixteen. In the meantime, a regent could be appointed of the tsar's choosing. The draft declared that Nicholas was abdicating according to the Fundamental Laws and was appointing his brother Michael as regent. The draft enjoined Alexei and Michael "to conduct the affairs of state in complete and inviolable union with the people's representatives in the legislative bodies and according to the principles established by them." It ended with an appeal to "all true sons of the Fatherland" to obey the tsar and help him, "together with the people's representatives," to lead Russia into victory and prosperity.

Nicholas revised the manifesto to leave the throne to Michael. He believed that his son's illness made it impossible for Alexei to live apart from his family. He also deleted the phrase "on the principles established by them." To the very end Nicholas refused to grant the Duma the authority to change the governmental system. He felt not disillusioned but betrayed. "All around there is treason, cowardice, and deceit," he wrote in his diary. In the midst of the turmoil, Michael renounced the throne his brother had conferred on him. The news reached the public at the same time as Nicholas's abdication. Michael declared, "I will accept the supreme power only if that be the desire of our great people, expressed at a general election for their representatives to the Constituent Assembly." The election, he stated, should adhere to the four-tail suffrage the liberals sought; that is, it should be universal, direct, equal, and employ a secret ballot.

---

[67] Wildman, *The End of the Russian Imperial Army*, 124–25.

[68] Gilliard reported that, during the tsar's and tsarevich's tour of the Odessa region in November 1915, Nicholas asked that the men on parade who had been in the war since its beginning raise their hands. Few hands were raised in some companies, none in others (Gilliard, *Thirteen Years at the Russian Court*, 154).

[69] The following account follows the description of Nicholas de Basily, *The Abdication of Nicholas II of Russia* (Princeton, N.J., 1984), 111–33, 151–53.

Thus, although Michael's renunciation of the throne was taken by all as an abdication, he left open the possibility of a constitutional monarchy. Michael, who had not been inculcated with the national myth as Nicholas had as heir, abandoned the realm of myth for the realm of politics. Nicholas viewed this act not as mere error or betrayal but as a profanation, an incomprehensible descent into political squalor. He wrote in his diary, "God knows who got him to sign such filth!" ("*Bog znaet, kto nadoumil ego podpisat' takuiu gadost'!*").[70]

---

[70] *Dnevniki Imperatora Nikolaia II*, 625. Nicholas's convictions were hardly shaken by the revolution. See Steinberg, "Nicholas and Alexandra," 14, 23, 25, 31, 36–37.

IT HAS BEEN a central argument of this study that Russian monarchy, guided by the overarching themes of myth, was an active and dominant force in shaping the political organization and culture of eighteenth- and nineteenth-century Russia. The political conflict of the early twentieth century took on its particularly violent and destructive forms in part because of the modes of thinking inculcated in the emperors and their advisers by the myth. The conquest motif, in particular, encouraged the intransigent use of force, the restoration of untrammeled authority, and an averseness to compromise. From the late 1870s the word *smuta* appears frequently in the writings of tsarist officials, conjuring the Time of Troubles in the early seventeenth century, a period of political breakdown, internecine social conflict, and foreign invasion. The alternative to absolute power was disintegration, anarchy, and international humiliation. The conquest motif expressed the domination of an imperial elite with foreign origins or associations that elevated them above the subject population, whether Russian or other nationality. It elaborated a heroic history for members of the elite. The people lived outside the myth, in the realm of the everyday.

The theme of conquest proved enduring and adaptable. It enabled Russian rulers to take on cultural and political forms—first of Byzantium, then of Western absolutism, and then of enlightened absolutism. The monarchs of Russia displayed dominant features of sovereignty, whether they reflected piety, reason, learning, or grace and elegance. The noble elite assumed their sovereigns' patterns of conduct and taste, elevating themselves with him over the subject population and associating themselves with an international culture of royalty. From the reign of Peter the Great the image of monarch was European, and the elite was presented as Westernized Russians, utilizing European learning and culture to justify the power of the absolute state.

The motif of conquest was thus assimilated to the European myth of Russian monarchy. Each monarch ascended the throne as conqueror, the bearer of new conceptions of Russian royalty, which he proceeded to display in his own setting, in his own scenario of the myth. The motif had a dynamic character, encouraging a rejection of tradition and demonstrative shows of change that distinguished the heroic monarch from what went before—the sad and tragic events of the previous reign. After Peter the Great, Russian emperors and empresses identified themselves with the Russian state and measured their achievements in terms of the expansion and transformation of the Russian state. The prowess of the ruler was displayed in programs of reform that applied Western ideas and institutional models to Russian institutions. Western concepts of law, administrative regularity and specialization, and economic development were identified with the success of the monarch in remolding Russian reality. The Russian sovereign was the embodiment of the Westernized absolute state.

The concept of nation, suggesting the involvement of a people in government, challenged the fundamental notion of an imperial ruling elite. But the official-nationality doctrine assimilated the concept of nation into the European myth and reconciled it with the conquest motif. The Russian people were distinguished by their devotion and loyalty to their Westernized rulers, in contrast to European peoples given to revolution and social conflict. Ceremonies and rhetoric made the people a figment of myth, a chorus acclaiming the dominion of the tsar and the state. Official nationality justified the authoritarian rule of Nicholas I. After the Crimean War, it provided the grounding for the Great Reforms of the reign of Alexander II. The abolition of serfdom, the court, and *zemstvo* reforms introduced elements of a European civil society, with the presupposition that the generous acts of a kind monarch would be rewarded with renewed gratitude and devotion of the people to monarchy. But the increased freedom and the refusal to consider representative government led instead to disaffection and revolution, culminating with the assassination of Alexander II in 1881.

The assassination brought a reassertion of the conquest motif in the form of a new national myth of Russian autocracy. Alexander III was presented as the highest embodiment of the Russian people, who were united with him organically by ties of nation and religion. No longer the Westernized Emperor, whose culture and associations placed him apart from the people, he was the most Russian of Russians. They in turn were partners in their own subordination. The myth disclosed a new foundation period in an idealized seventeenth century, borrowed from the Slavophiles, when the people's union with the tsar had not been impeded by Western institutions and ideals. The ruthless use of force would preserve the unity of tsar and people from the subversive and alien elements of the Westernized intelligentsia.

The national myth thus excluded educated society from the nation. The monarchy used its symbolic resources, religion, rhetoric, and art to preempt the concept of nation and to deny the term to the educated and professional classes that might form a nascent civil society.[1] If the European myth distanced the Westernized elite from the lower classes, the national myth, by evoking a fictive identity with the peasants, distanced the monarchy from the Westernized elite. Alexander III sought to define Russianness by his national

---

[1] Here I differ with the interpretation set forth by Geoffrey Hosking who argues that autocracy "was generated by the needs of empire, and had to be reinforced as that empire came increasingly into conflict with nation-building" (Geoffrey Hosking, *Russia: People and Empire, 1552–1917* [Cambridge, Mass., 1997], xxvi). He goes on to show how the Orthodox Church, educated society, and the intelligentsia failed to construct a concept of the Russian nation. But the monarchy was hardly a passive or dependent factor indifferent to the concept of nation. It actively discouraged or forbade the concept of a civic nation and by identifying the nation with the monarchy made it difficult or impossible for society to construct an independent concept of civic nationalism.

features and the unifying institution of the Russian Orthodox Church. He introduced measures to claim supremacy of Russian elements in the administrative elite, and the policies of Russification sought to demonstrate Russian political and cultural domination of national regions primarily in the western parts of the empire.

By presenting the emperor as the embodiment of the Russian people rather than the Russian state, the national myth redefined the relationship between monarch and state. Alexander III's physical image gave symbolic expression to the new goals and conceptions of this relationship. Michael Katkov had connected the idea of nationality with the state's capacity to wield force ruthlessly, without regard to legal or ethical restraints. Constantine Pobedonostsev, in his correspondence with Alexander III in the 1870s, had associated the weakness and indecision of Alexander II's officials with their alien, European character. The national myth attributed the assassination to this weakness, to the infection of the state apparatus with Western liberal ideas, borne by the officials who had supported the work of reform. Alexander III rejected the Petrine state apparatus, with its Western rationalistic orientation, and projected the image of a vigorous and authoritarian personal monarchy. He set himself against those state organs that were dominated by officials dedicated to legality and administrative regularity, particularly the State Council. His counterreforms reasserted a dynamic of change, trying to restore a direct personal authority of the tsar over the people, unmediated by institutions that enjoyed a degree of autonomy. Alexander sought to establish a truly Russian state administration, through the minister of the interior, which would tighten control over the *zemstva* and urban institutions, and, in the persons of the new appointive official, the land captains, strengthen administrative tutelage over the peasantry.

The counterreforms failed to eliminate these elements of institutional autonomy, but the national myth took hold, expressing a faith in the authority of the Russian emperor to rule forcefully and to strengthen the power of the monarchy at home and abroad. It bred an official arrogance and a sense of the unlimited potentialities of autocratic power. Influential figures harbored dreams of eastward expansion and the extension of Russian influence in the Balkans, to be realized after Russia overcame what they regarded as temporary fiscal and military problems. The myth also justified Sergei Witte's state-directed industrialization. Katkov and Witte could dismiss the traditional fears of a disruptive and rebellious proletariat by relying on the punitive authority of a powerful Russian national state. The efficacious use of force would quell dissatisfaction and preserve the unity between the Orthodox tsar and the Russian people.

Nicholas II came to the throne accepting the national myth as a given. But he had none of his father's faith in a transformed imperial state. Rather, he distrusted all officials and preferred to rely on familial and personal contacts. With the establishment of representative institutions in 1905 and 1906, his antagonism to the regular administrative order of the state only grew. As he became more distant from the state, he drew closer to the people. The imagined union between tsar and people became a personal one, a sense that he enjoyed a particular affinity with Russian peasants. This affinity was based on a common hostility to educated society and the intelligentsia and to a common belief in a direct mystical bond with God and holy men, venerated among the people. Alexander Mosolov, the chief of the Chancellery of the Ministry of the Court, remarked after the pilgrimage to Sarov that Nicholas began to speak of them at this time as if they were grown children.[2] Like children, they might err and cause trouble on occasion but they were sure to return contrite, and their views and demands were not to be taken seriously.

Convinced of his direct designation by God and a mission assigned to him by the national spirit and history, Nicholas accepted unquestioningly the Katkovian reliance on force. His petulant words at his wedding reception in 1895 made clear his position. When the constitutional movement arose in the first years of the twentieth century, he was prepared for confrontation. In short, the monarch was not a passive figure adopting defensive tactics at this point; he was a ruler seeking to restore autocratic prerogatives and deliver himself from the encumbrances that hampered his personal will in government and society. The revolutionary events of the early twentieth century should be visualized not as an irresistible force meeting an almost immovable object but as the convergence of two opposing forces on the existing state order. Nicholas undermined attempts to compromise with moderate elements and favored ministers of the interior who were disposed to repression and the use of force—Dmitrii Sipiagin, Viacheslav Plehve, Peter Durnovo, and, on the eve of the war, Nicholas Maklakov.

In the October Manifesto, Nicholas agreed to establish representative institutions, a State Duma elected from all classes of the population, and a partly elective, partly appointive State Council. But all his pronouncements made clear that he remained sovereign, that the Duma was his creation and had to win his approval if it wished to continue to exist. For him, this meant submissiveness, and none of the four Dumas were submissive. The 1907 change in the election law produced a conservative majority in the Duma and excluded most delegates from other nationalities. Peter Stolpyin sought through this measure to create a unity between the moderate, propertied elements and the monarchy. It is clear, however, that Nicholas regarded the new electoral system only as a first step toward the reaffirmation of his autocratic power. The assertiveness of the moderates in the Duma, their demands for reforms in the military and for a law on religious toleration, the recriminations about Rasputin challenged Nicholas's sovereignty and his vision of a triumphant restoration of absolute power.

The subsiding of the 1905 revolution and the restoration of order emboldened Nicholas to challenge the Duma's electoral mandate by demonstrating his own national democratic following. He used the occasions of the histori-

---

[2] Mosolov, *Pri dvore poslednego Rossiiskogo imperatora*, 119.

cal celebrations of Poltava, Borodino, and the election of the first Romanov tsar to associate himself with the great achievements of his ancestors and to demonstrate broad popular support. Rather than expressions of a broad national consensus, these celebrations distanced the tsar from the Duma. Meetings with peasants, in his mind, displayed his rapport with them and their acceptance of him as their trusted ruler.

The tercentenary of the Romanov dynasty represented the culmination of the historical celebrations and the beginning of a new stage in the definition of Nicholas's scenario. The festivities of 1913 convinced him of his role in the national myth as the successor to Tsar Michael and assured him of the triumph of his mission to restore personal autocracy. The ceremonial displays of the peasants' enthusiasm showed that they, like wayward children, had returned to their posture of devotion to their sovereign. The use of publicity confirmed his sense of being in touch with a mass democratic following. The celebration also revealed alternative conceptions of the past, which conceived of the early seventeenth century as a model for constitutional monarchy. But these were submerged by the color and acclaim of the ceremonies and the emphasis in monarchical literature on the figure of Michael himself. Nicholas felt that he enjoyed the mandate given to Michael and that he, like the first Romanovs, would restore an absolute monarchy after a period of anarchy and breakdown. In the fall of 1913 he made the first of two attempts to curtail the powers of the Duma, in violation of the October Manifesto. World War I provided him with additional opportunities to appear as leader of the nation. Initially wary of Russian involvement, he soon conceived of the war as another episode in the resurgence of absolute monarchy under his aegis.

Louis Marin wrote of Louis XIV, "The king is truly king, that is the monarch, only in his images. They are his real presence."[3] Marin was commenting on the separation between the physical and political body of the king in seventeenth-century France when the king's political body became a symbol of state. Nicholas also viewed his own images as his real presence, but they represented not the state but his own increasingly idiosyncratic image of the nation. By 1914 Nicholas saw the nation invested in himself and the numerous symbols of his personal life. The precincts of Tsarskoe Selo held a microcosm of Russia, as conceived of in his scenario. Easter eggs recalled his appearances as ceremonial embodiment of the nation. Hundreds of icons revealed his divine designation and personal attachment to national saints. The Feodorov village and cathedral enabled him to venture into a replica of an imagined seventeenth century where tsar and his family could pray in union with the Russian army.

[3] Louis Marin, *Le portrait du roi* (Paris, 1981), 12–13.

BIBLIOGRAPHY

ARCHIVAL SOURCES

*State Archive of the Russian Federation (Gosudarstvennyi Arkhiv
Rossiiskoi Federatsii) (GARF), Moscow*

Fonds: 601: Alexander Fedorovna; 640: Nicholas II; 641: Maria Aleksandrovna;
642: Maria Fedorovna; 660: Grand Duke Constantine Konstantinovich; 665:
Grand Duke Nicholas Aleksandrovich; 678: Alexander II; 677: Alexander III; 728:
Winter Palace Library; 826: V.F.Dhzunkovskii.

*Russian State Historical Archive (Rossiiskii Gosudarstvennyi
Istoricheskii Arkhiv) (RGIA), St. Petersburg*

Fonds: 472: Chancellery of the Ministry of the Court; 473, 474: Ceremonial Division
of the Ministry of the Court; 516: Kamer-Fur'erskii Journals; 797: Chief-Procurator of the Holy Synod; 878: S. S. Tatishchev; 1139: Bureau of Grand Duke Alexander Aleksandrovich; 1320: Committee for the Organization of the Tercentenary.

*Bakhmeteff Archive of Russian and East European Literature and History,
Rare Book and Manuscript Library (BAR), Columbia University*

Collections: Gershel'man-Shvarts, A. F. Giers, D. N. Liubimov, D. A. Obolenskii,
V. A. Kamenskii, I. M Shadrin.

Hesse State Archive, Darmstadt

Collection of Empress Maria Aleksandrovna.

*Manuscript Division of Russian National Library (Russkaia national'naia
biblioteka) (RNB), St. Peterburg*

V. S. Krivenko collection.

A. A. Bakhrushin State Central Theater Museum (TsTM), Moscow

M. V. Lentovskii fond.

PRINTED SOURCES

*4oe aprelia 1866g.: Polnyi sbornik izvestii, adresov, telegramm i stikhotvorenii po
sluchaiu chudesnogo spaseniia zhizni imperatora Aleksandra II.* Vol. 1. St. Peters-
burg, 1866.
Abrosova, Ekaterina. "Arkhitektor Vysochaishego Dvora Vladimir Aleksandrovich
Pokrovskii." *Tsar'ino: Pravoslavnyi istoriko-kraevedcheskii almanakh* 98, no. 4:
32–62.
Agulhon, Maurice. *Histoire vagabonde.* 2 vols. Paris, 1988.
Aksakov, I. S. *Biografiia Fedora Ivanovicha Tiutcheva.* Moscow, 1886.
———. *Sochineniia.* 6 vols. 1886–1887.
Al'bom 200 letnego iubileia Imperatora Petra Velikogo. St. Petersburg, 1872.
Al'bom kostiumirovovannogo bala v Zimnem Dvortse v fevrale 1903g. St. Peters-
burg, 1904.

Al'bom vidov tserkvei Estliandskoi gubernii, sooruzhennykh pod vedeniem Revel'skogo nabliudatel'nogo komiteta po postroike tserkvei, prichtovykh i shkol'nykh zdanii. Revel, n.d.

Alexander II. "Perepiska Aleksandra II s Velikim Kniazem Konstantinom Nikolaevichem," *Dela i Dni* (1920), 3:64–98.

Alexander III. "Dnevnik Naslednika Tsesarevicha Velikogo Kniazia Aleksandra Alexandrovicha, 1880g." *Rossiiskii Arkhiv* (1995), 6:344–57.

———. "Perepiska Aleksandra III s Loris-Melikovym (1880–1881gg.)." *Krasnyi Arkhiv* 1 (1925), 8:101–31.

———. "Pis'ma Tsesarevicha Aleksandra Aleksandrovicha k professoru A. P. Bogoliubovu." *Starina i Novizna*, no. 3, pt. 1 (1900): 1–13.

———. "Pis'mo Tsesarevicha Aleksandra Aleksandrovicha A.N. Stiuleru." *Starina i Novizna*, no. 6 (1903): 1.

———. *Souvenirs de Sebastopol (recueillis et redigés par s.m.i. Alexandre III, Empereur de Russie).* Paris, 1894.

Alexander Mikhailovich, Grand Duke. *Once a Grand Duke.* New York, 1932.

Ambler, Effie. *Russian Journalism and Politics, 1861–1881: The Career of A. S. Suvorin.* Detroit, 1972.

Anan'ich, B. V. "The Economic Policy of the Tsarist Government and Enterprise in Russia from the End of the Nineteenth through the Beginning of the Twentieth Century." In *Entrepreneurship in Imperial Russia and the Soviet Union*, ed. Gregory Guroff and Fred V. Carstensen. Princeton, N.J., 1983.

Anan'ich, B. V., and R. Sh. Ganelin. "Aleksandr III i naslednik nakanune 1 marta 1881g." In *Dom romanovykh v Rossii.* St. Petersburg, 1995.

———. "R. A. Fadeev, S. Iu. Vitte i ideologicheskie iskaniia 'okhranitelei' v 1881–1883gg." In *Issledovaniia po sotsial'no-politicheskoi istorii Rossii.* Leningrad, 1971.

———. "I. A. Vyshnegradskii i S. Iu. Vitte—korrespondenty 'Moskovskikh vedomostei'." In *Problemy obshchestvennoi mysli i ekonomicheskaia politika Rossii XIX-XX vekov*, ed. N. G. Sladkevich. Leningrad, 1972.

———. *S. Iu. Vitte—Memuarist.* St. Petersburg, 1994.

Anan'ich, B. V., and R. Sh. Ganelin, eds. *Nikolai Vtoroi: Vospominaniia, Dnevniki.* St. Petersburg, 1994.

Anan'ich, B. V., R. Sh. Ganelin, and V. M. Paneiakh, eds. *Vlast' i reformy: ot samoderzhavnoi k Sovetskoi Rossii.* St. Petersburg, 1996.

Anan'ich, B. V., R. Sh. Ganelin, et al., eds. *Krizis samoderzhaviia v Rossii, 1895–1917.* Leningrad, 1984.

Anan'ich, N. I. "Materialy lektsionnykh kursov N. Kh. Bunge 60–80-kh godov XIXv." In *Arkheograficheskii ezhegodnik za 1977 god.* Moscow, 1978.

Anon. *Bolezn' i smert' Aleksandra III: Pravdivye zametki.* London, 1900.

Anon. *Russian Court Memoirs, 1914–1916.* New York, n.d.

Applegate, Celia. *A Nation of Provincials: The German Idea of Heimat.* Berkeley, 1990.

Aronson, Michael. *Troubled Waters: The Origins of the Anti-Jewish Pogroms in Russia.* Pittsburgh, Pa., 1990.

Ascher, Abraham. *The Revolution of 1905: Authority Restored.* Stanford, 1992.

———. *The Revolution of 1905: Russia in Disarray.* Stanford, 1988.

Avrekh, A. Ia. *Tsarizm i IV Duma.* Moscow, 1981.

Baberowski, Jörg. *Autocratie und Justiz: Zum Verhältnis von Rechtsstaatlichkeit und Ruckständigkeit im ausgehended Zarenreich, 1864–1914.* Frankfurt am Main, 1996.

Baddeley, John F. *Russia in the "Eighties"; Sport and Politics.* London, 1921.

Baedeker, K. *Russland.* Leipzig, 1901.

Baker, Keith Michael. *Inventing the French Revolution.* Cambridge, 1990.

Bakhtin, M. M. *The Dialogic Imagination.* Austin, Tex., 1981.

Barkovets, Alia. "Photographs in the State Archive of the Russian Federation of the Last Russian Emperor and His Family." In *Nicholas and Alexandra: The Last Imperial Family of Tsarist Russia.* London, 1998.

Barrett, Thomas M. "The Remaking of the Lion of Dagestan: Shamil in Captivity." *Russian Review* 53, no.2 (July 1994): 353–66.

Barsukov, Nikolai. *Zhizn' i trudy M. P. Pogodina.* 22 vols. St. Petersburg, 1888–1910.

Bazhenov, I. "Prizvanie Mikhaila Feodorovicha k prestolu." In *Iubileinyi sbornik kostromskogo tserkovno-istoricheskogo obshchestva.* Kostroma, 1913.

Belcher, Margaret. "Pugin Writing." In *Pugin: A Gothic Passion*, ed. Paul Atterbury and Clive Wainwright. New Haven, 1994.

Bensidoun, Sylvain. *Alexandre III, 1881–1914.* Paris, 1990.

Berdiaev, Nicholas. *Dream and Reality: An Essay in Autobiography.* New York, 1962.

Beyrau, Dietrich. *Militär und Gesellschaft im vorrevolutionären Russland.* Cologne, 1984.

Bing, Edward J., ed. *The Secret Letters of the Last Tsar.* Toronto, 1938.

Birnbaum, F. P. "Iubileinyi rubl', medal'ernoe iskusstvo i Monetnyi Dvor." In *Faberzhe i Peterburgskie iuveliry*, ed. T. F. Faberzhe, A. S. Gorynia, and V. V. Skurlov. St. Petersburg, 1997.

Blackbourn, David. *Marpingen: Apparitions of the Virgin in Nineteenth-Century Germany.* New York, 1994.

Bogdanovich, A. V. *Tri poslednikh samoderzhtsa.* Moscow-Petrograd, 1924.

Bogdanovich, E. E. *Istoricheskoe palomnichestvo nashego tsaria v 1913 godu.* St. Petersburg, 1914.

———. *Strelki imperatorskoi familii.* St. Petersburg, 1899.

Bogdanovich, E. V. *Sila vsevyshniago chudodeistvenno iavlennaia 17 oktiabria 1888g.* St. Petersburg, 1889.

Bogoliubov, A. P. *Vospominaniia o v boze pochivshem Imperatore Aleksandre III.* St. Petersburg, 1895.

Bokhanov, A. N. "Velikii kniaz' Sergei Aleksandrovich." In *Rossiiskie Konservatory.* Moscow, 1997.

Bonnell, Victoria E. *Roots of Rebellion: Workers' Politics and Organizations in St. Petersburg and Moscow, 1900–1914.* Berkeley, 1983.

Borisova, E. A. *Russkaia arkhitektura vtoroi poloviny XIX veka.* Moscow, 1979.

Bovey, Kate Koon. *Russian Coronation, 1896.* Minneapolis, 1896.

Bozherianov, I. N. *Detstvo, vospitanie, i leta iunosti Russkikh Imperatorov.* St. Petersburg, 1914.

———. *Trista let tsarstvovaniia doma Romanovykh.* St. Petersburg, 1912.

Bratskii ezhegodnik: Pravoslavnye tserkvi i russkie zagranichnye uchrezhdeniia za granitseiu. Petrograd [sic], 1906.

Briusov, V. *Izbrannye sochineniia v dvukh tomakh.* 2 vols. Moscow, 1955.

Brooks, Jeffrey. *When Russia Learned to Read: Literacy and Popular Literature, 1861–1917*. Princeton, N.J., 1985.

Brumfield, William Craft. *A History of Russian Architecture*. Cambridge, 1993.

———. "The 'New Style' and the Revival of Orthodox Church Architecture, 1900–1914." In *Christianity and the Arts in Russia*, ed. William Craft Brumfield and Milos M. Velimirovic. Cambridge, 1991.

———. *The Origins of Modernism in Russian Architecture*. Berkeley, 1991.

Buchanan, Sir George. *My Mission to Russia*. Boston, 1923.

Buchanan, Meriel. *The Dissolution of an Empire*. London, 1932.

Bukhbinder, N. "Zubatovshchina v Moskve." *Katorga i Ssylka* 14 (1925): 96–113.

Bushnell, John S. "Miliutin and the Balkan War: Military Reform vs. Military Performance." In *Russia's Great Reforms, 1855–1881*, ed. Ben Eklof, John Bushnell, and Larissa Zakharova. Bloomington, Ind.

Buslaev, F. I. *Istoriia russkoi literatury; lektsii, chitannye Ego Imperatorskomu Vysochestvu Nasledniku Tsesarevichu Nikolaiu Aleksandrovichu, (1859–1860g.)*. Moscow, 1904.

———. *Moi dosugi*. Moscow, 1886.

———. *Moi Vospominaniia*. Moscow, 1897.

———. *Russkaia Khrestomatiia*. Moscow, 1904.

Butikov, Georgii. *The Church of the Savior on the Blood*. St. Petersburg, n.d.

Buxhoeveden, Baroness Sophie. *The Life and Tragedy of Alexandra Feodorovna, Empress of Russia*. London, 1928.

Byrnes, Robert F. *Pobedonostsev: His Life and Thought*. Bloomington, Ind., 1968.

———. *V. O. Kliuchevskii: Historian of Russia*. Bloomington, Ind., 1995.

Cannadine, David. "Splendor Out of Court: Royal Spectacle and Pageantry in Modern Britain, c. 1820–1977." In *Rites of Power: Symbolism, Ritual, and Politics since the Middle Ages*, ed. Sean Wilentz. Philadelphia, 1985.

Carlisle, Donald C. "V poiskakh propavshego 'mednogo vsadnika.' " *Obozrenie*, no. 9 (April 1984): 23–30.

Chakirov, Nikita, ed. *Tsarskie koronatsii na Rusi*. New York, 1971.

Charykov, N. "Karl Osipovich Khis." *Istoricheskii Vestnik* (April 1902): 422–36.

Cheremkhin, A. *Chest' i slava Tsariu osvobodivshchemu krest'ian ot krepostnoi nezavisimosti, 19 Fevralia 1861 goda*. St. Petersburg, 1863.

"Cherevin i Aleksandr III." *Golos Minevshego*, no. 5–6 (1917): 96–101.

Cherniavsky, Michael. *Tsar and People: Studies in Russian Myths*. New York, 1969.

———, ed. *Prologue to Revolution: Notes of A. N. Iakhontov on the Secret Meetings of the Council of Ministers, 1915*. Englewood Cliffs, N.J., 1967.

Chernukha, V. G. *Pravitel'stvennaia politika v otnoshenii pechati 60–70-e gody XIX veka*. Leningrad, 1989.

Chichakova, M. N. *Shamil' na Kavkaze i Rossii*. St. Petersburg, 1889.

Chicherin, B. P. *Vospominaniia: Moskovskii Universitet*. Moscow, 1929.

———. *Vospominaniia: Zemstvo i Moskovskaia Duma*. Moscow, 1934.

Chistov, K. V. *Russkie sotsial'no-utopicheskie legendy XVII–XIXvv*. Moscow, 1967.

Chizhov, S. "Iubileinye rubli 1912 i 1913 godov." In *Numismaticheskii Sbornik*. Moscow, 1915.

Clark, Katerina. "Political History and Literary Chronotope: Some Soviet Case Studies." In *Literature and History: Theoretical Problems and Russian Case Studies*, ed. Gary Paul Morson. Stanford, 1986.

———. *Petersburg: Crucible of Revolution*. Cambridge, Mass. 1995.

Colley, Linda. *Britons: Forging the Nation, 1707–1837*. New Haven, 1992.

Confino, Alon. "The Nation as a Local Metaphor: Heimat, National Memory, and the German Empire, 1871–1918." *History and Memory 5*, no. 1 (1993): 42–85.

Coquin, François-Xavier. "Le monument de Catherine II à Saint-Pétersbourg." In *Catherine II et l'Europe*, ed. Anita Davidenkoff. Paris, 1997.

Crews, Robert. "Civilization in the City: Architecture, Urbanism, and the Colonization of Tashkent." Unpublished conference paper.

Curtiss, John. *Church and State in Russia: The Last Years of the Empire*. New York, 1940.

Daly, Jonathan W. "Emergency Legislation in Late Imperial Russia." *Slavic Review* 54, no. 3 (fall 1995): 602–29.

Darby, Elisabeth, and Nicola Smith. *The Cult of the Prince Consort*. New Haven, 1983.

Davis, Richard Harding. *A Year from a Reporter's Notebook*. New York, 1898.

Del'vig, A. I. *Polveka russkoi zhizni*. 2 vols. Moscow-Leningrad, 1930.

Den', V. I. "Zapiski." *Russkaia Starina* 65 (1890): 577–608.

Diakin, V. S. *Burzhuaziia, dvorianstvo i tsarizm v 1911–1914gg.: razlozhenie tret'eiun'skoi sistemy*. Leningrad, 1988.

Dicstclmcicr, Fricdrich. *Soziale Angst: konservative Reaktionen auf liberale Reformpolitik in Russland unter Alexander II, (1855–1866)*. Frankfurt am Main, 1985.

Dixon, Simon. "The Church's Social Role in St. Petersburg, 1880–1914." In *Church, Nation, and State in Russia and Ukraine*, ed. Geoffrey A. Hosking. London, 1991.

Dubenskii, General-Maior D. N. *Ego Imperatorskoe Velichestvo Gosudar' Imperator Nikolai Aleksandrovich v Deistvuiushchii Armii*. 4 vols. Petrograd, 1916.

Dubnow, S. M. *History of the Jews in Russia and Poland*. 2 vols. Philadelphia, 1918.

Dubrovin, N. F. *Nikolai Mikhailovich Przheval'skii: biograficheskii ocherk*. St. Petersburg, 1890.

Dufferin, The Dowager Marchioness of, and Ava Dufferin. *My Russian and Turkish Journals*. London, 1917.

Dukhovetskii, F. *Dve nedeli v Peterburge; vospominaniia torzhestva pogrebeniia tela Imperatora Aleksandra III i svetlogo dnia brakosochetaniia*. Moscow, 1894.

Dumas, Alexandre. *Adventures in Czarist Russia*. London, 1960.

Durman, Karel. *The Time of the Thunderer: Michael Katkov, Russian Nationalist Extremism, and the Failure of the Bismarckian System, 1871–1887*. Boulder, 1988.

Dzhanshiev, Gr. *Epokha velikikh reform*. Moscow, 1896.

Dzhunkovskii, V. F. *Vospominaniia*. 2 vols. Moscow, 1997.

Eckardt, Julius. *Baltische Briefe aus zwei Jahrhunderten*. Berlin, n.d.

Edwards, [Henry] Sutherland. *The Russians at Home: Unpolitical Sketches*. London, 1861.

Efremov, V. "Otchego voina 1812 goda nazyvaetsia 'Otechestvennoi'?" In *Liubov' k otechestvu: istochnik sily narodnoi*, ed. V. Efremov and P. D. Zhukov. Ufa, 1912.

Elchaninov, A. *The Tsar and His People*. London, 1914.

———. *Tsarstvovanie Gosudaria Imperatora Nikolaia Aleksandrovicha*. St. Petersburg-Moscow, 1913.

Emmons, Terence. "The Peasant and the Emancipation." In *The Peasant in Nineteenth-Century Russia*, ed. Wayne Vucinich. Stanford, 1968.

Emmons, Terence. *The Formation of Political Parties and the First National Elections in Russia*. Cambridge, Mass., 1983.

———. *The Russian Landed Gentry and the Peasant Emancipation of 1861*. Cambridge, 1968.

Emmons, Terence, and Wayne Vucinich, eds. *The Zemstvo in Russia: An Experiment in Local Government*. Cambridge, Mass., 1982.

Engel'gardt, B. A. "Torzhestvennyi v"ezd v Moskvu gosudaria Imperatora Nikolaia II." In *Gosudar' Imperator Nikolai II Aleksandrovich*, ed. Sergei Zavalishin. New York, 1968.

Engelstein, Laura. *Moscow, 1905: Working Class Organization and Political Conflict*. Stanford, 1982.

Epanchin, N. A. *Na sluzhbe trekh imperatorov*. Moscow, 1996.

Ercolini, Michael. "An Introduction to the Stamps of the 1913 Romanov Issue." *The Journal of the Rossica Society of Russian Philately*, no. 122 (April 1994): 11–14

Faberzhe, Tatiana F., and V. V. Skurlov. *Istoriia firmy Faberzhe*. St. Petersburg, 1993.

Fallows, Thomas. "The Zemstvo and the Bureaucracy." In *The Zemstvo in Russia*, ed. Terence Emmons and Wayne Vucinich. Cambridge, 1982.

Fedotov, George P. *A Treasury of Russian Spirituality*. New York, 1965.

———. *The Russian Religious Mind*. 2 vols. Belmont, Mass., 1975.

Fehrenbach, Elizabeth. "Images of Kaiserdom." In *Kaiser Wilhelm II: New Interpretations*, ed. John C. G. Röhl. Cambridge, 1982.

Feodorovskii gosudarev sobor v Tsarskom Sele. Vol. 1: *Peshchernyi Khram vo imia prepodobnogo Serafima sarovskogo*. Moscow, 1915.

Feoktistov, E. M. *Vospominaniia E. M. Feoktistova: za kulisami politiki i literatury*. Leningrad, 1927.

Ferenczi, Caspar. *Aussenpolitik und Öffentlichkeit in Russland, 1906–1912*. Husum, 1982.

———. "Freedom of the Press under the Old Regime, 1905–1914." In *Civil Rights in Imperial Russia*, ed. Olga Crisp and Linda Edmondson. Oxford, 1989.

Fet, A. A. *Polnoe sobranie stikhotvorenii*. St. Petersburg, 1912.

Field, Daniel. *Rebels in the Name of the Tsar*. Boston, 1976.

———. *The End of Serfdom: Nobility and Bureaucracy in Russia, 1855–1861*. Cambridge, Mass., 1976.

Figes, Orlando. *A People's Tragedy: The Russian Revolution, 1891–1924*. New York, 1998.

Filaret (Metropolitan of Moscow). *Slova i rechi, 1859–1867*. Vol. 5. Moscow, 1885.

Filippova, T. A. "Petr Andreevich Shuvalov." In *Rossiiskie Konservatory*. Moscow, 1997.

Firsov, N. "Vospominaniia o tsesareviche Nikolae Aleksandroviche i Imperatore Aleksandre III v iunosti." *Istoricheskii Vestnik* (January 1909): 44–75.

Firsov, N. N. "Aleksandr II, lichnaia kharakteristika." *Byloe*, no. 20 (1922): 116–34.

———. "Aleksandr III; lichnaia kharakteristika, chast'iu po ego neizdannym dnevnikam," *Byloe*, no. 29 (1925): 85–108.

———. *Nikolai II*. Kazan, 1929.

Flier, Michael S. "At Daggers Drawn: The Competition for the Church of the Savior on the Blood." In *For SK: In Celebration of the Life and Career of Simon Karlinsky*, ed. Michael S. Flier and Robert P. Hughes. Berkeley, 1994.

———. "The Church of the Savior on the Blood: Projection, Rejection, Resurrection." In *Christianity and the Eastern Slavs*, ed. Robert P. Hughes and Irina Paperno. Vol. 2. Berkeley, 1994.

Florinsky, Michael T. *The End of the Russian Empire*. New York, 1961.

Flourens, E. *Alexandre III, sa vie; son oeuvre*. Paris, 1894.

Fon-Bradke, F. M. "Ocherk boevoi sluzhby Ego Imperatorskogo Vysochestva Gosudaria Naslednika Tsesarevicha i Velikogo Kniazia Aleksandra Aleksandrovicha vo vremia osvoboditel'noi voiny 1877–78 godov na balkanskom ostrove." *Starina i Novizna*, no. 15 (1911): 214–31.

Fon-Pfeil', Graf. "Poslednie gody imperatora Aleksandra II; iz vospominanii iz russkoi sluzhby, 1878–1881," *Novyi zhurnal literatury, iskusstva i nauki* (March 1908): 33–48.

Frank, B. "Iz neizdannoi perepiski imperatora Aleksandra III i Nikolaia II s V. P. Meshcherskim." *Sovremennye Zapiski* 70 (1940): 165–88.

Freeze, Gregory. "Subversive Piety: Religion and the Political Crisis in Late Imperial Russia." *The Journal of Modern History* 68 (June 1996): 308–50.

———. "Tserkov', religiia, i politicheskaia kul'tura na zakate starogo rezhima." In *Reformy ili revoliutsiia: Rossiia, 1861–1917*. St. Petersburg, 1992.

Frieden, Nancy Mandelker. *Russian Physicians in an Era of Reform and Revolution, 1856–1905*. Princeton, N.J., 1981.

Frumkis, T. "Kantata P. I. Chaikovskogo 'Moskva': (Ne)sluchainyi tekst v (ne)sluchainom kontekste." In *Moskva i moskovskii tekst russkoi kul'tury*, ed. G. S. Knabe. Moscow, 1998.

Fujitani, T. *Splendid Monarchy: Power and Pageantry in Modern Japan*. Berkeley, 1996.

Fuller, William C. Jr. *Civil-Military Conflict in Imperial Russia, 1881–1914*. Princeton, N.J., 1985.

———. *Strategy and Power in Russia, 1600–1914*. New York, 1992.

Galai, Shmuel. *The Liberation Movement in Russia, 1900–1905*. Cambridge, 1973.

Galitzine, Véra. *Reminiscences d'une émigrée*. Paris, 1925.

Garainov, A. *O vysochaishem puteshestvii i neskol'ko slov o poleznykh sobytiiakh*. St. Petersburg, 1855.

Gatrell, Peter. *Government, Industry, and Rearmament in Russia, 1900–1914: The Last Argument of Tsarism*. Cambridge, 1994.

Gautier, Théophile. *Oeuvres complètes*. 11 vols. Geneva, 1978.

———. *Russia*. 2 vols. Philadephia, 1905.

——— [Got'e, Teofil']. *Puteshestvie v Rossiiu*. Moscow, 1988.

Gavriil Konstantinovich, Grand Duke. *V mramornom dvortse*. New York, 1955.

Geertz, Clifford. *Negara: The Theatre State in Nineteenth-Century Bali*. Princeton, N.J., 1980.

Geinike, N. A. et al., eds. *Po Moskve*. Moscow, 1917.

Gellner, Ernest. *Nations and Nationalism*. Ithaca, N.Y., 1983.

Gendrikov, Vladimir, and Sergei Sen'ko. *The Cathedral of St. Peter and St. Paul: The Burial Place of the Russian Imperial Family*. St. Petersburg, 1998.

George, Martin. "Die 900-Jahr-Feier der Taufe Russlands im Jahr 1888 und die Kritik Vladimir Sergeevic Solovevs am Verhältnis von Staat und Kirche in Russland." *Jahrbücher für Geschichte Osteuropas* 36, no. 1 (1988): 15–36.

Gerschenkron, Alexander. "Agrarian Policies and Industrialization: Russia, 1861–1917." *Cambridge Economic History of Europe* 6, pt. 2 (Cambridge, 1966).

Gerua, B. V. *Vospominaniia o moei zhizni*. Paris, 1969.

Geyer, Dietrich. *Russian Imperialism: The Interaction of Domestic and Foreign Policy, 1860–1914*. New Haven, 1977.

Gilliard, Pierre. *Thirteen Years at the Russian Court*. New York, 1970.

Ginzburg, S. *Kinematografiia dorevoliutsionnoi Rossii* Moscow, 1963.

Girs, A. "Svetlye i chernye dni." *Chasovoi* 328 (March 1953): 9–10; (April 1953): 9.

Gleason, Abbott, *Young Russia: The Genesis of Russian Radicalism in the 1860s*. New York, 1980.

Glinka, V. M. *Russkii Voennyi Kostium XVIII-nachala XX veka*. Leningrad, 1988.

Glinskii, B. "Nastavnik tsarskikh detei." *Istoricheskii Vestnik* 63 (January 1896): 230–66.

Gluck, Carol. *Japan's Modern Myths: Ideology in the Late Meiji Period*. Princeton, N.J., 1985.

Gody ucheniia ego Imperatorskogo Vysochestva Naslednika Tsesarevicha (Sbornik Russkogo Istoricheskogo Obshchestva). Vol. 31. St. Petersburg, 1881.

Golder, F., ed. *Documents of Russian History, 1914–1917*. New York, 1927.

Golovin, F. A. "Zapiski." *Krasnyi Arkhiv* (1926), 6:110–49.

Golovin, K. *Moi vospominaniia*. 2 vols. St. Petersburg, 1910.

Gontar, Sergei N. "Alexander III's Reforms in the Decorative Arts." In *Maria Feodorovna: Empress of Russia*. Copenhagen, 1997.

Gorbunova, N. A. "1874–1880 v Livadii." *Nasha Starina* (July 1914): 648–65; (August 1914): 761–73; (September/October 1914): 837–45; (November 1914): 993–1008; (December 1914): 1052–68.

Gorky, Maxim. "On The Russian Peasantry." In *The Russian Peasant, 1920 and 1984*, ed. R.E.F. Smith. London, 1977.

Got'e, Iu. "K. P. Pobedonostsev i naslednik Aleksandr Aleksandrovich, 1865–1881." In *Publichnaia biblioteka SSSR imeni Lenina; sbornik II*. Moscow, 1929.

———. "Pobedonostsev and Alexander III." *Slavonic and East European Review* (June 1928): 30–54. (Translation of "K. P. Pobedonostsev i naslednik Aleksandr Alekandrovich.)

Grabar', I. *Istoriia Russkogo Iskusstva*. vol. 9. Moscow, 1965.

Graham, Stephen. *The Ways of Martha and the Way of Mary*. London, 1916.

Greenberg, Louis. *The Jews in Russia: The Struggle for Emancipation*. 2 vols. New York, 1976.

Grishchenko, A. *Russkaia ikona kak iskusstvo zhivopisi*. Moscow, 1917.

Grossman, Leonid. "Dostoevskii i pravitel'stvennye krugi 70-kh godov." *Literaturnoe Nasledstvo* 15 (1934): 83–162.

Grot, K. Ia. *Imperator Aleksandr III v otnosheniiakh svoikh k nastavniku svoei iunosti*. St. Petersburg, 1906.

Grunwald, Constantine de. *Le tsar Alexandre II et son temps*. Paris, 1963.

Guéry, Alain "La dualité de toutes les monarchies et la monarchie chrétienne," In *La royauté sacré dans le monde chrétien*, ed. Alain Boureau and Claudio-Sergio Ingerflom. Paris, 1992.

———. "L'état monarchique et la construction de la nation française." *Revue de la Bibliothèque Nationale*, no. 32 (summer 1989): 6–17.

Gurko, V. I. *Features and Figures of the Russian Past*. Stanford, 1939.

Guroff, Gregory, and S. Frederick Starr. "A Note on Urban Literacy in Russia, 1890–1914." *Jahrbücher für Geschichte Osteuropas* 19 (1971): 520–31.

Haimson, Leopold. "The Problem of Social Stability in Urban Russia, 1905–1917." In *The Structure of Russian History: Interpretive Essays*, ed. Michael Cherniavsky. New York, 1970.

Hamburg, G. M. *Boris Chicherin and Early Russian Liberalism, 1828–1866*. Stanford, 1992.

Hamilton, George Heard. *The Art and Architecture of Russia*. Harmondsworth, 1983.

Hermogen. Patriarch. *Tvoreniia Sviateishego Germogena; Patriarkha Moskovskogo i vseia Rossii*. Moscow: 1912.

Herzen, Alexander. "Pis'mo k imperatritse Marii Aleksandrovne." *Kolokol*, no. 27 (November 1858): 217–19.

Hobsbawm, Eric J. *Nations and Nationalism since 1780: Programme, Myth, Reality*. Cambridge, 1990.

———. "Introduction: Inventing Traditions." In *The Invention of Tradition*, ed. Eric Hobsbawm and Terence Ranger. Cambridge, 1983.

———. "Mass Producing Traditions: Europe, 1870–1914." In *The Invention of Tradition*, ed. Eric Hobsbawm and Terence Ranger. Cambridge, 1983.

Hoch, Steven. "The Banking Crisis, Peasant Reform, and Economic Development in Russia, 1857–1861." *American Historical Review* 96, no. 3 (June 1991): 795–820.

Holden, Anthony. *Tchaikovsky: A Biography*. New York, 1995.

Hosking, Geoffrey A. *Russia: People and Empire, 1552–1917*. Cambridge, Mass., 1997.

———. *The Russian Constitutional Experiment: Government and Duma, 1907–1914*. Cambridge, 1973.

Hull, Isabel V. "Prussian Dynastic Ritual and the End of Monarchy." In *German Nationalism and the European Response*, ed. Carole Fink, Isabel V. Hull, and MacGregor Knox. Norman, Okla., 1985.

Ignatii (Arkhimandrit). *17 oktiabria. Dva chuda: pervoe v Vologde, 1655 goda, vtoroe, pod khar'kovom, 1888g*. St. Petersburg, 1890.

———. *Zhizneopisanie arkhimandrita Ignatiia, (Malysheva), byvshego nastoiatelia troitse-sergievoi pustyni*. St. Petersburg, 1899.

Ikonnikov, A. V. *Istorizm v arkhitekture*. Moscow, 1997.

Illiustrirovannoe opisanie peremen v obmundirovanii i snariazhenii imperatorskoi russkoi armii za 1881 god. St. Petersburg, 1898.

Ilovaiskii, D. *Smutnoe vremia Moskovskogo gosudarstva*. Moscow, 1894.

Imperatorskii Moskovskii Arkheologicheskii Institut imeni Nikolaia II. *Vystavka drevne-russkogo iskusstva*. Moscow, 1913.

Ioann of Kronstadt. "Poslednie chasy Gosudaria Imperatora, Aleksandra III." NV, November 20, 1894, 2.

Iroshnikov, Mikhail, ed. *Nikolai II*. St. Petersburg, 1992.

Istoriia Feodorovskogo Gorodetskogo monastyria (Nizhegorodskaia guberniia) i postroenie v S-Peterburge khrama v pamiat' 300 iubileiia tsarstvovaniia imperatorskogo Doma Romanovykh. St. Petersburg, 1913.

Iubileinyi sbornik kostromskogo tserkovno-istoricheskogo obshchestva v pamiat' 300-letiia tsarstvovaniia doma Romanovykh. Kostroma, 1913.

Izvolsky, Alexander. *Recollections of a Foreign Minister*. Garden City, N.Y., 1921.

Jahn, Hubertus F. "For Tsar and Fatherland? Russian Popular Culture and the First World War." In *Cultures in Flux: Lower-Class Values, Practices, and Resistance in*

Late Imperial Russia, ed. Stephen P. Frank and Mark D. Steinberg. Princeton, N.J., 1994.

———. *Patriotic Culture in Russia during World War I*. Ithaca, N.Y., 1995.

Jelavich, Barbara. *St. Petersburg and Moscow: Tsarist and Soviet Foreign Policy*. Bloomington, Ind., 1974.

Jersild, Austin. "From Frontier to Empire: The Russification of the Causasus, 1845–1917." Unpublished manuscript.

Judge, Edward H. *Plehve: Repression and Reform in Imperial Russia, 1902–1904*. Syracuse, N.Y., 1983.

Kalinin, N. N., and M. M. Zelianichenko. *Romanovy i Krym*. Moscow, 1993.

Kallash, V. V., ed. *Tri veka; Rossiia ot smuty do nashego vremeni*. 3 vols. Moscow, 1912.

Kamenskii, E. "Naslednik Tsesarevich Aleksandr Aleksandrovich." *Istoricheskii Vestnik* (February 1917): 361–80; (March 1917): 633–66.

Kamenskii, E. "Ot detstva do prisiagi: iz zhizni avgusteishikh detei imperatora Aleksandra II." *Istoricheskii Vestnik* (February 1917): 427–58.

Kappeler, Andreas. *Russland als Vielvölkerreich; Entstehung, Geschichte, Zerfall*. Munich, 1992.

Karnovich, Evgenii. "Koronovanie Gosudarei." *Russkii Arkhiv* (1990), 1:33–63.

Kashchenko, S. G., and N. G. Rogulin. "Predstaviteli Doma Romanovykh—kavalery ordena Sviatogo Georgiia." In *Dom Romanovykh v istorii Rossii*. St. Petersburg, 1995.

Kassow, Samuel D. *Students, Professors, and the State in Tsarist Russia*. Berkeley, 1989.

Katkov, M. N. *Sobranie peredovykh statei Moskovskikh Vedomostei*. 14 vols. Moscow, 1897–98.

Katz, Martin. *Mikhail N. Katkov: A Political Biography, 1818–1887*. The Hague, 1966.

Kaufmann, Ingeborg. "Das dreihundertjährige Thronjubiläum des Hauses Romanov: Russland 1913." Masters thesis, Humboldt University. Berlin, 1996.

Kenez, Peter. "A Profile of the Pre-revolutionary Officer Corps." *California Slavic Studies* 7 (1973): 121–58.

Kennan, George F. *The Fateful Alliance: France, Russia, and the Coming of the First World War*. New York, 1984.

Kennedy, Janet. "The Neoclassical Ideal in Russian Scuplture." In *Art and Culture in Nineteenth-Century Russia*, ed. Theofanis George Stavrou. Bloomington, Ind., 1983.

Khlebnikov, Velimir. *Sobranie proizvedenii*. Leningrad, 1930.

Khomiakov, A. S. *Polnoe sobranie sochinenii*. 8 vols. Moscow, 1900–1907.

Kipp, Jacob W. "The Russian Navy and Technological Transfer." In *Russia's Great Reforms, 1855–1881*, ed. Ben Eklof, John Bushnell, and Larissa Zakharova. Bloomington, Ind., 1994.

Kirichenko, E. I. *Arkhitekturnye teorii XIX veka v Rossii*. Moscow, 1986.

———. *Khram Khrista Spasitelia v Moskve*. Moscow, 1992.

———. *Russkii stil'*. Moscow, 1997.

Kirikov, B. M. "Khram Voskreseniia Khristova (k istorii russkogo stilia v Peterburge)." *Nevskii Arkhiv: istoriko-kraevedcheskii sbornik* (1993), 1:204–45.

Kizenko, Nadieszda. "The Making of a Modern Saint: Ioann of Kronstadt and the Russian People." Ph. D. dissertation, Columbia University. New York, 1995.

Klassovskii, V. I. "Privetstsvie starogo vospitatelia Velikomu Kniaziu v den' ego sovershennoletiia." *Starina i Novizna*, no. 2 (1907): 1–9.

Kleinmichel, Countess M. *Memoirs of a Shipwrecked World.* New York, 1923.

Klimov, P. Iu. "Zhivopisnoe ubranstvo khrama Khrista Spasitelia." In *Khram Khrista Spasitelia*, ed. E. I. Kirichenko. Moscow, 1996.

Kliuchevskii, V. O. "Pamiati v Boze pochivshego Imperatora Aleksandra III." In *Chteniia v Imperatorskom Obshchestve Istorii i Drevnostei Rossiiskikh pri Moskovskom Universitete.* Vol. 4. Moscow, 1894.

———. *Sochineniia.* 8 vols. Moscow, 1956–59.

Knight, Nathaniel. "Ethnicity, Nationality, and the Masses," *Narodnost'* and Modernity in Pre-Emancipation Russia." In *Russian Modernity*, ed. David Hoffman and Yanni Kotsonis. London, 1999.

Kokovtsov, V. N. *Iz moego proshlogo.* 2 vols. Paris, 1933.

Komarov, V. *Sviashchennoe koronovanie Imperatora Aleksandra III i Imperatritsy Marii Fedorovny.* Moscow, 1883.

———. *V pamiat' sviashchennogo koronovaniia Gosudaria Imperatora Aleksandra III i Gosudaria Imperatritsy Marii Fedorovny.* St. Petersburg, 1883.

Kornilov, A. A. *Kurs istorii Rossii XIX veka.* 3 vols. Moscow, 1918.

———. *Obshchestvennoe dvizhenie pri Aleksandre I.* Paris, 1905.

Korol'kov, K. *Tsar-mirotvorets, Imperator Aleksandr III.* Kiev, 1904.

———. *Zhizn' i tsarstvovanie Imperatora Aleksandra III.* Kiev, 1901.

Koronatsionnyi al'bom v pamiat' sviashchennoi koronovaniia ikh Imperatorskikh Velichestv 14 maia 1896. St. Petersburg, 1896.

Koronatsionnyi sbornik: Koronovanie v Moskve; 14 maia 1896. St Petersburg, 1899.

Koronovanie ikh Imperatorskikh Velichestv. Moscow, 1883.

Korsakov, D. A. "Konstantin Kavelin; Materialy dlia biografii iz semeinoi perepiski i vospominanii." *Vestnik Evropy* (August 1886): 539–64.

Kostomarov, N. I. *Avtobiografiia.* Moscow, 1922.

Kostrikova, E. G. *Russkaia pressa i diplomatiia nakanune pervoi mirovoi voiny, 1907–1914.* Moscow, 1997.

Krasheninnikov, Arkadii. "Russkii zodchii Vladimir Nikolaevich Maksimov (1882–1942)." *Tsar'ino: Pravoslavnyi istoriko-kraevedcheskii almanakh*, no. 4 (1998): 63–83.

Krichinskii, S. "Khram v pamiat' 300 letia doma Romanovykh." *Zodchii* (1914): 122–23.

Krivenko, V. S., ed. *Obzor deiatel'nosti Ministerstva Imperatorskogo Dvora.* 2 vols. St. Petersburg, 1901.

Kropotkin, Peter. *Memoirs of a Revolutionist.* Garden City, N.Y., 1962.

Krukones, James, S. *To the People: The Russian Government and the Newspaper Sel'skii vestnik ("Village Herald"), 1881–1917.* New York, 1987.

Kryzhanovskii, S. E. *Vospominaniia.* Berlin, n.d.

Kurth, Peter. *The Lost World of Nicholas and Alexandra: Tsar.* Boston, 1995.

Kutepov, N. *Okhota na Rusi.* 4 vols. St. Petersburg, 1896–1911.

Lamzdorf, V. N. "Dnevnik." *Krasnyi Arkhiv* (1931), 46:3–37.

———. *Dnevnik, 1894–1896.* Moscow, 1991.

———. *Dnevnik.* 2 vols. Moscow-Leningrad, 1928–34.

Lanson, G. "Le tsar Nicolas II raconté par son ancien professeur." *Les annales politiques et littéraires* (September 1, 1901): 131–34.

Lant, Jeffrey L. *Insubstantial Pageant: Ceremony and Confusion at Queen Victoria's Court*. London, 1979.

LaPauze, Henry. *De Paris au Volga*. Paris, 1896.

Lappo, I. I. *Rech' proiznesennaia 21 fevralia 1913 goda*. Iur'ev, 1913.

Lathrop, Mrs. *The Court of Alexander III*. Philadephia, 1910.

Latynin, F. "Otryvochnye vospominaniia." *Istoricheskii Vestnik* (June 1909): 825–40.

Lavrova, N. N. "Imperator Aleksandr II i deti." *Istoricheskii Vestnik*, no. 139 (February 1915): 438–49.

LeDonne, John P. *The Russian Empire and the World, 1700–1917: The Geopolitics of Expansion and Containment*. New York, 1997.

Lear, Fanny [Blackford, Henrietta]. *Le roman d'une américaine en Russie*. Brussels, 1875.

Lebov, A. M. "Odin iz ubitykh ministrov." *Istoricheskii Vestnik* 107 (February 1907): 479–93.

Leger, Louis. *Moscou*. Paris, 1904.

Lemke, M. K., ed. *M. M. Stasiulevich i ego sovremenniki v ikh perepiske*. Vol. 1. St. Petersburg, 1911.

Leonov, A. E., ed. *Russkoe iskusstvo; ocherki o zhizni i tvorchestve khudozhnikov; seredina deviatnadtsogo veka*. Moscow, 1958.

Leont'ev, Constantine. *Sobranie sochinenii*. Vol. 7. Moscow, 1912.

Leyda, Jay. *Kino: A History of the Russian and Soviet Film*. Princeton, N.J., 1983.

Liashchenko, T. I. "Slovo v den' trekhsotletiia votsareniia Tsaria Romanovykh; Tserkov' Pravoslavnaia opora Prestola i Tsarstva Vserossiiskogo." *Trudy Imperatorskoi Kievskoi Dukhovnoi Akademii* (February 1913): i–x.

Lieven, Dominic. *Nicholas II: Emperor of All the Russias*. London, 1993.

———. *Russia and the Origins of the First World War*. London, 1983.

———. *Russia's Rulers under the Old Regime*. New Haven, 1989.

———. *The Aristocracy in Europe, 1815–1914*. Houndmills, 1992.

Likhomanov, A. V. *Bor'ba samoderzhaviia za obshchestvennoe mnenie v 1905–1907 godakh*. St. Petersburg, 1997.

Lincoln, W. Bruce. *In the Vanguard of Reform: Russia's Enlightened Bureaucrats*. De Kalb, Ill., 1982.

———. *Nicholas I; Emperor and Autocrat of All the Russias*. Bloomington, Ind., 1978.

Lindenmeyr, Adele. *Poverty Is Not a Vice: Charity, Society, and the State in Imperial Russia*. Princeton, N.J., 1996.

Lischke, André. *Piotr Ilyitch Tschaikovski*. Paris, 1993.

Lisitsyn, Protoierei Mikhail. "Pouchenie k narodu na den' trekhsotletiia tsarstvovaniia doma Romanovykh." *Tserkovnye Vedomosti*, February 9, 1913, 272–74.

Litvinov, N. P. "Iz dnevnika." *Istoricheskii Vestnik* (January 1907): 444–51.

Liubimov, D. N. "Otryvki iz vospominanii." *Istoricheskii Arkhiv* (November–December 1962): 69–84.

Lobanov-Rostovskii, Prince A. *Russia and Asia*. New York, 1933.

Lockhart, R. H. Bruce. *British Agent*. New York, 1933.

Loman, D. N. *Ko dniu sviashchennovo koronovaniia i muromazaniia Ikh Imperatorskikh Velichestv*. St. Petersburg, 1896.

———. *Tsar' osvoboditel', tsar'-muchenik, Imperator Aleksandr II; chtenie dlia naroda*. St. Petersburg, 1898.

Lopato, Marina. "Fresh Light on Carl Fabergé." *Apollo* (January 1984): 43–49.

Lotman, Ju. M., and B. A. Uspenskii, eds. *The Semiotics of Russian Culture.* Ann Arbor, Mich., 1984.

Lowe, Charles. *Alexander III of Russia.* New York, 1895.

Löwe, Heinz-Dietrich. *Antisemitismus und reaktionäre Utopie: Russischer Konservatismus im Kampf gegen den Wandel von Staat und Gesellschaft.* Hamburg, 1978.

Lukes, Steven. *Essays in Social Theory.* London, 1977.

Lukomskii, Georgii. "Khram v pamiat' 300-letia tsarstvovaniia doma Romanovykh." *Apollon* 5 (1914): 47–49

Lukomskii, V. Ia., and G. Ia. Lukomskii. *Kostroma.* St. Petersburg, 1913.

McDonald, David M. "The Durnovo Memorandum in Context: Official Conservatism and the Crisis of Autocracy." *Jahrbücher für Geschichte Osteuropas* 44, no. 4 (1996): 481–502.

MacDonald, Robert H. *Sons of the Empire: The Frontier and the Boy Scout Movement, 1890–1918.* Toronto, 1993.

Macey, David. *Government and Peasant in Russia, 1861–1917: The Prehistory of the Stolypin Reforms.* DeKalb, Ill., 1987.

McMillan, James, F. *Napoleon III.* London, 1991.

McNeal, Robert H. *Tsar and Cossack, 1855–1914.* New York, 1987.

McReynolds, Louise. "Mobilizing Petrograd's Lower Classes to Fight the Great War: Patriotism as a Counterweight to Working-Class Consciousness in *Gazeta Kopeika.*" *Radical History Review* 57 (1993): 160–80.

———. *The News under Russia's Old Regime: The Development of a Mass Circulation Press.* Princeton, N.J., 1991.

Maikov, A. N. *Polnoe sobranie sochinenii.* 4 vols. St. Petersburg, 1914.

Maiorova, O. E. " 'Ia zhivu postoianno v ramkakh . . .' " In *Kazan, Moscow, St. Petersburg: Multiple Faces of the Russian Empire,* ed. Catherine Evtuhov, Boris Gasparov, Alexander Ospovat, and Mark Von Hagen. Moscow, 1997.

———. "Tsarevich/samozvanets v sotsial'noi mifologii 1860-kh godov." Unpublished manuscript.

———. "Mitropolit moskovskii Filaret v obshchestvennom soznanii kontsa XIX veka." In *Lotmanovskii Sbornik,* 2. Moscow, 1997.

———. " '. . . Pishu Ia tol'ko dlia vas . . .': Pis'ma K. P. Pobedonostseva k sestram Tiutchevym." *Novyi Mir* (March 1994): 195–223.

Manning, Roberta Thompson. *The Crisis of the Old Order in Russia: Gentry and Government.* Princeton, N.J., 1982.

Marin, Louis. *Le portrait du roi.* Paris, 1981.

Marks, Steven, G. *Road to Power: The Trans-Siberian Railroad and the Colonization of Asian Russia, 1850–1917.* Ithaca, N.Y., 1991.

Maslova, E. N. *Pamiatnik "Tysiacheletiiu Rossii".* Leningrad, 1977.

Materialy dlia istorii uprazdneniia krepostnogo sostoianiia pomeshchich'ikh krestian' v Rossii v tsarstvovanie imperatora Aleksandra II. 3 vols. Berlin, 1860.

Maude, Aylmer [De Monte Alto]. *The Tsar's Coronation.* London, 1896.

Mayer, Arno. *The Persistence of the Old Regime: Europe to the Great War.* New York, 1981.

Maylunas, Andrei, and Sergei Mironenko. *A Lifelong Passion: Nicholas and Alexandra, Their Own Story.* London, 1996.

Medvedev, I. P. "Koronatsiia Nikolaia II glazami grecheskogo zhurnalista." In *Rossiia v XIX–XXvv.: sbornik statei k 70-letiiu so dnia rozhdeniia Rafaila Sholomonovicha Ganelina,* ed. A. A. Fursenko. St. Petersburg, 1998.

Merry, M. Mansell. *Two Months in Russia, July–September 1914.* Oxford, 1916.

Meshcherskii, Kn.V.L. *Moi vospominaniia.* 2 vols. St. Petersburg, 1897–98.

Metcalf, Thomas R. *An Imperial Vision: Indian Architecture and Britain's Raj.* Berkeley, 1989.

Mikhailov, A. D. "Teofil' Got'e—pisatel' i puteshestvennik." In Teofil' Got'e, *Puteshestvie v Rossiiu,* 5–13. Moscow, 1988.

Mikhailov, A. I. "Imperator Aleksandr Nikolaevich na zverinykh okhotakh (s 1849ogo po 1876 g.); Zapiski okhotnika ochevidtsa," *Russkaia Starina* 58 (1888): 103–24.

Miliukov, P. N. *Glavnye techeniia russkoi istoricheskoi mysli.* Vol. 1. Moscow, 1898.

Miliutina, D. A. *Dnevnik D. A. Miliutina, 1873–1875.* Moscow, 1947.

———. *Dnevnik D.A. Miliutin, 1878–1880.* Moscow, 1950.

Miller, Forrestt A. *Dmitrii Miliutin and the Reform Era in Russia.* Nashville, Tenn., 1968.

Miller, Liubov'. *Sviataia muchenitsa Rossiiskaia Velikaia Kniaginia Elizaveta Fedorovna.* Frankfort-am-Main, 1988.

Miloradovich, Gr. G. A. *Vospominaniia o koronatsii Imperatora Aleksandra II kamer-pazha dvora Ego Velichestva.* Kiev, 1883.

Morris, Peter. "The Russians in Central Asia." *Slavic and East European Review* 53, no. 133 (October 1975): 521–38.

Moskva v dni koronatsii: katalog vystavki. Moscow, 1996.

Moskvich, Grigorii. *Petrograd i ego okresnosti.* Petrograd, 1915.

Mosolov, A. A. *Pri dvore poslednego Rossiiskogo imperatora.* Moscow, 1993.

Mosse, W. E. *The Rise and Fall of the Crimean System, 1855–1871.* London, 1963.

Mouchanow, Marfa. *My Empress.* New York, 1938.

Moy, Carl Graf. *Als Diplomat am Zarenhof.* Munich, 1971.

Muntian, Tatiana N. "Life at the Court of Alexander III and Maria Feodorovna." In *Maria Feodorovna: Empress of Russia.* Copenhagen, 1997.

Muratov, P. "Vystavka drevne-russkogo iskusstva v Moskve," *Starye Gody* (April 1913): 31–38.

Narodnaia kartinka XVII–XIX vekov. St. Petersburg, 1996.

Narodnaia vera v sviatosti Patriarkha Germogena i plody etoi very, chudesa, sovershaiushchiiasia po Ego molitvam. Moscow, 1914.

Nasibova, Aida. *The Faceted Chamber in the Moscow Kremlin.* Leningrad, 1978.

Naumov, A. N. *Iz utselevshikh vospominanii, 1868–1917.* 2 vols. New York, 1954–55.

Nazanskii, V. I. *Krushenie velikoi Rossii i doma Romanovykh.* Paris, 1930.

Nechkina, M. V. *Vasilii Osipovich Kliuchevskii: Istoriia zhizni i tvorchestva.* Moscow, 1974.

Nekrylova, A. F. *Russkie narodnye gorodskie prazdniki, uveseleniia, i zrelishcha, konets XVIII-nachalo XX veka.* Leningrad, 1984.

Nelidov. A. I. "Zapiska A. I. Nelidova v 1882 o zaniatii prolivov." *Krasnyi Arkhiv* (1931), 46:179–87.

Nemiro, O. V. "Iz istorii organizatsii i dekorirovaniia krupneishikh torzhestv Doma Romanovykh: 1896–1917gg." In *Dom romanovykh v Rossii.* St. Petersburg, 1995.

Nemirovich-Danchenko, V. I. "Moskva v mae 1896 goda; pis'ma o koronatsii." *Niva*, April 27, 1896, 448–51; April 29, 1896, 496–507; May 10, 1896, 523–34; May 17, 1896, 561–72.

Nesin, Vadim. *Zimnii Dvorets v tsarstvovanie poslednego imperatora Nikolaia II (1894–1917)*. St. Petersburg, 1999.

Neverov, O. Ia. "Aleksandr II—tsenitel' i sobiratel' predmetov iskusstv." *Myzei Rossii* 4 (St. Petersburg, n.d.): 14–20.

Nevinson, Henry W. *The Dawn in Russia: Or Scenes in the Russian Revolution*. New York, 1906.

Nicholas and Alexandra: The Last Imperial Family of Tsarist Russia. London, 1998.

Nicholas II. *Dnevniki Nikolaia II*. Moscow, 1991.

———. *Polnoe sobranie rechei Imperatora Nikolaia II*. St. Petersburg, 1906.

———. *The Letters of the Tsar to the Tsaritsa*. London, 1929.

Nichols, Robert, L. "The Friends of God: Nicholas II and Alexandra at the Canonization of Serafim of Sarov, July 1903." In *Religious and Secular Forces in Late Tsarist Russia*, ed. Charles E. Timberlake. Seattle, 1992.

Nikitenko, A. V. *Dnevnik*. 3 vols. Leningrad, 1955–56.

Nikolaevna, Olga. *Son iunosti*. Paris, 1963.

Nikon, Episkop. "Vera Khristova ne terpit dvoedushiia." *Tserkovnye Vedomosti*, February 9, 1913, 282–91.

Nikonova, I. *M. V. Nesterov*. Moscow, 1984.

Nil'sen, V. A. *U istokov sovremennogo gradostroitel'stva Uzbekistana: xix-nachalo xx vekov*. Tashkent, 1988.

Nipperdey, Thomas. *Gesellschaft, Kultur, Theorie: Gesammelte Aufsätze zur neueren Geschichte*. Göttingen, 1976.

Nolde, Baron, B. E. *Peterburgskaia missiia Bismarka, 1859–1862*. Prague, 1925.

Norman, John O. "Alexander III as a Patron of Russian Art." In *New Perspectives on Russian and Soviet Artistic Culture: Selected Papers from the Fourth World Congress for Soviet and East European Studies, 1990*, ed. John O. Norman. New York, 1994.

O'Connell, Lauren, M. "A Rational, National Architecture: Viollet-le-Duc's Modest Proposal for Russia." *Journal of the Society of Architectural Historians* 52, no. 4 (December 1993): 436–52.

———. "Viollet-le-Duc and Russian Architecture: The Politics of an Asiatic Past." Unpublished conference paper.

Obol'ianinov, N. S. *Katalog russkikh illiustrirovannykh izdanii, 1725–1860*. 2 vols. Moscow, 1914–15.

Obolenskaia, S. B. *Franko-prusskaia voina i obshchestvennoe mnenie Germanii i Rossii*. Moscow, 1977.

Ocherk deiatel'nosti Ministerstva Imperatorskogo Dvora po prigotovleniiam i ustroistvu torzhestva sviashchennogo koronovaniia ikh Imperatorskikh Velichestv v 1896 godu. St. Petersburg, 1896.

Ofromisova, S. Ia. "Tsarkaia sem'ia (iz detskikh vospominanii)." *Russkaia Letopis'*, no. 7 (Paris, 1925): 227–51.

Okhota v belovezhskoi pushche. St. Petersburg, 1861.

Ol'denburg S. S. *Tsarstvovanie Imperatora Nikolaia II*. Washington, D.C., 1981.

Oom, F. A. "Vospominaniia." *Russkii Arkhiv* (1896), 2:427–52, 541–73; 3:34–58.

Opisanie sbora i zaniatii voisk pod Moskvoiu vo vremia sviashchennogo koronovaniia Ikh Imperatorskikh Velichestv v 1883 godu. St. Petersburg, 1883.

Opisanie sviashchenneishago koronovaniia Ikh Imperatorskikh Velichestv Gosudaria Imperatora Aleksandra Vtorago i Imperatritsy Marii Aleksandrovny Vseia Rossii. St. Petersburg, 1856.

Opisanie sviashchennogo koronovaniia Ikh Imperatorskikh Velichestv Gosudaria Imperatora Aleksandra tret'ego i Gosudaryni Imperatritsy Marii Fedorovny Vseia Rossii. St. Petersburg, 1883.

Orlovsky, Daniel T. *The Limits of Reform: The Ministry of Internal Affairs in Imperial Russia, 1802–1881.* Cambridge, Mass. 1981.

Otto, N., and I. Kuprianom. *Biograficheskie ocherki lits izobrazhennykh na pamiatnike tysiacheletiia Rossii vozdvignutom v g. Novgorode.* Novgorod, 1862.

Ouspensky, Leonid, and Vladimir Lossky. *The Meaning of Icons.* Crestwood, N.Y., 1982.

Pagden, Anthony. *Lords of All the World: Ideologies of Empire in Spain, Britain, and France, c. 1500–c. 1800.* New Haven, 1995.

Paléologue, Maurice. *Alexandra-Féodorowna, impératrice de Russie.* Paris, n.d.

———. *An Ambassadors' Memoirs.* 2 vols. New York, 1925.

Pamiat' milostivogo poseshcheniia gubernskoi zemskoi vystavki v oznamenovanii 300letiia tsarstvovaniia Doma Romanovykh v Kostrome. Kostroma, 1913.

"Pamiatnik Ekaterine II; 24 noiabria 1873g." *Russkaia Starina* 8 (1873): 638–48.

Pamiatniki arkhitektury prigorodov Leningrada. Leningrad, 1983.

Paperno, Irina. "The Liberation of the Serfs as a Cultural Symbol." *The Russian Review* 50 (October 1991): 417–36.

Papp, Robert. "The Road to Chervonets: The Representation of National Identity on Russian Money, 1896–1924." Unpublished manuscript. 1996.

Pares, Sir Bernard. *The Fall of the Russian Monarchy.* New York, 1961.

Parland, A. A. "Khram Voskreseniia Khristova," *Zodchii* (1907): 374–78.

———. *Khram Voskresenie Khristova sooruzhennyi na meste smertel'nogo poraneniia v Boze pochivshego Imperatora Aleksandra II na ekaterinskom kanale v Sankt-Peterburge.* St. Petersburg, 1909.

Paszkiewicz, Piotr. "The Russian Orthodox Cathedral of Saint Alexander Nevsky in Warsaw." *Polish Art Studies,* 14 (1992): 63–72.

Patkul, M. A. "Vospominaniia." *Istoricheskii Vestnik* 89 (1902): 38–66.

Pavlov, P. "Tysiacheletie Rossii." Supplement to *Mesiatseslov na 1862 god.* St. Petersburg, 1862.

Pazukhin, A. D. "Sovremennoe sostoianie Rossii i soslovnyi vopros." *Russkii Vestnik* (January 1885): 1–58.

Pearson, Raymond. "Privileges, Rights, and Russification." In *Civil Rights in Imperial Russia,* ed. Olga Crisp and Linda Edmondson. Oxford, 1989.

———. *The Russian Moderates and the Crisis of Tsarism, 1914–1917.* London, 1977.

Pearson, Thomas S. *Russian Officialdom in Crisis: Autocracy and Local Self-Government, 1861–1900.* Cambridge, 1989.

Pereira, N.G.O. "Alexander II and the Decision to Emancipate the Russian Serfs, 1855–1861." *Canadian Slavic Papers* 22, no. 1 (March 1980): 99–115.

Perets, E. A. *Dnevnik (1880–1883).* Moscow-Leningrad, 1927.

Perovskii, B. A. "Kratkii ocherk slov moikh Gosudariu Nasledniku Tsesarevichu." *Starina i Novizna,* no. 6 (1903): 344–46.

Perrie, Maureen. *The Agrarian Policy of the Russian Socialist-Revolutionary Party from Its Origins Through the Revolution of 1905–1907.* Cambridge, 1976.

———. *The Image of Ivan IV in Russian Folklore*. Cambridge, 1987.

Petrov, P. N. *Illiustrirovannoe opisanie torzhestv brakosochetannia Gosudaria Naslednika Tsesarevicha i Gosudaryni Tsesarevny*. St. Petersburg, 1867.

———. *Pamiatnik tysiacheletiiu gosudarstva rossiiskogo v Novgorode*. St. Petersburg, 1862.

Petrova, T. A., and T. A. Malinina. "The Private Rooms of the Imperial Family in the Winter Palace." In *Nicholas and Alexandra: The Last Imperial Family of Tsarist Russia*. London, 1998.

Petrovich, Michael Boro. *The Emergence of Russian Pan-Slavism, 1856–1870*. New York, 1956.

Petrovskii S. *Pamiati Imperatora Aleksandra III*. Moscow, 1894.

Pfeffer, Susanna. *Fabergé Eggs: Masterpieces from Czarist Russia*. n.p., 1990.

Pinchuk, Ben-Cion. *The Octobrists in the Third Duma, 1907–1912*. Seattle, 1974.

Pipes, Richard. *Social Democracy and the St. Petersburg Labor Movement, 1885–1897*. Cambridge, Mass, 1963.

Platonov, A. *Obzor deiatel'nosti obshchestva vozstanovleniia pravoslavnago khristianstva na Kavkaze za 1860–1910gg*. Tiflis, 1910.

Platonov, S. F. *Lektsii po russkoi istorii*. St. Petersburg, 1901.

———. " 'Vsia zemlia.' " In *Nachalo dinastii Romanovykh*, ed. P. G. Vasenko et al. St. Petersburg, 1912.

Pobedinskii, I. *Imperator Aleksandr III, Tsar'-mirotvorets (Ko dniu otkrytiia pamiatnika v Moskve)*. Moscow, 1912.

Pobedonostsev, K. P. *K. P. Pobedonostsev i ego korrespondenty*. Vol. 1. Moscow-Petrograd, 1923.

———. *Pis'ma Pobedonostseva k Aleksandru III*. Moscow, 1925.

Pobedonostsev, K. P., and I. Babst. *Pis'ma o puteshestvii gosudaria naslednika tsesarevicha po Rossii ot Peterburga do Kryma*. Moscow, 1864.

Podvor'e russkoi pravoslavnoi tserkvi v Karlovykh varakh. Prague, 1987.

Pogodin, M. P. *Istoriko-kriticheskie otryvki*. Moscow, 1846.

———. *Sochineniia*. vol. 4. Moscow, 1874.

Pokrovskii, I. M. "Russkoe dukhovenstvo, ego patriotizm i deiatel'nost' v zashchite Pravoslaviia i zakonnoi natsional'noi tsarskoi vlasti v smutnoe vremia i pri izbranii na russkii tsarskii prestol boiarina Mikhaila Feodorovicha Romanova." *Pravoslavnyi Sobesednik* (March 1913); 371–416.

Pokrovskii, N. V. "Kostromskii Ipat'evskii Monastyr'—kolybel' tsarstvuiushchego doma." In *Letopisnyi i Litsevoi Izbornik Doma Romanovykh: Iubileinoe izdanie v oznamenovanie 300-letiia tsarstvovaniia*, ed. M. S. Putiatin. Moscow, 1913.

Polovtsov, A. A. *Dnevnik gosudarstvennogo sekretaria A. A. Polovtsova*. 2 vols. Moscow, 1966.

———. "Dnevnik." *Krasnyi Arkhiv* (1923), 3:76–192; (1929), 2:170–203; (1931), 3:110–32; (1934), 6:169–86; (1923), 3:76–172.

Polunov, A. Iu. "Konstantin Petrovich Pobedonostsev—chelovek i politik." *Otechestvennaia Istoriia* (January–February 1998), 42–55.

———. *Pod vlast'iu ober-prokurora: gosudarstvo i tserkov' v epokhu Aleksandra III*. Moscow, 1996.

Pope, Barbara Corrado. "Immaculate and Powerful: The Marian Revival in the Nineteenth Century." In *Immaculate and Powerful: The Female in Sacred Image and Social Reality*, ed. Clarissa W. Atkinson, Constance H. Buchanan, and Margaret R. Miles. Boston, 1985.

Poselianin, E. *Iasnye dni. 17 oktiabria. 29 aprelia. 28 oktiabria.* Moscow, 1892.

Poznansky, Alexander. *Tchaikovsky: The Quest for the Inner Man.* New York, 1991.

Prazdnovanie deviatisotletiia kreshcheniia russkogo naroda. Kiev, 1888.

Prazdnovanie trekhsotletiia tsarstvovaniia Doma Romanovykh v Kostromskoi gubernii 19–20 maia 1913. Kostroma, 1913.

Preobrazhenskii, M. *Revel'skii Pravoslavnyi Aleksandro-Nevskii Sobor.* St. Petersburg, 1902.

Puteshestvie Gosudaria naslednika tsesarevicha i Gosudaryni tsesarevny v 1869 godu. Moscow, 1869.

Putiatin, M. S., ed. *Letopisnyi i Litsevoi Izbornik Doma Romanovykh: Iubileinoe izdanie v oznamenovanie 300-letiia tsarstvovaniia.* 2 vols. Moscow, 1913.

Quinn, Malcolm. *The Swastika: Constructing the Symbol.* London, 1994.

Rabenek, Lev. "Moskva i eia khoziaeva." *Vozrozhdenie,* no. 105 (1960): 101–4.

Radzinsky, Edvard. *The Last Tsar: The Life and Death of Nicholas II.* New York, 1992.

Radziwill, Ekaterina R. (Count Paul Vasilli). *Behind the Veil at the Russian Court.* New York, 1914.

———. *The Intimate Life of the Last Tsarina.* London, 1929.

Raeff, Marc. "The Romanoffs and Their Books: Perspectives on Imperial Rule in Russia." *Biblion* 6, no. 1 (fall 1997): 42–75.

Raun, Toivo, U. "The Estonians." In *Russification in the Baltic Provinces and Finland, 1855–1914,* ed. Edward Thaden. Princeton, N.J., 1981.

Réau, Louis. *Saint Petersburg.* Paris, 1913.

Rheims, Maurice. *19th-Century Sculpture.* New York, 1977.

Rheinstein, Max, ed. *Max Weber on Law in Economy and Society.* New York, 1967.

Richards, Thomas. *The Commodity Culture of Victorian England: Advertising and Spectacle, 1851–1914.* Stanford, 1990.

Rieber, Alfred J. *Merchants and Entrepreneurs in Imperial Russia.* Chapel Hill, N.C., 1982.

———. *The Politics of Autocracy: Letters of Alexander II to Prince A. I. Bariatinskii, 1857–1864.* The Hague, 1966.

Ritvo, Harriet. *The Animal Estate: The English and Other Creatures in the Victorian Age.* Cambridge, Mass., 1987.

Robbins, Richard. *Famine in Russia, 1891–1892: The Imperial Government Responds to a Crisis.* New York, 1975.

Robinson, Geroid Tanquary. *Rural Russia under the Old Regime.* New York, 1961.

Rodzianko, M. V. *The Reign of Rasputin: An Empire's Collapse.* London, 1927.

Rogger, Hans. "Nationalism and the State: A Russian Dilemma." *Comparative Studies in Society and History* 4 (1961–62): 253–64.

———. "Russia in 1914." *Journal of Contemporary History* (October 1966): 95–119.

———. "The Beilis Case: Anti-Semitism and Politics in the Reign of Nicholas II." *Slavic Review* 25, no. 4 (December 1966): 615–29.

———. "The Skobelev Phenomenon: The Hero and His Worship." *Oxford Slavonic Papers* 9 (1976): 44–78.

Roosevelt, Priscilla. *Life on the Russian Country Estate: A Social and Cultural History.* New Haven, 1995.

Rossiia pod skipetrom Romanovykh. St. Petersburg, 1913.

Rozanov, V. V. *Sredi khudozhnikov.* St. Petersburg, 1914.

Rubakin, N. A. *Rossiia v tsifrakh*. St. Petersburg, 1912.

Rumbold, Sir Horace. *Recollections of a Diplomatist*. 2 vols. London, 1902.

Rusakova, A. A. *Mikhail Nesterov*. Leningrad, 1990.

Russkii tsar' s tsaritseiu na poklonenii Moskovskim sviatynam. St. Petersburg, 1909.

Ruud, Charles A. *Fighting Words: Imperial Censorship and the Russian Press, 1804–1906*. Toronto, 1982.

———. *Russian Entrepreneur: Publisher Ivan Sytin of Moscow, 1851–1934*. Montreal, 1990.

S.A.T. *Vospominaniia o sviashchennom koronovanii ikh imperatorskikh velichestv v boze pochivshikh Gosudaria Imperatora Aleksandra Nikolaevicha i Gosudarynia Imperatritsy Marii Aleksandrovny*. Tver, 1882.

Sahlins, Marshall. *Islands of History*. Chicago, 1985.

Sapunov, B. V. "Nekotorye siuzhety russkoi ikonopisi i ikh traktovka v poreformennoe vremia." In *Kul'tura i iskusstvo Rossii XIX veka: Novye Materialy i issledovaniia*. Leningrad, 1985.

Schenk, Benjamin. "Aleksandr Nevskij und die russische Nation: Geschichtsbilder und Entwürfe kollektiver Identität, 1263–1917." Master's thesis, Free University of Berlin, 1997.

Schimmelpenninck Van Der Oye, David. "Ex Oriente Lux: Ideologies of Empire and Russia's Far East, 1895–1904." Ph.D. dissertation, Yale University. New Haven, 1997.

Schneiderman, Jeremiah. *Sergei Zubatov and Revolutionary Marxism: The Struggle for the Working Class in Tsarist Russia*. Ithaca, N.Y., 1976.

Schweinitz, General [Hans Lothar] von. *Denkwurdigkeiten*. 3 vols. Berlin, 1927–28.

Semennikov, B. P. *Nikolai II i velikie kniazia*. Leningrad-Moscow, 1925.

Semenov, N. P. *Osvobozhedenie krestian' v tsarstvovanie Imperatora Aleksandra II*. 3 vols. St. Petersburg, 1889–93.

Seton-Watson, Hugh. *The Decline of Imperial Russia, 1855–1914*. New York, 1964.

Shakhovskoi, Kn.V.N. *"Sic transit gloria mundi," 1893–1917*. Paris, 1952.

Shepelev, L. E. *Otmennennye Istoriei; chiny, zvaniia i tituly v Rossiiskoi imperii*. Leningrad, 1977.

Shevelev, A. A. "Puteshestviia po Rossii ego Imperatorskogo Vysochestva Naslednika Tsesarevicha Aleksandra Aleksandrovicha." *Russkoe Obozrenie* (July 1897): 52–92; (February 1898); 821–32.

Shliapkin, I. A. "Iz bumag odnogo iz prepodavatelei Aleksandra II." *Starina i novizna* 22 (1917): 3–17.

Shul'ts, S. *Khramy Sankt-Peterburga: istoriia i sovremennost'*. St. Petersburg, 1994.

Shumigorskii, E. S. "Iz zapisnoi knizhki istorika." *Istoricheski Vestnik*, no. 138 (November 1914): 624–31.

Shvarts, A. N. *Moia perepiska so Stolypinym; Moi vospominaniia o Gosudare*. Moscow, 1994.

Shvetsov, G. M. *Venok Tsariu-Velikomucheniku Gosudariu Imperatoru Aleksandru II blagoslovennomu: stikhotvoreniia prostoliudina G. M. Shvetsova*. St. Petersburg, 1882.

Siegelbaum, Lewis H. *The Politics of Industrial Mobilization in Russia, 1914–1917: A Study of the War Industrial Committees*. Oxford, 1983.

Silverman, Debora L. *Art Nouveau in Fin-de-siècle France; Politics, Psychology, and Style*. Berkeley, 1989.

Simonova, M. S. "Viacheslav Konstantinovich Pleve." In *Rossiiskie Konservatory.* Moscow, 1997.

Sinel, Allen. *The Classroom and the Chancellery: State Educational Reform in Russia under Count Dmitry Tolstoi.* Cambridge, Mass., 1973.

Sitwell, Sacherevell. *Valse des fleurs: A Day in St. Petersburg and a Ball at the Winter Palace in 1868.* London, 1941.

Sladkevich, N. G. *Ocherki istorii obshchestvennoi mysli Rossii v kontse 50-kh — nachale 60-kh godov XIX veka.* Leningrad, 1962.

Slocum, John W. "Who, and When, Were the *Inorodtsy?* The Evolution of the Category of "Aliens" in Imperial Russia." *The Russian Review* 57 (April 1998): 173–90.

Smith, Anthony D. *The Ethnic Origins of Nations.* Oxford, 1986.

Smolitsch, Igor. *Geschichte der russischen Kirche, 1700–1917.* Vol. 1. Leiden, 1964.

Snowman, A. Kenneth. *Carl Fabergé: Goldsmith to the Imperial Court of Russia.* New York, 1979.

Sobolev, V. S. *Avgusteishii Prezident: Velikii Kniaz' Konstantin Konstantinovich vo glave Imperatorskoi Akademii Nauk, 1889–1915 gody.* St. Petersburg, 1993.

Sobranie gosudarstvennykh gramot i dogovorov. Vol. 3. Moscow, 1822.

Sollogub, V. A. *Dnevnik vysochaishchego prebyvaniia za Dunaem v 1877 godu.* St. Petersburg, 1878.

Solov'ev, Iu. B. " 'Politicheskaia smert' P. A. Stolypina." In *Gosudarstvennaia deiatel'nost' P. A. Stolypina: sbornik statei.* Moscow, 1994.

———. *Samoderzhavie i dvorianstvo v 1902–1907gg.* Leningrad, 1981.

———. *Samoderzhavie i dvorianstvo v kontse XIX veka.* Leningrad, 1973.

Solov'ev, S. M. *Izbrannye trudy; Zapiski.* Moscow, 1983.

———. *Publichnye chteniia o Petre Velikom.* Moscow, 1984.

Sorenson, Thomas C. "Pobedonostsev's Parish Schools: A Bastion against Secularism." In *Religious and Secular Forces in Late Tsarist Russia: Essays in Honor of Donald W. Treadgold,* ed. Charles E. Timberlake. Seattle, 1992.

Spiridovitch, Alexandre. *Les dernières années de la cour de Tsarskoe-Selo.* 2 vols. Paris, 1928–29.

Starn, Randolph, and Loren Partridge. *Arts of Power: Three Halls of State in Italy, 1300–1600.* Berkeley, 1992.

Starr, S. Frederick. *Decentralization and Self-Government in Russia.* Princeton, N.J., 1972.

Stasov, V. V. *Izbrannye sochineniia v trekh tomakh.* 3 vols. Moscow, 1952.

Stavrou, Theophanis George. *Russian Interests in Palestine, 1882–1914.* Thessaloniki, 1962.

Steinberg, Mark. "Nicholas and Alexandra: An Intellectual Portrait." In *The Fall of the Romanovs: Political Dreams and Personal Struggles in a Time of Revolution,* ed. Mark Steinberg and Vladimir M. Khrustalev. New Haven, 1995.

Stolypin, P. A. *Rechi v Gosudarstvennoi dume i Gosudarstvennom sovete, 1906–1911.* New York, 1990.

Stone, Norman. *The Eastern Front, 1914–1917.* London, 1975.

Struve, P. V. "Intelligentsiia i revoliutsiia." In *Vekhi.* Moscow, 1909.

Subtelny, Orest. "The Hapsburg and Russian Empires: Some Comparisons and Contrasts." In *Empire and Society: New Approaches to Russian History,* ed. Teruyuki Hara and Kimitaka Matzuzato. Sapporo, 1997.

Sukhomlinov, V. *Vospominaniia Sukhomlinova.* Moscow-Leningrad, 1926.

Sultanov, N. *Pamiatnik Imperatoru Aleksandru II v Kremle Moskovskom.* St. Petersburg, 1898.

———. "Tserkov' v dome Moskovskogo General-Gubernatora." *Zodchii,* no. 2 (1893): 12–14; no. 3 (1893): 17–20.

———. "Vozrozhdenie russkogo iskusstva." *Zodchii,* no. 2 (1881): 9–11.

Suny, Ronald "The Empire Strikes Out: Imperial Russia, National Identity, and Theories of Empire." In *A State of Nations: Empire and Nation-Making in the Age of Lenin and Stalin,* ed. Ronald Suny and Terry Martin. Forthcoming.

Surguchev, Il'ia. *Detstvo Imperatora Nikolaia II.* Paris, 1953.

Sushkov, N. V. *Zapiski o zhizni i vremeni sviatitelia Filareta, Mitropolita Moskovskogo.* Moscow, 1868.

Suslov, I. M. *A. M. Opekushin; zhizn' i tvorchestvo.* Iaroslavl, 1968.

Suvorin, A. *Dnevnik.* Moscow, 1992.

Tager, A. S. *Tsarskaia Rossiia i delo Beilisa.* Moscow, 1933.

Tal'berg, F. A., and N. I. Podgornaia. *Kavalery imperatorskogo voennogo ordena sviatogo velikomuchenika Georgiia, I i II stepenei (1769–1916).* Riga, n.d.

Tanner, Marie. *The Last Descendant of Aeneas: The Hapsburgs and the Mythic Image of Emperor.* New Haven, 1993.

Tarasov, O. Iu. *Ikona i blagochestie: ocherki ikonnogo dela v imperatorskoi Rossii.* Moscow, 1995.

Tarsaidzé, Alexandre. *Katia: Wife before God.* New York, 1970.

Tatishchev, S. S. *Alexander II; ego zhizn' i tsarstvovanie.* 2 vols. St. Petersburg, 1903.

Thaden, Edward C. *Conservative Nationalism in Nineteenth-Century Russia.* Seattle, 1964.

———. *Russia's Western Borderlands, 1710–1870* Princeton, N.J., 1984.

———, ed. *Russification in the Baltic Provinces and Finland, 1855–1914.* Princeton, N.J., 1981.

Thompson, J. M. *Louis Napoleon and the Second Empire.* New York, 1983.

Tikhomirov, L. A. *Monarkhicheskaia gosudarstvennost'.* Buenos Aires, 1968.

———. *Vospominaniia.* Moscow, 1927.

———. "Znachenie 19 fevralia 1902 goda dlia moskovskikh rabochikh." *Byloe,* no. 12 (1912): 81–88.

Timofievich, Anatolii. *Prepodobnyi Serafim Sarovskii.* Spring Valley, N.Y., 1953.

Tiutchev, F. I. "Lettres de Th. I. Tjutsheff a sa seconde épouse née Baronne de Pfeffel." *Starina i Novizna* 19 (1915): 104–276.

———. *Polnoe sobranie sochinenii.* St. Petersburg, 1913.

Tiutcheva, Anna Fedorovna. *Pri dvore dvukh imperatorov. Vospominaniia, Dnevnik, 1853–1882.* 2 vols. Moscow, 1928–1929.

Toeplitz, Jerzy. *Geschichte des Films.* Vol. 1. Berlin, 1992.

Tolstaia, A. A. *Zapiski freiliny: pechal'nyi epizod iz moei zhizni pri dvore.* Moscow, 1996.

Tolstoi, I. I. *Dnevnik, 1906–1916.* St. Petersburg, 1997.

Toluzakov, S. A. *Podvig 300-letiia sluzheniia Rossii gosudarei doma Romanovykh.* St. Petersburg, 1913.

Topchii, A. T. "Romanovy, kazachestvo i osvoenie vostochnykh territorii Rossii." In *Dom Romanovykh v istorii Rossii.* St. Petersburg, 1995.

Trubinov, Iu. V. *Khram Voskreseniia Khristova (Spas na krovi).* St. Petersburg, 1997.

Tsarskoe prebyvanie v Moskve v aprele 1900 goda. St. Petersburg, 1900.

Tsivian, Yuri. "Censure Bans on Religious Subjects in Russian Films." In *Une invention du diable? Cinéma des premiers temps et religion*, ed. Roland Cosandey, André Gaudreault, and Tom Gunning. Sainte-Foy, 1992.

———. *Early Cinema in Russia and Its Cultural Reception*. London, 1994.

Turner, Victor, and Edith Turner. *Image and Pilgrimage in Christian Culture*. New York, 1978.

Tvardovskaia, V. A. *Ideologiia poreformennogo samoderzhaviia*. Moscow, 1978.

Ukhtomskii, Kn.E.E. *Puteshestvie na vostok ego Imperatorskogo Vysochestva, Gosudaria Naslednika Tsesarevicha, 1890–1891*. 6 vols. St. Petersburg, 1893–97.

Ulstrup, Preben. "Maria Feodorovna through Diaries and Letters." *Maria Feodorovna: Empress of Russia*. Copenhagen, 1997.

Unowsky, Daniel. "Creating Patriotism: Imperial Celebrations and the Cult of Franz Joseph." *Öesterreichische Zeitschrift für Geschichtswissenschaften* 9, no. 2 (1998): 269–93.

Uspenskii, B. A. *Tsar' i patriarkh: kharizma vlasti v Rossii (Vizantiiskaia model' i ee russkoe pereosmyslenie)*. Moscow, 1998.

Utrachennye pamiatniki arkhitektury Peterburga-Leningrada; katalog vystavki. Leningrad, 1988.

Vadbol'skii, Kn.A.P. "Iz vospominanii byvshego gvardeiskogo ofitsera." *Russkaia Starina* 114 (June 1903): 543–45.

Valk, S. N., ed. *Otmena krepostnogo prava; doklady ministrov vnutrennikh del o provedenii krest'ianskoi reformy, 1861–1862*. Moscow-Leningrad, 1950.

Valkenier, Elizabeth. *Russian Realist Art. State and Society: The Peredvizhniki and Their Tradition*. Ann Arbor, Mich., 1977.

Valuev, P. A. "8ogo sentiabria 1862 goda," *Russkaia Starina* 57 (January 1888): 1–16.

———. *Dnevnik P. A. Valueva*. 2 vols. Moscow, 1961.

Vasenko, P. G., ed. *Boiare Romanovy i votsarenie Mikhaila Feodorovicha*. St. Petersburg, 1913.

Vel'iaminov, N. A. "Vospominaniia N. A. Vel'iaminova ob Imperatore Aleksandre III." *Rossiiskii Arkhiv* (1994), 5:249–313.

———. "Vospominaniia N. A. Vel'iaminova o D. S. Sipiagine." *Rossiiskii Arkhiv* (1995), 6:377–93.

Velichenko, M. N., and G. A. Miroliubova. *Dvorets velikogo kniazia Vladimira Alekandrovicha*. St. Petersburg, 1997.

Venturi, Franco. *Roots of Revolution*. London, 1952.

Vereshchagin, V. A. *Russkie illiustrirovannye izdaniia XVIII i XIX stoletii*. St. Petersburg, 1898.

Verner, Andrew M. *The Crisis of Russian Autocracy: Nicholas II and the 1905 Revolution*. Princeton, N.J., 1990.

Veseliashchiisia Peterburg. St. Petersburg, 1994.

Veselovskii, I. I. *V. V. Grigor'ev po ego pis'mam i trudam, 1818–1881*. St. Petersburg, 1887.

Vesna krasna: allegoricheskoe shestvie ustroennoe na narodnom gul'iane v Moskve, 21 maia 1883g. Moscow, 1883.

Viazemskii, Kn.P.A. *Polnoe sobranie sochinenii*. vol. 12. St. Petersburg, 1896.

Vinogradoff, Eugene D. "The Russian Peasantry and the Elections to the Fourth State Duma." In *The Politics of Rural Russia, 1905–1914*, ed. Leopold Haimson. Bloomington, Ind., 1979.

Vinogradoff, Igor. "Further Russian Imperial Correspondence with Prince V. P. Meshcherskii." *Oxford Slavonic Papers*, no. 11 (1964): 101–11.

———. "Some Russian Imperial Letters to Prince V. P. Meshcherskii (1839–1914)." *Oxford Slavonic Studies*, no. 11 (1962): 105–57.

Viollet-le-Duc, E. *L'Art Russe*. Paris, 1877.

Voeikov, V. N. *S tsarem i bez tsaria*. Helsinki, 1936.

Voeikov, V. V. "Poslednie dni Imperatora Aleksandra II i votsarenie Imperatora Aleksandra III." *Izvestiia Tambovskoi Uchenoi Arkhivnoi Komissii* 54 (1911): 55–165.

Von Laue, Theodore H. *Sergei Witte and the Industrialization of Russia*. New York, 1969.

Vonliarliarskii, V. *Moi vospominaniia*. Berlin, 1939.

Von Solodkoff, Alexander. "History of the House of Fabergé." In *Masterpieces from the House of Fabergé*, ed. Alexander von Solodkoff. New York, 1989.

Vostorgov, Protoierei Ioann. "Ideinye zavety iubileia." *Tserkovnye Vedomosti*, February 9, 1913, 265–71.

———. "Uchastie tserkvi i dukhovenstva v velikikh sobytiiakh trista let tomu nazad." *Tserkovnye Vedomosti*, February 21, 1913, appendix, 329–32.

Vyrubova, A. A. *Stranitsy iz moei zhizni*. New York, 1923.

Warner, Marina. *Alone of All Her Sex: The Myth and Cult of the Virgin Mary*. New York, 1976.

Wcislo, Francis William. *Reforming Rural Russia: State, Local Society, and National Politics, 1855–1914*. Princeton, N.J., 1990.

Weeks, Theodore, R. *Nation and State in Late Imperial Russia: Nationalism and Russification on the Western Frontier, 1863–1914*. De Kalb, Ill., 1996.

Weidlé, Wladimir. *Russia: Absent and Present*. New York, 1961.

Wheatcroft, Andrew. *The Hapsburgs: Embodying Empire*. London, 1995.

Whelan, Heide. *Adapting to Modernity: Family, Caste, and Capitalism in the World of the Nineteenth-Century Baltic German Nobility*. Cologne, 1999.

———. *Alexander III and the State Council: Bureaucracy and Counterreform in Late Imperial Russia*. New Brunswick, N.J., 1982.

Whittaker, Cynthia H. "The Reforming Tsar: The Redefinition of Autocratic Duty in Eighteenth-Century Russia." *Slavic Review* 51, no. 1 (spring 1992): 77–98.

Wildman, Allan K. *The End of the Russian Imperial Army: The Old Army and the Soldiers' Revolt (March–April 1917)*. Princeton, N.J., 1980.

———. *The Making of a Workers' Revolution: Russian Social Democracy, 1891–1903*. Chicago, 1967.

Witte, S. Iu. *Konspekt lektsii o Gosudarstvennom Khoziastve*. St. Petersburg, 1914.

———. *Po povodu natsionalizma: Natsional'aia Ekonomiia i Fridrikh List*. St. Petersburg, 1912.

———. *Printsipy zheleznodorozhnykh tarifov po perevozke gruzov*. St. Petersburg, 1910.

———. *Vospominaniia*. 3 vols. Moscow, 1960.

Wortman, Richard S. "Ceremony and Empire in the Evolution of Russian Monarchy." In *Kazan, Moscow, St. Petersburg: Multiple Faces of Russian Empire*, ed. Catherine Evtuhov, Boris Gasparov, Alexander Ospovat, and Mark Von Hagen. Moscow, 1997.

———. "Moscow and Petersburg: The Problem of Political Center in Tsarist Russia, 1881–1914." In *Rites of Power: Symbolism, Ritual, and Politics since the Middle Ages*, ed. Sean Wilentz. Philadelphia, 1985.

Wortman, Richard S. "Statues of the Tsars and the Redefinition of Russia's Past." In *"Remove Not the Ancient Landmark"*: *Public Monuments and Moral Values*, ed. Donald Martin Reynolds. Amsterdam, 1996.

———. *The Development of a Russian Legal Consciousness*. Chicago, 1976.

———. "The Russian Empress as Mother." In *The Family in Imperial Russia: New Lines of Historical Research*, ed. David L. Ransel. Urbana, Ill., 1978.

Zaionchkovskii, P. A. *Krizis samoderzhaviia na rubezhe 1870–1880-kh godov*. Moscow, 1964.

———. *Otmena krepostnogo prava*. Moscow, 1968.

———. *Rossiiskoe samoderzhavie v kontse XIX veka*. Moscow, 1970.

———. "Russkii ofitserskii korpus nakanune Pervoi mirovoi voiny." In *P. A. Zaionchkovskii*, ed. L. G. Zakharova, Iu. S. Kukushkin, and T. Emmons. Moscow, 1998.

———. *Samoderzhavie i russkaia armia na rubezhe XIX–XX stoletii, 1881–1903*. Moscow, 1973.

———. *The Russian Autocracy under Alexander III*. Gulf Breeze, Fla., 1976. (Translation of *Rossiiskoe samoderzhavie*.)

———. "Vyshee voennoe upravlenie. Imperator i tsarstvuiushchii dom." In *P. A. Zaionchkovskii, 1904–1983gg. Stat'i, publikatsii i vospominaniia o nem*, ed. L. G. Zakharova, Iu. S. Kukushkin, and T. Emmons. Moscow, 1998.

———. *Voennye reformy 1860–1870 godov v Rossii*. Moscow, 1952.

Zakharova, L. G. "Alexander II." In *Rossiiskie samoderzhtsy, 1801–1917*. Moscow, 1994.

———. "Krizis samoderzhaviia nakanune revoliutsii 1905 goda." *Voprosy Istorii*, no. 8 (1978): 119–40.

———. *Samoderzhavie i otmena krepostnogo prava v Rossii, 1856–1861*. Moscow, 1984.

Zakharova, L. G., and L. I. Tiutiunnik, eds. *1857–1861: Perepiska Imperatora Aleksandra II s Velikim Kniazem Konstantinom Nikolaevichem; Dnevnik Konstantina Nikolaevicha*. Moscow, 1994.

Zander, Valentine. *St. Seraphim of Sarov*. Crestwood, N.Y., 1975.

Zelnik, Reginald. *A Radical Worker in Tsarist Russia: The Autobiography of Semën Ivanovich Kanatchikov*. Stanford, 1986.

Zhmakin, V. I. "Koronatsii russkikh imperatorov i imperatrits." *Russkaia Starina* 37 (1883): 499–538; 38 (1883): 1–36.

Zorkaia, Neia. *Fol'klor, lubok, ekran*. Moscow, 1994.

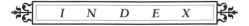

Note: Page numbers in italic type refer to illustrations.

Studies of the Harriman Institute

Abram Bergson, *Soviet National Income in 1937* (Columbia University Press, 1953).

Ernest Simmons, Jr. (ed.), *Through the Glass of Soviet Literature: Views of Russian Society* (Columbia University Press, 1953).

Thad Paul Alton, *Polish Postwar Economy* (Columbia University Press, 1954).

David Granick, *Management of the Industrial Firm in the USSR: A Study in Soviet Economic Planning* (Columbia University Press, 1954).

Allen S. Whiting, *Soviet Policies in China, 1917–1924* (Columbia University Press, 1954; paperback, Stanford University Press, 1968).

George S. N. Luckyj, *Literary Politics in the Soviet Ukraine, 1917–1934* (Columbia University Press, 1956).

Michael Boro Petrovich, *The Emergence of Russian Panslavism, 1856–1870* (Columbia University Press, 1956).

Thomas Taylor Hammond, *Lenin on Trade Unions and Revolution, 1893–1917* (Columbia University Press, 1956).

David Marshall Lang, *The Last Years of the Georgian Monarchy, 1658–1832* (Columbia University Press, 1957).

James William Morley, *The Japanese Thrust into Siberia, 1918* (Columbia University Press, 1957).

Alexander G. Park, *Bolshevism in Turkestan, 1917–1927* (Columbia University Press 1957).

Herbert Marcuse, *Soviet Marxism: A Critical Analysis* (Columbia University Press, 1958; paperback, Columbia University Press, 1985).

Charles B. McLane, *Soviet Policy and the Chinese Communists, 1931–1946* (Columbia University Press, 1958).

Oliver H. Radkey, *The Agrarian Foes of Bolshevism: Promise and Defeat of the Russian Socialist Revolutionaries, February to October 1917* (Columbia University Press, 1958).

Ralph Talcott Fisher, Jr., *Pattern for Soviet Youth: A Study of the Congresses of Komsomol, 1918–1954* (Columbia University Press, 1959).

Alfred Erich Senn, *The Emergence of Modern Lithuania* (Columbia University Press, 1959).

Elliot R. Goodman, *The Soviet Design for a World State* (Columbia University Press, 1960).

John N. Hazard, *Settling Disputes in Soviet Society: The Formative Years of Legal Institutions* (Columbia University Press, 1960).

David Joravsky, *Soviet Marxism and Natural Science, 1917–1932* (Columbia University Press, 1961).

Maurice Friedberg, *Russian Classics in Soviet Jackets* (Columbia University Press, 1962).

Alfred J. Rieber, *Stalin and the French Communist Party, 1941–1947* (Columbia University Press, 1962).

Theodore K. Von Laue, *Sergei Witte and the Industrialization of Russia* (Columbia University Press, 1962).

John H. Armstrong, *Ukrainian Nationalism* (Columbia University Press, 1963).

Oliver H. Radkey, *The Sickle under the Hammer: The Russian Socialist Revolutionaries in the Early Months of Soviet Rule* (Columbia University Press, 1963).

Kermit E. McKenzie, *Comintern and World Revolution, 1928–1943: The Shaping of Doctrine* (Columbia University Press, 1964).

Harvey L. Dyck, *Weimar Germany and Soviet Russia, 1926–1933: A Study in Diplomatic Instability* (Columbia University Press, 1966).

Harold J. Noah, *Financing Soviet Schools* (Teachers College Press, 1966).

John M. Thompson, *Russia, Bolshevism, and the Versailles Peace* (Princeton University Press, 1966).

Paul Avrich, *The Russian Anarchists* (Princeton University Press, 1967).

Loren R. Graham, *The Soviet Academy of Sciences and the Communist Party, 1927–1932* (Princeton University Press, 1967).

Robert A. Maguire, *Red Virgin Soil: Soviet Literature in the 1920's* (Princeton University Press, 1968; paperback, Cornell University Press, 1987).

T. H. Rigby, *Communist Party Membership in the U.S.S.R., 1917–1967* (Princeton University Press, 1968).

Richard T. DeGeorge, *Soviet Ethics and Morality* (University of Michigan Press, 1969; paperback, Ann Arbor Paperbacks, 1969).

Jonathan Frankel, *Vladimir Akimov on the Dilemmas of Russian Marxism, 1895–1903* (Cambridge University Press, 1969).

William Zimmerman, *Soviet Perspectives on International Relations, 1956–1967* (Princeton University Press, 1969).

Paul Avrich, *Kronstadt, 1921* (Princeton University Press, 1970).

Ezra Mendelsohn, *Class Struggle in the Pale: The Formative Years of the Jewish Workers' Movement in Tsarist Russia* (Cambridge University Press, 1970).

Edward J. Brown, *The Proletarian Episode in Russian Literature* (Columbia University Press, 1971).

Reginald E. Zelnik, *Labor and Society in Tsarist Russia: The Factory Workers of St. Petersburg, 1855–1870* (Stanford University Press, 1971).

Patricia K. Grimsted, *Archives and Manuscript Repositories in the U.S.S.R.: Moscow and Leningrad* (Princeton University Press, 1972).

Ronald G. Suny, *The Baku Commune, 1917–1918* (Princeton University Press, 1972).

Edward J. Brown, *Mayakovsky: A Poet in the Revolution* (Princeton University Press, 1973).

Milton Ehre, *Oblomov and His Creator: The Life and Art of Ivan Goncharov* (Princeton University Press, 1973).

Henry Krisch, *German Politics under Soviet Occupation* (Columbia University Press, 1974).

Henry W. Morton and Rudolph L. Tokes (eds.), *Soviet Politics and Society in the 1970's* (Free Press, 1974).

William G. Rosenberg, *Liberals in the Russian Revolution* (Princeton University Press, 1974).

Richard G. Robbins, Jr., *Famine in Russia, 1891–1892* (Columbia University Press, 1975).

Vera S. Dunham, *In Stalin's Time: Middle-class Values in Soviet Fiction* (Cambridge University Press, 1976; paperback, Duke University Press, 1990).

Walter Sablinsky, *The Road to Bloody Sunday* (Princeton University Press, 1976; paperback, Princeton University Press, 1986).

William Mills Todd III, *The Familiar Letter as a Literary Genre in the Age of Pushkin* (Princeton University Press, 1976).

Elizabeth Valkenier, *Russian Realist Art. The State and Society: The Peredvizhniki and Their Tradition* (Ardis, 1977; paperback, Columbia University Press, 1989).

Susan Solomon, *The Soviet Agrarian Debate* (Westview Press, 1978).

Sheila Fitzpatrick (ed.), *Cultural Revolution in Russia, 1928–1931* (Indiana University Press, 1978; paperback, Midland Books, 1984).

Peter Solomon, *Soviet Criminologists and Criminal Policy: Specialists in Policy-Making* (Columbia University Press, 1978).

Kendall E. Bailes, *Technology and Society under Lenin and Stalin: Origins of the Soviet Technical Intelligentsia* (Princeton University Press, 1978).

Leopold H. Haimson (ed.), *The Politics of Rural Russia, 1905–1914* (Indiana University Press, 1979).

Theodore H. Friedgut, *Political Participation in the U.S.S.R.* (Princeton University Press, 1979).

Sheila Fitzpatrick, *Education and Social Mobility in the Soviet Union, 1921–1934* (Cambridge University Press, 1979).

Wesley Andrew Fisher, *The Soviet Marriage Market: Mate-Selection in Russia and the USSR* (Praeger, 1980).

Jonathan Frankel, *Prophecy and Politics: Socialism, Nationalism, and the Russian Jews, 1862–1917* (Cambridge University Press, 1981).

Robin Feuer Miller, *Dostoevsky and "The Idiot": Author, Narrator, and Reader* (Harvard University Press, 1981).

Diane Koenker, *Moscow Workers and the 1917 Revolution* (Princeton University Press, 1981).

Patricia K. Grimsted, *Archives and Manuscript Repositories in the USSR: Estonia, Latvia, Lithuania, and Belorussia* (Princeton University Press, 1981).

Ezra Mendelsohn, *Zionism in Poland: The Formative Years, 1915–1926* (Yale University Press, 1982).

Hannes Adomeit, *Soviet Risk-Taking and Crisis Behavior* (George Allen & Unwin, 1982).

Seweryn Bialer and Thane Gustafson (eds.), *Russia at the Crossroads: The 26th Congress of the CPSU* (George Allen & Unwin, 1982).

Roberta Thompson Manning, *The Crisis of the Old Order in Russia: Gentry and Government* (Princeton University Press, 1983).

Andrew A. Durkin, *Sergei Aksakov and Russian Pastoral* (Rutgers University Press, 1983).

Bruce Parrott, *Politics and Technology in the Soviet Union* (MIT Press, 1983).

Elizabeth Kridl Valkenier, *The Soviet Union and the Third World: An Economic Bind* (Praeger, 1983).

Sarah Pratt, *Russian Metaphysical Romanticism: The Poetry of Tiutchev and Boratynskii* (Stanford University Press, 1984).

John LeDonne, *Ruling Russia: Politics and Administration in the Age of Absolutism, 1762–1796* (Princeton University Press, 1984).

Diana Greene, *Insidious Intent: A Structural Analysis of Fedor Sologub's "Petty Demon"* (Slavica Publishers, 1986).

Richard Gustafson, *Leo Tolstoy: Resident and Stranger* (Princeton University Press, 1986).

William Chase, *Workers, Society, and the State: Labor and Life in Moscow, 1918–1929* (University of Illinois Press, 1987).

John Malmstad (ed.), *Andrey Bely: Spirit of Symbolism* (Cornell University Press, 1987).

David A. J. Macey, *Government and Peasant in Russia, 1861–1906: The Prehistory of the Stolypin Reforms* (Northern Illinois University Press, 1987).

Leopold H. Haimson in collaboration with Ziva Galili y Garcia and Richard Wortman (eds.), *The Making of Three Russian Revolutionaries: Voices from the Menshevik Past* (Cambridge University Press, 1988).

Zenovia A. Sochor, *Revolution and Culture: The Bogdanov-Lenin Controversy* (Cornell University Press, 1988).

Frank Miller, *A Handbook of Russian Verbs* (Ardis Publishers, 1989).

Gerald D. Surh, *1905 in St. Petersburg: Labor, Society, and Revolution* (Stanford University Press, 1989).

Elizabeth Klosty Beaujour, *Alien Tongues: Bilingual Russian Writers of the "First" Emigration* (Cornell University Press, 1989).

Theodore H. Friedgut, *Iuzovka and Revolution, Volume I: Life and Work in Russia's Donbass, 1869–1924* (Princeton University Press, 1989).

Ziva Galili, *The Menshevik Leaders in the Russian Revolution: Social Realities and Political Strategies* (Princeton University Press, 1989).

Marcus C. Levitt, *Russian Literary Politics and the Pushkin Celebration of 1880* (Cornell University Press, 1989).

Robert L. Belknap (ed.), *Russianness: In Honor of Rufus Mathewson* (Ardis Publishers, 1990).

Mark von Hagen, *Soldiers in the Proletarian Dictatorship: The Red Army and the Soviet Socialist State, 1917–1930* (Cornell University Press, 1990).

Elizabeth Valkenier, *Ilya Repin and the World of Russian Art* (Columbia University Press, 1990).

Robert L. Belknap, *The Genesis of "The Brothers Karamazov"* (Northwestern University Press, 1990).

Jane Gary Harris (ed.), *Autobiographical Statements in Twentieth-Century Russian Literature* (Princeton University Press, 1990).

Frank Miller, *Folklore for Stalin* (M. E. Sharpe, 1990).

Irina Reyfman, *Vasilii Trediakovsky: The Fool of the "New" Russian Literature* (Stanford University Press, 1990).

Michael Sodaro, *Russia, Germany, and the West from Khrushchev to Gorbachev* (Cornell University Press, 1990).

Francis William Wcislo, *Reforming Rural Russia: State, Local Society, and National Politics, 1855–1914* (Princeton University Press, 1990).

Greta N. Slobin, *Remizov's Fictions, 1900–1921* (Northern Illinois University Press, 1991).

Thomas C. Owen, *The Corporation under Russian Law, 1800–1917: A Study in Tsarist Economic Policy* (Cambridge University Press, 1991).

Paul R. Josephson, *Physics and Politics in Revolutionary Russia* (University of California Press, 1991).

Stephen Lessing Baehr, *The Paradise Myth in Eighteenth-Century Russia: Utopian Patterns in Early Secular Russian Literature and Culture* (Stanford University Press, 1991).

Alexander J. Motyl (ed.), *Thinking Theoretically about Soviet Nationalities: Concepts, History and Comparison in the Study of the USSR* (Columbia University Press, 1992).

Alexander J. Motyl (ed.), *The Post-Soviet Nations: Perspectives on the Demise of the USSR* (Columbia University Press, 1992).

Judith Deutsch Kornblatt, *The Cossack Hero in Russian Literature: A Study in Cultural Mythology* (University of Wisconsin Press, 1992).

Ellen Chances, *Andrei Bitov: The Ecology of Inspiration* (Cambridge University Press, 1993).

Robert Weinberg, *The Revolution of 1905 in Odessa: Blood on the Steps* (Indiana University Press, 1993).

Heather Hogan, *Forging Revolution: Metalworkers, Managers, and the State in St. Petersburg, 1890–1914* (Indiana University Press, 1993).

Cathy Popkin, *The Pragmatics of Insignificance: Chekhov, Zoshchenko, Gogol* (Stanford University Press, 1993).

Marcia Morris, *Saints and Revolutionaries: The Ascetic Hero in Russian Literature* (State University of New York Press, 1993).

Theodore H. Friedgut, *Iuzovka and Revolution, Volume II* (Princeton University Press, 1994).

Robert A. Maguire, *Exploring Gogol* (Stanford University Press, 1994).

David L. Hoffmann, *Peasant Metropolis: Social Identities in Moscow, 1929–1941* (Cornell University Press, 1994).

Richard S. Wortman, *Scenarios of Power: Myth and Creation in Russian Monarchy. Volume I* (Princeton University Press, 1995).

Catharine Theimer Nepomnyashchy, *Abram Tertz and the Poetics of Crime* (Yale University Press, 1995).

Adrian Wanner, *Baudelaire in Russia* (University Press of Florida, 1996).

Michael David-Fox, *Revolution of the Mind: Higher Learning Among the Bolsheviks, 1918–1929* (Cornell University Press, 1997).

Deborah Martinsen (ed.), *Literary Journals in Imperial Russia* (Cambridge University Press, 1997).

Olga Meerson, *Dostoevsky's Taboos* (Dresden University Press, 1998).

DATE DUE